Convention Sales and Services
Sixth Edition

Milton T. Astroff
Marketing Consultant

James R. Abbey, Ph.D.
Professor
College of Hotel Administration
University of Nevada, Las Vegas

Waterbury Press

Disclaimer

This publication is designed to provide accurate and authoritative information in regard to the subject matter covered. It is sold with the understanding that the publisher is not engaged in rendering legal, accounting, or other professional service. If legal advice or other expert assistance is required, the services of a competent professional person should be sought.
— *From the Declaration of Principles jointly adopted by the American Bar Associaqtion and a Committee of Publishers and Associations.*

Copyright © 2002
Waterbury Press
1605 Iron Ridge Dr.
Las Vegas, NV 89117
Tel: 702-254-1530
Fax: 702-254-3824
E-mail: Waterburypress@hotmail.com

Printed in the United States of America

ISBN 0-9620710-4-8

Contents

Introduction ix

Part I Convention Sales

1 Introduction to the Convention, Meetings and Trade Show Industry

The Convention and Meetings Industry Today 3
The Scope of Today's Meetings Market 7
  Types of Meetings, Who Holds Meetings, Emerging Types
  of Meeting Facilities
Other Trends in the Meetings Industry 18
  Globalization, Second-Tier Cities, The Growth of Convention
  Centers, Third-Party Meeting Planners, Increased Use of
  Technology, Revenue Management

2 Developing a Marketing Plan

The Difference Between Sales and Marketing 33
The Importance of Marketing 34
The Marketing Plan 35
The Four Steps of the Marketing Plan 37
  Step #1 Conducting Marketing Research,
  Step #2 Selecting Target Markets and Positioning the Property,
  Step #3 Establishing Objectives and Action Plans,
  Step #4 Reviewing and Monitoring the Marketing Plan
Putting a Marketing Plan into Action 60

3 Organizing for Convention Sales

Sales Structures 69
  The Sales Office, How the Sales Office Interfaces with
  Other Departments
The Sales and Marketing Staff 73
  Positions Within Sales, Supplemental Sales Staff
Managing the Sales Effort 83
  Standard Operating Procedures, Sales Meetings, Assigning
  Account Responsibility, Evaluating the Sales Effort
Sales Records and Filing Systems 87
  Hotel Filing Systems, Control Books and Sales Forms
Sales Office Automation 101
  Advantages of Automation, New Advances in Hotel Computer
  Systems, The "Virtual" Office, Additional Uses of Automation

4 Selling the Association Market

Revenue Producers 113
Requirements for Association Meetings 115
Kinds of Association Meetings 117
    Annual Conventions, State and Regional Conventions,
    Conferences, Seminars and Workshops, Board and Committee
    Meetings
Characteristics of Association Meetings 122
    Cycle and Pattern, Geographic Restrictions, Lead Time, Kind
    of Sites, Voluntary Attendance, Convention Duration, Price
Association Meeting Decision Makers 127
    Association Director, Association President and Officers,
    Committee Chairperson, Board of Directors, Other Influences
Sources for Finding Association Business 131
    Directories, Databases, Specialized Periodicals, Hotel Records

5 Selling the Corporate Meetings Market

Requirements for Corporate Meetings 141
Kinds of Company Meetings 145
    National and Regional Sales Meetings, New Product/Dealer
    Meetings, Professional/Technical Meetings, Management
    Meetings, Training Meetings, Stockholder/Public Meetings,
    Incentive Meetings
Characteristics of Company Meetings 149
Corporate Meeting Decision Makers 157
    Full-time Meeting Planner, Company President, Marketing
    and Sales Executives, Advertising and Sales Managers,
    Other Corporate Executives, Passenger Traffic/Corporate
    Travel Managers, Training Director, Meeting Specialists/
    Third-Party Planners
Sources for Finding Corporate Business and Decision Makers 161
    Special Meetings Publications, Trade Directories, Trade
    Associations, Internet Sites, Convention and Visitors
    Bureaus, Lateral Referral and Account Penetration

6 Selling Other Markets

Nonprofit Organizations 169
The SMERF Groups 170
    Social Groups, Military and other Reunions, Educational
    Meetings, Religious Meetings, Fraternal Meetings
Government Agencies 179
Labor Unions 182
Incentive Meetings 182
Insurance Meetings 187
Medical Meetings 188

7 Selling to the Meetings Market

Personal Sales Calls 195
     Pre-call Planning, Opening the Sales Call, Getting Prospect
     Involvement, Presenting Your Property, Handling Objections,
     Closing and Follow-up
Telephone Selling 203
     Telephone Techniques, Screening Prospects, Setting
     Appointments by Phone, Telephone Sales Call Follow-up,
     Handling Inquiries, Telemarketing
Sales Blitz Selling 209
Trade Show Selling 211
Selling with Convention Bureaus 213
Site Inspection Selling and Familiarization Tours 217

8 Advertising to the Meeting Planner

Print Advertising 223
     Trade Magazines, Hotel Directories
Using Technology for Advertising 229
     The Internet, E-mail Advertising, Fax Transmissions
Collateral Materials 232
     Brochures (Convention Brochures, Video Brochures, CD-ROMs),
     Other Collateral Materials, Specialty Items
Direct Mail Advertising 237
Planning an Advertising Strategy 243
     Reach, Frequency, Timing and Consistency, Exchange Trade
     Advertising, Cooperative Advertising and Strategic Partnerships,
     Advertising Agencies
Public Relations and Publicity 251

9 Negotiations and Contracts

Negotiations 259
Letter of Agreement/Contract 260
     Names of Organization and Hotel, Official Dates, Number and
     Kinds of Rooms, Rates, Arrival Pattern, Public Space,
     Complimentary and Reduced Rate Rooms, Prior Visits,
     Working Space, Registration Control, Exhibit Space, Food
     Functions, Refreshment Breaks, Liquor, Audiovisual
     Equipment, Union Regulations, Master Account and Credit
     Procedures, Method of Payment, Termination/Cancellation
     Clauses, Damage Clause: Liquidated or Mitigated Damages,
     Gratuities and Service Charges, Attrition Clause, Arbitration,
     Warranty of Authority, Insurance/Indemnification
Contract Standardization 276
Multiple-Meeting Contracts 278

Part II Convention Services

10 The Service Function

Service is the Key 285
Who Services 288
    Convention Service Manager, Increased Recognition,
    Convention Service Staff
The Transition 297
Importance of Communication 301
An Overview of the Service Function 302

11 Guestrooms

Reservation Systems 311
    Postal Reply/Fax Response Cards, Toll-Free Telephone
    Numbers, Hotel Internet Site Reservations, Rooming Lists,
    Convention Center Housing Bureaus, Third-Party Housing
    Companies, Tally Sheets
Room Assignment 321
    Rate Structures, Complimentary Arrangements, Priorities,
    Room Types, Release and Confirmation Dates, Arrival/
    Departure Pattern, Other Hotels
Managing Room Blocks 327
    No-Shows/Overbooking, Historical Performance
Check-in/Check-out 332
    Check-in Procedure, Check-out Procedure
The Computer Influence 333
    Reservations, Registration and Room Assignment, Check-out
    and Billing, Reports and Analysis Applications

12 Preparing for the Event

Pre-Convention Meeting 341
    Key Personnel Roster
The Specification Sheet (Resume) 343
The Function Sheet (Banquet Event Order) 347
The Importance of Communication 350
Communicating Details Electronically 350
The Importance of Follow-up 352

13 Function Rooms and Meeting Setups

Function Rooms 361
    Types of Function Rooms, Function Room Size and
    Layout, Meeting Room Plans, Timetable for Setup and
    Breakdown

Managing Function Rooms 370
    *Sales Restrictions on Function Space, Function Room
    Charges, Release Dates, Several Meetings Simultaneously,
    Use of Meeting Rooms by Others, Employee Procedure Manuals*
Meeting Setups 376
    *Function Room Furniture, Basic Meeting Setups, Setups
    with Tables*
Meeting Rooms of the Future 387
Monitoring Function Room Usage 387

14 Food and Beverage Service

Food Service 393
    *Types of Food Functions, Themed Events, Changing Tastes,
    Types of Service, Pricing Food Functions, Attendance,
    Attrition, Function Rooms, Control Procedures, Staffing,
    Uniserve or Duoserve*
Beverage Service 408
    *Types of Setups, Hospitality Suites, Brands, Pricing Methods,
    Beverage Control*
Post-Function Actions 414
In-House Coordination: Large vs. Small Properties 415
    *Role of the Catering Manager, Servicing and Selling,
    Communication and Cooperation*

15 Audiovisual Requirements

Outside or Inside? 423
    Audiovisual Specialists, In-House Equipment
Types of Audiovisual Equipment 427
    *Sound Systems, Lighting, Lecterns, Screens, Slide Projectors,
    Overhead Projectors, Rearview Projection, Motion Picture
    Film Projectors, Videotape Projectors, Projection Systems
    for Computer Presentations, Projector Stands, Multimedia
    Presentations, Simultaneous Interpretations, Virtual
    Conferencing, Spare Parts, Other Presentation Devices*
Charging for Audiovisual Equipment 446
Union Regulations 446
Signs and Notices 447
    Hotel Rules, Sign Responsibility, Price Schedule, Locations

16 Admission Systems and Other Services

Convention Registration 453
Convention Security 454
    *Controlled Admission, Ticket Arrangements, Uncontrolled
    Admission, Exhibit Security*
Other Services 458
    *Convention Headquarters Room, Convention Hospitality
    Suites, Guest Packages, Telephones, Printing and Duplication,
    Decorations, Entertainment, Preferred Suppliers*

Guest/Companion Programs 463
 Building Guest/Companion Attendance, Activities for
 the Attendee's Guests (Shopping Trips, Sightseeing and
 City Tours, Guest Lectures, Other Activities), Activities
 for Children
Checklists 468

17 Exhibits and Trade Shows

The Scope of Exhibits and Trade Shows 475
 Types of Exhibits, Exhibit Assignments
Exhibit Planning 478
 Key Trade Show and Exhibit Personnel (The Trade Show
 Manager, Exposition Service Contractors/Decorators,
 Exhibitors), Scaled Drawings, Layouts, Photo File,
 Timetable, Show Hours and Room Assignments, Labor
 Regulations, Insurance
Exhibit Billing Procedures 490
 Hotel's Rental Charge, Exposition Service Contractor's Fee
Convention Shipping and Receiving 492
 Exhibit Shipping, Recommended Address Terminology,
 Shipping Methods, Incoming Shipping Costs

18 Convention Billing and Post-Convention Review

Convention Billing 503
 The Master Account, Time of Payment, Guest Credit, Tips
 and Gratuities, HSMAI's Suggested Payment Schedule
Post-Convention Review 513
 Comparison with Projections, Function Attendance,
 Special Services, Individual Comments, Post-Convention
 Reporting, Final Appraisal

Appendix I

Directory of U.S. Trade Organizations and Publications 525

Appendix II

Directory of Canadian Trade Organizations and Publications 529

Index

Index 531

Introduction

Much has happened in the hotel-convention business since the first edition of this text. The sweeping changes taking place in this booming industry and the growing impact of the convention business to properties of all sizes have prompted the sixth edition of this manual.

Convention Sales and Services was designed to serve as a primer and guide to those who are already involved in this exciting segment of the hospitality field. The first five editions of this book were tested on the firing line in university classrooms and in hotel sales offices throughout the world. Most gratifying have been the critiques of seasoned industry professionals who have commented, "Yes, this is just the way it's done... large or small, those properties that are successful follow the procedures as laid out in your text."

To maintain that level of credibility, the contents of this sixth edition have been substantially updated. Based on the suggestions of professors, students and industry professionals, a number of improvements have been made in this text. The discussions of many topics have been rewritten to update them and to make them more comprehensive. These revisions are based on current trade journal articles, seminar notes, book reviews, and input from industry leaders. New or expanded sections, providing the latest research information and current industry practices, have been added to every chapter, and new photographs and forms enhance the content.

Part I offers practical insight into the different kinds of meetings and conventions, the types of organizations that stage such events, and the people who hold the key to site selection. It also provides advice and suggestions on how to reach and sell to these important groups and people. Material also includes how to analyze a hotel property to determine which segments of the market may be sold and serviced successfully and how to organize a staff to go after desired business. Practical advice is also given on how to finalize an event through negotiations and letters of agreement.

Part II deals with the convention service itself. Once the client has been sold on holding his or her event in a hotel, its staff must ensure that the event flows smoothly. Each convention is a custom production, and skilled, knowledgeable people are needed for its execution. Repeat business is essential for the success of any hotel, and professional convention service is absolutely necessary for a hotel to compete for its share of business.

Text Features

Our purpose through this book is to present convention management in a readable style. Each chapter contains numerous cross-referenced illustrations, actual industry examples, and quotes from successful hotel sales and service managers to enhance comprehension and encourage retention of the text material. Several case studies are also included in the text to illustrate the practical application of principles presented and provide ample opportunity for group "brain-storming."

It is our goal to make this material readily understandable and usable. Toward that end, we have added several industry examples and periodic sections on "Putting It All Together." The initial "Putting It All Together" sections provide case study examples of how concepts discussed in the text can be used to create successful sales and marketing strategies and to execute successful functions. In later chapters, students will be given the opportunity to test their knowledge, using the concepts discussed in the chapter to solve hypothetical problems themselves.

End of Chapter Material

A chapter summary and study questions follow each chapter. The questions help the reader pull together and integrate the basic concepts of the chapter. In addition, these questions give the reader an opportunity to see how his or her own values will affect the way management principles will be applied.

The "Key Terms" that appear at the end of the chapter have been set in bold type in the chapter text. These terms are defined at the end of the chapter

A listing of "Internet Sites" has been added to the end of each chapter to enable students to obtain additional information (and industry examples) from the firms and organizations discussed in the chapter. The Web addresses listed are current as of the writing of this text. Addresses may change, however; if a site is not available at the address given, a search engine can be used to access its new location.

Instructional Support Package

A comprehensive Instructor's Manual to assist teachers in the classroom use of the text is available. Each chapter in the Instructor's manual includes a review outline, a list of key terms, a suggested lecture outline, and a test item file.

Transparency Masters

A complete series of transparency masters has also been prepared for the instructor. To a large degree, the study of convention sales and service is a study of forms. The charts, exhibits and figures from the text have been enlarged and reproduced in a separate manual available to educators.

Successful hotel executives must have a complete grasp of convention sales and service, which offers an opportunity to go after *desired* guests, not just numbers. No one can progress to executive ranks today without a full understanding of the role meetings and convention business plays in hotel profitability, so this lucrative market merits careful study by both students and those already in the field.

Convention Sales and Services will detail how the hospitality industry is responding to this market, and show you how selling to or servicing the conventions and meetings market offers the opportunity for you to enjoy an exciting and rewarding career with practically limitless potential.

James R. Abbey, Ph.D., CHA
Las Vegas, Nevada

In Memoriam

The first editions of this book were co-authored with Milton T. Astroff. Milt, known throughout the hospitality industry as an innovator, was the founder and first publisher of such publications as *Meetings & Conventions*, *Travel Master,* and *Training*. He also wrote a number of articles and shared his immense knowledge — and sense of humor — at hospitality industry seminars and conventions and at seminars on management development, sales training and meeting development. Milt, who later held chief executive and marketing positions in several prominent communications companies and specialty trade newspapers, not only contributed his invaluable knowledge and insights to *Convention Sales and Services*, but he also personally typeset and designed the layout of the text's fifth edition.

The industry experienced a great loss when Milt passed away in the spring of 2000. And I personally lost a special friend and business partner. This book is dedicated to Milt, who so profoundly influenced so many of today's hospitality professionals.

Convention Sales and Services

Part I

Convention Sales

Learning Objectives:

This portion of your text introduces you to the nature and scope of today's growing and changing meetings market. When you have studied this chapter, you will:

- Be able to identify the types of meetings held and tell when and why each is typically used.

- Know the types of organizations that hold meetings and detail specific requirements of each.

- Be aware of the current trends that are impacting the meetings industry.

Outline

The Convention and Meetings Industry Today

The Scope of Today's Meetings Market

- Types of Meetings
- Who Holds Meetings
- Emerging Types of Meeting Facilities

Other Trends in the Meetings Industry

- Globalization
- Second-Tier Cities
- The Growth of Convention Centers
- Third-Party Meeting Planners
- Increased Use of Technology
- Revenue Management

The Meetings Market: Types of Meeting Customers

Keith Patrick
Director of Convention Services
Pinehurst, Inc., North Carolina

"Meeting terminology is important...Those in the hotel business who aspire to be true professionals seek to understand the differences in order to help the meeting planner produce a successful event...As a convention sales or service professional, you'll be working with an ever-increasing professional group of people referred to as meeting planners or convention managers...Only by knowing the groups and the purpose of their meetings can you service them toward the accomplishment of their goals...."

1 Introduction to the Convention, Meetings and Trade Show Industry

O nly three decades ago, the hospitality industry looked at servicing the conventions and meetings market as a "necessary evil," and meetings and convention business was regarded as a fairly insignificant market segment. Except for a few resort destinations, such as Miami Beach, Las Vegas and a handful of premier hotels in the nation's larger cities, there were few locations suitable for large meetings. The available facilities were usually limited to ballrooms designed for social functions. Lighting was more conducive to dining and dancing than meetings; meeting facilities were limited and scattered throughout the property. Audiovisual equipment, if available at all, was minimal, and contracts between properties and meeting planners were practically nonexistent.

Few hotels had convention departments to assist in meeting planning or to solicit convention business, and the position of convention service manager was a rarity. Most meetings business was handled by the property's sales department, which handled sporadic requests from non-professional meeting planners, such as secretaries or clerical support staff.

The few meetings held were typically conventions or small business meetings. Convention delegates were usually white males attending primarily for the food and fun. Activities for spouses—who were usually wives—were scarce, and since people didn't travel much, the convention was looked upon as a "perk"—a mini-vacation of sorts.

The Convention and Meetings Industry Today

The conventions and meetings industry is vastly different today. Projections based on the most recent study commissioned by the Convention Industry Council (CIC) discloses that the average association delegate spends $232 per day and that approximately $115 billion dollars annually is generated directly from meeting, conventions, expositions and incentive travel (see Figure 1.1).[1] And, this figure is only a fraction of the $315 billion—supporting nearly four million jobs—generated indirectly from the convention business; local transportation companies, hotel suppliers, retail stores and other businesses all benefit (see Figure 1.2).

While leisure travelers may represent larger numbers for the hospitality industry, meeting attendees—who frequently travel on an expense account—bring in the lion's share of revenue in addition to benefiting properties by filling "soft spots" and generating word of mouth business. Therefore, the lucrative convention and meetings market is becoming an increasingly important—and competitive—target market (see Figure 1.3).

To take advantage of the profitable meetings and conventions market, it is important to become aware of the trends that have affected it over the past few years.

One of the most important factors impacting the convention industry has been the increase of female business travelers. As a result of the growth of this market segment, which is generally more discriminating and security conscious than the typical male business traveler, many properties have offered additional amenities. Premium shampoos and lotions, hair dryers and makeup mirrors, all-female floors accessed by special keys or cards, improved lighting in parking lots and additional security measures are just some of the services now offered to meet the female traveler's needs. Areas such as open atrium lobbies and business floors with conference space have been added to provide female business travelers an alternative to meeting with male clients or associates in their rooms or a hotel bar. Hotel bars, too, have changed. Many have adopted an open format in lobby areas, making them more inviting for casual patronage and providing a more secure and relaxed setting for business contacts.

Figure 1.1 WHERE ASSOCIATION DELEGATES SPEND MONEY.

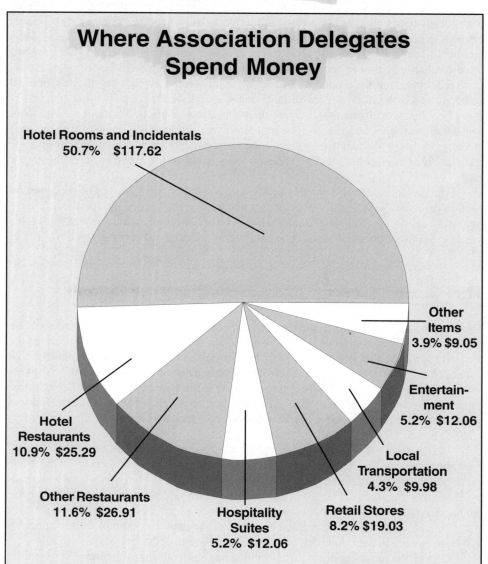

The International Association of Convention and Visitors Bureaus determined that the average association meeting delegate spent approximately 232 dollars per day at national and international conventions. It is important to note that this survey includes only association delegates; corporate delegates can be expected to spend an additional ten to twenty dollars per day more, as many are on expense accounts and usually entertain potential clients while attending meetings and conventions. **Source: Adapted from the International Association of Convention and Visitors Bureaus' Delegate Expenditure Study. Used with permission.**

tions are offered by a number of other organizations as well. Certified Association Executives (CAE) are trained by the American Society of Association Executives (ASAE), while the International Association for Exposition Management (IAEM) offers the Certified Exposition Manager (CEM) program. Also, professional groups such as Meeting Professionals International (MPI), the Society of Corporate Meeting Professionals (SCMP), the Professional Convention Management Association (PCMA), and the Society of Incentive Travel Executives (SITE) have been formed—and joined in force by meeting planners—for additional training and networking. A Certified Meeting Manager (CMM) program, for example, is offered by Meeting Professionals International (MPI). This program, begun in Europe at the request of meeting planners who wanted a more comprehensive educational program, was recently approved for the U.S. Viewed as a graduate curriculum for meeting planners, the CMM program provides senior-level certification on a global scale.

The increased sophistication of independent meeting planners—and the rise of professional meeting planning intermediaries, such as convention service companies and the entry of travel agents into the field—make it imperative for properties to service meeting planners at a highly professional level. Most properties today operate convention sales departments to service this most important market segment, with a corresponding interest in education and an upsurge in creativity on the part of those in the hospitality industry to enable convention service professionals to effectively compete for and service such lucrative bookings.

The Scope of Today's Meetings Market

Despite rising costs for transportation and hospitality services, more and more meetings are being held. They are held for a variety of purposes: to keep abreast of today's ever-changing technology; to keep sales goals on track; to meet for group motivation and rewards; and many more. No longer are meetings limited to a few annual conventions that simply require a large ballroom for a general session and a few food functions or small business meetings where attendees are informed by a speaker armed only with a flip chart and a few marking pens. Today's attendees—and planners—expect a lot more. Hotel business centers, that are complete with computers, fax machines and sophisticated communications equipment have become commonplace; state-of-the-art audiovisual equipment is expected; and many conventions have taken on the appearance of lavish productions—complete with exotic foods and decor—to attract attendees. Picture an event on the scale of a Broadway production with an anticipated run of just a week or even a few days, with a professional cast and production people, and the budget committed to accomplish a presentation on this level, and you then have an idea of the scope of many of today's meetings.

This boom is a far cry from the meetings picture during the recession of the early 1990s. During that time, properties were willing to make a number of concessions to attract meetings business.

In today's booming meetings market, however, the supply cannot keep pace with the demand. Beverly Kinkade, vice president and director of association sales for the Sheraton Corporation, says,

> "Small meetings are up, and so is training activity...Convention attendance is up in all industries...There is greater demand across the board."[2]

Now planners are seeing how economic cycles play a vital role in how hotels respond to group business. The greater demand, which is due in part to there having been virtually no growth in the upscale and luxury property category, has resulted in:

- tighter availability of rooms, especially at peak times
- the need for longer lead times
- stricter enforcement of cancellation and attrition penalties
- a higher premium on "all hold" meeting space
- fewer concessions on food and beverage functions
- less flexibility in "comp" allotments; and
- tougher negotiations of other amenities

Bruce Harris, president of Conferon, the nation's largest independent meeting planning company, says,

> "When the economy got better, the pendulum switched to a sellers' marketplace. Prices went up, and the need to make concessions went down. Hotels are putting an end to some of the 'ridiculous' concessions, certain things they felt they had to do to book business despite the fact that they hurt their ability to be profitable."[3]

Although more convention hotels are being built, it is still a seller's market, and contracts and negotiation issues favor hotels. Planners continue to face higher rates, longer lead times, reduced flexibility with dates and stiffer penalties if they fail to fill space. But, the industry is highly cyclical, and a wise hotelier knows that business lost today may be business lost tomorrow, when it is needed. Hotels are looking to hold on to future group business by working with planners, often suggesting flexibility with dates; groups looking for value as well as availability, for example, are urged to consider shoulder seasons rather than peak periods for their meetings.

You still face a great deal of competition in selling your site and facility for today's meeting. If you land a piece of business, you remain very much involved. You have a strong vested interest in the success of the convention. If it goes well and you gain the approval of the event sponsors and attendees, you stand a better chance of getting the repeat business and recommended business which is so very important in the career of anyone in the hospitality business. To successfully compete in the marketplace, it is important to know:

- the types of meetings held
- who plans and holds meetings, and
- the types of properties that can successfully accommodate different meeting groups

Types of Meetings

In the interest of simplicity, we will use the term *convention business*. But we are actually dealing with an entire spectrum of meetings of all types. It would be simpler if all events were just called *meetings*; after all, that's what they basically are. But that's not the way it is. There are a number of not-quite synonyms for the term, with nuances of difference.

Convention. The most commonly used term in the field is **convention**. The dictionary tells us that a convention is a meeting of delegates for action on particular matters. These may be matters of politics, trade, science, or technology, among others.

Today's convention usually involves a general session and supplementary smaller meetings. Conventions are produced both with and without exhibits. Most conventions have a repetitive cycle, the most common of which is annual. Giving market reports, introducing new products, and mapping of company strategy are some common objectives of a convention. The general session usually requires a ballroom or large auditorium for the whole group. Specific problems are discussed in smaller groups, using a number of small breakout rooms.

Conference. A *conference* is a near-synonym for a convention, usually implying much discussion and participation. The word convention is used in trade circles for regular meetings of a general nature. The term conference is used frequently in technical and scientific areas, although it is used in trade as well. The differences are those of semantics rather than execution. A conference program commonly deals with specific problems or developments and may or may not have smaller breakout meetings. Conferences may be small or large in attendance.

Congress. The term *congress* is most commonly used in Europe and in international events. It usually refers to an event similar to a conference in nature. Oddly enough, only in the United States is the term used to designate a legislative body. Attendance at a congress varies a great deal.

Forum. A meeting featuring much back-and-forth discussion, generally led by panelists or presenters, is often called a *forum*. Much audience participation is to be expected, with all sides of a question aired by both panelists and the audience. Two or more speakers might take opposing sides and address the audience rather than each other.

A moderator will summarize points of view and lead the discussion. The audience is usually allowed to ask questions, so a number of microphones must be supplied by the hotel.

Symposium. A *symposium* is similar to a forum, except that conduct seems to be more formal in a symposium. Whether by individuals or panels, the method is one of presentations. Some audience participation is anticipated, but there is generally less of the give-and-take that characterizes a forum.

Lecture. The *lecture* is even more formal or structured, using individual presentation, often by just one expert. It may or may not be followed by questions from the audience. Lectures vary widely in size.

Seminar. The *seminar* format tries to get away from the idea of a presenter or presenters addressing an audience from a platform. A seminar usually involves much participation, much give-and-take, a sharing of knowledge and experience by all. It usually is under the supervision of a discussion leader. This format obviously lends itself to relatively small groups; when such a meeting grows, it generally changes to a forum or symposium.

Workshop. The *workshop* format calls for general sessions involving only small groups that deal with specific problems or assignments. Whether or not the term is used, the workshop format is commonly used by training directors for skill training and drills. The participants actually train each other as they share new knowledge, skills, and insights into problems. Obviously, it is characterized by face-to-face dealing, with a great deal of participation by all.

Clinic. Used a great deal in training activity, the *clinic* offers drills and instruction in specific subjects. It is almost always limited to small groups interacting with each other on an individual basis.

Retreat. A *retreat* is usually a small meeting, typically in a remote location, for the purpose of bonding, intensive planning sessions, or simply to "get away from it all."

Institute. Conferences, seminars and workshops are often offered by an *institute*, which is frequently established within a trade or profession to offer extended educational and training opportunities. The term is often used to suggest further meetings on the same topic. For example, an institute might offer continuing training programs every quarter of the year.

Panel. The *panel* calls for two or more speakers offering viewpoints or areas of expertise. It is open for discussion among the panelists, as well as with the audience. A panel is always guided by a moderator and may be part of a larger meeting format.

Exhibitions and Trade Shows. An *exhibition* usually describes an event held in conjunction with another meeting, such as a convention. The exhibition format is used for display, usually by vendors of goods and services, and has a built-in audience since it is held as part of a convention (see Figure 1.4).

The term **trade show** is used to describe a show that is held for its own sake. In Europe such exhibits, generally held without any type of program, are called *trade fairs*.

Another term used interchangeably is *exposition*. Most industrial, professional, and scientific trade shows are not open to the public. When large scale exhibitions are open to the public, they are referred to as *consumer shows* (examples are home shows, flower and garden shows, auto shows and boat shows) and a modest admission fee is typically charged. Because consumer shows are designed to attract a local clientele, they do not generate a large amount of room revenue for community hotels.

But the trade show concept is often attractive to meeting planners, whose meeting costs can be defrayed by the revenues generated from exhibitors, who are charged for their booth or table space. And, the concept of a "marketplace" showcasing a vast array of new equipment, technology, and ideas often boosts delegate attendance. An interesting convention program coupled with the showcase of the trade show combines to form a strong magnet, drawing increased delegate attendance benefiting show organizer, exhibitor and attendee.

In the past few years, trade shows have increased in scope, with some—such as the annual COMDEX computer show—attracting over a hundred thousand attendees. This growth has resulted in a new industry substructure which includes trade show planning specialists, convention planning services, and auxiliary firms supplying trade show equipment and labor.

Persons and companies who sponsor and manage trade shows often hold membership in the International Association for Exposition Management (IAEM). IAEM has over 3,000 members who plan nearly 5,000 shows and expositions annually.

A trend that is likely to fuel this market segment is the "piggybacking" of meetings—meetings and exhibitions planned in conjunction with those held by others in the same field or related enterprises (see Figure 1.5). This pooling of resources is beneficial to both exhibitors and attendees for a number of reasons:

Figure 1.4. TRADE SHOW EXHIBITION.

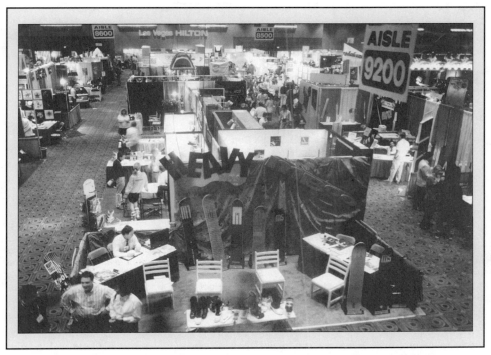

This floor at the Las Vegas Hilton shows a typical trade show exhibit. The convention service manager and the meeting planner have created a master layout that the decorator follows to partition areas for each exhibitor. Such exhibits are of extreme importance to the financial well-being of the trade association.

- access to convention facilities requiring a large minimum amount of exhibit space
- a wider audience base for exhibitors
- a more diverse mix of exhibitors, which would likely draw additional attendees, and
- greater clout for the organizers in hotel negotiations

For the "piggybacking" to be most effective, it is important that all parties "mesh" well. There must be a synergism between products and/or services offered that is readily apparent to attendees, making it more worth their while to attend, and the co-sponsors of events should have enough in common to enable them to work well as a group.

Meetings. All the terms we've defined represent meetings of a sort. When none of the terms seems to apply, the event can always be called simply a *meeting*. This is particularly true when all the attendees are members of a single organization, meeting to discuss organizational affairs, such as stockholder meetings, board of directors meetings, etc. These can attract both a local and an out-of-town clientele, and range from a few attendees to large groups. It is important to understand these various differences in terminology in order to grasp the kind of event the client is trying to produce and to help the meeting planner to effectively carry it out. Much of it has to do with the projection of a desired image. While meeting descriptions are not scientific terms, but loose, often interchangeable ones, proper terminology can help people work together to achieve a tone or image for an event, and in that sense terms are important. For example, a *seminar* connotes something more cerebral

Figure 1.5. PIGGYBACKING.

Conventions and Trade Shows

	Dates	Attendance	Hotels
Bakery Equip. Manufacturers Assn.	Sep 13-15	6,000	Conv. Center
Food Service Consultants Soc. Int'l.	Sep 13-17	200	Alexis Park
N. Amer. Assn. of Food Eqip. Mfrs.	Sep 14-17	15,000	Conv. Center

Source: Las Vegas Convention and Visitors Authority

"Piggybacking" or co-sponsoring of meetings and exhibitions at the same time and site for attendees in related fields can help to boost attendance and allow a greater number of exhibitors to show products and services to a wider audience. For example, three different but related groups held simultaneous conventions in Las Vegas: The Bakery Equipment Manufacturers Association, Food Service Consultants Society International, and the North American Association of Food Equipment Manufacturers.

than a *convention*. A *conference* in Chicago may be termed a *congress* in Geneva. A *conference* conjures up a picture of a small group in shirt-sleeves, while a *lecture* promises a more formal presentation to a passive audience. Accurate communication is needed in the convention business, and the ability to use proper terminology is important. Those in the field should understand the various terms used to describe meetings and use them correctly to achieve the professionalism expected by today's more sophisticated meeting planners.

Who Holds Meetings

Once you have determined that convention business, whatever the terminology, is worth going after, the next question deals with determining who holds meetings. Corporations and associations represent the two major types of meeting sponsors. But nonprofit organizations, such as governmental agencies, labor unions, and fraternal and religious organizations also hold conventions, meetings and trade shows. For convenience, we have broken today's convention business into three major categories:

- Corporations
- Associations
- Nonprofit organizations

Corporations. The corporate meeting is of extreme importance. Such meetings can be likened to an iceberg. A small tip protrudes above the surface while a huge mass floats beneath it. Companies have no need or desire to publicize their meetings, but meet they do. And often. They hold small meetings, large meetings, and middle-sized meetings. Business executives stress communications, and one of the most fundamental methods of intra-company communications is the meeting. Company meetings are a prime part of the market and growing rapidly.

Attending conventions and conferences is very definitely a part of professional and business activity. Such expenses as transportation, lodging, food, entertainment of clients, and registration fees are tax-deductible as business or professional expenses. Companies that stage meetings for dealers or their own staffs may deduct the cost of such events as business expenses. This has been a strong stimulant to meetings and conventions. It is also a strong factor in site selection, as those who attend look to such business trips as quasi-vacations.

Insurance companies are important to the hotel sales manager because they are such prolific meeting sponsors. There are continuing training programs for personnel. The prize, however, is the incentive trip for their top salespeople. These deluxe events are produced in various sizes and durations. Such trips are free to the attendee but are not planned exclusively for recognition and recreation. Most insurance companies schedule training and sales technique workshops in conjunction with such trips. Incentive trips are promoted a year in advance and therefore require more advanced planning. However, so many insurance company meetings are produced in such a variety of sizes and types that the insurance company meeting planner is a prime contact for hotels from the large property to the small inn.

Associations. The most visible convention organizers are the many associations throughout the country—indeed throughout the world because many of them are truly international. Associations vary in size and nature. Their scope ranges from small regional organizations through statewide associations to national and international ones. Perhaps the best-known group to hotel sales managers is the American Society of Association Executives (ASAE). This group's membership consists of key decision makers who play major roles in the selection of cities and hotels for their own associations' conventions. Associations can be divided into several general categories:

- Trade associations
- Professional and scientific associations
- Veterans and military associations
- Educational associations
- Technical societies

Trade Associations. Trade associations are usually considered the most lucrative form of meeting business because their members are composed mostly of executives who have made it in business. Such conventions are often held in conjunction with exhibits.

A good example of such a group in the hospitality industry is the National Restaurant Association, which meets annually in Chicago with more than 110,000 in attendance. Big industrial suppliers of kitchen equipment and restaurant supplies do a great amount of entertaining during the convention.

It is a rare trade that doesn't have at least one association. Many have several national ones, involving different levels of the trade. It is common for the manufacturers in a trade to have their own association; the wholesalers and distributors to have theirs; and the retailers, still a third.

The photographic industry shows this pattern. There is the Photographic Marketing Association, whose members are retailers and photofinishers. They hold an annual convention of national status followed by a regional one six months later. The National Association of Photographic Manufacturers is a smaller group made up exclusively of domestic manufacturers. Its members meet once a year, while its boards and committees meet more frequently. The Photographic Manufacturers and Distributors Association has the broader membership base made up of foreign and domestic companies. In addition, there are a number of regional associations of independent camera dealers that hold regional exhibits and meetings. All of these organizations are trade associations.

Professional and Scientific Associations. The numerous associations in the professional and scientific fields are also inveterate meeting holders. Their subject matter ranges far and wide, but they all share a love for meetings. Each profession has its national association as well as state chapters.

The American Medical Association and the American Bar Association are well known to almost everyone. The Hospitality Sales Marketing Association International (HSMAI) is a good example in the hospitality industry, meeting annually for a major get-together and holding a number of regional and state workshops throughout the year.

Veterans and Military Associations. Meetings are held by both "active-status" and veterans reunion groups of the military associations. These groups have been known to get quite rowdy but are often good spenders. Such groups have large annual conventions and are usually interested in a resort-recreation site.

Educational Associations. Elementary, high school and college teachers and others affiliated with academe are prime sources of business. They hold many national meetings, and every state has a teachers' association of some sort as well. Even educators in the lodging and food service industry have their own association, the Council on Hotel, Restaurant and Institutional Education (CHRIE).

One aspect of the educational group business that makes it particularly attractive to many hotels is the time of year these groups meet. While not excessive spenders, they frequently meet during the slow summer months.

Technical Societies. Associations also are found among technical professions. The Society of Motion Picture and Television Engineers holds two national conventions a year. The Professional Photographers of America holds a national event annually, and most states have chapters that hold annual conventions of their own. In addition, there are specialty groups such as wedding photographers and newspaper photographers that have their own associations and conventions. Think of any profession or career and you'll find at least one association. Librarians, teachers, hospital administrators, engineers—all have associations.

Nonprofit Organizations. There are many nonprofit organizations that just don't fit into the above slots, but they take no back seat when it comes to meetings.We have all seen political conventions on television. The camera shows the main floor, but think of the demand for smaller meeting rooms, suites, food functions, and so on. The story is repeated on a more modest scale on the state and regional level. All add to the market.

Hotels house weekend seminars on sex and marital problems, women's roles in the world, and social problems, to mention a few. The meetings of nonprofit organizations are just like those of other associations, and should be sold and serviced just like them.

Government Agencies. Many branches of the government have a need to hold meetings off government premises for government employees or with the public. The Department of Agriculture, the Department of Commerce, the World Health Organization, and the United Nations affiliates are prolific meeting planners.

These agencies are funded in a variety of ways. Chambers of Commerce are usually membership organizations that are privately funded. The Department of Agriculture, of course, spends public money. The labels are not important so long as you understand how they operate, what their meeting needs are, and how you can sell and serve them efficiently.

(A word may be in order here. There is a love for acronyms among associations and governmental agencies that can drive the outsider up the wall. Each association seems to feel that the world is focused on it and that everyone knows what XYZ stands for. It also leads to crossed lines. Take AMA. It can refer to the American Medical Association or the American Management Association, both prolific meeting holders. It takes a bit of caution. Listen carefully and take good notes. Take nothing out of context. Soon, you'll talk in acronyms, too.)

Labor Unions. Labor unions have become one of the most important economic forces in the world. The largest unions are in the construction, manufacturing, mining, and transportation fields.

Labor unions are organized on four levels: local, state and regional, national, and international. Each level represents countless meetings and conventions, providing a fertile market for hotels. Most union members spend slightly less than the average convention delegate, but they still provide hotels with a sizable piece of business.

Large labor union conventions are similar to political conventions. They are held annually or biannually and include committee meetings, debates, speeches, and guest speakers.

SMERF Groups. The industry has coined an acronym for certain nonprofits—the term SMERF (which stands for social, military, educational, religious and fraternal) has come to represent a major market segment for many properties because of the large number of room nights these groups occupy each year—largely during property slack times.

SMERF groups have three common characteristics: they are very price sensitive; they are more likely to book meetings during the hotel's off-season; they very often have nonprofessional planners who change from year to year.

Religious groups, for example, are not traditionally big spenders, but they are a viable market. Denominations hold regional and national meetings as well as seminars and ministerial workshops. Their events frequently begin on Monday and close on Thursday, providing weekend resort properties with midweek business.

Although price sensitive (attendees tend to double and triple up in rooms, eat most meals off-property, and spend little money in lounges), SMERF groups are proving to be increasingly important for properties.

Barbara McDonald, national account manager for Sheraton Corporation's Chicago sales office says:

> "SMERF business used to be the lowest rated business. The perception has been that these meetings are groups like fraternity chapters coming to have a beer brawl in your hotel, and that's just not so. The SMERF market is just as important as the corporate and other markets because the SMERF groups fill our down time. It's that simple. Also, small SMERF business can lead to much larger business. If a CEO comes in with his fraternity and likes the hotel, you could have just landed another piece of business."[4]

According to Warren Breaux, assistant vice president of national sales for Hyatt Hotels Corporation:

"Hotels must have at least 70 percent occupancy to get a return on the investment of building the property. The four-and-a-half months worth of weekends, holidays, and seasonally distressed times are very difficult to fill, but this is a market that can help fill it. We would certainly rather fill our rooms at a reasonable, yet lower, rate than let these rooms go vacant. But we can't use that philosophy 365 days a year."[5]

SMERF groups do not follow a normal business schedule, and shop for the best rates, but they provide an excellent source of revenue during slack times. A property that can offer discount rates—and is willing to assist the largely nonprofessional meeting planners—can find that SMERF groups may make a considerable impact on the property's revenues.

Emerging Types of Meeting Facilities

The demands of the meetings market have changed greatly over the past decade. Hospitality facilities that wish to continue to enjoy a share of the meetings market must be aware of current trends, such as an increase in smaller meetings and an increasing cost-consciousness as associations and corporate planners demand a greater return on their meeting investments. The hospitality industry has met the changing needs of meeting planners in a number of ways, with some of the greatest changes taking place in the emergence of all-suite hotels and conference centers.

All-Suite Hotels. All-suite hotels were originally positioned to attract two market segments: business travelers who wanted "more than a room" and the relocation market. All-suite hotels, with their separate living rooms, complimentary "perks" such as breakfasts and cocktail hours, and homey atmospheres serve as "temporary residences," and are especially attractive because their features are available at rates competitive with standard hotel rooms.

One of the reasons that prices are competitive is that all-suite hotels eliminate many costly features, such as lavish lobbies, a wide choice of restaurants and entertainment facilities, and extensive meeting space. While meeting planners look for these amenities—especially for large meetings—many are attracted by the features offered by the all-suite hotels.

First, all-suite hotels are ideal for board meetings and small training sessions as each suite can serve as a small breakout room, and the atmosphere is conducive to conducting both business and personal conversations. Second, all-suite hotels solicit the smaller markets that are virtually ignored by the larger properties; larger properties are often perceived to be more interested in serving groups of 200 or more, while groups of 50 or less seemed to get far less of the hotel staff's attention. Third, the worries about room assignments are eliminated—every attendee is offered a suite and therefore receives VIP treatment. In addition, meeting planners of small, regional meetings find that attendees are willing to pay for the perceived value of a suite over a conventional hotel room.

Many chains are targeting the small meetings market by developing all-suite properties. Embassy Suites, a forerunner in the development of all-suites properties, has formed a national group and meeting planning service department and offers a toll-free number to planners arranging meetings for groups of 300 or less (see Figure 1.6). Marriott also offers all-suite properties (with approximately 3,000 sq. ft. of meeting space) to accommodate groups of 300 or less to attract small corporate meetings.

Conference Centers. **Conference centers** differ from hotels in several ways. First, the *design* of conference centers typically differs from meeting facilities offered by hotels and resorts. Meeting rooms are situated away from high traffic areas to minimize distractions, and offer conveniently located breakout areas that are constantly refreshed. Since many conference sessions run for several hours, meeting rooms are designed for endurance and comfort and are equipped with commonly used audiovisual equipment (see Figure 1.7).

In addition, dining rooms often offer buffet meals for greater flexibility and to eliminate the hassles of developing set menus. Dining areas are often equipped with half walls, large plants and other decor that offers privacy for small groups. Guest rooms are usually roomier to provide work and study space, and additional facilities, such as small offices, libraries and computer centers, are usually included in conference center design. Most conference centers also offer a "concierge" concept. Secretarial personnel provide information, typing, transcribing, fax, copying and mailing services to ensure smooth meetings.

A significant difference between hotels and conference centers is the *pricing policy*. Most conference centers offer their own version of the *Full American Plan*. This *package* price, available either per day or per person, includes rooms, meals, breaks, meeting rooms, audiovisual equipment and other needs (see box titled "Conference Center Pricing"). This "one-stop shopping", for a **complete meeting package** eliminates unexpected charges and is considered a real value by many meeting planners.

Another important factor is that conference center *bookings* can be made on a 24-hour basis. If a meeting runs longer than expected, the group doesn't have to be concerned about incurring additional, often exorbitant, rental costs or having to vacate to accommodate another group.

Today's largest independent conference centers are Dolce International, which operates conference center resorts in the United States, Canada and France, and Benchmark Hospitality, but many hotels have gotten into the conference center business. Hilton, which recently purchased Promus Corp, acquired the Harrison Conference Centers and now has 17 facilities (and plans to add more), while Marriott opened 20 conference centers in 2000 and plans to double that number by 2005. Starwood Hotels does not have dedicated conference centers, but houses conference center facilities within some of their hotels.

The International Association of Conference Centers (IACC) was founded to assist properties in targeting the conference center market. IACC members include conference centers and related firms and suppliers. To qualify for membership in the IACC, a property must derive a minimum of 60 percent of its business from meeting-related activities and must offer a "total and balanced meeting environment."

Nearly every property—large or small—can handle some type of meeting. Throughout this book, the term *property* is used within the context of hotels. We recognize, however, that hotels come in many styles and shapes, and that many different names are given to properties that house meetings and conventions. In addition, traditional hotels are not the only types of facilities chosen by the meeting planners. Meeting sites may be found in the following:

- resort hotels
- downtown hotels
- suburban hotels
- airport hotels

- large motels and motor hotels
- condominium resorts
- cruise ships

- universities
- company meeting rooms
- specialized meeting centers
- convention centers

The concepts presented throughout this book may be applied to any of these facilities.

Figure 1.6. ALL-SUITE HOTELS.

FINALLY, A HOTEL THAT UNDERSTANDS EVEN SMALL MEETINGS ARE BIG MEETINGS.

At over 145 Embassy Suites® hotels, every meeting will receive our full attention, no matter how big or small. Whether you meet in one of our fully equipped meeting rooms, host a luncheon in our atrium or convene in a conference suite, you'll enjoy quality accommodations and a responsive, efficient staff. We always do whatever it takes to make sure your meeting is a success—all backed by our Meetings Guarantee. After all, just because you're having a small meeting doesn't mean it should be treated that way.

EMBASSY SUITES®

Call 1-800-634-0066
or
visit www.embassy-suites.com
to plan your next meeting.
Circle # 444 on Reader Service Card

© 1999, Promus Hotels, Inc.

This advertisement promotes the benefits of Embassy Suites to meeting planners. Once simply characterized as offering two-room suites and a free breakfast, all-suite hotels have expanded to meet the needs of meeting planners. Embassy Suites, for example, promotes its fully equipped meeting rooms, conference suite, and the attention of its staff to both large and small meetings.

Other Trends in the Meeting Industry

The expanding convention business has been—and will continue to be—impacted by a number of recent trends. Properties and managers who wish to continue to successfully compete for the meetings dollar should be aware of the impact of the following trends:

Figure 1.7. MARKETING A CONFERENCE CENTER TO THE MEETINGS MARKET.

This advertisement for the Hickory Ridge Conference Centre highlights the special meetings amenities offered by the facility. Unlike hotels, which must keep function space flexible, conference centers are dedicated to meetings, and can offer 24-hour holds on meeting rooms and focus on the special needs of meeting planners, such as the PC hookups and cork strips for hanging visual aids mentioned in this ad.

Globalization

The unprecedented events of the early 1990s—the breakup of the former Soviet Union, the opening of trade in European bloc countries, the passage of the North American Free Trade Agreement, and the establishment of the European Economic Community, to name just a few—opened up a vast new market for the convention industry. Potential business was no longer limited to 240 million Americans, but a global village of five billion people with

Conference Center Pricing

Many conference centers offer a Full American Plan pricing policy. This policy, which includes everything involved in the conference—rooms, meals, meeting facilities, and even supplies—allows for a single group billing and enables the meeting planner to stay entirely within budget.

Sample Conference Plan Per Person Per Night

	SINGLE	DOUBLE PER PERSON
Dinner	$18.00	$18.00
Breakfast	8.00	8.00
Lunch	12.00	12.00
Refreshment breaks	10.00	10.00
	$48.00	**$48.00**
15% service charge	7.20	7.20
Conference department	25.00	25.00
Guestroom	119.80*	74.80*
Per Person Price	**$200.00**	**$155.00**

Sample Day Guest Plan Per Person Per Day

Lunch	$12.00
Refreshment breaks	10.00
15% service charge	3.30
Conference department	24.70*
Per Person Price	**$50.00**

*With the Day Guest Plan, any change in the price normally increases or reduces the conference allocation, and allocations to other departments remain constant.

growing economies. **Globalization** has impacted the convention industry in two significant ways.

First, despite a generally sluggish economy, the lifting of restrictions ushered in a boom in world tourism and business travel, increasing attendance at more meetings and conventions at domestic properties.

Second, the economy was ripe for foreign hospitality interests to buy domestic properties. This means there is additional competition for both foreign and domestic convention business, resulting in the need for more creative marketing on the part of domestic properties to attract international business—and keep domestic meetings and conventions.

Second-Tier Cities

As costs for hotel rooms and transportation continue to rise in many major cities, budget conscious meeting planners search for more economical sites. Milwaukee, Wisconsin; Birmingham, Alabama; and Charlotte, North Carolina, are just a few examples of what has become known in the industry as **second-tier cities**.

Meeting planners who face the challenge of "selling" attendees on these seemingly less exotic locations usually find attractive incentives. In Charleston, West Virginia, for example, delegates can go white water rafting or take a cruise on the *West Virginia Belle* during their free time—activities that cannot be enjoyed in Chicago or New York. Attendees for the most part have responded favorably to these diverse activities, and have also noted the friendliness of the people living in second-tier cities. And, all of this is usually enjoyed at a much lower cost than attendees would pay to meet in a larger city.

In addition to lower room rates—and often lower transportation expenses—second-tier cities often offer better service. Besides being enthusiastic about new business, and "rolling out the red carpet," hotels in many second-tier cities often focus on one meeting at a time.

The growth in the choice of second-tier cities has led to the building of convention centers in many of these cities to better serve smaller association and corporate business meetings with larger facilities and up-to-date communications and audiovisual equipment.

The Growth of Convention Centers

The nation's exhibit and meeting space has doubled over the past ten years, largely due to new or expanded convention centers. First-tier cities, including Chicago, Orlando, San Diego, Las Vegas and Los Angeles, have expanded or built additional, modernized facilities. Second-tier cities, such as Mobile, Alabama; Providence, Rhode Island; and suburbs of New York, New Orleans and Atlanta have also built new centers to attract state and regional groups and national groups with local connections (see Figure 1.8).

Most convention centers are publicly owned and are supported by taxes on hotel rooms. Known as hotel occupancy, room or bed taxes, these fees vary considerably. High room taxes are often a factor in site selection, and can price a city out of a planner's budget.

Other convention facilities are privately owned. The Sands Expo and Convention Center in Las Vegas, for example, is the largest privately owned facility in the nation. It already boosts over 900,000 square feet of exhibit space and 23 meeting rooms, and additional expansion is planned.

There are, of course, differences in how public and private convention centers operate and how they solicit and service business. In Chapter 7, we will discuss how hotel salespeople can work with convention centers to increase business for their properties.

Third-Party Meeting Planners

Today, it is not always easy to identify the meeting decision maker. While hotel salespeople formerly dealt almost exclusively with corporate and association meeting planners, third-party planners (either independents or meeting management firms) are becoming more prevalent in the industry.

Corporate downsizing, the increased complexity of negotiations in a seller's market, and increased use of Internet technology has many organizations looking outside their staffs for meeting planning services. Since these intermediaries are hired "out-of-house," a

Figure 1.8. MARKETING A CONVENTION CENTER TO MEETING PLANNERS.

These ads promote the New Orleans Ernest N. Morial Convention Center. The ad campaign was designed to favorably compare the facility to facilities available in other cities and to promote the convention center's easy access to the city's attractions and first-class accommodations.

Many second-tier cities have built all-new convention centers to target state and regional groups or national groups with local connections. These convention centers are "user friendly," with visual appeal and flexibility. Most can host a wide range of events, are equipped with the latest in audiovisual and communications technology, and offer a number of services, including on-call exposition contractors and completely staffed business centers and food service facilities.

To make these centers more attractive and convenient, many are attached to an "anchor" hotel. The Pennsylvania Convention Center in Philadelphia, for example, envisioned an attached hotel in its development plan, and an attached 1,200 room Marriott opened in 1995, just two years after the Convention Center. The adjacent hotel, easily accessed by skywalk, added an additional 38,500 square feet of exhibit space and a 33,000 square foot grand ballroom to the city's new facility. The Minneapolis Convention Center connects four major hotels by skywalk, ensuring accessibility even in inclement weather.

NEW ORLEANS IS PUTTING THE SQUEEZE ON FLORIDA

...by peeling away event after event from our southern neighbor. Here's why. In New Orleans, you won't shuttle your budget away. Everything your attendees want at a convention is within walking distance of our 1.7-million-square-foot Morial Convention Center: world-famous restaurants, jazz clubs, quaint paddlewheelers, the incomparable French Quarter and 16,000 first-class hotel rooms.

This great package has made New Orleans America's #1 Convention City.* Our attendance-building magic will get your juices flowing.
Call 504/582-3023.
Fax 504/582-3088.
*Metropoll IV

ERNEST N. MORIAL CONVENTION CENTER
NEW ORLEANS®
FORMERLY NEW ORLEANS CONVENTION CENTER

NEW ORLEANS IS THE REASON CHICAGO PLAYS THE BLUES.

In the old days, a big show had no other choice than Chicago. That tune won't play anymore. New Orleans has 700,000 gross square feet of contiguous exhibit space (soon to grow to 1.1 million) on one floor, under one roof. Blend in our 25,000 citywide hotel rooms and 20,000 airline seats per day.

Then compare our reasonable work rules and lower labor costs and add in New Orleans' attendance-building magic.

That's a combo that'll jazz up your bottom line.

Call 504/582-3023.
Fax 504/582-3088.

ERNEST N. MORIAL CONVENTION CENTER
NEW ORLEANS®
FORMERLY NEW ORLEANS CONVENTION CENTER

SHERMAN WAS ONLY THE FIRST TO BURN ATLANTA.

Why are more and more conventions marching to New Orleans? Because New Orleans has hot entertainment, world-famous restaurants, quaint paddlewheelers and the charming French Quarter — all within walking distance of 16,000 first-class hotel rooms and the 1.7-million-square-foot Morial Convention Center.

Win the bottom-line battle. Make New Orleans your weapon.
Call 504/582-3023.
Fax 504/582-3088.

ERNEST N. MORIAL CONVENTION CENTER
NEW ORLEANS®
FORMERLY NEW ORLEANS CONVENTION CENTER

new industry buzzword— *outsourcing*—has been coined. These third-party planners can be broken down into several categories:

- Independent Meeting Planners
- Association Management Companies
- Destination Management Companies
- Incentive Travel Houses
- Travel Agents

Independent meeting planners. *Independent meeting planners* are private contractors (firms or individuals) who provide planning services directly to a client. Increasingly, planners are leaving their associations and corporations to set up shop as independents. Such planners are generally easy to work with because they are experienced. They function as intermediaries, and are paid a fee, which can vary. Some independent meeting planners simply assist corporate in-house meeting planners; others are responsible for the entire execution of the meeting. Interestingly, these companies often employ former hotel salespeople who know how to negotiate with hotels.

The largest of the meeting management companies are Conferon and HelmsBriscoe. These companies often team up with similar businesses (especially Internet companies) to offer a more comprehensive package of planning, housing, and reservations. Conferon, for example, has licensed the technology of Passkey.com, a large housing company that is replacing many convention and visitor center housing bureaus, to enable them to more easily interface with the hotel community.

Meeting management companies search out hotel sites and aid their clients in conducting meeting programs. These third-party planners make their money by charging a flat fee to the meeting organization or by seeking a commission from the hotel.

In years past, hotels only paid commissions (usually 10 percent of the room rate) to travel agents. However, in the early 1990s, when hotels were struggling to fill rooms, many properties agreed to pay commissions to meeting management firms. In today's sellers' market, hotels are reluctant to pay commissions to these third parties, but will do so during slow periods when business is needed.

John S. Parke, CMP, Vice President - National Accounts for Marriott International, says that escalating commissions paid by hotels have led to a glut of new third-party providers and thinks that it is time for industry associations to establish guidelines for third parties. He says:

> "If organizations that plan meetings and conventions along with the
> hotel community call for the implementation of a third party certifica-
> tion, they would initiate the process of viewing third party providers as
> ethical and professional product experts."[6]

Association management companies. *Association management companies* work for smaller associations that do not employ a full time professional staff. In most cases, employees of these firms work through the board of directors of associations to manage meetings and plan conventions and other activities. Often these firms provide management services for two or more associations.

Destination management companies. These firms offer convention and meeting services at the host city. **Destination management companies** may arrange for room accommodations, restaurant reservations, airport shuttle service, entertainment, technical services (teleconferences, audiovisual presentations, etc.), and special programs for attendees and spouses.

Most destination management companies remain "behind the scenes," assisting the meeting planner with the details of the meeting. This type of firm knows the host city, and can provide in-depth information on the destination, both in terms of suppliers and extra convention activities (special sight-seeing tours, etc.)

Incentive travel houses. *Incentive travel houses* deal directly with arranging incentive travel packages for corporations wishing to reward or motivate their staffs or their customers. These packages are usually "first class," and involve an exotic or popular resort location. They typically include a number of "perks" and special amenities not commonly associated with regular hotel and travel packages.

Travel agents. Some travel agents have expanded their traditional role of selling package tours, transportation and guestroom services to offer meeting planning services to corporate accounts. Mega travel agencies, such as BTI America (with 100 meeting planners), McGettigan Partners (150 planners in three offices) and American Express (48 planners) plan everything from board meetings to trade shows.

This transition came naturally, as travel agents were able to keep abreast of changing airline price structures and routes, and many corporate meeting planners are now turning to travel agents to arrange everything from transportation to rooms to meeting space. Since not all travel agents are experienced in meeting planning, corporate clients must carefully select those who have this expertise, and properties may have to work more closely with those who are just learning the meetings field. This association can prove extremely profitable, however, both in terms of meetings business and other individual and group bookings at the property.

A highly controversial subject between hotels and travel agents is the question of commissions on convention business. Generally, a hotel will pay a commission of approximately 10 percent to an agent who books an *independent* or *tour guest* into the hotel. However, *convention rates* are usually quoted *net* and not commissionable further.

What this means is that the hotel will not pay a commission to a travel agent for booking a convention delegate. The airline and ground handler, on the other hand, do pay a 10 percent commission for a convention air tour package.

Increased Use of Technology

New advances in computer, telephone and video technology have radically changed the ways hotels do business and communicate with clients. This new technology includes:

- The Internet
- Fax capability, including Broadcast fax and fax-on-demand
- E-mail
- Video Conferencing
- In-room Technology
- Bar Coding

Internet. Leading this trend is an increasing use of *the Internet,* a worldwide system of computer networks providing easy access to thousands of "pipelines" of database information. The Internet is being used by properties, meeting planners and other property business sources.

Meeting Planner Profile

Today's meeting planners spend thousands of hours a year planning events from simple training meetings to huge conventions involving thousands of participants and hundreds of exhibitors. It is an exciting and varied career, and one which is constantly evolving. So who is the "typical" meeting planner of today?

According to a survey conducted by *Meetings & Conventions* magazine, today's professional meeting planner fits the following profile:

- Male (54% versus 46% female)
- Works in a department with about 11 other people
- Has been at the same job for 8 years
- Earns $52,400 a year (salaries range from $20,000 to $90,000 or more;

(50% of all meeting planners make $30,000 to $59,999)

Duties typically include: budgeting; site selection; negotiating with hotels, airlines and vendors; program planning; trade show and exhibit planning; food and beverage selection; hotel and ground transportation arrangements; and post-meeting evaluation, including surveys of participants and an evaluation of the facility and service provided at each function.

In order to stay on top of market conditions, most belong to one or more professional associations, and find the following skills most useful for their profession: excellent oral and written communication and organizational skills; leadership qualities; flexibility; and the ability to handle pressure.

Meeting planners now use the Internet to search for properties that meet their requirements, "tour" properties, and even auction their event for the best price. At Plansoft.com, for example, meeting planners can search a database of more than 14,000 meeting venues and then forward a RFP (request for proposal) to the desired property. Other sites offering searchable databases can be found at the end of this chapter. Some sites offer meeting facilities only, while others offer direct access to other service providers, such as transportation companies and other key suppliers.

While many meeting planners still rely on site visits to make a final decision, an increasing number are viewing properties through the "virtual tours" offered on hotel web sites. These tours, which vary in their degree of sophistication, are replacing brochures (including video brochures) and even CD-ROMs as an effective way to present a property. If the planner likes what he or she sees, it only takes the click of a mouse to contact the hotel for additional information or a RFP.

One of the newest Internet applications is auctioning meetings. Two companies, EventSource.com and StarCite Inc., offer auctions in which hotels bid on business descibed by planners during a 15-minute on-line auction. At the end of the auction, the planner can select a hotel from among the bidders or the lowest bid wins (the outcome depends on the auction's format). EventSource, which held its first auction in October 1999, reported that participating meeting planners saved an average of 10-32 percent over opening bids -- which opened 25-40 percent below current market prices.

Hotels are also using the Internet to create a presence for their properties, link to other sources of meeting planning business, and conduct market research. Hotel chains use corporate web sites to link their properties; a meeting planner can log on to the corporate site and call up a number of locations. But even small properties, realizing that they are now advertising to a global market, are developing web sites.

In addition to the value of having an individual presence on the Web, many hospitality properties are benefiting from alliances with other entities that service the meetings market. Hotels can be featured on or linked to web sites hosted by their destination cities, their local convention and visitors bureau, or other firms and organizations that offer services to the meetings industry, such as Expedia (expedia.com). A detailed discussion on how the Internet is used to market properties will be presented in Chapter 8.

Last, but certainly not least, the Internet can be used as a powerful research tool. Hotels can use the Internet to research their competition, their target markets, and current economic trends that impact business. Logging on to a competitor's web site provides a wealth of information on its facilities and ability to service meetings. Accessing a particular corporation or association can yield contact information and pertinent facts about meeting history. As an added benefit, the Internet can provide the names of businesses and associations that were not even previously considered by the property.

To keep pace with the changes brought about by technology, today's hotel salespeople are expected to be computer literate. Not only will they be using the Internet for research and bookings, they will most likely use computerized applications for most aspects of the sales and service process (see Chapter 3).

Fax capabillity, Broadcast Fax and Fax-on-demand. While some thought *fax transmissions* would become obsolete due to the popularity of e-mail, fax is still a powerful tool for communicating with meeting planners. *Broadcast fax* is used to send updates on the property and other announcements to meeting planners at regular intervals. *Fax-on-demand* provides a source for meeting planners for meeting room specs, open dates, banquet menus and other meeting-related information by simply dialing a property's fax number. Fax is still an easy and fast way to transmit an existing document.

E-mail. *E-mail* (electronic mail) is becoming increasingly popular for communicating both inter-office and inter-property and with meeting planners and other possible sources of business. The advantage of e-mail over fax (which is simply a copy of a document) is that e-mail can be edited; a meeting planner can be e-mailed a copy of a contract, for example, edit it and return it to the hotel with a minimum of effort. Further information on applications of both fax and e-mail will be presented in Chapters 3 and 8.

Video conferencing. *Video conferencing*, also called *teleconferencing*, has been in use for some time, using satellites to link groups and speakers. New technology has greatly enhanced transmission quality and sound, and has led to other improvements, including multimedia presentations, video-enhanced speakers, instant replay, and "live projection" (projecting a close-up image of the speaker onto a large video screen to bring him or her "closer" to the audience). Additional information on audiovisual technology is provided in Chapter 15.

In-room technology. *In-room technology* already includes the availability of fax machines, voice mail services and computer hookups in guestrooms. Some hotels are offering a separate Internet connection that will not tie up the room telephone line. Other applications include in-room video checkout, voice or electronic control of thermostats and lighting levels, in-room television channels that offer "tours" of the property and display convention programs and other pertinent information to guests, and other innovations.

Brian Beamish, a supplier of voice-processing systems, states,

> "Soon the widespread telephone technology will be linked to computer networks on the information superhighway. I can see an E-mail message from the Internet triggering the light on the telephone to indicate there's a message waiting. Similarly this could also work voice-to-text. Someone could send out a message over the Internet by simply speaking into the phone."[7]

Bar coding. *Bar coding* is currently being used to "code" room keys and for ease in convention registration and accessibility, and it is increasingly being used for inventory control of audiovisual and other convention related equipment (see Chapters 15 and 16).

Revenue Management

Over the past few years, hotels have joined the ranks of airlines and cruise ships in using yield management -- setting room prices based on demand. With today's technology, prices can be revised instantaneously as availability and demand warrant (this concept will be discussed further in Chapter 3).

While this strategy has proven effective in filling rooms, hotels generally realize revenue from a number of sources. Hotels today are interested in more than rates, dates, and space. They are basing pricing on demand, but applying the approach to all the property's profit centers, not just guestrooms. Hotels are now evaluating a group's spending patterns and potential before booking them.

Kostas Trivizas, Director of Revenue Management for the Savoy Group, London, explains:

> "Hotels receive combined requests for meeting rooms, food and beverage, guest rooms, and all of these requests come with a different profit margin, so you want to find the right mix that optimizes the one profit margin at the end for all the departments together. This requires specific forecasting -- demand for guest rooms with meeting rooms, meeting rooms with banqueting rooms, or banqueting rooms alone, or meeting rooms alone...Often what happens is that yield managers end up trying to do tactical optimizing -- last minute close up of rates...revenue management gets to the root, such as correctly formulating pricing issues."[8]

Mr. Trivizas feels that revenue management is one of the most challenging aspects in the industry, and predicts that Revenue Management Director positions, which are marketing driven, will become more commonplace.

Already, hotel chains are evaluating convention and meeting groups with revenue management software. Salespeople input estimates of room revenue and catering revenue in dollars per night, suite and hospitality revenues, arrival and departure patterns, room to function space in square feet per night, and date requirements of prospective meetings. The software then evaluates the business according to what is already on the books, historical trends, and forecasts of potential bookings. Meeting groups are assessed on their ability to meet revenue expectations in food and beverage, audiovisual, recreational usage, telephone revenues, and even retail spending.

Chapter Summary:

As you can see from this overview of the convention and meetings industry, there are a number of factors that must be taken into consideration after the decision has been made to solicit this lucrative market segment. To successfully compete for meetings business, you must have a working knowledge of the various types of meetings and the groups that typically hold them, be aware of the types of facilities that can best sell and service the various segments within the meetings market, and stay abreast of trends impacting the industry to enable you to develop effective strategies for attracting meetings business.

In the next chapter, we will take a look at the most important factor in successfully obtaining meetings business—planning—and learn how to successfully market a property. Subsequent chapters will detail establishing a sales office for maximum efficiency, will outline specific strategies for reaching each of the subsegments of the meetings market, and will discuss the issues most important to meeting planners today.

Endnotes:

1. Peter Shure, "P.S.: Production Notes," *Convene*, June 2000, p. 4.
2. Amy Tiebel, "What Buyers Need to Know in a Seller's Market," *Convene*, June 1995, p. 33.
3. Ibid.
4. Dara Wilson, "SMERF GROUPS: Second-Class No Longer," *Association Management*, February 1990.
5. Ibid.
6. Correspondence with John Parke, V.P. National Accounts for MARRIOTT International
7. Deborah McKay-Stokey, *Future Hotelier*, March/April 1995.
8. "Profit Performance: A primer for mastering revenue management," *World Hospitality*, February 2000, p. 4.

Additional References:

- Meeting News Handbook — Selecting a Meeting Site. www.meetingnews.com/handbook.htm
- Professional Meeting Management, 3rd Edition, Edward Polivka, Professional Convention Management Association. www.pcma.org

- "Utilization of the Internet: The Meetings Industry" — Independent study by J.D. Powers and Associates for Meeting Professionals International. www.mpiweb.org
- "Recommendations for Industry Best Practices," Professional Convention Management Association Task Force on Third-Party Practices. www.pcma.org

Internet Sites:

For additional information on the firms and organizations discussed in this chapter, visit the following Internet sites. The Web addresses listed are current as of January 2001. Addresses may change, however; if a site is not available at address below, a search engine can be used to access its new location.

Allmeetings - www.allmeetings.com
Benchmark Hospitality - www.benchmark-hospitality.com
Conferon - www.conferon.com
Convention Industry Council (CIC) - www.c-l-c.org
Dolce International - www.dolce.com
EventSource - www.eventsource.com
Helms Briscoe - www.helmsbriscoe.com
Hilton Hotels - www.hilton.com
International Association of Conference Centers (IACC) - www.iacconline.org
International Association of Convention and Visitors Bureaus (IACVB) - www.iacvb.org
Meetings Industry Mall (MIM) - www.mim.com
Meeting Professionals International (MPI) - www.mpiweb.org

Study Questions:

1. As a convention sales or service manager, what are the types of meeting planners you might be working with? How are these planners different?
2. Why is it important for hotel people to understand the differences between various types of meetings? After all, aren't all the definitions synonymous?
3. Distinguish between a congress and a conference, a symposium and a workshop, a trade show and a consumer show.
4. How do conference centers differ from hotels?
5. Why are many meeting planners choosing second-tier cities for their conventions?
6. What are the characteristics of SMERF groups?
7. Describe the competitive advantages of all-suite hotels in the meetings industry.
8. Briefly describe the important and changing role of third party meeting planners in the meetings market.
9. Explain how technology is reshaping the relationship between meeting planners and hotel salespeople.

10. What is revenue management and how is it affecting the way hotels sell and service the meetings industry?

 Key Terms:

All-suite hotel. A hotel that features rooms larger than typical guest rooms, with a living or working space separate from the bedroom(s).

Complete meeting package. An all-inclusive pricing plan offered at conference centers.

Conference center. A property specifically designed to handle group meetings. Conference centers are often located outside metropolitan areas and may provide extensive leisure facilities.

Convention. A meeting of delegates for action on a particular matter. Usually involves a general session and supplementary smaller meetings. Conventions are produced with and without exhibits.

Destination management companies. Professional management companies specializing in the design and delivery of convention events, activities, tours, staffing, and transportation, utilizing local knowledge, expertise, and resources.

Globalization. The international consolidation of big business and the growing trend for countries to allow free transfer of goods and services across national boundaries.

Second-tier cities. Smaller cities and suburbs of major cities that offer the meeting planner an attractive location and at the same time provide less costly accommodations and transportation.

Trade show. An exhibition with displays, generally held within a trade industry or discipline. May be independent or in conjunction with a convention. Not open to the general public.

Learning Objectives:

This portion of your text covers the importance of developing a marketing plan in order to compete successfully in the meetings market. When you have studied this chapter, you will:

- Be able to explain the difference between sales and marketing and tell why marketing is essential to the success of hotels and restaurants.
- Be familiar with the ideas, terminology and steps associated with developing and implementing a marketing plan.
- Be familiar with such marketing concepts as market segmentation, positioning and target marketing.

Outline

The Difference Between Sales and Marketing

The Importance of Marketing

The Marketing Plan

The Four Steps of the Marketing Plan

　Step #1 Conducting Marketing Research

　Step #2 Selecting Target Markets and Positioning the Property

　Step #3 Establishing Objectives and Action Plans

　Step #4 Reviewing and Monitoring the Marketing Plan

Putting a Marketing Plan into Action

Charles Walhaven
Director of Convention Services, Meetings.com
Nashville, TN

"Knowing what aspects of your meeting facility are most important to meeting groups is essential...The foundation of any marketing plan is the property analysis...A property analysis is a written, unbiased self-appraisal used to assess the strengths and weaknesses of your hotel...Experience your property from a meeting planner's point of view...Your creativity and knowledge of your properties capabilities will help you meet the needs of your target markets."

2 Developing a Marketing Plan

I n Chapter 1, we saw that the convention business is a potentially lucrative market segment that can be serviced by almost any type of property. But this does not mean that a hotel should just plunge headlong into attempting to capture all the convention business it can handle. Going after convention business without a sense of what the property can deliver may lead to costly mistakes, including misdirected advertising, fruitless sales calls or, worst of all, poor service.

Serious consideration must be given to a property's overall goals and how the convention business fits into them. A true managerial approach to marketing should lead to realistic objectives that can be measured. A good plan, in fact, *demands* clearly defined objectives, with careful thought given to methods, policies and procedures.

In this chapter, we will present a practical step-by-step approach to planning a marketing program. This analysis will help you to determine whether convention sales are actually a viable piece of business for your property. The marketing plan will be our base. We will refer to it often, so it is necessary for the reader to grasp the concept thoroughly.

The case study of the Rolling Green Resort will be used to explain key marketing concepts. Many of the figures and examples in this chapter are related to this case study, so it is important that you not only read the text but also review these examples for a better understanding of each application.

The Difference Between Sales and Marketing

Before we explore the foundation for convention sales and marketing, there is an important question that needs to be addressed: What exactly is **marketing**? Some people think that marketing and **sales** are synonymous. Others think that marketing is no different than the age-old sales and promotion concept; they consider the combination of sales, advertising, promotion and merchandising to be marketing. Neither is correct.

There is a clear distinction between marketing and sales. The terms are not synonymous, and sales and marketing are *not* equal; marketing is more than sales. Being market-minded is much broader than being simply sales-minded. Marketing is strategic and directive. It is goal-oriented, and the goals are concise and measurable. It is the groundwork, the research, the *plan* on which sales promotion is based (see box titled "The Difference Between Sales and Marketing").

The practice of marketing—combining, blending, integrating and controlling all of the factors that have an influence on sales—is not new. Many firms have recognized the importance of their customers and have successfully catered to their changing needs. The conscious application of marketing theory, however, is relatively new to the hospitality industry. Until recently, hotel marketing was never thought of in the same light as industrial marketing. It was not considered that a hotel might be similar to a consumer product.

In the early days of innkeeping, the demand for hotel rooms was far greater than the supply; there simply were not enough rooms to go around. It didn't matter what type of rooms were built; the customer had no alternative choices. A marketing plan that was customer-oriented was not needed to sell the product.

But the hospitality industry of today is far different. The city that once had a single inn now has four or five new hotels, each of them unique. Where formerly the demand exceeded the supply, the reverse is now true in many markets.

Now, the lodging industry is realizing that its problems are not unlike those of companies specializing in tangible products. Thus, many hotels are attempting to come to grips with what marketing means in an effort to apply marketing management principles. Hotels that wish to effectively compete must become marketing-oriented. The future belongs to those who are customer-oriented, those who are in the business of meeting the changing needs of the public -- not just in the business of maintaining hotel rooms.

THE DIFFERENCE BETWEEN SALES AND MARKETING

MARKETING	SALES
Focuses on market analysis, planning and control of changing market variables.	Focuses on field work and desk work to sell to the consumer.
Focuses on long-term trends and creating new products, markets and strategies for future growth.	Focuses on short-term considerations—today's products, markets, consumers and strategies.
Focuses on profit planning, including determining the optimum market segment mix.	Focuses on volumes and quotas, current sales, bonuses and commissions.

The Importance of Marketing

While properties still sell rooms and meeting space through their sales departments, increased competition has resulted in an increased need to apply marketing principles to develop successful sales techniques and strategies. Marketing, which focuses on the researching of trends and variables in the marketplace, is an essential part of gauging consumer preferences and developing plans which will enable the property to meet its sales goals.

Like other industries, the hospitality industry is subject to both controllable and uncontrollable variables that will affect sales efforts. External variables, such as weather conditions, fuel shortages and airline strikes, are largely uncontrollable. Other market variables, however, are inherent to all properties and can be controlled through marketing strategies to attract and retain new and repeat business.

These controllable variables, called the **marketing mix**, consist of "four Ps"—product, place, promotion and price. *Product*, in the hospitality industry, consists both of physical facilities—guest rooms, banquet space, meeting facilities and recreational amenities—and of more intangible factors—such as service and the vacation or meeting experience itself. Since a large part of the hospitality product is intangible (you are often selling a property's atmosphere), most marketing strategies will emphasize *benefits* rather than the more tangible physical *features* offered by a property (this concept will be discussed in greater detail in the sales chapter of this book). *Place* refers to the accessibility of the products to its consumers. Hospitality products, of course, do not have to be distributed to the consumer; instead, the consumer must travel to them. This accessibility may be facilitated by marketing strategies which involve intermediaries, such as meeting planners, tour operators and travel agents.

Promotion includes both persuasion (getting the consumer to buy) and communication (developing a relationship with the client). In the hospitality industry, communication plays an especially important part in determining exactly what a meeting planner wishes to purchase and is just as important as the actual promotion of the property. *Price,* the fourth factor, is one of the crucial concerns of the marketing mix. Since price is often an important consideration when dealing with the meetings market, this variable should be taken into consideration when establishing room rates for the varying market segments (see Figure 2.1).

Many properties employ a *marketing manager* to plan, direct and control all of these factors. It is his or her job to establish programs, policies and objectives to adapt to changing customer needs. The marketing manager must know and understand such concepts as capital markets, break-even analysis and cost control, as his or her function includes establishing long- and short-range sales goals.

The marketing manager's job begins with planning. He or she must constantly plan new ways and activities to adapt to the changing needs of the customer while providing continuity to the hotel and improving its image and salability.

The Marketing Plan

While the fast-paced and ever-changing nature of the hospitality industry seems to be better suited to short-term sales efforts rather than long-term marketing strategies, there are many advantages to long-range marketing planning. Having a detailed, written plan creates an awareness of the problems and obstacles faced by the property and helps managers to think ahead to make better use of the property's resources. In addition, a written **marketing plan** sets responsibilities, coordinates efforts and helps evaluate the results of marketing and sales efforts. As an added bonus, the research done in the early stages of developing the marketing plan can identify opportunities to increase revenues in some market segments and point out previously ignored segments.

To be most effective, a marketing plan should cover a three-year period. While many properties feel that a yearly marketing plan is enough, a twelve-month plan may restrict sales efforts to already established guest bases. Many corporations and associations make commitments well beyond one year, and short term sales goals may eliminate the opportunity to capture a larger share of the lucrative conventions and meetings business.

A three-year plan, of course, may be broken down into yearly segments with specific goals for each time period. Periodic review of the plan is essential, especially if there are drastic changes in the economy or personnel, enabling advertising and direct sales efforts to be adjusted to adapt to these changes.

The marketing plan will serve as the property's "road map," and should include programs to attract business to each of the property's revenue centers—rooms, banquet facilities, restaurants, and so on. Because these programs should complement rather than compete with one other, it is important to define specific objectives for each revenue center, and to be sure that these objectives—and strategies for attaining them—are understood by each staff member.

Figure 2.1. THE IMPORTANCE OF PRICE IN PROMOTING THE HOSPITALITY PRODUCT.

Many sources of group business, including associations, government groups and small corporations, are especially price-sensitive. This ad addresses the consumer's concern over price — while still promoting the services offered by the property at an affordable cost.

While the director of sales or the marketing manager is ultimately responsible for the property's marketing plan, many properties have recognized the benefit of a team effort in the development of effective sales strategies. In a marketing team, or "sales committee" approach, representatives from each revenue center provide detailed information on the workings of their departments and offer specific strategies for review. This type of team effort not only gives the director of sales or marketing manager better insights on how to best promote or improve day-to-day operations, but also provides an excellent way to sell the entire property.

The Four Steps of the Marketing Plan

No matter what approach is taken, a marketing plan consists of four basic steps (see Figure 2.2):

- Conducting market research
- Selecting target markets and positioning the property
- Establishing objectives and action plans
- Reviewing and monitoring the marketing plan

To ensure a better understanding of these steps, we will be using the fictitious Rolling Green Resort as a case study (see Rolling Green Resort Case Study).

Figure 2.2. THE FOUR STEPS OF THE MARKETING PLAN.

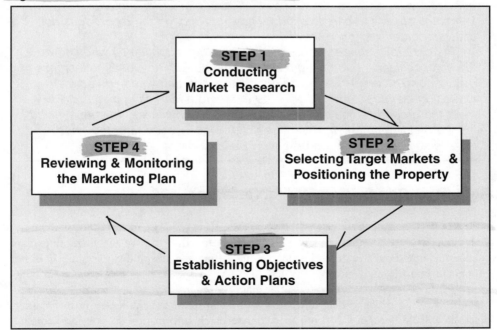

In today's highly competitive hospitality industry, it is essential to have a systematic approach for increasing sales. A well-developed marketing plan serves as a blueprint for the sales effort, and provides an effective sequence that minimizes wasteful effort. Marketing plan development, therefore, is a never-ending process. After one marketing plan cycle has been completed, results are evaluated and the process returns to the research portion of the marketing cycle to ensure that up-to-date sales guidelines and strategies are employed.

> ### *The Rolling Green Resort Case Study*
>
> *The 320-room property is located forty miles north of St. Louis, a metropolis of over three million people. Situated on the banks of the Pritchard River, it is in a renowned vacation area featuring high wooded hills, picturesque fruit and dairy farms, country estates, historic battlefields and a national cemetery. A small community nearby, Forest Glen, serves as a shopping center for the approximately 1,200 rural residents of the valley.*
>
> *The resort is about two miles off U.S.16, a main four-lane north-south highway which is fairly heavily traveled by tourists going south in the winter and north in the summer. This transient trade constitutes the bulk of the resort's business, which is good in the peak summer months and for a few weeks in the winter. But business is generally poor in the spring, fall and late winter months.*
>
> *The Rolling Green Resort's revenues currently consist primarily of room sales to individuals and a minimal amount of banquet business—despite the fact that the property has an excellent dining room and boasts a ballroom that can accommodate 600 people on the second floor. Both the first-floor dining room and the ballroom overlook the river, and both feature charming outside patio/balcony areas. On the lower level, there are several rooms of varying sizes which are now being used only for storage.*
>
> *Property recreational amenities include a large swimming pool, three lighted tennis courts and riding stables. The resort is in close proximity to a number of riding, hiking and biking trails, and bicycle rentals are available in Forest Glen. In addition, there is a small dock that is adequate for three or four small boats and can be used for fishing, although the resort does not offer any organized river activities.*
>
> *The general manager of the resort is an elderly gentleman who knows the hotel business, but he is unable to come up with any ideas to increase occupancy. The property's board of directors has appointed you as their marketing manager, and it is your job to create a marketing plan that will meet the property's goals of attracting additional business—perhaps including the meetings market, which has not previously been targeted—and increasing occupancy during the slow periods.*

Step #1 — Conducting Market Research

Before you sell any product, you must know its strengths and weaknesses in order to determine how to best promote it. This is where the first step of the marketing plan, conducting market research, is invaluable. In selling the hospitality product, it is not enough to know what your property has to offer; you must also determine what competition you face and what trends in the marketplace may affect future sales and marketing efforts. In order to determine how to best position your property in the marketplace, it will be necessary for you to gather research information so you may conduct a:

- Property analysis
- Competition analysis
- Marketplace analysis

The findings from these three types of research will be used as the foundation to plan the most effective marketing strategies for your property, and will set the stage for the targeting of specific market segments and the development of marketing strategies designed to sell the property to each.

Property Analysis. A **property analysis** involves an honest appraisal of exactly what a property has to offer. Since this analysis will form the base of information from which virtually every marketing and advertising decision will be made, any error in judgment here will almost certainly result in mistakes in your marketing and advertising strategy. In order to most objectively judge a property, input can be solicited from variety of sources, including employees and guests. You might also try to picture the property as if you are seeing it for the first time—become a guest yourself and experience the property from a guest's perspective. Later, as you analyze other parts of the property, put yourself in the place of a meeting planner seeing the property for the first time.

While it may seem superfluous, this analysis should always be done in writing (even if you feel you know the property inside and out), and should include all of the property's revenue centers. This analysis should detail the property's strengths and weaknesses, and provide space for comments on areas that need improvement (see Figure 2.3).

The first place to start is with the property's physical appearance. Since customers, including meeting planners, form a negative or positive first impression from the appearance of the property, and appearance often plays a large part in sales promotion, a hotel with a neat eye-catching appearance (see Figure 2.4) is a step ahead of a more lackluster competitor.

First, the entrances, grounds and exterior construction should be assessed with a critical eye for improvement. What is the overall general appearance? Is there ample parking? Are outside areas well-lighted and secure? The exterior of the property should be evaluated in terms of traffic flow, accessibility, eye appeal and compatibility with local surroundings.

Next, make a detailed, room-by-room and facility-by-facility inspection. Are rooms clean and in good repair? What type of dining facilities are offered by the property? Are kitchen facilities modern and up to code? Do you have an on-premise lounge or nightclub? Does it offer entertainment—and what type? What is the condition of the common areas—are they clean, inviting and well-lighted?

Put yourself in the place of the meeting planner. In terms of facilities, what do you offer? Location? Adequate transportation? Ample meeting space and up-to-date audiovisual equipment? Meeting rooms that are free from distraction? A highly trained staff? A well-lighted and secured environment that will make women attendees feel more comfortable?

Hotels vying for convention business should assess their function space and what equipment they have available or can obtain from local suppliers. It is wise for a hotel to prepare a printed list of its group function business equipment, including the kind and quantity available and the locations of the specific pieces of equipment. This itemization can serve both as a selling tool when presented to a meeting planner and as an inventory list for the property.

In some cases, properties wishing to target a specific market segment, such as the meetings market, have designed special facilities to appeal to their target markets (see box titled "Facilities that Meet the Needs of the Meetings Market"). While this type of renovation may not be practical for all properties, the property analysis can give valuable clues as to what property modifications are needed to attract specific business.

Figure 2.3. SAMPLE PROPERTY ANALYSIS FORM.

PROPERTY ANALYSIS - ROLLING GREEN RESORT			
AREA	**STRENGTHS**	**WEAKNESSES**	**RECOMMENDATIONS**
Exterior	Attractive and appealing, newly designed entrance Clean, good repair, freshly painted	Lack of seating/relaxing area near entrance Dumpster area visible from west wing	Veranda entrance could be more inviting with addition of comfortable chairs Construct fence to conceal trash area
Meeting rooms	Ballroom can accommodate 600 persons Ballroom overlooks river	Rooms on main level are not utilized	Convert storage rooms to meeting and function space
Parking	Convenient to rooms Lot has perimeter fence and landscaping	Driveway is in need of repair Perimeter fence is too low for security purposes Very narrow driveways at hotel entrance Difficult to enter driveway because of traffic	Repair asphalt cracks in drive Research feasibility of widening entrance
Rooms	Comfortable, modern decor Easy to keep clean Cable television Easily accessible Refrigerator in each room Effective air-conditioning	Not entirely secure Little consistency in door locking systems Small bathrooms	Install stronger window locks Install high quality door latch mechanisms Rent out less desirable rooms last
Reputation	Friendly, clean hotel, modern, charming Courteous staff Moderate priced rooms	Positioning is as an average facility More individual than group business Not a well known property	Use slogan or marketing strategy Involve hotel in more community support
Location	Riverfront Accessible to Expressway Popular vacation/resort area	Far from downtown and airport Two miles off main road	Develop shuttle system for groups Billboard advertising on highway

In order to provide the best source of information possible about a property, a property analysis should be written out, and include an objective look at the property's strengths and weaknesses. This is only one of several pages in the Property Analysis. Similar comparisons should be done for every area that can affect the property's profitability, including restaurants, lounges, room service, catering, convention services, shops, recreational amenities, housekeeping, bell staff, reservations, and accounting and billing, as well as other influences, such as local attractions, pricing and brand awareness. This type of analysis provides a means of taking stock of what the property has to offer, what areas need to be upgraded, and what steps can be considered to improve weaknesses.

FACILITIES THAT MEET THE NEEDS OF THE MEETINGS MARKET

William Cox, the architect for the Boca Raton Hotel in Boca Raton, Florida, conducted a study to determine an ideal design and layout for function rooms at convention-oriented properties. His research showed that a different type of facility was needed for servicing groups than for catering to individual guests, and he recommended the following design guidelines to the Boca Raton management:

1. A large hall capable of seating and feeding at one time the total number of guests the house is designed to accommodate.

2. Meeting rooms for groups ranging in size from 20 to 100. The total area of these rooms should equal or exceed that of the banquet hall.

3. Large and small meeting rooms that can be partitioned easily and quickly to adapt to individual group requirements.

4. Built-in audio and visual aids in each meeting room, with individual control stations in each possible subdivision of the space. The speaker should be able to control lights, sound and projection from a single station.

5. Stage facilities in the main banquet room for a single performer or production of musical shows.

6. Exhibit space with adequate electrical service, water and gas. Another special requirement: doorways must be high enough and wide enough to accommodate a tractor-trailer.

Cox's recommendations can be applied by any property seriously considering the convention business.

Source: William Cox, "Design Guidelines for Convention Resorts" (highlights from speech at meeting of the American Hotel & Motel Association's Resort Committee).

And what about recreational amenities? Do you have indoor/outdoor swimming pools? Do you offer easy access to golf and tennis? Do you have an exercise facility? How good are your recreational amenities in relation to those of your competitors?

Your inspection of the Rolling Green Resort has shown the exterior to be charming and in good repair, although the wide veranda could be made even more inviting with the addition of comfortable chairs. The guestrooms, ballroom and kitchen facilities are modern and adequate, but you are determined to make better use of the wasted space on the lower level.

Your tour of the grounds has shown that the driveway to the property is in need of minor repair—and perhaps widening—and that parking facilities are minimal. The pool area is large and clean, but is probably underused; its size and convenient proximity to the kitchen facilities offer excellent possibilities for food and beverage functions.

In addition to taking stock of the physical aspects, the property analysis also takes into consideration such intangible factors as the property's reputation and quality of service. Reputation includes how the property is perceived — is it classified as an inn, hotel,

Figure 2.4. CONVENTION HOTEL CONSTRUCTION.

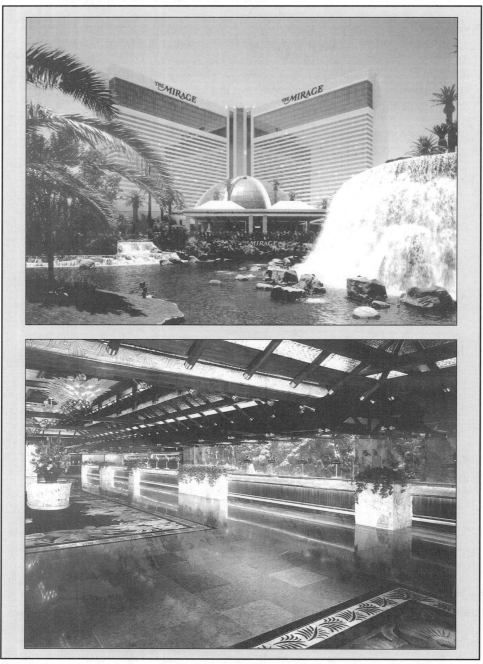

Today's convention hotels are a far cry from the traditional choices of the past. The Mirage Hotel & Casino in Las Vegas, for example, attracts meeting goers with its multiple lagoons, waterfalls, and a 54-foot "volcano," and is also recognized for its 90-foot high glass enclosed atrium, a popular feature in many of today's new convention hotels. In addition to its visual appeal, the property has addressed the needs of the meetings market with a large lobby, enhanced by a 20,000 gallon saltwater aquarium. The lobby has multiple windows to ensure efficient check-in. And, meeting rooms are situated away from transient traffic and accessed by two separate lobbies that provide convenient places to meet before and after individual sessions. One lobby features a large counter that can be used for registration and message service. (Courtesy of MGM-Mirage).

resort? Is it considered upscale, budget, family-oriented? How would guests describe the atmosphere — relaxing, bustling, business-like?

As far as the Rolling Green Resort's reputation, it is perceived as modern yet charming, but —unfortunately—the property seems to be a well-kept secret. Aside from a directional sign on the highway, nothing has been done to promote the property. There is a definite need for you to get the word out.

A property's location can also be a selling point. Is it within easy access to major highways or airports? Are there other historic or scenic attractions or major amusement centers close by? Are there annual events that draw people to the area?

The Rolling Green Resort has the advantage of being located in a particularly popular vacation area—and can capitalize on a number of scenic attractions. Its location on the river can also be a selling point. Two drawbacks come immediately to mind—it is a considerable distance from the nearest airport, and, because of its location off the highway, may not be accessible year-round in inclement weather.

The last part of your property analysis helps you assess your property's current position in the marketplace by examining the property's sales history and current guest base. This part of your research, known as the **business status and trends summaries**, traces the property's past, present and potential operating statistics, including sales patterns over a three-to-five-year period (see Figure 2.5). Such analysis helps to track the "soft spots"—low business periods—inherent to hospitality sales, and can disclose sales areas that need improvement.

These charts show the history of occupancy and activity by month for all profit centers. Without this, it is difficult to determine objectives and action strategies for the coming year.

In addition to looking at room statistics, it is also necessary to determine the makeup of your property's customer base (see box titled "Guest History Analysis"). How old are they? Are they singles, married couples, families? Middle-income, high-income? Sports-minded? Good drinkers? This information, which is extremely useful in planning marketing strategies, can be obtained by designing a guest questionnaire and perhaps offering an incentive (a free dinner for two, a week-end at the property, etc.) to ensure guest participation.

Another key area for research is the *geographic origin study*. Not only is it important to know who your guests are, but also where they come from. Identifying "feeder cities" or "catchment areas" can result in a more effective use of time and money. And, the smaller the geographic area used as categories the better. It is more useful to know, for example, that a guest came from Chicago than to know that a guest came from Illinois. This breakdown by cities and even zip codes can help the property to direct advertising to those areas which are most likely to produce guests.

Geographic and zip code information can come from a number of sources, beginning with the guest registration card. Other sources of information include responses from advertising or direct mail campaigns. This information should be updated regularly to avoid a confrontation with thousands of guest registration cards at the end of the year and to ensure that the correct areas are being targeted.

Competition Analysis. In addition to analyzing your own property, it is of prime importance to know your competitors and evaluate their strengths and weaknesses in comparison to your own. First, you must know who your competitors are — let's define them as properties in the immediate area which offer similar facilities and room rates, and service similar markets (see Figures 2.6 and 2.7).

To completely and effectively assess your competition, fact sheets should be prepared to compare: guest room and function room rental rates; banquet menu pricing; func-

Figure 2.5. THE BUSINESS STATUS AND TRENDS SUMMARIES.

MONTHLY OCCUPANCY AND AVERAGE RATE

Month	2000		2001		2002	
	Average Rate	Occupancy Percent	Average Rate	Occupancy Percent	Average Rate	Occupancy Percent
January	69.00	50.5	74.50	46.7	86.70	59.6
February	61.50	52.4	71.00	52.6	85.45	62.0
etc.						

BANQUET FOOD AND BEVERAGE REVENUE (in thousands)

Month	2000		2001		2002	
	Food	Beverage	Food	Beverage	Food	Beverage
January	7691	761	6541	531	14126	1646
February	10250	1614	4694	1911	17120	3361
etc.						

RESTAURANT FOOD AND BEVERAGE REVENUE (in thousands)

Month	2000		2001		2002	
	Food	Beverage	Food	Beverage	Food	Beverage
January	15461	8761	18640	7640	21013	9641
February	20911	11411	22611	11311	23415	11421
etc.						

FUNCTION ROOM REVENUE (in thousands)

Month	2000		2001		2002	
	Food	Beverage	Food	Beverage	Food	Beverage
January	1290	330	1700	410	2690	491
February	810	240	1423	467	2870	502
etc.						

Figure 2.5 continues on the following page

tion room square footage and quality of meeting space; typical number of guest rooms allocated to groups (called the group room allotment); and services offered to meeting groups, i.e., audiovisual, airport shuttle, express check-in, and so on.

A **competition analysis** should be done at least quarterly, and information gathered from a variety of sources. The most useful source is a firsthand look at the com-

Figure 2.5 (cont. from preceding page) THE BUSINESS STATUS AND TRENDS SUMMARIES.

GEOGRAPHIC ORIGIN OF GROUP BOOKINGS

Missouri	Number by City	Total by State	State Percent
Kansas City Springfield Joplin Jefferson City	51 36 32 24		
TOTAL		143	34 percent
etc.			

GROUP ROOM NIGHTS BY MARKET SEGMENT

Segment	Jan	Feb	Mar	Apr	May	Jun	
Corporate Group							
Insurance	621	541					
Computer	29	59					
Incentive	43	122					
Other	—						
Association							
National	330	461					
State and Regional	461	296					
Other	69	—					
SMERF							
etc.							

This market research, which is also called an occupancy and activity analysis, traces the property's past and present operating statistics and aids in forecasting future activity. While most properties keep guest room statistics, it is also important to monitor the activities of other profit centers, such as restaurants and banquet operations, and to determine where the property's customer base is coming from — and when. These statistics make it easier to develop effective marketing strategies to both existing and new markets.

petitor. Stay there, or walk through, pick up literature and study their advertising. Get literature from convention and visitors' bureaus and the chamber of commerce. Check the telephone directories, hotel chain directories and travel guides to try to determine just what features are being promoted and to whom. Internet searches can also yield extensive information. Most convention hotels host Internet sites that you can access for a fast, comprehensive analysis of competitive properties.

This analysis of the competition can help to point out market segments that are not being serviced at your property and can provide valuable clues as to how you can change your own marketing strategies to generate additional business.

As far as the Rolling Green Resort is concerned, there is obviously no local competition for rooms, but this is a rare case in the hospitality business. In most locations — even small towns — there is at least one other competitor (and often times many more), who may offer a different type of product or may target a market segment that your own property is overlooking. The Rolling Green Resort has identified the Arrowhead Conference Center and the Hilton Inn as competitors. Both are located in the outskirts of St. Louis.

A Guest History Analysis:
A Valuable Key for Building Business

X Hilton Inn St.George.Utah

PLEASE PAY LAST AMOUNT

1450 HILTON INN DRIVE
ST. GEORGE, UTAH 84770
(801) 628-0463

GUEST REGISTRATION 34725

Names_____

Address_____

City or Town_____ State_____ Zip_____

Firm_____

MAKE OF CAR	LICENSE No.	MODEL	STATE

MY ACCOUNT WILL BE PAID BY
☐ CASH   ☐ CHECK   ☐ CREDIT CARD_____
TYPE AND NUMBER

I AGREE TO THE CORRECTNESS OF THIS STATEMENT AND PERSONALLY ASSUME LIABILITY

SIGNATURE
X_____
REMARKS

NOTICE TO GUESTS: SAFETY DEPOSIT BOXES ARE PROVIDED FOR DEPOSIT OF VALUABLES. THE HOTEL IS NOT RESPONSIBLE FOR VALUABLES NOT DEPOSITED

ARRIVED	DEPARTED	ROOM	RATE	CLERK	NO. GUESTS

Guest market research is an invaluable tool for both protecting a property's current customer base and for developing strategies to increase new and repeat business. While other guest market research, such as geographic origin, may be obtained from responses to advertising or direct mail campaigns or from post-departure guest surveys, one of your most valuable resources can be found in-house: guest registration cards. Guest registration cards are an effective way to determine the geographic origin of a property's guests, and offer a wealth of other information, including:

- the number and type of guests (individual business travelers, family leisure travelers, group commercial business, etc.)
- the source of the reservation (travel agent, meeting planner, guest direct, etc.)
- reservation date (which will help to determine the lead time required)
- length of stay
- room rate and revenue generated (room, food and beverage, gift shop, valet, etc.)
- personal information, including name, address, city, state and zip code (a ready-made mailing list)

This knowledge helps a property to determine which market segments (and guests) are sources for the most business, and, by learning what zip codes are producing the most business, the property can direct advertising (or rely on repeat business and target other geographic areas).

By determining guest origins, patterns, and needs, a property can develop strategies and programs to increase potential business. If, for example, guest market research reveals that 80% of the property's business comes from within the state and that these in-state guests travel an average of three week-ends a year, the property could consider quarterly mailings offering special packages to these guests to entice repeat business. A fishing tournament, a "Get-Away" week-end, etc., are just two examples of possible strategies. And, besides offering a great potential for repeat business, former satisfied guests are an invaluable source for building additional business through word-of-mouth advertising. Such referrals make it even more important to keep in touch with customers. It is costly to get a guest the first time; it is vital to get business again.

Figure 2.6. COMPETITIVE RATE ANALYSIS.

COMPETITIVE RATE ANALYSIS

Hotel / Rates	Rolling Green			Arrowhead Conference Center			Hilton Inn		
	Single	Double	Suite	Single	Double	Suite	Single	Double	Suite
Rack	84-92	94-102	130+	100-105	105-110	160	102-116	102-118	140+
Corporate	80	80	120	98	104	140	88	88	130
Tour	62	72	—	—	—	—	85	92	—
Convention	78-90	88-100	120+	85-100	90-105	140	88-98	94-104	130+
Club Floor	90	100	—	—	—	—	115	125	—
Government	68	78	—	85	90	—	85	90	—

This form compares the rates of your property against those of the competition. Note that ALL types of rates are included — rack, corporate, convention, tour, club floor and government. In addition to benchmarking rates, hotels also gauge competitor activities in areas such as occupancies, group bookings, guest relations, promotional programs, use of advertising, selling methods, market penetration, and market segmentation mix. To monitor these areas, fact sheets are often prepared on each competitor. This comprehensive type of analysis can point out specific areas in which your property differs from the competition and can help you to determine how to set your rates in order to better compete for specific market groups.

Marketplace Analysis. The **marketplace analysis**, also known as a *situation analysis,* evaluates the environment in which the property operates (see Figure 2.8) and the property's operating status in that environment. The marketplace analysis identifies factors that can affect business, such as the cost of travel and government regulation, and also includes research on the environment around the property. This latter research can include the population and projected growth of the local community, the economic trends being experienced by local industry, the traffic counts for nearby highways and airports, recreational amenities and attractions in the area, and unique area activities — such as fairs, festivals, rodeos, etc. — that attract crowds. All of these strengths can be incorporated into property promotion.

Data for the marketplace analysis can be found in census information, industry reports, periodic updates from the chamber of commerce and even the local newspaper. Becoming involved in community affairs is another way to learn what is going on in the area and how trends may affect business.

In the case of the Rolling Green Resort, the marketplace analysis may reveal that there is little going on in terms of population growth and projected changes in the economy. If you were to find out that a light industrial park was proposed nearby, however, that information would greatly impact your property.

While the research phase of the marketing plan is very important, the crucial exercise is not to merely collect data but to *interpret* property, competition and marketplace information. The key is to "boil down" the statistical information gathered in order to select appropriate market segments and to help form strategies for reaching them.

In the case of the Rolling Green Resort, for example, your research has shown that you could indeed service at least some portion of the meetings market if you were to formulate a plan to better utilize the "wasted" space on the main level. It may be viable to

Figure 2.7. COMPETITIVE ANALYSIS — NEED FULFILLMENT BY MARKET SEGMENT.

COMPETITIVE ANALYSIS NEED FULFILLMENT BY MARKET SEGMENT				
Needs and Wants of Target Markets	COMPETITORS			
	Rolling Green Resort	Hilton Inn	Arrowhead Conference Center	Comments
Corporate Meetings Market				
AV equipment	1	3	3	Our access to outside AV firms is limited
Security	3	2	2	
Training atmosphere	2	2	2	Our secluded location is a benefit to corp planners
Space on short lead time	3	2	3	
Soundproof meeting rooms	2	2	1	
Master account billing	3	2	3	
Efficient check-in, check-out	2	2	2	
Wake-up, message service	2	2	2	
Quality food service	2	2	3	
Association Meetings Market				
Comp. room policy	3	2	2	We offer 1 comp for 40, rather than 1 comp for 50 rooms booked
Exhibit space	1	3	1	
Accessible location	1	3	2	
Overflow arrangements	1	3	2	
Assistance with housing	2	2	2	
Spouse programs	2	3	2	
Reasonable room rates	3	2	2	
Recreational amenities	3	1	1	Key: 3 = superior 2 = average 1 = poor
Convention coordinator	3	2	2	

A competitive analysis can take many forms, including just a simple feature-by-feature comparison of the competitors' facilities with one's own. The most pertinent information can be gained by evaluating how one's property "stacks up" in specific market areas. This is one type of form used to compare the services offered to each market segment. Market segmentation is the practice of targeting segments of customers within the overall marketplace. Isolating target markets and determining how well your property fills the needs and wants of each segment is extremely helpful in finding your competitive advantages. Once determined, these advantages can be used to differentiate your property in the form of positioning. This form illustrates just two market segments. You should assess the needs and wants of all market segments you are targeting — the corporate individual traveler, the travel agent market, the incentive group market, the family market, and so on. The key is to find a difference that makes a difference to each targeted customer.

turn one or two rooms into attractive conference rooms, or to add a business center or other facilities — such as an exercise room or childcare center — to attract this additional business.

Step #2 — Selecting Target Markets and Positioning the Property

After an honest self-appraisal, set reasonable, reachable targets. Be realistic because sales efforts are costly and, if done sincerely, are emotionally exhausting and the price is too high to be wasted.

How do you choose your **target markets**? The obvious first step is to target groups you are already serving. The information obtained from room reservation cards may show that a majority of your guests come from metropolitan St. Louis. If so, direct advertising there.

Next, chart the number of room nights you are currently selling to each market segment by month (see Figure 2.9). If you are realizing a high occupancy from associations or sports teams, for example, expand your efforts to those market segments.

Then, determine what other markets you may adequately service (see box titled "Selecting Target Markets"). A property such as the Rolling Green Resort would be an attractive destination for market segments such as honeymooners, business travelers and families. Its location and atmosphere would be ideal for "murder mystery weekends" or special educational seminars or retreats.

The conventions and meetings industry has been shown to be a lucrative market segment that should be targeted. While this particular property is probably inadequate to handle large conventions, what other segments within the convention and meetings industry can it service? What specific needs of meeting planners does it meet (see Figure 2.10)? Your location away from the bustle of the city may be an inducement to St. Louis businesses wishing to hold training sessions in a quiet, yet convenient, location. And, many small meetings and seminars do not require large facilities — or even have a food function. Are there state or regional associations that can be targeted? SMERF groups? Other groups that you can adequately serve?

Due to its historic setting, the Rolling Green Resort might also appeal to historical societies, educational groups and veterans' groups. And, the nearby city of Forest Glen should not be overlooked as a potential source of business from wedding receptions, awards banquets and other community functions. Perhaps the resort could promote regional activities, such as a dairy festival, or sponsor a sports team to attract visitors to the area.

Once you have selected your target markets, you must then determine how to best *position* the property to each of them. **Positioning** refers to the perception of a property by the guest. It is a composite of the property's reputation, what it stands for and how it differs from the competition. In short, it is the property's image or uniqueness — which gives you the wherewithal to sell it to your guests. To effectively sell a property, your perception of it and your customers' perception of it must match (see box titled "Positioning Your Property"). An example of success in positioning is the Cadillac automobile. The name immediately conjures up the image of a luxury car.

The property's positioning plays an important role in advertising. It enables you to create the advertising which will project the image you want for the property.

You may, for example, wish to position the Rolling Green Resort as an attractive small meetings destination. Or, you may wish to "play up" the historical significance or the tranquility of the area to attract associations or retreat business.

Figure 2.8. THE MARKETPLACE ANALYSIS.

Part I	MARKETPLACE ANALYSIS
OPPORTUNITIES	**EFFECTS ON BUSINESS**
The St. Louis Airport is expanding and bringing in two new regional carriers.	Easier accessibility to the city. These airlines service several of our feeder cities.
The local college has made arrangements with several companies to hold seminars and workshops on electronics this spring and fall.	Possible room nights from students and instructors, and meeting space for meetings, classes and seminars.
Archaeological dig in Majestic Canyon has uncovered an ancient Indian burial ground. An influx of scientists and historians have begun a major investigation of the area. etc.	Possibility of room nights from those not wishing to sleep on site and day rooms from those who wish to shower and clean up after the dig. Also increased business in food and beverage areas.

Part II	
PROBLEMS	**EFFECTS ON BUSINESS**
The highway from St. Louis is scheduled to be repaired in May.	Guests will experience some delays during May. However, when construction is finished the repairs and additional lane will make access to our resort easier and faster. Also a possibility of increased restaurant business from the workers.
A new Sheraton Hotel has been proposed. Construction is to commence late next year. etc.	This property is to be located midway between our property and St. Louis. If developed, this will be increased competition; and Sheraton is strong in the corporate market and has a good established reputation.

This marketplace analysis looks at the environment in which your hotel operates and assesses the effects of political, economic, sociological and technological factors (these are often termed the "uncontrollable variables"). The marketplace analysis generally consists of two parts, one titled "Opportunities and Effects on Business"; the other is titled "Problems and Effects on Business." These studies detail influences (both positive and negative) that may have an effect on your business and provide a way to determine how these opportunities and challenges can impact your property. You should use this environmental scanning to monitor your environment in order to design strategies that will help you to avoid potential problems while taking advantage of the opportunities provided in your marketplace environment.

Figure 2.9. STATE AND REGIONAL ASSOCIATIONS OCCUPANCY CHART.

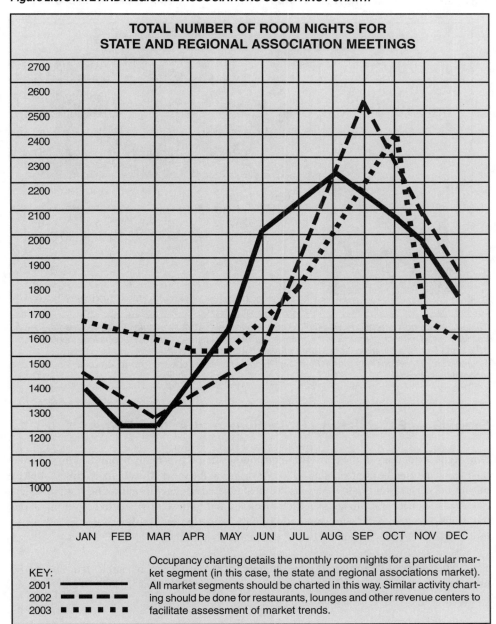

In order to determine the most effective marketing strategies, properties should chart the number of room nights they realize from each market segment they serve. This occupancy chart for the state and regional associations market sub-segment provides such information as the number of guests and peak months of occupancy, and is useful to forecast trends and direct advertising.

Figure 2.10. TARGET MARKETS: MEETING THE NEEDS OF THE SMALL MEETINGS MARKET.

This ad shows how a property with limited guest rooms can target the small meetings market. The ad
implies that the meeting planner's small group is important to the resort and will receive individual attention.
This is the type of ad that would be used to reflect the positioning of the Rolling Green Resort.
Source: "Small Meetings - Hands On Planning Guide", a special supplement from Corporate Meetings and
Incentive magazine.

Step #3 — Establishing Objectives and Action Plans

One of the attractions of the convention business is that it fills many rooms at a time — and
business can often be controlled to fill those rooms at the most advantageous times, such as
during the off-season or slow periods. To best take advantage of marketing opportunities,
however, it is necessary to set specific objectives and to develop plans to help bring about
the desired results. And, since marketing goals cannot be met without sales, it is wise to
look at each revenue-producing center and set goals for each.

Marketing Objectives. At the beginning of each year, research data should be
used to set specific goals for each market segment. To arrive at these goals, certain
questions need to be answered:

- When are the property's peak periods? In what months does business
  need to be increased?
- What revenue centers need more sales effort? Does the restaurant
  do more business during some months? Would offering family rates
  help to boost room occupancies?
- What market segments can be reached to increase business?
  What priority should each be given?
- What steps can be taken to generate additional revenues in each segment?

Marketing objectives should be set for each market segment, revenue center and revenue-producing service (the property's laundry, valet parking, gift shop, and so on). These goals must be clearly defined *in writing* so that every one involved gets the same information. In addition, the goals must be realistic yet challenging; if a property is currently experiencing an average occupancy of 65 percent, it is unrealistic to expect to set a goal of 100 percent — but the sales staff can shoot for a more reachable, yet challenging, goal of 80 percent during certain months.

Setting specific goals helps in the monitoring process. Room nights can be tracked and restaurant covers counted periodically to ensure that marketing goals are being met.

Developing Action Plans. Once objectives have been outlined, **action plans** must be developed to meet those objectives. This is the real meat of the marketing plan. There should be detailed action plans for each market segment and revenue center, and, since action plans can be compared to "mini" marketing plans, they should incorporate the following six areas:

1 *A description of the market segments or types of business to be solicited.*
   Will the plan target business travelers? Local associations? Honeymooners?
2 *A specific description of the target customer.* If the target segment is
   local associations, this portion of the action plan will include the names,
   addresses and telephone numbers of local contact persons.
3 *Rates, special plans or promotions that will be offered.* This should
   include any discounted rates for association groups, a possible free
   room for a tour operator, special package rates (rooms, food service,
   entertainment) for groups.
4 *Specific Objectives.* Here, the objectives are clearly spelled out. The
   plan should not just call for "increasing room occupancies," but rather
   should specify the room night and revenue goals by month for the entire
   year. These types of objectives enable the sales department to plan
   strategies to meet its goals.
5 *Action Steps.* This portion of the action plan involves the actual steps
   that should be taken to carry out the marketing objective. Perhaps some
   promotional literature will be developed. An "open house" may be held
   to introduce the local meeting planners to your facilities. In the case of
   the Rolling Green Resort, you may plan an advertising campaign directed
   to those leisure travelers within a two-day drive of the property
   (see Figure 2.11.).
6 *Budgeting.* It is not enough to simply set goals. Enough money has to be
   allocated to help achieve them. You should go through each strategy and
   action step to determine what each will cost.

As you can see, action plans are specific and therefore require personalized attention. It is highly recommended that the action plans for each revenue center be assigned to specific individuals who can oversee their part of the total marketing effort and monitor the progress of their department's objectives. The Chapter Appendix provides a detailed description of how each of the six areas discussed in the marketing plan are applied in the Rolling Green's market segment plan for increasing corporate meetings.

Budgeting. As we mentioned in the discussion on developing action plans, there needs to be a specific budget set for each revenue center and for each market segment

Selecting Target Markets

The primary purpose of the research phase of marketing planning is to identify three to five priority needs for the property and ways to meet those needs. The study of the property, competition and marketplace (the business status and trends summaries, in particular) assist the marketing team to identify areas needing sales activity and when specific business is needed.

Once a property's priorities are identified, market segments can be selected that can meet these priorities. Hotels are always looking for ways to improve their customer mix; they must periodically evaluate their customer mix in order to drop or replace low rated segments and boost business from segments that are more profitable.

Noted industry marketing consultant Tom McCarthy suggests that properties ask the following five questions to best determine which market segments to target:

- Does the property meet the needs of this segment?
- How does the competition meet the needs of this segment? The number and quality of competitors in the area weighs heavily in determining whether or not to solicit a specific segment.
- Does this segment meet the property's needs? Look at the list of property's needs and determine whether the segment will provide the kinds of business that will satisfy those needs.
- How much business is the property getting from this segment at present? If it is getting some business from this segment, there is likely to be more out there.
- How much time and money will it take to solicit this segment vis-a-vis its long-term potential?

In today's favorable market, properties are being more selective, not only in regard to the market segments they are targeting, but even as to the particular customers they are booking. Transients pay higher rates than groups, so in periods of high demand, some meetings business is given "back burner" treatment. The type of group is also being closely scrutinized; those with substantial banquet business, for example, are of more value to hotels.

Barbara Best, National Accounts Director for Hyatt Hotels says, "Smart hoteliers want to have a mix of business, but we are trying to learn how to best manage that mix." Because of high demand, hotels can indeed be more selective—but their selectivity is often at the expense of the meetings industry. Lynn Tiras, president of International Meetings Managers in Houston, TX, says, "Hotels are looking at the whole picture to see if a particular piece of business is of value to them, and they are turning away business that doesn't have enough food and beverage or whatever.

"In some cases I can understand it, like when they don't want to tie up all their meeting space for a group that may not need any sleeping rooms or F&B, but they are going way beyond what's reasonable in some cases too.

Continures on page 55

Obviously, a property must make sound business decisions, but it must be careful, too, not to jeopardize future business. Weighing out a property's priorities, current business relationships with the meetings industry, and market trends is essential to help a property to effectively manage its customer mix without jeopardizing future business.

To illustrate how these strategies are put into practice, let's go back to our case study of the Rolling Green Resort. The property's marketing team, for example, has decided not to solicit the individual government business because the segment is too rate conscious, and also determined that there is no substantial room night volume from the leisure sport fishing traveler. The marketing team instead decided on the following priorities and selected the marketing segments listed in the accompanying chart to meet the property's needs.

Market Segments Targeted to Fill Priorities

Priorities	Market Segments to be Given Emphasis to Solve Priorities
Priority #1 **Midweek Business** **Year Round** This is our area of greatest opportunity for significant increases. We have some corporate individual travelers, but if this can be expanded and coupled with the corporate meetings market targeted, we will be able to create a strong corporate base to fill this need.	• Corporate Individual • Corporate Meetings • Intensive Training Meetings
Priority #2 **Shoulder and Value Season Group** Early fall and late spring are our shoulder periods, with winter being the off season. The association market (particularly state and regional groups) have been our strongest in the past. We will concentrate our efforts in this market and also with the SMERF market to target groups into the shoulder and value seasons.	• State and Regional Associations • Educational Groups • Government Groups • Religious Groups in Preparation for Christmas and Easter Pageants • Medical Associations • Veterans Groups
Priority #3 **Banquet Business** Has not been pursued actively in the past. Efforts will be directed to maintain current customer base with increases in average check, banquet beverage revenue and to target into the weekends.	• Local Corporate Groups • Weddings - Bridal Fairs • Reunion Business • Civic Groups

Positioning Your Property

Positioning is essentially the name recognition of your property by the public, and is critical to a property's success. Just as the "golden arches" are immediately linked to McDonald's, it is imperative for a property to establish a readily recognizable image in today's competitive hospitality industry.

One example is the Peabody Hotel in Memphis, TN, whose mallard ducks have been an integral part of the property's marketing plan since the 1930s. Each day, at 11:00 a.m. and at 5:00 p.m., one drake and four mallard hens march in and out of the hotel's lobby fountain to the strains of John Philip Sousa's "King Cotton March." The ritual is so popular that the ducks have come to symbolize the property. So, although the ducks themselves generate no revenue, they are an invaluable tool in promoting the property—they appear on the property's logo, and on gift items, and are used in advertising (the ad shown here uses the ducks to detail the varied types of meetings that the hotel services).

But positioning is more than just catchy symbols or logos. In today's competitive marketplace, proper positioning enables you to:

1. Identify possible competitive advantages.
2. Select the *right* competitive advantages, and
3. Deliver your property's chosen position to carefully selected target markets.

To effectively position your property, the following factors should be taken into consideration:

- *Physical Attributes* — Is your property a "classic" hotel with a colorful history? Does it feature unique construction or features — formal gardens, waterfalls, etc.? How is it different from other properties in your area?
- *Service* — How efficient is your check-in and check-out service? How long is the wait at your restaurant? Do you offer specialized service needed by guests (computers, FAX service, children's programs, etc.)?
- *Personnel* — How are your customer contact people perceived? Are they courteous and friendly? Can they communicate well and respond to guest needs?
- *Location* — Where is your property located — beachfront, mountain, mid-city, airport, etc.? Is it conveniently located (or, conversely, remote)? What aspect of your location gives you an advantage over the competition?
- *Image* — How is your property perceived by the public — luxury, family, business traveler friendly? Do you have a distinctive image that differentiates you from your competition? Does your property live up to its perceived image?

Continued on page 57

Your property's projected image must effectively meet the needs and wants of each of your targeted market segments. You must find opportunities to determine and promote what each segment needs. What benefits do they seek? What needs are currently unmet — and what needs can be met or improved? What innovations are needed to attract unreached market segments? And, most important, are those additional segments worth going after?

The famous ducks introduced at the Peabody Hotel in Memphis, TN, in the 1930s have become an integral part of the Peabody Hotel Group's advertising campaigns. This ad associates the immediately recognizable ducks with the diverse organizations that have held meetings at the Peabody Orlando. Courtesy of Peabody Hotels and Turkel Schwartz & Partners.

(see Chapter Appendix, Part VI). This type of fiscal planning ensures that there are enough dollars spent in the most effective areas.

While there are several types of budgeting, one of those most commonly used is **zero-based budgeting**. This method of allocating money is based on a "task method;" money is budgeted at levels to get the job done, but each expenditure must be justified.

Since this budget is based on the tasks that need to be done, it can only be completed after an action plan has been developed. In this way, the property can be sure that there has been enough money allocated to meet the objective. If, for example, you have determined that an extra six sales calls a month are needed in the St. Louis area, you can easily determine the amount of money needed to take care of that portion of the action plan.

Another advantage of this system is that once money has been committed to a certain department or market segment, there is some room for adjustment. If advertising costs less than estimated, for example, you may opt to increase advertising or divert the excess money into additional sales calls. In order to readily see what is available, however, a budget form must be developed that provides instant access to information (see Figure 2.12.).

The use of computers in hotel sales offices has greatly facilitated the budgeting process. Computers can forecast based on previous and current expenditures, and provide instant printouts to let you know where you stand on dollars allocated for your marketing strategies.

Figure 2.11. TARGETING PROSPECTIVE CUSTOMERS.

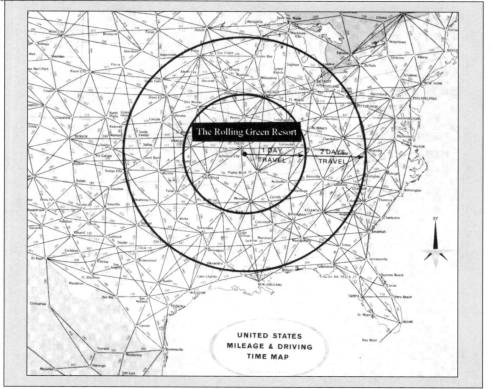

A map such as this can be used to target customers with a one- or two-day driving time from a property. This part of an action plan can be incorporated into either a direct mail or print advertising campaign to target the business or leisure travelers most likely to visit the resort. (Map by permission of Rand-McNally).

Figure 2.12. SAMPLE MARKETING BUDGET FORM.

A summary budget should be prepared combining the budgets developed for each of the market segment plans. This format is especially helpful when developing a marketing budget because it lists anticipated and actual amounts expended the previous year, provides a variance column and allocates the current budget into targeted market segments.

Step #4 — Reviewing and Monitoring the Marketing Plan

Despite the best planning, outside influences (an energy crisis, a natural disaster, etc.) or inherent weakness in the marketing plan (unrealistic goals, lack of provision for personnel turnover, etc.) make it imperative to periodically review the marketing plan. This evaluation should be done at regular intervals — each month, each quarter or at the end of an advertising program — to ensure that marketing goals are "on track" and that money is not being wasted on strategies that are not producing the desired results.

Goals that have been clearly spelled out are easier to monitor and revise, if necessary. For example, if specific goals have been set to increase room occupancies in the winter months by 15 percent or to cater an additional ten wedding receptions during the month of June, it is a simple matter to count room nights and banquet activity. Other types of monitoring can include the recording of room nights by market segment, charting and comparing room nights or restaurant covers before and after an advertising campaign, and determining what zip codes are producing the most business.

In the case of the Rolling Green Resort, for example, you may have coded newspaper advertising to determine which cities are responsible for generating additional business. If you see that there is little response from the Chicago area, you may opt to channel advertising dollars being spent there into more lucrative areas, such as the St. Louis market, or try for a better response by advertising in travel guides or specialty magazines instead.

Before "scrapping" a part of the marketing plan, however, you must ascertain if the strategy was given enough time to work (as we have learned, some corporations and associations make booking commitments years in advance and a one-time direct mailing may not bring immediate results) and determine if there could be other reasons for a lack of response (inclement weather in the Chicago area, for example, may have prohibited people from traveling). Sometimes, all it takes is a little corrective action — such as targeting a market segment during a month in which they are more likely to book — for a strategy to bring about increased business. In other cases, an evaluation may show that a more effective marketing strategy is needed to reach a particular segment. Perhaps rooms are priced too high to attract a price-sensitive group or a specific benefit offered does not have enough appeal. A periodic evaluation will point out these weaknesses and give the property an opportunity to either revise strategies or goals or to focus its marketing efforts in other directions.

This process of monitoring, evaluating and correcting is the final phase of a marketing cycle that returns once again to the research stage in order to keep abreast of market trends and new ways to reach and retain business.

Putting a Marketing Plan Into Action

The marketing plan is not developed to sit on a shelf collecting dust; it should be an integral part of sales and promotional efforts and referred to often. Once the marketing plan has been prepared, it should be distributed to each department, and its objectives and how to meet them explained to all of those who are involved in particular parts of the marketing effort. Juergen Bartels, president of Westin Hotels, says of his chain's marketing plan, "It's not a dead plan, it's a lively plan; we work from the plan everyday."

Since the marketing plan is the foundation for sales efforts, it is important that the entire sales team become especially familiar with the goals and objectives outlined. From these goals and objectives, sales goals and quotas are set and specific market segments are targeted. It is important that the sales team thoroughly understand their role(s) in the marketing effort, and utilize the research collected to position the property to potential sources of business.

In addition to the sales department, the implementation of the marketing plan will impact everyone on property. Each department should be appraised of department goals — and the strategies for achieving these goals — and should be made aware of the integral part that the department plays in the overall success of the property's sales efforts. If a marketing team approach was used to develop the marketing plan, each department's representative can serve as a "team leader" to ensure that his or her department remains on track.

 ## Chapter Summary:

Today's meeting planner has a myriad of choices, so competition for the meetings market has become fierce. Attracting and keeping customers requires a planned, carefully researched and thought-out effort, and a written marketing plan is a must for every hospitality establishment. In this chapter, we have discussed the four steps inherent to each marketing plan and how to implement the marketing plan.

Although the marketing effort will involve the entire staff of the property, the main thrust begins in the sales department. In the next chapter, we will discuss how putting together an effective sales team, implementing workable sales procedures and organizing an efficient sales office can help the property to remain competitive and meet its marketing goals.

Additional References:

Marketing Leadership in Hospitality, Third Edition, Robert Lewis and Richard Chambers, John Wiley and Sons, 2000.
www.hospitality@wiley.com

Hospitality Marketing Management, Third Edition, Robert Reid and David Bojanic, John Wiley and Sons, 2001.
www.hospitality@wiley.com

Internet Sites:

For additional information on the firms and organizations discussed in this chapter, visit the following Internet sites. The Web addresses listed are current as of January 2001. Addresses may change, however; if a site is not available at address below, a search engine can be used to access its new location.

Association for Convention Marketing Executives (ACME) - www.acmenet.org
Hospitality Sales and Marketing Association International (HSMAI) - www.hsmai.org
Peabody Hotel - www.peabodymemphis.com
Mirage Hotel and Casino - www.themirage.com
Boca Raton Resort and Club - www.bocaresort.com

Study Questions:

1. What is the difference between sales and marketing?
2. The marketing plan should cover what time frame?
3. List the four steps in developing a marketing plan.
4. Research should be conducted in what areas before developing action plans?
5. What factors should be considered when selecting target markets?
6. What is meant by zero-based budgeting?

7. Choose two lodging properties and assess how each has positioned itself in the marketplace. Include a discussion of the following factors: physical attributes, service, personnel, location and image.

Key Terms:

Action plans. The specific steps taken to achieve marketing objectives.

Business status and trend summaries. Reports that assess the property's current position in the marketplace by examining the property's sales history and current guest base. Part of the property analysis.

Competition analysis. An evaluation of competition in order to identify their strengths and weaknesses in comparison to your own. Part of the market research step.

Marketing. The practice of combining, blending, integrating and controlling the factors that influence sales.

Marketing mix. The combination of the four "Ps" of marketing — product, price, place and promotion — used to achieve marketing objectives for a target market.

Marketing plan. A written guide detailing sales, advertising and promotion programs used to attract business to the property's revenue centers.

Marketplace analysis. An evaluation of the environment in which the property operates. Assesses both opportunities and problems in the marketplace, and determines how they impact the property. Part of the market research step.

Positioning. A strategy to develop the product and service as distinct in the minds of consumers. Positioning attempts to distinguish a firm from any of its competitors.

Property analysis. An evaluation of a business' facilities, services and programs to determine strengths and weaknesses. Part of the market research step.

Sales. Direct efforts through face-to-face calls, telephone calls and mailings.

Target markets. Market segments that a property singles out as having the greatest potential, and toward which marketing activities are directed.

Zero-based budget. A budget that starts at zero and requires planners to justify expenditures for each activity.

Chapter Appendix

Sample Marketing Plan

This excerpt from a hotel marketing plan illustrates a detailed market segment plan for the corporate meetings market. The Rolling Green Resort would prepare detailed action plans for each market segment and revenue center. This third step is the core of the marketing plan. The statistics gathered on the property, the competition, the marketplace, and the target customers in the first two steps might encompass more pages in the plan, but success is based on how well the action plans are developed and implemented.

As you read this action plan, note how complete and specific it is, providing a "road map" for the coming year. The strongest marketing plans result from the input of people from all areas of the property. Therefore, brainstorming sessions with key personnel are essential to developing effective action plans.

Market Segment Plan

Corporate Meetings

I. Description

The Rolling Green Resort will aim at expanding its share of the corporate meetings market. Types of meetings sought will include: corporate sales, training and development, distributor and dealer, executive conferences, product presentations, stockholder, board and management meetings. Our property should target local, statewide and national corporations who have yearly meetings in our area.

II. Target Customers

    A. Present local files.   98

    B. Priority accounts — present high volume accounts and   5
       those in the area not using us at present, but are known
       to produce high volume business.

- Pritchard Data Services
- Harper and Associates
- Stewart Group
- Stubs Real Estate Investment
- Adam and Bre Corporation

    C. St. Louis Prospects

- Companies of over 50 employees within selected SIC   120
  numbers in following zip codes:
  63111, 63137, 63128, 63104, 63121

- Companies of over 100 employees within selected SIC numbers in all other zip codes within metropolitan area ... 70

D. Tri-County-St. Louis Area (other than above zip codes)

All companies with 100+ employees plus the following companies if they have less than 100 employees:

- Top 10 law firms, stockbroker-investment firms, leasing firms, relocation firms, insurance companies, advertising agencies, real estate main offices ... 200

- All branch and regional offices of Fortune 500 companies ... 24

- All companies of 50+ employees moving in from outside Montcalm County ... 73

E. Kansas City, Springfield, Chicago (within one day drive)

- All manufacturing and insurance companies with 100+ employees ... 55

- All branch and regional offices of Fortune 500 companies ... 62

- MPI (Meeting Professionals International) and SCMP (Society of Corporate Meeting Professionals) members in these cities ... 325

F. Four-State Region

- Top 30 seminar companies ... 30

- Fortune 500 company home offices ... 150

- ASTD (American Society for Training and Development) members in the four-state region. ... 917

Total Target Customers ... 2026

III. Rates, Special Plans, Packages and Promotions

A. Seminar/Training/Corporate Group Package:
Available on selection of specific dates.
Minimum of 25 sleeping rooms include:

	Single	Double, Per Person
Room (per person)	$80.00	$40.00
Tax (7%)	5.60	2.80
Meeting Room	4.00	4.00
Continental Breakfast	3.50	3.50
Lunch	7.50	7.50
AM/PM Refreshment Breaks	3.00	3.00
All Food Tax (7%)	.98	.98
All Food Service (15%)	2.10	2.10
	$106.68	$63.88
Above package including dinner		
Dinner	15.00	15.00
Tax	1.05	1.05
Food Service	2.25	2.25
	$125.00	$82.18

B. Extended Stay/Early Arrival

If stay is extended to include Saturdays, free unlimited use of the championship golf course and tennis facilities, along with free champagne brunch will be provided. For new bookings arriving on Sundays rather than Mondays, free welcome cocktail parties will be organized and tickets given to a local show or performance.

IV. Objectives and Goals

Based on a review of our property, the competition and marketplace, we have identified fall and spring as our most important priorities for the coming year. The corporate market is targeted as one segment to fill this need. Our objective is to increase our corporate group rooms business from 6% to 10% of our total rooms business. And to increase our annual room sales revenue from $622,542 to $669,400 (7% increase) and increase average daily rate from $72 to $79 for this segment. Monthly targets are identified below:

Room Nights and Revenue Goals From Corporate Meetings												
	J	F	M	A	M	J	J	A	S	O	N	D	Totals
Room Nights	700	850	900	800	700	600	550	550	600	750	900	600	8500 room nights
ADR	78	78	80	80	80	75	75	75	78	82	82	78	$78.75
Room Rev (000)	54.6	66.3	72.0	64.0	56.0	45.0	41.3	41.3	46.8	61.5	73.8	46.8	$669.40

V. Action Steps

A. Sales/Direct Mail

Step No.	Method	Target Customers	No.	Details	Qtr.	Sales Days	Resp.
1	Telephone	Present local files	98	Survey their satisfaction over the telephone. Give comp one-night stays to any who were dissatisfied.	1	5	AH JM
2	Telephone	Priority accounts	5	Have contact with these accounts a minimum of once a month. Include entertainment at hotel, sporting events or other local activities to build relationship.	1,2,3,4	20	AH JM
3	Personal Blitz	St. Louis prospects and those in Tri-County St. Louis area	287	Personal visits by sales staff to outline our services and deliver small gifts such as a business pen.	2,4	15	TS AH JM
4	Phone Blitz	Planners in key feeder cities of Chicago, Kansas City, Springfield and Four-State Region	1539	Promote our package and familiarize the company with our product.	1,3	25	AH TS JM
5	Direct Mail	Previous corporate meeting customers	250	Send personal thank you letters for their past business and ask them to rate satisfaction by returning post-paid questionnaire.	1	4	AH JS
6	Telephone	Previous corporate meeting customers (not returning questionnaire)	70 (est)	Survey satisfaction over the phone. Provide comp room night to any who were dissatisfied.	1	3	AH JS
7	Telephone	Tri-County St. Louis, Kansas City, Springfield and Chicago areas of of over 100 employees	340	Call for initial qualification to determine if file should be set up (at least 30 room nights per year). Set up appointments.	2	6	JM TS
8	Direct Mail	ASTD members in Four-State region	1000	Promote our package and familiarize with our product special rates, etc. Mail-in response card enclosed.	2	25	TS JM AH
9	Telephone	ASTD members in Four-State region	100	Respondents to mailing.	3	25	JM AH

B. Advertising

Media
The Trade Journal Magazine (2 col x 5 ") 12 times
Corporate Market Review (5 col x 8 ") 6 times
The St. Louis Directory — Annual

C. Merchandising
   Development of the following brochures and flyers:

	Total
Meeting Planners Informational Brochure, 4p4c	1,500
Hotel Fact Sheet (group) 8"x11" 2c	5,000
Meeting Package 4p4c	5,000

D. Public Relations and Publicity
   Contact local TV stations, major newspapers, and the Convention
   Authority announcing prominent corporate meetings.

VI. Budget

A. Sales
   Dues and Subscriptions

The Trade Journal Magazine	$500	
Corporate Market Review	350	$850

B. Advertising
   Media

The Trade Journal Magazine		
2 Col x 5" @ $800 x 12x	9,600	
Corporate Market Review		
5 col x 8" @ $750 x 6x	4,500	
The St. Louis Directory		
Annual	1,000	$15,100

   Direct Mail
   American Society for Training and
   Development (ASTD) $3,000

Brochures and Flyers		
Informational Brochures	1,650	
Hotel Fact Sheets	1,200	
Meeting Packages	2,400	
		$5,250
Production costs (ads and brochures)		$5,000
Other Selling Aids — Gifts for Blitzes		$6,000
Total Corporate		$35,200

Summary

Corporate meetings business is one of our priorities for the coming
year. The estimated 8,500 room nights is 10% of total rooms business, and the $35,200 is 9.2% of total marketing budget.

Learning Objectives:

This portion of your text discusses how sales departments are organized within the hotel framework. We will cover both the function and physical layout of a sales office, look at positions within sales and see how sales efforts are managed, and discuss standard operating procedures used in today's hotel sales office. We will also discuss how automation has changed the way salespeople do business and how revenue management has resulted in more effective sales efforts. When you have studied this chapter, you will:

- Understand the function of the sales office and how the sales office interfaces with other departments in the hotel.

- Be able to describe the various positions within the sales department and the duties of each.

- Be familiar with the procedures used by sales offices to follow a sale through from prospecting to execution of the event and understand how sales office automation is being used to enhance the sales effort.

Outline

Sales Structures
- The Sales Office
- How the Sales Office Interfaces with Other Departments

The Sales and Marketing Staff
- Positions Within Sales
- Supplemental Sales Staff

Managing the Sales Effort
- Standard Operating Procedures
- Sales Meetings
- Assigning Account Responsibility
- Evaluating the Sales Effort

Sales Records and Filing Systems
- Hotel Filing Systems
- Control Books and Sales Forms

Sales Office Automation
- Advantages of Automation
- New Advances in Hotel Computer Systems
- The "Virtual" Office
- Additional Uses of Automation

Organizing the Sales Office

Beverly W. Kinkade, CHME, CMP
Vice President Industry Relations
Starwood Hotels and Resorts

"The role of the sales department in pursuing the convention business is vitally important. With today's competitive hotel environment, it is imperative to have sales policies and procedures in place to smooth the communication both within the sales office and other areas of the property. In order to reach occupancy and revenue goals, the sales office must not only be organized and staffed with enthusiastic, knowledgeable people but also have an efficient filing system, written operating procedures and an effective system for monitoring both function room and guest room bookings."

3 Organizing for Convention Sales

According to a study by Laventhol and Horwath, a consulting firm to the hospitality industry, approximately 50 percent of the lodging industry's total receipts are derived from the meetings market. But in today's highly competitive marketplace, it is simply not good enough to send salespeople out into the field to solicit meetings business. Tapping this lucrative market requires an efficient, organized sales endeavor.

This chapter deals with how to organize the sales effort by creating a sales office — both the physical plant and the personnel in it — that maximizes a property's potential to sell to and service the convention and meetings market. We will also discuss some of the positions within sales, and see how sales efforts can be structured and managed for optimum results.

Sales Structures

Two trends have greatly impacted the way hotel sales departments do business. First, acquisitions, mergers, and consolidations have occurred in the lodging industry at a record pace as companies realize the value of acquiring multiple brands and the cost savings from combining departments. Since 1997, some 75 acquisitions have taken place, including Marriott's purchase of Renaissance and Ritz Carlton; Starwood's take over of Sheraton and Westin; and Hilton's acquisition of Doubletree, Red Lion, Embassy Suites, Hampton Inns and the Harrison Conference Centers.

Today, a handful of firms own nearly 100 brands. To increase efficiency, these hotel companies are consolidating their operations and relying more on regional and national sales offices. Rather than having a dozen individual properties call on a potential client for meetings business, chains are assigning a single salesperson to represent every brand in the hotel company's portfolio to the client. This concept will be discussed in greater detail later in this chapter.

Second, marketing functions have increasingly been incorporated into sales. More hotels today are focusing on the overall bottom line, not just revenue from meetings business. While rates, dates and space are still important, more properties are evaluating a group's spending patterns and potential for revenue property-wide before booking them. This trend, called revenue management, has led to revenue management positions and departments within many sales offices, and revenue management is expected to expand throughout the industry. A detailed look at revenue management will be provided later in the chapter.

All hotels, whether they are large or small, should have some kind of sales department from which sales efforts are directed. At small properties, a salesperson usually handles all types of business. He or she may call on meeting planners, travel agents, tour operators and other sources of potential business. Still smaller hotels may have to combine sales operations under another department or even have the general manager direct the sales effort, with the GM often designating one day a week for personally making sales calles.

Regardless of size, every hotel has "non-sales" employees who could be recruited to assist in the sales effort. If a food service employee and two front desk people, for example, would each make five calls per week to qualify new prospects, fifteen calls per week -- 750 calls a year -- could be made!

Larger properties generally have a specialized sales staff and operate out of a separate sales office. It is best, if at all possible, to have full-time sales specialists for convention sales. In the largest organizations, the degree of specialization is carried still further, with salespeople assigned to market segments. One sales staffer may go after association business; another goes after corporate meetings business; still another focuses on incentive programs. Obviously, such concentration is practical only for chain operations. It is not essential to successful selling to break down the task so finely, but this should tell you that each segment of the market has its own appeal.

To be effective, sales offices must be structured so that business is handled profitably, while conforming to the guidelines in the marketing plan. A number of factors must be taken into consideration before determining the actual structure of a property's sales office:

- Unity of command
- Authority commensurate with responsibility
- Span of control

Unity of command provides accountability by ensuring that salespeople answer to only one person, whether that be a sales manager or the director of sales. Salespeople who have two or more bosses may be given conflicting orders, greatly hampering the sales effort.

Authority commensurate with responsibility means that the salesperson, sales manager or director of sales has the authority to make decisions within his or her realm of responsibility. A salesperson, for example, may be given rate guidelines, enabling him or her to negotiate with a prospect rather than be limited by a fixed rate. Or, a sales manager may be given the authority to develop new techniques to increase personal or group productivity.

Span of control refers to the number of employees that a supervisor can adequately manage. If supervisors are given too large a number of salespeople to handle, they may not be able to adequately monitor the overall sales effort or assist individuals in problem areas.

The Sales Office

The sales office is often the first contact a client has with the property, and first impressions can make the difference between sales success or failure. To be effective, the sales office (and effort) must be properly organized. This organization should include both a sales philosophy as well as a physical office layout conducive to generating sales.

The Function of the Sales Office. As we have said, the sales office must be established and organized to enable it to meet the overall goals and objectives of the property's marketing plan. The sales department should be structured so that group business is not only solicited but also properly serviced by being given authority over other departments that will be involved in servicing group business (see Figure 3.1).

However the sales office is organized, it is crucial that all employees understand their roles in meeting the goals set forth in the marketing plan. Property salespeople should be professional, knowledgeable and service oriented. And, all property employees, whether they be field salespeople or the receptionist at the sales office, should be aware of their importance in the marketing effort. Walk-in clients, for example, should be greeted

Figure 3.1. TYPICAL CONVENTION HOTEL ORGANIZATION CHART.

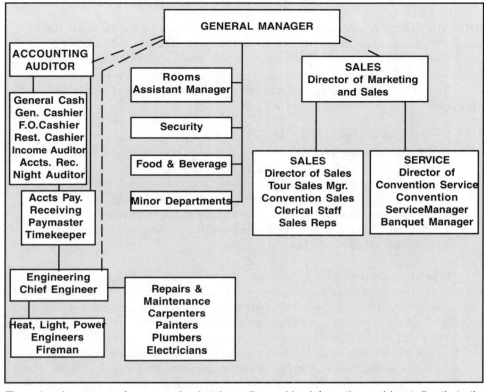

The sales department of a convention hotel usually provides information and input directly to the general manager. It is important to note, however, that the sales department, especially in convention hotels, is increasingly being given authority over other departments, such as the front desk, reservations, catering, and housekeeping, to enable it to deliver what it promises to clients.

promptly and made to feel at home, and the receptionist or secretary should be able to answer any immediate questions a visitor may have. At smaller properties, reception duties can be handled by front desk personnel who have been trained to answer client questions; larger properties may depend on a specially trained receptionist, secretary or sales associate to handle client greeting.

The Physical Layout of the Sales Office. Both the location and the appearance of the sales office are important. Sales offices should never be hidden away in the basement or an unused guest room; nor should they be located in "goldfish bowl" areas off the main lobby. Ideally, a property selling meeting and banquet facilities should locate the sales office adjacent to these areas.

The sales office should appear tasteful and professional, with a minimum of clutter, be well-lit and ventilated, and have comfortable seating and reading material available. Property information sheets and brochures, sample menus and perhaps albums of past events or news clippings about the property are informative — and good pre-sale tools. Sales office decor can also include photographs of guest and banquet rooms and the sales and managerial staff as well as awards received by the property. This type of decor helps to familiarize the client with the property's facilities, and can also help to develop confidence in the property.

How the Sales Office Interfaces With Other Departments

Before the hospitality industry became more marketing-oriented, the sales department was usually a separate entity responsible only for filling guest rooms and function space. Today, however, it has become imperative for not only the director of sales but also his or her staff to move into the mainstream of the day-to-day operations of the property.

Ronald Hughes, former general manager of the Palmer House in Chicago, stresses this viewpoint:

> "We have a responsibility to our salesmen and saleswomen that they become more involved in the day-to-day hotel operations, not only for the training benefit, but even more important so that their input and suggestions are built into the operation. The hotel that is market-oriented is a giant step ahead of its competition. To develop this marketing concept, the senior salesman, and especially the sales director, must be involved when we do our long range budgeting, short range forecasting, and many other basic planning functions."

In other words, management must indicate that the sales effort has a high priority and see that the director of sales has been delegated sufficient authority. To function well, the sales manager must have full authority over the banquet department, the convention services staff, advertising and sales promotion, a supporting clerical staff, and, of course, the sales staff itself. In many hotels, the reservations department is also considered an important area in relationship to sales, especially since reservationists are the first to have contact with potential clients (this relationship can be so important that some hotels, such as the Hyatt chain, have structured their reservations departments under the sales department). Negotiations between the sales staff and clients generally result in promises made. Such promises must be kept. The difference between a successful convention property with many repeat bookings and a less successful one usually reflects on the determination to live up to commitments.

This is especially true in dealing with convention and group meetings business. In addition to ensuring that guest rooms are available, it is imperative that the director of sales and his or her sales staff work closely with a number of other departments, especially the convention services and banquet/catering departments.

Convention Services. As we will see in the second part of this book, a good convention services department is essential for repeat bookings. Meeting planners must be satisfied with meeting space, the handling of functions, the availability of equipment and the service attitude of the staff in order to book repeat business or to recommend the property to others (see Figure 3.2).

The convention service manager serves as the on-the-scene contact between the convention organizer and the hotel. He or she is the one who sees that all provisions of the contract are carried out, and is the one who must be prepared to cope with the requests — and emergencies — that come up as the convention nears and during the event itself.

This position is a very crucial one and should never be downgraded. The convention service manager must have sufficient stature and authority to cope with the unexpected (see Figure 3.3).

Banquet/Catering Department. Although some people feel that the banquet/catering department does not belong under the authority of the sales department, we feel that control of all function space should be overseen by one person — the director of sales. This eliminates confusion and communication problems, since choices must sometimes be made regarding who will get a function room on a certain night. This decision must be made with an eye toward the overall scheme of things, and this falls within the responsibility of the sales executive.

For the sake of argument, let us take a look at what would happen if this were not the case. This partial organization chart has the banquet manager reporting indirectly to the assistant manager. When a client requests banquet space, the banquet manager will book one of the hotel's banquet rooms. While this action seems efficient enough on the surface, the sales department often needs the function rooms should any convention group be booked.

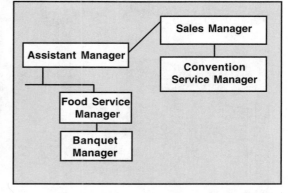

This could happen in the event of a communication breakdown. If the banquet department booked a function room and the sales department unknowingly booked the same room for a training seminar, the hotel would be placed in an embarrassing position and would most likely lose business.

The Sales and Marketing Staff

The sales staff is the first contact that many people have with a hotel. The corporate planner and the association meeting planner first establish contact through the sales office. Their first impressions are formed by the warmth, personality and public contact of the sales staff.

Positions Within Sales

While the sales effort itself should be coordinated by one person, the director of sales, there are a wide variety of positions within the sales department. While each individual on the sales staff is given certain responsibilities, it is important to remember that sales is a *team effort*. The efforts of each member must be coordinated with those of the others on the sales team for maximum results.

The Director of Marketing. The director of marketing spearheads the sales effort by setting objectives and monitoring the action plans. He or she works closely with the director of sales to ensure that goals are being met and that the sales effort is kept within budgeted limits.

The Director of Sales. The director of sales, who may be called the sales director or vice-president of sales at some properties, is responsible for executing the marketing plan formulated and accepted by top management. It is his or her job to coordinate and direct the efforts of the sales staff. All sales promotional programs must be channeled through him or

Figure 3.2. THE IMPORTANCE OF THE CONVENTION SERVICE DEPARTMENT

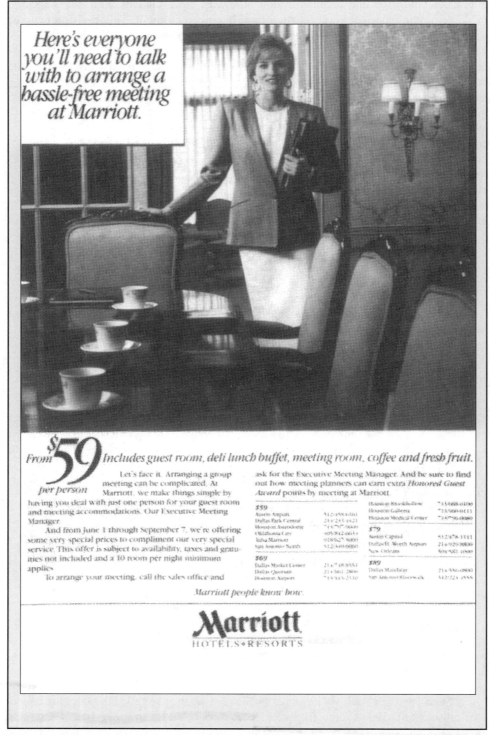

This advertisement shows the importance of a good convention service department, especially when dealing with inexperienced meeting planners. It promises a "hassle-free meeting" to attract meeting planners to the Marriott.

her for approval. He or she works closely with the general manager or director of marketing to determine target markets and to set the budget appropriations for each market segment.

While the scope of this position is often argued, it is our belief that the director of sales should be given all the authority necessary to ensure that sales goals are met. This may include becoming involved in a number of areas, including advertising and public relations, budgeting and any other function of the hotel that directly or indirectly affects the sales effort. The salary for this position will vary depending on the type of hotel (see box titled "Typical Salaries and Bonuses for Directors of Sales").

The Director of Revenue Management. With today's trend toward combining sales and marketing efforts, revenue management has become increasingly important to hotels. Properties that previously relied on the director of marketing and the director of sales to realize maximum profit potential are now creating a specific position dedicated to forecasting supply and demand and researching the potential profitability of groups.

Swissôtel, for example, employs a revenue manager to decide price structure based on the date, season, day of the week, competitive situation, and the potential of the group. A state of the art computer system is at the heart of the revenue manager's decision making process, and predictions can be made for weeks -- even months -- ahead. While the position is fairly new and can be expected to change, the HSMAI expects that the position will be firmly integrated into hotel sales offices by the year 2010.[1]

Sales Managers. Depending on the size and type of property, there may be a number of additional sales managerial positions. The *convention sales manager* is responsible for soliciting convention trade for the hotel (see Figure 3.4). It is his or her job to identify and

Figure 3.3. THE COMMUNICATION ROLE OF THE CONVENTION SERVICE MANAGER

THE COMMUNICATION ROLE OF THE CONVENTION SERVICE MANAGER

The convention service manager is the intermediary between the promises made by the sales manager, the expectations of the meeting planner and the execution of the event by the hotel operating departments. The immediate conclusion from the chart below is that this individual must be very detail-oriented and tolerant of high degrees of stress during an event.

| SALES MANAGER | CONVENTION SERVICE MANAGER | MEETING PLANNER |

HOTEL OPERATING DEPARTMENTS
FRONT OFFICE
HOUSEKEEPING
CATERING
UNIFORM SERVICES
RECREATION
SECURITY
ACCOUNTING
RESERVATIONS

The convention service manager acts as the on-site connection between a meeting group and the host property.

TYPICAL SALARIES AND BONUSES FOR DIRECTORS OF SALES

Type of Property	Median Base Salary	Median Bonus
All-suite/Extended Stay	$56,268	$ 3,360
Commercial-Transient Hotel with limited meeting space	$75,641	$ 8,932
Conference Center - Meeting and Convention Oriented Properties	$84,216	$ 705
Resort Properties Targeting Leisure and Convention Guests	$89,320	$10,386

The above figures show the median annual salary and bonuses earned by the Director of Sales at various types of properties. These figures are based on assumed annual increases of five percent. Compensation for this position varies based on a number of factors, including property revenues and geographical location as well as type of property.
Source: Salaries are adjusted from the 1997 Compensation Survey of Hospitality Sales Executives. HSMAI Marketing Review, Fall 1997, p 40.

contact the associations, corporations and fraternal organizations that could use the hotel for their conventions. Convention sales are generally made through personal visits, so the convention sales manager must build a relationship of confidence with the prospective client. Due to long lead times, a convention sales manager may need three to five years to get specific convention business.

The *convention service manager,* while not always considered an actual member of the sales team, works hand in hand with the convention sales manager. His or her job is to coordinate and service the conventions booked by the property. The convention service manager takes over after the sale has been made and begins to work out the fine details with the convention group. In addition, any problems that arise during the convention will be directed through convention services. The convention service manager must work closely with all departments, coordinating the efforts of the food and beverage departments, the front office, and the banquet setup crew to see that things run smoothly in the exhibit area.

A *tour and travel sales manager* is responsible for developing group and charter business for the hotel. He or she works closely with travel agents, tour wholesalers, tour operators and transportation companies. This person is generally instrumental in putting together tour packages and must have expertise in the pricing and promotion of group packages. The tour and travel sales manager may also put together group incentive packages.

Some properties may also employ a *director of advertising and public relations* whose job it is to coordinate all promotional materials and public relations and to make the final decision on advertising media (radio, television, magazines, newspaper, billboard, direct mail).

Sales managers are responsible for directing, supervising and evaluating the efforts of the sales staff. Their responsibilities may include hiring and training salespeople, developing departmental policies and procedures, setting specific goals for individual sales-people and monitoring the progress of sales team goals.

The Sales Staff. The property's salespeople are the key to sales success. These are the people who prospect, set appointments and make personal calls on prospective clients. They must be professional, knowledgeable about the property, the competition, and their markets, and must possess excellent organizational and verbal and written communication skills. Today's sales professionals must also be computer literate as most hotels utilize computerized sales systems, and long-distance communication is often an integral part of the sales function.

Ironically, the increased use of technology sometimes impacts relationships between salespeople and clients. The use of the Internet by meeting planners to research possible sites, "virtual tours" of properties, and other technology, such as electronic transmittal of contracts have sometimes minimized face-to-face contact between meeting planners and hotel salespeople.

This makes it all the more important for salespeople to commit to building long-term relationships with customers. **Relationship marketing** -- the building and maintaining of lasting relationships with customers -- is important in today's competitive environment. Meeting planners are more likely to feel comfortable with a salesperson who has performed well in the past, and may even take familiarity and trust into consideration over other factors, including price.

Unfortunately, meeting planners are sometimes unable to work with the salesperson who assisted with a past function. The turnover of sales personnel in the hotel industry is considerably higher than turnover in other industries. According to a recent Dartnell's Sales Force Compensation Study, the annual turnover in all industries is 14.1 percent; in the hospitality industry, turnover more than doubled at 30.5 percent. And, the percentage may actually be considerably higher, as hotels do not consider transfers within the company as employee turnover.

The compensation structures employed by some hotels may be contributing to the problem. Some hotels opt to reward salespeople for performance, paying a commission rather than a salary, so there is a tendency for salespeople, especially younger sales people, to opt for compensation from the generation of new business rather than commit to building relationships with current customers.

But good convention salespeople are especially important to a property's success if it has targeted the group meetings market, and prior experience in sales is often desired. In many cases, students begin getting exposure to this sales area while still in school by participating in sales blitzes coordinated with a convention property.

According to a survey by David C. Bojanic and Elizabeth A. Dale:

> "In the hotel industry, most sales training is done internally, with empha-sis on field training. Then, as one gains experience, more classroom train-ing is provided. Convention salespeople tend to progress through the ranks, enabling them to gain an in-depth knowledge of the hotel's prod-ucts. However, one's sales training is mostly on-the-job training, working with smaller clients under close supervision" and "most hotels are requir-ing sales experience for new hires in convention sales."[2]

Some salespeople are trained to handle specific accounts, such as local corporate business or regional associations, and may spend a great deal of time outside the hotel as well as handling routine office duties, such as following up on previous clients to generate repeat business.

Figure 3.4. SAMPLE JOB DESCRIPTION FOR CONVENTION SALES MANAGER POSITION

Job Title:	Convention Sales Manager
Department:	Marketing
Reports to:	Director of Sales
Basic Functions:	Reviews with Director of Sales the marketing strategy that will obtain maximum occupancy levels and average rate. Responsible for all convention group business related to the market segments as they relate to annual revenue projection.
	Consults daily with the Director of Sales concerning the defined territory and how it relates to the marketing success of the hotel through effective merchandising, prospecting, solicitation and booking of business.
Scope:	Sales manager will be the primary person for booking of long term convention group business with long term being more than six months out.
Work Performed:	Initiate prospecting and solicitation of new accounts; manage current accounts to maximize room nights from the account in relation to the hotel marketing plan; responsible for administrative efforts necessary to perform the aforementioned.

1. Quotas for this position are:

Room nights per month	1200
Soft spot percentage	20
Phone calls per week:	
Trace:	20
Prospecting:	25
Personal calls per week	10
New accounts per week	10

Individual to supply weekly, monthly and annual reports supporting productivity standards.

2. Probe for customer needs: rooms, suites, desired dates, day of week pattern, program agenda, food & beverage requirements and degree of flexibility in each of the aforementioned areas.

3. When available obtain information on the group's past history, i.e., previous rooms picked-up, arrival/departure pattern and double occupancy percentage.

4. Review availability of client's REQUIRED DATES AND ANY ALTERNATE DATES which should be offered. The dates presented to the customer should satisfy the customer's needs while allowing the hotel to maximize occupancy and average rate.   (continued)

Figure 3.4. (continued)

5. Negotiate with the customer: day/day of the week pattern, day by day room block, group rates (within guidelines as set by DOS), comps and function space.

6. Tentatively block rooms and function space in accordance with office policy.

7. Confirm in writing all aspects of the meeting. Check to ensure they received the signed contract.

8. Alert all necessary departments of pending tentative: i.e.; front office and credit.

9. Upon receiving the signed contract, process definite booking ticket, definite function room outline and credit application.

10. Oversee, manage and track the way in which reservations are to be made, the pick-up of the group block, adherence to the cut-off date, and any subsequent adjustment to the room block (positive or negative).

11. To periodically contact the customer while in-house to be certain all is in order and going well. To handle any last minute needs as they arise.

12. Conduct an exit interview with the customer to determine their level of satisfaction and ask for additional business.

13. Send letter of appreciation to customer. (Letter should include actual room night consumption and the letter should be tailored to previous exit interview discussions.)

14. Individual is to attend extracurricular activities, meetings, and accept any responsibilities or projects as directed by the Director of Sales.

Supervision Exercised: Supervise and share one secretary with another individual.

Supervision Received: Primary supervision from the Director of Sales. Initial training, and retraining as needed, also received from the Director of Sales, as well as direction as to room merchandising.

Responsibility & Authority: Upon satisfactory completing rooms merchandising and operational training, the individual will have the authority to make decisions and confirm dates, room blocks and rates to the clients. (continued)

Figure 3.4. (continued)

Minimum Requirements:	Bachelor of Arts or Science degree — preferably business, hotel or restaurant administration. Individual must also be professional in appearance and approach.
Experience: Sales Competencies:	Minimum of two years experience in hotel sales.

1. Ability to negotiate.
2. Accounts strategizing.
3. Ability to prospect.
4. Ability to judge profitablility of new business.
5. Knowledge of product.
6. Knowledge of competition.
7. Ability to make presentations.
8. Ability to organize and plan.
9. Ability to utilize selling skills.
10. Ability to overcome objections.
11. Ability to problem solve and make decisions.
12. Ability to write effectively.

A job description is a detailed listing of the function and organizational relationship of each employee. This job description for the convention sales manager shows the many facets of this important job and details the qualifications required for the position. Note that under "Work Performed" both room night and activity goals are stated. Top salespeople like to have their efforts measured against predetermined goals. Quality of calls is more important that quantity; therefore, room night/revenue goals are most important. However, maintaining activity goals such as number of phone calls, personal sales calls, and new accounts per week leads to more room nights booked and more revenue.

Clerical Support. To enable salespeople to handle the most important aspect of their jobs — selling —it is essential that a property employ a good clerical staff that can maintain careful and detailed records, make intelligent use of this data and assist in follow-up. While responsibilities may vary from property to property, the main function of the clerical staff is to provide support at the home base and to handle walk-in clients in the absence of sales personnel.

It would be penny-wise and pound-foolish to foot the considerable expense of fielding a sales staff only to skimp on the support at home. The period of sales effort before signing a convention can be very long, and salespeople must be continually in touch with the meeting planner. With today's high cost of sales calls, a follow-up system of letters and phone calls generated by a well-trained clerical staff is essential. The clerical staff will also maintain careful, detailed records of your prospects' convention activities, personnel changes and other data that may help win the sale.

Supplemental Sales Staff

It is often impractical and uneconomical for hotels to cover all the market bases with their in-house staff. To gain representation nationwide, chain properties supplement their staffs' sales efforts with *regional and national sales offices,* while independent properties turn to *independent hotel representatives* to help them with regional and national sales efforts.

Regional and National Sales Offices. Another trend taking place in the hospitality industry is the reorganization of the sales function from a property basis to a regional basis. National chains, including Marriott, Hilton and Starwood, are merging sales departments from several properties into one central location. As this happens and the number of "unassisted" sales continues to grow as planners take advantage of Internet virtual tours and electronic transactions, individual salespeople in the future will only sell to their property's larger accounts, and sales staffs at the property level will be reduced in favor of regional sales reps.

One of the reasons for the success of regional and national offices is their use of *corporate sales staffs* in regional sales offices. The **regional sales office** serves as an intermediary between meeting planners and individual properties by providing a central information point that directs meeting planners to the property that best fits their needs.

The corporate staff solicits business for any hotel in the chain, and there are a number of advantages in this approach. First, a customer who has experienced good service and a successful meeting in one hotel of the chain might be induced to stay within the chain for their next meeting. Even when convention organizers have to move around the country to increase attendance, they may be sold on staying within the chain. Secondly, it is easier for a meeting planner who is scheduling ten similar meetings in many parts of the country to book all of them at once with a single salesperson. Once a salesperson has broken through to close a sale, the way to booking additional locations is easier. And, still another advantage comes into play when a meeting planner cannot get a free date at one hotel. The chain may be able to offer another hotel on that date, whereas an independent property loses out when firm dates cannot be met.

Several hotel chains, including Sheraton, Hyatt, and Red Lion Hotels and Inns, have developed computer systems that link their convention hotels with their regional and national sales offices. These systems give instant electronic access to group booking data, including availability, rates and dates and, in addition, track client histories and account activity chainwide. With such information at their fingertips, many regional sales representatives are now empowered to block space, print out proposals for any hotel on the system, and book business on the spot. The hotel's director of sales is then notified by electronic mail for approval of the agreement. And, regional sales offices also serve the properties within a chain's region by providing promotional materials and public relations.

Independent Hotel Representatives. Many hotels do not feel they can adequately cover all of their market bases with an in-house sales staff; they often supplement the staff with an **independent hotel representative**. These outside individuals or firms represent the property as a "long arm" of the sales department.

Because hotels have different needs, the services provided by independent hotel representatives vary widely. In some cases, the representative may be hired simply as a field salesperson, soliciting clients who are impractical for the hotel's in-house staff to reach. Other hotels may use larger representation companies, whose services include consulting, market analysis, advertising and public relations in addition to sales.

Because of economics, independent hotel representatives usually represent more than one property. This causes many hotels to balk at the notion of being represented by such firms. Quite logically, they question having a competitor represented by the same firm. Hotel representatives answer this criticism by saying they represent properties of different sizes and market emphasis, not similar clients seeking the same clients.

Should a hotel use an independent hotel representative? If you can afford to field your own staff and it performs satisfactorily, that's fine. If you can afford only limited sales efforts, a representative may offer another dimension. What counts is the amount of sales generated.

A hotel should investigate the benefits offered by an independent hotel representative firm. Such firms usually specialize in a particular market, while overlapping to other sources of business. If your target market is the convention trade, be selective, since few firms actually specialize in this area. And, since the majority of association and trade convention groups are headquartered in Washington, DC, Chicago or New York, your chances of reaching the convention market are greatly increased if your representative has an office in one of these locations. Just two examples of such firms include the Krisam Group, headquartered in Washington, DC, and The Leading Hotels of the World, Ltd., based in New York City.

There are a number of factors that you will want to consider in making your decision (see box titled "How to Choose an Independent Hotel Representative"). In addition, you may wish to consult similar-sized properties who are using a representative you are considering. Ask them about the effectiveness of the representative, especially in regard to areas in which you feel you may have difficulties.

If you opt to go with an independent hotel representative, it is important to remember that they are generally hired on a contract basis, usually paid a fee and receive a set percentage of the volume of business they directly book for the hotel. They must be given clear guidelines on what type of business the property is soliciting and what rates the property will accept.

In other words, the hotel representative should work within the framework of the property's marketing plan, and, as an extended member of your sales force, should be thoroughly familiar with the property's facilities, rates and operating procedures. Personal visits and tours by the management should be encouraged. The representative should be given organizational charts, operating manuals and materials detailing charges for meeting rooms, guest rooms and other facilities. And, most importantly, the representative should be

---

HOW TO CHOOSE AN INDEPENDENT HOTEL REPRESENTATIVE

Choosing an independent hotel representative is not to be taken lightly. Take the same care in hiring a hotel representative as you would in hiring an in-house executive. Here are questions to help you to determine whether an individual or firm would be an asset to your sales operation:

1. How many hotels does the firm represent? Has it extended itself so much that it may not be able to meet your needs?
2. Does the firm represent competing properties? If so, how will this affect its handling of your account?
3. Does the representative specialize in that targeted market you are seeking? Does he or she have knowledge of the group and convention business? Is the firm doing business with organizations you have targeted?
4. Does the firm have offices in the cities that are your major market areas?
5. Is the representative's staff knowledgeable about your type of operation? Does his or her staff have a hotel background?
6. How does the representative regard service? Do you want him or her to be an extension of your sales staff? Is he or she willing to be part of your team?
7. Can he or she deliver needed supporting services and advise you on brochures and other printed materials?

given a copy of the property's marketing plan — with specific objectives spelled out for him or her to meet.

Managing the Sales Effort

While hiring good salespeople, whether they be in-house staff or independent hotel representatives, is an important step toward achieving sales goals, the sales effort itself must be structured and managed properly for maximum effectiveness. Managing the sales effort involves a number of areas: the development of standard operating procedures (SOPs) for salespeople and convention staff; periodic sales meetings to discuss goals and problems; the prioritizing of accounts; keeping accurate records; and, most important, the monitoring and evaluating of progress.

Standard Operating Procedures

An effective sales effort begins with standardized guidelines for each step of the sales and servicing process. Each salesperson should be made aware of the sales office's **standard operating procedures (SOPs)**. These are instructions explaining how recurring business activities should be handled. Written SOPs presented together in a manual provide a constant reference for sales and banquet personnel, and are an essential training tool for new employees.

Areas that might be included in a SOP manual include:

- function book control and procedures
- guest room control book procedures
- booking policies
- rate guidelines for high and low demand periods
- credit/deposit/cancellation policies
- policies regarding V.I.P. and complimentary rooms
- meeting room rental fees and procedures
- banquet and room reservation cut-off dates
- convention service standards and procedures
- the organizational chart and specific job descriptions for the sales department

The sales department's SOPs can be added to or amended as situations warrant, but it is important that each person involved in the sales effort be made aware of any changes. These written SOPs help to eliminate costly errors by ensuring that each member of the sales team follows the same procedures when booking and servicing groups.

Sales Meetings

Just as written procedures are important, good communication is also essential to an effective sales effort. Sales meetings are an excellent way to ensure that all people involved in the sales effort have the same information and can help to eliminate potential problems by identifying and dealing with them early.

While the number and type of sales meetings may vary, the most commonly used meetings are weekly and monthly staff meetings, weekly function meetings, marketing team meetings and periodic (usually annual or semi-annual) sales meetings for all employees.

Weekly and monthly sales or staff meetings are usually headed by the coordinator of the sales effort; this may be the director of marketing, the director of sales or the sales manager at larger properties, or the general manager at small properties. Held to discuss any changes in the sales or promotional effort, the progress on certain accounts, new and tentative bookings, sales goals and potential problems, these meetings are usually attended by all sales personnel and the heads of any departments affected by the sales efforts (convention services, banquet/catering, front desk, etc.). Since the mutual exchange of ideas and information is vitally important to any sales effort, these regularly scheduled sales meetings should also include a period of open discussion or a brainstorming session.

Weekly function meetings generally include only the department heads involved in selling to and servicing the convention market. These meetings ensure that every area of the property is adequately covered when making commitments to groups, and help to ensure that specific business is understood and properly handled.

Many properties hold an annual or semi-annual sales meeting for all the property's staff. The marketing plan—and each employee's role in it—is presented, and specific information, such as advertising and promotional efforts and the affect on individual departments and employees is discussed. This benefits both employee and management, providing an opportunity to obtain ideas and suggestions from employees working in day-to-day operations.

Assigning Account Responsibility

Keeping the sales staff abreast of current information and goals is only part of the management of the sales effort. It is the responsibility of the director of sales or other leader of the sales effort to ensure that accounts are being distributed and handled in the most productive and cost-effective manner for optimum results.

There are many variables in assigning responsibility. Some directors of sales feel that accounts should be assigned by market segment; if he or she has three salespeople, for example, one will be assigned to corporate meetings, one to association business and one to incentive travel. While this may seem practical on the surface, there may be drastic imbalance within the market segments. The salesperson assigned to corporate meetings, for example, may end up with more accounts than he or she can handle.

The director of sales may see this imbalance, and assign two people to cover the property's most lucrative segment. This approach, too, may present problems, since most corporations find it more comfortable to deal with only one contact person at a property.

One solution is to assign specific accounts, rather than market segments, to each of the salespeople; one salesperson would be responsible for all the business generated by a particular organization. This type of account assignment is beneficial to both the salesperson and the client; it provides one contact person and helps to build rapport that may generate future business. If this approach is taken, it is important to distribute accounts with particular attention to the number of accounts, their geographic area and the market segments into which they fall. In terms of numbers, it is usually considered best to assign accounts equally; if, for example, a property expects to target 900 accounts over the coming year, each of the hotel's three salespeople should be given 300 of them.

This number can vary based upon the location of the accounts. If, for example, a property can target a nearby industrial park, it is easier for a salesperson to handle these accounts than it would be for a salesperson to adequately cover accounts spread over a two state area. In this case, the salesperson covering the local area can be assigned a larger number of accounts.

The market segment factor comes into play when determining just how much business will be generated by each account. A salesperson assigned to a large corporate account, for example, can expect to cover a great deal more business — meetings, award ceremonies, the annual convention, etc. — than a salesperson assigned to an association that stages just one annual convention. In this case, or in the case of the salesperson who shows particular expertise in servicing a specific market segment, accounts can be redistributed for the best results.

Key Account Management. Once accounts have been assigned, the typical salesperson may find that he or she is looking at 300 to 400 sources of potential business. Selling to and servicing these accounts will involve making cold calls, setting appointments and following up — all activities that will generate a mountain of paperwork. So how does a salesperson decide how to handle the monumental task of effectively selling to his or her accounts? The solution is **key account management**.

Key account management involves prioritizing accounts based on their profit potential. This is important because, generally, 20 percent of a salesperson's accounts generate 80 percent of the business. Look at accounts individually to determine which ones have the highest potential for generating business and organize your time to sell and service these accounts. Key account management, then, involves ranking accounts. This is usually done on five levels:

- *Level 1* consists of all new and established accounts with a high potential for business. These are the accounts that will warrant your highest attention. As a general rule, a minimum of five personal calls and five telephone calls should be allocated to these accounts annually.

- *Level 2* consists of high potential accounts that are already providing a good share of business. Of course you want to continue to follow up on these lucrative accounts, but they don't require the same amount of personal attention and they can usually be serviced by four personal and four telephone calls annually.

- *Level 3* consists of new accounts with medium potential and established accounts that are not generating the medium potential expected of them. These accounts generally require three personal and three telephone calls each year.

- *Level 4* consists of accounts with medium potential providing an acceptable level of business. These accounts are normally followed up with two personal and two telephone calls annually.

- *Level 5* consists of low potential new and established accounts that do not warrant a great deal of time. These accounts require little more than token attention, such as a personal visit while on a sales trip to a more lucrative account or a telephone call after all the other business has been handled.

The level of each account can be determined by preparing an account "spread sheet" (see Figure 3.5) and by discussing questionable accounts with the director of sales. When setting account levels, however, remember that your priorities may change as your accounts and prospects change. Perhaps a company that had a low potential level because of its distance from the property may expand into your area or an association that had previously met at another hotel chain may have become dissatisfied and is now looking for another meeting place. These scenarios, which are not that uncommon, show the necessity

Figure 3.5. KEY ACCOUNT MANAGEMENT SPREAD SHEET

KEY ACCOUNT MANAGEMENT SPREAD SHEET

Name of account and key contact	# of times account was called on last year	# of times we expect to call on account this year	Estimate of room night potential from account
Stubbs Insurance Mark Steward	4 Personal calls 4 Telephone calls	5 Personal 5 Telephone	25 r.n. x 12 mo. @ $75 = $22,500 20 r.n. x 12 mo. @ $80= $19,200 30r.n. x 2 days x 4 @ $72=$17,280 125r.n. x3 days @ $75 = $28,125 Total $87,105

KEY ACCOUNT MANAGEMENT SPREAD SHEET

Estimate of food and beverage potential	Estimate of meeting room revenue potential	Total potential dollar value of account	Level of account priority (Level 1 through Level 5)
40% of Room Revenue = $34,842	4 Workshops - Complimentary function space Product Showcase - 1.00 per square foot for exhibit hall = $10,000	Rooms $86,105 Food & Beverage $34,842 Meeting Space $10,000	Level 1 — High Potential Account

Prioritizing accounts can be accomplished easily if a salesperson takes a look at all of his or her accounts and judges them by the same criteria. A spread sheet, such as this one, provides a place for necessary data and enables the salesperson to see the profit potential of each account at a glance. Since each of a salesperson's 300-400 accounts are assessed, the Director of Sales can review the spread sheets with salespeople on a periodic basis (usually the end or beginning of a year) to reassess priorities.

for personally reviewing your accounts to determine how much time and effort should be spent to realize maximum sales potential.

It is also important to note that the goals set for a salesperson will affect how he or she manages accounts. Some properties set goals for high and low periods, for example. In this case, a fairly low priority account may provide the business needed during a slow period -- and help achieve an individual sales goal. It is also important to maintain a balance between maintaining good customer relations and prospecting for new customers. In some cases, salespeople will have sales goals based on business from current customers and business to book from new accounts. All of these variables will figure into managing accounts for maximum benefit.

file should be placed in the file drawer in place of the file. This enables the sales staff to keep track of the file's whereabouts.

The **tickler file**, also known as a *trace file, bring-up file* or *follow-up file*, is an effective follow-up tool. Tickler files may come in various forms; some are card files with monthly dividers and card separators marked 1 through 30 or 31 (see Figure 3.9), others are accordion-style files with multi-pockets. And, there are systems designed to fit within a letter-sized file cabinet. In all of these systems, cards are filed by month and day.

The tickler file, used properly, works very well, costs little and takes little time to implement. It works this way: you make contact with a prospect who indicates that no meeting plans will be finalized until October. Obviously, you want to contact the person before then — perhaps by the middle of September — so you place a card or note or a copy of some correspondence in the pocket marked September 15. This type of system eliminates reliance on memory, and ensures good follow-up — *if* you remember to remove everything in the pocket on each day of the month!

A variation of the tickler file uses colored tabs on the tops of the cards in the file. Each color represents a month — perhaps the groups that meet in November or on weekends. The tab system works well to categorize prospects and to encourage you to make additional cold calls each week on suitable prospects.

Of course, all records should be updated when a booking has been made. And outdated copies should be removed from the follow-up file. This will avoid an automatic follow-up letter being sent. The same procedure should be taken if the association has made a booking with another hotel.

Several computerized versions of the tickler file are available. Specialized hotel software, such as Delphi, not only reminds salespeople of important dates, but also offers additional sales tools. The computerized trace report show in Figure 3.10, for example, breaks down the day's business into several categories. The salesperson can take advantage of this to prioritize his or her work and schedule each day to make the most of sales opportunities. But even salespeople who do not have access to hotel-specific software can utilize other programs, such as Microsoft Outlook, to help organize their work. The Outlook program features a daily calendar and task list.

Control Books and Sales Forms

In addition to files, the sales office utilizes a number of forms and control books in selling to and servicing the group sales business.

Control Books. In selling public and banquet space to convention groups, for example, the salesperson must be sure that the assigned space will be available. Overbooking is eliminated by the use of a hotel **function book** (see Figure 3.11).

The function book serves as the hotel's "bible" when it comes to booking meeting and banquet space, so there should only be one book to prevent mismatched entries or double bookings.

The most common type of function book is a large book with a page for every day of the year. The function book has a number of vertical columns, providing space for such information as:

- the name of the organization or person requesting space
- the contact person (name, title, address, telephone)
- type of function

- time required for the event
- total time required (for setup, breakdown, cleanup)
- number of attendees
- type of setup required
- rates charged
- contract status
- other remarks

There should be at least one section for each meeting or function room, with space to cover specific time periods in each day. To ensure the most efficient use of the function book, all bookings should be made in pencil, the name of the group should be recorded exactly as it appears on the file to facilitate future referencing, and the starting and ending times should be recorded to enable the property to book another event if possible.

To eliminate possible errors, only one person should be given control of the function book. This may be the convention sales manager, or, at properties with a large staff, the senior sales executive. Single person control of the function book is essential; convention space cannot be sold efficiently without this control.

Figure 3.8. SAMPLE ACCOUNT FILE.

The account file is usually kept in a standard file folder and contains all of the group's information, including sales call reports, tentative and definite booking information, function sheets from past business, and correspondence generated relating to the booking. Information is placed in the file in chronological order (with the newest on top)) and secured with clips to prevent loss. Like the master file, account file folders may be color coded to call attention to specific characteristics of the group.

Figure 3.9. SAMPLE TICKLER (TRACE) FILE.

NATIONAL LIVESTOCK DEALERS ASSN. N-02197
PA

Trace:

DATE	INL.	DATE	INL.
Jan. 12	M.A.		
June 15	M.A.		

Divided into months and days of the month, the tickler file helps with account follow up. Salespeople use the tickler file to remind themselves of calls to be made or correspondence to be sent on a specific date.

There may be instances in which the same space is desired by two groups. In this case, sales managers will try to determine the best "fit" for both the hotel and the group. Factors to be considered are the likelihood that the space will actually be filled, the estimated profitability of each group, the status of the group (regular client or new business), the likelihood of repeat business, the long-term profitability of each group, the possibility that one group would consider an alternate date, and the group's convention history. Only after a decision has been made will the group's name be entered into the function book.

In addition to controlling meeting space, it is also necessary to control guestrooms. Properties use a **guestrooms control book** for this; at some properties this book is referred to as the *rooms control bible.* This ensures that rooms are available for groups. This book is used by the sales department to stay aware of the number of rooms it can sell, as hotels often stipulate a maximum *group allotment* — the number of rooms available for sale to groups — to ensure that a proper market mix of group, tour and travel, and individual guest business is maintained. Demand fluctuates by time of year and by day of week so the group room allotment varies considerably. For example, the summer months are generally soft convention months, so a 400-room hotel might only do 25 percent of its business with meeting groups and 75 percent with individual travelers.

Although these percentages may be reversed in the typically busy convention periods of spring or fall, hotels rarely, if ever, will sell the entire hotel to convention groups. Individual corporate and leisure travelers are consistent year-round producers, and selling out to a convention will alienate travelers displaced by convention groups.

The guestrooms control book's format usually consists of monthly report sheets with space for the group's name and guest room commitment by day. These "forecast sheets" are dated and bound in book form, providing projections several years ahead.

As with the function book, all entries should be made in pencil. Often, definite bookings are listed on the upper half of the page, while tentative bookings are entered on the lower half. This technique indicates the negotiating period of convention sales.

Figure 3.10. COMPUTERIZED TRACE REPORT.

The Durham Resort
Morning Report for Ralph Johnson
September 21, 1999

Rooming List Due

Group Name	Date	Day	Room Type	Agree	Block	Pickup	New Block
Mt. Hope Radiology Dept.	2/ 2/ 00	Wed	Run of House	25	25	_____	_____
	2/ 3/ 00	Thu	Run of House	25	25	_____	_____
	2/ 4/ 00	Fri	Run of House	300	300	_____	_____
	2/ 18/ 00	Fri	Run of House	25	25	_____	_____

Deposits Due

Group Name	Arrival Date	Trace Date	New Status/ New Trace Date
Acorn Dry Cleaning	3/ 20/ 00	1/ 10/ 00	_____ ___ /___ /___

Verbal Definites - Contract Due

Group Name	Arrival Date	Trace Date	New Status/ New Trace Date
Jacobs Wedding	9/ 1/ 00	1/ 15/ 00	_____ ___ /___ /___

Tentatives - Decision Due

Group Name	Arrival Date	Trace Date	New Status/ New Trace Date
Automobile Travelers Assn	3/ 24/ 00	11/ 20/ 99	_____ / ___ / ___ /
Arizona Building Company	4/ 30/ 00	12/ 20/ 99	_____ / ___ / ___ /

Leads - Decision Due

Group Name	Arrival Date	Trace Date	New Status/ New Trace Date
Balloon Industries	2/ 1/ 00	11/ 1/ 99	_____ / ___ / ___ /

Source: Delphi Newmarket Software Systems, Inc., Durham, New Hampshire

This report not only replaces the cumbersome manual tickler file, but also offers additional sales tools to the salesperson. The trace report, for example, breaks down the day's business into several categories. The salesperson can take advantage of this feature to prioritize work and schedule each day to make the most of sales opportunities.

Figure 3.11. FUNCTION BOOK RESERVATION SHEET.

U.S. Grant
HOTEL

FUNCTION BOOK RESERVATION SHEET

Group Name _____   Comments _____

Contact _____   _____

Address _____   _____

Phone _____   _____

Dates In House _____   _____

A G E N D A

DAY/DATE	TIME	FUNCTION	SET-UP	# OF PEOPLE	ROOM NAME

Meeting Space Charges:

Sales Rep _____

Date _____

Option Date _____

Date Entered _____

Entered By _____

The sales or catering manager must fill out this form and submit it to the person responsible for monitoring the hotel's function space. In addition, one copy of this form will go into the account file and another copy to the salesperson's reader file.

It is extremely important for the hotel sales office and the front desk/reservations department to have good communication and contact with one another. Because both are booking business, it is imperative that room sales are not overlapped. Traditionally, reservations has reported to the front office manager, but reservations are increasingly being placed under the sales department in many convention-oriented hotels.

Most hotels also computerized their function and guestrooms control books (see Figure 3.12). This method still provides control, since only authorized personnel can add or change information (while information is being changed, the system goes into a "read only" mode until the information is updated). However, the information is readily available to salespeople, either in-house or from a remote location.

Before Hyatt Hotels updated their function books, Gordon Kerr, Hyatt's senior vice president of Management Information Systems, said:

> "Each hotel kept this giant diary with function room bookings written in it. If a customer called Hyatt headquarters in Chicago to book a function room in San Francisco, for example, the manager of the San Francisco hotel had to be called to check availability. Customers eager to book space would wait hours, or even days, to receive a reply. By that time, many would-be customers had found space elsewhere. With the computerized system, Hyatt users can check availability and book function rooms at any connected hotel from any hotel in the network."[3]

Wendy Bonvechio, director of sales and marketing, Sheraton Seattle Hotel & Towers, says:

> "Automation is very important to our business. Customers have seen a drastic change in how quickly their requests are processed since we automated several years ago.
>
> "A problem that has been completely eliminated is the inevitable double booking that occurred with the manual systems. With automation, the computer won't allow you to double book. Our customers demand automation because it is quicker, makes us more efficient and virtually eliminates mistakes. It's no longer an option, but a necessity in order to compete in today's market."[4]

Sales Forms. Once a sales commitment has been made, there are a number of forms used to follow the sale to the final execution of the function. The *tentative booking sheet* (or report) is used if a date has not been confirmed or if details have not been worked out (see Figure 3.13).

In the normal sequence of events, a convention organizer may inquire about the availability of the property on certain dates. Requirements are discussed, but perhaps there are circumstances that must be resolved before setting a definite date. Perhaps board approval is needed or, in the case of a corporate meeting, a supervisor must be consulted. The meeting planner then asks for an *option* on the space, and a *hold* is placed on the room(s).

This means that the hotel has agreed to hold the space pending final confirmation by the client (this agreement may be verbal or by letter). Some properties are cautious about tentative bookings; they do not want to lose out on other business while protecting a tentative account that may not "go definite." That is why it is important to limit the length of the hold by designating an *option date*. An option date is the date by which the client must confirm the order or release the space. If this period is too long, the hotel has severely

Figure 3.12. *COMPUTERIZED FUNCTION AND GUESTROOMS CONTROL BOOK.*

THE RIVERVIEW HOTEL

Date printed: October 1, 2000   Time printed: 11:59 AM

DELPHI — Function Space Profile   Page: 1

Report for Oct 1 2000 to Oct 31 2001

Room Name	Time Period	We 1	Th 2	Fr 3	Sa 4	Su 5	Mo 6	Tu 7	We 8	Th 9	Fr 10	Sa 11	Su 12	Mo 13	Tu 14	We 15	Th 16	Fr 17	Sa 18	Su 19	Mo 20	Tu 21	We 22	Th 23	Fr 24	Sa 25	Su 26	Mo 27	Tu 28	We 29	Th 30	Fr 31
WASHINTN	M				D	D	D	D				D	D						T	T	T											
	L				D	D													T	T	T											
	A				D														T	T	T											
	E																		T	T	T											
ADAMS	M																		DD	DD												
	L																															
	A																						DD	DD								
	E				T	T	T		T	T																						
JEFFERSON	M				D	D	D		VD	VD	VD	VD	VD	VD																		
	L											VD	VD	VD																		
	A																															
	E																															
MADISON	M											T	T	T												T	T	T				
	L								VD	VD					T	T	T			DD	DD	DD				T	T	T				
	A								VD	VD																						
	E																															
MONROE	M																		T	T	T											
	L																		T	T	T											
	A																		T	T	T											
	E																		T	T	T											
JACKSON	M								VD	VD	VD	D	D	D																		
	L								VD	VD	VD	D	D	D																		
	A																															
	E																															

Many hotels are using computerized function and guestrooms control books to provide instant access to information by sales personnel, who must often provide an immediate answer regarding the availability of function space or rooms. These reports are very similar to the manual reports kept by some hotels. The main difference is that the computer generates these reports automatically by using booking information already entered into the system. These sample reports were generated by Delphi System, software specifically designed to meet the needs of the hotel industry.   (continued)

limited its freedom to seek another customer, but the date should be long enough to enable the client to secure the necessary approval.

A *definite booking form* is used after business has been confirmed (see Figure 3.14). It is processed when a contract or letter of agreement has been signed and when the business is scheduled for a specific date. The form includes a number of details needed to properly service the function, such as the number of attendees, setup requirements, etc. The date and details will be penciled into the function book (and guestrooms control book, if required).

Once a group "goes definite," establish a **working file** for the event. This file differs from the account file. The working file contains only the information relevant to the event. It is the file from which the convention service department works. Once the event concludes, the working file is broken down and appropriate materials are returned to the

Figure 3.12. COMPUTERIZED FUNCTION AND GUESTROOMS CONTROL BOOKS.

THE RIVERVIEW HOTEL

Date printed: August 27, 1996   Time printed: 11:41 AM

DELPHI — Group rooms Control Report for 1997 June

	1 Sun	2 Mon	3 Tue	4 Wed	5 Thur	6 Fri	27 Fri	28 Sat	29 Sun	30 Mon	Total Rooms	Total Guests	Ave. Rate	Room Revenue	Decision Date	RT	SRC	Stat	Date Entered
DEFINITES for CORP.																			
D.E.C.											500	500	124.00	62,000.00	8/27/96		TRB	D	8/27/96
Mass Bay Co											200	200	118.00	23,600.00	8/27/96		TRB	D	8/27/96
I.B.M.											90	90	125.00	11,250.00	8/27/96		TRB	D	8/27/96
Coastal Inc.											15	15	128.00	1,920.00			TRB	D	2/13/96
CORP.	0	0	0	0	0	0	0	0	0	0	805	820	122.69	98,770.00				D	
TENTATIVES for CORP.																			
Lotus Dev. Co.			5	5	5	5					20	40	145.00	2,900.00	8/27/96		SB	T	8/27/96
Crimson Trvl						6					24	48	118.00	2,832.00	8/27/96		RWH	T	8/27/96
Eastern Inc.											35	70	130.00	4,550.00	8/27/96		RWH	T	8/27/96
Lotus Dev. Co.											15	30	121.00	1,815.00	8/27/96		RWH	T	8/27/96
Intel Corp.											9	27	121.00	1,089.00	8/27/96				
Eastern Inc.											4	4	145.00	580.00	8/27/96				
CORP.	0	0	5	5	5	11	0	0	0	0	107	223	128.65	13,766.00				T	
DEFINITES for Assoc.																			
Travel Assoc.	25.	25	25								75	75	108.00	8,100.00	9/30/96		KL	D	3/10/96
N.A.F.E.											30	60	127.00	3,810.00	8/12/96		CRW	DD	8/12/96
U.S.ASSOC.											120	240	120.00	14,400.00	8/1/96		TS	D	8/10/96
U.S.ASSOC.							7	7	7	7	63	126	112.00	7,056.00			TS	D	8/10/96
U.S.ASSOC.							5				20	20	120.00	2,400.00					
ASSOC.	25	25	25	0	0	0	17	7	7	7	308	521	116.12	35,766.00				D	
TENTATIVES for ASSOC.																			
Vets Assoc.	2	2	2								6	12	121.00	726.00	8/25/96		TRB	T	8/25/96
N.A.R.R.P.	10	10									20	40	120.00	2,200.00	8/25/96		TRB	T	8/25/96
Data Systems			6	6	6	6					48	96	131.00	6,288.00	8/25/96		TRB	T	8/25/96
D.P.A.			10	10	10						30	60	145.00	4,350.00	8/25/96		TRB	T	8/25/96
Mutual Assoc.					3	3					24	48	131.00	3,144.00	8/25/96		TRB	T	8/25/96
Mont Ward Co.											40	80	100.00	4,000.00	6/24/96		EP	T	6/24/96
Newsweek											16	32	131.00	2,096.00	8/25/96		RWH	T	8/25/96
N.A.F.E.											36	72	127.00	4,572.00	8/12/96		TRB	T	8/25/96
Int'l Assoc.											8	16	118.00	944.00	8/25/96		TRB	T	8/25/96
Womens Assoc.											4	8	110.00	440.00	8/25/96		TRB	T	8/25/96
Manufact. Assn											48	96	127.00	6,096.00	8/25/96		TRB	T	8/25/96
N.A.T.C.O.							45				270	540	234.00	63,180.00	8/25/96		TRB	T	8/25/96
Dental Assoc.								2	2		4	8	110.00	440.00	8/25/96		TRB	T	8/25/96
Central Assoc.									30	30	60	120	120.00	7,200.00	8/25/96		TRB	T	8/25/96
US Yacht Club									4	4	8	16	131.00	1,048.00	8/25/96		TRB	T	8/25/96
ASSOC.	12	12	18	16	19	9	45	2	36	34	622	1244	171.58	106,724.00				T	

(Continued from preceding page). Tentative and definite bookings in the function book and guestroom control book are monitored on a regular basis. At the weekly sales meeting, discussion will center on booking activity and how to best manage the guestroom and function space inventory. The computerized function and guestrooms control books will help the sales team to look at business on the books and manage it for the benefit of both the hotel and meeting planners.

account file. Some hotels file the folders chronologically, but because the function book already lists all events in such order, you may be more comfortable filing alphabetically. It doesn't matter so long as there is some chronological system to remind the hotel of pending events.

After the convention is booked, other forms may also be necessary. In some cases, details such as a date, room requirement or guest room figure may change. It is then necessary to complete a *change form* to ensure that these changes are made. There may be many times when a piece of business which was considered definite is cancelled. In such a case, a *cancellation form* must be filed. Since there may be a number of reasons for the cancella-

Figure 3.13. TENTATIVE BOOKING FORM.

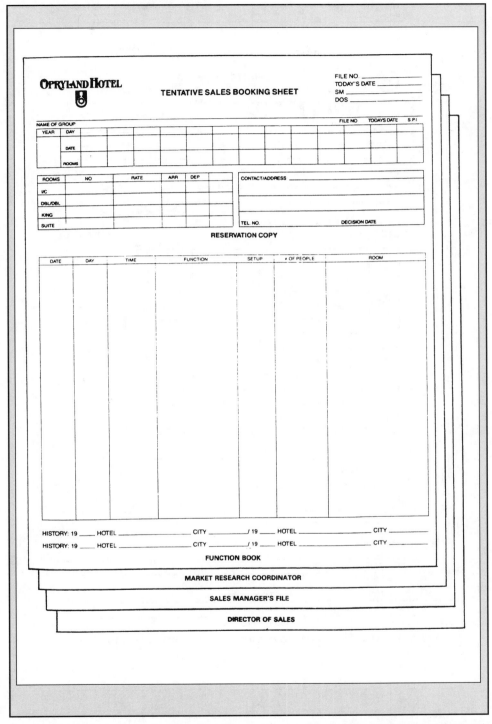

This form is used pending final confirmation of an event or function. Tentative bookings are often made when a client is interested in the space but needs to work out additional details or get approval. Using this form, tentative details are entered into the function book in the event that the function is confirmed (note the space for the *option date, the date by which a final decision must be made*).

Figure 3.14. DEFINITE BOOKING FORM.

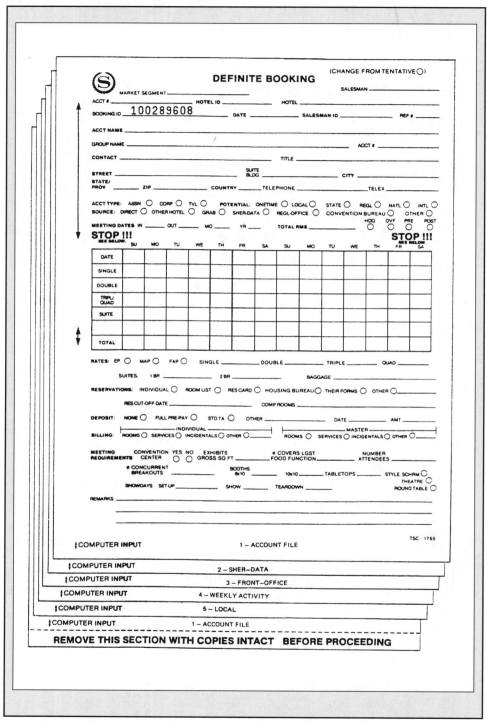

This form is processed when a contract or letter of agreement is signed. At that time, the information on the form is entered into the function control book. Note that the form includes details of the function to enable plans to be made to service it effectively.

tion, some properties follow up the cancellation form with a *lost business report* that details the reason for the cancellation.

Some properties use a general form that eliminates the use of several of these forms. And, in addition to these general sales office forms, salespeople also utilize a number of forms for their individual use to track their progress in selling to accounts. These forms will be discussed in Chapter 7, where we take a look at specific selling techniques.

Sales Office Automation

Over the past several years, there have been dramatic changes in the way hotels do business. Today's advanced technology has eliminated much of the "drudge work" that was an inherent part of the sales effort. Paperwork that used to be done by hand (notes about sales calls and account requirements, for example), taking hours to prepare, update and analyze, is now readily available by calling up a screen on a computer terminal. In this section, we will take a look at how today's computer is drastically changing the face of the sales office — how it is not only helping to eliminate time-consuming paperwork, but how it is being used to personalize presentations, create lists of potential contacts, and forecast future demand for guest and meeting rooms.

Advantages of Automation

Hospitality industry professionals agree that up to 70 percent of a salesperson's time can be spent on non-sales activities, such as call tracing, checking the availability of rooms, blocking rooms and space — and simply running back and forth to filing cabinets to retrieve information. The computer has changed all that. No longer is it necessary to search for lost files or prepare reports by hand; this data is readily available on individual computer terminals.

In addition, the computer frees salespeople from the office. If a salesperson is out making calls, information can be accessed by other salespeople or the clerical staff if immediate action is required. And, pertinent information (often in the form of reports) is instantly available to other departments requiring it (the banquet/catering department, reservations, etc.).

Computers make it easy to "personalize" important documents such as contracts and correspondence. They also simplify mass mailings, generating mailing labels (often by zip code or group type) in a fraction of the time it would take a secretary to sort through records and type labels to specified target groups. Sales management uses computers to evaluate both individual and departmental performance — the computer can provide detailed reports of sales calls made, the amount of business booked and the potential area for future efforts.

New Advances in Hotel Computer Systems

While hotels have used computer systems for booking reservations for several years, only recently have sales offices been automated to provide up-to-date information to salespeople and sales management. Tim Grover, Regional Director of Sales and Marketing for Starwood Hotels and Resorts Worldwide states:

"For any hotel sales force automation is critical. Delphi (software for hotel sales and catering) controls more than 80 percent of the market; it is considered the 'Microsoft' of hotel sales and catering systems. They have a Windows-based version for managing sales contracts, group room blocks and catering space. It is also user-friendly and can generate a variety of reports. Delphi software also functions as an excellent contact manager. Every conversation with a client about an event is documented and accessible to our entire sales team. And, finally, it helps us manage our revenue more efficiently. Knowing what's on the books at any given time for both room sales and catering is a valuable asset that benefits both the customer and the hotel."[5]

In addition to the access to this information, we have also seen how computers are being used to eliminate the large amount of paperwork generated by the sales department. One of the most important ways in which a computer is being used, however, is to assist the sales department in organizing and analyzing information about meeting groups. Database management programs provide a way to keep a service history of all client bookings, including the expected and actual number of attendees, the number of guest rooms booked, the types of functions booked, average room rate and average check, etc. **Database marketing** becomes a simple process. If a salesperson wishes to target groups that meet in the western regions of the country, for example, the computer will produce a list of accounts that meet that criteria for the salesperson to contact (see box titled "The Hidden Opportunities with Database Marketing").

The "Virtual" Office

Besides eliminating much of the drudgery of keeping records and accessing the information necessary to sell to and service meetings business, computers are playing an increasing role in improving the efficiency of property salespeople. No longer does it take days to answer inquiries or check date availability. Nor do salespeople have to sell from their own property. Many of today's salespeople are using technological advances to create "virtual offices" — armed with a laptop computer, a cellular phone, and an e-mail address, they are free to go where the business is — while still maintaining close contact with their home property (see box titled "The Virtual Sales Manager"). Not only does this mean working while away on business; a number of hotel salespeople are now home-based. Sheraton, for example, estimates that about half of its 100 salespeople selling its Starwood brand are home-based, and this trend is expected to continue.[6]

Laptop computers are the main component of a virtual office. While they are portable enough to be carried in a briefcase, they provide the capability of tapping into the property or chain's computer system to check for room availability, rates and other information needed by potential clients. Most are equipped with FAX modems, enabling the salesperson to check availability, generate a reply or proposal for the meeting planner, and immediately FAX the document to the customer.

Swissôtel, a hotel chain with properties in the United States, Europe, Asia and the Middle East, was one of the first hospitality firms to "go virtual." Their United States national account team is equipped with laptop computers and accompanying cellular phones which enable salespeople to get immediate availability and rate information. The laptops are also used to send and receive faxes and, since they store property photos and detailed information about guestrooms and meeting space, they can be used to create customized presentations for meeting planners.

Swissôtel president and CEO Andreas Meinhold says of the system:

> "In a sense, Swissôtel has packed its bag and taken itself on the road using specially adapted laptops and connectivity links. Because our salespeople are tapped into the property-management system, they're able to operate out of their virtual office as if they were behind the front desk of any Swissôtel.
> "Our account managers will be able to spend their time just selling, not focusing on administrative tasks. They can work when they want and where they want, and really spend their time focusing on our customers' needs."[7]

Electronic mail (e-mail) offers a number of advantages to salespeople. First, is its speed. No longer does it take days to send correspondence to a client and wait for a reply. With e-mail, the salesperson can send off a message or proposal, get a reply, and respond to the reply within a short period of time (unlike telephone messages, e-mail can be directly responded to as soon as it is received; there is no need to talk to the home office, hang up the phone, and look for and dial the client's number). Second, although it is private, a number of the same messages may be sent to different contacts at one time (if a salesperson wants to get the word out about a new promotion, for example, the message can be generated once and e-mailed to several potential customers). Third, e-mail allows for flexibility. A number of messages — either the same or different — can be generated at one sitting and one or all can be sent at the same time. Conversely, an e-mail recipient can pick up all of his or her e-mail messages at once and respond as time and priorities allow. Last, but certainly not least, is the versatility of e-mail. E-mail communications can range from a short note requesting specific information to a large file of text and graphics, and even software applications can be transferred via e-mail.

While it is becoming increasingly common for salespeople to have an e-mail address, the medium has not yet replaced the need for other high-tech communications devices, such as *cellular phones*, which enable salespeople to make calls to and from remote locations. Cellular phones are often used in conjunction with laptop computers to contact clients and to keep in touch with the home office. Using a cellular phone eliminates the necessity of having to look for a phone after meeting with a client, and provides the added convenience of minimizing "down time" — calls can be made while waiting for a client, in a cab on the way to the airport, and so on.

Still other salespeople rely on voice mail services and pagers to keep in touch with the home office and clients. *Voice mail services*, which offer a "private" telephone number, can be checked frequently for calls and have the advantage of 24-hour availability (even when the sales office is closed). *Pagers* can be an important tool for salespeople working a local area. Some pagers offer two-way message capabilities while others simply "beep" the recipient in the event of an incoming call or message and display either a telephone number or a short message for responding.

Other technological advances that have made it easier for today's hotel salespeople to concentrate their time on selling include computerized Rolodexes, "memo" machines, personal organizers, and electronic dictionaries, spelling checkers and translation devices. These advances can enhance efficiency and professionalism and will give the salesperson more time do what he or she was hired to do — sell rooms and meeting space by going where the business is and focusing on the needs of potential clients.

THE HIDDEN OPPORTUNITIES WITH DATABASE MARKETING

Database marketing allows hotels to develop personal long-term bonds with customers. Sometimes called relationship marketing or loyalty marketing, this approach departs from the mass marketing that has long been used to reach meeting planners. Few industries maintain the information about their customers that hotels keep — files that not only indicate guest requirements but make it easy to identify customers for future communications. Every hotel has account files, including information on past groups and registration cards from individual guests. The most frequently asked question is, "How long do we keep these records?" A more important question is, "What can the information in these files do for us?" The history in these files is the foundation for database marketing.

As competition has heated up in the past five or ten years, hotel operators have scrutinized marketing expenditures more carefully than ever. What they have learned is that it's five to seven times more expensive to acquire new guests than it is to retain existing ones. Your best customers are those who have purchased recently, purchase frequently, and deliver the greatest contribution to revenue.

Guest folios, registration cards, and group history on meeting planners form the core of your database; they allow you to personalize service to meet guest needs, thereby improving the guest experience and reinforcing loyalty.

Hotels typically use database marketing to analyze travel and spending patterns of market segments. Database programs allow you to easily trace and maintain customer controls, call up any customer record quickly, generate call-back schedules, follow-up letters and mailings as well as mail merge to individual or a large number of customers.

Establishing relationships and a dialogue with customers is fast becoming a requirement for survival in the hotel industry. Whether a hotel continues to rely solely on its guest history system or decides to invest the time and money in a more sophisticated database system, one thing is certain: Hotel managers who know the most about customers and are able to harness resources for quick response to threats and opportunities will enjoy a tremendous advantage in the competitive decade ahead. If you cannot move quickly enough, your competitor across the street surely will.

Contributed by Cindy Estis Green, President, Driving Revenue

Additional Uses of Automation

In addition to automating sales records and enhancing the effectiveness of the property's salespeople, the computer and other facets of today's technology are being used to boost productivity and increase efficiency by:

- Generating daily, weekly, and monthly reports
- Providing rooms and equipment inventory
- Generating mailing lists
- Using word processing functions to generate contracts, proposals, routine correspondence, and so on.

Personalization. In terms of word processing, the computer age has also ushered in an age of personalization. Today's meeting planners want to be more than an account number. Computer data banks make it easy to personalize correspondence and even routine contracts to meet this need.

The Virtual Sales Manager

Many hotel managers feel chained to their properties, overseeing the day-to-day operations of their sales staffs and ensuring that meeting arrangements are met, — but not Michael Mulcahy, a sales manager for the Sheraton City Centre in Washington, DC. Four days a week, Mulcahy is in New York City, soliciting business for the hotel and communicating with the property through his laptop computer and cellular phone.

The arrangement, which has proven highly profitable for the hotel, came about by chance. While Mulcahy and Yale Feldman, the GM of the hotel, were in New York booking a client, a business representative from another firm who happened to be in the office asked for information on the hotel. Although the pair eventually "accidentally" booked a $60,000 piece of business, the sale produced its share of frustration. It took an entire afternoon of calling back and forth to the Washington sales office to finalize the details, leading to Feldman's resolve to create a paperless office that could serve clients in their own environment.

Sheraton bought $55,000 worth of Delphi hardware and software and spent another $5,000 to train staffers to utilize it. The property's staff serves as a support team to Mulcahy, who now spends four days of his five day work week in Manhattan, keeping in contact with his staff through his laptop computer and cellular phone.

Mulcahy's laptop unit requires an electrical outlet and one telephone line. It has a built-in modem that allows Mulcahy to fax documents to the property and receive contracts and other documents in return. His cellular phone not only enables him to check messages on his voice mail, but also provides the capability to set appointments while he is in transit — whether it be in a taxicab or aboard a commuter flight.

Mulcahy feels that the arrangement is beneficial to both the property and the client: "At the bottomline, I'm giving them more personal service by being here and meeting with them, so it is to their advantage...There's nothing like being there and reviewing room availability onscreen with the client. And not only that, but taking it a step further and generating the contract and having them sign before you leave. The level of immediacy is far greater."

Sources: "Have Laptop, Will Travel: DC Sheraton Executive Telecommutes from NYC," Toni Giovanetti, *Hotel Business*, Aug. 1994, pps. 3 and 42; "A Satellite Salesperson," Joy Auer, *Lodging*, June 1994, pps. 23 and 24.

Some of the advantages of using word processing, with a special emphasis on personalization, include:

- Letters need to be written only once and can be stored on file for future use.
- Spelling can be verified with the system's dictionary, and most systems offer a grammar check as well.
- Mailing lists for meeting planning organizations can be merged with in-house lists (duplicate entries are purged, resulting in a single, clean file).
- Standard paragraphs can be recalled for insertion into proposal letters and contracts.
- Information from a previous function can be used in a follow-up letter, for example, "Do you wish to use the Monte Carlo room for your awards banquet again this year?"
- Filing is correctly done accurately, automatically and quickly, eliminating the most hated clerical job in the office.

Simple mass mailings can be effectively personalized with the name of the contact person and his or her group. This information can be merged into a routine sales letter to give the impression of a personal touch. And, as with computerized sales records, this type of automation frees the sales department's clerical people to pursue other, more productive duties, such as setting appointments or following up on accounts for salespeople.

Yield and Revenue Management. Another vital use of the computer has been in the area of market analysis. **Yield management** is becoming an increasingly important tool in filling both meeting and guest rooms — while increasing profitability for the hotel. Yield management is based on the forecasted demand for function space and rooms. Prices, of course, tend to rise when demand exceeds the supply and fall when the opposite is true. Yield management is a tool that takes the factors influencing business into account to predict when a property can sell space and rooms at higher rates.

Using computer data, the hotel sales department can forecast demand by analyzing booking lead time, anticipated pick up of room blocks, anticipated walk-ins at rack rate, and past experience for that particular time of year. The computer will flag high demand days to signal restraint in negotiation, while highlighting projected low occupancy periods. Armed with this information, salespeople can steer meeting planners that have flexible dates toward low demand dates. Best of all, any forecast can be updated instantly in light of actual activity.

Although yield management has been used by airlines and cruise ships for a number of years (rates have long been based on the customer's willingness to pay), the hospitality industry was relatively slow to capitalize on this concept. With software programs designed specifically for hotels now on the market, however, yield management is becoming an increasingly important tool in determining how to fill rooms for the most profitability.

Revenue management takes yield management a step farther by not only assessing a group's potential for rooms revenue but also looking at the group's projected impact on the property's overall bottom line. Revenue management takes into consideration the size of the group, its spending history (not just in terms of rooms, but overall spending at the property's other revenue-producing outlets, such as restaurants and recreational facilities), and future revenues for the hotel (additional bookings by the group and individuals, referrals, and so on).

Chapter Summary:

Organizing for sales is essential if a property is to capture its share of the lucrative meetings and convention market. In this chapter, we have discussed how sales are structured on a number of levels. We have detailed the importance of the physical layout of the sales office as well the relationship of the sales department with other property departments that will be involved in servicing a group's business, discussed the various positions within sales, and introduced types of supplementary sales staff, including regional sales offices and independent hotel representatives.

Managing the sales effort at any level involves utilizing a number of forms to successfully follow up on business booked and to ensure successful execution of a group's events. We have looked at a number of these forms, including the function and guestrooms control books, as well as forms that enable salespeople to manage their time and enable them to focus on key accounts. We have also seen how the computer has changed the way in which salespeople do business, making it far easier and more efficient to reach and service their customers. In the next three chapters, we will take a look at the primary sources of meetings business and see how sales efforts are specifically organized to sell to and service each segment.

Endnotes:

1. Lalia Rach, Ed.D, "The Current and Future Marketing Professional," *HSMAI Marketing Review*, Fall 1998, p. 22.
2. David C. Bojanic and Elizabeth A. Dale, "A Survey of Convention Sales Career Opportunities," *Hospitality & Tourism Educator*, Fall 1993, pps. 41 & 43.
3. Courtesy of Hyatt Hotels Corporation Sales Automation System, *Datamation*.
4. William Duncan, "Booking Streamlined by Next Generation of Hospitality Software," *Convene*, November 1994, p. 40.
5. "How Technology is Refining Hotel Operations," *Convene*, December 1999, p. 124.
6. Beth Rogers, "Working at Home," *HSMAI Marketing Review*, Spring 2000, p. 34.
7. Laura Ross-Fedder, "Computers Empower Swissôtel Sales Staff," *Hotel & Motel Management*, May 8, 1995, p. 4.

Additional References:

• <u>Hospitality Sales: A Marketing Approach</u>, Margaret Shaw and Susan Morris, John Wiley and Sons, 2000.

- *Journal of Convention and Exposition Management,* K.S. Chon, The Haworth Press, Inc.
www.haworthpressinc.com

Internet Sites:

For additional information on the firms and organizations discussed in this chapter, visit the following Internet sites. The Web addresses listed are current as of January 2001. Addresses may change, however; if a site is not available at the address below, a search engine can be used to access its new location.

Delphi/Newmarket Software - www.newsoft.com

Hospitality Sales and Marketing Association International (HSMAI) - www.hsmai.org

Hospitality Industry Technology Exposition and Conference - www.hitechshow.org

International Association of Hospitality Accountants (IAHA) - www.iaha.org

Perfect Meeting - www.perfectmeeting.com

Best Practices:

SWISSÔTEL: Implementing a Global Sales Effort

The Practice: Swissôtel has established a global sales effort for key accounts, facilitated by a proprietary, computerized global sales data system. This practice places a global team leader in the area from which the bulk of the key account's business is generated; regional team leaders for the same key account are located in other geographic sectors. This sales team cross-sells the key account to drive account sales by using the information on the key account contained in the global sales system.

Why the Practice Was Developed: Shortly after Steve Houser accepted the position of vice president of sales and marketing - The Americas, he learned that North American salespeople were selling only North American properties. He and the senior vice president of sales and marketing initiated a needs assessment program. The findings revealed that no cross-selling was being done anywhere in the organization. That is, key accounts were handled strictly in the region where they were located. In addition, the study indicated a strong need for an integrated global sales system. This need was dramatically evident based on Swissôtel's plan to more than double in size by the end of the year 2000.

The Approach for Implementation: For two months, the sales staffs worked on acquiring information about their various accounts to determine if the account provided at least 300 room nights per year in at least two locations, the amount of data available on the account, and the account's decision-maker at the corporate and local level. The information was fed into the chain's computer system, where it could be used to qualify accounts and determine the value of new accounts. Swissôtel also initiated a global sales team effort for qualified key accounts that designates a global team leader and regional team leaders for each account. As a result, the sales organization became an account-driven agency rather than an occupancy-driven one and has been very successful, garnering a 25 percent revenue increase totaling $9 million from 150 accounts since the program's inception.

Source: *The Key to Best Practices in the U.S. Lodging Industry* **by Drs. Laurette Dube, Cathy A. Enz, Leo M. Renaghan and Judy A. Siguaw. This research, conducted by The Center for Hospitality Research, School of Hotel Administration, Cornell University, was funded by American Express in partnership with the American Hotel Foundation.**

Study Questions:

1. How is the sales department perceived within the organizational structure of the hotel? Why is it necessary for the sales department to assume authority over other departments?
2. What three elements are crucial in structuring a sales office? Why is each important?
3. Sketch job descriptions for the various positions within the sales department. How will these vary between large and small properties?
4. What is an independent hotel representative? What considerations are important in choosing an individual or firm to effectively represent your property?
5. What are the key elements of a sales office filing system? Why is each important?
6. Discuss the importance of the function book and guestrooms control book. Why is it important that only one person control these books when a manual system is used?
7. How has computer technology changed the sales office? How is automation being used to enhance the sales effort?

Key Terms:

Account file. A standardized folder holding the information needed to serve a client.

Database marketing. The process of using guest folios, registration cards and group history of meeting planners to develop relationships and dialogue with customers.

Function book. Master control of all banquet space, broken down on each page or screen by banquet rooms, with a page or screen for each day of the year.

Guestrooms control book. A book or computer screen used to monitor sleeping room allocations to groups.

Independent hotel representative. An individual or firm that acts as an addition to the hotel's internal sales staff.

Key account management. Prioritizing of accounts based upon their individual profit potential.

Master card. An index card that contains a summary of everything needed for a sales effort, including the organization's name, the decision maker(s), key contacts, addresses, telephone numbers, and so on. Cards may be color coded to accent key factors. Many properties today use the computerized version of the master card.

Reader file. A file containing copies of internal and external correspondence generated by a salesperson. Useful for reviewing the performance of the sales staff.

Regional sales office. Sales offices for chain properties that are located in places other than the property. Help promote and sell individual properties.

Relationship marketing. Marketing that views customers as assets and emphasizes retaining customers by nurturing and sustaining relationships with them.

Revenue management. The practice of assessing a group's overall profitability on the property's bottom line. Not only is the group's impact on guestrooms and meeting space revenues assessed, but also its spending in other areas (from restaurants to retail) as well as its potential for future business.

Standard operating procedures (SOPs). Written instructions explaining how business activities should be handled.

Tickler file. A follow-up file used to remind salespeople of correspondence, telephone calls sales calls or other business activities that must be handled on a particular day. A computerized version is commonly used by today's hotel salespeople.

Working file. A file set up as soon as a booking is definite, containing information relevant to the event.

Yield management. A technique used to maximize the revenue/profit of the hotel by basing prices for guestrooms and banquet space on supply and demand.

Learning Objectives:

This portion of your text takes an in-depth look at the association market. We will discuss the types of meetings held by associations, their typical patterns, requirements for meetings, how site decisions are made and by whom, and ways to reach this lucrative market segment. When you have studied this chapter, you will:

- Be able to describe the kinds of meetings held by associations and the characteristics of each.

- Know the key decision makers for association meetings and what they look for in determining a meeting site.

- Be able to identify the most effective sources for finding association business.

Outline

Revenue Producers

Requirements for Association Meetings

Kinds of Association Meetings
- Annual Conventions
- State and Regional Conventions
- Conferences
- Seminars and Workshops
- Board and Committee Meetings

Characteristics of Association Meetings
- Cycle and Pattern
- Geographic Restrictions
- Lead Time
- Kind of Sites
- Voluntary Attendance
- Convention Duration
- Price

Association Meeting Decision Makers
- Association Director
- Association President and Officers
- Committee Chairperson
- Board of Directors
- Other Influences

Sources for Finding Association Business
- Directories
- Databases
- Specialized Periodicals
- Hotel Records

The Importance of the Association Market

Kathy Dixon Leone
Vice President of Sales
Boca Raton Resort and Club

"The association market provides a tremendous base of business, both in the meetings the market holds, and the meetings it can generate through the exposure a property gains by hosting its corporate membership. If serviced properly, it can provide a base of business that can be the foundation of a property's success for years to come."

4 Selling the Association Market

In the first three chapters, we've studied the importance of the convention business and the trends impacting it, the marketing plan—the cornerstone of sales—and the organization and operation of the sales office. In the next three chapters, we will take a look at the major meetings market segments in detail. The two most prominent target markets, the association and corporate meetings segments, will follow a similar outline: what planners look for in selecting sites, the kinds of meetings held and the characteristics of each type, key decision makers, and how to locate sources for business. Other markets, including nonprofit organizations, government agencies, and other small meetings market segments will be covered in Chapter 6.

According to a Convention Industry Council study, associations spend more than $77.97 billion a year on meetings (see Figure 4.1). It comes as no surprise then that hotel chains such as Hilton, Marriott, Hyatt, Radisson, and Starwood have convention properties in major cities and look to association meetings to fill 30-40 percent of their rooms annually. The Boca Raton Resort and Club attributes approximately 65 percent of its annual sales volume to groups and meetings. Forty percent of their sales from meetings are realized from the association market. That's a lot of business, and it warrants careful study of the kinds of meetings that associations hold and how you can capture your share of this lucrative market.

Revenue Producers

The convention is of extreme importance to the **association**. It is the single largest source of associations' non-dues revenue (see box titled "The Principal Sources of An Association's Income"). Membership dues range from twenty-five dollars or so to several thousand dollars annually in more affluent associations, but almost every association views its convention, meetings, and exhibits as prime sources of revenue.

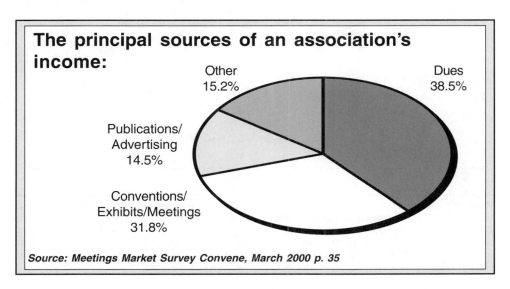

The principal sources of an association's income:

- Other 15.2%
- Dues 38.5%
- Publications/Advertising 14.5%
- Conventions/Exhibits/Meetings 31.8%

Source: Meetings Market Survey Convene, March 2000 p. 35

Figure 4.1. ASSOCIATIONS ARE THE MOST VISIBLE CONVENTION ORGANIZERS.

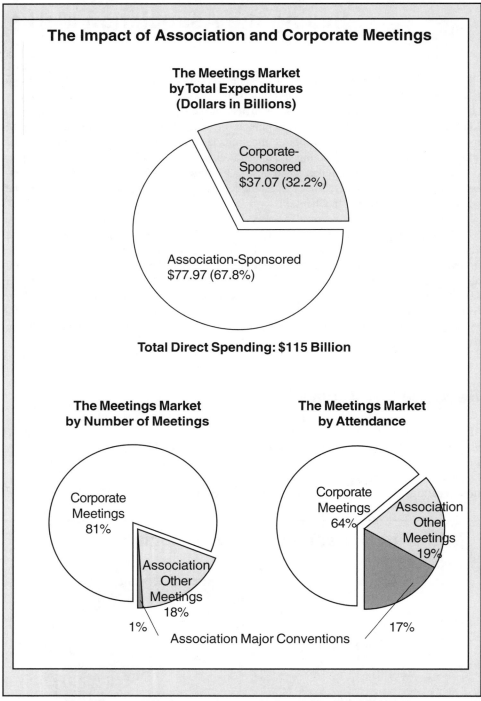

The Impact of Association and Corporate Meetings

**The Meetings Market
by Total Expenditures
(Dollars in Billions)**

Corporate-
Sponsored
$37.07 (32.2%)

Association-Sponsored
$77.97 (67.8%)

Total Direct Spending: $115 Billion

**The Meetings Market
by Number of Meetings**

Corporate
Meetings
81%

Association
Other
Meetings
18%

1%

Association Major Conventions

**The Meetings Market
by Attendance**

Corporate
Meetings
64%

Association
Other
Meetings
19%

17%

While corporations provide a larger market in total number of attendees and meetings, the spending of associations is approximately two and one-half times that of corporations. The principal reason for this difference in spending is that associations generally include a trade show as part of their conventions.
Source: Updated from "The Economic Impact of Conventions, Expositions, Meetings and Incentive Travel Study" conducted by the Conventions Industry Council and the 2000 Meeting Market Study conducted by Meetings and Conventions Magazine.

Associations earn money from conventions in several ways. One is with exhibits. The group may rent the exhibit hall of a hotel or convention center for one to three dollars per square foot depending on demand and season. The association then subleases the space to exhibitors for considerably more -- up to fifty dollars per square foot in some cases.

Registration fees at such events also add to the association's coffers. When a convention "package" includes a number of meal functions, it is not uncommon for the package to cost the delegate several hundred dollars. The hotel is paid only for the actual number of meal tickets collected or the number of meals the meeting planner guarantees, which adds more to the profits of the convention since not every person attends every event.

Associations earn additional money from the advertising in their publications and programs. And when a participating company sponsors a segment of the program and picks up the tab, the association's costs are further reduced.

Thus, when you consider how important conventions are to membership retention and to revenue production, it becomes apparent that these events are absolutely essential for the well-being of an association. They constitute a major effort on an association's part, and they are planned and conducted as such.

Requirements for Association Meetings

Site selection is crucial to the success of a convention. Mike Welch, executive director of the Credit Union Executives Society of Madison, Wisconsin, has said:

> "We look for good facilities, pleasant weather, an attractive location, and a city that's near the largest concentration of members. We also consider

Figure 4.2. FACTORS CONSIDERED IMPORTANT TO ASSOCIATION MEETING PLANNERS IN THE SELECTION OF A FACILITY/HOTEL.

Association Planners

Factors Considered Very Important	For Major Conventions	For Other Meetings
Number, size, quality of meeting rooms	83%	68%
Negotiable food, beverage and room rates	75	67
Cost of facility/hotel	75	72
Quality of food service	71	63
Number, size and quality of sleeping rooms	68	48
Efficiency of billing procedures	57	48
Meeting support services and equipment	55	42
Assignment of one staff person to handle all aspects of meeting	53	48
Efficiency of check-in and check-out procedures	52	41
Availability of exhibit space	47	16
Previous experience in dealing with facility and its staff	41	36
Proximity to shopping, restaurants, off-site entertainment	27	18

Although the purpose of a meeting ultimately determines the facility selection criteria, the table above gives insight into general factors of importance to the association meeting planner. Negotiable rates continue to be an important aspect of hotel selection for conventions and meetings.
Source: The 2000 Meetings Market Study conducted by Meetings and Conventions magazine.

who else is going to be there and when. For instance, when our annual convention is taking place in a city, we don't want to go there for a seminar for a year or two."

Figure 4.2 details some of the other factors that meeting planners take into consideration when making a site selection. These considerations include:

Adequate Meeting Space. The organizer is always concerned about your ability to house the general assembly and smaller sessions. He or she is interested in space for workshops and committee meetings, as well as your ability to handle food functions expertly without encroaching on the meetings.

Enough Guestrooms. We don't know a single convention organizer who doesn't prefer to house the entire group in one hotel. Suites are needed in addition to singles, twins and doubles. When a single hotel can't house the entire group, two or more hotels in close proximity are the most desirable.

Adequate Exhibit Space. Exhibits mean money for the association and are an attraction for the members. Planners look for adequate exhibit space, located conveniently to housing. Hotels with exhibit facilities have an advantage. When larger exhibits require exhibition halls, the preference is for setups near the hotel. Delegates prefer not to travel between hotel rooms and convention areas.

An Attractive Location. A location need not be a resort to attract different groups. Chicago gets lots of business because of its central location. That's very important to many busy groups.

Other groups may like to combine the show with other business. Your city may be in the heart of their business world. Attendance is also easier to stimulate if people don't have to travel too far. Easy driving distance may mean an extra ten percent registration. Many associations do like resort locations. You may be able to offer that, or perhaps you are

Figure 4.3. SUMMARY OF TYPES OF ASSOCIATION MEETINGS OTHER THAN MAJOR CONVENTIONS.

Type of Meeting	Total Meetings	Average # Planned	Average Attendance	Average # Days Duration	Average # of Months Lead Time
Board Meetings	40,300	4.0	36	1.9	5.6
Educational Seminars	61,800	7.4	99	2.4	7.0
Professional/Technical	33,900	6.0	97	2.3	7.1
Regional/Local Chapters	29,200	6.7	104	1.8	6.1
Other Meetings	9,000	4.2	188	2.6	9.9
Total/Average	174,200	14.7	90	2.2	7.1

The average association meeting planner works on over 14 meetings per year.
Source: The 2000 Meetings Market Study conducted by Meetings & Conventions magazine.

located in great tourist country. Put simply, you have to offer something attractive to each group.

Service. Last, but probably most important, the meeting planners look for service. They want some assurance that you have an experienced staff that is interested in doing a good job. Each convention event is a custom job and many things can, and do, go wrong. Convention planners live with such hazards and justly feel that your staff should have the expertise and the desire to keep the show moving. Service is what brings repeat and recommended business.

Kinds of Association Meetings

The first kind of association meeting to come to mind is the *annual convention.* Certainly this is the most visible, and the largest, but there are many other occasions for associations to meet. For example, lots of planning is required in staging a convention. *Board and committee meetings* are often scheduled for this very purpose, as well as at other times for many other purposes, and may require a meeting room at a hotel property. In addition, *regional conventions, conferences, seminars and workshops* are conducted through the year by most associations (see Figure 4.3). These are all sources of good business for hotels. It is a rare property that cannot handle some kind of association business. You may not necessarily be able to handle the major events but there are many others that you can service.

Annual Conventions

Almost every association has an annual convention. The annual convention is a ritual in associations of all types—international, national, state and regional.

Attendance varies, of course. Some conventions are truly huge affairs. The Chemical Society draws between 20,000 and 30,000; others have fewer than 100. The mean attendance is about 850 people. Conventions vary only in scale, maintaining similar philosophy and motivation.

The most recent market study conducted by *Meetings & Conventions* magazine reports attendance figures as follows:

Delegate Attendance at Annual Convention	% of Associations
Fewer than 100	14%
100-149	23
150-299	15
300-499	14
500-1,999	13
1,000-1,999	9
2,000 or more	12
	100%

Average delegate attendance: Male 515

Female 331

846

Since 66 percent of all national meetings and trade shows have an average attendance of 500 or less, even small properties can take advantage of this lucrative market. And,
small properties can benefit from the large conventions by making arrangements with
neighboring properties to handle overflow business generated by large groups.

Exhibits are a major part of association meetings, especially trade and technical
societies. Two-thirds of the annual association conventions are held in conjunction with a
trade show or exhibit. These conventions attract 130 exhibitors using an average of 21,000
square feet of exhibit space. Exhibits are a source of essential income to associations, and
very important to exhibitors, too.

There are conventions without exhibits, of course, and it is also not unheard of for a
convention to stage a major program with exhibits in one hotel and another program
without exhibits in another. And sometimes, an event may be held in a city because of the
presence of another convention with an exhibit.

Most conventions include a **general session** attended by everyone and a number of
smaller meetings. These smaller meetings are often termed **breakout sessions**, where the
group divides into smaller meetings, and **concurrent sessions**, where meeting sessions on
different topics are scheduled at the same time. Sometimes, the general session runs concurrently with the exhibit hours; sometimes they run tandem so as not to compete for members'
attention.

It is a rare convention without food functions. Many groups sell a complete convention package for their event. The package includes registration fees and prepaid tickets to
all food functions and special events.

You can see at this point that a convention, especially a large one, calls for a number
of rooms of different kinds. Large rooms are needed for the general assembly, the exhibit,
and the food functions; smaller rooms for committee and board meetings, workshops, and
smaller food functions; and suites and similar rooms for hospitality centers.

Often a hotel cannot handle an entire convention because of its size, so several hotels
may band together to sell an association as a team. The hotel business is odd in that strong
competitors often become partners in a project, and both can enjoy additional business as
a result. Even a piece of a convention event may be profitable, as well as giving the hotel a
foot in the door for future business (see the Copley Connection advertisement in Figure
4.4).

There is another variation of the national convention—the exhibit without convention program. These events, often called *exhibitions*, *expositions*, or *trade shows*, sometimes are not even sponsored by an association but by individual entrepreneurs or companies. These events can bring you business even if you cannot house the exhibit itself. Many
an exhibition becomes the focal point of the industry or trade it serves and gives exhibitors
the opportunity to hold sales meetings and dealer meetings in conjunction with the event.

State and Regional Conventions

The major difference between a regional convention of a national organization and one
staged by a state or regional association is sponsorship. A state association usually holds an
annual meeting for its members within the state, although in recent years state organizations have ventured beyond state borders on occasion. Many national associations, even

Figure 4.4. THE COPLEY CONNECTION.

In this example of cooperative advertising, The Westin Hotel and the Boston Marriott, both at Copley Plaza, have teamed up to attract conventions and large meeting business. The properties, normally competitors, provide a range of integrated services to attract large groups.

those with affiliated state chapters, hold regional conventions to supplement their national ones. Of interest is the recent growth in regional association meetings. When finances are short, many association members skip the big annual conventions, and attend smaller, shorter meetings that are closer to home. As a rule, the regional event is smaller than the national one both in attendance and size of the exhibit. Again, some regional conventions have exhibits and others don't. There is no rule of thumb.

The major difference, as far as hotel people are concerned, has to do with who makes the decisions about when and where the event will be held. Both state and regional conventions are an important source of business for both large and small hotel properties (see Figure 4.5).

According to the *Association Meeting Trends* report, only ten percent of all state and regional conventions had an attendance of more than 1,000; 17 percent had attendance of 500 to 1,000, and 75 percent had less than 500 attendees, making this an ideal market for smaller properties.

And, since chapters of national associations meet within the state or regional boundaries, it is a market that can be reached relatively easily. Sources for locating state and regional business include:

- Chambers of Commerce and Convention Bureaus.
- The Yellow Pages of telephone directories for capital cities.
- Newspapers from capital cities or feeder cities.
- The American Society of Association Executives (ASAE). Hotel salespeople can join such groups as the Washington Society of Association Executives (WSAE) or the California Society of Association Executives (CSAE) as allied members.

Once a group has been located, it is important to remember that in many cases the meeting planners may be committees or inexperienced planners and that lead time is usually fairly short. A property that shows a willingness to assist with meeting planning will gain an edge over the competition.

Another way to solicit this market's business, which is an important source of revenue for off-peak periods, is to offer inexpensive room rates. Many attendees pay their own expenses, making room rates especially important to them. And, because spouses usually attend, a property that offers a single/double occupancy flat rate for these groups is especially attractive to this lucrative market.

Conferences

Associations have become frequent stagers of conferences, primarily to supplement the annual convention program with a specific program made timely by new developments. The 2000 election, which resulted in concern over ballot counts, precipitated a number of conferences, for example.

The number of conferences held within an industry varies, of course. They have become commonplace in the technical, scientific and professional worlds. A breakthrough in an electronic process or medical treatment or a change in corporate law or tax structure brings on a rash of conferences.

Figure 4.5. STATE AND REGIONAL ASSOCIATION MARKET AT A GLANCE

State and Regional Association Market at a Glance

Location

This segment of the association market is usually an offshoot of the national or international association. Groups usually rotate their convention among the major cities within the state or region and rely heavily upon local support for invitation. They meet four to six months before or after their affiliated national convention.

Facilities

Preferred facilities include free and ample parking as a high percentage of attendees drive. Access to means of public transportation is not critical; therefore, suburban hotels are often used. Most conventions require ballrooms for plenary sessions or banquets as well as several breakout rooms for seminars.

Price

Double occupancy is common so hotels should consider a flat rate, perhaps a compromise between the single and double rates. Attendance is voluntary so the decision maker is price-sensitive. They often will schedule their meetings during a hotel's off-periods and will schedule a Thursday arrival/ Sunday departure or Friday arrival/ Sunday departure.

Services

Preferred services include business services, such as fax machines, office copiers, typing and word processing. Other services include audiovisual equipment necessary for presentations and occasionally exhibit halls for table-top exhibits.

Decision Makers

These groups usually do not have a paid staff or a permanent office, but rather are administered by volunteers and committees on a part-time basis. The local chapters frequently submit bids or invitations to host a regional or state meeting. Because volunteer staff changes annually, it is important to actively solicit and update files frequently to determine decision makers.

Best Ways to Reach Market

Check the yellow pages under associations in all major cities (most are headquartered in capital city due to lobbying efforts). Most states have an affiliate of the American Society of Association Executives (ASAE) and publish a list of their members. Local convention and visitors bureaus and chambers of commerce will normally supply a listing of professional associations in their area. Personal contacts and direct mail are the most effective means to reach the decision makers.

Seminars and Workshops

Closely allied to the conference, but on a more modest basis, is the seminar. Association seminars are usually tied in with training and continuing education, such as the training of apprentice craftsmen, the updating of scientific and engineering personnel, or the presentation of marketing developments within an industry. Such seminars are presented around the country to small groups. Such business is within the scope of almost any hotel property.

Board and Committee Meetings

Association business regularly calls for smaller meetings. The board of directors may meet on a regular basis, not necessarily in the city of the association office. These meetings are often set in attractive locales as a way of encouraging outstanding people to serve, since they are not paid. Attendance at board meetings may range from ten to twelve to up to two hundred. The hotel chosen for such meetings is in a prime position to sell the property for the national convention, and for business emanating from the board members' own organizations.

Committee meetings may range in size from ten to fifty people and are held at varying rates of frequency. These events, too, can be serviced by hotels of any size as long as they are geared for meetings.

Figure 4.6. MONTHLY AND DAILY MEETING PATTERN OF ASSOCIATIONS.

When they are held

Rated by the *number of events*, these are the most active convention months in order of importance:
• October • May • April
  • June • September

Rated by the *number of attendees*, these are the most active convention months in order of importance:
• October • September • March
  • February • January

Starting Day of Meeting
Percentage of Total Market

Sat 8.3%
Fri 16.0%
Sun 21.1%
Thurs 17.5%
Mon 12.6%
Wed 15.0%
Tues 9.5%

Source: By permission of Successful Meetings magazine.

Characteristics of Association Meetings

Association meetings of all types follow similar patterns; understanding these patterns will help you sell them intelligently.

Cycle and Pattern

Conventions are held on a regular time cycle. The most common is annual, although there are associations that hold two conventions a year and some that convene only every two years. The one-year cycle is often supplemented in a national organization with one, two or even three regional conventions on a smaller scale.

Conventions most frequently begin on Sunday and run through Wednesday or begin on Thursday and check out on Sunday (see Figure 4.6). The reason for this pattern is the airfare savings realized with a Saturday night stayover. These Saturday night stayovers, required by most airlines to qualify for reduced airfares, have boosted the occupancies of many downtown hotels that previously saw weekends as their slowest periods. Meetings and conventions that previously began on Mondays have moved registration to Sundays whenever possible so attendees can take advantage of the lower airfares. For some resort properties, however, the Saturday overnight requirement has had a negative effect, driving conference business to the end of the week. Jim Tierney, Vice President of Marketing, Amelia Island Plantation Resort, says:

> "With the drastic reduction in airfare when people stay overnight on Saturday, demand for conference business has—during the last few years—shifted to the weekends. This costs my resort and other resorts like us significant room revenue. Conferences that are booked on group rates that are lower than our daily rate take the place of social or transient guests that generally pay a higher room rate on weekends. Then to attract conference business Sunday through Thursday, we find ourselves having to negotiate deeper discounts than we might normally offer because the airfares are higher and that adds significantly to the meeting planners' overall costs. We, therefore, lose revenue at both ends of the week."[1]

A strong geographic pattern is also indicated. Most associations alternate between the East and West in site selection. The most popular variation calls for a midwestern city every two years, with eastern and western cities alternating during the other two years. Typical examples follow:

	1999	2000	2001	2002	2003
National Conventions					
ABC Assn.	New York	Los Angeles	Washington	Denver	Boston
XYZ Assn.	Chicago	New York	St. Louis	Las Vegas	Milwaukee
Regional Conventions					
ABC Assn.	San Diego	Atlanta	Phoenix	Miami	San Francisco
	Cleveland	Kansas City	Cincinnati	St. Louis	New Orleans
XYZ Assn.	Los Angeles	Dallas	Philadelphia	Boston	Miami
	Atlanta	Seattle	San Diego	Detroit	Los Angeles

The important factor is the area of the country, not the specific city. The pattern may call for a Midwest location, which would be St. Louis, Chicago, Cincinnati or others. The Southeast could be served with Atlanta, Miami, Tampa or Memphis. Much depends on the geographic interests of the association members. If there is no special interest factor, the site selectors attempt to provide an interesting place to serve as an additional attraction.

The scheduling of regional events calls for a frank recognition that some members will not travel too far for the event. One association executive told us that his records show a hard core of regulars come to the convention every year no matter where it is held. This group is supplemented by members who come from within three hundred miles. Obviously, he holds regional conventions to keep his members involved. Perusal of the meeting pattern should show you when the group would next consider your part of the country.

Geographic Restrictions

Many state organizations, as part of their constitutions, have limited site selections to within their own states. This is also true of regional associations. There may be further restrictions because of the narrow interests of the program or the nature of the association's business.

There has been some deviation from such rigid limitations in recent years. One device that association executives have used to break out of the pattern is a reciprocal agreement with another state organization. Thus a Colorado chapter might meet in Massachusetts one year and the Massachusetts chapter would meet in Colorado. This satisfies the political aspects of catering to local businesses while providing a novel site to stimulate attendance.

Lead Time

Association conventions are planned well in advance, with a **lead time** of two to five years the norm for the annual meeting and somewhat less than a year for other types of association meetings. Even decisions finalized two years in advance are the result of research and discussion that took up to five years. The larger the convention, the greater the lead time. Meeting planners are well aware that every hotel is not suitable for their convention. They want time to visit the site, check with past clients, and check other alternatives before making the decision.

This long lead time can be frustrating for the new hotel or the new hotel sales manager, but it is the pattern for associaton conventions. And the clear pattern enables you to decide when you can best propose your property to have the best chance of success.

Kind of Sites

Association business does not all go to the same kind of property. This is hardly surprising, considering the many kinds of associations and societies and the many types of meeting events they hold. Requirements and preferences could scarcely be expected to be uniform, but it is a rare hotel property that cannot serve some sort of association event.

Meetings are held in various types of facilities, depending on the size, nature and duration of meetings. Types of meeting facilities commonly used by associations include downtown hotels, airport hotels, suburban hotels, resorts, convention centers, conference centers, college/university campuses and the association's headquarters (see box titled "Types of Facilities Used").

The kind of site selected generally reflects the group size, degree of sophistication and members' affluence. Obviously, a 200-room hotel would not be considered for a 500-person convention, unless it is in cooperation with other hotels. The basic requirements must be met—an auditorium for the main assembly, exhibit space if needed, support rooms for committees' and exhibitors' meetings.

We have discussed geographic considerations. Add to that ease of transportation and how the association executive feels about it. It is hard, for example, to find a more acces-

Types of Facilities Used

	For Conventions	For Other Association Meetings
Downtown hotels	60%	65%
Resort hotels (not including golf resorts)	23%	25%
Convention centers	12%	20%
Suburban hotels	21%	35%
Suite hotels	10%	9%
Airport hotels	11%	25%
Golf resorts	10%	18%
Gaming facilities	3%	6%
Residential conference centers	2%	6%
Nonresidential conference centers	1%	9%
Cruise ships	1%	2%
Other facilities	4%	35%
Did not use overnight accommodations	3%	5%

Source: Meetings & Conventions' 2000 Meetings Market Report

sible place than the hotels near O'Hare Airport at Chicago. If the executive believes that such a site would draw more attendance, he or she may choose it.

There are other geographic factors involved. Many convention organizers want the vacation element working for them. How many extra registrations can a site such as Toronto or Las Vegas or Colorado Springs draw? That's the name of the game. There are many ways to enliven a regularly scheduled convention. Good, stimulating programming is the ideal way, but it's very hard to execute. It is often easier to stage the event at a lovely resort and keep your people happy by exposing them to "the good life."

Sports also play a role in site selection. Golf, tennis, swimming and boating are factors considered by convention planners as they analyze their people. Some fervent golfers on the board may very well swing the decision to a property with a famous course and favorable climate.

Voluntary Attendance

It should be clear by now that the association convention planner has to *attract* members to the annual event. One might think that business and professional interests would suffice as a magnet. Undoubtedly they do draw a certain number, but there are an indeterminate number of fence sitters. Should they go this year or should they skip it? This is where site attraction plays such an important role, and the meeting planner is aware of it.

The option to attend is the member's own. He or she may demand that both business needs and vacation desires be satisfied. If your property or region has tourist attractions, you should make sure that these are all part of your presentation. Whether it is the opera at the Lincoln Center or shopping at Saks Fifth Avenue, antique hunting in the Poconos, or gaming in Las Vegas, a hotel's attraction is more than just its decor and facilities. Learn what positive aspects of your property you can project. Sales may depend on it.

As a bonus, records show that spouses come too when the site is attractive. That results in double occupancy revenues and longer stays. Vacations with tax-deductible expenditures also help turn out the members.

Figure 4.7. AVERAGE DURATION OF ASSOCIATION MEETINGS.

Length of Meeting
(Percentage of Total Market)

3 Days
36.2%

4 Days
22.6%

2 Days
16.5%

5 Days
12.8%

1 Day
4.4%

6 Days
4.5%

Source: By permission of
Successful Meetings magazine.

7 Days
2.0%

8 Days
1.0%

Convention Duration

The average duration of a convention is three to five days (see Figure 4.7). This is generally true for national events, although smaller affairs may last only two or three days. Seminars, committee meetings and the like can last just a day or two. Most conventions with exhibits meet no fewer than three days. There is quite a lot of additional business to be picked up as a result of such conventions as many exhibiting firms hold sales meetings just before the event. This is true, too, for the association's board of directors and many committees. Look also for small associations among delegate groups who meet each year at the major convention.

Price

Your rate schedule is an important consideration for the association executive. We refer to your guestroom rates, not so much to your charges for meeting rooms, food functions, etc., although they will be reflected in the overall registration fee and charges for individual events. Guestroom rates must be aligned with the kind of people expected to attend. This is where the full range of hotels comes into play.

Many a convention organizer sticks with the traditional downtown hotels because of price. The older properties, built years ago at lower costs and lower mortgages, often can offer lower rates. That means nothing to some associations. But to others, it can mean the difference between choosing your property and rejecting it. Price can be a factor. Keep in mind that it is not always the most important one, even though it is always brought up.

Here, too, some study of where the group has met will help. If its history discloses successful years at places such as the Fairmont in San Francisco and the Plaza in New York, you can feel pretty sure that the convention organizer wants the best places for his or her people and that they are accustomed to paying the price. On the other hand, one convention organizer told us that her people were middle-level employees who traditionally paid their own way to the convention. When she booked at a more expensive place, she invariably received an increased number of complaints from members.

There is no right price level. It must suit the group you are trying to sell. Or, more accurately, it must suit the picture the association executive has of his or her people.

Association Meeting Decision Makers

Selection of the convention site—both city and hotel—is a two-step process. The first is screening all suggestions and solicitations; the second is the final approval. We have separated the two because not all people are active in both phases.

Association Director

Almost every association has a permanent executive person. The title may be executive secretary, executive vice president or executive director. Usually, he or she is the administrator of the association, and a very important person to hotel people. Your sales effort starts with this decision maker. A well-run sales staff of a hotel or convention bureau will treasure a file on each association and its key people; the list always starts with the executive director (see Figure 4.8). Note: Any "he" in this discussion is purely for convenience. The executive director may be a woman, and female executives are by no means restricted to associations with primarily women members or activities. If an inquiry comes in from a female "executive director," never assume that she is a clerical assistant. Those days are long gone.

The executive director is a key person for the initial screening of suitable convention sites and swings great influence over the final selection as well (see box titled "Executive Directors Speak Out About How Sites Decisions are Made"). After all, this executive enjoys a continuity in office that the elected officials do not have. The elected officials may serve for a year or two and then pass on the reins to the next team. But the executive director continues in office, and does so with the backing of the key members of the association.

The executive director doesn't work alone, however, especially in larger organizations. Since most of the administrative work has nothing to do with the convention activities, the executive director often has a staff member specifically assigned to convention planning. In the largest organization, this person may have a staff of his own. This convention planner thus is another person you should consider as very important when you make your presentation. He or she reports to and works closely with the executive director. Often

Figure 4.8. TYPICAL JOB TITLES OF ASSOCIATION DECISION MAKERS.

Job Title	Association Planners
Events/Conventions/Conference Planner/ Coordinator/Manager/Director	34%
President/Executive Vice President	25
Meeting Planner/Coordinator/Manager/Director	13
Assistant to Executive	13
Treasurer	3
Director of Education	2
Marketing Director/Coordinator/Officer	2
Board Member	1
Other	7
Total	100%

Source: The 2000 Meetings Market Study conducted by Meetings & Conventions magazine.

the executive appoints a site selection committee to do **site inspections**. This group visits cities and hotels and is responsible for securing convention space arrangements for the association.

Executive Directors Speak Out About How Site Decisions are Made

Garis Distelhorst, National Association of College Stores:
"Our process is collaborative. The meetings staff screens proposals and pre-pares a list of four or five cities. At that point, my role is to determine if there are any that wouldn't work and to suggest any destination not on the list that we might want to do additional research on. We try to follow and East/West/ Central rotation. We focus on second-tier cities that are going to treat our meeting as a big deal...."

Ron Moen, American Association of Orthodontists:
"Preliminary screening is the responsibility of the director of meetings. Actual site reviews of two or three cities on the short list are conducted by the direc-tor, myself, and the member of the board who will be president in the year that the meeting will be held. A committee of the board rubber stamps our recommendation...when it's unanimous...."

Dan Weder, Institute of Food Technologists:
"The recommendation comes to me. I visit cities in the running and make the site decision. While it ultimately goes to the executive committee for approval, in 30 years they've never failed to ratify a selection."[2]

Small associations often cannot afford a full-time executive and are serviced by **multiple association management organizations**. These organizations function as the executive and office staff for a number of associations that otherwise would have to make do with volunteers. In this way the associations enjoy professional management at costs they can afford.

There are approximately 200 association management organizations in business today, managing the affairs of over 500 national associations and more than 1,000 state and regional associations. In such cases, you may find yourself dealing with one man or woman responsible for several convention bookings. The advantage to you is that when selling to these organizations you are not talking about a group coming back in four or five years. One of their clients may be interested in your property later in the same year. Many of these management organizations specialize in one or two industries. If your hotel's history shows a concentration of certain types of associations, such as automotive or computer groups, it would be wise to link with those association management organizations that represent these types of associations.

The trade association representing multiple association management organizations is called the Institute of Association Management Companies (IAMC). This group holds an annual meeting and trade show, and is an ideal target market for smaller lodging properties (see Appendix I for their address).

There are independent companies that fill this role as well. Convention management companies work either for a negotiated fee or a percentage of the registration fees as an incentive to stimulate attendance. Such management firms obviously are important. They influence site selection and are also the people who work with the hotels to execute the meeting. They are also a factor in getting other business.

Association President and Officers

The power of the president varies greatly among associations. As mentioned, the president usually serves for a year or two. He or she may serve as an honorary figurehead or may flex a great deal of muscle. You really have no choice but to pay a lot of attention to this key person. In almost all cases, keep in mind that he or she shares in the initial screening of a selection site and is certainly in on the final decision.

When you build your files on association personnel, take notes on the vice presidents and secretary/treasurers as well. These officers are future years' presidents. A recent study suggests:

> "It is not uncommon in associations to have a new chairperson every year. Often, this chairperson has substantial power over staff and other members...Such power may include the ability to affect the list of sites initially being considered and one that is eventually chosen as the convention location in the future. Because of the lead time necessary to plan major conventions or trade shows, many of these meeting sites are picked years in advance. At the same time, many associations also know in advance who the association president will be in any given year. Either tradition or bylaws regulate much of the decision power on site selection to the person who will be president during the year of a particular convention. Therefore, marketing strategies not only need to be aimed at the current chair or president, they need to identify and court future leaders. A long term relationship between the hospitality marketer and the asso-

ciation chair(s)-to-be can impact how they use their influence in your favor for the year they are in power."[3]

Committee Chairperson

Certain committee heads get involved in the initial suggestions and screening. This depends on the nature and structure of the organization and the subject of the event. They most definitely are a factor in site selection for seminars dealing with the committee's subject matter.

You can see that a fair number of hands get involved in creating the original list of proposed places and in the preliminary screening to narrow down the choices. If you are eliminated in the final selection, it may mean loss of business that year, but you may well be in line for a booking when the cycle brings the association back to your part of the country. There may also be some consolation prizes in the form of selection for lesser events such as committee meetings or seminars.

Board of Directors

The final list is usually presented to the board of directors for the final selection. It is worth emphasizing that the recommendations of the executive director usually are accepted. Some get their way all the time; some must deal more politically and tactfully. But the executive director remains the single most important person you must sell to get association business. He may not rule autocratically, but he manages to get his way most of the time. You may lose the business at the directors' meeting, but without the support of the executive director, you never even get that far. Generally, *all* the finalists meet with the director's approval.

Other Influences

It is common practice in many scientific and technical societies for local chapters to make an **association bid** for the national event. That is not to say they *bid* in the sense of offering money. Rather, they request the honor of playing host to the national group and offer their efforts to make the convention a success. This is especially true with international societies; an invitation from a national chapter is required before a location is considered.

Hotel salespeople are aware of this practice. We know of cases in which a local delegate to an international congress has been approached by a convention bureau or hotel. An appeal is made to his local pride and to any other emotions that can be brought to bear. It is not uncommon in such cases for the bureau or hotel to bear the costs of the delegate's travel, a hospitality suite and the presentation to the board. It is wise to assure the delegate that the bureau or hotel would supply clerical support to enable the delegate to fulfill his role of host.

It doesn't always require such effort. Appeals to local delegates or chapters often bring results merely because of civic pride and a willingness to help local businesses. Look around your city and make friends with people in local association chapters. At the very least, you may pick up a local banquet or one-night meeting.

It is important when you enlist the aid of local members to impress upon them that you and your establishment are fully capable of handling the business. They may very well feel uncertain about the wisdom of getting involved and perhaps fear the embarrassment of a debacle at the national convention. But then you have to convince any prospect at any level that you and your staff are competent and interested in doing a good job. Those are the two key points you must make over and over — that your staff has the *expertise* and the *desire* to do whatever must be done to execute the meeting properly.

In addition to the decision makers who have direct involvement in their association, *third-party planners* have become increasingly influential in site selection. As we discussed in Chapter 1, many of today's meetings are planned by third-party intermediaries, including meeting management firms, independent meeting planners, and travel agents (both individuals and mega-agencies). In many cases, these third-party planners are involved in searching out hotel sites and, due to their familiarity with the industry, their recommendations highly influence their association clients -- especially when the intermediaries will be coordinating and executing the event.

Many of these third-party planners, however, seek a commission from the hotels they recommend. When hotels were struggling to fill rooms in the early 1990s, it became customary to pay a ten percent commission (the percentage of the room rate traditionally paid to travel agents) to meeting management firms. In a good economy, however, an increasing number of properties are balking at paying commissions. This issue is expected to remain a volatile one in the early years of the 21st century, and its final resolution will likely affect the role and impact of third-party meeting planners.

Sources for Finding Association Business

Associations are readily located, fortunately. The national ones seem to be clustered in a relatively few cities. New York, Washington and Chicago lead in the number of associations. Other major headquarter cities include Philadelphia, Austin, Indianapolis, Los Angeles, Milwaukee, Oklahoma City and Richmond.

Directories

Several volumes offer detailed listings of associations. One is *Who's Who in Association Management,* published by the American Society of Association Executives, 1575 Eye Street, NW, Washington, DC 20005. It lists approximately 7,000 associations. The list is available for sale and, under certain circumstances, for direct mail rental. It is a valuable reference.

Other directories include the *National Trade and Professional Associations of the United States* and its companion publication, *State and Regional Associations of the United States.* Each offers over 7,000 listings. The publisher is Columbia Books, Inc., 1212 New York Avenue NW, Suite 330, Washington, DC 20005. The publisher will rent the list for direct mail use and will supply various breakdowns and services at prices quoted on request.

The *Encyclopedia of Associations* (and its companion, *Geographic Index of Associations*) is published by Gale Research Company, 835 Pnobscot Building, Detroit, MI 48226. Contact the publisher for prices.

National Associations of the United States lists all the national associations, membership totals, and officers and addresses. It may be obtained by writing to the Superintendent of Documents, U.S. Government Printing Office, Washington, DC 20402.

Successful Meetings magazine publishes two directories. The *Directory of Conventions* lists more than 19,000 coming events in the convention field. It offers such excellent details as convention sponsor, dates, whether there is an exhibit, estimated attendance, headquarters facilities, name, title and address of the executive in charge and reports on the scope of the meetings. The second directory, *The Exhibit Schedule*, includes more than 11,000 listings of major events around the world. It includes full data, as in the *Directory of Conventions*. Contact the publisher for prices and more information on either of these products at Successful Meetings, 633 Third Ave., New York, NY 10017.

The Salesman's Guide publishes directories of association, corporate and incentive meeting planners (see Figure 4.9). Each listing includes the names and titles of the meeting planners, their addresses, number of conventions and meetings held, past and future sites, months held, and the type of facility utilized. These directories can be ordered from Reed Reference Publishing, P.O. Box 31, New Providence, NJ 07974 (phone 1-800-521-8110).

Databases

A number of databases are available to assist hotels in target marketing to the association planners. Associations, publications and independent organizations are making important facts and figures available to enable interested hotels to better identify true prospects for their particular property.

Successful Meetings magazine offers a useful marketing service for the hotel field called the *SM/Databank*. The magazine has stored data on the history of more than 300,000 meetings held by some 28,000 associations over the past twenty-five years. The database includes information on events planned by associations. You may obtain information about prospects that fit your preferred client profile, such as the time of the week in which a group meets, time of year, geographic pattern, size of the group, whether it has exhibits, where it has met previously and where it is scheduled to meet in the future.

The Professional Convention Management Association (PCMA) has developed their new *American Meetings Databank* (see Figure 4.10). This database functions as a centralized source of meetings information for both meeting planners and suppliers.

Most recently, the International Associations of Convention and Visitors Bureaus (IACVB) has ended its code of confidentiality regarding information provided by member bureaus. All historical and demographic meeting information in its meeting information network (*CINET*) is now accessible through their local bureaus. This database contains some 21,000 meeting profiles going back over the past four years and the future site-selection information for nearly 11,500 organizations. The report includes the decision maker's name, history of past meetings, start and end dates, registered attendance, number of guest rooms used, number of meeting rooms used and square footage of exhibit space required. Approximately 1,500 new histories are added yearly. This information is invaluable, providing a factual convention operations history of these leading convention organizations.

Most meeting planners are eager to verify information for these databases on their organizations' meetings for two reasons. First, this history provides them with information useful in negotiating with hotels. Second, planners recognize that database information allows hotels to target their prospects, eliminating misdirected efforts and reducing the number of cold calls from suppliers who do not have enough rooms and/or meeting space for their meetings.

Databases provide a valuable service in building your prospect file for sales campaigns. One subscriber to databases says, "We feel it is an innovative way to find pre-

Figure 4.9. SAMPLE OF INFORMATION PROVIDED BY DIRECTORIES.

36   **CALIFORNIA – HUNTINGTON BEACH**

Column headers (rotated): ■ TYPE OF MEETING | † NO MEETINGS PER ANNUM | MONTHS HELD | NO OF DAYS | ★ NO OF ATTENDEES | O TYPE OF FACILITY

ASSOCIATION	MEETING PLANNERS	CONVENTION BOOKINGS	■	†	MONTHS	DAYS	★	O
UNITED STATES LIFESAVING ASSN (USLA) PO BOX 366 HUNTINGTON BEACH, 92648 714-536-5263/FAX: 714-374-1500	**BILL RICHARDSON** (Pres) *Speaker* *Exhibit Space*	05/93 Florida Keys 11/93 Chicago 05/94 Seattle Booked 6 mos in advance	C			3	B	DAR
WESTERN ECONOMIC ASSN INTL (WEA) 7400 CTR AVE # 109 HUNTINGTON BEACH, 92647 714-898-3222/FAX: 714-891-6715	**ELDON J DVORAK** (Exec Vp) **VERONICA M DVORAK** (Dir Of Conf)	06/91 Seattle 06/94 Vancouver 07/92 San Francisco 07/95 San Diego 06/93 Lake Tahoe *Far East* Booked 1 yr in advance *South Pacific* OC	C M	1		3-4	E	DRC
WYCLIFFE BIBLE TRANSLATORS (WBT) P O BOX 2727 HUNTINGTON BEACH, 92647 714-969-4600/FAX: 714-969-4661	**RON OLSON** (Assoc Dir) **GERALD ELDER** (Treas) *Speaker*	OC	M	12	V	3	A	
THE ELECTRICAL MANUFACTURING & COIL WINDING ASSN INC PO BOX 278 IMPERIAL BEACH, 91933 619-575-4191/FAX: 619-575-5009	**CHARLES E THURMAN** (Exec Dir) *Speaker*	10/91 Boston 10/93 Chicago 09/92 Cincinnati 09/94 Chicago 06/93 Hong Kong *Far East* Booked 2-3 yrs in advance OC	C M	2-3		3-4 3	E A	AC
AMERICAN COLLEGE OF TRIAL LAWYERS (ACTL) 8001 IRVINE CTR DR STE 960 IRVINE, 92718 714-727-3194/FAX: 714-727-3894	**ROBERT A YOUNG** (Exec Dir)	Booked 2-3 yrs in advance						
INTERIOR DESIGN EDUCATORS COUNCIL (IDEC) 14252 CULVER DR SUITE A331 IRVINE, 92714 714-551-1622	**CANDEE ERWIN** (Exec Secy) *Exhibit Space*	04/92 Alexandria	M	6	4	4	C	D
MOTORCYCLE INDUSTRY COUNCIL (MIC) 2 JENNER ST SUITE 150 IRVINE, 92718 714-727-4211	**PAMELA AMETTE** (Vp) **CATHY WILSHIRE** (Asst Prog Dir) *Speaker*	02/94 Cincinnati 02/95 Cincinnati Booked 2 yrs in advance	C M	1	10	1 3	A U	C C
MULTI LEVEL MARKETING INTL ASSN. (MLMIA) 119 STANFORD CT IRVINE, 92715 714-854-0484/FAX: 714-854-7687	**DORIS WOOD** (Pres.) *Exhibit Space*	09/91 Toronto 08/92 Orange County *Canada* 02/93 Orange County *Europe* *Far East* Booked 3-5 mos in advance OC	C M	4	1, 4, 7, 10	4-5 2-3	B U	AR
NATIONAL ASSN OF NAMEPLATE MANUFACTURERS (NAME) 17300 RED HILL AVE STE 100 IRVINE, 92714 714-261-9588/FAX: 714-261-2594	**JAMES A KINDER** (Exec Vp) **LINDA BRADY** (Dir Of Educ) *Speaker* *Exhibit Space*	03/93 Naples 10/94 St Louis 09/93 New Orleans 03/95 Palm Springs 03/94 Scottsdale *Mexico* Booked 2 yrs in *Caribbean* advance OC	C M	1		1-2 4-5	D B	D DR
NATIONAL MIDAS DEALERS ASSN (NMDA) 14795 JEFFREY RD STE 202 IRVINE, 92720 714-551-1289/FAX: 714-551-0621	**MYRON P GORDON** (Exec Dir) **FRANK MAGLIOCCO** (Assoc Exec Dir) *Exhibit Space*	10/91 Las Vegas 09/94 Boca Raton 11/92 New Orleans 10/93 Colorado Springs *Canada* Booked 2-3 yrs in advance OC	C M	10	1, 2, 3, 4, 5, 6, 7, 8, 9, 10, 11, 12	4 1-4	C U	DR A

■ TYPE OF MEETING   (C) Convention Data (M) Smaller Meetings & Seminar Data
† MONTHS HELD   (1) Jan (2) Feb (3) Mar (4) Apr (5) May (6) June (7) July (8) Aug (9) Sept (10) Oct (11) Nov (12) Dec
  (P) Spring (S) Summer (F) Fall (W) Winter (V) Various
★ NUMBER OF ATTENDEES   (U) Under 50 (A) 51-100 (B) 101-200 (C) 201-500 (D) 501-1000 (E) 1001-5000 (F)Over 5000
O TYPE OF FACILITY   (D) Downtown (A) Airport (R) Resort (C) Convention Center

The Nationwide Directory of Association Meeting Planners, *available from The Salesman's Guide, lists the names and titles of over 10,000 meeting planners from over 6,500 major associations. The directory details the number of meetings held annually, the months in which they are held, the approximate number of attendees, and the geographic location of the meetings. Of special interest to hotel salespeople: the type of facilities used by each group.*
Source: Salesman's Guide.

qualified profiles and a really efficient way to pursue business. By receiving the profiles, we save hours of time that would otherwise be spent on cold calls."

Specialized Periodicals

There are a number of periodicals that serve the market. Some go only to association personnel; others are distributed to both association and corporate personnel. Their advertisers are hotels, convention bureaus, airlines and other suppliers in the convention industry.

Association Management is published monthly by the American Society of Association Executives. Its circulation consists of the members of this prestigious organization. The list is available for rental for direct mail under specific circumstances. The Association Directory & Buying Guide lists members with address and telephone numbers which makes it most useful. Vendors may join the society as associate members.

Association Meetings is published six times a year. It is circulated to full-time managers of societies and associations as well as volunteer/member part-time managers, and others. A sales lead service is available to advertisers.

Convene is published ten times annually by the Professional Convention Managers Association (PCMA).

Meeting News is a monthly tabloid newspaper. Its circulation includes association personnel. The tabloid provides a reader service card to key ads and to supply sales leads. Its New Names service offers the names of meeting planners in that function for less than one year.

Meetings & Conventions is a monthly publication whose circulation also contains association personnel. Its circulation is available for rental for direct mail. Advertisers get a reader service card system plus a sales lead service in the association and corporate fields.

Medical Meetings magazine, published eight times annually, concentrates on a specific segment of the field. The circulation is formed from medical societies and associations, biomedical corporations, hospitals and medical centers, and government and foundation organizations. They, too, offer a reader sales lead system.

Successful Meetings, a monthly magazine, also includes association personnel in its circulation, as well as corporate planners. Advertisers receive the SM Convention Research Bulletin published weekly. It provides information about groups planning meetings. *Successful Meetings* publishes SM Tip Flash, which supplies advertisers with sales leads. Their list may be rented for direct mail.

These are prominent publications but not the only ones. Others are listed in Appendix I. Information as to the particular segment each serves should be obtained from the publishers.

Hotel Records

If you are newly assigned to a hotel convention sales staff, one of the first things to do is to closet yourself with the function books and other records from the past few years. Much can be learned from them. How many groups met in your house but never returned? It is amazing how many times business is lost because no one followed up and pressed for more business.

Your hotel records will also offer clues to personnel changes. If a group didn't return, a new executive director could offer another chance. You could call and indicate that his

Figure 4.10. SAMPLE OF DATABANK INFORMATION.

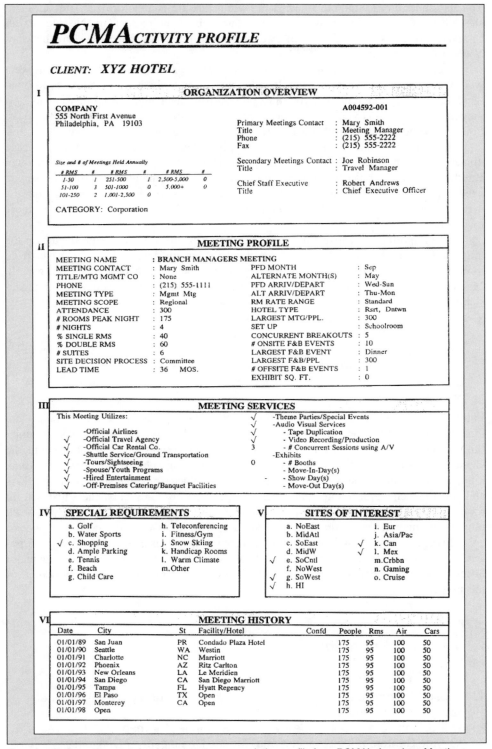

PCMACTIVITY PROFILE

CLIENT: XYZ HOTEL

I. ORGANIZATION OVERVIEW

COMPANY
555 North First Avenue
Philadelphia, PA 19103

A004592-001

Primary Meetings Contact	: Mary Smith
Title	: Meeting Manager
Phone	: (215) 555-2222
Fax	: (215) 555-2222

Size and # of Meetings Held Annually

# RMS	#	# RMS	#	# RMS	#
1-50	1	251-500	1	2,500-5,000	0
51-100	3	501-1000	0	5,000+	0
101-250	2	1,001-2,500	0		

Secondary Meetings Contact	: Joe Robinson
Title	: Travel Manager
Chief Staff Executive	: Robert Andrews
Title	: Chief Executive Officer

CATEGORY: Corporation

II. MEETING PROFILE

MEETING NAME	: BRANCH MANAGERS MEETING		
MEETING CONTACT	: Mary Smith	PFD MONTH	: Sep
TITLE/MTG MGMT CO	: None	ALTERNATE MONTH(S)	: May
PHONE	: (215) 555-1111	PFD ARRIV/DEPART	: Wed-Sun
MEETING TYPE	: Mgmt Mtg	ALT ARRIV/DEPART	: Thu-Mon
MEETING SCOPE	: Regional	RM RATE RANGE	: Standard
ATTENDANCE	: 300	HOTEL TYPE	: Rsrt, Dntwn
# ROOMS PEAK NIGHT	: 175	LARGEST MTG/PPL.	: 300
# NIGHTS	: 4	SET UP	: Schoolroom
% SINGLE RMS	: 40	CONCURRENT BREAKOUTS	: 5
% DOUBLE RMS	: 60	# ONSITE F&B EVENTS	: 10
# SUITES	: 6	LARGEST F&B EVENT	: Dinner
SITE DECISION PROCESS	: Committee	LARGEST F&B/PPL	: 300
LEAD TIME	: 36 MOS.	# OFFSITE F&B EVENTS	: 1
		EXHIBIT SQ. FT.	: 0

III. MEETING SERVICES

This Meeting Utilizes:

	-Official Airlines	√	-Theme Parties/Special Events	
√	-Official Travel Agency	√	-Audio Visual Services	
√	-Official Car Rental Co.	√	- Tape Duplication	
√	-Shuttle Service/Ground Transportation	√	- Video Recording/Production	
√	-Tours/Sightseeing	3	- # Concurrent Sessions using A/V	
√	-Spouse/Youth Programs		-Exhibits	
√	-Hired Entertainment	0	- # Booths	
√	-Off-Premises Catering/Banquet Facilities	-	- Move-In-Day(s)	
			- Show Day(s)	
			- Move-Out Day(s)	

IV. SPECIAL REQUIREMENTS

	a. Golf		h. Teleconferencing
	b. Water Sports		i. Fitness/Gym
√	c. Shopping		j. Snow Skiing
	d. Ample Parking		k. Handicap Rooms
	e. Tennis		l. Warm Climate
	f. Beach		m. Other
	g. Child Care		

V. SITES OF INTEREST

	a. NoEast		i. Eur
	b. MidAtl		j. Asia/Pac
	c. SoEast	√	k. Can
	d. MidW	√	l. Mex
√	e. SoCntl		m.Crbbn
	f. NoWest		n. Gaming
√	g. SoWest		o. Cruise
√	h. HI		

VI. MEETING HISTORY

Date	City	St	Facility/Hotel	Confd	People	Rms	Air	Cars
01/01/89	San Juan	PR	Condado Plaza Hotel		175	95	100	50
01/01/90	Seattle	WA	Westin		175	95	100	50
01/01/91	Charlotte	NC	Marriott		175	95	100	50
01/01/92	Phoenix	AZ	Ritz Carlton		175	95	100	50
01/01/93	New Orleans	LA	Le Meridien		175	95	100	50
01/01/94	San Diego	CA	San Diego Marriott		175	95	100	50
01/01/95	Tampa	FL	Hyatt Regency		175	95	100	50
01/01/96	El Paso	TX	Open		175	95	100	50
01/01/97	Monterey	CA	Open		175	95	100	50
01/01/98	Open				175	95	100	50

Sample of information contained in a prototype association profile from PCMA's American Meetings Databank.

group had met successfully at your hotel and perhaps persuade the group to book again. You also should try to find out where the previous director is now located. After all, he or she selected your hotel previously and may be amenable to doing so again. No sales staffer should rely on a past customer's memory to bring him or her back. Sales life is not that easy. You must go after business.

Keep in mind that the easiest prospect is a satisfied past customer. If the meeting went well, you have an excellent prospect. If it did not go smoothly, it is imperative to find out why. It could be something that you must prevent from happening with other clients or it may be something that you have already corrected and you could then press for business. Some of the best business relationships result from clearing up past grievances.

Hotel records may also lead to other prospects gleaned from local small bookings. A dinner meeting handled solely by the banquet manager may indicate only a local chapter. But this small bit of business of dinner for twenty or so may be just the Trojan horse you need to penetrate the state or national parent organization. Much can be learned from the members themselves. At least, a follow-up phone call will increase the chances for more local business.

It is important to realize that much association business must be cultivated over the long haul, so don't get discouraged. The road to that major booking may have to go through many minor bits of business before you score the big one, or before scoring at all. Maintain a good follow-up system; keep after target associations, and you'll get your share.

 ## Chapter Summary:

In this chapter, we have discussed the importance of the associations market to hotels and identified some of the factors that hospitality firms need to consider if they wish to target this market segment. It is essential to know the types of meetings that associations hold, the characteristics of these meetings (cycle and pattern, geographic restrictions, lead time, kinds of sites desired, and price considerations), and to determine the key decision makers and how to reach them. A hotel that "does its homework" can attract business that will fill rooms and bring revenue to the property's other facilities in what would normally be slack months and may generate significant repeat business from association meeting attendees.

In the next chapter, we will discuss the corporate meetings market. While some corporate meetings may seem similar to those held by associations at first glance, there are major differences to consider that will enable your property to target this primary source of meetings business.

 ## Endnotes:

1. "Resort Committee Seeks Members to Address Saturday Overnight Airfare Issue", *HSMAI Update*.
2. Drs. J. Dana Clark, Catherine Price, and Suzanne Murrmann, "Collaborative 'Buying Centers': How Associations Choose Destinations," *Convene*, December 1997, pages 58 & 59.

3. J. Dana Clark, Michael R. Evans, and Bonnie J. Knutson, "Selecting a Site for an Association Convention: An Exploratory Look at the Types of Power Used by Committee Members to Influence Decisions," *Journal of Hospitality & Leisure Marketing, Vol. 5(1),* 1997, p. 91.

Additional References:

- Destination Marketing For Convention and Visitors Bureaus, Second Edition, Richard Gartrell, Kendall/Hunt Publishing.

- Contemporary Hospitality Marketing, William Lazer and Robert Layton, Educational Institute, AHLA. www.ei-ahla.org

Internet Sites:

For additional information on the firms and organizations discussed in this chapter, visit the following Internet sites. The Web addresses are current as of January 2001. Addresses may change, however; if a site is not available at address below, a search engine can be used to access its new location.

American Society of Association Executives (ASAE) - www.asaenet.org
Association Management - www.asaenet.org/publications/amcurrent/index/html
Association Meetings - www.meetingsnet.com
"Association Management Companies" (directory) - www.asaenet.org/
AMCDirectory/AMCresults.cfm
Convene - www.pcma.org/pub/convene.rtm
Convention Industry Council (CIC) - www.conventionindustry.org
International Association of Association Management Companies - www.iamc.org
International Association of Convention and Visitors Bureaus - www.iacvb.org
International Society of Meeting Planners - www.iami.org/ismp.html
Meetings and Conventions - www.meetings-conventions.com
Meetings in the West - www.meetingsweb.com
Professional Convention Management Association (PCMA) - www.pcma.org
Successful Meetings - www.successmtgs.com

Study Questions:

1. Conventions are extremely important to associations for financial reasons. Explain why.
2. What kinds of meetings do associations hold? What type of facilities are best suited to each?

3. How do state and regional association meetings differ from the national association meetings?
4. Identify the monthly and daily meeting pattern of association meetings.
5. Attendance for association conventions is voluntary. How important is price to association executives? What implications does this have on a hotel's sales efforts?
6. What individuals in the association make the site selection decision?
7. List sources for locating associations.

 Key Terms:

Association. A group of people joined together for a common purpose.

Association bid. A regional chapter requests the honor of hosting a national convention.

Breakout session. Small group sessions within the meeting, formed to discuss specific topics.

Concurrent session. Meeting sessions on different topics scheduled at the same time.

General session. The main meeting attended by the majority of the association members.

Lead time. The time between the booking and the actual meeting date.

Multiple association management organizations. Firms that function as the executive and office staff for a number of associations.

Site inspection. Tour of the property conducted by representatives of the association or corporation in order to determine whether the hotel is suitable to host the meeting/event.

Learning Objectives:

This portion of your text takes a look at the corporate meetings market. We will discuss the kinds of meeting held by corporations and what factors are considered in staging corporate meetings, the key decision makers for company meetings, and how to locate sources of corporate business. When you have studied this chapter, you will:

- Be able to describe the types of meetings held by companies and tell how these meetings differ from meetings staged by associations.

- Know the characteristics and requirements for company meetings of all types.

- Be able to identify key corporate decision makers and detail ways in which sources of business can be located.

Outline

Requirements for Corporate Meetings
Kinds of Company Meetings
- National and Regional Sales Meetings
- New Product/Dealer Meetings
- Professional/Technical Meetings
- Management Meetings
- Training Meetings
- Stockholder/Public Meetings
- Incentive Meetings
Characteristics of Company Meetings
Corporate Meeting Decision Makers
- Full-time Meeting Planner
- Company President
- Marketing and Sales Executives
- Advertising and Sales Managers
- Other Corporate Executives
- Passenger Traffic/Corporate Travel Managers
- Training Director
- Meeting Specialists/Third-Party Planners
Sources for Finding Corporate Business and Decision Makers
- Special Meeting Publications
- Trade Directories
- Trade Associations
- Internet Sites
- Convention and Visitors Bureaus
- Lateral Referral and Account Penetration

Selling to the Corporate Meetings Market

Helmut Knipp
President and Chief Operating Officer
Lexington Management Corporation

*"**Qualify** and **Quantify** are two of the most important steps in the solicitation of any account. You have to know the potential an account has before you can make intelligent rate and solicitation decisions. With our salespeople, we stress the importance of doing research on our customers...Two other areas require mentioning. One is to take outstanding care of the customers you have...It is much more costly and time-consuming to find new customers than it is to take care of existing ones...The second area is that of prospecting. A salesperson must make new contacts all the time...The more contacts you make, the more prospects you talk to, the more business you're going to book. Ask your existing customers for other contacts in their business or trade. Read the newspapers and trade journals with open eyes. These publications are full of leads and prospects...."*

5 Selling the Corporate Meetings Market

oday's corporation is a complex organization. The geographic marketing range has grown to the point that most companies now market nationally or internationally. The structure of larger companies is more detailed and multifaceted than ever before. Modern executives who received their training with such companies in mind are keenly aware of the vital need for *communication*. Meetings remain a most basic form of communication within companies. You are concerned solely with those company meetings that take place off company premises, and there are enough of them to satisfy any enterprising hotel sales staff.

If the association convention business represents the best-known and most visible segment of the meetings field, corporate meetings offer the greatest potential for growth. A recent study by *Meetings & Conventions* magazine found that more than half of the corporate planners surveyed expected to hold more meetings than they previously held in past years. Although the volume of corporate business is greater than that of the association segment, corporate business is not as visible. Since company meetings are varied and are controlled by a wider variety of personnel, they are harder to dig out. But they offer a great deal of group business potential that no hotel should ignore.

Fortunately, hotel marketing people do not have to decide which segment of the market — associations or corporations — to sell. The two are a digestible mix, and a successful property enjoys its share of both kinds. The ratio of each really reflects upon the kind of property you have, what you are equipped to handle, and where you are located. While some hotel features and benefits appeal to both markets, there are significant differences (see Figure 5.1). Examine your hotel with an eye to what corporate meeting planners want and the kinds of meetings they hold.

Requirements for Corporate Meetings

The factors that make a hotel attractive for association events hold true for most corporate meetings too. Keep in mind that corporate meetings vary a great deal in size, scope and purpose. It is important, therefore, to match the planner's needs with the hotel's facilities.

Quality Food Service. Food and beverage functions are major contributors to the success or failure of corporate meetings. Long after other meeting details are forgotten, corporate attendees remember an elegant banquet, a unique refreshment break or an unusual theme party.

Corporate meeting planners consistently rate quality of food service as very important in choosing a hotel or facility (see Figure 5.2). The planner of today is continually encouraging the staff to surpass a previous year's convention program. To gain its share of repeat business, a hotel must continue to upgrade menus, contribute to the uniqueness of each event and create an occasion that will be long remembered.

Adequate Meeting Space. It is hard to hold a meeting efficiently if the meeting rooms are too small—or too large (although surplus area may be screened off). When you go after

Figure 5.1. COMPARISON OF ASSOCIATION AND CORPORATE MEETING GROUPS.

COMPARISON OF ASSOCIATION AND CORPORATE MEETING GROUPS

FACTOR	ASSOCIATION	CORPORATION
Attendance	Voluntary	Mandatory
Decision making	Decentralized; often committee	Centralized
Number of meetings	Fewer, but larger attendance	More, but fewer attendees per meeting
Potential for Repeat Business	Some, but must rotate sites	High
Room Block	Must track reservation pickup closely	Stable
Spouse Attendance	Common	Seldom
Exhibits	Frequent; heavy demand for hospitality suites	Less frequent
Site Selection	Need to build attendance with attractive locations; sometimes political	Seek convenience, service and security
Geographic Pattern	Rotate geographically	No set pattern
Lead Time	Long (usually two to five years)	Short (often less than one year)
Billing Format	Individual Folios	Master Account
Risk of Cancellation	Minimal	Higher; penalty clauses and advance deposits are common
Arrival/Departure	More likely to have early arrivals	Few early arrivals or departures
Price	More price conscious; generally good negotiators	Less price-sensitive
Convention and Visitors Bureau Involvement	Frequently utilize convention bureaus, especially with city-wide conventions	Seldom contact convention bureau
Reservation Procedures	Generally use postal reply cards or Housing Bureau	Frequently provide a rooming list

company business, discuss room requirements in detail. The main room may need support from a number of small rooms. If your layout shows these nearby, you have a strong selling point. The traffic flow pattern of the meeting is very important.

Service. Companies meet for good reason, and they don't want problems. They want service — good service. They want what was promised, and on time. The reward is repeat business. Except for incentive programs, corporate meetings promise the most repeat business. Many planners mention good service first when asked what they look for in a meeting site.

Enough Guestrooms. No company likes to split up at a meeting, chancing the "loss" of attendees during the walk or cab ride to the meeting site. They prefer to house everyone under one roof. This is a difficult problem to overcome if you can't offer it but your competitor can. Hotels combine presentations to large groups but the first choice is invariably a single hotel housing all attendees.

Convenient Location. Location is very important to the corporate meeting planner. Travel means company money. Time spent traveling and at the meeting itself means time off the job. That's a prime factor. A convenient location is a strong sales asset. Company planners use downtown hotels, airport hotels, and suburban locations, especially for regional meetings and training sessions.

Business Class Rooms

In response to the increasing number of business travelers, hotels began offering business centers equipped with computer equipment, FAX machines, copiers and secretarial services. The drawback to business centers, however, was that many were not accessible on a 24-hour basis, making it difficult for individual business travelers and corporate meeting attendees to attend to business after hours.

Some hotels met this need by creating business floors with 24-hour access to office equipment and supplies, while some hotel chains designed guestrooms specifically for business travelers and corporate meeting attendees, who often retreat to their rooms at the end of the day's sessions to work. These "business class" rooms usually include large desks (often stocked with business amenities such as paper clips, writing implements, Post-it notes, etc.), in-room computer hookups and FAX machines, a desk telephone, enhanced lighting and ergonomic desk chairs.

Among the chains offering rooms with these special features are Hyatt (the Hyatt Business Plan), Clarion (Biz Class Office Rooms), Sheraton (Corporate Club Rooms), Westin (the Guest Office), and Delta (Business Zone Guestrooms). These rooms are usually available at a slightly higher charge than regular sleeping rooms, but are becoming increasingly popular with business travelers and are an attractive advantage when marketing a property to the corporate meetings market.

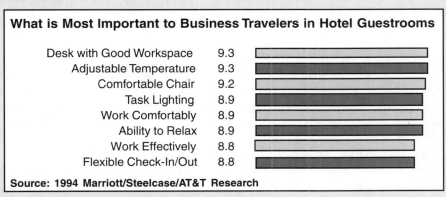

What is Most Important to Business Travelers in Hotel Guestrooms

Desk with Good Workspace	9.3
Adjustable Temperature	9.3
Comfortable Chair	9.2
Task Lighting	8.9
Work Comfortably	8.9
Ability to Relax	8.9
Work Effectively	8.8
Flexible Check-In/Out	8.8

Source: 1994 Marriott/Steelcase/AT&T Research

Attractive Location. Business officials have a clear image of their company, and they want to meet in a hotel consistent with that image. This does not necessarily mean a posh place, but an attractive place.

For incentive trips, it goes without saying that the hotel and the area must have tourist attractions. The basic concept is to reward those who meet targeted goals. The prize selected must stimulate extra effort. The approach for incentive meetings is quite different from that of sales meetings, but the two are often intertwined. A working sales meeting requires solely a *suitable* hotel site; an incentive meeting requires a most *desirable* one.

Security. Corporate meetings are private affairs to a far greater extent than most conventions. The discussions are not meant for the ears of people outside the com-

Figure 5.2. FACTORS CONSIDERED IMPORTANT TO CORPORATE MEETING PLANNERS IN THE SELECTION OF A FACILITY/HOTEL.

Factors Considered Important in Selection of a Facility Hotel

Factors Considered "Very Important"	Corporate Planners
Cost of hotel or meeting facility	75%
Negotiable food, beverage and room rates	75
Number, size, and quality of meeting rooms	74
Quality of food service	73
Number, size and quality of sleeping rooms	65
Efficiency of billing procedures	60
Availability of meeting support services and equipment, such as audiovisual equipment	55
Efficiency of check-in and check-out procedures	55
Assignment of one staff person to handle all aspects of meeting	54
Previous experience in dealing with facility and its staff	48
Convenience to other modes of transportation	39
Proximity to airport	35

Corporate austerity programs, coupled with a greater awareness of the size of meeting expenditures, has caused corporate planners to rank the cost of a hotel or meeting facility and negotiable food, beverage and room rates as the most important factors in booking hotels. The quality of food service, which was formerly their first priority, dropped to fourth place on the list, after the number, size and quality of meeting rooms.
Source: The 2000 Meetings Market Study conducted by Meetings & Conventions magazine.

pany, and, because of the increasing competition in the marketplace — especially in the computer and other high tech fields, security has become an even more important issue for corporate meeting planners. If your property understands this need for additional security and can offer viable solutions, you will have a far greater chance of securing corporate meetings business.

Folding vinyl partitions and meeting rooms right off busy lobbies leave corporate planners cold. As does unrestricted access to meeting rooms and areas in which equipment and displays will be stored. In some cases, the planner may even worry about communications sent to the property's FAX machine or the security of the property's phone system.

If you hope to handle this type of high-level meeting, you must be prepared to answer these concerns. First, offering a layout of the traffic pattern of the property can be an asset if the group's meeting and storage facilities will be isolated from the main flow of traffic. Second, you may offer additional security measures, such as one or two trusted employees to freshen meeting rooms and watch over unoccupied facilities. Third, the business may be so attractive that you will want to go to the extra expense of hiring outside security guards or setting up a dedicated FAX line for the group. If the company will be the only group meeting in the hotel at that time, you have an additional selling advantage. This is an asset for the smaller properties, turning what may be considered a liability (small size) into a positive attraction. This is also a strong selling point for resort properties; the remoteness of a location may be an additional sales point for the security conscious client.

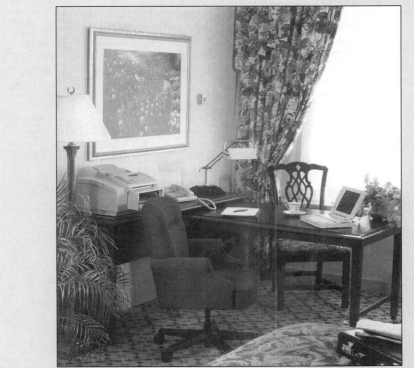

Sheraton's New Club Rooms. Responding to customer research, ITT Sheraton has introduced a guestroom with more flexible work space. The workspace includes the HP Office Jet, a combination fax/copier/printer.

Kinds of Company Meetings

Corporate meeting business has been increasing more rapidly than any other market. Hundreds of thousands of meetings are held all over the country throughout the year, and the spectrum of meetings attended is broad. Among the prevalent types of company meetings are:

- National and regional sales meetings
- New product introduction/dealer meetings
- Professional/technical meetings
- Management meetings
- Training meetings
- Stockholder/public meetings
- Incentive meetings

Each will be considered in detail but Figure 5.3 summarizes several key characteristics. The most widely attended meetings are for professional/technical purposes and training, each type totaling over 8 million attendees. On average, the highest attendance is at national sales meetings (141 attendees) and the lowest at training (64) and management

Figure 5.3. SUMMARY OF TYPES OF CORPORATE MEETINGS.

Summary of Types of Corporate Meetings					
Type of Meeting	Off-premise Meetings	Average # Planned	Average Attendance	Average # Days	Average # of Months Lead Time
Management Meetings	157,000	5.4	34	2.6	3.5
Incentive Trips	105,200	4.4	90	4.7	8.2
Training Seminars	229,700	7.4	64	2.9	3.7
Regional Sales Meetings	98,700	5.4	65	2.5	3.8
National Sales Meetings	43,000	5.4	141	3.5	6.8
Professional/ Technical Meetings	80,500	4.4	79	2.8	5.3
New Product Introductions	52,500	4.4	121	2.3	3.7
Stockholder Meetings	15,000	2.6	93	2.0	5.2
Other Meetings	10,600	7.3	89	3.2	9.1
Total/Average	835,900	13.8	61	2.9	5.5

Note that the average lead time for corporate meetings is less than one year, the attendance is generally less than 100 persons, and the duration of most corporate meetings is two to three days.
Source: The 2000 Meetings Market Study conducted by Meetings & Conventions magazine.

meetings (34). The average number of off-premise meetings planned yearly by corporate planners is 13.8.

The kinds of companies holding meetings are diverse. Insurance, banking and investment groups, automotive and other industrial and manufacturing concerns are just a few of the prospects for the corporate meeting business. It would be more difficult to find any sizable organizations that do not hold meetings — and lots of them.

National and Regional Sales Meetings

The best-known company meeting, and one of the largest sectors of the corporate meetings market, is the **sales meeting**. The nature of a national sales organization makes it a natural for meetings. These events are scattered throughout the country. With new products and new sales developments appearing all the time, there is constant need to meet face to face with the sales team, at every level. There are national sales meetings with everyone present, meetings of regional sales managers, and regional sales meetings run by regional sales managers.

Attendance at national sales meetings averages about 150 for three to four days. Regional sales meetings are smaller, averaging 65 in size over two to three days.

The reasons for the sales meetings are many, often dealing with several objectives. The annual sales meeting may involve new product introduction, new company policy and suggested sales techniques to overcome problems, or it may simply be a morale builder and stimulator to cap a successful year and to start work on the next one. Sales meetings come in all sizes, at any time of the year, and all mean good, regular, repeat business for hotels.

Sales meetings are generally staged and controlled within the sales and marketing departments of each division of a company.

New Product Introduction/Dealer Meetings

Sales executives often hold national and regional events to meet with dealers or distributors. New product introduction is very important in these meetings too. The introduction of new sales and advertising campaigns calls for carrying the message out to the hinterlands. The very heart of the sales and marketing philosophy is to sell your own staff first and then your distributors and dealers and their staffs, and to work them up to new levels of enthusiasm. This approach results in many meetings around the country.

As in the case of the sales meetings, **dealer meetings** can be very small, such as a cocktail reception for a dozen or so one evening, or great affairs involving thousands and running three to five days. The Ford Motor Company spent several million dollars for a live Broadway-type stage show, combined with multimedia presentation, at the large Las Vegas Convention Center. The affair called for several days of rehearsals and two weeks of back-to-back charter flights from all parts of the country. The production was worthy of any on Broadway, yet had a run of only two weeks. If the objective of the meeting is achieved, the meeting is a success and the cost accepted as necessary and worthwhile.

Dealer meetings, in addition to being attended by sales personnel, also attract top company management, stockholders and the press. Since these meetings are often "gala affairs," they provide an excellent opportunity to "show off" the property and to book additional business from both the company personnel and from "outside" attendees. There is no better sales presentation than a successful execution of a meeting on premises. This is the opportunity to display your hotel at its best.

Professional/Technical Meetings

The need to update technical personnel increases every year. The volume of technical development and innovation is hard to envision. In only the last 100 years — just four generations — man has created the automobile, the airplane, the spaceship, the laser, and the transistor. An engineer or scientist cannot afford to stop learning or he or she will soon be obsolete. To give you some idea of the scope, General Electric has some 30,000 engineers, representing an enormous investment in technical talent that requires constant updating. It is a resource that needs to be safeguarded against personnel obsolescence.

Company **professional/technical meetings** often take the seminar and workshop formats. Independent consultants, educators and even vendors are invited to demonstrate and lecture.

Management Meetings

Just as sales and technical personnel meet, so do all levels of executives. Far-flung organizations mean that there is a need even at the top for executives to get together for discussion.

Such meetings may be regular events, such as board meetings, or may be called in response to a special situation. These are usually small meetings, but they call for the finest in accommodations and service. An important characteristic of such meetings for hotel salespeople is that each attendee is a potential customer for meetings within his or her own division or company.

Management meetings most commonly last for two days and follow no special locations rule, ranging from convenient downtown or airport locations to remote resorts and lodges.

Training Meetings

Training of personnel on all levels is an important activity of the larger corporations. Companies may conduct training in technical skills such as welding, machinery repair and maintenance. Computer systems result in more training sessions. Sales personnel receive training, as do executives.

About half of training directors conduct programs off company premises. These **training meetings** are held on a regular basis and usually run about three days. Attendance is usually small. Most training groups number fewer than 50, and most are nearer 30 (see Figure 5.3). Groups of ten to 15 are not at all rare, so even small hotels can handle these meetings.

That is not to say that training directors are satisfied by just any facility; they have firm criteria. They do, however, deal with small groups that are easily accommodated. They want meeting rooms with permanent walls instead of screen dividers, rooms good for audiovisual use, easy access to meeting rooms without distraction from other hotel activities, and prompt service for food functions such as refreshment breaks and lunches. Well-lighted and well-ventilated rooms with adequate space for either classroom or U-shaped seating (there is often a preference for extra-wide 24- or 30-inch tables), and guestrooms with well-lighted work space (desks or large tables) are especially attractive to training meeting planners.

Training directors do not need prestigious locations and impressive surroundings. They are more likely to choose hotels that are convenient to airports, highways and parking. Training directors have no need to change locations to stimulate attendance or interest. They make excellent customers because they tend to come back to hotels that have worked out well. Dependability, reasonable prices and good service all count a great deal toward repeat business.

Many hotels and motels have done well with this kind of business, to the point of having almost permanent commitment of certain meeting rooms and a constant use of a minimum number of guest rooms by a single company. Chains, too, find such business good because trainers often call for similar setups by a team in central locations around the country.

Regular business bookings can also be picked up when personnel become acquainted with a property while attending a training session.

An odd characteristic of training meetings is the frequent reluctance to use the term *training*. At lower levels, employees look for training and will regard it as an added benefit and frequently stick with an employer that offers it. But sales and middle-level people at times resent the thought that they *need* further development. The situation is dispelled by tact, so don't be surprised to see *workshops, seminars,* or *management development* or simply *meetings* being booked by training directors.

The position of training director has broadened in many companies over the years. Today, you may find your key decision maker under a title reflecting involvement with *human resources.*

Stockholder/Public Meetings

Companies find it necessary at times to hold meetings for non-employees. These typically fall into the category of **stockholder/public meetings**. The annual stockholders meeting can range from a mere formality attended by a handful to a fairly active one-day event involving a goodly number, with lunch and refreshment breaks. These seem to vary with the economic climate.

Public relations and industrial relations departments also hold meetings and exhibits to tell their stories. They, too, add their bit to the growing number of corporate meetings.

Incentive Meetings

Each year, as millions of people exceed their business goals or quotas, many are rewarded by a trip — trips that collectively mean close to $6 billion to the travel industry. Up to 45 percent of that figure is spent on hotels alone. Meetings are included in 80 percent of all incentive trips and those meetings are called **incentive meetings**.

Incentive travelers may be suppliers, dealers, customers, salespeople or other employees. They must qualify in some way to participate.

What do incentive customers want? Above all, they look for first-class service. Companies offer these trips as rewards to top performers, so they want them treated in a special way.

For hotels that can deliver what these customers want, the benefits are substantial. First, bookings are guaranteed. This means easy forecasting and a break-even factor that's minimal compared to other markets. Second, incentive participants typically make use of all hotel facilities, such as restaurants, bars and room service. Third, incentive meetings mean high-dollar revenues. Average room rates are usually higher, with double occupancy most common, and they spend more on banquets than do many other meeting segments. Because this market is so lucrative, an extended discussion is included in the next chapter.

Characteristics of Company Meetings

Any meeting should have a clear objective, a logical attendance group, and a site and structure to suit the event. When we discuss characteristics of company meetings, keep in mind that we are talking about many different *kinds* of meetings — all sizes and shapes, instigated by many causes, planned and executed with rare exception by a variety of people.

But this very difficulty in describing a "typical" meeting should be most encouraging to hotel staffs. It is a most unimaginative hotel salesperson, or a particularly primitive

Figure 5.4. WHEN CORPORATE MEETINGS ARE HELD.

Source: 2001 State of the Industry Report by Successful Meetings magazine.

hotel property, who cannot come up with some part of this market that can be sold and serviced well. This is the time to ignore what facilities you may lack and concentrate on what you *have*. Select that portion of the market that you can target and call your own. Think in terms of your own sales campaigns and the kinds of hotel properties that can handle the situations discussed in this chapter.

Time Cycle

Figure 5.4 shows that corporations tend to meet midweek and throughout the year. Company meetings seem to follow a demand schedule instead of the fixed-time cycle that is common with associations. A meeting is planned and executed as need arises. After all, a company meeting doesn't require the time needed by associations to build attendance. A simple directive from the top brass is all that is needed to ensure that everyone will attend the meeting.

Lead Time

The planning period for company meetings is relatively short, rarely longer than a year. In the case of incentive trips, some consideration about general area may be made some eight months to a year in advance, and, in the case of great numbers, the time may stretch to two years. But that is still much shorter than the lead time of associations.

The annual sales meeting is usually planned eight to twelve months prior to convening. Corporate structure in this decision making is simple. Some middle-level person, or perhaps two, will suggest, investigate and screen properties and pass along the recommendation to one executive who generally makes the final decision. In some companies, one person does it all, which certainly can shorten lead time. There are many variations, of course.

Most other company meetings have a very short lead time -- less than three months is becoming typical. Due to changes in the economy, the introduction of new products and companies, mergers and acquisitions, and breakups or expansions, businesspeople meet more often on short notice (see box titled "Shrinking Lead Times"). Short lead times are especially prevalent in the technology and pharmaceutical industries due to product breakthroughs. Nearly every company meeting planner can recall instances when it seemed like the meeting was needed for the next day. There is one kind of company meeting that we

---

SHRINKING LEAD TIMES

According to a study by *Meetings Today*, 74 percent of all corporate meetings held in 1999 were classified as short term, having a turnaround time of 90 days or less. Rich Del Colle, the Boston-based meeting planner for Hewlett-Packard Co., explains:

> "Today's pace has picked up from 10 years ago. Before, business used to be five days a week, but now it's 24 hours a day, seven days a week. That's what people expect, and you need to keep customers happy and get your products out there." [1]

Another contributing factor is the increased use of technology. Internet virtual property tours, electronic requests for proposals, and instant communications through e-mail and fax have enabled corporate planners to act more quickly. Technology has replaced the numerous telephone calls, letters, and in-person site inspections formerly inherent to corporate meeting planning, and hotels that wish to capture their share of this market must have the technology and flexibility to respond to today's corporate needs.

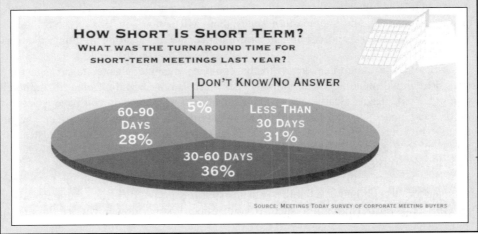

HOW SHORT IS SHORT TERM?
WHAT WAS THE TURNAROUND TIME FOR SHORT-TERM MEETINGS LAST YEAR?

DON'T KNOW/NO ANSWER

60-90 DAYS 28%
5%
LESS THAN 30 DAYS 31%
30-60 DAYS 36%

SOURCE: MEETINGS TODAY SURVEY OF CORPORATE MEETING BUYERS

refer to as a *crisis* meeting. That follows when someone says, "Let's get everyone together as soon as possible and talk this thing out!"

It is too late to start selling your property at that point. If you had been in there selling, or had enjoyed some business from that company before, you might get a chance at this business. Certainly, there is no time for anyone to shop around. The situation calls for fast action and the meeting generally goes to a place the company has used before or to some wide-awake salesperson who had been in there pitching at the time.

It is such types of corporate business that must fill the gap when the convention function book is less than filled. The unexpected sales meeting, the crisis that calls for facing dealers or distributors, the new modification for which service personnel must be trained — all these bring opportunities for business meetings. These are meetings executives don't discuss when you talk to them. You must sell them on the idea of using your facility when the need next arises, and hope you made enough of an impression that they'll remember.

Geographical Patterns

There is no general geographic pattern for company business. To begin with, there is often no reason to vary sites to attract attendance, as in the case of associations. When the vice-president of sales calls a meeting in Chicago at the first of the month, it is not surprising to find the sales staff in Chicago at that time.

There is also no reason not to go back to the same hotel if it performed satisfactorily. The main reason for another selection may very well be mere boredom on the part of the meeting planner or his or her boss. It really depends on the kind of meeting. The annual meeting, with much hoopla and singing of the company song, may call for a variety of sites from year to year, but the hastily organized meeting doesn't. In fact, a strong case can be built for repeating at a hotel proven dependable by the last meeting, or at least for some hotel that had been pushing for the business.

Training directors, in particular, prefer to deal with the same hotel on a consistent basis. Some feel that with only small meetings to offer, they reach the status of *important customer* only through the promise of repeat business. Most training directors feel the need for distraction-free, classroom-type isolation, with a good supply of audiovisual equipment and service. Once having worked out such an arrangement with a suitable facility, they are understandably loathe to change.

There is some geographic factor involved, but it is the most obvious one. An Atlanta hotel obviously will have a better chance at getting a regional sales meeting for a staff covering the southeastern states than will a hotel in Boston or St. Louis. Time, the cost of transportation and convenience are all factors affecting the geographic location.

Imagine the assignment given to the company meeting planner to arrange for a series of regional meetings for a national sales staff. He or she might plan to use hotels in New York, Chicago, Seattle, Los Angeles, Dallas and Atlanta. If you have a hotel in any of these general areas, geography will work for you and give you a chance at the business in your sector. But the planner is also free to meet in Houston instead of Dallas, in St. Louis or Milwaukee instead of Chicago, in Boston or Philadelphia instead of New York.

This is where selling comes in. The hotel sales staffer must present the hotel positively and turn what might be a liability into an asset. If Kansas City is less glamourous than New York, it is more centrally located. If your property is not downtown, it offers fewer

Figure 5.5. TYPES OF FACILITIES USED BY CORPORATE MEETING PLANNERS.

TYPES OF FACILITIES USED BY CORPORATE MEETING PLANNERS

Urban/Midtown Hotels	63%
Suburban Hotels	50%
Resort Hotels	44%
Airport Hotels	28%
Private Conference Centers	17%
Suite Hotels	18%

Total is greater than 100% due to multiple mentions.

Urban/midtown hotels are most popular with corporate planners, followed by suburban hotels and resort hotels. The key criteria is generally the purpose of the meeting.
Source: The 2000 Meetings Market Study conducted by Meetings & Conventions magazine.

distractions, easier access by automobile and free parking. If it is downtown, it offers more opportunities for entertainment. A salesperson should concentrate on the property's positive factors, instead of being haunted by its shortcomings.

Company meetings, unlike many association meetings, rarely have regulations against meeting anywhere. The company president or board may favor some types of sites and frown on others in keeping with the image they want to project, but that's not the same as restrictions written into a constitution or bylaws.

Kinds of Sites

What kind of hotel does a company prefer? The answer has as many variations as there are companies and kinds of meetings (see Figure 5.5). A meeting planner should select a site to benefit from its locale and the hotel's attractions. The hotel that would be good for an incentive trip or annual dealer meeting may not be the wisest choice for that crisis meeting or training session.

For a successful sales and marketing career, help your customer achieve the kind of meeting he or she wants. Try to get those meetings that go well in your establishment. Let the ones that get away be those that really should be held in some other type of hotel.

Give careful thought to the kind of meetings most suitable for your hotel. Is yours a downtown hotel? Then stress its convenient location, especially when some people participate in only part of the program. Comfortable and familiar, the downtown hotel is a frequent choice.

Is yours a suburban hotel/motel? It offers easy access by auto and free parking. Stress its informal atmosphere. Will the meeting be the only one in the house? That is considered by many corporate planners to be so important that it may be the very factor that swings the business to you.

Airport location? The obvious advantage is convenience when air transportation is used, plus all the features of the suburban hotel. Once small properties, airport hotels come in all sizes today.

Resort? This is the obvious choice for incentive meetings, but is also often chosen to get away from the distractions of the city. Resorts in the off-season offer excellent rates, charm, exclusivity, industrial security, physical beauty and a good image.

Conference center? As mentioned in Chapter 1, conference centers are growing in popularity with corporate meeting planners, and many major hotel companies, including Marriott, Hilton, and Sheraton have noticed this shift and are becoming key players in the conference center segment. While the few conference centers of past decades had a "going back to school" stigma, today's state of the art facilities are often the choice of corporate planners looking for high-tech presentation equipment and locations that minimize distractions.

These are but a few benefits and characteristics of each type of property. You should be able to add others and to present your property positively as the one that best fits the meeting planner's event.

Attendance

One characteristic of corporate meetings that makes them popular with hotel people is the predictable attendance. Whether attendees come alone or with their spouses, attendance is nearly always mandatory. A rooming list submitted before the event is usually accurate. Barring mishap or illness, no-shows are minimal. Nancy Holder, RJR/Nabisco's conference planner says,

> "In corporate planning, if you book 200 rooms, you're going to use 200 rooms, unless there's an emergency. In other areas of planning (associations), you have to convince people to come. In the corporate world, if the CEO tells you to show up, you're going to show up."[2]

While attendance at corporate meetings is mandatory, one problem associated with corporate meetings is the risk of cancellation of the entire event. Poor financial returns or unexpected delays may result in a corporate official changing or cancelling the meeting. For this reason, most hotels now require nonrefundable deposits and have included stringent cancellation clauses in their contracts with corporate groups (cancellation clauses are explained and illustrated in Chapter 9).

Care should be taken to get a VIP list. It can be embarrassing to everyone to have the fledgling sales trainee assigned to the fine corner room and the vice-president of sales in a minimum single. If no VIP list is submitted, bring up the subject yourself and help your customer create one. If no need exists for him or her, fine. But check it out and at least flag a few names for preferred treatment. Those executives' comments may determine whether you get the group again.

Duration

Most corporate meetings are short. Some are limited to a single day and others may run as long as five days, but three days are about the most common. Arrival on the previous evening is popular so that the meeting can start early the next morning. Cocktail receptions and/or brisk action at the hotel bars add to the profits to be derived from corporate business.

Take care to coordinate the final day meeting program with your policy on check-out time. Plan ahead. If you can't gracefully extend the normal check-out time, perhaps you can arrange to check all the luggage with the bell captain or arrange for all luggage to be placed in just a few rooms before the check-out deadline. If you don't look ahead and decide how you will cope with the many requests at the last minute (or even with the entire group checking out late without even discussing it with you), your staff will be forced to improvise. And they may not always handle it as you would like.

Bring the matter up with the meeting organizer even if he or she doesn't. State your policy and suggest how to arrange matters. You can arrive at an agreed-upon arrangement. At the very least, you have alerted the planner to a potential problem.

Exhibits

The exhibit is a trademark of the association for the most part. Corporate meetings, however, frequently have exhibits too. It is not uncommon, for example, for such meetings to display new products or to use live presentations on a grand scale. Thus you can expect requests for stage facilities and exhibit space when servicing corporate events.

larger, repeat bus.

Meeting Room Requirements

There is a need for large and small meeting rooms, varying from event to event. Some meetings call for small committee-type rooms. In many training set-ups, the main group breaks into units of as few as ten people who meet separately for awhile, then reconvene in the main meeting room. Most meeting organizers prefer such *breakout* rooms to be right at hand.

If your hotel has such rooms in the same wing of the building, you have an edge when you solicit such business. It leaves something to be desired if the group has to huddle around a few tables in different parts of the main meeting room. It certainly is difficult to attract such a group under those circumstances if the competition can offer more suitable arrangements.

One Meeting, One Check

It is nice for a hotel to have most group business paid for with one check. That's one appeal of corporate business. Many companies pay all the expenses for their employees; others have different guidelines. Discuss with the meeting planner what he or she will approve for payment on the master account and what the individual must pay for upon checkout. Your front desk must be informed. Your credit manager may want to do some homework on the customer-corporation and may propose a schedule of payments, beginning with a deposit. As a general rule, corporate business is paid for en masse.

Figure 5.6. HILTON NATIONAL SALES OFFICE MAXIMIZES MULTI-BOOKING POTENTIAL.

In an effort to market its chain, Hilton's national sales office offers Hilton Direct U.S.A. This chain-wide meeting site search is offered to meeting planners at no charge. The meeting planner's specifications are matched against more than 2,000 Hilton hotels and its new brands, and information on availability and prices is provided to the planner within 24 hours. This service is just one example of how chains are turning to national sales offices to market properties to meeting planners.

Multiple-Booking Potential

Hosting company meetings offers the opportunity to promote other business. Each person attending the meeting has sampled your hotel. If the impression is favorable, you may become the first choice whenever that person stops in your city on business trips. Or you may benefit from recommendations to others both in and out of the organization. Remember that most association boards include businesspeople who hold their own organizational meetings.

Help to execute a smoothly functioning meeting and you can pick up future business from the company as well. What appears to be a single meeting may be repeated in several parts of the country. This is a great situation for hotel chains. One person may order meetings in a number of locations, and that person may handle the logistics of all those meetings. There is often enough flexibility in the designation of the cities to be used that a chain may sell dates in a number of different properties (see Figure 5.6).

The appeal to the meeting planner is achieving the status of a more important customer and he or she has only to explain his or her needs once and have them duplicated in different hotels.

What does this mean to a single-location hotel? In order to compete with a chain effort, the individual hotel must present a good case for being the best choice in the city. Ideally, that image would be so strong that a meeting planner normally using a chain for the entire group of meetings would break that pattern when it comes to your city.

Many wise hotel salespeople cooperate with their counterparts in independent hotels in other cities. They try to get the meeting planner to buy from independents as often as possible, and make it easy for that to happen by recommendations and the passing of the sales lead to each other. Independent hotels in different cities recognize that they function as true allies in the sales competition with chains. This concept has helped in the development of the hotel representative who, with a stable of independent hotels, can offer the same kind of "one-stop shopping" as the chains.

Corporate Meeting Decision Makers

We have already discussed how difficult it can be to reach the corporate decision maker. No sales effort succeeds unless it is directed at the person or persons with the authority to make the decision. The convention sales picture is no different. Your story may be a good one, but it will be to no avail unless it is told to the right person.

Who is the *right* person? Not only does it vary from company to company, but it may vary from year to year within the same company. But some titles do keep coming up and they certainly represent a starting point for sales penetration (see Figure 5.7).

To find the decision maker, you have to ask the right questions. "Who coordinates your meetings?" is not a good question; the person who coordinates the details of a meeting may not be the actual decision maker. It is far better to ask, "Who is responsible for deciding which hotels your company uses for meetings?" With this approach, you will be able to make immediate contact with the decision maker or recommender rather than having to deal with one or more "go-betweens," saving valuable time and effort.

Another approach, which may require slightly more time and effort, but which may also prove profitable, is to start at the top of the company and work downward. While speaking with the president of a company may not result in an immediate booking, this

Figure 5.7. MEETING PLANNERS CORPORATE POSITIONS.

Meeting Planner's Corporate Position

Job Title or Position	Corporate Planners
Corporate Administration	51%
Sales/Marketing	25
Meeting/Exhibit Planning	10
Advertising/Sales Promotion/Public Relations	6
Personnel/Training and Development	5
Other	4

Many corporations do not have professional meeting planners. Therefore, in prospecting for business, it is wise to know the common job titles for corporate decision makers. These are summarized above.
Source: The 2000 Meetings Market Study conducted by Meetings & Conventions magazine.

contact can prove valuable in two ways: you won't be referred to someone below the decision making or recommending level and a referral "from above" is a great door opener.

Once the key contact is determined, you should pay attention to tomorrow's decision makers. As the account is worked and information is secured on the organizational structure, "star performers" should be identified and relationships with them cultivated. Knowing the people who are likely to succeed present decision makers can pay dividends in the future.

Full-Time Meeting Planner

When companies have centralized meeting planning activity, you deal with a full-time meeting planner. Hopefully, this should make your job easier because you deal with an experienced, knowledgeable pro who knows what he or she wants and how to go about getting it.

It is easier to deal with someone who knows what he or she wants. It can protect you from overlooking something in the arrangements. Both parties want the same thing — a smoothly run meeting — and it helps if both parties are expert. Build a reputation for competence and fair dealing and you are on your way to a successful sales career in the convention field.

There are several organizations of active corporate meeting planners, including the Society of Corporate Meeting Professionals and Meeting Professionals International. SCMP is a small group, but its membership, which are all full-time planners, boasts larger companies, including Dow Chemical, 3M Companies, and State Farm Insurance. Membership in MPI is much larger, but members are mostly part-time planners.

Company President

Smaller companies seldom have enough meeting activity to warrant a full-time meeting planning employee. In many such companies, the decision maker is the president or some counterpart, such as a partner or chairman. It is understandable that the president of a large corporation such as General Motors will not be involved in such decisions, but the president of a company employing several hundred people might get involved in the national sales or dealer meeting. Never worry about making contacts too high up the corporate ladder. If he or she isn't involved personally, a president is seldom hesitant about naming the right person. And the recommendation of the president does you no harm when you deal with subordinates.

Marketing and Sales Executives

Marketing and sales executives are key people. The exact title may be *vice president, sales* or *marketing director* or *manager* or *product manager.* They may operate on a national, international or even a regional basis. The bulk of corporate meetings involves the important areas of sales and marketing, so it makes sense to zero in on these people.

Such executives don't join meeting planning societies. They don't think of themselves as meeting or convention planners. But they do plan many of them, or, more accurately, are involved with them. They call the meetings, control the kind of meetings they want, and most often have the most important voice as to where and when they will take place. That makes them very important people for you to contact.

Advertising and Sales Promotion Managers

One step down the corporate ladder is the *advertising* or *sales promotion manager.* One person may carry both titles because the work is interrelated. In addition to usual duties, such middle executives frequently handle meeting planning functions. There is no relationship in such assignment to the size or type of company. If the company does not have a full-time meeting planner, the task is assigned to some departmental or divisional manager, and since it involves marketing activity, the advertising or sales promotion manager is often selected.

At the very least, such middle managers get involved in the initial screening of a site and the planning and execution of a meeting. They could be your first hurdle. You need them to recommend your property. In some cases, that is sufficient; in others, the final selection is made by their boss — the vice president, director or manager of sales and marketing. Some people freely admit when their authority is limited, but some find it too painful to do so.

It helps you to know who the final decision maker is, but you have to pay attention to the level that screens, too, or you may never get to the final selection stage. Make sure that your presentation summarizes your strong points very clearly so that they may be passed along in discussion with others.

Other Corporate Executives

Not all meetings stem from marketing divisions. Other executives get involved with staging meetings and therefore site selections. They carry titles such as *manager of corporate relations, public relations, industrial relations,* or *communications.* Such personnel may very well be active in sales and marketing, too. Corporate organization charts seldom indicate anyone as meeting specialists, yet many executives are. The executive in charge of meetings may have that assignment for a period of time and then it may pass on to another.

The role of meeting planner is often a part of the career path for upward bound middle management.

Passenger Traffic/Corporate Travel Managers

Many companies maintain a travel desk, which handles arrangements for employee business travel. When plane or hotel reservations are needed, they are requisitioned through the passenger traffic personnel. Sometimes these travel offices or departments get into meetings activity; it is surprising that this does not happen more frequently. In any case, such personnel commonly negotiate with a hotel or hotel chain for a *commercial rate*, a rate guaranteed to their personnel.

The National Business Travel Association (NBTA), an organization of corporate traffic managers, sponsors an annual trade show in August and the Association for Corporate Travel Executives (ACTE) holds its meeting in February. Both are good shows and well attended by hotels seeking to build corporate group travel business.

Training Director

Training directors use a wide variety of hotel types. Airport and other suburban locations are popular because of ease of access and parking. Small resorts are used in the off-season, especially when executive development programs call for more prestigious sites. With lower budgets, training directors make good use of secondary hotels, off-season rate breaks and all-cost packages.

Training departments usually handle their own meetings, even in cases where the company already has a setup for sales meetings. You may sell the sales department for their meetings but still have to sell another group for training sessions.

Training directors' requirements do not differ from those of most small meetings, but they are less likely to be permissive about such things as audiovisual equipment, permanent dividing walls, low-hanging chandeliers and nearby distractions in the hotel. Actually, these specifications are similar to those that any good meeting planner would want (see Figure 5.8).

Meeting Specialists/Third-Party Planners

Just a few years ago, nearly all corporate meetings were planned by in-house departments. Due to downsizing, many companies, like associations, are looking outside their own organizations for meeting planning services. Some of these **third-party meeting planners** only get involved in larger meetings. Others select hotels, airlines, destination management companies and other meeting services. They conduct site searches, negotiate rates on behalf of the companies and associations they represent, and assist in conducting meetings and conventions. Travel organizations are called in at times, especially for incentive programs. These organizations are important sources of business.

As mentioned in the opening chapter, companies such as Conferon and Helms Briscoe have become prominent sources of meetings business. But, other independent meeting planning companies will likely grow in size as hotel chains continue to consolidate. Hotel chains now focus their efforts on deriving their business from the biggest clients and have justified this approach based on the rationale that 80 percent of

Figure 5.8. ADVERTISING TO PLANNERS OF SMALL MEETINGS.

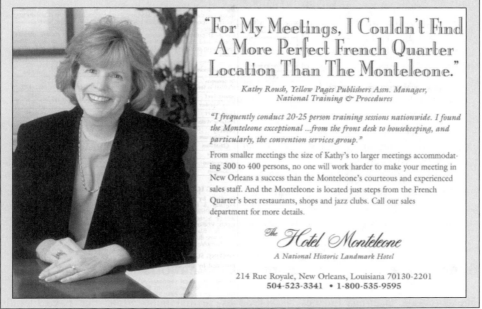

This ad for The Hotel Monteleone in New Orleans promotes its commitment to servicing small meetings. The ad focuses on how the hotel works hard to make a meeting a success, and adds to its credibility by featuring a testimonial from a meeting planner who typically holds small meetings of 20-25 persons.

group business comes from 20 percent of their clients. Therefore, third-party leads will grow in importance.

Steve Armitage, vice president of sales and managing director of Hilton Hotels, says:

> "We want to increase our market share with key accounts, and the more business we get from an organization, the better positioned we can be to partner with them on the rates they need for an event to be successful."[3]

Third-party companies make their money by charging a management fee to the meeting groups they represent or by charging the hotel a commission on the room rate. Obviously, hotels would prefer that these third-party planners secure their fee from the groups they represent, but, recognizing the volume of business provided by third-party planners, hotels are increasingly willing to pay commissions.

Many smaller associations and corporations have limited bargaining power when negotiating with hotels. But when they outsource their meetings to a large third-party planner they often realize the advantage of volume savings. To get more personal attention -- and perhaps greater concessions from hotels -- it is likely that more planners will turn to third-party meeting management companies to locate and negotiate facilities for their meetings.

Sources for Finding Corporate Business and Decision Makers

It's a great big business world out there, and while you may be eager to just get out there and knock on doors, that isn't the recommended use of time. Tom McCarthy, a veteran of hotel sales, believes prospecting should be more calculated:

"A salesperson might have a territory that includes 35,000 companies. If a salesperson can qualify 20 new prospects a week, it doesn't take much figuring to determine that the salesperson can qualify about 1,000 accounts a year.

"Wouldn't it make more sense to work with a list broker and pick 1,000 companies in advance that would be assigned the salesperson (based on proximity, size, and type of business), rather than just telling the person to 'hit the bricks'? Do we think the person will call on the best 1,000 out of the 35,000 by chance?

"Here we are working with computers and sophisticated software and still living in the 19th century when it comes to the most basic principles of prospecting."[4]

In today's competitive environment, prospecting for new business is essential, but going up and down the street knocking on doors is not the way. Once you know the kind of corporate executives you want, there are a number of ways for you to reach them effectively.

Special Meetings and Business Publications

The corporate meetings business is served by several publications that have literally done your job of sorting out those executives interested in meetings. It is hardly a surprise, therefore, to find that advertising appearing in these publications seems to be an industry rundown of the leading convention hotels. These magazines also offer advertisers sales lead services, providing the names of and data about likely prospects.

The four leading publications are *Successful Meetings, Meetings & Conventions, Meeting News* and *The Meeting Professional*. Most of their circulation is to readers in the corporate area. A list of trade magazines and their addresses are given in Appendix I.

There are other publications of interest to hotel marketing people, although they do not specialize in conventions; they either deal with related editorial subjects or reach the executives likely to make meeting decisions. Most relevant is *Sales and Marketing Management*. As its name implies, the publication is directed to sales and marketing executives who are frequently involved with meetings.

General business publications can be considered as well. Although these publications are not directed specifically to executives who are involved with meeting decisions, their circulations reflect profiles similar to those of meeting planners. Hotels with adequate advertising budgets can promote their meeting facilities in such publications as *The Wall Street Journal, Business Week*, and *Fortune*.

Trade Directories and Publications

It is possible to develop sales leads by working your way through a specific industry. If your records indicate meetings of similar companies, it may be that industry is a fertile field for more business. The insurance industry, for example, is a prolific meeting group. There is even an association of meeting planners solely within that field. Other individual trades and industries may offer names of companies similar to those that have met in your hotel.

Dun and Bradstreet's Million Dollar Directory lists the nation's largest businesses and their officers. It is published by Dun and Bradstreet, 99 Church Street, New York, NY 10007.

Standard and Poor's Register of Directors and Executives is a similar publication. The *Register* alphabetically lists over 60,000 companies and provides addresses and basic information on numbers of employees, revenues and key personnel. The address for this publication is Standard and Poor's, 25 Broadway, New York, NY 10004.

Ward's Business Directory lists over 135,000 of America's largest companies and provides the same information as *Dun's* and the *Register*. However, Ward's sorts the geographic listings by zip code, and ranks headings under SIC Code of Sales. Wards also provides separate lists for 1,000 of the biggest private companies and 1,000 of the biggest public companies in the U.S. The publication is available from Gale Research Company, 835 Pnobscot Building, Detroit, MI 48226.

Meeting Professionals International Membership Directory is available to members and allied members of Meeting Professionals International (MPI), 1950 Stemmons Freeway, Dallas, TX 75207. To obtain a copy of this guide — the best-known source of corporate meeting planners — hotel people must join the organization along with a meeting planner.

Scientific and Technical Societies in the U.S. and Canada is published by Canadian Business Magazine, 300 St. Sacrament Street, Montreal, Quebec, Canada.

The *National Associations of Businesspersons* is published by the U.S. Department of Commerce. Listed are the names, addresses and chief executives of associations of business firms. The publication is available from the Superintendent of Documents, U.S. Government Printing Office, Washington, DC 20401.

Best Insurance Reports, published by A.M. Best Company, Ambest Rd, Oldwick, NJ 08858, lists some ten thousand executives of insurance firms.

The *Directory of Corporate Meeting Planners* lists 12,000 meeting planners, with address, phone number, number of meetings, and when and where meetings are held. It is available from Douglas Publications, Richmond, VA (1-800-223-1797).

Trade Associations

If you feel that specific industries might be worth following, call on the executive directors of their trade associations. *You should be calling on them anyway for their own association business*, but they can also be a prime source of leads. They can pinpoint the larger companies in the trade and those in your part of the country. Their trade directories could be a good source of leads and a good addition to your mailing list.

Many meetings are held in the principal locale of the sponsoring company. It makes sense, therefore, to study directories of businesses within your city, state or area of the country. Chambers of commerce could also supply such lists.

The local library, chamber of commerce, and state industrial commission are also excellent sources for local leads. Most offer publications that list businesses according to Standard Industrial Classification (SIC), developed by the federal government. In many cases, your property may already have a breakdown of businesses booked by SIC code; this makes it particularly easy to target other businesses from the same category.

Don't neglect to solicit the local branches of national organizations. You may be told that meeting decisions are made at the national headquarters, but don't ignore the local firms. It is common for a corporate meeting planner to ask a local district manager about a suitable hotel in the area. The order may come from corporate headquarters, but the important input could come from your own area.

In addition, local branches often hold meetings of their own, albeit smaller ones. Local dealer meetings, training sessions and regional sales meetings are often within the responsibility of the regional sales manager. Going after the regular commercial business of a branch sales office may give you a chance at some group business as well.

Internet Sites

Another effective way to find meeting planners is to visit Internet sites that provide membership information and search services. One of the largest is MPIWeb, the Web site of Dallas-based Meeting Professionals International. MPI has more than 58 chapters in 51 countries, including 30 in North America, and you can click on MPI Chapters to find chapters in specific geographical areas. The site offers a free search service (a hotel salesperson does not have to be a member or associate member of MPI to use the search feature) that allows you to select such items as "Meeting Consultant/Independent Planner." By entering a specific city and state, you will be provided with a list of updated names and contact information.

This is just one of the many sites available on the Internet. A hotel salesperson can search for companies by name, access financial data and find key executives through financially-oriented sites, and access vendors that serve the conventions and meetings industry for leads without leaving the comfort of the sales office.

Convention and Visitors Bureaus

Many hotel salespeople are also finding that working with their city's convention and visitors' bureau can be an excellent way to build corporate business. While CVBs formerly dealt with associations business, many are now targeting smaller corporate markets and can provide leads for your property.

Just a few years ago, the International Association of Convention and Visitor Bureaus held its first Destinations Showcase event in New York City to promote CVB services to corporate planners. While many corporate decision makers had not previously used CVBs, interest in using them as "one-stop shopping" venues has increased. If a corporate meeting planner is interested in booking space in Orlando, for example, he or she need make only one call to the CVB; the CVB will respond with information on only those hotels that meet the planner's needs.

And, properties can also find additional leads by participating in the destination marketing efforts of CVBs. Many of them participate in trade shows promoting their destination city, and participating properties may either send salespeople to meet with show visitors or make promotional materials available at the CVBs booth (selling with CVBs is explained in detail in Chapter 7).

Lateral Referral and Account Penetration

Many hotel people are content when they get meetings business from a large corporation. But hosting company meetings offers the opportunity to promote even more business. Just help to execute a smoothly functioning meeting and your hotel will have an edge on the competition when it comes to additional business from the firm.

Some companies are so large that employees in one division have little or nothing to do with those in other sectors. If your meetings business comes from a product manager in one division, give serious thought to following up with everyone who has the title of product manager in that and other divisions of the company.

The operating structure of the company may be uniform throughout, and if the product manager in one instance has the meetings responsibility, it is likely that others would too. If not, the manager will likely be able to point you to a decision maker. Your case is stronger if you can get a recommendation from your original product manager customer. Even if he or she doesn't know the others personally, an endorsement from someone within the firm should open some doors.

Such lateral referrals and complete **account penetration** of all sectors of a large firm is the sign of a successful hotel sales manager. Think of the large companies in your area as a multi-divisional entity simply loaded with business potential.

This will also help your prospects for business in other companies. You will gain an insight into corporate structure that will help you analyze other companies in the same industry. The structures are generally similar. It certainly provides you with a good starting point by knowing the titles you are seeking. Understanding the corporate setup and who most likely has the meetings chore gives you a big leg up to penetrating and selling corporate business.

Other opportunities await at the property level. Local suppliers, such as your produce wholesaler, dairy operator, insurance agent and other suppliers of products and/or services are potential sources of meetings business. Even if a property's suppliers do not require meeting space for themselves, many belong to trade, professional or civic organizations or social or religious groups. The property's suppliers, then, could very well be in a position to recommend the property as a meeting site for future meetings of their respective organizations.

Employees of a property are also good sources of meetings business. Many employees belong to organizations (bowling teams, garden clubs, the P.T.A., religious groups, etc.) that meet regularly or have need of function space for special occasions such as installation dinners, awards nights and other events. Property employees could very well influence the choice of "their" property for those events.

 ## Chapter Summary:

In this chapter, we have taken an indepth look at the corporate meetings segment. We have discussed the kinds of meetings held by corporations and the characteristics of the various company meetings. We have determined who the key corporate decision makers are likely to be and how to find them. This lucrative market segment is becoming increasingly important to hotels, and hotel salespeople who understand the requirements of corporations and can match these requirements to their properties can successfully target the corporate market. In the next chapter, we will take a look at the third segment of the group meetings market, the varied nonprofit groups.

Endnotes:

1. Chris Davis, "Exclusive Short Term Meetings Survey: Lead Times Shrinking," *Business Travel News*, March 22, 1999, pp. 23 & 24.
2. Michael Adams, "Career Jumping," *Successful Meetings*, February 1996, p. 36.
3. "Hilton Makes Fast Progress Absorbing Promus," *Meetings News*, March 20, 2000, p. 53.
4. Tom McCarthy, "Get Your Sales Management Ready for the 21st Century," *Hotel and Resort Industry*.

Additional References:

*   "Meetings Today," Chris Davis, *Business Travel News*
    www.btnonline.com

*   "The Information Revolution in Hospitality: A Guide to Intelligent Marketing 2000-2020," Cindy Estis Green, *The HSMAI Foundation Research Review*
    www.hsmai.org

Internet Sites:

For additional information on the firms and organizations discussed in this chapter, visit the following Internet sites. The Web addresses listed are current as of January 2001. Addresses may change, however; if a site is not available at the address below, a search engine can be used to access its new location.

Association for Corporate Travel Executives (ACTE) - www.acte.org
Business Travel Net - www.business-travel-net.com
Meeting Broker - www.MeetingBroker.com
Meetings and Conventions magazine - www.traveler.net/m&c
Meeting News magazine - www.meetingnews.com
Meeting Professionals International (MPI) - www.mpiweb.org
National Business Travel Association (NBTA) - www.nbta.org
Society of Corporate Meeting Professionals - www.scmp.org
Successful Meetings magazine - www.successmtgs.com

Study Questions:

1. There are many similarities between association meetings and corporate meetings, but there are also clear distinctions. Contrast the two considering lead time, attendance, and kind of site required.
2. Company meetings come in many sizes and shapes. If you were the sales manager of a small property with limited meeting facilities, what types of company meetings would you target?
3. Discuss the multi-booking potential of corporate meetings.
4. As with associations, finding the key decision maker is of utmost importance. Why is this problem so acute in the corporate meetings market? List probable decision makers within the corporate structure.
5. What role do local chapters or business offices play in the determination of meeting sites?
6. Discuss how hotels are upgrading guestrooms with extra services and "perks" to meet specific business traveler needs.
7. List the six major sources for finding corporate meetings and tell how each is used to develop a client base.

Key Terms:

Account penetration. The process of determining new sources of business within an organization.

Dealer meetings. Meetings held on a regional and national basis for dealers and distributors. Usually held to introduce new sales and advertising campaigns and new products.

Incentive meetings. Meetings held during incentive trips given to employees, distributors and dealers as a reward for top performance.

Management meetings. Relatively small meetings consisting of top management. Often request upgraded accommodations and services.

Professional/technical meetings. Meetings held in order to update the company's technical personnel. Usually take the form of seminars/workshops.

Sales meeting. Often a meeting dealing with such company objectives as product introduction, sales policies, company goals, discussion of sales techniques, or to boost morale.

Stockholder/public meetings. Meetings for non-employees.

Third-party meeting planners. Outside individuals or firms who handle meeting planning for companies. Services may include site selection, negotiations, and assisting in all phases of staging the meeting.

Training meetings. Meetings held to update personnel in new company policies, methods or procedures. Usually fairly small in size.

Learning Objectives:

This portion of your text introduces you to the third major source for meetings business, nonprofit organizations. While this segment is smaller than the associations and corporate markets, it is equally important to hotels wishing to fill space during typically slow periods. Also included in this chapter is a discussion of incentive meetings, insurance meetings, and medical meetings. While these groups are not nonprofit, they merit special attention as a source for meetings business. When you have studied this chapter, you will:

- Be able to identify the types of nonprofit organizations that provide extensive meetings business.

- Be able to describe the types of meetings held by each and the factors that influence site decisions.

- Know who makes the decisions for these meetings and how to best reach the decision makers for these groups.

Outline

Nonprofit Organizations

The SMERF Groups
- Social Groups
- Military and Other Reunions
- Educational Meetings
- Religious Meetings
- Fraternal Meetings

Government Agencies

Labor Unions

Incentive Meetings

Insurance Meetings

Medical Meetings

Successfully Targeting SMERF Groups

Lyn Matthew, CHSE
Director of Sales and Marketing
Embassy Suites Resort, Scottsdale, AZ

"The remaining group market segments, commonly referred to as SMERF (Social, Military, Educational, Religious and Fraternal) as well as government, union, medical, insurance and incentive markets are by far the most diverse and challenging...Research is critical in determining which groups can best be served by the property... Since a property can be perceived in many different ways by targeted prospects, it is important to communicate the benefits that highlight the planner's needs and wants...Meeting needs vary widely...The astute sales executive must carefully match property capabilities with the needs of the conference planner. By selling the benefits of the property relative to the conference needs and wants, the sales executive has the opportunity to become a top producer while at the same time satisfying the needs of the meeting planner and paving the way for future bookings."

6 Selling Other Markets

While many properties place their emphasis on selling to associations and corporations, there are several other sources of meeting business that can prove profitable to properties that seek them out (see box titled "Convention Income Survey"). While the structures of these organizations can be similar to those of associations and corporations, they possess unique characteristics and are worth special mention.

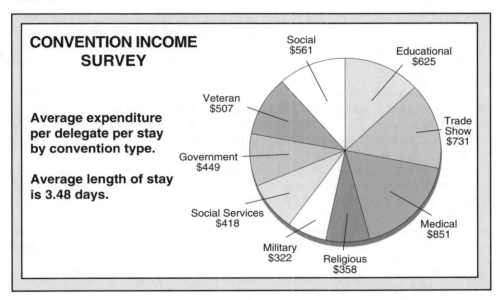

CONVENTION INCOME SURVEY

Average expenditure per delegate per stay by convention type.

Average length of stay is 3.48 days.

Social $561
Educational $625
Veteran $507
Trade Show $731
Government $449
Social Services $418
Medical $851
Military $322
Religious $358

Nonprofit Organizations

Although many organizations cannot be termed associations, they are structured in similar fashion. They have members, are nonprofit and were created to accomplish some common purpose. Some, such as the Red Cross and the Boy Scouts and the Girl Scouts, promote charitable causes. In addition to meetings business, these types of organizations, which exist through fund-raising, may be excellent sources of business for your banquet department. Others of this category include political clubs and parties, which need hotel meeting accommodations for their regular conventions and frequent meetings. Still others include social, military, educational, religious and fraternal (SMERF) groups and the government agencies, labor unions and medical groups, which will be discussed in greater detail in this chapter.

Selling to these organizations is much the same as selling to trade associations, although it is difficult to find a central source that identifies these organizations since they are so varied. The records of a convention or tourist bureau may be of some help, and there are also directories from which a list of nonprofit meeting groups can be compiled. The

Guide to American Directories, published by the Klein Company in New York City may provide leads in your targeted categories.

Another particularly good avenue for reaching nonprofit, cost-conscious groups is HSMAI's Affordable Meetings Exposition and Conference. The event includes a 650-booth trade show as well as seminars for planners and hospitality suppliers, and meeting planners can attend both the trade show and educational program free of charge. Most planners attending this show are not members of traditional planners associations such as MPI or PCMA; they are volunteer meeting planners or those whose titles don't imply meeting planning. These people plan such events as hobby conventions, military reunions, educational, religious and fraternal meetings, and government meetings.

Once you have determined which of these groups you can best service, you can start by soliciting local chapters of national groups (always stay alert for autonomous local groups). Generally, most nonprofit organizations are staffed by permanent employees and volunteers and overseen by a board of directors. Site selection processes will vary, but recommendations are usually passed along to a board of directors for a final selection. Lead time tends to be shorter than that of most trade associations; a lead time of one to two years is most common.

Since most local committees are made up of volunteers, it is a good policy to assure them of your aid should they succeed in getting the national organization to schedule its event at your property. If you offer to extend help for the chores associated with being the host chapter, this may encourage them to push for consideration of your locale as a meeting site.

As a further selling point, don't be reluctant to point out the many economic benefits to the community when a convention is held there. Research has indicated that delegates to regional and state conventions account for expenditures of about $145 a day for three or four days.

Once you are past the local chapters and have penetrated the national organization, you will usually find that there are experienced meeting planners on the staff. Some of these national organizations do a great deal of convention work. They will work with you in the manner of association staffs, especially if you have been successful in getting the local chapter to request the position of host chapter.

The SMERF Groups

One of the most important subsegments in the nonprofit organizations market are the **SMERF groups**. This acronym represents the collective group of social, military, educational, religious and fraternal groups. These groups, though typically price-conscious, are economically viable to properties (large and small) both because of their sheer numbers and their ability to fill "soft spots" as most meet during the typically slow summer months (see box titled "Typical Monthly Meeting Patterns").

Social Groups

People are avid "joiners," and there are groups for almost every interest. Just looking through the "Groups and Organizations" listing in a local telephone directory may yield such prospects as chess clubs, ethnic groups (Italian-American clubs, etc.), garden clubs and bowling leagues. These organizations may be local, or they may be part of a regional or national organization. No matter what their size, these social groups should not be over-

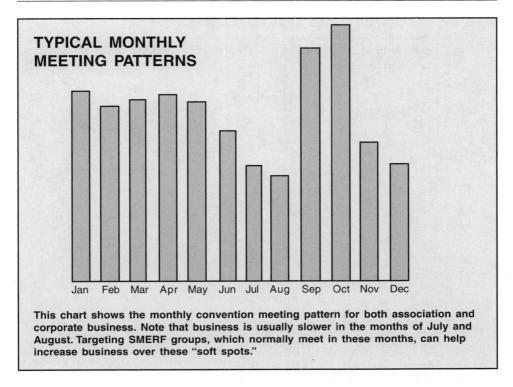

TYPICAL MONTHLY MEETING PATTERNS

Jan Feb Mar Apr May Jun Jul Aug Sep Oct Nov Dec

This chart shows the monthly convention meeting pattern for both association and corporate business. Note that business is usually slower in the months of July and August. Targeting SMERF groups, which normally meet in these months, can help increase business over these "soft spots."

looked as potential sources of business. Even a small local group may require meeting space or can generate meals business, while large groups can be an excellent source of banquet and convention business. Many social clubs hold awards banquets or fund-raising functions or can be a source of business for annual events such as Christmas parties and installation ceremonies. Groups such as garden and craft clubs often host local shows or fairs, which not only result in meeting space sales, but may bring in out-of-town business and generate publicity for your property.

Military and Other Reunions

The reunions market, which consists of family, class and military reunions, is a rapidly growing market segment. This segment is an excellent source of flexible weekend business.

In recent years, military reunions in particular have paved the way for an entire new industry that assists in planning these nostalgic events. Bob Brooks, president of THE Reunion Network, Inc., estimates the military reunion market to be worth $15 billion a year in air travel, hotels, food, drink and entertainment.

In the past, military reunions, which typically draw 100 to 300 people or more, were planned by nonprofessionals. Because of the rising demand, however, several resources were developed to assist inexperienced meeting planners.

THE Reunion Network, established to provide assistance and training publishes a newsletter, *TRN News,* that offers tips for planning a successful reunion and provides additional services to planners, such as offering lists of "reunion friendly" hotels. Military reunion planners can also look to other publications, such as *Reunions Magazine, Military Reunion News,* and *The Reunion Handbook: A Guide for Reunion Planners,* for assistance in planning their meeting. In addition to these resources, *Service Reunions,* a registry

Figure 6.1. SOURCES FOR FINDING REUNIONS BUSINESS.

Properties wishing to target the lucrative reunions market can utilize a number of sources to find leads:

Publications

Reunions Magazine
P.O. Box 11727
Milwaukee, WI 53211-0727
414-263-4567

Reunion Research
Publisher of:
Family Reunion Handbook
Reunion Handbook:
A Guide for School &
Military Reunions

Reunion Research
40609 Auberry Road
Auberry, GA 93602
209-855-2101
www.reunited.com/tomstips

Reunion Planning

The Reunion Desk
188 W. Randolph Street,
Suite 1700
Chicago, IL 60601
800-634-2153

Professional Reunion
Management Instruction
P.O. Box 5040
Colorado Springs, CO 80931
800-500-6304

Reunion Network
2450 Hollywood Blvd.
Hollywood, FL 33020
800-225-5044

Books on Reunions

How to Locate Anyone
Who Is, or Has Been,
In the Military
by Lt. Col.
Richard S. Johnson
800-937-2133

Reunions for Fun-
Loving Families
by Nancy Funke Bagley
Brighton Publications
P.O. Box 120706
St. Paul, MN 55112
800-536-2665

Let's Have a Reunion:
A How-To-Do-It Guide
by Philip A. Hannema

In addition, hotels can join such organizations as THE Reunion Network. This group publishes *TRN News*, a free newsletter for reunion planners, and offers help — including lists of "reunion friendly" properties — to inexperienced meeting planners. In addition to being included on THE Reunion Network's list of contact properties, your hotel can advertise to meeting planners in the newsletter.

listing over 9,000 military units, helps planners in the most difficult part of their jobs: locating members. This service, which lists planners by state, military service, size of meeting, and month of meeting, also provides telemarketing lists, making it an invaluable resource for properties that wish to target this lucrative market. There are also a number of other resources for hotels wishing to target military reunions (see Figure 6.1).

Military reunion business has several notable characteristics (see Figure 6.2). For the most part, reunions are held in September and October, and occupancies run from Thursday or Friday through Sunday. Most groups meet annually or biennially, and many will seek your professional expertise in setting up their meeting.

Most military reunion programs include a Saturday night banquet and a memorial service, and a short business meeting. Room occupancy is usually 75 to 150 per night, although this can go higher for larger reunions. Since many are on fixed incomes, paying their own way, they are extremely price-conscious. Attendees often share rooms with spouses or friends.

Hotels with planned spouse programs have a competitive edge in attracting this market. Attendees are typically male, but spouses have a strong voice in the decision to attend. One meeting reunion planner states:

> "All of the men have something in common, but almost none of the women do. If you do the job right, the wives will send the check in the day the registration notice arrives."[1]

Figure 6.2. THE MILITARY REUNION MARKET AT A GLANCE.

Location:	Family and/or military-oriented destinations that can offer a combined vacation/reunion. Past destinations have included San Diego, California, Daytona Beach, Florida, San Antonio, Texas. Almost any city with popular local attractions or a good climate, however, can compete for this market.
Facilities:	Programs usually consist of a short business meeting, a memorial service and a Saturday night banquet. Requirements include limited audiovisual equipment, but there must be enough banquet space to seat the entire group and their spouses at one time. A hospitality room is usually required.
Price:	Since many attendees are on fixed incomes, this group is very cost-conscious. Properties that offer low rates, free or low-cost meeting space or discounts to local attractions are especially inviting.
Services:	Properties targeting this group can expect to assist with the planning of functions, as many military reunions are planned by nonprofessionals. Some groups will also require special meal menus.
Decision Makers:	Contact must be made with individual military unit or group to determine the decision maker.
Best Ways To Reach Market:	Join THE Reunion Network, and advertise in THE Reunion Network News. Other advertising opportunities include *Reunions, the Magazine*, and *Military Reunion News*. Find contacts through the *Military Reunion Handbook*, and purchase lists or labels from Service Reunions National Registry. Attend military reunion training conferences and organize fam trips for military reunion planners.

Military towns also have an edge as veterans like to visit their old haunts and tour bases, ships and museums. The Pensacola, FL Convention and Visitors Center, for example, touts its history as "The Cradle of Naval Aviation." And the Montgomery, AL Chamber of Commerce estimates that military reunions have a $10 million annual impact on the local area economy because the Air Force keeps its historical records at a base there.

Class and family reunions differ from military reunions in terms of size, meeting frequency, and types of programs. Recreational amenities are considered very important, and there may be several food and social functions but little in the way of meeting space needed. Like military groups, however, these groups pay their own way, and usually provide a good number of double occupancy rooms.

Class reunions are the largest in terms of numbers of events and number of attendees. However, attendees stay an average of just one night in a hotel. Family and military reunions, on the other hand, draw fewer people but the attendees stay for a longer period of time -- an average of two nights in the case of family reunions and 2.5 nights at military reunions.

Although most family reunions are hosted by nonprofessionals, there are a growing number of trained class reunion meeting planners. The National Association of Reunion Planners (NARP) is an organization that offers meeting planning training and networking. In addition, exhibiting at the African-American Family Reunion Conference, held annually at Temple University in Philadelphia, is an excellent way to reach potential customers. According to the National Coalition of Black Meeting Planners (NCBMP), African-Americans are an excellent source of reunions business, especially if your city can offer points of interest relative to the black heritage (museums, entertainment, etc.) and your property is sensitive to African-American issues.

Other ways to target the class and family reunions market are to advertise in *Reunions Magazine*, a Milwaukee-based monthly publication, and to work closely with your local convention and visitors bureau or chamber of commerce. These organizations are often contacted by individuals or groups wanting information about "reunion friendly" hotels.

Educational Meetings

The educational meetings market is an excellent market segment for filling rooms during slow summer occupancy periods. Elementary, high school and college teachers and others affiliated with academic programs are prime sources of convention business. They hold a number of meetings, and every state has a teachers' association of some sort as well. In addition, most states have continuing education requirements that necessitate periodic seminars and classes for teachers.

Most educational meetings are relatively short (sometimes lasting only a day), and meeting planners look for accessibility and value. Since most attendees come at their own expense, they are extremely price sensitive. Properties that are located close to major transportation arteries or an educational center (college, university, etc.) and can offer reduced room rates are especially attractive.

Since this market is so diverse, there are many potential contact persons. Cooperative extension services often sponsor seminars, and the state director is the decision maker (a county agent's directory is an excellent source of contact names). Alumni offices and divisions of continuing education at local colleges and universities are sources of leads for meetings business, and admissions offices can provide transient business from visiting parents and prospective students. Other leads can be obtained through the administrative offices at a local educational institution or board of education. Personal contacts and referrals are often available from college professors and teachers who belong to professional associations.

A pamphlet specifically keyed to the educational meetings market is *Educational Associations and Directories*. Providing the names and addresses of educational offices, it can be obtained from the Superintendent of Documents, U.S. Printing Office, Washington, DC 20401. The *National Directory of College Athletics* identifies personnel in the athletic departments of universities and colleges throughout the United States. This directory can be secured by writing the Collegiate Directories Inc., P.O. Box 450640, Cleveland, OH

44145. Or, you may wish to utilize the Blue Book of College Athletics, published by Athletic Publishing Company, P.O. Box 931, Montgomery, AL 36101.

Religious Meetings

Religious groups are an excellent source of business for gatherings both small (board meetings, committee meetings, seminars and workshops) and large (area and regional meetings and conventions). Large conventions of 10,000 to 45,000 attendees are a common annual occurrence, and a property that understands the unique needs of religious groups can take advantage of this opportunity to fill "soft spots" — most groups meet during the summer months (usually over a three day to two week period).

Most large religious meetings are "family affairs," and meeting planners tend to choose locations that are family oriented (Orlando, Anaheim, Dallas). Since most attendees pay their own way, they are price sensitive, usually opting for double occupancy rooms.

One reason that religious meetings can be profitable to a hotel is that they do not displace corporate or association business. Because these groups are value conscious, religious meeting planners negotiate lower rates by booking on holidays and weekends and seeking shoulder or valley periods. Vaughn Hall, director of convention sales and marketing for the Santa Clara, CA Chamber of Commerce/Convention and Visitors Bureau, says, "We've targeted the religious market because our weekends are slow and it's a good filler market for us."[2]

There is another very good reason to target this market. Many religious groups do community service projects when they visit a city. In Indianapolis, for example, 2,000 meeting attendees helped local neighborhood associations rehabilitate ten houses and clean up city parks. Other groups work at soup kitchens or run blood drives. The Jehovah's Witnesses even have built a clause into their contract with convention centers saying that *they* will clean the center at the convention's end.

Many of the larger religious meetings are planned by professional meeting planners, many of whom belong to the Religious Conference Management Association (RCMA). This group was founded in 1972 and has approximately 800 meeting planner members and 2,100 associate members that represent hotels, convention bureaus, and other suppliers. RCMA members are responsible for over 2,000 meetings a year, and represent more than 250 denominations and religious organizations.

RCMA's Annual Conference and Exposition is an ideal arena for direct sales to this market. The group also publishes a quarterly magazine, *Highlights,* and a membership directory. Properties seeking the religious market would find associate membership in the organization to be an excellent investment.

Fraternal Meetings

Fraternal organizations can be broken down into two categories: "The Greeks," which are the familiar college campus societies, and fraternal and service groups, such as the Benevolent Protective Order of Elks, the Fraternal Order of Eagles, and the American Legion, to name a few.

National fraternities and sororities, which number 55 and 26 respectively on college campuses across the country, typically meet during the summer months at events planned by a paid executive. The activities of this vast market are coordinated by three major groups: the National Interfraternity Conference (NIC), which represents 48 fraternities; the

Religious Meetings at a Glance

Attendance: Consists of hundreds of organizations from dozens of denominations throughout the United States and the world; may range in size from small board meetings to mega-conventions of up to 75,000 (see photo). May consist of clergy, lay people, or both; are often family affairs.

Location: Favor family-oriented cities such as Orlando, Anaheim, and Atlanta. Also prefer second and third tier cities, generally in the South or Midwest, such as Birmingham, Indianapolis, and St. Louis. Mark McCulley, CMP, festival administration manager for the Worldwide Church of God, evaluates each city for facility size and quality; affordability of hotel and convention facilities; area attractions and amusements; friendliness of the city; and, overall entertainment value of the region.

Facilities: Need a wide selection of meeting and convention space — small meeting rooms for seminars, workshops, and meetings; large convention halls to hold large crowds. Often require numerous breakout rooms and have many, often simultaneous meal functions.

Services: Restaurant availability is a high priority. According to April McWilliams, V.P. of Sales for the Greater Birmingham CVB, "Whenever people finish up with a meeting, they're always hungry. They want a place to eat, so it's important that hotels or centers have restaurants open for them, even if it's just for pie or coffee." Some religious groups will require special menus as well (i.e., Jewish Kosher foods).

Price: Middle- to low-budget hotels are preferred since most pay their own way. Double occupancy is norm. Property offered discounts and complimentary transportation are valued.

Decision Makers: Most national events are planned by professional meeting planners. Local and regional events planned by a committee or the leader of the organization.

Best Ways To Reach Market: The RCMA (Religious Conference Management Association) is a national organization representing over 250 denominations and religious organizations. They publish a quarterly magazine, *Highlights*, and a membership directory.

Religious groups, such as the Promise Keepers, a men-only ministry based in Boulder, CO, generate over 7,200 conventions and meetings internationally and represent 30 million nights of hotel accommodations annually.

Panhellenic Conference, the female counterpart of the NIC; and the Fraternity Executives Association (FEA), whose membership is made up of paid executive officers from a number of fraternities (see box titled "Sources for Reaching the Fraternal Market").

The size of most general membership meetings, held during the months of June through August, ranges from approximately 150 to 800 or more. Multiple occupancy rates are high, since spouses or fellow students often share rooms. Meeting agendas typically include a banquet lunch, so properties wishing to service this market must have ample facilities to seat the entire delegation at one time. Lead time is typically two to three years.

Sources for Reaching the Fraternal Market

Fraternal Executives Association

Attendee Profile: College fraternity executives (executive directors and national presidents) from the top college fraternal organizations in America.
Program: Fraternity-related suppliers from the hospitality industry can socialize with executives and participate in a trade show.
Contact: Fraternity Executives Association, www.fea-inc.org

National Panhellenic Conference

Attendee Profile: College sorority executives (executive directors and national presidents) from the top women's fraternal organizations in America.
Program: Geared mainly toward hospitality industry suppliers, the best opportunity for business development occurs during the trade portion of the event.
Contact: National Panhellenic Conference, P.O. Box 90264, Indianapolis, IN 46268 (317) 255-4379

National Interfraternity Conference

Attendee Profile: National fraternity executives and college fraternity advisors from throughout the country.
Program: Mainly fraternity related; the trade show portion of the event offers the best opportunity for business development.
Contact: National Interfraternity Conference, Inc. 3901 West 86th Street, Suite 390, Indianapolis, IN 40268-1791 (317) 872-1112

In addition to general meetings, sororities and fraternities hold educational retreats and leadership training institutes, which are usually held during the school year to train newly elected officers. While some of these meetings are held on college campus for cost-effectiveness, properties that can offer discounted rates may be able to capture some of this business.

Other possibilities for business include national board or council meetings, which usually consist of the governing boards of sororities and fraternities. Since group size is small, ranging from six to 125 people, and meetings are shorter, these meetings are often held on weekends (usually during the months of October and February). Airport facilities and properties close to the campus can often draw this type of business.

A subsegment for special consideration is African-American fraternal organizations. Consisting of eight major fraternities, these groups have annual or biennial conventions of 2,000 to 20,000 people. Besides generating high attendance, the advantage of servicing this market is that the membership is generally older and more affluent than the typical collegiate fraternity member. Alumni chapters play active roles in these organizations, and attendees tend to have more disposable income than their college counterparts — which translates to higher entertainment, catering, and alcoholic beverage revenue for hotels.

In addition to the traditional Greek societies, there is another group of professional or honorary societies that should also be included in this category. Some examples include Alpha Omega, a professional dental fraternity, Sigma Delta Chi, a professional journalism society, and Delta Epsilon Sigma, a scholarship honorary society. Some of these host large conventions, meeting on an 18-month rotational basis in the months of August and December. The December conventions, held between Christmas and New Years Day, are an excellent way to fill this traditionally slack time. These groups can be reached through related professional associations or through contact with the American Society of Association Executives (ASAE), since many of these meeting planners belong to that association.

Service groups also hold a number of meetings and special events throughout the year. While many of these (such as the Elks and the American Legion, for example) have their own meeting facilities, they can be excellent sources of business for special occasions, including fund-raising events and annual functions such as Christmas parties. This group may also play host to regional and national conventions or generate rooms business from out-of-town guests attending local functions.

Both fraternal and service groups' regional and national meetings are usually family affairs and are often presented to delegates — who pay their own way —as a vacation-convention combination. Planners, therefore, look for recreational amenities as well as value.

There are a number of ways to reach this lucrative market segment. *Leland's Annual Fraternity-Sorority Directory* is issued each January by Leland Publishers, Inc. It lists the officers of national sororities and fraternities. Sororities and fraternities can also be reached by contacting college campuses and their alumni associations or by contacting the national governing groups mentioned in this section. Service groups may be found in local telephone directories or through chamber of commerce listings.

To solicit this market on a larger scale, you may wish to consider participating in three events held by major fraternities and sororities. The Fraternal Executives Association (FEA) holds a meeting and vendor trade show during the first two weeks of July, while the National Interfraternity Conference (NIC) holds a larger event during the first week of December. While this event also includes a trade show, it is less hotel specific than FEA's. The National Panhellenic Conference (NPC), which is held in October, also features a trade show and gives vendors the opportunity to meet with the executives and staff members of 25 attending sororities.

Government Agencies

Another frequently overlooked — but potentially lucrative — nonprofit market segment is government meetings business (see Figure 6.3). This market segment can be an excellent source of conventions business, especially when agencies deal with business groups. The Department of Agriculture and the International Food Organization of the United Nations are two examples of this type of agency.

Figure 6.3. THE GOVERNMENT MEETINGS MARKET AT A GLANCE.

Location:	Preferred locations are those that are easily accessible. Cities to which airlines offer direct flights and discounted fares are given priority. Government planners must be sensitive to the public appearance of booking a resort or elegant location.
Facilities:	Preferred facilities offer double-double guest rooms and reasonably priced restaurants. Most meetings involve training, so quality meeting rooms and audiovisual support are prime concerns.
Price:	Generally are cost conscious. Planners must deal with a strict bid process and sparse per diems. Hotels bidding must know how to fit within government per diem guidelines; rates quoted must include taxes.
Services:	All "low-cost" or "no-cost" services that the property can provide are solicited by planners, i.e. free shuttle van from airport, complimentary coffee breaks, and waived meeting room rental. Require flexible payment schedules as the government is often slow in paying.
Decision Makers:	Meetings are planned at the local, state and federal levels. Key contacts include the agency director, training officer, contract specialist and procurement officer.
Best Ways To Reach Market:	Join the Society of Government Meeting Professionals. SGMP's monthly chapter meetings, national newsletter, directory, and annual conference are excellent for identifying and contacting prospects. List your property in the *Official Airline Guide Government Edition* and subscribe to the *Commerce Business Daily*, a publication listing requests for meeting proposals.

It is difficult to generalize about the kind of business that comes from government agencies. It varies a great deal, as does interest in different parts of the country. We are strong believers in "fishing expeditions." Go into any local government office and ask the supervisor about meetings held by his department or any emanating from the national or state office. This takes patience and hard work, but you may be able to add a number of prospects to your lists. And don't overlook chambers of commerce. Some are funded by local governments while others are independent membership organizations; in either case, local chambers can be excellent sources of meeting business.

If the people expected to attend meetings are government employees, it would help if you learned what the current **per diem** allowance, the fixed amount of money allowed for government employees for each day of travel away from the office, is for your city. It is seldom a generous sum, and employees often add to it out of their own pockets. If you can offer a meeting package of lodging and meals that is covered by the per diem allowance, you will be more likely to attract this market segment.

When going after government business, you will find that it is not too different from dealing with corporations. You deal with the strata of executives. When you get to the person of authority, you can close the deal. You can expect many small meetings, on short notice, just as you do in corporate business.

The majority of government meetings are held for training purposes, and there are several key needs that must be met in order to attract this business. First, accessibility is important; direct flights at discounted rates are a major factor in the choice of locations. Second, most agencies look for free meeting space; a property that hopes to secure government business must make this concession in exchange for room business. Third, government meetings are on a tightly controlled per diem basis; a property that can offer a rate within government guidelines has a distinct advantage in attracting this market. Government agencies are also often slow in paying (it can take as long as 45 days to receive payment); a property must be able to work within government payment schedules. Since lead time is short (less than one year), government agencies often keep files on properties that meet their requirements and can book meetings on short notice.

Since most meetings are training meetings, the meeting planner is often a training officer, contract specialist or procurement officer. Although properties will usually work with one of these people in regard to meeting details, site selection is often based on two distinct types of price submission: Invitation for Bids (IFB) and Request for Proposals (RFP).

The IFB procedure uses sealed bids that are mailed or hand-delivered to the requesting government office in sealed envelopes until a preset bid opening date. All prices are announced during the bid opening. The RFP is a confidential method of selection. The government is free to negotiate with a supplier who meets government standards. Once a final selection is made, the property must prove that it can provide the contracted services (physically and financially).

There are several sources for locating government business (see Figure 6.4). Local legislators can also be invaluable contacts; often, the suggestions of a legislative committee will result in a booking. Direct mail contact may also be made with various government agencies and officials. A direct mail package might include a government rate sheet, third-party endorsements from government groups that have met at your property, and an offer for a member of the agency to visit your hotel. Advertising is another option frequently used to reach the government market.

The Internet can also be used to reach this market. Allmeetings.com, an online meeting planning site that matches planners with hotels, now has a special area for government planners. Planners input their meeting specifications (number of attendees, budget constraints, etc.) and allmeetings returns only the hotels that meet the strict requirements of

Figure 6.4. SOURCES FOR LOCATING GOVERNMENT TRAVEL BUSINESS.

Information Publications

Official Airline Guide - Government Edition
Reed Travel Group
Secaucus, NJ 07096
(201) 902-1988
Fax: (201) 319-1761

Features include contract air and car listings, all qualifying noncontract hotels, per diems by location, policies, procedures and other information needed by a government employee for travel.

United States Government Manual
Superintendent of Documents
U.S. Government Printing Office
Washington, DC 20402
(202) 783-3238
Stock #69-000-00015-1

Includes listing of executive agencies and department functions, guide to boards, commissions and committees, complete explanation of government structure by branch, unilateral organizations, federal region map, independent establishments and government corporations, and commonly used abbreviations and acronyms.

Commerce Business Daily
c/o Superintendent of Documents
U.S. Government Printing Office
Washington, DC 20402
(202) 783-3238

Features on-line database service, lists all government contract opportunities over $25,000, and lists the names and locations of federal agencies buying products or services, description of requirements, contract supervisor and ordering process. On subscription basis.

Government Services Administration Traffic and Travel Zone Offices:

EASTERN ZONE
Federal Supply Service Bureau
75 Spring Street S.W.
Atlanta, GA 30303
(404) 331-5121

CENTRAL ZONE
Federal Supply Service Bureau
1500 East Bannister Road
Kansas City, MO 64131-3088
(816) 523-6029

SOUTHWEST ZONE
Federal Supply Service Bureau
819 Taylor Street
Ft. Worth, TX 76102
(817) 334-2737

WESTERN ZONE
Federal Supply Service Bureau
525 Market Street
San Francisco, CA 94015
(415) 974-9292

NATIONAL CAPITAL ZONE
Federal Supply Service Bureau
7th and D Streets SW
Washington, DC 20407
(202) 472-2003

Media

Government Executive
1730 M Street NW
Washington, DC 20036
Edited to help top government managers perform their jobs.
Governing
2300 N Street NW Suite 760
Washington, DC 20037
Edited for state and local government executive, providing "how-to" information.

Organizations

Society of Government Meeting Professionals
908 King St
Alexandria, VA 22314
(703) 549 - 0892
www.sgmp.org

Society of Travel Agents in Government
6935 Wisconsin Circle NW
Washington, DC 20815
(301) 654-8995

government travel policies and per diems. And, two key organizations can assist a property in obtaining business from this lucrative market: the Society of Government Meeting Professionals and the Society of Travel Agents in Government.

Labor Unions

The labor union meetings market has become so important that many properties employ sales personnel to specifically target this category. There are over 150 unions in the United States, and most hold meetings fairly regularly. In addition, most unions stay with a property with which they have been satisfied, providing an excellent opportunity for repeat business.

Union meetings, which are usually held only at hotels that are unionized, fall into three general categories: national conventions; regional conferences; and executive and committee meetings.

National conventions are usually held every two years, with site locations shifting between the eastern and western regions of the United States. National conventions typically generate:

- high spouse attendance
- high per person expenditures
- a number of social programs
- several sponsored functions, providing good food and beverage revenue

Because of their size, national conventions are held at larger properties that can provide the rooms and meeting space needed to accommodate the delegates and their spouses. The general session, which typically takes on a political atmosphere, is the focal point of the convention and is usually attended by all of the delegates. Sophisticated audiovisual equipment is often required, as is media accessibility, since prominent political speakers are often part of the program.

In addition to the large amount of space needed for the general session, sufficient space is needed for the various social functions in the program. These may range from banquets for the entire contingent to breakfast meetings for key leaders to a number of hospitality suites.

Regional conferences are usually held in central locations. Meetings typically last two to three days and draw attendances of 200 to 500 delegates. As in the case of national conventions, meeting planners seek out properties that can accommodate all of their delegates and offer sophisticated audiovisual equipment.

Executive and committee meetings, which number as many as four a year, are usually held in the union's headquarters city. Since participants are key union people, attendance is smaller (15 to 20 people). These meetings are important to a property, however, as the success of a small meeting may lead to the booking of larger meetings and conventions.

Contact persons for union business include the general secretary of a union for national conventions and the secretary-treasurer for executive and committee meetings. Meeting planners are professional and well-disciplined, and the selling process must include a sense of trust based on personal relationships and the ability to meet the meeting planner's needs.

Incentive Meetings

While incentive travel is a part of the corporate meetings market, this important market segment is sufficiently different to deserve special mention, especially due to its growing impact and importance to resort properties.

What is **incentive travel**? It is a travel award — often a deluxe tour package — offered as motivation to employees and customers to put forth extra effort and meet criteria established by the program sponsors. Since the trip is a reward for selling (or buying), incentive meeting planners seek first-class accommodations and service, and look for locations that offer good weather, sight-seeing, recreational facilities, entertainment and a choice of restaurants (see Figure 6.5).

The economic environment has a great impact on the degree of incentive travel. When times are tough, it becomes critical to motivate employees and customers. Incentives have been proven to increase employee and distributor participation in moving products and services. Travel incentives, which are recognized as effective motivators, have been used to improve morale, reduce turnover and achieve special sales targets. They have also been used to get dealers to concentrate on specific brands and to increase purchases.

Travel award programs are frequently established for automobile dealers, appliance distributors, insurance salespersons, and other employee and customer groups. The insurance, auto parts and electronics industries are the heaviest users of incentive travel (see Figure 6.6).

Most incentive trips last five days to a week (occasionally longer), and have an average attendance of approximately 125 people to ensure that everyone involved gets special attention. While most incentive trips have typically been group affairs, *individual incentive travel* is a trend that has been gaining momentum. Many qualifiers prefer to take an individual trip with a significant other.

Figure 6.5. FACTORS IMPORTANT TO INCENTIVE TRAVEL PLANNERS.

Factors Considered "Very Important"	Incentive Trips
Safety and security of destination	75%
Availability of recreational facilities such as golf, swimming, tennis, etc.	65%
Climate	65%
Sightseeing, cultural and other extracurricular attractions	58%
Glamorous or popular image of location	58%
Availability of hotels or other facilities suitable for meetings	68%
Transportation costs	65%
Ease of transporting attendees to/from location	66%
Distance traveled by attendees	56%
	Total is greater than 100% due to multiple mentions

Since incentive travel is largely motivational — a "reward" for a job well done — incentive travel planners have different requirements than general corporate meeting planners. Interestingly, while the availability of recreational facilities, such as golf, swimming, tennis, etc., once ranked number one on the list, the safety and security of the destination is now the top concern.
Source: The 2000 Meetings Market Study conducted by Meetings & Conventions magazine.

Figure 6.6. THE TOP 10 USERS OF INCENTIVE TRAVEL.

TOP 10 USERS OF INCENTIVE TRAVEL
(BY INDUSTRY, IN MILLIONS)

Industry	Amount
Insurance	$342.9
Auto parts, Accessories	$203.2
Electronics, Radios, TV	$189.5
Automobiles and Trucks	$149.8
Heating and Air Cond.	$123.3
Farm Equipment	$108.6
Office Equipment	$101.6
Appliances	$78.0
Building	$75.7
Toiletries	$66.7

Percentage of Field
Represented by Top 10 **56%**

This graph shows the industries that rely most on incentive travel to motivate their staffs and promote sales and gives an idea of the scope of this lucrative market segment. Properties wishing to target these groups may wish to invest in the Director of Premium, Incentive and Travel Buyers. *This directory, available from the Salesman's Guide, Inc., is organized by industry and contains a list of corporate buyers along with buyer profiles to help qualify them.*
Source: Society of Incentive Travel Executives.

Why is incentive travel so important to hotels? Typical per person costs for a group incentive trip average about $2,500. Also of importance is that many incentive travel trips include spouses. The presence of spouses not only contributes to increases in the double occupancy figures of a property (which, in itself, has a favorable effect on operating results), but is also a factor in increased spending. The award winners will often spend their own money on "extras," such as gift items, recreation, and entertainment options not included in the award package.

Obviously, incentive trips call for a desirable vacation setting. All the tourist attractions come into play here — be it a natural attraction, an ideal climate, excitement or even some tie-in with the industry or company. The experienced incentive planner will analyze his or her people carefully to decide what type of site and program will draw the greatest number of people. It may be a big-city trip, a trip abroad, a cruise or an exciting visit to a playground such as Las Vegas or Hawaii. At the Hilton Waikoloa, for example, the lobby of the hotel features a lagoon populated by dolphins, and guests are transported to their rooms by boat. This type of "fantasy resort" is extremely popular among incentive meeting planners. A Pocono resort, a ski lodge in Colorado or a country club with a famous golf course may be just the thing for a smaller group.

Much less is called for in the way of meeting facilities for incentive groups than for a convention or conference as the meeting business that is conducted is much less complex.

Figure 6.7. SAMPLE INCENTIVE TRAVEL AD.

WHAT BETTER INCENTIVE THAN A PALACE IN BEIJING?

Within the ancient imperial boundaries of Beijing, a short stroll from the Forbidden City and the main shopping district, stands the magnificent Palace Hotel. Part of the renowned Peninsula Group, it is famous for incomparable levels of service–making it the perfect reward for excellence.

All 530 rooms and suites are superbly appointed and offer all modern conveniences, including satellite television.

A wide range of recreational facilities are at your disposal, including a well-equipped health club and swimming pool, plus a variety of world-class restaurants featuring international cuisine and regional Chinese delicacies.

For a memorable banquet, The Palace offers a selection of exciting ballroom theme parties and spectacular outdoor catering events at the Great Wall, Prince Gong Mansion and many other unique venues.

And because every detail is carefully planned by the hotel's highly experienced staff, the success of your event is assured–leaving you and your top performers feeling like emperors.

Circle #311 on Free Information Card

王府飯店
THE PALACE HOTEL
Beijing

Managed by THE PENINSULA GROUP

8 Goldfish Lane, Wangfujing, Beijing 100006, P.R.C. Tel: (86-10) 6512 8899; Fax: (86-10) 6512 9050
The Peninsula Group Regional Sales Office in U.S.A.: Los Angeles, Tel: (310) 278 8777; Fax: (310) 278 2777;
Chicago, Tel: (312) 263 6069; Fax: (312) 263 3744; New York, Tel: (212) 489 9568; Fax: (212) 397 0360
The Peninsula Hong Kong • Manila • New York • Beverly Hills • Quail Lodge Resort & Golf Club Carmel • The Palace Hotel Beijing • The Kowloon Hotel Hong Kong
E-mail: rph@peninsula.com Website: www.peninsula.com or CONTACT YOUR TRAVEL PROFESSIONAL

This ad, targeting the lucrative incentive travel market, focuses on giving top performers a break to reward them. Unlike ads directed to meeting planners looking for value, this ad features the resort's exotic location and luxurious atmosphere.

Usually a general assembly hall and banquet facilities will suffice. The accent is on the vacation activities, and the business connection is definitely of the soft sell variety. Almost any resort property should be able to handle this type of business.

If your property could be considered a candidate for incentive travel, you would greatly benefit by developing a marketing strategy to reach incentive travel planners.

INCENTIVE TRAVEL HOUSES

E. F. MacDonald is generally regarded as the innovator in incentive travel. Working as a stock boy in a luggage factory, he observed an NCR representative picking up merchandise. He learned the luggage was intended as incentive prizes for dealers. He conjectured that if luggage could be used as an incentive, so could travel. From this was born the specialized incentive travel agent. E. F. MacDonald (now Carlson) was soon joined by other firms. S and H Travel Awards, Maritz, Business Incentives and others have moved in to capture a share of this growing market. At one time incentive travel was planned exclusively by the company, but the tremendous growth in incentive travel created a demand for full-time professional incentive travel companies (houses). These organizations fall into three basic categories.

1. *Full-service incentive houses* — These organizations offer clients a wide range of services from program planning and development to implementation. This type of firm handles both travel and merchandise fulfillment, and offers specific measurement criteria, promotional materials and sales campaigns based on each company's goals.

2. *Travel fulfillment companies* — These organizations handle the travel planning while the corporate clients design and operate their own incentive programs.

3. *The travel agency with an incentive division* — This type of firm does not offer marketing services, but has personnel that specialize in incentive trips.

These companies see to the details of the incentive program. They negotiate with airlines and hotels and then package the transportation, lodging and meeting accommodations, meals, tours and entertainment. They often prepare the promotional literature and may even get involved in setting the goals of the program. Before the group arrives, the agent visits the site and reviews with the hotel the arrangements for servicing the group. The agent sees the group through its stay, serving as the liaison between the group and the hotel. In essence, then, the agent serves as a bona fide meeting planner, seeing to the needs of the group he or she represents. Minneapolis, Chicago and St. Louis are the locales of the top incentive travel companies in the country. Large hotel chains and convention bureaus often schedule an "incentive house blitz" to these cities to solicit these companies.

There are a number of ways to reach this market segment. Contacts and leads can be developed through the Society of Incentive Travel Executives (SITE). SITE publishes an annual directory of incentive travel executives and also sponsors an annual trade show called the Incentive Travel and Meeting Executives Show, where incentive travel suppliers such as hotels, attractions and airlines can exhibit their products.

The international marketplace (primarily Europe, Asia and Canada) has also become an attractive area. Convention bureaus and hotels can attend key international shows such as the Canadian Travel Expo (held in Toronto), the Asian Business and Incentive Show (in Singapore) and the European Incentive Business Travel Meetings Expo (staged in Geneva, Switzerland).

Still another option is dealing with **incentive travel houses** (see box titled "Incentive Travel Houses"). While repeat business from groups is rare because destinations are varied each year, incentive travel houses, which represent several different companies, can provide repeat potential; they often will return different groups to a property that they have successfully dealt with in the past.

Advertising is yet another way to reach this market. Unlike ads to corporate meeting planners, which stress a property's professionalism in handling meetings, incentive travel ads must stress the desirability of your location and the recreational and entertainment amenities available (see Figure 6.7). The two principal trade publications for reaching incentive planners are *Corporate Meetings and Incentives* and *Corporate and Incentive Travel* (see Appendix I for addresses).

Insurance Meetings

While the insurance companies fall into the corporate market category, they deserve special attention because they spend more money — roughly $2 billion annually — on meetings than any other industry. In addition, insurance meeting planners anticipate an across the board increase in incentive, sales and training meetings in the future as insurance companies are consolidating and merging at a significant pace. A recent study reports that one in three have acquired another company within the last two years. These mergers mean more meetings as field forces and home offices must learn each others' culture and practices.

There are over 6,000 insurance companies in the United States, and each holds about 20 meetings a year, ranging in size from 20 attendees at small workshops, to conferences of 200, and major conventions of 3,000 or more. These national conventions are the largest, held annually for three to five days and planned a minimum of a year in advance.

Regional meetings are smaller and held more frequently than national meetings, and tend to be sales oriented. While expenditures per person are typically less, resorts are considered for this type of meeting. Convenience and accessibility, however, are the important factors in site selection, and lead times average six to nine months.

Local meetings are usually held in hotels, and are primarily training seminars and board meetings. Local meetings may have a lead time of as short as two weeks, and proximity to the home office is a prime consideration in site selection, as is quality of service and facilities.

Although the insurance industry sells two basic types of insurance, life insurance and casualty insurance, most business comes from the life insurance segment. Life insurance companies employ large sales forces with regular training meetings and conferences. This segment also holds a large number of incentive meetings to keep its sales staff motivated.

Whether large or small meetings are planned, this group is not overly price conscious, and the availability of recreational amenities often plays a role in site selection. The agenda of a small meeting usually calls for business meetings in the morning and afternoon and scheduled recreational or social activities in the evening. At larger meetings, business sessions are held in the morning, recreational activities are offered in the afternoon, and social functions figure prominently in the evening. Since spouses are usually invited to larger regional and national meetings, the availability of spouses' and guests' programs is an added plus when attempting to solicit insurance company business.

To solicit this lucrative market, you should start at the company's home office. There may be a number of decision makers within the company (see box titled "Insurance Com-

---

Insurance Company Decision Makers

A recent survey by *Insurance Conference Planner* magazine determined the principal job titles for insurance company decision makers were:

Job Title	Insurance Planners
Vice President	28%
Director of Meetings	26%
Marketing/Administrative Executive	25%
Meeting Planner	16%
President	5%
	100%

pany Decision Makers"). Many large insurance companies have their own travel departments, often staffed by five to seven meeting planners. When selling to this market segment, it is important to remember that even the persons responsible for meeting planning of smaller companies are highly skilled professionals who are good negotiators who demand the same quality in their suppliers.

As in other meeting market segments, third party planners are increasingly being used by the insurance industry. Approximately one-third use incentive travel houses and/or meeting management companies to assist in site selection and program planning.

When targeting insurance meeting planners, a professional, well-prepared, and sincere approach is the best, whether you are reaching them through advertising or direct sales. They typically conduct their own site inspections, and detailed letters of agreement are important to them. The better you understand their needs for each meeting and demonstrate how your property can meet the high standards of the meeting planner, the better chance you will have in securing their business.

Most insurance executives and meeting planners belong to trade associations, the two most well-known being Meeting Professionals International (MPI) and Insurance Conference Planners Association (ICPA). The Life Insurance Marketing Research Association (LIMRA) is also a key life insurance trade organization (its members write more than 90 percent of all life insurance). Allied membership is available in most associations serving this market, and this would be a worthwhile investment in gaining insurance groups meetings business.

According to a recent survey, insurance meetings planners are also turning to technology to search potential sites. Some 88 percent said that they researched hotel chains' Web sites while conducting an online search, while such online resources as Allmeetings, EventSource, PlanSoft, and StarCite were also used.[3] Establishing a Web presence, then, can greatly enhance your chances of tapping into this lucrative market.

Medical Meetings

Last, but certainly not least, is the medical meetings market. While this market segment may be part of the associations market, this dynamic and rapidly growing segment merits additional attention.

Today's ever-changing technology and healthcare reforms make it mandatory for medical professionals to keep abreast of how the latest trends impact their profession. It is estimated that medical and healthcare groups currently hold over 35,000 meetings annually, and this number is expected to grow dramatically for a number of reasons:

- Medical professionals must stay current on new treatments, potential cures and the latest surgical procedures and medical techniques.
- Modern advances such as lasers, ultrasound and electrodiagnostic machines are changing the way medicine is practiced. Trade show exhibitors and product demonstrations provide opportunities to introduce medical professionals to the latest technology.
- Doctors and other healthcare professionals must earn Continuing Medical Education (CME) credits to maintain certifications. The most popular places to earn CME credits are forums sponsored by medical societies, associations, universities and private providers.
- The constant emergence of new medical specialties (and subspecialities) has spawned a number of new medical organizations. This trend will create additional continuing education needs.

- Globalization has also impacted the medical profession. Record numbers of international attendees have been reported at the medical meetings held in the United States, and more American medical professionals are attending meetings abroad.

Most medical meetings are small (the majority have 200 or less in attendance) and are usually held in sites close to major medical facilities. While most meet during peak periods (fall and spring), some groups also meet during traditional "soft spots" (summer and winter months). And, since many medical groups plan several meetings a month, there is a great potential for repeat business.

Medical meetings require a high level of presentation. Technical presentations, in which demonstrators can interact with the audience and take questions from all over the world, are sometimes done via satellite. One medical meeting planner explains:

> "We show live surgeries on a big screen...our camera work allows for close-ups and instant replays...busy physicians are drawn to medical meetings with new techniques and new knowledge."[4]

Requirements for medical meetings also include several breakout rooms for small group discussion and good message service. For larger medical meetings, exhibit space with adequate electrical outlets will be needed. Since most meetings are technical meetings, most medical groups prefer to meet in a quiet location; a meeting booked near rooms used for a college reunion or a bowling league will lose future business.

One difficulty with medical meetings is that the amount of function space they require is incredibly high relative to the number of guestrooms typically used. Therefore, they are sometimes not a good piece of business for a hotel, particularly during high demand periods. Meeting planners have responded to this dilemma with a space-saving technique that is becoming increasingly used for medical and scientific group meetings: *poster sessions* rather than formal verbal presentations. Using horizontal corkboards, presenters can post a visual summary of their findings, experiences, or opinions instead of giving an oral presentation from a platform.

It is fairly simple to reach this lucrative and growing market segment. The typical medical meeting planner is an experienced professional; most belong to the Professional Convention Management Association (PCMA), a trade association originally formed for medical meeting planners and now open to all association planners. This association holds an annual meeting in January, and is an opportunity for hotel salespeople to interact with planners. You can also place print ads in the numerous medical periodicals and journals published for doctors, dentists, and the scientific community.

Summary of Sources for Reaching Meeting Planners

Meeting Planning Associations	Number of Members	Composition of Members
American Society of Association Executives www.ASAEnet.org	25000	84% association executives 16% suppliers (hotels, convention bureaus)
Insurance Conference Planners Association www.ICPA.org	470	All insurance planners, full or part ime. Suppliers cannot become members but can attend meetings
International Association for Exposition Management www. IAEM.org	3300	54% trade show managers 46% suppliers. Suppliers may join as associates
Meeting Professionals International www.mpiweb.org	1700 in 42 countries	50% meeting planners (45% corporate, 19% assoc., 19% independent, 8% other), 50% suppliers
National Coalition of Black Meeting Planners www.mcbmp.com	1500	Professional meeting planners, suppliers and contractors
Professional Convention Management Association www.pcma.org	4800	60% suppliers, 40% meeting planners
Religious Conference Management Association www.meetingsnet.com	2900	Meeting planners, contractors, suppliers of religious organizations or denominations
Society of Corporate Meeting Professionals www.SCMP.org	200	49% corporate, 49% convention service managers, 2% students
Society of Government Meeting Professionals www.SGMP.org	2700	51% suppliers contractors, 49% meeting planners
Society of Incentive Travel Executives www.site-intl.org	2000	Hotels, airlines, cruise lines, tour operators, travel agents, official tourist organizations as well as supporting organizations

Membership Restrictions	Convention	Publications
Active members must be executives of non-profit associations. Suppliers may be associate members	Annual meeting and exposition in August	*Association Management* magazine
Must be employed by an insurance company or insurance association	Two: Annual in November, summer forum in June	*Insurance Conference Planner* newsletter
Trade show managers. Suppliers may join as associates	Two: Mid-year in June, annual meeting and expo in December	Weekly newsletter
Open to all meeting executives. The number of supplier members must be matched by the number of planners	Two: Trade show in July, education conference in January	*The Meeting Professional* magazine, newsletter to chapter leaders, newsletters from Special Interest Groups
Only professional meeting planners with at least one year experience	2 annual meetings: one in spring, the other in fall	*The NCBMP Newsletter*
Members responsible for meetings of nonprofit associations. Affiliate members may be vendors or independent planers	Annual convention held in January	*Convene* magazine and *PCMA Perspectives*
Restricted to religious organizations	Annual meeting held in January or February	*Religious Conference Manager* magazine
Only one member from each organization	2 annual meetings: one in June, the other in October or November	Newsletter *Update*
Restricted to government meeting planners, suppliers and contractors	Annual meeting in May	*The Society Page* newsletter plus the *Membership Directory*
Application needs approval, letter of recommendation	Annual meeting held in December	Monthly newsletter as well as *Insite* magazine

Chapter Summary:

In this chapter, we have detailed the types of meetings held by nonprofit organizations and specialized segments of the corporate meetings market. We have seen how nonprofits, though largely price sensitive, can add to a property's bottom line by filling typically slow periods and providing potential repeat business. And we have seen how other segments, such as labor unions and incentive travel, can be lucrative for specific types of hotels. In this chapter, as in the two previous chapters, we have determined:

- Each segment's characteristics and needs.
- The kind of meetings they hold.
- What they look for when selecting a property.
- The decision maker for each market segment.
- How to locate key sources of potential business.

These crucial factors are essential in determining what type(s) of group business your property can handle. In the next two chapters, we will see how these factors also play a key role in determining the most effective ways to sell and advertise to each segment of the meetings market.

Endnotes:

1. Fred Gebhart "Reunion Meetings", *Meeting News*, April 12, 1999, p. 10.
2. June Norman, "Moving toward the Mainstream", *The Meeting Manager*, December 1995, p. 32.
3. Alison Hall, "Meetings Made Us", *ICP* (www.meetingsnet.com), January/February 2001, p. 49.
4. Joseph Dabrian, "The Changing Pulse of Medical Meetings", *The Meeting Professional*, July 1999, p. 69.

Internet Sites:

For additional information on the firms and organizations discussed in this chapter, visit the following Internet sites. The Web addresses listed are current as of January 2001. Addresses may change, however; if a site is not available at the address below, a search engine can be used to access its new location.

African-American Fraternities/Sororities: The Natl. Pan-Hellenic Council - www.nphc.org
Fraternity Executives Association - www.fea-inc.org
Insurance Conference Planners Association - www.icpa.org
National Interfraternity Conference - www.greeklife.org/nic

National Panhellenic Conference - www.greeklife.org/npc
Professional Convention Management Association - www.pcma.org
Religious Conference Management Association - www.meetingsnet.com

 ## Study Questions:

1. What are SMERF groups? Why are they an important market segment? What SMERF market segments show the most potential for future growth?
2. How does dealing with government agencies differ from dealing with other meetings groups? What types of hotels are best suited for the various types of government meetings?
3. What types of meetings do labor unions typically hold? What factors are important to planners booking labor union meetings?
4. What makes the incentive market different from the corporate market in general? What types of properties are best suited to handling this market segment? What types of amenities would you stress if you were trying to attract the incentive market?
5. What are the characteristics of insurance meetings? What types of hotels might be most attractive to this type of business?
6. Cite several reasons why the medical meetings market segment is likely to grow.
7. Who are the key decision makers for each of the segments discussed in this chapter? How can each type of meeting planner most effectively be reached?

 ## Key Terms:

Incentive travel. Travel financed by businesses as an employee or dealer reward for outstanding performance.

Incentive travel houses. Full-time professional travel companies that make arrangements for companies that wish to offer incentive trips. Usually represent several different firms.

Per diem. The fixed amount of money given to government representatives for each day of travel away from home.

SMERF groups. An acronym for the nonprofit organization market segment made up of social, military, educational, religious and fraternal groups.

Learning Objectives:

This portion of your text discusses direct selling to meeting planners. In the chapter, we will cover personal sales calls, telephone sales calls, and the other most commonly used methods of selling to planners. When you have studied this chapter, you will:

- Be able to describe the six steps of a personal sales call and be able to explain why each is important.

- Know how to most effectively use the telephone to sell to planners, handle inquiries, and follow-up on your accounts.

- Be able to detail other methods of direct selling and know the advantages and disadvantages of each.

Outline

Personal Sales Calls
- Pre-call Planning
- Opening the Sales Call
- Getting Prospect Involvement
- Presenting Your Property
- Handling Objections
- Closing and Follow-up

Telephone Selling
- Telephone Techniques
- Screening Prospects
- Setting Appointments by Phone
- Telephone Sales Call Follow-up
- Handling Inquiries
- Telemarketing

Sales Blitz Selling

Trade Show Selling

Selling With Convention Bureaus

Site Inspection Selling and Familiarization Tours

Common Sense Strategies for Convention Sales

Charlotte St. Martin
Executive Vice President Operations and Marketing
Loews Hotels

"Salespeople close sales...They do their research; they follow-up; they are consistent and persistent; they do what they say they will do and they deliver what they say they will deliver...I firmly believe that establishing that relationship [with a customer] is the single most important thing a salesperson can do to make a sale... Research and planning are critical to any discipline in the sales process... whether it be personal sales calls, sales blitzes, booth selling at industry trade shows, site inspections, or telephone sales."

7 Selling to the Meetings Market

The size and diversity of the meetings market makes it a viable target market for all types and sizes of hospitality properties. However, reaching meeting planners and securing meetings business is too important to be done haphazardly. Capturing a share of the meetings market requires carefully planned strategies that fall within the guidelines of the property's marketing plan while meeting the needs of meeting planners.

There are two basic ways to reach this lucrative market: *selling* and *advertising*. Advertising techniques will be discussed in Chapter 8. In this chapter, we will take a look at some of the most effective direct sales tools used by properties today:

- Personal sales calls
- Telephone selling
- Sales blitz selling
- Trade show selling
- Site inspection selling and familiarization tours

While it is impossible to cover each of these areas in great depth in this book (volumes have been written on personal sales calls, for example), we have covered the essentials, giving an overview that will demonstrate the importance of direct selling to meeting planners.

Personal Sales Calls

The most effective tool in convention sales, or any other kind of sales, is the personal sales call. This type of face-to-face selling works well with both professional and non-professional meeting planners. The personal sales call offers the opportunity to present your case in a detailed manner, to answer questions immediately and to read the reaction of the prospect so you can gain a better understanding — and take remedial action if necessary.

The personal sales call consists of six essential steps (see Figure 7.1). Each of these steps is vitally important in presenting your property effectively to the meeting planner, and we will cover each of them in the following sections.

Step #1: Pre-call Planning

While getting out there and selling is the best way to ensure that you will generate meetings business for your property, there is another — quite logical — step that should always precede the selling process: *pre-call planning*. While this planning (and the research inherent to it) may seem time-consuming and tedious, knowing your property, knowing your competition and knowing your prospect are the keys to effective selling.

Knowing your property can help your sales effort in two ways. First, you will know exactly what you have to sell. You will know your property's strengths and weaknesses — and how to showcase or downplay them as needed. Second, and just as important, knowing basic facts about your property will give you the confidence you need for making a sales

Figure 7.1. **THE SIX STEPS OF A SALES CALL.**

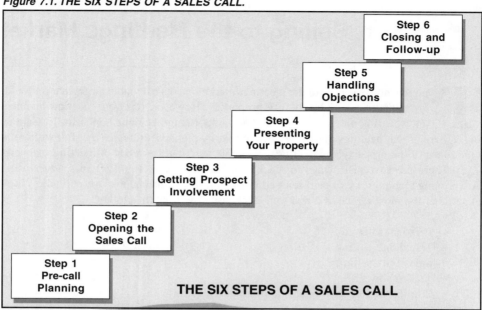

The sales process is a systematic series of actions that directs the meeting decision maker toward a buying commitment.

call. You won't have to worry about what questions a prospect will ask — you will already have the answers to most of his or her concerns (how many rooms are available, the size and capabilities of meeting rooms, audio visual equipment available, etc.).

Since it is virtually impossible to memorize every detail about your property, many hotels prepare a *property fact book* (see Figure 7.2) to assist their salespeople (old and new) to know enough about the property to properly present it. This information can be updated as necessary and serves as an excellent tool for the selling process.

Knowing your competition can also help you to better sell your property. If you know a competitor's rates are slightly lower than yours, for example, you may expect a prospect to raise an objection — and you can be prepared to justify your additional cost by pointing out your property's special amenities, free parking space or some other feature that the meeting planner may perceive as well worth the rate difference.

The third phase of pre-call planning, *knowing your prospect,* is essential for tailoring presentations to meet the needs of meeting planners. David Scypinski, vice chairman of development and senior vice president, industry relations of the Starwood Hotels and Resorts believes that hotel salespeople must know the customer as never before:

> "It's not enough to know your customers' products, services and objec-
> tives. You have to know everything about their business and industry.
> Hotel salespeople should understand how the organization they are try-
> ing to book makes money and how large their budget is...there's no sub-
> stitute for knowing your customers' organization, business needs, and
> objectives."[1]

Many properties — even those that utilize mailing lists to develop new sales leads — send out surveys or make telephone calls to gather information about potential prospects (see Figure 7.3). And, don't forget the benefit of obtaining information right under your

Step 1. Pre-Call Planning

In order to best sell your property, you must know what your property has to offer and how to best present it to interest a potential client. Conducting a property analysis, competition analysis, and prospect analysis, then, should always precede your sales presentations. Good pre-call planning also includes making sure you have the materials you will need for each sales call, managing your sales calls to ensure the best use of your time (combining an appointment call with a cold call in the same area, for example), and ensuring that you are projecting a professional image.

Step 2. Opening the Sales Call

Prepare an introduction, a statement regarding the purpose of the call, benefit statement (what the prospect can expect to gain), and bridge statement (asking for permission for the salesperson to continue) that will be interesting and appealing enough for the prospect to want to hear more about your property.

Step 3. Getting Prospect Involvement

Build rapport and get the client to discuss his or her needs and concerns. This involves projecting a professional image, using — and interpreting — body language, and listening skills. This step may make or break your sales presentation — if you can't develop rapport or get the prospect involved, he or she will have little interest in your presentation; on the other hand, a prospect who likes and trusts you will be far more open to what you have to say.

Step 4. Presenting Your Property

The "meat" of the sales presentation, this step explains the property's facilities and services — and should always be structured to show how the property's *features* can *benefit* the client. The presentation itself may include visual aids and collateral materials, but if the client sees little benefit to his or her organization, it will be difficult to close a sale.

Step 5. Handling Objections

This step gives the salesperson an opportunity to answer the concerns of the prospects — and can actually be instrumental in making the sale...if the salesperson is seen as a problem-solver concerned with the needs of the organization. You should always anticipate objections (most are over price or some aspect of your product), and be prepared to offer solutions that will satisfy the client's needs.

Step 6. Closing and Follow-up

A successful close is the ultimate objective of a sales call, but, incredibly, some salespeople don't even ask for the sale! Trial closes can be used during various stages of the presentation, but it is essential that you ask for a sale before leaving your prospect's office. Once a sale has been made, it is important to follow-up immediately. Follow-up demonstrates your property's commitment to service, and is an essential part of building rapport — as well as future repeat business and possible word of mouth referrals from the meeting planner.

Figure 7.2. OUTLINE FOR PROPERTY FACT BOOK.

OUTLINE FOR PROPERTY FACT BOOK

GUESTROOM INFORMATION	RESTAURANTS & LOUNGES	MEETING AND BANQUET FACILITIES
Priority I Number of rooms Number of singles/doubles/ suites Size of rooms — square footage Number of floors Phones in rooms Fire alarms/detectors in rooms Handicapped rooms Non-smoking rooms Amenities in rooms	**Priority I** Seating capacity Number of tables and types Atmosphere/interior design Non-smoking sections Dress requirements Pricing by restaurant Restaurant positioning	**Priority I** Location of meeting rooms Square footage/seating capacity Utilities available Exhibit space Meeting room rental rates
Priority II Room rates Check-in/check-out times	**Priority II** Menu style/theme Types of food by restaurant	**Priority II** Function room furniture Audiovisual capabilities
Priority III Customer mix Average occupancy by day of week Average length of stay by segment Sales budget Profitability by segment Group check-in/check-out procedures Front desk staffing	**Priority III** Entertainment Reservation policy Cocktails available Wine cellar/list Food served in lounge Special promotions Opening/closing times	**Priority III** Banquet seating capacities Banquet menu Theme parties Outside services Types of banquet specialties Beverage service Banquet staffing levels

New salespeople cannot learn everything about a property in their first week. To help them gain knowledge in a logical order, questions about each area (guestrooms, restaurants and lounges, meeting and banquet facilities, etc.) should be arranged by priorities. At the end of week one, a salesperson should master all Priority I questions; and each week, master another priority level. The Director of Sales should assign the responsibility of updating and maintaining the property fact book to one specific person in the sales department.

own roof; talk to meeting planners currently using your property and ask them about potential leads (and their requirements).

Once you decide that a prospect is indeed a valid one, you must make contact to try to sell. Sales calls in which you initiate the contact without any degree of interest indicated by the prospects are called **cold calls**. The anticipated percentage of success in these cases is understandable lower than when you are dealing with past customers or recommendations. It is often a problem just getting in to see the right person.

You can increase the efficiency of such efforts if you precede your visit with some sort of preliminary campaign. You might send your convention facilities brochure to the contact person, along with a personal letter. Follow up with another letter if you hear nothing within a few weeks. Then call for an appointment. If you fail to get an appointment, try again.

Figure 7.3. SAMPLE SALES PROSPECT CARD.

Date of Contact _____ Trace Date _____

Name of Contact _____ New Prospect ☐ Yes ☐ No

Company Name _____ Type of Business _____

Address _____ Telephone _____

_____ Fax _____

Prospect's estimated sales potential:

Room nights _____

Meetings/Banquets _____

Dollars _____

Facilities/services needed:

_____

_____

_____

Background information on prospect and company:

_____

_____

_____

Salesperson's Name _____

To make the most of a sales call, it is helpful to have some basic information about the needs of a prospect. A sales prospect card can help the salesperson to determine how to best structure his or her presentation to appeal to the needs of the client.

Your most effective calls will likely be **appointment calls**, where you have prearranged a visit with the prospect, but don't completely rule out calling without an appointment. When you are already in the area for another appointment, a cold call is worth a try. Cross index your prospect list geographically. Mixing cold calls with your appointments will increase your number of sales calls. Cold calls sometimes work, but even if you cannot get in to see the right person at that time, you stand to lose little except a few minutes time. Sales success, to use an analogy from baseball, is accomplished not so much from achieving a high "batting average" as from your total number of hits. More "turns at bat" (sales calls) mean the chance for more "hits" (sales).

Once you have completed the research phase of your pre-call planning, assemble the materials needed to make an effective presentation. A well-organized and professional *sales kit* should include only that information pertinent to each prospect's needs. Fumbling through too many materials in a sales kit may result in a loss of presentation momentum.

Most sales kits contain basic information such as a general property information sheet, a meeting and banquet room information sheet, a convention brochure and other visual aids, including color photographs, a map of the property, etc. If you plan to include third-party endorsement letters, make sure they are relevant to your prospect. A letter from an association meeting planner praising your theme party, for example, would have little significance for a corporate meeting planner wishing to hold a training session.

Step #2: Opening the Sales Call

Selling is essentially helping someone to buy. Open your sales call in such a way that it puts the customer at ease so that he or she can build rapport with you. Your opening should consist of an introduction, a statement of the purpose of your call (and its benefit to the prospect), and a bridge statement that leads into the actual presentation. You can start by introducing yourself and your property ("Good afternoon, Mr. Jones. I'm John Doe from the Golden Gate Resort in San Diego, California."), while offering a brief but firm handshake. You may also wish to add a few words at this time to show your interest in the prospect. For example, "I've heard so much about what your firm has been doing in the area of microcomputers, and I'm looking forward to hearing more about your innovative uses of microchips." But take care not to get so immersed in discussion about the company that you neglect your objective.

As soon as possible after the introduction, state the purpose of your call. Can you offer the prospect additional meeting space or are you there to try to win back former business? After stating your purpose, you should present a benefit or two that will give the prospect a reason to listen to you. Once you have stated your property's benefits, lead into the body of the sales presentation with a bridge statement. This statement basically asks the prospect for permission to continue, and is usually in the form of a question: "Would you be interested in learning how other associations used one of our theme parties to increase attendance?" or "May I show you just a few examples of our state-of-the-art audiovisual system?" If the prospect gives a positive response, you have the green light to continue. If the prospect is not interested, thank him or her for their time and ask for an appointment in the future.

Step #3: Getting Prospect Involvement

Involve the prospect in the sales process to determine his or her needs. Do it by asking questions, and always ask *before* making your presentation. Two types of questions are generally used: closed-ended questions and open-ended questions.

Close-ended questions require a specific reply. These include such queries as "How many training meetings do you stage each month?" or "What is your average attendance at your annual convention?" **Open-ended questions**, on the other hand, give the prospect an opportunity to express his or her feelings. Open-ended questions such as "Why do you think last year's meeting was so successful?" or "What factors are most important to you in selecting a resort?" will provide clues into what is important to the prospect and can help you to adjust your sales presentation to meet those concerns.

Effective questioning is among the more critical aspects of selling. Decide what information you need from the prospect in advance, and use it as a checklist for asking questions during your sales call.

Step #4: Presenting Your Property

While every salesperson should have a prepared and rehearsed sales presentation that addresses the needs of each market segment, you increase your chances of a sale if you custom-tailor this general presentation for specific clients. Most clients are really interested only if what you offer will benefit them. Rather than being a product-seller, become a problem-solver; always present your property's features as benefits to the client (see Figure 7.4).

Figure 7.4. TURNING FEATURES INTO BENEFITS.

Feature		Benefit
All of our breakout rooms are adjacent to the room where your general session will be held	SO THAT	no time will be wasted between sessions and you will be able to keep your meeting on schedule.
We offer 24-hour room service	SO THAT	those attendees who must check-in late may still enjoy a late meal in the comfort of their room.
Every room has a desk	SO THAT	your meeting attendees will have plenty of room to review and work on handouts they receive during the daily meeting sessions.
We have a health club and spa	SO THAT	your trainees can relax and unwind after a day of intensive educational meetings.
Benefit		**Feature**
Those attendees who check-in late may still enjoy a late meal in the comfort of their room	BECAUSE	we offer 24-hour room service.

Salespeople who present only features rely on their prospects to interpret how those features can benefit them. Instead, salespeople should try to influence the interpretation by always linking features with benefits and explaining to prospects how the features will benefit them and enhance their meetings. To assist you in thinking "benefits," the words "so that" can be used to tie the two. The selling sentence can also be reversed, using the word "because" to link the benefit to the feature.

Your presentation should directly address the client's needs — and should include visual aids, such as pictures, charts and graphs, to enable the planner to envision how your property will work for his or her meeting. Many salespeople today use more sophisticated visual aids — slide presentations or video brochures (see Chapter 8) — but the important factor is how these presentations relate to the client.

When presenting, use testimonial letters and publicity reprints to increase your credibility. Prospects are more likely to believe the good things their peers and unbiased reviewers have to say about your property than what a salesperson might say. Third-party endorsements from meeting decision makers in the same segment as your prospect are best;

use association-related letters when selling to association meeting planners, corporate letters when presenting to corporate decision makers, and so on.

Once your presentation is completed, make a transition statement (which can be as simple as asking "Do you have any questions?") that may lead to a close — or to what is often the next phase of the sales call, overcoming objections.

Step #5: Handling Objections

It is a rare meeting planner who will not have some questions or objections. It is important, therefore, to anticipate the most likely areas of concern and to be able to respond immediately.

The most common objections involve concerns over price or product, or simply a lack of interest. *Price* objections ("Your competitor has cheaper rates") can often be overcome by pointing out a compensatory benefit ("Perhaps. But our meeting package includes free meeting and function space as well as free golf and tennis facilities.") Whenever possible, try to get the focus off price ("Putting price aside for the moment, do you have any other concerns?"). This tactic may work if you can demonstrate how your property meets the client's needs so well; then, price diminishes in importance.

Product objections ("Your property may not be as attractive to our attendees as the new resort in your area") may be handled in a number of ways. Try restating the objection and offer a positive response: "I gather that you don't feel our property is modern enough. Although we are an older property, our rooms and meeting space have been completely renovated and we offer all amenities found at new properties in our area. Clients tell us our property has a great deal of character and charm."

Lack of interest objections ("We are happy with our present hotel") can be overcome by finding out why the client is satisfied and offering comparable —and additional — benefits. Or, you may point out that a change of site may prove to be stimulating to the attendees. Then a change in site could then be considered acceptable to the planner; by you having offered an alternative without the implication that the selection of the previous property was wanting in any way. If nothing changes the client's mind at that time, it is still a good practice to ask to be considered for a meeting or function in the future. There are many factors that may come into play at some future date that may open the door for you.

When handling objections, it is vital that you *never* knock your competition. At best, this is unprofessional; at worst, the meeting planner may feel that your words reflect on his or her judgment — and you may lose any possibility of booking a sale at that time or in the future.

Step #6: Closing and Follow-up

While many salespeople enjoy presenting their product, some hesitate when it comes to asking for the sale! The skill of closing, however, can be learned, and can be more comfortable when salespeople realize that clients *expect* to be asked to book at the property.

There are two types of closes: trial closes and major closes. **Trial closes** are used to elicit responses from the client, and are generally used to build an "agreement staircase." In other words, the salesperson periodically asks for positive client response ("Don't you agree that our audiovisual equipment will greatly enhance your training sessions?" or "Don't you think our ballroom would make an elegant setting for your awards banquet?" or "Don't you find our golf course to be one of the finest in the state?"). Positive responses, repetition of benefits by a client, and positive nonverbal signs (frequent smiles, the client leaning forward, etc.) are excellent indicators that the salesperson can proceed with his or her major close.

The **major close** is the question or statement that asks for the sale. It should be attempted as soon as the client has reached a peak of excitement, and should elicit a commitment. This close should be as direct as possible ("May I reserve space on a definite basis?"), and after making it, you should stop talking and give the client a chance to respond. Avoid the temptation to keep talking — you may inadvertently say something that brings up concerns the client had not previously considered!

Once your call is completed, leave as soon as is politely possible. And, whether you have made a sale or not, always follow up your sales call promptly with a "thank you" letter. This gesture shows your commitment to customer service and may result in future sales.

If a commitment has been made, follow-up is even more important. You will want to service your client with frequent post-sale contacts, including keeping him or her informed on the progress of preparations for the function. It is also important to check with the planner during the function. Arlene Sheff, CMP, a planner for Boeing Company, recently held a meeting and said she:

> "...never saw the salesperson once on site. I spoke to him on the phone
> several times before the meeting, but while the meeting was going on, he
> never came by even once to see how things were going. If a hotel sales-
> person wants my repeat business, they need to track me down and check
> on my meeting. It's all about building a relationship with me." [2]

Contacting the client after the function to ensure that all went according to plan is also essential. This type of commitment leads to customer rebookings and word-of-mouth referrals for additional business.

Telephone Selling

One of the problems with personal calls is that they are getting increasingly expensive. Many properties are cutting down on the expense of personal calls by stepping up their use of the telephone, especially as a tool to screen prospects and to set appointments with clients.

Although telephone calls should not be a substitute for as many personal visits as you can manage, you should become proficient in using the telephone as a means to increase customer contact, screen prospects to make personal calls more effective, and offer immediate assistance to clients in the event of urgent situations.

Telephone Techniques

Since using the telephone is much more impersonal than talking face to face with a prospect, it is important that you and your salespeople develop techniques to make the most efficient use of this sales tool. As with a personal sales call, *preparation* is the key word. Before making a call, you should have an outline of what you are going to cover. A clearly typed topical outline will help you maintain control of your thoughts and maintain a logical flow in your conversation. You can even use a prepared presentation — as long as it doesn't sound "canned." Along with your outline or presentation, you also want to keep

SAMPLE SCRIPT FOR A TELEPHONE APPOINTMENT CALL

There are three steps in making a telephone appointment call once you have reached the decision-maker: opening the call; the presentation; and setting the appointment. Sample statements include:

Opening the Call

"Hello, Mr. Stubbs. My name is Diane Street, sales manager of the Oakbrook Hotel, the new hotel just down the street from your offices. Since we are neighbors and so convenient, I thought you would be interested in hearing about our hotel and the affordable meeting package we have just designed for local businesses."

The Presentation

"Mr. Stubbs, from my research, I've learned that you schedule intensive training meetings lasting two or three days with several evening working sessions. We have developed a 24-hour meeting program for companies with needs such as yours. The program reserves your meeting rooms on a 24-hour basis so that you will not be inconvenienced with removing training materials each evening and resetting equipment the next morning. In addition, our copying equipment is available to you 24 hours a day for any timely additions or changes in your handout materials."

Setting the Appointment

"I know you'll be impressed with our state-of-the-art meeting rooms and our convention service staff who will assist you in staging successful training meetings. When could we meet for lunch to discuss your upcoming employee development seminars?
"Would you prefer the beginning or later part of the week? Is 11:30 or 12:00 most convenient for you?
"Great. I'll see you Thursday at 12 noon at our concierge desk. I'll have my name tag on so you can recognize me.
"Thank you for your time, Mr. Stubbs. I'm looking forward to meeting with you personally. Have a good day."

Note that the salesperson clearly identified herself and her hotel, stated the purpose of her call and how the prospect would benefit from an appointment, appealing to his need for convenient meeting facilities. Note that in setting the appointment, she asked forced-choice questions, giving the planner a choice between two positive alternatives .

---

pertinent backup information — room rates, function room sizes and capacities, availability, and so on —at hand so that you never have to fumble while searching for it. Also, keep paper and pencil handy to jot down notes or to remind yourself of information requested by the client.

It is easy to dismiss a voice on an impersonal electronic instrument so you will want to make your telephone time as productive as possible. Set aside times when you will not be interrupted; a prospect is likely to be annoyed if you put him or her on hold. At many properties, salespeople are given specific blocks of telephone time in which to make their calls.

Using the telephone involves the mastery of several simple techniques. Always hold the receiver slightly away from your mouth and speak slowly and distinctly. Immediately identify yourself and your property. Put your personality into the call — be cheerful yet professional — and always be willing to listen to the prospect's view. Don't be reluctant to ask the prospect to spell his or her name if it isn't clear. No one minds repeating or spelling their name.

Screening Prospects

The telephone makes it easy to prequalify prospects before making appointments for personal calls. Many properties use sales lead services, often referred to as *tip sheets* (see Figure 7.5), to analyze information about frequent convention and meeting planners. All of

Figure 7.5. SAMPLE "TIP SHEET."

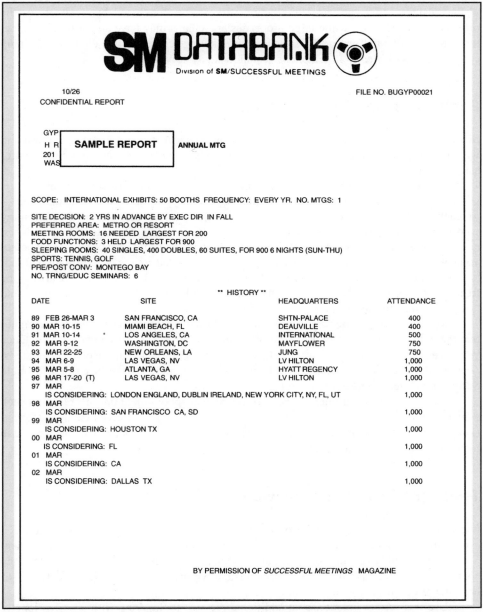

Tip sheets allow you to "do your homework" before making a sales call. Perhaps the most common complaint planners voice about hotel salespeople is their failure to take time to research a prospect's business. Planners resent the waste of their time when given a sales pitch by a salesperson from a property wholly unsuited to their requirements. Tip sheets can be used to screen prospects and then follow up with a telephone call or letter asking for an appointment. They are also an invaluable tool for customizing a telephone appointment call and the actual sales presentation.

these names will not be high-priority prospects; they must be scanned to determine those who best fit into your marketing plan. But, since other hotels are receiving the same tip sheet, you must take quick action after an initial screening. Since you already have basic information about each lead, you can tailor your telephone calls to these prospects.

Other prospects can be interviewed directly by salespeople, who will enter information that could be helpful in a sales presentation on a **call report** (see Figure 7.6). This form can help the salesperson to determine the needs of the prospect — if the prospect represents viable business. In some cases, marketing surveys are conducted by members of the property's clerical staff, while large properties and chains may have an entire department that surveys potential prospects (see the telemarketing section in this chapter). Training clerical staff specifically in telephone techniques pays dividends.

Setting Appointments by Phone

Since cold-calling is less effective than calling on prospects who are already interested in what the property has to offer, the telephone is a useful tool for setting appointments for sales presentations.

One of the most challenging tasks in using the telephone to set appointments is getting by the intermediaries — the receptionist, secretary, administrative assistant, etc. — to reach the decision maker. The intermediary is often your contact person in determining who makes the decision for holding meetings and can be your best friend — or worst enemy; his or her response and level of assistance can make the difference between whether you get an appointment or not! These people can be an added source of information, too. It is important, then, to build rapport with these support people. They should always be treated with respect, and, for best results, should be told the objective of your call — and how it will benefit their boss.

Meeting planners are usually busy, and their time is scarce, so you should remember that the objective of your call is to simply set an appointment — not to make a sale. Once you have reached the decision maker, the telephone appointment call involves three steps: opening the call, the presentation, and setting the appointment (see box titled "Sample Script for a Telephone Appointment Call").

Be careful that your telephone effort to make an appointment doesn't turn into such a detailed telephone "visit" that the prospect feels he or she has received enough information to withhold the appointment. It is better to be there in person. Stress that you have material, such as an audiovisual presentation, that must be shown.

Telephone Sales Call Follow-up

It is just as important to follow up on your telephone calls as it is on your personal calls, especially since a telephone call does not leave as lasting an impression as a personal visit. Since you are either looking for information or an appointment when you make telephone contact, you should take the time to write a friendly note thanking the prospect for his or her time or confirming an appointment date.

Use this further contact as an additional pre-sale tool. Along with a professionally typed letter, include requested information (room rate sheet, menus, etc.) or some hotel brochures to familiarize the prospect with your property before you arrive. Then, a few days later, you can call the prospect to verify that they received your materials.

Figure 7.6. SAMPLE CALL REPORT.

RED LION INNS.

CALL REPORT

FIRST CALL

REPEAT CALL

FILE NO.

COMPANY / ORGANIZATION:

STREET ADDRESS

CITY   STATE   ZIP

CONTACT: PHONE:

DOES YOUR COMPANY HAVE MEETINGS?   ☐ NO   ☐ YES   HOW OFTEN?

SIZE   CONTACT

WHEN IS YOUR NEXT MEETING?   WHERE

DO YOU NEED GUEST ROOMS?   ☐ NO   ☐ YES   HOW MANY

WHO MAKES THE RESERVATIONS?

DO YOU NEED OUT OF TOWN RESERVATIONS? ☐ NO ☐ YES   WHERE?

DO YOU HAVE SUCH THINGS AS:

- CHRISTMAS PARTIES

- AWARDS BANQUETS

- OTHER

ARE YOU OR ANYONE ELSE IN YOUR
COMPANY AFFILIATED WITH AN ASSOCIATION?

COMMENTS:

SALESPERSON   DATE

FORM NO. 001-S47 (4/86)

Call reports are used by salespeople to survey the needs of a potential contact and to trace the follow-up on each account. At some properties, surveys are taken by support staff and the names of qualified prospects are passed on to the salespeople for follow-up.

This type of follow-up not only keeps you in the prospect's mind, but also demonstrates your property's commitment to customer service. Meeting planners, especially those who are nonprofessionals or those with limited experience, are more likely to choose a property that has demonstrated its willingness to work closely with its clients.

Handling Inquiries

In today's high tech world, many meeting planners prefer doing business via e-mail, and sales departments without e-mail will find themselves left behind. Inquiries about your property also come via requests for proposals on the Internet or your hotel's web site, by fax, telephone calls or mail and from walk-ins. Walk-ins should always be immediately referred to a hotel salesperson; other inquiries require an immediate follow-up by telephone.

A large number of properties use voice mail systems. While these systems are convenient, many planners are put off by them. They want a timely response, so sales department phones should be answered by a live person. Not only does this show that a property is interested in the planner's business, it provides the opportunity for the salesperson to determine the prospect's needs.

Inquiry calls should be handled like sales calls, and all inquries -- no matter what their source -- should be followed up by a phone call. Salespeople are not simply order takers. During the call, the salesperson should ask enough questions to be able to present the property effectively. By getting to know the prospect and his or her needs, even if the property cannot handle the business at that time, a relationship has been built and there is a greater potential for future business.

Telemarketing

Besides individual telephone calls, the hospitality industry is making extensive use of **telemarketing** — large-scale telephone qualifying and research — to identify potential prospects. While the larger chains have used telemarketing for some time, the practice has become more widespread. Smaller properties have found that telemarketing can be an invaluable tool to reach prospects before sending salespeople out on expensive sales calls.

Telemarketing falls primarily into two basic categories: qualifying and market research. When a property simply wishes to obtain information, smaller properties can utilize additional staff — secretaries, front desk personnel, etc. — to assist in a telephone effort. It should be noted, however, that this type of "telephone blitz" is not true telemarketing — which is a specialized program backed by technology which offers instant access to information.

For large-scale efforts, a professional telemarketing staff is trained to work from prepared scripts. Using such a script, an experienced telemarketer may reach 50 or more prospects a day, either to obtain information or to present the property and close a sale. Reduced sales budgets have caused many properties to increase telemarketing efforts through to final sales. This is especially true when dealing with prospects in distant areas that you cannot get to economically.

A good telemarketing script must be short enough to keep the prospect on the line, but long enough to get the desired information or sale. It should also be specific, with benefits to the client spelled out early. It should be structured to draw the prospect into the conversation and offer the opportunity for him or her to become involved by expressing views and needs. When pressing for an actual sale, follow the same steps as you would in a personal sales call.

Telemarketing is also used for market research, to determine exactly what meeting planners are looking for. Such information is used to upgrade facilities and services, making it easier for salespeople to present the property as meeting the needs of meeting planners.

No matter what type of telemarketing program is implemented, is it essential that it be as disciplined as any other form of selling. The staff should be thoroughly trained, and there should be clear-cut goals and follow-up to ensure that goals are being met.

Sales Blitz Selling

A **sales blitz** focuses on contacting potential clients in a concentrated area over a brief period of time (usually three days), and is an effective tool for both reaching and qualifying new business. A sales blitz may consist of simply "cold calling" on businesses and associations in an area, but unannounced, random sales calls on meeting planners are usually not a good idea. Planners often feel such calls are intrusive and discourteous. Instead, hotels should carefully plan and identify prospects prior to a sales blitz -- and, ideally, send prospective clients a letter advising them of the coming visit.

Other sales blitzes may be more elaborate. A new property, for example, may wish to use the sales blitz technique to introduce itself to the community; the blitz would serve as a way to invite potential clients to attend a special property presentation. If a sales blitz is used to introduce a new property or to promote a special property presentation, however, extensive planning is needed. The program may include audiovisual presentations, property tours, and food and beverage functions. In many cases, notables such as local or national celebrities or political figures are invited to stimulate interest and lend credibility to the property. No matter what type of program is planned, however, its ultimate purpose should be to demonstrate a property's ability to handle meetings business. It is of obvious importance, therefore, to get as many of the prospects to attend the event and receive the special presentation.

Still other properties join up with their local convention and visitors bureau to conduct a sales blitz. In this case, several entities are involved (the CVB, area hotels, destination management companies, and area attractions) in a coordinated sales effort to attract a specific market.

Whether a sales blitz will lead to a property presentation or will be used simply to survey potential clients, most properties begin planning several weeks in advance. Sales letters are often sent out to prospective clients to advise them of the coming visit. This strategy leads to "warm calls" — contacts with planners who have some idea of what the property can offer. Proper preparation is important as it will result in the sales blitz participant getting in to see more prospects and create an atmosphere conducive to selling.

When planning a sales blitz, a city directory is used to map out specific target areas. Providing each participant with a list of prospects in a concentrated area greatly reduces the traveling time involved, enabling a sales blitz participant to make 75 to 90 calls over a three-day period.

In most cases, the sales blitz is used simply to collect information, qualify prospects, or invite prospects to that special property presentation, so it is not always necessary to tie up the property's sales staff in a sales blitz effort. Some properties hire a temporary sales blitz staff or utilize sales-oriented college students for blitzes over break periods.

Each person involved should clearly understand the purpose of the blitz, including how many calls he or she is expected to make and what questions he or she can answer (if using an outside blitz team, participants are usually instructed to refer contacts to a member of the property's sales staff). Sales blitz participants should be given an adequate supply of survey sheets (see Figure 7.7) and collateral materials, such as property business cards, convention brochures, and low-cost specialty items imprinted with the property's name and telephone number to keep the property's name in front of the prospect.

Figure 7.7. SAMPLE SALES BLITZ SURVEY SHEET.

Sales Blitz Survey Sheet

Organization_____

Address_____

_____ Zip_____ Phone_____

Contact_____ Title_____

Contact_____ Title_____

1. How many meetings do you have a year?_____ When?_____
   Size_____ Who plans them?_____

Contact_____ Title_____

When is your next meeting? _____

Where are meetings usually held? _____

2. Do you have incoming visitors that require sleeping accommodations?

   Yes_____ No_____ How many per month?_____

   If yes, where are they housed?_____

   Do you reserve the room? Yes_____ No_____ (If not, who does?)

   Contact_____ Title_____

3. Does your organization plan such things as:

   ___Christmas Parties?   ___Retirement Dinners?
   ___Award Dinners?   ___Other Social Events?

   Are you the organizer, or is there a social chairman?
        Yes_____ No_____ Contact_____

4. Are you, or any of your associates, affiliated with any other organizations or associations that might have need for meeting or banquet space? Yes_____ No_____

Name_____ Contact_____

Comments:

Taken by: _____ Date Taken_____

Source: Howard Feiertag, "Blitzes and Sales Calls: Indispenable Selling Tools," *HSMAI Marketing Review.*

During a sales blitz, survey sheets are used to record prospect information. Once qualified, the prospects with the highest potential for business will merit additional contact.

Trade Show Selling

Trade shows provide an opportunity for a property to reach meeting planners (see Figure 7.8). One of the advantages of trade show participation is that you will meet people who are buying. Another advantage is the relatively low cost. While trade show participation requires effort and expense, it can be cost-effective. A personal sales call typically costs about $300, while, according to research by the Center for Exhibition Industry Research, the average cost of a new client contact at a trade show is only $185. And, if your convention bureau is exhibiting in a trade show, it may be posible for your property to share booth space and expenses with them. In addition to these benefits, trade shows also provide excellent opportunities to see what your competition is doing!

Figure 7.8. TRADE SHOWS FOR REACHING THE MEETINGS MARKET.

Exhibit Shows	Number of years	Number of exhibitors	Usual attendance
1. American Society of Association Executives Annual Meeting & Expo	45	800	5,000
2. Incentive Travel & Meetings Exec Show	31	963	14,319
3. Religious Conference Management Association Annual Conference	27	688	1,250
4. Meeting Professionals International Annual Meeting	17	350	1,700
5. Health Care Convention & Exhibitors Association Annual Meeting	42	130	600
6. International Association for Exposition Management	6	125	1,000

Twenty years ago, the only major industry trade show was the American Society of Association Executives Expo. Today, there are a number of shows aimed at different segments of the meetings industry. Above is a brief listing of national and regional exhibit shows, the number of years each show has been held, and recent attendance figures. When selecting a show at which to exhibit, keep in mind your primary target markets and plan your trade show strategy specifically for these markets.

There are also some disadvantages to selling through trade shows. First, there is the initial cost and transportation of a property's display; these expenses are especially prohibitive for small properties that must compete with the elaborate displays of larger competitors. Secondly, your competition is likely to be participating in the same show and wooing the same target markets you are trying to attract. And, lastly, your booth time may be taken up by a number of meeting planners who will not generate business for your property.

To make the most of trade show selling, planning is again the key (see Figure 7.9). A pre-show action plan identifying potential clients and a strategy for contact and follow up is an excellent way to ensure that the maximum benefit is derived from trade show participation. Strong potential business should be targeted, and your representatives should find

Figure 7.9. EXHIBITING AT TRADE SHOWS.

Exhibiting at Trade Shows

Before

- When choosing trade shows, ask show management for a rating ratio of meeting planners to salespeople.
- Contact previous exhibitors; ask about attendance and quality of prospective buyers.
- Use pre-show promotions. Target important prospects by mail or phone. Arrive early to make sales calls in the area prior to the show.
- Be prepared with meeting planner kits for distribution at the booth.
- Meet with the sales team to clarify team objectives, set individual goals. Train salespeople with written sales scripts. Role play different sales situations — using a sales brochure, qualifying prospects and securing information from prospects.

During

- Set up the booth in advance and assign salespeople to no more than three hour shifts before a break.
- Ask quick, qualifying questions to help determine interest. Be courteous and friendly but discontinue discussion when the visitor is not a prospect.
- Smile; act and look knowledgeable; stand, don't sit; don't smoke, eat or drink in the booth.
- Use prospect's business card to take notes of specific needs for follow-up.
- Schedule sales team meetings before and after each day of the show to discuss problems and solutions and to coach the sales team.

And After the Show

- The sixty days after the show are most critical. Assign responsibility for following up on leads and appointments; establish deadlines for follow-ups.
- Review exhibit objectives to see if goals were attained. Each dollar invested should return ten dollars in sales.

Used with permission of Howard Feiertag, CHSE, CMP.

To make the most of trade show exhibiting, the above list details what to do before, during, and after a trade show.

out where these planners are staying; this enables your reps to see planners that don't make it to the property's booth. It is best, therefore, to allow at least two days to make calls before the show opens and to allow at least one day after the show to follow up on new local contacts made through the show.

Both your booth and personnel should adequately reflect your property's image and professionalism. Personnel should always be friendly, courteous and informative, and the booth should be arranged in a manner that involves the prospects. Rather than setting tables across the booth, it is more effective to place tables along the sides and back to draw people into the display. Giveaway materials should be kept to a minimum; it is a mistake to offer too many giveaways. Most meeting planners prefer to "travel light" and do not wish to be overwhelmed by too many materials. It is far better to show a video brochure and/or give live presentations at scheduled times. These can be enhanced by one or two pieces of concise, informative material accompanied by your business card.

No matter how simple or elaborate your display, it is important to always remember your purpose: selling. It is important to qualify prospects. If your property is a resort, for example, it would have little appeal for a meeting planner seeking airport hotels at which to hold training meetings. While you shouldn't discount these prospects entirely — they may have contacts who can use your property or may have use for your property at a later date — it is important to deal primarily with meeting planners who offer a high potential for business for your property. In other words, you must quickly qualify prospects to determine how much time you should spend with them. A survey sheet or questionnaire is an excellent way to determine if a booth's visitor is a good prospect. If he or she is unlikely to have a need for your property, be polite but brief and move on to a better qualified prospect as soon as possible.

Trade show selling is not complicated if you have set clear-cut goals for before and during the show and have established guidelines for follow up. The contacts made at a trade show should be followed up as quickly as possible after the show to keep your property fresh in the contact's mind. This interest and demonstration of your property's commitment can result in both business from your trade show contacts and referral business in the future.

Selling with Convention Bureaus

Even if you represent a large property with extensive convention facilities, a local convention bureau can be an invaluable partner in selling to the meetings market, even serving as an extension of your property's sales staff. Bill Snyder, past president of the Anaheim Convention and Visitors Bureau states:

> "A Bureau's function is to bring conventions, trade shows and tourists to its respective area. A secondary objective is, of course, to offer those services which necessarily follow the attraction of conventions, trade shows and tourists.
> "A Bureau should be the nucleus for the sales effort in the visitor industry for that community and should also represent the point of "one stop shopping" for any prospect or client contemplating holding a convention or trade show in that city. A Bureau must be impartial in its representation of its facilities if it is to be successful."[3]

Convention bureaus are structured in different ways. Some are membership organizations to which hotels, transportation companies, restaurants and local merchants turn to organize efforts to bring in convention business. Others are funded through room taxes and work to promote general tourism (see Figure 7.10). In some cases, they operate exhibition halls that were built with public funds.

The convention bureau's sales office is set up similarly to a hotel sales office, but on a larger scale. Its job, sometimes called **destination marketing**, is to sell the city, bring conventions to the area and to make the group's stay productive and enjoyable (see box titled "Destination Marketing"). When a bureau receives a letter or phone call from a meeting group saying the city has been selected for its convention, the bureau sends out a

Figure 7.10. FUNDING OF CONVENTION AND VISITORS BUREAUS.

FUNDING OF CONVENTION AND VISITORS BUREAUS

Bed Taxes in Selected Trade Show Cities

City	Bed Tax
Houston	15%
Chicago	14.9%
Los Angeles	14%
New York City	13.25% + $2.00 per night
Atlanta	13%
Anaheim	11%
Las Vegas	9%

Las Vegas boasts far and away the largest bureau budget, double that of Hawaii, which in turn is nearly double that of Reno.

Annual Bureau Budgets (in millions)

City	Budget
Las Vegas	$124,000,000
Hawaii	$62,600,000
Reno	$32,200,000
Orlando	$25,700,000
Los Angeles	$22,000,000
Kissimmee	$20,000,000
Atlanta	$16,700,000
Miami	$15,600,000
San Diego	$15,200,000
San Francisco	$14,300,000

Hotel room taxes are often the largest source of revenue for convention and visitors bureaus. These taxes, also known as bed or pillow taxes, are levied on a percentage basis of room rate, and nationally account for over 60 percent of the typical convention and visitors bureaus' budgets. These taxes sometimes generate controversy, however, as they are not always used to promote the city as a convention, group meeting and vacation destination. In some cities, these taxes are instead diverted to fund community programs.

convention lead form to local hotels (see Figure 7.11). The hotel may then contact the group.

In addition to providing leads to area hotels and convention support firms, the bureau also assists in executing conventions, often supplying registration clerks, guides, spouses' program personnel, and so on. Most important for hotels, most convention bureaus also provide a housing bureau for placing delegates in the city's hotels when large conventions are booked.

If your area has a convention bureau, it most likely is a member of the IACVB, the International Association of Convention and Visitors Bureaus. If so, you are fortunate,

Figure 7.11. SAMPLE CONVENTION LEAD FORM.

SAN FRANCISCO
CONVENTION & VISITORS BUREAU
1390 MARKET STREET, SAN FRANCISCO, CALIFORNIA 94102

CONVENTION LEAD FORM

Date ___xxx___

TO All major hotels

FROM Matt Miller

GROUP XYZ CORPORATION

CONTACT Mr. John Jones   **TITLE** Convention Manager

ADDRESS 6000 K Street N.W.

CITY Washington, DC 20097   **PHONE** (202) 123-4567

ATTENDANCE 500   **NO OF ROOMS** 350

EXHIBIT SPACE NET SQ FT 4000

REQUESTED DATES February 3-6, February 10-13, 2004
arrivals 2/2 or 2/9; departures 2/7 or 2/14

MEETING REQUIREMENTS

2/2 or 2/9	6 p.m. reception for 300 people
2/3 or 2/10	8 a.m. breakfast for 150
	12 noon lunch for 500
	9:00-5:00 general session for 500 theatre style
2/4 or 2/11	9:00-12 noon 5 workshops for 100 each theatre style; afternoon free
2/5 or 2/12	9:00-12 noon general session for 500 theatre style
	12 noon reception & lunch for 500
	2:00-5:00 5 workshops for 100 each
2/6 or 2/13	9:00-12 noon general session for 500 theatre style
	7 p.m. reception & dinner dance for 500 people

San Francisco is definite; hotel selection within three months

Please copy the Bureau on all your correspondance

History

2001	New Orleans	476 registered; 327 rooms used
2002	Las Vegas	498 registered; 319 rooms used

This is an example of a form sent by the San Francisco Convention & Visitors Bureau to hotels in the city advising them of an upcoming convention. Note that the form includes the group's requirements (number of rooms, types of functions that will be held, room space requirements, etc.) to enable hotels to decide if they can realistically service the business.

because the IACVB offers a wealth of detailed, confidential information to assist you in your selling efforts. Each IACVB member receives and files reports dealing with convention performances and characteristics of all associations that convened within the member's city. This data includes promised attendance and actual attendance figures, prices paid,

DESTINATION MARKETING

Over a century ago, in 1895, Detroit hotelier Milton J. Carmichael presented an idea of promoting the city as a whole to help build individual hotel business. The concept proved to be so successful that the Detroit hoteliers created the nation's first convention bureau. Before long, the idea spread to other cities, and today hundreds of such bureaus exist around the world.

The convention bureaus' primary objective is *destination marketing* — promoting their respective areas as a whole to attract meetings and convention business. To do so, convention bureaus engage in advertising campaigns, participate in trade shows, and offer a number of services to meeting planners, including general desination information, centralized housing of convention delegates, and registration services.

Once given a meeting's requirements — dates, rates and space — bureaus go to work for planners. The bureau usually arranges site inspection visits. After a group is booked, the bureau's focus shifts from marketing to service.

While the scope of services offered by bureaus depends largely on staff size and budget, some bureaus have become very innovative. The Chicago Convention and Tourism Bureau utilizes its in-house telemarketing department to help planners build attendance at conventions. Using a prepared script and a database of the convening group's members, the bureau's staff makes up to 2,500 calls free of charge. This service is credited with increasing convention attendance in the Windy City by as much as 16 percent. With each additional attendee representing an average of $800 in spending, such effort benefits both planners and local businesses.

concessions granted, and almost everything else you would want to know about a prospect. When you track a convention over a period of five years, a pattern emerges that enables you to decide whether or not you have a good chance to get such business — and how to go after it.

In addition to maintaining records on major associations and corporations, bureaus also subscribe to key association and corporate publications, such as the *Encyclopedia of Associations* and *The Directory of Corporate Meeting Planners,* and make them available to local hotels for research. These publications, among others, are invaluable in securing the meetings market, but are often too expensive for individual properties to purchase.

The most important facet of working with convention bureaus, however, is the advantage of pooled resources. The convention bureau serves as a coordinator when the size of an event makes it mandatory to present the sales proposal as a group and to house the delegates in a number of hotels. And, since the convention bureau's function is to promote the area as a whole, its efforts — exhibitions at trade shows, print advertising and direct mail efforts — will directly benefit your property and serve as an additional marketing resource in helping you to obtain a share of business.

Site Inspection Selling and Familiarization Tours

One of the best ways to show exactly what your property has to offer is to invite the meeting planner to visit it personally. This can be done in two ways: on an individual basis *(site inspection selling)* or in a structured group setting *(familiarization tours)*, which offer a number of planners the chance to experience what the hotel has to offer.

Many meeting planners will not book a site unless they have had the opportunity to see it personally, and site inspection selling can be an effective sales tool if certain guidelines are followed:

- Always schedule a visit when the property is busy. This will give the planner an opportunity to see your efficient service in action — and will give credibility to your claims of excellence.
- Don't be too busy, however, to devote time to the planner. He or she should be greeted like a guest, and should have the opportunity to meet those people with whom he or she will be dealing (the catering manager, convention services manager, and so on).
- Alert the staff of the impending site inspection. If possible, post a photograph of the meeting planner and provide pertinet information to enable employees to greet the planner by name.
- A welcoming note from the general manager upon the planner's arrival and a brief visit with the general manager sometime during the visit are good gestures. Many planners indicate they can tell a lot about how a hotel is run by meeting the general manager.
- Feature only those items of interest to the planner. Don't waste everyone's time showing your state-of-the-art audiovisual equipment to a planner whose focus will be social functions or recreational activities.
- Train a number of staff personnel to serve as "tour guides" in the event a salesperson is away. These staff members should be able to answer questions — and sell features as benefits. It is also helpful if they can offer supplemental material, such as photographs of past successful events, third-party endorsements, and so on, to capture the planner's interest.

- Remember the purpose of suggesting a site inspection: selling. Knowing your property, competition, and prospect are keys. Follow the six steps of personal selling discussed in the opening of this chapter. Laura Anevedo, meeting planner for Alder Droz, Inc. says:

> "My favorite part about site inspections is being able to visualize my next meeting taking place at the prospective property. Usually the salesperson is putting his/her best foot forward in order to capture the busines and is really excited about showing off the property. If the salesperson has done homework on my past programs, he/she can really be influential in my ultimate decision to book a program at that property."[4]

Familiarization (fam) tours require more planning than individual site inspection visits, and, since they can be expensive for the property, involve qualifying prospective visitors. Michael Smith, Director of Convention Sales for the Portland (OR) Visitors' Association, states:

> "We do not invite people just because they happen to plan meetings. Unless they are seriously thinking of meeting in Portland, they are not invited. Our members need to know that the people we are bringing in are legitimate and the trip is an investment."[5]

George Mittler, Director of Sales at the Sheraton San Marcos in Chandler, Arizona, also believes in qualifying prospects, and achieved remarkable results from his semiannual fam tours. He explains:

> "At the Sheraton San Marcos Resort, we have found the formula to successful fam trips. After spending $40,000 on our two semiannual fam trips, we booked $900,000 in business as a direct result of the trips. Resorts generally strive for ten times the return on the money invested in a fam tour, by we consistently come back with more than 20 times the investment. In fact, on every fam tour we've organized in the past two years, we've booked business while meeting planners were still on-site.
>
> Competition in our area is stiff, so you have to develop a niche. Ours has been to go above and beyond what the competitors offer. We sell service and successful meetings. We train our people, and everybody from the general manager to the busboys sells the resort. Our philosophy of involving the entire staff as salespeople is the reason we convert so many fam trippers into clients.
>
> To fascinate the fam trippers, we stage three major events while they're here: a 'Meeting Planners Invitational Golf Tournament,' 'Dinner in the Desert,' and a '50s Night' or a 'Casino Theme Night' dinner-dance. The whole point of these extravaganzas is to demonstrate to planners how the San Marcos can plan and carry out theme events.
>
> Since it costs about $400 to $500 per person, not counting airfare, to host fam-trip guests, we pre-qualify fam trippers. The days of 'Come eat my shrimp and drink my booze' are long over, so we make sure these people are qualified. To cut costs, we also co-sponsor with a local airline."[6]

Qualified meeting planners may be contacted either by mail or telephone, and should be given a reasonable lead time to make plans (four to six weeks is the norm). If a group tour, planners invited should have similar professional needs. One planner stated:

> "I hate to go on fams where everyone is an association planner and I'm the only corporate planner. They show you everything from an association standpoint, and there's a big difference."

The property should let attendees know exactly what the fam tour involves: its duration; what is included (meals, transportation, etc.); and whom the invitation includes (spouse, other members of the selection committee, etc.). When the meeting planners arrive for the tour, they should be greeted individually and given a schedule of events. Events should be planned to show prospects exactly what the property can offer. Staff members usually handle property tours, although an outside person (a member of the local Convention and Visitors Bureau, for example) may conduct off-property tours of the area's leisure and cultural activities.

As with individual site-inspection selling, property salespeople should try to get a meeting commitment before the guests leave the property. If this is not possible (in some cases, for example, the planner must report back to the site selection committee), the fam tour should be followed up as soon as possible. Many properties include a questionnaire in their follow up letter, asking what the participants liked and disliked. This type of questionnaire not only can assist the property to plan better fam tours, but can also be used to provide insights into the needs, likes and dislikes of the individual participants.

Fam tours not only bring business from the participants, but can influence their peers as well. Today, a number of properties are using technology to make their fam tours available to a wide audience of meeting planners. A fam tour, marketed to a specific segment of planners, is videotaped and is made available on tape and on the property's web site. This not only enhances the experience for the participants but also provides a "virtual tour" of the property -- and feedback from the attendees -- to other meeting planners.

Chapter Summary:

As you can see, personal selling — whether it be an individual effort, such as a face-to-face sales call or telephone call, or a strategy to sell to groups at a trade show — plays a key role in booking meetings. But direct selling is not the only way to introduce your property to meeting planners. In the next chapter, we will see how *advertising* can supplement your sales efforts. We will take a look at how this sales tool can work hand-in-hand with personal selling to help generate lucrative meetings market business for your property.

Endnotes:

1. "A New Approach to Selling," *The Meeting Professional*, February and April 2000, pp. 43 & 46.
2. Becky Cumming and Melina Legos, "Squaring Off," *Successful Meetings*, June 1999, p 37.

3. From correspondence with Bill Snyder, past president, Anaheim Convention and Visitors Bureau.
4. "In the Trenches," *Meetings in the West*, July 2000, p. 6.
5. Suzanne Miller and Ross Weiland, "Planners Want Better Fam Trips," *Meeting News*, April 1993, p. 57.
6. From correspondence with George Mittler, Director of Sales, Sheraton San Marcos

Additional References:

Destination Marketing, Richard Cartrell, Kendall Hunt Publishing, Dubuque, Iowa.

Hospitality Sales: A Marketing Approach, Margaret Shaw and Susan Morris, John Wiley and Sons, 2000.
www.hospitality@wiley.com

Hospitality Sales and Advertising, James Abbey, Educational Insitute, AHLA, 1998.
www.ei-ahla.org

Internet Sites:

For additional information on the firms and organizations discussed in this chapter, visit the following Internet sites. The Web addresses listed are current as of January 2001. Addresses may change, however; if a site is not available at the address below, a search engine can be used to access its new location.

Chicago Convention and Tourism Bureau - www.chicagoil.org
Hospitality Sales and Marketing Association International - www.hsmai.org
Loews Hotels - www.loewshotels.com

Study Questions:

1. Identify the steps in making a personal sales call. Why is each important?
2. List the steps in making a telephone appointment call. Why is follow-up especially important after making telephone contact? What kind of follow-up can be done?
3. In what other ways is the telephone used to sell to and service customers?
4. What is a sales blitz? Why can a sales blitz be a cost-effective sales tool?
5. What is a trade show? How can a property make the most of its trade show exhibit?

6. What are the advantages of working with a convention bureau to secure business?
7. What is a "fam" tour? What steps should a property take to ensure that a "fam" tour is successful?

 Key Terms:

Appointment call. A prearranged appointment with a prospect to introduce the features and benefits offered by a property. During this visit, the salesperson may or may not attempt to close the sale.

Call report. A document, usually resulting from some personal contact, that provides general information about an account (address, contact person, etc.) as well as remarks on the needs of the group and any action steps that can be taken to sell the hotel's products and services to the group.

Close-ended question. A question requiring a specific answer that often can be given in just a few words.

Cold call. A fact-finding call on a prospect with whom there has been little or no previous contact; often made without a definite appointment.

Destination marketing. Promotion of a particular location as a meeting site and/or tourist attraction.

Familiarization (fam) tour. Free or reduced-rate trip given to meeting planners, travel agents, travel writers and other sources of potential business to acquaint them with a property or destination.

Major close. A question or statement at the end of a sales presentation that asks for a definite commitment on the prospect's part.

Open-ended question. A question that gives a prospect the opportunity to express his or her feelings and knowledge.

Sales blitz. Concentrated canvassing of a selected geographic area over a specific time period in order to gather information on potential leads.

Telemarketing. The systematic use of the telephone for marketing or sales purposes.

Trial close. A statement or question posed by the salesperson during a sales presentation that seeks to evoke a positive response from the client.

Learning Objectives:

In this chapter, we will discuss the types of advertising most commonly used to reach the meetings market. We will focus on print ads, collateral materials, direct mail, and the newest medium for business-to-business marketers, the Internet. In addition, we'll look at how to plan an advertising strategy and discuss how public relations and publicity can be used to project an image that will attract meeting planners to your property. When you have studied this chapter, you will:

- Be able to describe the various types of media used to advertise to meeting planners.

- Know what factors are involved in developing an effective advertising strategy.

- Be able to explain the difference between public relations and publicity and tell how each is used to project the desired image for your property.

Outline

Print Advertising
- Trade Magazines
- Hotel Directories

Using Technology for Advertising
- The Internet
- E-mail Advertising
- Fax Transmissions

Collateral Materials
- Brochures
  - Convention Brochures
  - Video Brochures
  - CD-ROMs
- Other Collateral Materials
- Specialty Items

Direct Mail Advertising

Planning an Advertising Strategy
- Reach, Frequency, Timing and Consistency
- Exchange Trade Advertising
- Cooperative Advertising and Strategic Partnerships
- Advertising Agencies

Public Relations and Publicity

The Planners' Perspective on Advertising

Ed Griffin, Jr., CAE
Executive Vice President/CEO
Meeting Professionals International
Dallas, Texas

"Advertising wins when the meeting planner understands both the benefits and the unique qualities of a product or service. The hotel must explain how the product will satisfy the planner's needs. In order to do that, the advertiser must know what's important to the planner. Planners want to know about such things as room capacities, pricing, guarantees, restrictions and value seasons. Advertisers increasingly compete for the planner's time vs. the planner's wastepaper basket...it is essential for messages to be direct, simple and concise. The ad copy must be directed specifically at the planner, with a view to planner benefits rather than product features."

8 Advertising to the Meeting Planner

Advertising can play a key role in your sales effort since its primary function is to generate interest in your property. Advertising supplements your sales effort. It is an invaluable tool for targeting meeting planners who have not previously been reached and offers additional information to those who are aware of your facilities.

When a property advertises, its message is seen by a vast audience, generating potential leads that can be followed up by the sales staff. Marketing efforts, then, should be supported by an advertising and promotional strategy that is carefully planned and executed.

One of the benefits of advertising is that it, like sales presentations, can be "tailored" to meet the needs of potential customers. For example, properties can target the corporate segment, whose meetings are often staged by inexperienced planners, with one type of ad, and target the association segment, which looks for a desirable location as well as meeting planning assistance to increase attendance, with an ad promoting those benefits (see Figure 8.1).

While there are a number of media available, including newspapers, trade magazines, travel guides, direct mail, collateral material, outdoor advertising, television and radio, not all are used to reach meeting planners. You will have to make very specific choices based on your target customers, marketing goals and budget.

Print Advertising

One of the most effective ways to reach meeting planners is through **print advertising**. Most meeting planners look for information. Advertising in printed media most likely to be seen by meeting planners can increase your property's chances of generating meetings business.

While some properties advertise in such newspapers as the *Wall Street Journal* and magazines including *Fortune* and *Time*, which are often read by meeting planners, the most promising media in which to advertise is *trade magazines*, especially the specialized meetings publications that we discussed in Chapters 4, 5 and 6.

Trade Magazines

Magazine advertising offers several advantages. First, ads can be printed in color and photographs reproduced with good quality. Second, many magazines have a long reading life. Back issues of some magazines are kept and reread, often passed on to others, giving ads a longer life. Third, and most important, magazine advertising gives the hotel an opportunity to key its convention promotion efforts to a select group of readers.

Once you have opted to use print advertising, you will need to develop effective print ads. Good print ads don't just happen. They are carefully thought out and targeted toward a specific audience (see Figure 8.2).

The most effective ads follow the AIDA principle, which focuses on *attention, interest, desire* and *action.* To attract *attention*, your ad must stand out from the rest. In most

Figure 8.1. *TAILORING ADVERTISING TO THE NEEDS OF THE MEETINGS MARKET.*

The needs of corporate and association planners often differ greatly. Corporate meeting planners, especially those inexperienced in planning events, want assurance that they will have help in staging a successful meeting. Association meeting planners have an additional concern — selecting a site that will appeal to the greatest number of members as attendance is largely voluntary. These print ads are tailored to address the needs of each segment. The San Francisco Hilton ad promotes the property's experience in successfully handling all details for the meeting planner. The ad developed by the Hawaii Visitors Bureau Meetings & Conventions Department promotes Hawaii as a popular destination site for meetings, both corporate and association.

cases, this is done through the use of a headline or eye-catching illustration. If an illustration is used, it must tie in with the copy of the ad. Whenever possible, use *color* to attract attention. If your budget prohibits using full-color ads, even a property with limited funds can use black plus one other color to draw attention to key points.

To keep the reader *interested*, your copy should be specific and to the point. Don't be reluctant to use plenty of white space and large or bold type for easy readability. Use bulleted lists for key points. Keep the copy simple, using short sentences and words that are easy to understand. Make your ad quick to read and easy to comprehend.

To build *desire*, the text should present your features as benefits and tell the reader why your property is different. If you offer special services to the meeting planner, tell them so — and offer this as a benefit to them. You may also want to include photographs of your expertise in action. But don't make the mistake of including a photograph of an empty room — nothing looks more sterile; portray action by including people in your meeting or function room photographs.

Last, but certainly not least, you will want to create an ad that stimulates *action* on the part of the reader. Since the primary purpose of your ad is to generate a response, offer a way to do so. In many cases, ads are accompanied by a reply card or include a coupon (or, at the very least, an address) to enable the respondent to request additional information.

Figure 8.2. SAMPLE PRINT AD.

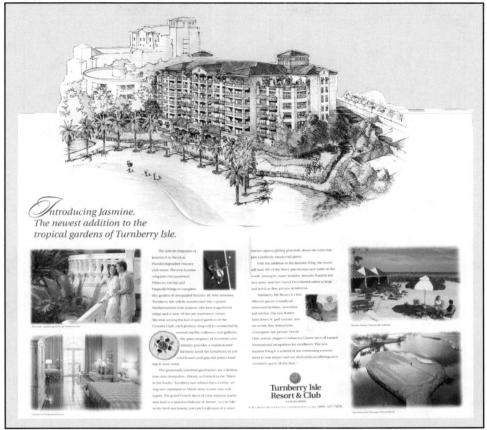

This four-page ad appeared in several meetings magazines, including Successful Meetings, Meetings and Conventions, *and* Corporate Meetings and Incentives. *While the costs of production and additional insertion costs (for placement in the center of the magazine) are high, the stopping feature of the pop-up feature grasps the attention of meeting planners.*

Today, most properties offer toll-free numbers, fax numbers, and e-mail addresses to encourage prompt responses (see Figure 8.3).

Always be sure your ad includes your property's name, address and your *logo*. It is highly effective to have ads that are readily identifiable, and, since your logo is distinctly yours, it should be used in all media efforts (it generally appears toward the bottom of the ad).

Once you have developed the components of your ad, you will have to decide on how you want it positioned in the magazine. Magazine space is sold in a variety of sizes (see Figure 8.4). You will have to determine which size and placement will work best for your ad.

The positioning of your ad is important. Studies have shown that the reader's eye is drawn initially to the upper part of the right hand page. For an ad smaller than a full page, the position on the upper right hand page might mean more readership. It is even more preferable to have your ad positioned in the editorial section of the magazine and, when possible, ask that your ad be the only hotel ad on the page. The magazine's placement of your small ad next to competing ads may reduce its efficiency. Sometimes you can negotiate to avoid such circumstances; sometimes an additional fee will guarantee it. Good position, facing editorial copy, will help your ad do the job.

Figure 8.3. ADVERTISING CONTACT NUMBER.

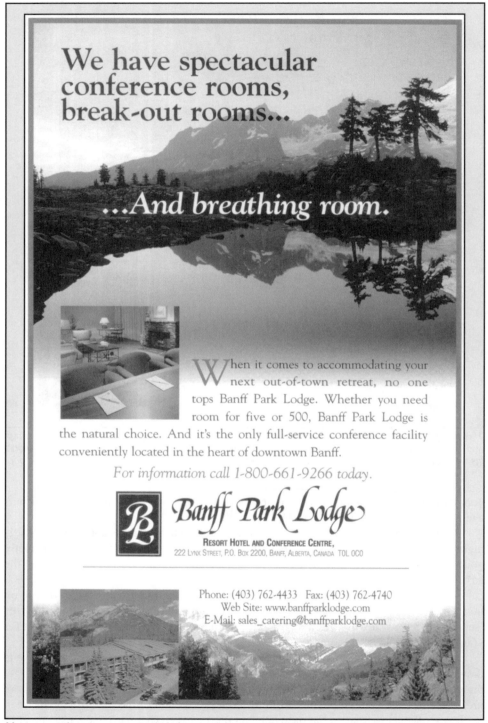

Most properties now promote their fax numbers, e-mail address(es) and their web sites address in addition to the toll-free numbers common in ads of the past. Note that the e-mail address goes directly to the sales department. This type of response mechanism connects the planner directly to a department that deals with meetings as well as enabling the planner to respond to an ad quickly.

Figure 8.4. MAGAZINE SPACE OPTIONS.

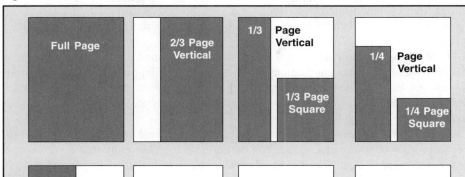

The standard magazine page is 7 x 10 inches. Tabloid publications are larger. A popular tabloid size is 10 x 14 inches, but tabloids do vary in dimension. The ad sizes offered by tabloid publications are, of course, a full tabloid page, a junior page (which is usually 7 x 10 and is positioned like the half-page island in a magazine), and smaller ads which usually follow the sizes and designations of the magazine format like above. There are many variations and combinations that can be used; for example, two 1/2 page horizontal ads running across two facing pages. These shown are the most common and universally accepted by publications. Bleed is the term used when the ad extends beyond its usual border out to the very edge of the paper. Most publications make an additional charge for bleed ads.

Magazine ad space is sold by the page or fraction of a page, and ads can be positioned in standard layouts in a variety of ways. These are some of the sizes and placements most commonly used.

The size and frequency of your ad is largely dependent on your budget (see box titled "Magazine Advertising Rates"). While some properties can afford full-page color ads, other properties have to opt for smaller ads if they are to place them frequently. Ads are like sales calls; frequency is important. Your prospects may require several exposures to your advertising before they respond. Advertising gurus advise you to run ads at least every other month throughout the year. If, in your eyes, a publication doesn't warrant six ads a year, perhaps you ought to rethink your decision to advertise in it at all. Frequency is important for effective advertising.

Hotel Directories

In addition to trade magazines, hotel directories (especially those directed to meeting planners) and other business directories are excellent media for reaching meeting planners. These directories list property information in a standard format (see Figure 8.5). The meeting planner has the opportunity to "comparison shop" various factors such as location, facilities, transportation and price. And while your property is presented exactly as all others in these editorial listings, most directories offer advertising space for your property's print ad.

Other directories to consider are those for meeting planners, executives in business and industry and any other publications for your specific target markets (education, military reunions, etc.). While these directories primarily list information for and about their members, most offer display advertising space through which you can directly target your market.

It is important to note, however, that advertising in these types of directories will differ from your standard advertising. You do not have the continuity that comes with a series of ads in a periodical. You have just the one time ad in which to make your sales pitch. Readers of directories turn to them for *facts*. Take a leaf from their book and load your ad with details. Your ad should supply all the information necessary to generate an inquiry — and a means for the meeting planner to respond, doubly so if the publication does not have a built-in ad inquiry reader service card system.

Magazine Advertising Rates

Listed below is a sampling of *Meetings and Conventions* magazine's 2000 advertising rates. Costs for print advertising vary depending on a number of factors. For example, the use of color is more expensive, but color ads have a greater "stopping power" than black and white advertising. The position of an ad is also a factor; the inside and back covers are the most expensive placements because of their higher exposure. Hotels also have the option of using special inserts for a higher rate. While rates will vary from publication to publication, most magazines offer discounts to frequent advertisers.

A. Black & White

	1x	4x	7x	13x	26x
One Page	$17,015	$16,955	$16,310	$14,955	$14,390
2/3 Page	12,290	12,205	11,780	10,790	10,465
1/2 Page*	9,655	9,570	9,220	8,435	8,195
1/3 Page	6,745	6,725	6,445	5,920	5,790

*Island 1/2 Page plus: $655

B. Color

2-Color: B/W earned rate plus	$1,935
Match Color: B&W earned rate plus	2,545
Match Color Spread: B&W earned rate plus	4,425
4-Color: B&W earned rate plus	5,095
4-Color Spread: B&W earned rate plus	8,895
5-Color: B&W earned rate plus	7,385

C. Covers

	1x	7x	13x
Inside: 2-Color	$24,870	$23,200	$21,095
4-Color	27,955	26,330	24,300
Back: 4-Color	29,340	27,655	25,540

D. Inserts

	1x	7x	13x
2 pages	$16,940	$16,280	$14,960
4 pages	30,495	29,305	26,930
6 pages	41,170	39,565	36,355
8 pages	49,405	47,480	43,630

E. Commission and Credit Policy

15% to recognized agencies. Net 30 days. It is understood that all orders are accepted for space subject to our credit requirements. There are no additional discounts for cash payments.

Figure 8.5. HOTEL DIRECTORIES.

OFFICIAL MEETING FACILITIES GUIDE

Planning meetings is complicated enough without worrying about where to find the right facilities with the best accommodations and support services. That's why you need OMFG—the comprehensive directory of more than 1,500 convention centers, hotels, and resorts in the US, Canada, and the world. OMFG's five big sections are chock-full of information on site location . . . accommodations and current rates . . . dining, entertainment, and recreational facilities . . . meeting rooms, ballrooms and exhibit space . . . conference equipment and support services . . . access to airports and transportation . . . even the facts on local climate, attractions, and shopping.

Packed in OMFG's 1,100 information-filled pages, you'll find just about everything you need to help you choose the right facility at the best price. So your chances of having a flawless meeting are greatly enhanced—every time.

Published semiannually, OMFG is the complete source meeting planners turn to first.

OFFICIAL MEETING FACILITIES GUIDE EUROPE

Created especially for the European meeting planner, with complete descriptions of over 300 premier meeting sites throughout Europe and around the world. A complimentary subscription is available to qualified meeting planners in Europe.

THE ESSENTIAL GUIDEBOOK
FOR TRAVEL, MEETING,
AND CONVENTION PLANNERS

Hotel directories provide detailed information that meeting planners need to screen properties. Using directory information, planners can compare properties with regard to location, meeting facilities, amenities, recreational activities and costs. In addition to the Official Meetings Facilities Guide, other directories commonly used by meeting planners include Meetings and Conventions *magazine's Gavel,* Successful Meetings' SourceBook, *and The Hotel Guide.*

Using Technology for Advertising

Over the past few years, a number of new technologies have made a difference in how hotels market themselves to the meetings market. While print advertising is still an important way to get a property's message out, these new technologies make it even easier for a property to reach new and existing customers and to interact with them in exciting new ways.

The Internet

The Internet (also known as the "Net") is becoming an increasingly powerful tool in marketing to meeting planners and other sources of group and transient business. Today, meeting planners and other decision makers can directly access a variety of travel services over the Internet, and are finding it indispensible for comparing properties and services. According to the 2000 Meetings Market Study conducted by Plog Research, some 81 percent of association planners used the computer to help plan meetings (this includes the use of e-mail) and 59 percent used the Internet for meeting planning purposes.

Meeting planners cite a number of benefits to using the Internet, including 24-hour availability, a wealth of up-to-date information on potential meeting sites not only locally but around the world, and the ability to "interact" on most sites. Using the Internet can save time and money and make the planner's job easier. Cathy Shurety, meetings and events coordinator at Aluma Systems in Concord, Ontario, Canada, says:

"The Internet definitely makes it easier for me to do my job. Now when a department comes to me with a meeting request, I can come up with a list of potential venues based on their criteria within half a day. Before the Internet, we mostly looked at local venues. Now I can easily inspect properties anywhere in the world."[1]

Meetings related magazines have made the planner's job easier by featuring popular hospitality and planning sites and giving tips on how to use the Web. Loews Hotels jumped on the "information bandwagon" by developing a 44-page "Meeting Planners' Guide to Using the Web" advertising supplement that appeared in *Meeting News* in July 2000. The guide featured tips on using search engines and listed top industry sites in addition to promoting the chain's own site and properties.

There are basically two ways in which properties can use the Internet to reach prospects. The first is for a property to set up its own Web site, allowing meeting planners and other clients to directly access a chain's site or information on specific properties. According to the 2000 Meetings Market Study, 17 percent of association planners accessed individual hotel sites to make a meeting decision. The Internet enables hotels to create high-quality presences via computer. No longer does a property have to rely on constantly updating its color brochure or getting the word out about a new product or service — using the Internet, it can create a graphic presentation featuring full-color images with sound and video, and even offer a "virtual" tour of the property.

Hotels using the Internet to market their properties to meeting planners can instanteously provide them with the following:

- A listing of meeting facilities and floor plan diagrams
- The name and telephone number of a contact person
- A form to fill out about their upcoming meetings that can be faxed or e-mailed to the property with the click of a button
- A reservations system that lets the planner guarantee rooms by using a credit card

Features also include interactive electronic brochures, enabling planners to "tour" the facilities or talk to the chef and then tap into the hotel's computer to book function space for banquets and meetings as well as book their guestrooms. Most hotels now have an interactive request for proposal, and it is now possible for meeting planners to do virtually all their meeting business with a property on-line.

To promote a property, a hotel must first set up its "web site," which includes its own "address." These sites will vary significantly, depending on the property and the services it promotes, but all start with a "home page" or directory to subsequent pages or "web pages." The home page typically includes the property's name, logo, and a "menu" of information from which to select. If a chain services a number of market segments, it is best to provide links to information of specific interest. Sheraton, for example, offers a "Meeting Facilities" section, Hilton has a "Meetings & Groups" link, Marriott features a "Meeting Planning" section, and Inter-Continental Hotels and Resorts offers a "Global Meetings Portfolio" on its homepage.

The best, most effective home pages are visually attractive and should project the company's image or positioning. Subsequent Web pages should be designed to be as interactive, informative and convenient to the user as possible. The Web pages should include all pertinent information required by a user (room rates, square footage of meeting space, a biography of your chef, etc.), interesting graphics (photos, charts and graphs, etc.), and up-to-date information.

Most sites now offer the opportunity for planners to search for specific meeting criteria. The planner enters specifics and the computer will search for a "match" for his or her requirements within the chain. And, as we have said earlier, RFPs are usually available. But sites should also include a direct link to the property sales office or reservation system as well as pertinent e-mail addresses and your property's toll-free and fax telephone numbers.

The second way to reach meeting planners is to "*link*" your property to other meetings-related sites, such as a CVB site (used by 13 percent of association meeting planners), city site (cited as being used by five percent of meeting planners), meeting planner services, or the sites of other firms to which planners turn for information. *Convene* magazine publishes an annual "Web Site Directory" that provides the addresses of national and international Convention and Visitors Bureaus, conference and convention centers, hotel chains, hotels and resorts, convention services, and airlines and car rental agencies. By linking with one of these entities, you are likely to reach prospects looking specifically for meeting services. A meeting site service, such as Allmeetings.com, Eventsource.com, Plansoft Network, or a host of other companies that are accessed as directories to convention-oriented hotels can also prove effective.

A property may also choose to *advertise* on other sites likely to be visited by its targeted segments. One of the most popular choices is a "banner ad" that appears when a site is accessed. Linking and advertising costs vary widely, so it is a good idea to determine the overall benefit. One disadvantage is that many of your competitors may also be linked to the same site, so you will want to promote a unique benefit if you choose to link with other sites or buy space on sites that feature other hotel advertising.

E-mail Advertising

According to the 2000 Meetings Market Study conducted by Plog Research, 78 percent of meeting planners use **e-mail** for planning purposes. Over half (51 percent) use e-mail for facility search/site selection, while 46 percent negotiate with vendors by e-mail. Hoteliers who want to get the word out about their products and services are finding e-mail an inexpensive and effective way to advertise. Buggsi Patel, President and CEO of Buggsi Hospitality Group, says:

> "We still do direct mail, but we're finding e-mail to be an extremely effective use of our time and money. The Internet is changing the way properties go to market. It's the medium that everyone who is looking ahead is looking to leverage."[2]

As with other advertising, however, planning is needed before sending out e-mail messages. First, using e-mail requires building a database of qualified prospects. Second, content must be developed that will appeal to your various targeted segments. And, last but certainly not least, e-mail must be welcomed by your prospects.

Time and privacy are important to planners, and sending "spam" -- the electronic equivalent of unsolicited "junk mail" -- may drive potential customers away. Today's successful e-mail marketers are using *permission marketing* to ensure that their messages make a favorable impression. This strategy involves asking a planner's permission before sending an e-mail about your property. Most planners would welcome information to help make their jobs easier, and your property could structure its e-mail campaign to alert the planner of seasonal rate changes, special offers, or other items of interest that may make a meeting decision easier (the expansion of your meeting rooms, the addition of a gourmet chef, etc.).

E-mail advertising typically yields responses up to 15 times greater than those generated from direct mail and also has the advantage of doubling as a lead qualifying tool. Hoteliers are also seeing the value of e-mail as a new way to communicate on a regular basis. E-mail is seen as an effective way to nurture customer relations by demonstrating the hotelier's commitment to staying in touch and serving the planner's future needs.

Fax Transmissions

Fax (facsimile) transmissions are useful to provide meeting planners with up-to-date information on new products and services. Faxes provide a copy of the original document — a letter, proposal, advertisement, special announcement, etc. — and are advantageous in that they are instantaneous and that meeting planners make them a priority to read. There are two ways in which fax transmissions are commonly used: fax-on-demand and broadcast fax.

Fax-on-demand offers the latest in property information directly to a meeting planner via a special fax number. This information can be accessed at any time, even when the sales office is closed, and can be updated as required to supply the latest information.

Broadcast fax provides simultaneous transmission of information to a data base of interested or qualified prospects. Special announcements, changes in services offered, or other information can be sent to a number of planners at once.

Will technological developments, such as the Internet, e-mail, and fax transmissions (as well as the CD-ROMs we will discuss in the next section), replace personal site visits or diminish the role of the hotel salesperson? A recent study by Meeting Professionals International (MPI) and PlanSoft Corporation found that while technology is a useful tool for initial screening, it cannot replace in-person visits to investigate space for meetings. The large majority of respondents to the survey say that personal contact and building relationships are still essential to the meetings process.[3]

Collateral Materials

Collateral material is supplementary advertising pieces used along with direct mail, magazine advertising and other promotional efforts. This includes a vast array of promotional materials such as convention and rack brochures, newsletters, postcards, menus, tent cards, matchbooks and many other items.

The greatest distinction between collateral material and other advertising devices is the directness of collateral pieces. Newspaper advertising takes a shotgun approach; collateral material is more specific and is often directed right to the decision maker.

Brochures

Perhaps one of the most familiar collateral materials is the brochure. Most convention hotels use two brochures: a standard *rack brochure,* which is directed to the leisure market, and a *convention brochure.* As with other advertising, the focus of these brochures will differ widely; the rack brochure usually promotes rooms, restaurants and recreational amenities, while the convention brochure provides detailed information regarding function space, food and beverage service and convention services.

Convention Brochures. The convention brochure may be prepared in a number of ways. It can be a standard three or four-fold type, loose-leaf pages bound in an attractive cover, or presented in booklet style. Whatever style you choose, remember that it should fit in with your property's overall advertising and project your property's image. In addition, no matter what type is used, it should always contain pertinent information.

When planning your brochure, start with the assumption that your prospect has never seen or even heard of your hotel, and certainly has never been informed of its convention capability. Image yourself as a meeting organizer looking for a suitable hotel for your next event. The information you would want should be presented clearly and concisely. A

BASIC CONVENTION BROCHURE INFORMATION

Your property's convention brochure should provide all the information a meeting planner needs to make a decision on a meeting site. Effective convention brochures should include most — if not all — of the following information:

- Your property's name
- Your property's address and, when possible, an area location map detailing proximity to airports, major highways and area attractions.
- Your property's telephone number (a toll-free number encourages responses) and name of contact person, if applicable (convention services manager, convention coordinator, etc.)
- Your fax number. Fax usage is increasing rapidly
- Photographs, diagrams, or *complete* descriptions of exhibit space (dimensions, scaled drawings, floor load, ceiling height)
- Audiovisual equipment available
- Other meeting services available (teleconferences, fax service, personal computers, clerical and/or registration help, business center)
- Special services and facilities (photographic services, flowers, entertainment)
- Banquet and beverage arrangements
- Theme party arrangements
- Guestroom information (descriptions, floor plans, room block policy, reservations, rates, arrival/departure information)
- Special procedures (billing procedures, shipping and receiving procedures, signs and notices policy, etc.)
- Recreation and amenities (hotel attractions, spouse entertainment, area attractions)
- Transportation (parking facilities, shuttle service, tours, taxis, public transportation)
- Other general information (climate, dress, gratuities, the availability of room service, etc.)
- References from past conventions
- Checklists and planning guides for the meeting planner

common complaint from planners is the lack of good, accurate descriptive material from hotels.

A brochure will give the planner enough basic data for preliminary planning (see box titled "Basic Convention Brochure Information").

The larger meeting rooms should be diagrammed, if possible, or at least described adequately. "Large" is not a very accurate phrase. How many people will the grand ball-room accommodate? In what sort of setup (auditorium-style offers greater capacity than seating at round tables, for example)? A good brochure will give enough information so it can be used as a tool by meeting planners to narrow down a field of contestants for meeting functions.

One of the primary sources for ideas for preparing a convention brochure is, of course, existing pieces. Begin collecting brochures. There are some excellent ones in the field. Start a reference file of brochures you admire for one reason or another. They'll give you many ideas you may want to incorporate into your own brochure.

The best brochures show scaled outlines (blueprints) of all major rooms. One meeting planner stated,

> "I like to receive a meeting planner's kit, not general information about the hotel. I need to see a floor plan with specific seating capacities. It takes time and it's expensive for a hotelier to send out information; it should be useful."

The brochure need not be so utilitarian that it fails to present your property in a good light. A facility is not chosen merely for its ability to house the event. The beauty of the structure and surroundings, the convenience of the location, and the expertise of the staff are all important. But such data should not be included at the expense of basic facilities information. Always include your usual hotel brochure along with your convention brochure.

Design your material to enable your contact to present your case completely and favorably. Good brochures will work for you in sales presentations, mailings and trade shows, and through intermediaries such as convention bureaus, airlines and convention specialists.

Video Brochures. In addition to printed brochures, many properties produce video brochures. Video is both inexpensive and versatile, and a videotape can show a property's selling points in a way that no printed piece can (see Figure 8.6).

A video brochure can show the property at various times of the year, and is an excellent resource for the meeting planner who is unable to visit the property in person. Video brochures can show a property at its best, in a variety of setups (both meeting rooms and banquet facilities), and can also show other important selling points, such as seasonal attractions.

Most video brochures are fairly short, running four to six minutes in length, and must present the property's best points in that short time. Many properties, therefore, enlist the services of a firm that specializes in hotel video brochures before attempting to shoot one on their own. This may cost slightly more, but the benefits of the expertise of the professional firm (and high quality shooting techniques) are worth the additional time and expense. The brochure is presenting your property just when the potential buyer is researching it and therefore calls for professional expertise.

CD-ROMs. Like the video brochure, **CD-ROMs**, computer discs that can store a great amount of data (including text, pictures and sound), can be used to give meeting planners

Figure 8.6. SAMPLE HOTEL VIDEO BROCHURE.

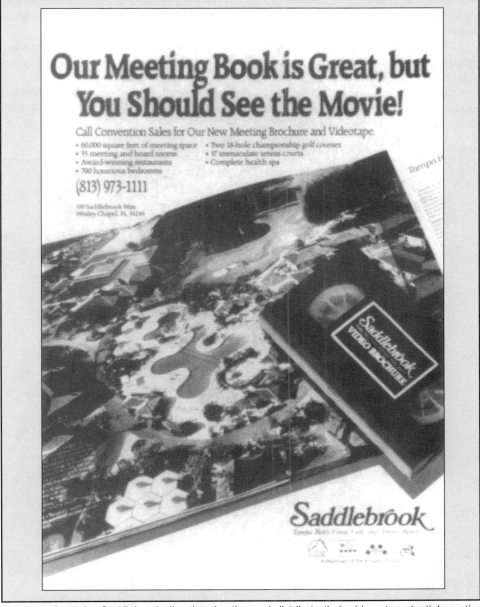

Hotels such as the Saddlebrook directly advertise and distribute their videos to potential meeting clients. Video brochures are also used for in-house presentations to meeting planners and at trade shows and conventions. Video brochures directed to meeting planners often combine live action with animated graphics of meeting room configurations.

a "tour" of the property. Often used in conjunction with Internet advertising, CD-ROMs can be sent to meeting planners for use on their own personal computers for a "virtual" look at a property or area. According to the 2000 Meetings Market Study, 23 percent of meeting planners used a CD-ROM for meeting planning purposes.

CD-ROMs offer several advantages over video brochures. First is their format: CD-ROMs typically offer 650 million characters — or approximately 160,000 pages of text);

they are durable (with a shelf life of approximately 100 years); cannot be erased by magnetic fields; and they can be easily and inexpensively reproduced and mailed. In addition, a growing number of meeting planners utilize personal computers, and most of these computers are equipped to use CD-ROMs.

In many cases, CD-ROM presentations are duplicates of those on Internet web sites, greatly reducing the cost of production. And, CD-ROMs can be used on a personal computer even if a meeting planner does not have access to the Internet.

CD-ROMs are currently in use by a number of properties and Convention and Visitors Bureaus, including those in San Antonio, TX, and Santa Clara, CA (see Figure 8.7). Radisson Hotels distributed CD-ROMs that include a directory of Radisson properties,

Figure 8.7. "VIRTUAL" SANTA CLARA ON CD-ROM.

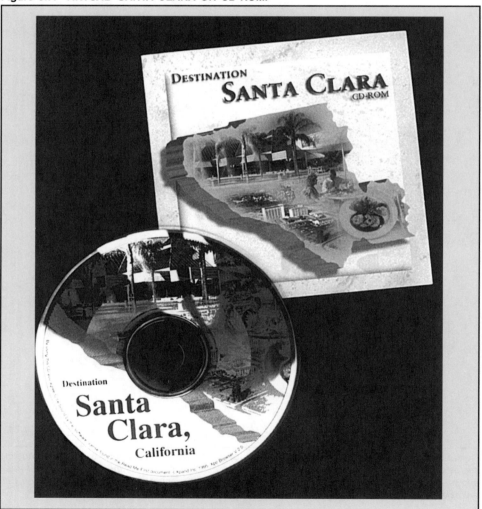

One of the first on-line site inspections designed for meeting planners, Destination Santa Clara *is available on the Web and on CD-ROM. The virtual presentation was developed by the Santa Clara (CA) Convention & Visitors Bureau to provide meeting planners with interactive information on the city's meeting facilities. The CD-ROM version is available in three formats: fact sheets (electronic brochures complete with pictures), overviews presented in two-minute "infomercials," and a "virtual walk-through." Vaughn Ball, director of sales and marketing for the CVB, says: "Because we are located in Silicon Valley and making an effort to target high-tech groups, it's essential that we use technology to reach our market both nationally and internationally."*

including floor plans of all the chain's hotels, to meeting planners in addition to its Internet directory. And, Sheraton is adapting its Meeting Facilities Guide to CD-ROM. According to Kay Heder, director of corporate sales, North America, "It will allow the user to virtually go into a hotel and browse" (eliminating any concern over the location of ballroom pillars, etc.).

As with other types of advertising, CD-ROM presentations should project the desired image for your property and should meet the needs of meeting planners by offering pertinent information. The detailed floorplans mentioned above are an excellent selling point, as are interviews with key convention services personnel, a "tour" of the property (preferably when there are groups in-house), testimonials by satisfied clients, and so on. Many properties opt for professional assistance when creating their first CD-ROM, especially if it will be used in conjunction with an Internet marketing program.

Other Collateral Materials

In addition to brochures, collateral materials may include such diverse pieces as postcards, fliers, maps, menus, tent cards and newsletters (see Figure 8.8). These materials not only serve to keep your property's name and its features in the prospects' minds, but also can be used by salespeople to enhance their sales presentations.

As with brochures, all pieces used should be carefully planned and integrated into the property's overall marketing and advertising strategy. All pieces should be attractively designed and, as in print advertising, list the benefits offered by your property as well as its features. And, most importantly, printed collateral materials should be targeted to the conventions market (separate newsletters should be developed for the meetings market and the leisure travel segment, for example).

Specialty Items

Collateral materials also include **specialty items** (sometimes called **premiums**) that are marked with the property's name and toll-free number. These may include such inexpensive items as matchbooks or keychains, or "signature" items, such as glassware, plush toys, or sportswear featuring the property's logo.

Chain properties have the advantage of ordering specialty items from the chain's catalog at greatly discounted rates. But even small properties can take advantage of this advertising tool — which, according to the Specialty Advertising Association (SAA), boasts a recall factor of up to 40 percent even after six months. It is fairly easy to find suppliers of specialty items, and costs can be kept down by ordering in quantity and staying with the same imprint.

Select items that reflect the image of your property, not necessarily the cheapest. It is far more cost-effective to choose items that a meeting planner will probably use (keeping your property's name constantly in his or her mind), such as a desk calendar or a coffee mug.

Direct Mail Advertising

Another popular tool in the promotion person's kit is **direct mail advertising**. Direct mail can be used to screen prospects (see Figure 8.9), to follow up on advertising leads, and to make a printed sales presentation in great detail to many prospects at once — at far less a

Figure 8.8. SAMPLE PROPERTY NEWSLETTER.

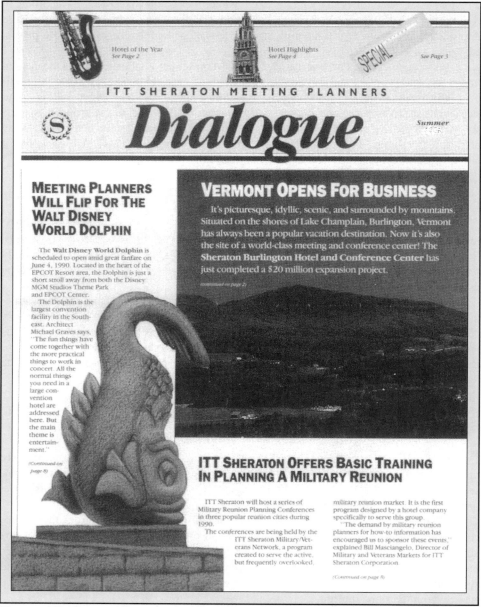

The newsletter is an excellent — and relatively inexpensive — way to convey property information to meeting planners. Newsletters may be produced at the property level or as part of a chain's effort to introduce its properties to meeting planners. Newsletters typically contain such features as property statistics, articles and/or photographs of successfully staged events, personnel profiles, special offers, and general meeting information. Newsletters are typically used in convention kits, enclosed with sales letters, or used in direct mail campaigns.

cost than for print or broadcast advertising. Direct mail preselects the client and reaches him or her personally and privately. No other media can do this as effectively.

Unfortunately, there are also disadvantages to direct mail. The cost of direct mail efforts has increased over the years, especially due to increasing postal rates. Another

Figure 8.9. SAMPLE DIRECT MAIL SURVEY.

mount airy lodge

Mount Pocono, Pennsylvania 18344
Telephone: 717-839-8811

FREE DIRECT LINES
New York City: 212-966-7210
212-226-0841
Philadelphia Area: 215-561-5650

DIRECT TOLL FREE NUMBERS
From Eastern Pa. (Area Codes 215 & 717)
1-800-532-8271
From N.Y., N.J., Md., Del.
1-800-233-8116

GROUP & CONVENTION FORM

In order that we may up date our files and supply you with accurate information, we would appreciate your completing this form and returning it in the self addressed envelope. Thank you.

1. Name of Organization:_____

   Your Name:_____Phone Number_____

   Address:_____City:_____State:_____Zip:_____

2. Are you planning any function? ( ) yes   ( )no

3. Would you be interested in Mount Airy Lodge? ( ) yes ( ) no

4. If yes, for what function: ( ) Convention   ( ) Seminar

                             ( ) Incentive Program ( ) Social Outing

                             ( ) Board Meeting   ( ) Conference

Month:_____Days of Week:_____Year:_____Any Specific Dates:_____

Number of Persons:_____Number of Rooms:_____

5. Have you ever held a function in the Poconos? ( ) yes ( ) no

6. Are there any reasons why you cannot hold a function in the Poconos?

   ( ) yes ( ) no If yes, please state reason_____

7. Do you have a copy of our full color 24 page convention brochure?

   ( ) yes ( ) no If no, would you like one? ( ) yes ( ) no

8. What do you look for in a convention site?_____

   _____

9. What convention publications do you read?_____

   _____

10. If you can supply any additional information regarding your

    requirements, it would be greatly appreciated:_____

    _____

    _____

In addition to promoting a property, direct mail can be used to solicit information and qualify leads. Surveys such as this one are an invaluable resource for obtaining "hot leads" — prospects with a definite interest in the property — and provide salespeople with client information that can be used in a follow-up letter or sales call.

disadvantage of direct mail is that pieces frequently end up in the wastebasket. An efficient program that will overcome these difficulties, however, can be produced at almost any budget level.

One factor in the success or failure of direct mail is ensuring that you are advertising directly to your target market. Whom are you trying to reach? If your objective is to increase your convention market share by 10 percent, then direct mail should be directed to

WRITING EFFECTIVE SALES LETTERS

Effective letter writing is a skill than can be developed. Here are a few fundamental techniques that should be used:

- Use the correct titles of hotel personnel and the person with whom you are dealing.
- Be informative but brief. Stick to the facts.
- Be yourself; write like you speak. Write as if the client were with you in the office.
- Emphasize key points by underlining them or using bold-faced lettering.
- *Always ask for the sale* — and provide a means for the client to respond (a reply card, toll-free number, etc.)

Keep in mind that you should always write in the client's language; avoid the use of hotel terms that may confuse or mislead. Don't give the sales copy second billing in direct mail pieces. Be specific, and make your correspondence meaningful and convincing.

meeting planners, not travel agents. Therefore, a direct mail campaign is only as good as the mailing list used. If your hotel does not have a mailing list, start one immediately. Begin by compiling a list of people who have met in your hotel in the past. Keep in mind that we are a mobile business society and lists must be updated frequently. Expect many returns and changes of names and addresses after each mailing, and remember to budget for postage due on returned pieces. It is vital to delete the undeliverables and note the changes of addresses on your list so that expensive printing and postage are not wasted in subsequent mailings.

As we have discussed, there are also several directories and a number of publications that supply the names, addresses and phone numbers of most association, corporation, incentive, fraternal and other meeting planners. It is also possible to rent names from the circulation lists of suitable magazines.

Convention bureau notices from past years can also be a source of prospects for your mailing list, since major city-wide conventions are channeled through the bureau. Groups that have met in years past may hold smaller meetings that you may be able to attract. The convention bureau list might also show some groups have a repeat pattern for the city. These groups should be given a high priority in your sales campaign.

It is a good policy to develop two lists: a *general* one of all prospects you feel reasonably sure are relevant and a *preferred* list of screened prospects and past customers. You will probably mail more frequently to the second list than to the first.

Before sending any mailings, you should also decide on a follow-up method. Ideally, your direct mail efforts will give you a list of "hot" leads to follow up. The list of new leads generated through direct mail will be wasted if these prospects are not attended to promptly. You may wish to have follow up literature readily available, or forward responses directly to your salespeople for an immediate personal contact.

Direct mail, only one part of a hotel's total advertising effort, should be carefully planned for maximum results. The direct mail campaign must be integrated into the hotel's overall sales objectives, and mail pieces should blend with the property's other media advertising.

Some of the most commonly used direct mail pieces include sales letters, surveys and postcards, but more creative and elaborate visual aids may also be used (see Figure 8.10).

When deciding what types of materials would be most effective to use, several factors must be considered such as the purpose of the mailing, its scope and the costs involved.

Figure 8.10. DIRECT MAIL "NOVELTIES".

Direct mail sometimes includes novelties or gifts to stimulate interest. A series of three novelty mailings were used to introduce the Registry Hotel at the Minneapolis/St. Paul airport. The items — a rubber sandwich, a baseball and glove, and a balsa wood airplane — were keyed to fliers stressing the hotel's proximity to the airport and a sports center. The campaign won a first-place award in the HSMAI's annual advertising contest.

Sales letters are the meat of any direct mailing. Their function is to convince and to sell. Time does not permit a salesperson to make personal calls on every prospect, so the message must be communicated through the written word.

It is effective to use well-written personal letters, with convention brochures as enclosures. Seemingly personal, individually typed letters can be produced using your in-house word processing system or local letter shop services. If you want to create more ambitious direct mail programs, use your advertising agency or local creative services to produce the mailing pieces. But don't underestimate the power of personal letters addressed to a person by name. The high cost of brochures and postage make it advisable to polish your techniques (see box titled "Writing Effective Sales Letters").

Many properties find that a number of mailings must be used to achieve best results. A one-time mailing is not too effective unless it is a birthday or holiday greeting or an answer to an inquiry. Direct mail *campaigns*, then, should be a part of your direct mail efforts.

When using more than one mailing, the frequency, as well as the content, is important. There is no hard and fast rule, but the maximum interval between mailings is considered to be about two months. Obviously, multiple mailings must never be the same. The first letter must be an attention-getter. Its content must be appealing and retain the reader's interest. Future mailings should be built around the theme presented in the first one, but the information and point of the letters should be different. In some cases, you may want to build on each letter sent. The point of your message may be the same, but the content should be stated differently and creatively or the reader's interest is sure to wane (see Figure 8.11).

Figure 8.11. SAMPLE DIRECT MAIL SERIES.

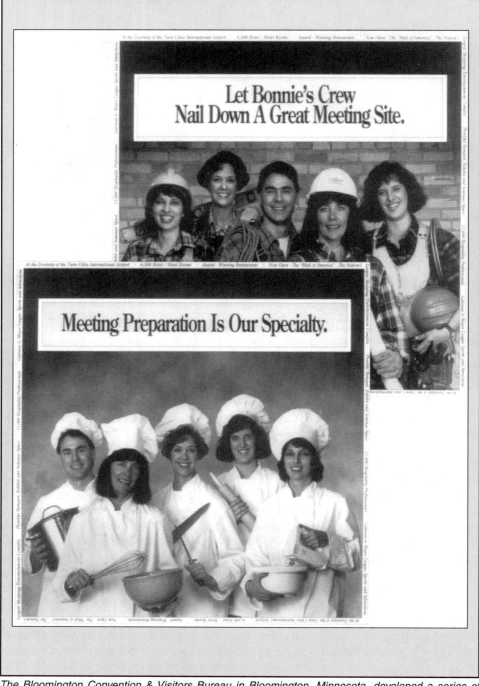

The Bloomington Convention & Visitors Bureau in Bloomington, Minnesota, developed a series of mailings to introduce its Executive Director, Bonnie Carlson, and her staff to meeting planners. Each mailing in the series featured people who would actually help planners in staging their functions, creating an atmosphere of familiarity and trust long before the function was held. Each three-fold mailing had an illustration, a copy panel and a tear-off reply card. This type of series reinforces your property's message in the minds of meeting planners. If done correctly, planners will actually look forward to additional mailings.

Direct Mail Marketing

Carolyn Hamilton-Proctor
President
Graphic Communications, Las Vegas NV

"Direct mail is a powerful weapon in your sales arsenal. Studies show repeatedly that the direct mail package outpulls any other printed format. Properly used, direct marketing will make your marketing plan more targeted — and more profitable.

Direct mail makes advertising accountable. Direct mail to meeting planners does not replace journal or directory advertising, rather it complements them. Proper integration of general advertising and direct mail will have a synergistic effect on your profits.

A solid list of names and current addresses of your guests is worth its weight in gold. Direct mail requires the maintenance of a guest database which includes both demographic and psychographic profiles of your guests. The more specific the guest profile in your database, the more successful your direct mail campaigns can be. Compiled lists that match your guest profile, rented from outside sources, will yield respondents who also can be added to your existing database. Increasing and updating your in-house guest database is an ongoing process."

Planning an Advertising Strategy

As you can see, there are a number of ways to reach meeting planners, and you must develop a strategy that will work best for your property (see box titled "Selling Sheratons to the Meetings Market"). Developing such a strategy, of course, means working within the marketing plan — and budget — established for your property, and structuring your efforts accordingly.

Some of the factors you will want to consider in devising your strategy include whom you wish to target, what media you will use, and how much money you can spend. Many properties prepare a media chart (see Figure 8.12) to plan advertising placement and expenditures over the course of a year. Annual planning is much more effective than last-minute, haphazard efforts. When you plan on an annual basis, keep in mind that you can schedule your advertising expenditures to match your property's fiscal or budget year. Publications compute frequency discounts on a consecutive twelve month period. You can, if it suits your purpose, schedule your advertising from March 2002 through February 2003, for example. Also, it is helpful, if you can manage it, to set aside a sum for special situations that crop up during the year.

Reach, Frequency, Timing and Consistency

When planning your advertising strategy, four key factors should be taken into consideration: reach, frequency, timing and consistency.

Reach refers to the number of different individuals who are exposed to your message during a specific period. This, of course, is determined by the media you select. When

Figure 8.12. SAMPLE HOTEL MEDIA CHART.

Client number: BM100-3   MEDIA SCHEDULE 01/01/01 THRU 12/31/02
Media: MEETINGS

Publications	January	February	March	April	May
Association Management Pub Number Issued Circulation AS700-6A Monthly 21,120 96 Rates 15th of 2nd Month Publication Total $8,372.50				Page 4/C $4,186.00 Or Pg 4C	
Business Travel News Pub Number Issued Circulation BTN15-8A Bi-Weekly 51,046 Jr Pg or 1/2SPD 3 Weeks Prior Publication Total $34,000.00			Jr Pg 4/C $6,800.00 Mtgs Today 22 +BRC	Jr Pg 4/C $6,800.00 Mtgs Tday 19	Jr P4\C $6,800.00 Mtgs Tday 10 +BRC
Corporate & Incentive Travel Pub Number Issued Circulation C0605-6A Monthly 49,698 One Month Prior Publication Total $4,764.00		Page 4/C $4,764.00 DSTNTN Colorado			
Executive Memo **Colorado Soc. Of Assn Executives** Pub Number Issued Circulation COSAE-6A Monthly 250 One Month Publication Total $12,605.50				Page BW $500.00	
Executive Update - GWSAE Pub Number Issued Circulation EU478-6A Monthly 9,000 33% DSCNT Publication Total $12,605.50					Page 4/C $3,740.00 SPGNTME PK
Forum (CSAE) Pub Number Issued Circulation For 10-9 11X/Yr ½ SPD or Pg 6 weeks Prior Publication Total $6,262.37				Page 4/C $1,789.25	
Incentive Pub Number Issued Circulation IN150-6A Monthly 40,281 15th, 2 Months Prior Publication Total $39,467.80				Page 4/C $4,911.30 +BRC	Page 4/C $4,911.30
Insurance Conference Planner Pub Number Issued Circulation IN500-6A Bi-Monthly 7,451 1st of Month Preceding					Page 4/C $2,622.25 Incentive

All listed rates are based on applicable rate card as of the date of preparation and are subject to change.

In order to plan an effective advertising strategy, many properties prepare an annual media chart that lists such data as name and type of publication to be used, size of ad (or length of spot), and advertising expenditures, both for production and space costs. This approach provides an at-a-glance overview of the property's advertising, controls budget commitment, and can also be used to measure the effectiveness of advertising. This sample shows data from January- May; a complete chart would extend through December.

targeting the conventions market, for example, you are focusing on a smaller number of specific prospects than if you were targeting the transient market. You should select the media that will be most effective in reaching them (a specialized trade journal, for example) rather than opting for indiscriminate media (a television spot). You are interested in how many potential customers you can reach for each dollar spent.

Frequency refers to the number of times your target audience sees or hears your message. As with sales, advertising is rarely effective on a "one-shot" basis; it is usually necessary to expose your prospects to your message on a frequent basis — and often in a number of ways, such as the combination of trade journal advertisements and direct mail efforts. It is beneficial to expose your prospect to your message a number of times.

Timing, then, is an important factor. Some properties prefer to advertise or send out mailings on a *continuing* basis, timing their advertising to appear once a month, for example. There are times, however, when you can take advantage of a *pulsing* approach. Pulsing is used to promote business over slow periods. A property, for example, may wish to

---

SELLING SHERATONS TO THE MEETINGS MARKET

When the Sheraton Corporation sought to position itself to attract meeting planners, it went directly to the source, conducting extensive research with clients to learn what was important to them and what was needed to help make their job easier. The result was the Sheraton Master Plan for Meeting Planners, which responded to the meeting planners' request for more information to ensure professionalism in the industry.

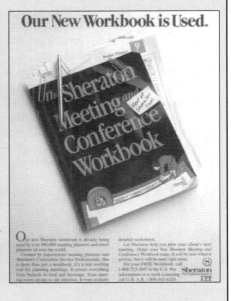

The Sheraton/PCMA Showcase I is a program for new meeting planners (and serves as a refresher course for full-time professionals). These workshops cover the basics of meeting planning, including site selection, working with properties, room setup, food and beverage planning, etc.

The Sheraton/PCMA Showcase II is more comprehensive, exploring new trends in the industry, and offers in-depth information on subjects such as negotiations, contracts and liability, meeting specification preparation, and program design, among others. Like Showcase I, it is offered free to meeting planners, along with a complimentary continental breakfast and lunch.

In addition to these workshops, Sheraton developed a comprehensive free meeting planning manual. The manual plays an important part in the chain's advertising, showing its willingness to assist meeting planners and its commitment to successful meetings.

To further enhance its professionalism, Sheraton also launched the industry's most comprehensive training program for its own Convention and Conference Services Managers — a strategy that has generated tremendous interest within the industry and adds credibility to the chain's advertising, which positions the Sheratons as both dedicated to maintaining high standards of professionalism and being "meeting planner friendly."

MAKING THE MOST OF EXCHANGE TRADE ADVERTISING

Exchange trade advertising can be a viable advertising tool if it is used properly. Bob Stein, a senior vice-president of an advertising agency and author of <u>Marketing in Action for Hotels/Motels/Restaurants</u>, offers these recommendations for negotiating exchange trade agreements:

1. Consider some variations on the "one-for-one" arrangement, especially when the publication or station approaches you. You could receive $1.50 or $2.00 of advertising for every dollar of hotel facilities, especially if food and/or beverage are included in the arrangement. When such is the case, point out that food and beverage represent an out-of-pocket cost to you, whereas available publication space or radio and TV time ordinarily do not.
2. Consider these limitations, all of which mean money in your pocket: For commercial hotels and motels, (a) rooms only, and then only during periods when you don't expect to be at capacity, or (b) food only, rather than food and beverage. For A.P. (American Plan) or M.A.P. (Modified American Plan) resorts, the room portion only.
3. Bring your advertising agency into the picture and require the publication or station to pay the customary 15 percent commission. Your ad agency will undoubtedly handle the placement of the advertising, and if it receives the commission, you will not be required to pay it.
4. Include as a condition of your reciprocal deal that your facilities are limited to use by certain individuals (publisher, station manager, key executives, employees), and secure in advance a list of those persons.

Reprinted courtesy of *Lodging Hospitality Magazine*, a Penton/IPC publication.

---

offer special rates during its valley periods of early fall and midwinter, and would advertise over a predetermined time prior to these periods. Similarly, *flighting* (advertising only when managers feel it necessary, with no regular pattern) can be used when it is necessary to promote special packages or events. Perhaps the area will be host to a local festival or special event; advertising can promote the property's participation or proximity to the action.

Most convention publications run special editorial sections throughout the year dealing with meetings in certain geographic areas, such as a city or state, or specific types of properties, including golf resorts, airport hotels, conference centers, etc. Editors and publishers will usually supply the schedule of such features for the full year. When you plan your advertising, you might be able to take advantage of such targeted sections by placing your ad in them while still maintaining your objectives in timing and frequency. There are additional advantages to appearing in editorial sections describing your specific area.

No matter what approach is used for timing, **consistency** in advertising is vital. Your advertising must develop distinguishing characteristics — a logo, special colors or design, etc. —to stand out from the rest. Your prospects should be able to identify your property's ad at first glance.

Since the purpose of your advertising is to become known and patronized, your advertising strategy should also include a program of follow up and monitoring and evaluation. *Follow up* is extremely important, especially in the conventions and meetings market. Most planners are "comparison shopping" and if they have responded to your ad or mailing it is likely they have responded to others. Your prompt handling of an inquiry will demonstrate your commitment to provide efficient service.

Inquiries should be followed up with a personal letter and information that was requested at the very least. Whenever possible, especially if the respondent has included his or her telephone number, make a personal call of thanks and request an appointment. This can lead to an immediate sale.

To develop the most cost-effective program, however, you must carefully *monitor and evaluate* your program periodically. Determine which ads or direct mail pieces seem to attract the most interest; check to see which publications are generating the most leads; and monitor the number of conversions from inquiries. And, take steps to determine the actual cost per conversion from each type of inquiry. If your ad series is costing $35,000, for example, but you have only generated $15,000 in business, take another look at your ad program.

Exchange Trade Advertising

To cut advertising costs, many properties have looked for alternatives, such as trading out goods and services or sharing advertising expenditures. **Exchange trade advertising** is an arrangement in which the hotel exchanges its services (rooms, food, beverage, use of recreational amenities, etc.) for advertising (newspaper, magazine, outdoor space, radio and television spots). Such arrangements are also referred to as *reciprocal advertising* and *trade-out advertising,* and can be very worthwhile as long as the hotel fully understands the procedure. It is important to realize that exchange trade advertising is not free; there is a cost to the hotel, and this cost must be budgeted, just as print advertising costs are. And, whether you are paying cash or exchanging services, your hotel's advertising efforts must be directed to your target markets. If you are trying to build group meeting business, for example, a trade exchange with a billboard specialist would not be the wisest use of your money.

Exchange trade advertising does offer some real advantages to a convention hotel, and its possibilities should be investigated. As with any advertising strategy, there are factors that should be considered and guidelines to follow in order to utilize this type of arrangement for your maximum benefit (see box titled "Making the Most of Exchange Trade Advertising").

The use of exchange trade advertising does require increased record keeping, but it also affords yet another benefit — the opportunity to build relationships with media firms. A friend in the media can be a real asset when it comes to editorials and publicity about your hotel (and, the hotel is in a position to extend extra courtesies to the media's important clients). In the final analysis, exchange trade advertising can be mutually beneficial if a fair arrangement is negotiated.

Cooperative Advertising and Strategic Partnerships

Cooperative advertising also provides an additional way to save on advertising costs. In a cooperative arrangement, several properties — or a property and several related entities, such as a convention and visitors bureau, an airline or car rental company or local area attractions — advertise together to both save on costs and maximize results.

Cooperative advertising can be used as either a "one shot" promotion, or, as is done more commonly, in an advertising campaign that promotes the services and attractions available in an area. This type of advertising provides meeting planners with more information, and options, and can also prove beneficial to your property. If your property has limited meeting facilities, for example, you can advertise with a full service meeting hotel, offering your rooms to accommodate meeting overflow.

Strategic partnerships are another form of cooperative agreement. These alliances are relationships between independent parties that agree to cooperate in advertising but still maintain their separate identities. A common example is several hotels combining

Figure 8.13. SAMPLE COOPERATIVE ADVERTISING.

Cooperative advertising provides the opportunity for two or more properties and/or related services to share advertising space and costs. In this example, ten hotels at Knoxville's airport and the Smoky Mountain Visitors Bureau have teamed up to promote a number of features, including their ability to host meetings and their convenience to area transportation and attractions, from shopping to the Great Smoky Mountains National Park.

forces with each other (and often the city's CVB and/or other attractions) to offer a "one-stop shopping" alternative to compete with larger cities (see Figure 8.13).

Susan Henrique is director of sales and marketing for Coastal Fairfield County, Connecticut, which is located near New York City. In 1999, her CVB as well as those in Arlington, Virginia (near Washington, DC), Prospect Heights, Illinois (near Chicago), and Irving,

Texas (near Dallas), formed an "Edge City Alliance" to promote themselves to meeting planners. She says:

> "In an ever-changing economy, meeting planners seek affordable alternatives for their meetings. The program illustrates that there are alternatives, which include accessibility and benefits of the larger destination cities without the bigger price tag. We all need help for weekend occupancy and have similar budgets for meetings marketing. The real key is that we are all on the outside looking at a first-tier city."[4]

Members of the alliance see their consolidated efforts as a way to bring their resources to the notice of meeting planners who might not have considered alternatives just across big-city borders. Their strategic partnership also allows individual participants to stretch their advertising dollars; with their participation in the "Edge City Alliance," each property and CVB can get maximum exposure at less cost, enabling them to save money for their own promotional efforts to their other targeted market segments.

Advertising Agencies

A hotel that has its own advertising department should make special efforts to develop material and advertising dealing solely with the convention market. In smaller properties, the sales manager may be his or her own advertising manager. At larger properties, a full creative and production department may be employed.

Such efforts may be supplemented by an outside advertising agency. A properly selected — and properly utilized — agency adds skilled specialists to the work force of any advertising department. Even smaller hotels can afford an arrangement with smaller ad agencies (it is difficult to work without one, in fact). Advertising agencies are not a substitute for your own sales efforts, but they have the skills and the resources to back up the sales department with the required promotional material.

What services can you expect from an agency? That depends on the type of agency. *Full service agencies* are appropriately named; they provide a full range of services, from creative design to the production of materials to the media placement of completed ads and spots. Many also offer research and assistance in planning campaigns — and offer the benefit of having branch offices across the country. The agency's commission — 15 percent — is usually paid by the media in which the ad or spot is placed; the property pays for print space or air time and production costs.

A la carte agencies, also called *modular services* and *creative shops*, are usually smaller in scope than full-service agencies and work on a negotiated fee basis. These agencies are often used for one-time advertising assignments, such as an ad or brochure production or in the placement of an advertisement. Payment, therefore, is on a per-job basis.

Media-buying services buy space for submitted promotional materials. These services do not usually produce materials, but can be helpful in placing advertising created by the property's in-house advertising department.

Many convention hotels have found it advantageous to use advertising agencies, but it is extremely important that when a hotel uses an advertising agency both are in agreement as to the direction of the advertising campaign. Naturally, a hotel is more familiar with its strengths than the outside agency. The hotel must communicate its positioning and goals to its agency representative to ensure that the advertising creates the image a property

Figure 8.14. HOW TO WRITE A PRESS RELEASE.

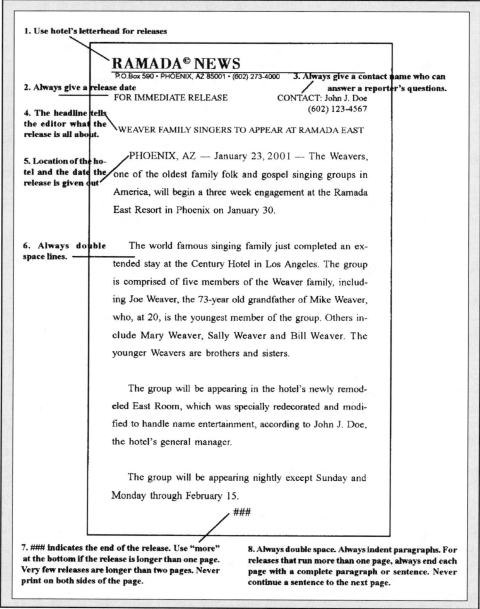

Press releases are used to inform the media of special events, property and personnel changes, and property involvement in community affairs. The press release should always be double-spaced and contain pertinent, newsworthy information. Today, press releases commonly include the fax number and e-mail address of the property's contact person in addition to his or her telephone number .

wishes to project and is aimed at its target market(s). To ensure that the property and the agency can work well together, it is important to select an agency carefully (see box titled "Selecting an Advertising Agency"). A properly functioning agency offers you an experienced and objective view of your property's promotional efforts.

SELECTING AN ADVERTISING AGENCY

Before you select an advertising agency, you should evaluate your property's needs. Will you need full services or just assistance in placing your own promotional material? How would an advertising agency be utilized — as a supplement to your in-house advertising department, occasionally as needed for research or production, as an extension of your advertising and sales effort? How much can you afford to spend on outside services?

Once you have established guidelines, informal meetings should be held with representatives of agencies of interest to you. Each representative should provide the answers to the following questions:

1. How long has the agency been in business? Does it have a proven track record in the hospitality industry?
2. Does the agency represent competitors? If so, how will this affect the handling of your account?
3. What services can the agency provide? Does it offer full creative services? market research? media placement?
4. Who will be assigned to your account? How much time can he or she spend learning about your property and its needs? In the event "your" account person is not available, who will be assigned to handle your account?
5. How will costs be handled? Is the agency willing to work within the property's budget?

Public Relations and Publicity

While advertising is a powerful method of reaching target markets, you can do more to keep your hotel's name before your potential customers. Advertising coupled with public relations and publicity can form a stronger combination to reach planners.

Public relations is a broad term that encompasses a number of methods of communicating favorable information about a property. Its purpose is to create a positive image about the property. Loews Hotels, for example, began a model program -- and won an award -- with its Good Neighbor Policy. This community outreach program seeks to address a number of concerns, such as homelessness, illiteracy, and environmental preservation, and mobilizes not only the chain's properties but meeting planners as well. The hotel's contracts include an offer for meeting planners to donate surplus products and materials to a local charity. Donations have ranged from clothing to items from food shows to basic supplies (poster board, masking tape, etc.) that are donated to area preschools.

As with advertising, a good public relations plan must be developed — and people trained to implement it. While every employee — from general manager to front desk personnel to a valet attendant — plays a role in developing and maintaining a positive image for the property, it is essential that a professional public relations person or staff be employed to oversee the property's efforts in this important area. Small properties may employ one person or work with an outside public relations firm. Large properties may also utilize an outside public relations firm or engage a multi-talented public relations staff. In either case, public relations people or firms will be called upon to perform a variety of duties: acting as the property's spokesperson, contacting the media about the property, maintaining contacts with past guests, and so on.

One of the public relations staff's most important responsibilities is dealing with the media to obtain favorable publicity for the property. *Publicity* is the gratuitous mention of your hotel in newspapers, magazines and over the airwaves. When you advertise, you pay for space or air time and control what is said about your hotel and its services. Many readers or listeners may be apprehensive about whether you can or will deliver on your promises. Publicity, however, which comes from an impartial third party, lends credibility to a property.

In the hospitality industry, there are many opportunities to generate good news that is of interest to meeting planners. Some of it just happens — a celebrity stays at the property, the property wins a prestigious award, a trade magazine does a story on a particular area, and so on. Much of it, however, is created — the hotel sponsors a festival or creates innovative theme parties. Or, the property can get its name in the news through its expansion and renovation programs or the involvement of its staff members in community affairs.

Meetings magazines — one of your best resources for reaching meeting planners — are always interested in stories of interest to meeting planners. Innovative meeting techniques, reports on new methods used to service successful meetings, renovations programs that will impact the meetings industry (the opening of additional facilities, etc.) and personnel changes are all of interest. "Meeting Calendars" listing hotels that are hosting major meetings are also published; these are excellent vehicles for a free listing for your property. Make a strong effort to get photographs of meetings in progress at your property. Meetings magazines are always looking for such illustrations. In addition, the organization sponsoring the meeting may use your photographs in their own publicity efforts, giving you additional exposure at the same time. It is not by accident that hotel lecterns carry the hotel's logo prominently across the front panel so that all photos of the speaker show the logo as well.

Trade magazines, such as those listed in earlier chapters, are spearheaded by an editor who makes the decisions about the subjects of articles and when they will run. They also have a managing editor who coordinates the makeup of the magazine. These people should be on your mailing list to receive publicity materials (press releases, newsletters, personal letters and invitations, etc.), as should editors of major newspapers in your property's target markets. The news generated about your property must meet their requirements of editorial interest, timeliness and accuracy to be considered for publication.

There are two basic ways to communicate your property information to the media: finished pieces and press releases. Some properties employ staff writers to write articles and features for submission to trade magazines and newspapers. If you want to improve your chances of having such articles accepted for publication, you should study the publication to emulate their editorial style. Also, an editor is more inclined to accept a story if the thrust of the story is on the meeting that was held, with the property getting its publicity with some subtlety through photographs and mentions of the meeting site.

Almost all properties send out *press releases* about events of importance (see Figure 8.14). Press releases are usually printed on stationery with the property's logo and name, address and telephone number, and include basic information (time, place and other pertinent details) and the name of a property contact person. Press releases should always be sent well in advance of a deadline, but it is important to note that there is no guarantee that your material will be featured — or that it will be presented as written. You are not paying for space and you have no control over editorial content or its presentation.

It is important, then, to plan your press releases to ensure the maximum coverage possible. Since your press releases will be aimed at meeting planners, consider those events and personnel changes most likely to get them thinking about your property. The development of a state-of-the-art audiovisual system, for example, is of interest and is likely to make it to trade magazines. As is news of expansions (again, think how you can best word your release to appeal to the meeting planner — present a benefit in your copy), personnel changes (especially if the staff member is well-known in the meetings field), and special events held by your property — your innovative execution of an elaborate function will appeal to other meeting planners.

Since your submissions will result in additional interest — and require a prompt response — it is advisable to have follow up information readily available. In addition to promotional material to send to respondents, most properties with a planned public relations and publicity strategy prepare a **press kit** to both introduce the property to the news media and to provide back-up information. Press kits generally feature a property information sheet, the property's brochures, biographies of key personnel, and, when available, previous press clippings. Press kits should be updated as necessary and targeted for your property's market segments; a press kit for meetings magazines, for example, would contain different material than a press kit directed to travel writers.

In today's high-tech world, the computer is also being used to get the word out about a property. In January 1999, the Walt Disney World Swan and Dolphin hotels launched a new "media only" website to provide journalists with immediate access to press releases, photographs, logos, hotel specifications, dining and entertainment options, and other information on-line. Information is continually updated, and the site is "user friendly," enabling writers to cut and paste a press release (or a portion of it) directly into the writer's document. Other methods of contacting the press include "breaking news" features; e-mails sent to a database of journalists that have requested to be contacted in the event of a newsworthy event. These options are usually less expensive than sending traditional press releases and preparing press kits, but can be just as effective if the effort is carefully planned and targeted.

A good public relations and publicity plan does not just seek to get your property's name in the media. To be effective, the plan should be integrated into the overall hotel marketing strategy, targeted toward specific market segments, and scheduled to coincide with the property's slow periods. It should be planned to not only showcase your property to best advantage, but also to show its commitment to its customers through hiring the most capable staff, offering first-class facilities and getting involved in the community in which it is located.

Chapter Summary:

As you can see, a good advertising strategy coupled with a carefully planned public relations and publicity plan can greatly enhance the sales effort and actually "pre-sell" the property by creating awareness and a positive image in the meeting planner's mind. These tools can help the salesperson to close a sale and begin the second phase of his or her job — helping to coordinate the meeting planner's function. In the next chapter, we will take a look at what happens after a meeting planner commits to a property. We will discuss how negotiating skills and contracts can help to forge long-term business relations in the lucrative meetings market segment.

Endnotes:

1. Anne Dimon, "Are You E-Planning Savvy?," *Meetings and Incentives*, June 2000, p. 24.
2. Marty Whitford, "You've Got Mail," *H&MM*, August 14, 2000, p. 34.
3. Lauren Shababb, "In-Person Inspections, Please," *Successful Meetings*, August 2000, p. 14.
4. Ruth A. Hill, "A United Front," *Lodging*, December 1999, pp. 27-28.

Additional References:

- Event Web Newsletter, Doug Fox, Publisher and Editor.
  www.eventweb.com

- Editor and Publisher, Database of media contacts. Includes Web site links.
  www.mediainfo.com

- Hospitality Sales and Advertising, James R. Abbey, Educational Institute, AHLA, 1998.
  www.ei-ahla.org

Internet Sites:

For additional information on the firms and organizations discussed in this chapter, visit the following Internet sites. The Web addresses listed are current as of January 2001. Addresses may change, however; if a site is not available at address below, a search engine can be used to access its new location.

The following websites provide meeting site services that allow hotels to post availability and property descriptions for meeting planners. The companies listed earn subscription (listing) and transaction (commission) fees from participating hotels.

Allmeetings - www.allmeetings.com
EventSource - www.eventsource.com
Hot Dates Hot Rates - www.hotdateshotrates.com
Meeting Path - www.meetingpath.com
PlanSoft - www.plansoft.com

The following websites have been developed by hotel chains to specifically reach meeting planners.

Hilton Hotels - www.hilton.com
Site offers online hotel directory that features group value dates and floor plans.

Hyatt's Meeting Planning Index - www.hyatt.com
Site contains a facilities guide and meeting services and planning information.

Marriott - www.marriott.com
Site offers a hotel search of Marriott convention hotels

 ## Study Questions:

1. What is print advertising? What elements should always be included in print ads? Where can print ads be placed to effectively reach meeting planners?
2. Why is the convention brochure an important sales tool for the meetings market? What information should be included in a convention brochure?
3. Why is direct mail an effective tool for reaching meeting planners? What are the elements involved in an effective direct mail campaign?
4. Why is it necessary to plan an advertising strategy? What factors should be considered?
5. What are exchange trade and cooperative advertising? What are the advantages and disadvantages of each?
6. Why do some properties use advertising agencies? What types of advertising agencies are available and what services does each offer? What factors should a property consider when selecting an advertising agency?
7. What is the difference between public relations and publicity? How can each be used to enhance the property's advertising efforts?

 ## Key Terms:

Broadcast fax. A function that transmits fax messages to a selected group of recipients.
Collateral material. Supplementary advertising materials, including brochures, tent cards, key rings, matchbooks, postcards, and video brochures.
Cooperative advertising. A pooling of marketing dollars by several tourism businesses for promotional purposes in order to increase market impact and/or reduce costs.
Consistency. In advertising, refers to the design of advertising messages for a similar look or sound to enhance audience recognition and greater cumulative impact.
CD-ROM. A read-only-memory compact disk used to hold data, including printed text and graphic images.
Direct mail advertising. Advertising sent via mail to prospects' residences or places of business. Contains copy to motivate the reader to purchase a product or utilize a service and usually includes a means to respond.
E-mail. Electronic mail messages sent via computer.

Exchange trade advertising. An arrangement in which the hotel exchanges rooms, meals, recreational amenities, etc. for advertising space or time. Also called reciprocal advertising.

Fax-on-demand. A function that provides an immediate response to information requests via fax transmission. In most cases, information is requested through a toll-free number.

Frequency. The number of times advertising appears in print or on the air.

Press kit. News releases, fact sheets, photographs, news clippings and other material, often attractively packaged, designed to give the news media background information about a property.

Print advertising. Advertising appearing in print in such media as newspapers, magazines, and directories.

Public relations. The systematic effort of a company to create a favorable image in the minds of various segments of the population.

Reach. The percentage of different locations or people exposed to a media message at least once during a specific period of time.

Specialty items (Premiums). Supplementary advertising items, such as coffee cups, t-shirts, beach towels, and so on, that bear the name of the business and other advertising and contact information.

Strategic partnerships. Relationships between independent parties that agree to advertise cooperatively but still retain their separate identities.

Timing. In advertising, refers to the scheduling of ads.

Learning Objectives:

This portion of your text introduces the factors that must be considered and the necessary steps that need to be taken when negotiating contracts for functions with meeting planners. When you have studied this chapter, you will:

- Know how to negotiate contracts with meeting planners that benefit both the hotel and the group.

- Be able to describe the various areas that are included in a typical hotel contract.

- Know the importance of standardizing contracts and be able to detail how multiple-meeting contracts are negotiated.

Outline

Negotiations
Letter of Agreement/Contract
- Names of Organization and Hotel
- Official Dates
- Number and Kinds of Rooms
- Rates
- Arrival Pattern
- Public Space
- Complimentary and Reduced Rate Rooms
- Prior Visits
- Working Space
- Registration Control
- Exhibit Space
- Food Functions
- Refreshment Breaks
- Liquor
- Audiovisual Equipment
- Union Regulations
- Master Account and Credit Procedures
- Method of Payment
- Termination/Cancellation Clauses
- Damage Clause: Liquidated or Mitigated Damages
- Gratuities and Service Charges
- Attrition Clause
- Arbitration
- Warranty of Authority
- Insurance/Indemnification

Contract Standardization
Multiple-Meeting Contracts

Negotiations and Contracts

David C. Scypinski
Senior Vice President of Industry Relations
Starwood Hotels

"The most successful salespeople take a long-term approach to negotiating contracts by looking to develop an agreement that benefits both the hotel and the customer. A one-sided contract may bring in much-needed revenue in the short-term, but may make it impossible to re-book the business. And in this business, as in any other, the key to profitability is repeat business...This is not to say you shouldn't seek to negotiate the most profitable contract possible; but you should be professionally aggressive in your negotiations, looking to balance the financial goals of your hotel and the customer's objectives."

9 Negotiations and Contracts

I n today's competitive "sellers' market," hotels largely book business based on its maximum profitability. With the growth of individual business and leisure markets, which tend to pay higher rates than the group meeting segment, properties have become stricter in terms of room rates and contract negotiations for meetings business. But wise hoteliers know that their relationship with planners is equally if not more important. Charging exorbitant rates simply because demand is high may produce revenue in the short-term, but may adversely affect future business -- both from the planner and from potential word-of-mouth referrals.

Today's hoteliers must negotiate contracts that provide optimum benefits to both the property and the planner. In this chapter, we will see how contracts are negotiated, the areas of concern taken into consideration and included in the contract to ensure the successful execution of a function, and detail how hotels use specific clauses to protect themselves financially. This process begins with negotiations.

Negotiations

Negotiations involve two or more parties coming together to reach an agreement for their mutual benefit. This process should be viewed as a friendly, problem-solving partnership, not as a fearful or uncomfortable situation. Negotiating can result in a win-win situation for both your property and the meeting planner when handled properly.

The first step involves preparation by gathering information. Knowledge is power and good negotiation skills begin by researching three key areas: your product, your competition and the prospect.

Product knowledge begins by studying the *property fact book*. It is nearly impossible to effectively sell features and benefits or to demonstrate how your property is best equipped to meet the prospect's needs without thorough knowledge of your property (see Chapter 7).

In addition to knowing your property's features, you must also understand *when* your property needs group business, the optimum guest mix, and the average daily rate for each market segment. The bargaining position of meeting planners will vary depending on your hotel's level of business, which can be divided into three categories:

- *Peak* — this is the period when demand for a property and its services is highest and the highest prices can be charged.
- *Valley* — this period, also known as the "value season," characterizes times when demand is lowest. Reduced prices are offered to meeting planners during valley periods to attract business.
- *Shoulder* — this period falls between a peak and a valley. Rooms are available and a mid to high rate can be charged. The shoulder period is the time when many properties concentrate their sales and marketing efforts.

You must know as much about your competitor's product as your own in order to successfully sell against them. When negotiating, emphasize the strengths of your property where you know the competition is weak.

There are several factors to consider when evaluating your prospect's position:

- **Budget.** Knowledge of the meeting planner's past and present budget gives you an indication of how much they may be willing to spend on similar events and if price is a major concern.

- **Purpose of the meeting.** Every property has its appeal. If a meeting is for training, a small suburban property can offer the group the option of being the only meeting in the house, which pleases some planners.

- **Dates.** When is the meeting scheduled? How flexible is the group? Do your competitors have the preferred dates open? You are negotiating from a position of strength when you know your competitors don't have the desired dates open.

- **Hot buttons.** What are the meeting planner's key concerns and what are the most important buying factors? Is it the availability of special services, such as express check-in/check-out, extra staffing at the front desk, or special meals? Key concerns tell you what to emphasize and also give clues to the importance of price. Obviously, planners who mention VIP service and extra amenities as crucial to their meeting are going to be less price resistant.

- **Past problems.** Did the planner experience problems with another property? If poor food service is mentioned more than once, then price may not be as important a consideration as quality food at next year's event.

When negotiating it is essential to look at the "life time value" of the account. Would offering concessions for a minor function for the client today result in additional, long term lucrative business tomorrow? Trade-offs are a part of negotiating, but you should sell value and offer concessions only when absolutely necessary. Successful negotiating is a give and take process — the end result is that both parties are satisfied. The planner can look forward to a successful meeting within budget, while your hotel benefits from a profitable piece of business and from the positive relationship that may lead to additional business in the future.

Letter of Agreement/Contract

While contracts are now the norm, the word *contract* frightens many people — people who readily enter into an agreement made formal by a letter. Most business people would not dream of drawing up a contract without legal counsel, but will sign a letter that lists the terms of an agreement. For all practical purposes, a letter of agreement and a contract function the same way, the difference being one of semantics.

Much has to be discussed when a meeting planner indicates a willingness to consider a hotel for a particular event. The essential elements of a contract are (a) an agreement (an offer by one party and an acceptance by the other), (b) an obligation on the part of one or more of the parties, and (c) consideration (usually expressed in monetary terms, but could be expressed as mutual promises).

A **letter of agreement/contract** should include, in simple language, all arrangements that have been negotiated and agreed to. This protects the client and the hotel, but it also does something else of extreme importance. By itemizing all matters to be covered, the letter of agreement is essentially a clearly stated checklist of what is expected of either party. This is vital because most misunderstandings reflect a lack of communication and a lack of experience by either the hotel executive or the client or both.

The letter of agreement should cover each point clearly in a separate paragraph. Each point should be documented. Nothing should be left to verbal agreement. The parties that negotiated the deal may no longer be employed by the hotel or the client when the convention actually takes place. In any case, memory is decidedly fallible. Everything should be included *in writing*. This will eliminate many misunderstandings when the time comes to settle up the accounts, and even prevent malfunctions during the meeting itself.

It is also sound practice to contact a hotel that was previously used as a convention site by the group. This contact can be made by using an **inquiry questionnaire**, which asks a group's former hosts to critique the group for the benefit of a prospective host property (see Figure 9.1). This information is helpful intelligence data to use during negotiations.

Cooperation of this kind is commonplace among hotels. Such inter-hotel conversations will not only make you aware of possible pitfalls with a group, but can also keep you abreast of current practices and trends throughout the hotel industry. Some discretion should be exercised not to make inquiries from a hotel — or a hotel within a chain — that is in a position to make a last minute bid to book the business. But with some care, past sites of the group could be valuable sources of helpful data.

Before offering a letter of agreement, many hotels send a **proposal letter** to the meeting planner. This proposal letter should spell out exactly what the customer will receive at the hotel. Proposal letters usually follow a standard format, including much of the same information included in the letter of agreement/contract, but they are usually not as detailed. Remember, your written proposal is a selling document and should present your key features and benefits. Include convention brochures, fact sheets, complimentary letters from past groups, and other promotional materials with your proposal letter. The conclusion to your proposal letter should always ask the prospect to take action -- to do business with you. Be sure to establish a trace date to follow up every proposal letter.

A proposal letter is normally initiated from a site inspection or a **request for proposal (RFP)** from a meeting planner (see Figure 9.2). A written RFP from a planner includes the group's desired dates, guestroom and meeting space requirements, and the group's meetings history. Since planners often send out a RFP to several hotels at the same time, your response should be timely. Planners expect to receive information on availability and pricing within a day or two of their request.

Should the group accept your proposal, you should send a letter of agreement along with a note of thanks. It is customary for this letter to be sent in duplicate, and to request that it be countersigned by a responsible person from the association (or other sponsoring organization) and returned. As we explained, this constitutes a legal contract whereby both parties have agreed to the terms and arrangements. An alternative to the duplicate-copy method might be a letter from the meeting planner stating that the letter of agreement is correct and accepted.

In any case, certain information must be recorded and points negotiated and recorded. We will list all that should be covered in the letter. It is worth repeating that a soundly written letter of agreement helps both parties execute a successful meeting and prevents misunderstanding by stating what is to be done, by whom, and at what price. Nothing is part of the agreement that is not included in the letter.

Names of Organization and Hotel

Name both parties to the agreement. Both the organization and the hotel should be clearly indicated, along with the intent to select the hotel as the site for the meeting. The meeting should be identified by name or any other designation.

Figure 9.1. INQUIRY QUESTIONNAIRE.

U.S. Grant HOTEL

AN ATLAS HOTEL

Post Office Box 80098
San Diego, California 92138
(619) 232-3121

Dear Colleague:

The U.S. Grant Hotel is working with:

We understand this group met with you. At your convenience we would sincerely appreciate receiving the following information:

1.

Date								
Original Room Block								
Actually Used								

Meeting Requirements (Program if available):

2.

	Persons	Set-up
General Session	_____	_____
Breakouts	_____	_____

Catered Functions:

3.

	No. of Functions	Persons
Breakfast	_____	_____
Lunch	_____	_____
Dinner	_____	_____
Receptions	_____	_____

4. Comments: _____

_____

Thank you in advance for your cooperation. We will be happy to reciprocate at any time.
Sincerely,

_____
Signature

It is sound practice to track the historical performance of meeting groups. A questionnaire such as this one requests a post-convention critique from hotels used by the meeting group in the past. This information is extremely valuable in negotiations as it gives the hotel an early sense of whether the group meets its commitments. While it is acceptable practice for competitor hotels to exchange basic information on groups (such as rooms blocked, actual pickup, percentage of double occupancy, number of food functions and the like), it is a violation of antitrust law and a criminal offense to exchange pricing information (such as room rates or banquet charges).

Figure 9.2. SAMPLE REQUEST FOR PROPOSAL.

Date: 3/1/2002

REQUEST FOR PROPOSAL

2004 Plastic Surgery Senior Residents Conference
Sponsored by the Plastic Surgery Educational Foundation
Galveston, TX

Only possible dates:
April 14-18, 2004
April 21-25, 2004
May 5-9, 2004

EVENT PROFILE:

This meeting provides a forum for third-year residents to present their papers and helps to prepare them for medical practice.

ORGANIZATION PROFILE:

The PSEF is the educational arm of the American Society of Plastic and Reconstructive Surgeons, which is a 6,000 member national medical association representing 97% of all plastic surgeons in the U.S. The ASPRS/PSEF sponsors approximately 40 meetings/year throughout the U.S. and abroad.

ATTENDEE PROFILE: Third-year medical residents; average age early 30's
                          From all over U.S.
                          70% male, 30% female
                          15% traveling with spouse

PROPERTY TYPE NEEDED: City location close to restaurants and nightlife.

GUEST ROOM REQUIREMENTS:

Arrival	Tuesday night	5 rooms
	Wednesday night	120 rooms
	Thursday night	130 rooms
	Friday night	130 rooms; 2 suites
	Saturday night	110 rooms; 2 suites
Depart	Sunday	5 rooms

Notes: Need flat single/double rate. 85% sgl, 15% dbl. 85% non-smoking. Rate-sensitive group.

Concessions: 2 1BR suite upgrades for Assn. Presidents
               1/50 comp
               2 reduced rate staff rooms.

MEETING SPACE REQUIREMENTS:

Day	Time	Function	Attendance	Budget
Wednesday	3:00pm-7:00pm	Registration	2 6' tables	
	6:30pm-7:30pm	Reception	200 people	$30/p
	7:00pm-24 hrs	Exhibit Setup	25 6'tables plus 20 double-sided posters	

The RFP provides general information about the requesting organization and event, including specifics about the group's space requirements, a history of the group, and its decision date. The RFP may be mailed, faxed, e-mailed, or, as is becoming increasingly common, sent via the Internet to hotels. In most cases, meeting planners not only request proposals from hotels, but from a number of other suppliers as well, such as service contractors (companies that set up exhibits), security companies, audiovisual suppliers, tour shuttle firms, florists, and housing companies if the event is outsourced. This particular RFP includes three sheets; only the first is shown. Page two lists daily functions, meeting room requirements, the group's meeting history, and a space hold request; page three provides special requirements, a response date, information on the group's decision date, and the name and contact numbers of the meeting planner.

Official Dates

It sounds basic, but make sure the exact dates of the event are listed. They are often referred to as the *official dates.* It is wise to indicate the dates for moving in and moving out as well.

Not only the date, but also the hour of beginning and ending should be specified. This protects the hotel against the meeting tying up a room beyond the cutoff time. You don't want a breakfast ending too late to set up the room for a luncheon or training session later in the day.

Number and Kinds of Rooms

Specify the number of guestrooms to be held, spelling out the number of suites, single, double and twin rooms. Sometimes a client will want the location of the rooms specified, as in the case of a multi-room structure. If you agree to it, specify the number of rooms in Building A and the number in Building B.

Also include a reservation **cutoff date.** Attendees who make their reservations after the cutoff date are not guaranteed a room or the negotiated convention rate. If this is the case, attendees must pay the "market rate" for available rooms. A typical clause might read: "*A cutoff date of thirty days prior to the opening of the convention is established. This cutoff date is May 1, 2002. After this date, any of your unused room commitment will be released to the general public. After the cutoff date, we will continue to accept your group's reservations on a space-available basis.*"

Specify the method by which room reservations will be made: by mail using a pre-printed reservation reply card; by rooming list; through the Housing Bureau of the Convention and Visitors Bureau; to the hotel directly or to an "800" number.

Rates

Specify clearly the rates for each type of accommodation. If a range is agreed to, list rates from the lowest to the highest. If a flat rate is negotiated, state it clearly. If rooms are to be priced differently in different sections of the hotel, it may be wise to list such rates separately. And when listing rates for suites, be sure to note that the suite includes a parlor and a number of guestrooms, such as a parlor and one bedroom or a parlor and two bedrooms.

Arrival Pattern

It is important that you know when the guests will arrive. If 400 rooms are being held, it is unlikely that all 400 room occupants will arrive on the same day. You should develop a **flow chart** to reserve rooms in accordance with the agreement. The agreement, for example, might call for 100 rooms for arrival on Monday, January 10, 200 rooms for arrival on Tuesday, January 11, and the remaining 100 on Wednesday, January 12. It is also wise to indicate the breakdown of the rooms into singles, doubles, twins and suites. You may find arrival dates easier to secure than check-out dates, but these too are of great importance to you.

Public Space

The experienced convention planner will want you to hold all your public rooms until he or she has firmed up the program and the resultant traffic flow pattern. If the event is far in the future and if it will not occupy the entire hotel, this may be difficult. You need public space to sell other meetings. Keep in mind that while eye-catching events are the big ones, most meetings do not fill the hotel; usually there are several in the house at once. The second or third meeting in the hotel at the time, albeit smaller ones, represent important income, as well as opportunities to serve repeat customers.

How much of your public space to hold is a point to be negotiated, but it is reasonable to hold all rooms that might possibly be used for the event. A date must be set by which the program will be completed to the point that unused public space can be released. If you agree to hold rooms without setting an option or **release date**, you may find yourself unable to use them to solicit other meetings or banquets.

Many meeting planners prefer specific meeting rooms to be named in the contract. This limits your flexibility. If possible, avoid naming the specific function rooms and include a clause to indicate how and when meeting space may be released. For example:

We have reserved function space based on the requirements described to us. The meeting group will provide the final program to the hotel nine months before the meeting. At that time, all space not being used will be released back to the hotel. The specific names of the function rooms will be furnished to you when you are ready to print your program. This allows time for attendance figures to be well established.

Another consideration is the guestroom to public space ratio. Groups and transients are both part of the hotel's overall room demand. Groups book well in advance, so hotels can generally offer them lower rates for a guaranteed block of rooms. The booking cycle for transients is much shorter (a week or two) and they pay higher rates. Depending on demand, a hotel's group room allotment differs daily throughout the year.

Consider a 400-room hotel with a **group ceiling** (targeted number of group rooms) of 300 rooms over a given period and an expected transient demand of 100 rooms. The property is effectively a 300-room group hotel. Revenue is lost if the hotel assigns all its public space to a 200-room group as that leaves no meeting space for the remaining 100 group rooms.

Complimentary and Reduced Rate Rooms

It is commonplace in the convention industry for hotels to supply some complimentary rooms, but the number varies a great deal. A hotel may be more generous if the meeting is scheduled during an off-time of the week or season. A more successful hotel may be tougher when it comes to concessions. A very common rule of thumb is one complimentary guestroom for every fifty rooms used. No matter what formula is used for complimentary rooms, it should be clearly spelled out. If charges are to be made for meeting rooms, the rooms and the rates should be specified. Such charges are usually made in the event that few guestrooms are used.

A hotel and a client may also agree to a number of reduced rate rooms. This is done for staff members, speakers and performers. This is subject to negotiation, of course, and should not be taken for granted. A contract clause on complimentary rooms might read:

We will be pleased to furnish one complimentary guestroom for every fifty room nights utilized. The complimentary commitment will be provided on a cumulative basis for the length of the meeting. The hotel offers a choice of accounting procedures for compli-

mentary rooms. A bottom line dollar credit on the Master Account will value each unit at the daily average guestroom rate generated by the group, or guestrooms/suites can be reserved on a complimentary basis prior to arrival.

Prior Visits

A hotel often will not charge for guestrooms used by the meeting organizer and his or her staff during visits to the hotel before the event to make preliminary arrangements. This is often done on a *space-available* basis. It is wise to set a specific limit on the number of rooms made available for this purpose.

Working Space

Offices, press rooms and similar working space should be discussed. If a charge is to be made for them, specify the rates. If no charge is to be made, specify this clearly, but also spell out the maximum number of rooms to be used for this purpose. Many meeting planners insist upon indicating the location of such rooms to make sure the locations are convenient to the meeting sessions.

Registration Control

In the case of association conventions, hotels usually agree to clear all requests for accommodation from people of that particular industry with the convention organizer. You need to do this in order to credit the association with the total number of rooms used in conjunction with the convention. All such rooms should be applied against the guaranteed number of rooms. In addition, a convention organizer often wants to control the use of suites as hospitality centers or even as setups which circumvent the exhibit itself and its booth space and decorating costs.

Exhibit Space

If a charge is to be made for the exhibit hall, say so clearly and state what is to be included in the charge. Items to be considered are hours the exhibit is to be open, electricity, air conditioning or heat, carpeting and the number of tables and chairs. List what the hotel is to furnish and what must be contracted for with a show decorator.

Some hotels charge on the basis of the number of booths sold by the association. The charge is usually a per booth rate by day for the duration of the convention including move-in and move-out days. However, this ties the hotel's rental income to the show manager's ability to attract exhibitors and so normally hotels levy a flat charge. A fee of one to two dollars per square foot for each exhibit day is quite common.

Food Functions

Specify how much notice you require for guarantees on food functions. Most common is 48 hours advance notice. If you need more time, and you may over weekends, negotiate it and include it in your letter of agreement. Menus have to be priced and approved. Most hotels will agree to set tables for a percentage above the number guaranteed in order to accommodate additional guests. Many set for an additional ten percent, others hold it to five percent, and still others base the percent on the number of persons to be served. For example, a paragraph such as this might be used:

A 48-hour guarantee is required on all meal functions. Your catering manager must be notified of the exact number of attendees for whom you will guarantee payment. For functions scheduled on Sunday or Monday, the guarantee must be received by noon on the preceding Friday.

The hotel will set up as follows:

20-100 persons set	*5% over guarantee*
101-1000 persons set	*3% over guarantee*
1001 persons and over	*1% over guarantee*

In the event a guarantee is not received, the original estimated attendance count will be prepared and billed.

Refreshment Breaks

It is amazing how many arguments stem from refreshment break arrangements. Many meeting organizers think in terms of coffee shop standards. They do not understand the conditions under which the hotel operates. As a result, much resentment is evidenced, and it is important to explain all that is involved when the hotel supplies refreshment breaks. Spell out the costs and labor required for all refreshment breaks. Include prices for cakes, soft drinks and juice, too. It is important to the hotel that its clients have faith that the hotel charges are fair.

Liquor

Spell out the hotel's policy on liquor service. Most hotels prohibit meeting planners from bringing in food or liquor from outside the property. State your policy on this matter clearly so that no misunderstandings arise during the meeting. A typical contract clause might state:

No food or beverages of any kind will be permitted to be brought into the hotel from the outside without the written permission of the hotel. The hotel reserves the right to assess a service charge for any food and beverages brought into the facility in violation thereof. If any alcoholic beverages are to be served on the premises (and/or elsewhere under the hotel's alcoholic beverage license) the hotel will require these beverages to be dispensed by hotel servers and bartenders. The hotel's alcoholic beverage license requires the hotel to (1) request proper identification (Photo ID) of any person of questionable age and refuse alcoholic beverage service if the person is either under age or proper identification cannot be produced and (2) refuse alcoholic beverage service to any person who, in the hotel's judgment, appears intoxicated.

If you charge by the bottle, an arrangement should be made for inventory control and credit given for unopened bottles after the convention. It is important both for the hotel and the client to identify the person authorized to tally the inventory with your staff. The credit could be issued at that time.

THE CONVENTION INDUSTRY COUNCIL

The best customers are the ones who really know their business. And they like to do business with vendors who know theirs. It is amazing how rapidly and steadily the convention business grew, with very little done to expand areas of knowledge and expertise. Fortunately, leaders of four associations met in 1949 to come to grips with the situation. This group —including both vendors and buyers — formed a council to establish a set of commonly accepted trade standards.

The Convention Industry Council, as it is now known, adopted four basic objectives:
1. to bring about a sympathetic understanding and acceptance among these organizations of the responsibility of each to the other.
2. to create a sound and consistent basis for handling convention procedures and practices through a program of study and education.
3. to conduct educational and activities of mutual interest to participating organizations.
4. to acquaint the public with the fact that conventions are essential to industry and to the economy of the community and nation.

The four original organizations were the American Hotel and Motel Association, the American Society of Association Executives, the Hospitality Sales Marketing Association International, and the International Association of Convention & Visitor Bureaus.

Today, 29 organizations comprise the Council, about half representing seller groups and half representing buyer organizations.

Through the years the Council has been the educational leader for the industry. It created the Certified Meeting Professional (CMP) program. In 1961 it published the *Convention Industry Council Manual*. This manual presented detailed responsibilities of each of the three groups involved in a convention — the sponsoring organization, the hotel and the convention bureau — and how they were interrelated. This manual, now in its seventh revised edition, contains useful checklists, forms and an industry glossary. Recently, the CIC published an economic-impact study of the meetings industry.

29 ORGANIZATIONS COMPRISING THE CONVENTION INDUSTRY COUNCIL

Air Transport Association of America
American Hotel and Lodging Association
American Society of Association Executives
Association of Conference and Events Directors International
Association for Convention Marketing Executives
Association for Conventions Operations Management
Association of Destination Management Companies
Center for Exhibition Industry Research
Exhibit Designer and Producers Association
Exposition Service Contractors Association
Healthcare Convention and Exhibitors Association
Hospitality Sales and Marketing Association Int'l
Insurance Conference Planners Association
International Association for Exposition Management
International Association of Assembly Managers
International Association of Conference Centers
International Association of Convention & Visitors Bureaus
International Association of Speakers Bureaus
International Special Events Society
Meeting Professionals International
National Association of Catering Executives
National Coalition of Black Meeting Planners
National Speakers Association
Professional Convention Management Association
Religious Conference Management Association
Society of Corporate Meeting Professionals
Society of Government Meeting Professionals
Society of Incentive Travel Executives
Trade Show Exhibitors Association

Audiovisual Equipment

Some hotels supply audiovisual equipment from their own inventories; others use local dealers. In either case, it is important to show the rate structure for equipment and services, or to indicate that it is the convention staff's responsibility to make its own arrangements. You may prefer to supply the names of local service companies that deal directly with and bill to the client. Some hotels will accept the local dealer's bills and rebill the convention. It is important, then, that there be a clear understanding as to who has the responsibility to provide the necessary equipment so that the client receives the service needed.

Union Regulations

Convention organizers are accustomed to union help and regulations, but you should list the basic workday, rates and overtime charges. You should also state any out-of-the-ordinary union requirements in your labor contract. Making your client aware of them eliminates much aggravation.

Many astute meeting planners will not sign confirmations or agreements without first checking out union conditions. The hotel has a responsibility to alert the meeting planner to the possibility of local labor contracts terminating before the meeting, any likely labor rate increases, or possible labor disputes.

Master Account and Credit Procedures

The meeting planner will have a master billing account. He or she must furnish the hotel with a list of people authorized to sign for charges that are to be placed on the **master account**. The client must also indicate which charges the convention organizer will pick up for such people as speakers and performers. The client may choose to pay room rate only and let the individuals pay all incidental charges. In the case of a corporate meeting, the arrangement may have to be clarified for each attendee. Make it clear that the master account will have to be verified and initialed before the client leaves after the meeting.

Before extending credit to a corporate group or an association, hotel sales executives frequently request a completed credit application (see Figure 9.3). Calls also may be made to colleagues at properties where the group has met previously. These references combined with Dun and Bradstreet credit checks are used to determine the credit limit extended to the meeting group.

Method of Payment

Specify how the group's bill is to be paid. If you want a deposit, say so and give the date that it is due. Also negotiate any additional sum to be paid, as well as the final payment.

Most convention organizers prefer to go over the master account before they leave the hotel, but some hotels cannot have it ready that quickly. It is a common practice to leave some portion of the account unpaid, should there be some items that require negotiations or that aren't ready for final accounting. But most hotels do insist that the master account be approved by the client before leaving, while all matters are fresh in the mind and the staff is available for consultation. A statement such as the following might be included:

The hotel will be expending money immediately in labor and services to ensure the most successful meeting for you. Therefore, it is our policy to ask for 75 percent of the master account to be paid prior to your departure from the hotel. The remaining 25 percent will be direct billed.

Termination/Cancellation Clauses

A **termination clause** should be included in the agreement for cases when either party might cancel because of circumstances beyond its control. Termination means that both parties are excused from performance without liability. For example, the hotel should not be held responsible for nonperformance in the event of a strike, lockout, fire or failure of

Figure 9.3. APPLICATION FOR DIRECT BILLING.

MARRIOTT'S
Camelback Inn
RESORT GOLF CLUB & SPA
P.O. BOX 70 • SCOTTSDALE, AZ 85252 • (602) 948-1700

CREDIT APPLICATION

Direct billing privileges are not automatically extended. To apply for direct billing privileges, please complete and return this application to the hotel. Should you have any questions regarding the status of your application, please call the Credit Manager at (602) 948-1700, ext. 7715 or your Sales Representative.

Name of Group: _____

Address: _____

City: _____ State: _____ Zip: _____

Telephone: _____ Date(s) of Event: _____

References:
Hotel Reference: _____ Contact: _____

Address: _____ Phone: _____

Date(s) of Event: _____ Amount Billed: _____

Hotel Reference: _____ Contact: _____

Address: _____ Phone: _____

Date(s) of Event: _____ Amount Billed: _____

Bank Reference: _____ Officer: _____

Address: _____

Telephone: _____ Account #: _____
(please indicate the acct. # from which payment will be drawn)

Items to be Billed: (Please check)
All Room Charges ( )
Some Room Charges ( ) please specify
Restaurant Charges ( ) please specify
Banquet Charges ( )
Recreational Facilities ( )
Other ( ) please specify
Other ( ) please specify

Estimated Value _____

I have completed this application in behalf of this group and believe all information contained to be correct. I understand that the extension of direct billing privilege is conditional upon our agreement to pay our account in full within thirty days of receipt of the hotel's statement.

Signed: _____ Date: _____

Title: _____

Accounting Department Approval _____

Many hotels do not automatically issue credit to new clients. Meeting groups that do not have a credit history with the hotel must fill out a credit application form. Note that both hotel and bank references are requested on this form.

heat, light, power or natural disasters. Planners might terminate if there is a change in ownership, hotel chain affiliation, management company or bankruptcy proceedings by the hotel.

The next paragraph after the termination clause should be the **cancellation clause**. Cancellation means that one party elects not to perform, which ordinarily requires the payment of damages. Many conventions are planned a number of years in advance, so occasions do arise that call for a cancellation of the event. The cancellation clause should spell out what it will cost the hotel and/or the group if either party should cancel for reasons not identified in the termination clause. Cancellation clauses in hotel contracts often establish cancellation fees on a sliding scale with the amount increasing the closer the cancellation is to the anticipated date (see Figure 9.4). Planned food and beverage functions might also be factored into the scale. Since cancellation fees are based on lost profits, not lost revenues, the percentage of revenue received by the hotel cannot exceed its profit margin (generally 60-75 percent for sleeping rooms and 20-30 percent for food).

Figure 9.4. SAMPLE CANCELLATION POLICIES OF FOUR HOTELS.

Anatole Hotel Cancellation Policy

In the event that you have to cancel your meeting within _____ of the actual date, you will be asked to pay a cancellation fee of half the anticipated room revenue. This fee will be used to recuperate loss of revenue which cannot be replaced. In the event we are able to resell all or part of your block, an adjustment will be made.

In the event of a national emergency or an act of God, where you had no control over the circumstances, the above paragraph is null and void. If you are able to rebook the meeting or one with similar requirements within one year of the cancellation date, we will be pleased to apply the cancellation fee to this meeting.

Any controversy or claim arising out of, or relating to the cancellation of the contract or the breach thereof, shall be settled by arbitration in accordance with the rules of the American Arbitration Association, and judgment upon the award rendered by the Arbitrator(s) may be entered in any court having jurisdiction thereof.

South Seas Plantation Cancellation Policy

Cancellation Notice Received	Cancellation Charge
0-60 days prior to scheduled arrival date	Full payment on rooms for the duration of the dates agreed upon
60-90 days prior to scheduled arrival date	75% of above
90-120 days prior to scheduled arrival date	50% of above
120-180 days prior to scheduled arrival date	Forfeit deposit

NOTE: Same cancellation policy applies in the event the agreed upon length of stay of days is reduced.

It is further provided there shall be no right of termination on your part for the sole purpose of holding the same meeting in another city or facility. Neither does South Seas Plantation have the right to cancel your room block if another larger group requests the same space and dates.

Opryland Hotel Cancellation Policy

In the event that it become necessary for you to cancel your conference with us, we would be in a difficult position to try to resell your room nights and the cancellation would, no doubt, result in additional lost revenue for our Hotel. We will, however, attempt to resell the room nights that were reserved for you and would only assess a cancellation fee for those room nights not resold over the initially agreed upon dates. This fee would be based upon the unsold room nights multiplied by your established group rate for that period.

Hotel Del Coronado Cancellation Policy

In the unfortunate event that the Group cancels the meeting due to extraordinary and unforeseeable circumstances, the Group agrees (1) to pay one night's rent for the number of rooms confirmed if the cancellation occurs within one year of the scheduled dates, the night paid for being the night the largest number of rooms had been confirmed, and (2) to pay for the entire number of rooms confirmed if the cancellation occurs less than three months prior to the scheduled dates of the meeting.

(Used with permission of the Anatole Hotel, Opryland Hotel, South Seas Plantation Resort and Hotel Del Coronado Legal Department, Timothy R. Binder, General Counsel)

Damage Clause: Liquidated or Mitigated Damages

To protect themselves in the event of cancellation, most hotel contracts include either a **liquidated damage clause** or a **mitigation of damage clause**. A liquidated damage provision is an agreement by both planner and hotel in advance as to the penalty for cancellation. Damages are collected upon cancellation. With a mitigation of damages clause, the penalty is not predetermined — the hotel must wait until the convention dates actually pass and then prove its loss. Tracking and reporting the use of space following a cancellation is inconvenient, difficult, and requires waiting much longer to recover damages, so most hotels prefer a liquidated damage clause.

A liquidated damage clause allows the parties to agree in advance as to the amount and method for calculating damages that might be paid in the event of cancellation. The amount of liquidated damages is less than what a hotel might have received from mitigating damages, but it is a "sum certain." The liquidated damage clause sets the limits of damages well in advance of the meeting. If the hotel resells some of its rooms, there is no reimbursement to the meeting group.

A liquidated damage clause is generally stated in a sliding scale tied to a percentage of anticipated profits and/or to a specific dollar amount. The amount would be low for cancellations two or three years out and higher for cancellations closer to the meeting date. For example:

Under the terms of this Agreement, the Hotel is reserving for your use the room block and public space requirements described herein. In the event these reserved facilities and related services are not used, the Hotel will experience significant monetary losses.

Notwithstanding any other provision of the Agreement, you shall have the right to cancel this Agreement without cause upon written notice to the Hotel at any time prior to the event and upon payment of an amount based on the following scale:

*Notice and payment received on or before 12/15/02 - $183,060
(15 percent of total anticipated revenue)
Notice and payment received on or before 11/15/04 - $366,120
(30 percent of total anticipated revenue)
Notice and payment received on or before 11/05/05 - $854,280
(70 percent of total anticipated revenue)
Notice and payment received after 11/05/05 - $1,220,400*

Carolyn Colton, assistant general counsel for Marriott International, cautions that in calculating a liquidated damage amount the hotel should consider other profit centers beyond sleeping rooms. She says:

> "When a group cancels an event, the hotel also experiences substantial damages in lost food and beverage/banquet sales and/or lost fees for use of function space. In addition, the hotel suffers losses in other aspects of its business, such as lost restaurant and gift shop sales, movie purchases, and room service."[1]

Most meeting planners will favor a mitigation of damage clause. Such a clause requires the hotel to try to minimize its damages by working to find business to replace the business lost by cancellation. Hotels that agree to mitigate damages must wait until after the meeting dates have come and gone before determining damages and then are faced with the difficulty of computing damages.

Gratuities and Service Charges

Gratuities and service charges should be discussed in advance of the meeting and should be spelled out in the letter of agreement. Most meeting planners view gratuities as part of convention costs, and even though a touchy area, no problems should arise if guidelines are clearly established at the outset. For example, a gratuity clause might read:

Bellperson gratuities of $3.00 per person round trip are mandatory on group arrivals. Maid gratuities of $1.00 per room, per night, are optional, but suggested.

A service charge statement might read:

All catered food, beverage and related service charges will be subject to the current sales tax. Each catered function will automatically reflect a service charge of 17 percent.

Attrition Clause

An attrition clause (also called a slippage or under performance clause) is relatively new and may be unfamiliar to many meeting planners. Until recently, it was industry practice for hotels to accept the risk of low pickup by agreeing to hold a block of rooms for a group until a specific cutoff date (generally 30 days). After that date, the unusued rooms reverted to the hotel for resale with no additional liability to the group.

Although some hotels still adhere to this practice, most, especially in periods of high demand, have altered their contracts to include attrition clauses. An attrition clause allows the hotel to collect damages if the actual sleeping rooms used are significantly fewer than the group's **block**, the number of rooms originally reserved for the meeting. Guestrooms that are used are referred to as **pick-up**; unused rooms are known as **slippage.**

Attrition clauses protect hotels from excessive losses due to slippage. John Foster, an attorney specializing in meeting law, states:

> "Slippage clauses are making planners a little sharper in their forecasting. You're better off in today's climate to underbook your convention than overbook. It's always easier to go back to the hotel and ask for more rooms than to decrease your block."[2]

The number of rooms for which a planner must pay attrition is negotiable. Kristy Sartorious, Director of Sales for Wyndham Hotels in Dallas, says that they allow a group twenty percent attrition off their room block before penalties are assessed. In contrast, Westin Hotels adjusts the percentage from city to city and by type of property: resort versus downtown.

For example, the Westin St. Francis in downtown San Francisco allows a ten percent slippage while the Westin La Paloma Resort in Tucson allows only five percent. The reason for the difference is that downtown properties can more easily resell rooms to business travelers while the resort hotels primarily rely on vacationers.

Attrition fees are generally based on a sliding scale: the fewer the rooms occupied, the greater the penalty. Attrition fees are best negotiated as an exact dollar amount, and should provide several option dates to review the room block with an agreed-upon percentage of reduction. For example:

From one year to nine months prior to arrival, the group will be allowed to reduce their room block by twenty percent without penalty. For reduction over twenty percent, a fee of ___ dollars per room will be assessed. From six months to three months prior to arrival, the group will be allowed to reduce their room bock by ten percent without penalty. For reduction over ten percent, a fee of ___ dollars will be assessed.

In addition to attrition fees for sleeping rooms, some hotels are requiring planners to pay penalties for meeting space and food and beverage that are not picked up because the group did not meet its guestroom commitment. A food and beverage attrition clause might read:

The number of catered food and beverage functions and the attendance figures for such functions have been taken into consideration in establishing the room rates for this convention. Should any food and beverage functions be cancelled, the Group will be responsible for 50 percent of the estimated food and beverage revenue lost, based on the minimum catering prices in effect at the times of the meeting times the number of scheduled attendees.

The attrition clause clearly spells out what is required of the group and the specific penalties that will be levied should the group fail to live up to its contract. Many meeting planners are vocal against these clauses, claiming that attrition clauses force them to look into a crystal ball. Richard Granger, meeting planner for Allmerica Financial, explains:

> "Five years ago you didn't see attrition clauses. Now you're lucky to be permitted ten to fifteen percent shrinkage. Attrition clauses are not only tougher, but broader. They used to cover only room slippage, but now include food and beverage costs too."[3]

Hotels, citing their need to be financially accountable, feel that such clauses are justified and prevent the unethical practice of meeting planners overestimating room counts to obtain additional concessions.

Arbitration

Arbitration clauses are often used because **arbitration** provides an efficient, timely and relatively inexpensive alternative to litigation. An arbitration rather than a court action is usually in the best interests of both the hotel and the meeting planner. A typical arbitration clause might read:

Any controversy or claim arising out of or relating to this agreement, or the breach thereof, shall be settled by arbitration in accordance with the Rules of the American Arbitration Association, and judgment upon the award rendered by the Arbitrator may be entered by any court having jurisdiction thereof.

The Convention Industry Council created the Alternative Dispute Resolution (ADR) as an alternative to lawsuits and arbitration. This program is designed to provide a streamlined, but nonbinding, means to resolve disagreements. The ADR program is designed to allow hotels and meeting planners to submit a written statement of claims and to present their case at an oral hearing before a three member panel composed of individuals from within the industry. Contracts must include a provision that the ADR program will be used if a dispute arises. Each party must agree to submit its dispute to the Convention Industry Council.

The following paragraph is typical of the language that may be used in a contract between the hotel and the meeting planner:

Any unresolved dispute related to this contractual agreement shall be initially submitted for review to the Convention Industry Council Alternative Dispute Resolution Program, in Washington, DC. By signing this contract, both parties agree that they are voluntarily submitting all of their disputes that arise under this contract to the Convention Industry Council Alternative Dispute Resolution Program.

A hearing is held within thirty days after the statements are filed. Each party has three hours in which to present its case and is limited to three witnesses who may be cross-examined. Lawyers may not be present at the hearing, but may assist in drafting complaints and preparing answers. All rulings by the panel are nonbinding, unless the parties to the dispute agree otherwise.

Warranty of Authority

The principles of agency law specify that if both parties are authorized to sign a contract for a meeting, the contract is still binding on both the hotel and the meeting group if one or both of the signers is no longer with their employer. A warranty of authority clause states that the signers have been granted authority by their respective organizations to enter into an agreement. Such a clause is especially relevant given the turnover of both hotel sales people and meeting planners and in light of the considerable time frame between the signing of the agreement and the execution of the event.

A warranty of authority clause might read:

The Group Name and the person signing this Agreement on its behalf represent and warrant that the undersigned person is an authorized and appointed agent of the Group Name, fully empowered to bind the Group Name to all provisions contained in the agreement, and that no further action is required on the Group Name's part to enter into this agreement.

This agreement shall be binding upon the Group Name and its successors and assigns.

Insurance/Indemnification

Many hotels stipulate that the meeting group must agree to carry adequate liability insurance that protects the hotel against claims arising from the group's activities conducted in the hotel during the convention. In doing business with associations and trade shows, a hotel incurs specific liability in its relationship with trade show exhibitors. Although exhibitors sublease hotel space from the association or trade show, the hotel should require the exhibitor to sign a "hold harmless" or liability agreement that confirms that the hotel is not responsible for damages or theft of material or equipment. Some hotels extend this to deny accountability for accidents occuring in public areas that are not the result of negligence by the hotel.

Convention hotels also request that a copy of the meeting group's exhibitor contract be submitted to the convention services department prior to its printing and distribution. The reason for this is to ensure the meeting group and the hotel are protected.

An insurance clause might read:

The group acknowledges that the hotel and its owners do not maintain insurance covering property brought into the hotel by exhibitors and that it is the sole responsibility of the exhibitor to obtain insurance covering such losses. The group shall give written notice of such to any exhibitors. The group is responsible for submitting to the hotel an executed release of liability from each exhibitor.

Indemnification is a word found in many meeting contracts. To indemnify means to protect. An **indemnification clause** provides mutual protection. The hotel and the meeting group indemnify each other. A typical indemnification clause might read:

Each party agrees to indemnify and hold harmless the other from any and all loss, damage, or expense (including attorneys' fees) arising from the negligence or willful misconduct of the indemnifying party, its agents and employees in the performance of its duties and responsibilities under this agreement.

This clause states that each party will be responsible for its own negligence and that each party agrees to hold the other party harmless if the actions of one party cause the other party to be sued or suffer loss.

If doing business by letter of agreement/contract seems complex and detailed, think of this format as a checklist or order form. Arranging for a convention requires more than ordering a certain number of guestrooms. Your letter of agreement shows you, the hotelier, what the client expects and also shows the client his or her responsibility. It works out well when thought and time are given to each detail.

The first letter of agreement/contract may be the hardest to write. After you get it polished, save it as a sample. It will save much work if that polished letter and its various clauses are individually stored in a word processor file so that they may be used when you are formulating new contracts or letters of agreement.

It will help you also if you list details in such a manner that they can be transposed directly onto function setup sheets. That makes the meeting easier to service and errors less likely to occur. Do keep in mind that some details just cannot be supplied when the letter of agreement is signed, so provision may have to be made to add a supplementary agreement later on.

Contract Standardization

To facilitate the formerly time-consuming process of contract negotiation and to meet the requests of meeting planners for more consistency when dealing with properties, the industry has responded with an important trend: the standardization of contracts and other meetings-related paperwork. Following the introduction of the Marriott Meetings Network (see Figure 9.5), a number of chains have developed their own standardized forms and services (see box titled "Contract Standardization").

Standardized contracts, which are most prevalent in the area of small meetings due to their short lead time, essentially provide a heightened degree of communication by standardizing language and covering all relevant issues, and most meeting planners are very receptive to them. Blanca Diaz, manager of corporate event planning at McGraw-Hill in New York, says:

> "If I receive a contract that is not that customer friendly, I have to run it by
> the legal department and it delays the signing of the contract. In the past,
> it was nightmarish. Now I'll approve some of the contracts on sight."[4]

There are drawbacks, of course. Some meeting planners, especially independent ones, prefer to use their own forms. Their point of view is that every event is unique and no one form can handle all individual group needs. But their perspective is being overshadowed by the sea of planners who welcome not only standardized contracts, but other standardized forms and services as well — event resumes, banquet events orders (BEOs), and billing procedures and computerized access to such areas as rooming lists. Diana Johnson, conference administrator for 28 events in different cities across the nation, says:

Figure 9.5. STANDARDIZED SERVICES FOR THE MEETINGS INDUSTRY.

In response to meeting planners' needs for consistency when negotiating with hotels within its chain, Marriott developed the Marriott Meetings Network after two years of intensive customer research. This computerized system enables properties within the chain to standardize contracts and eliminates the need for meeting planners to update contracts. Since a group's paperwork is stored in the chain's computer system, it can be easily retrieved and previous histories can be checked to ensure that the group's requirements are met.

"Once you've read the standard BEO you know the format. You know right where to look to find the same things; meeting setups, guarantee policies, set menus. You don't have to scrutinize it as much."[4]

The standardization of these previously time-consuming pre-convention documents and procedures enables both the meeting planner and the convention staff at individual properties to concentrate on servicing the event and offers yet another benefit besides saving time and money — meetings clout. Jack Breisacher, vice president of group sales for Renaissance Hotels and Resorts, explains:

"After all, the customer is often spending a few hundred thousand dollars with us, and all they want to know is how much money was spent in each area. Then they'll take that information to a property next year and say, "Here's what we did, and based on that here's what we need at this time.' It becomes a solid negotiating tool."[4]

Contract Standardization

Hilton: A leader in standardization, with development of a standardized group resume 20 years ago, the chain now offers standardized contracts and general meeting forms at 52 corporate-owned and managed properties.

Hyatt: Developed Meeting Connection program featuring standardized contract for groups of fewer than 100; now, 104 properties have standardized contracts for larger groups as part of The Standard. Also mail out their standardized resume on microsoft disks, enabling planners to enter meeting specs into the program and mail or e-mail documents back.

Marriott: Lead the industry in meeting paperwork standardization with the Marriott Meetings Network, a computerized network system providing standardized contracts, master-billing forms, group resumes, and post-convention reports (see ad). Thirty-six of the chain's properties in the United States, Mexico and Canada offer this service.

Ritz-Carlton: All meeting-related paperwork — contracts, group resumes, banquet event orders, billing formats, and post-convention reports — are standardized at 30 Ritz-Carlton properties.

Sheraton: Developed ITT Sheraton Connections, providing standardized contracts, banquet event order forms, and billing formats, at 27 domestic convention properties.

Renaissance: Offers standardized meeting paperwork (contracts, billing formats, group resumes, and post-convention reports) at 49 Renaissance properties in the United States.

Westin: Provides standardized forms and offers Grouplink, a computerized system which enables planners to enter group rooming lists themselves.

Multiple-Meeting Contracts

Negotiating multiple-meeting contracts is becoming commonplace in the hospitality industry. These contracts, which schedule business over a period of one to several years, have grown in popularity -- especially with corporate meeting planners, who laud them as time- and cost-saving. A planner from a healthcare organization, for example, says she signs a multiple-meeting contract with a major hotel chain for her group's 200 educational seminars held every year around the country. The contract guarantees a price that is a percentage off the rack rate at each hotel and saves time, eliminating the need to negotiate separate contracts.

Disadvantages for meeting planners are the difficulty of accurately predicting meeting attendance, unless attendance is mandatory; future developments, such as company downsizing or mergers; or being "locked in" by contracts. If the meeting planner becomes aware of another property that can provide services at a lower rate, he or she is bound by a previously negotiated multi-meeting contract.

For hotels, multiple-meetings contracts offer the advantage of guaranteed business, but there is also a major disadvantage: perhaps another group comes along that would generate more rooms or food and beverage revenue for the property. If the space is tied up, the property has no recourse but to let the new business go. It is imperative, therefore, that hotels consider multiple-meeting contracts carefully, weighing the proposed multiple-meetings business while maintaining a degree of flexibility in these contracts, especially those that are a year or more out. Other factors, such as the history and stability of the group or possible business developments on either the part of the group (a possible merger in the group's future, for example) or the property (perhaps the obtaining of new, more lucrative business) should also be considered before entering into multiple-meetings contracts.

Chapter Summary:

As you can see, the hotel industry is working hard to deal with meeting planners on a highly professional basis and to make the process of securing profitable meetings business easier through the development of "win-win" contracts and the standardization of meetings-related services. In the next section of this book, we will take a look at the various areas involved in actually executing the meetings and conventions secured through excellent salesmanship and effective negotiating.

Endnotes:

1. Carolyn Cotton, "Liquidated Damage Provision Reflects Compromise on Hotel's Part," *Convene*, May 1996, p. 33.
2. Mary Ann Mc Nulty, "Be Prepared for a Slippage Clause," *Meeting News*, September 1993, p. 27.
3. Melinda Legis, "Killer Contracts," *Successful Meetings*, May 1999, p. 50.
4. Kenneth Hein, "Standardization Efforts Paying Off," *Meeting News*, April 1996, p. 11.

Additional References:

- <u>Meeting Manager Standards and Meeting Coordinator Standards</u> by the Meeting Professionals International Canadian Council and the Government of Canada, The Department of Human Resources Development
  www.mpiweb.org

- Resolving Disputes in the Global Marketplace, Arbitration Seminar, American Bar Association
  www.abanet.org

- <u>Hospitality Law</u>, Steven Barth, John Wiley and Sons, 2001.
  www.hospitality@wiley.com

Internet Sites:

For additional information on the firms and organizations discussed in this chapter, visit the following Internet sites. The Web addresses listed are current as of January 2001. Addresses may change, however; if a site is not available at the address below, a search engine can be used to access its new location.

American Bar Association Alternative Dispute Resolution Section - www.abanet.org/dispute/drlinks.html

Convention Industry Council - www.conventionindustry.org

Hospitality Sales and Marketing International (HSMAI) - www.hsmai.org

PCMA Toolbox (Model Contracts) - www.pcma.org/toolbox

Study Questions:

1. Distinguish between a proposal letter and a letter of agreement (contract).
2. What elements should be considered when developing a contract?
3. What is the master account? In what ways is this account billed?
4. What is a damage clause? An attrition clause? What is the difference between a termination clause and a cancellation clause? How extensively are each of these clauses used?
5. What is the Convention Industry Council? What groups make up its membership and what is their role in the convention industry?

6. What are standardized contracts? What types of properties typically use them? What are the pros and cons of using standardized contracts?
7. What are the advantages and disadvantages of negotiating multiple-meetings contracts?

 Key Terms:

Arbitration. The settling of a disagreement by the review and decision of an arbitrator rather than using the courts.

Attrition clause. Allows the hotel to impose a penalty if the actual guestrooms used are significantly less than the rooms blocked.

Block. The number of guestrooms reserved for a group.

Cancellation clause. Provision in the contract that specifies damages that apply for both parties should either party terminate the agreement.

Cutoff date. The designated date when the buyer (upon request) must release or add to their function room or guestroom commitment.

Flow chart. Indicates the arrival and departure pattern of the meeting participants.

Group ceiling. The maximum number of guestrooms that can be allocated to groups on a particular day. Sometimes referred to as the hotel's group room allotment.

Indemnification clause. Contract clause that specifies compensation for injury, loss or damage. Also referred to as a hold harmless clause.

Inquiry questionnaire. Questionnaire requesting a post convention critique from hotels used in the past by specific meeting groups.

Letter of agreement/contract. Letter from the buyer accepting the proposal. No legal agreement/contract exists unless both parties have accepted the proposal.

Liquidated damage clause. A contract clause that specifies in advance the exact amount of money parties agree to pay in the event of breach of contract.

Master account. One folio for the group on which all charges are accumulated. Also called the master folio.

Mitigation of damage clause. A contract clause that requires parties to determine damages after the dates of the canceled event.

Pick-up. Number of guest rooms actually used out of a room block.

Proposal letter. A letter sent before the letter of agreement or contract which spells out exactly what the customer will receive.

Request for proposal (RFP). Action initiated by the meeting planner for an offer or bid for hotel services.

Release date. The date beyond which the hotel is free to rent the unused function space to other groups.

Slippage. The number of guestrooms not used from the original reserved block.

Termination clause. Contract clause that limits liability should the convention be prevented due to circumstances beyond either party's control. Sometimes referred to as an Act of God clause or a force majeure clause.

Convention Sales and Services

Part II

Convention Services

Learning Objectives:

This portion of your text looks at the role of the convention service manager and his or her staff in ensuring that the property delivers all that was promised to the meeting planner. When you have studied this chapter, you will:

- Be able to describe the role of a convention service manager at a number of types of properties.

- Know how the convention service staff helps to ensure a smooth meeting.

- Be able to describe how group business is turned over to the convention service department from the salesperson and the different ways in which salespeople are involved after the sale.

Outline

Service Is the Key

Who Services?
- Convention Service Manager
- Increased Recognition
- Convention Service Staff

The Transition

Importance of Communication

An Overview of the Service Function

The Role of Convention Service Professionals

Devon Walter, CMP
Convention Services Manager
Sheraton El Conquistador
Tucson, Arizona

"Convention service professionals have only one job, and that is to give the meeting professional the best meeting ever... The keys to producing a great meeting are communication and planning...The convention services and meeting professional become a team, and communication between team members is critical...Pre-planning is so important to the success of the meeting. There will always be some little glitch when the meeting is on-site, and that is so much easier to deal with when everything else is running smoothly — because it has been PLANNED...A convention services professional can expect to spend over 40 hours a week at the facility when there is a group in house... Depending on a group's evening activities, the convention service manager may be at the facility quite late checking on a reception, dinner, or dance... But when the meeting professional and you sit down to conduct the post-convention evaluation and the former says it was the best one ever, that is tremendously rewarding...For those who enjoy working with new people daily, learning about new organizations, working hard, multi-tasking, delegating, administering, coordinating, juggling, creating, and working with details, this is the PERFECT job!"

10   The Service Function

S ecuring a convention is only the beginning; once business has been booked, you must deliver what was promised. How a convention goes out of a hotel is equally -- or even more -- important as obtaining the group's business. A hotel salesperson does not sell just guestrooms, meeting space and complicated audiovisual equipment -- his or her most important product is reassurance; reassurance that the hotel is capable of handling the group's business. To a great extent, the meeting planner's job depends on how well the hotel does its job.

Hard work and many dollars are invested in advertising and promotional material in an effort to recruit group business. Yet, satisfied meeting planners and delegates are the best and most economical advertising medium. If the hotel performs well, the meeting planner will likely return to the property. Delegates are well traveled today and expect more from hotels. If your hotel has made a favorable impression, planners may recommend it to their peers and delegates may stay with you on return visits -- and recommend that their business associates and friends do the same.

Since nothing attracts another piece of group business more than a satisfied convention, it is crucial that all promises made in the selling process be fulfilled. An indelible impression will be made when the hotel provides service that is above and beyond the preconvention promises.

Service Is the Key

Sometimes, the service follow-through is regarded as an afterthought to the heavy emphasis placed on selling a convention or meeting. But failure in the essential service phase can be costly. A meeting planner evaluates the success of his or her convention on the extent to which the hotel's commitments were kept. Lack of communication, poorly trained or indifferent employees, failure to heed details and rude responses to requests are all detriments that may result in lost future business.

How might the hotel better serve the convention group? Most important is a well trained and courteous staff with a service attitude. The hotel industry is essentially a people business and it is important to communicate the property's willingness to assist the meeting planner during both the selling and servicing process (see box titled "Selling and Servicing Small Meetings"). Hotel staff members should be made aware of the importance of convention delegates and should be trained to understand that nothing short of top performance is expected.

One person is usually designated to direct the convention staff and serve as liaison between hotel personnel and the meeting planner. This individual's primary responsibility is to coordinate the group's activities and see that all events function smoothly.

You can build good will in other ways — make arrangements with labor if exhibits are used, obtain any official permissions that are required by local government departments, such as police or fire, and assist with transportation needs. Help convention delegates schedule their time and keep them informed about the facilities in the hotel. Book special entertainment, arrange tours to points of interest, and provide the highest quality food and beverage service possible. In short, give convention delegates every reason for staying at your property -- and returning in the future.

SELLING AND SERVICING SMALL MEETINGS

A single hotel contact person and easy accessibility to a source of assistance are of prime importance to planners of small meetings. The Marriott Corporation addressed this need with the introduction of a new position, the Executive Meeting Manager. This person, who is responsible for booking and servicing small meetings and catering functions, is viewed as a one-stop shopping source to simplify planning for the small group client.

Other chains followed suit, either designating individuals to work one-on-one with meeting planners or developing programs designed to help planners of small meetings. Hyatt, for example, introduced the "Hyatt Meeting Connection," which offers a toll-free number, a fax number and a web address to enable a meeting planner to get in touch with the hotel quickly. After providing pertinent details on the date and size of the meeting, the planner is contacted by a Hyatt Meeting Connection Manager who assists with meeting details.

Hilton's program, "Hilton Direct," is targeted to inexperienced meeting planners, as is Sheraton's "One Stop" program. These sources simplify planning to set the stage for suggestive selling and creative presentations, which, in turn, built repeat business and revenues.

With Renaissance Hotels and Resorts' "Meetings Express" service, a sales manager handles meeting details for planners, including guest rooms, function rooms, and audiovisual services. Other programs include Westin's "Westin One Call," Omni's "Omni Express," and Wyndham Hotels' "Wyndham One."

Radisson's "Meeting Solutions" provides on-line requests for proposals, a toll-free meetings desk help line, and faxing of guestroom confirmations to meeting planners. Canadian Pacific Hotels guarantees small groups a 24-hour turnaround of availability and rate confirmations, and each hotel has a "one-stop" shopping salesperson.

Stuck Planning A Small Meeting?

HYATT **MEETING CONNECTION**
Making Small Meetings A Big Success

1-800-543-1818
or fax your meeting requirements to (402)593-4030
or visit our Web site at www.hyatt.com.

HYATT
HOTELS & RESORTS

Just attach this sticker to your Rolodex.
Then call Hyatt Meeting Connection and leave the details to us (see inside).

History of Convention Services

1940s — *Meeting planners worked with the individual department heads.* Conventions were small and meeting planners would contact the food and beverage manager, the rooms division manager, accounting and others in the hotel on their own.

1950s — *Salesperson serviced.* Dealing with a number of different people in the hotel became more and more of a headache for the planner, especially as the size of convention groups grew. Meeting planners looked to their salesperson to coordinate their meetings within the hotel.

1960s — *Beginning of the convention service position, but with limited authority.* Salespeople were now confronted with the problem of spending a considerable amount of their time servicing groups. Feeling the need to concentrate more time on the selling of the hotel and its facilities, many sales managers turned servicing over to either the sales secretary or the lowest level salesperson.

1970s — *Role of convention service manager increased in importance.* As the number and complexity of the meetings held grew annually, so did the importance of the convention service manager. This increased recognition was advanced by the Society of Corporate Meeting Professionals, which opened its membership ranks to convention service managers.

1980s — *Gained industry respect.* Convention service managers formed their own association (seven hundred strong) called the Association of Convention Operations Management (ACOM). Meeting planners came to rely on the dedication, knowledge and hard work of the convention service department.

1990s — *Elevated to the Hotel's Executive Committee.* Now most of the major hotel chains have a corporate level position for convention services. Within the hotel, convention service managers generally report to marketing, occasionally to food and beverage or catering, and now increasingly directly to the general manager. In hotels that look to conventions for a major portion of their room nights, the Director of Convention Services is part of the hotel's executive committee.

2000s — *Serve as Meeting Consultants.* The role of the convention service manager has expanded beyond delivering meetings service. Increasingly, meeting planners look for partners who can consult and present customized solutions to their problems. Most hotel chains have raised the bar, requiring their convention service managers to become certified with the same education and training as the customer.

Regardless of how smoothly a program is planned, snags and slipups inevitably occur. If your hotel helps meeting planners solve these problems, future business is nearly always assured. It may be necessary to shuffle meeting rooms around, help find a last-minute substitute speaker or prepare a special entree for the wife of the chairman of the board. The attitude with which you accept these common occurances will, to a great extent, determine the location of next year's convention. The professionalism your staff demonstrates is the hotel's best promotion for future business from the convention organizer and it increases the likelihood of business referrals. If you conquer any crisis that threatens the flow of the meeting, the parting handshake may well be accompanied by the meeting planner's promise, "We'll see you next year."

Who Services?

One of the frequently discussed issues in convention management is the extent to which the salesperson should be involved in the servicing process. The structure of the hotel staff is based on how this issue is resolved.

Some hotels say that a salesperson is just that, and that he or she shouldn't become involved in servicing the client. They claim that the service function is a specialty, distinct from selling, and that there is a more efficient use of staff and a higher rebooking percentage when salespeople spend 100 percent of their time selling. Others hold that the convention salesperson should handle the sales and servicing completely. They suggest that the sales representative should follow up all hotel visits, write up the actual bookings and coordinate the servicing of the group during its stay at the hotel. These are diametrically opposed points of view. Which should you follow?

Resort Management, a lodging and foodservice publication, asked the managers at three hotels how they handled sales and servicing. Their comments on how they handle this controversial issue are presented in Figure 10.1. Judging from this discussion, there seems to be basically three approaches to the question: "Who services?"

The Tamarron's position is that the sales manager should sell, arrange and work with the meeting from beginning to end. They feel that the salesperson who does not get involved in servicing may be concerned only with putting business on the books, thus perhaps making hasty promises that are impossible to keep.

Opposed to this view is the Kingsmill, with the opinion that once the sale is made the salesperson should step aside in favor of the in-house conference coordinator, who then documents the client's needs, draws up the letter of agreement and follows through to the end of the meeting.

A third, middle-of-the-road, approach is practiced at Jug End. There, the salesperson meets the group as it arrives, but then steps out of the picture until the function is nearly completed. He or she then returns on closing day to attempt to sell upcoming meetings.

Which approach should you practice? Our experience says "the best approach is the one that works." No one procedure is best for all situations. If the size of the hotel justifies an in-house convention service manager, we support separation of sales and service.

The Convention Service Manager

Throughout the text, we have taken the position that the servicing responsibility is handled by the convention service manager. Such a practice assures the association or corporate executive that whatever his or her requirements — reservations, banquet, meeting room setup — there is one individual with complete authority and responsibility for his or her meeting.

The title *convention service manager* has not been adopted by all hotels. Many use such other titles as conference or convention or service coordinator, convention manager,

Figure 10.1. VIEWPOINTS ON WHO SHOULD SERVICE MEETINGS.

TAMARRON

Located in the Rocky Mountains about thirty miles from Durango, Colorado, the Tamarron is a resort owned by Golf Hosts International. It offers 415 guest rooms and 7,000 square feet of meeting space.

I find that both direct sales and service selling have very valid points. However, I feel that the points in service selling far exceed those in direct sales. The advantages of direct sales do give the opportunity to the sales staff to concentrate their total effort in the booking business, and do not tie them up in the laborious task of accumulating the multitude of details that it always takes to conduct a successful conference. But when you have a sales department whose only responsibility is getting meetings on the books, they seem to lose contact with the other departments and see their responsibilities as only that of putting business on the books.

I am a strong believer in service selling with modifications. I believe there is a definite need for a conference coordinator to assist in the many details that are involved in successful conferences. However, conference coordinators should never eliminate any of the responsibilities of the salesperson who actually sells the group.

I think the salesperson who is instrumental in booking business has got to be kept involved from beginning to end. By doing this, it builds the association executive's confidence in the hotel, makes the salesperson more aware of the strong and weak points of his people and, consequently, makes the salesperson better in booking other groups and puts him or her in an excellent position to rebook meetings. It also helps the salesperson tremendously in building his or her own reputation with the meeting planners because they understand the promises and assurances that were made when the booking was made, and the planners see that he is always available and visible during the conference to see that these promises are carried out.

Salesperson Services

KINGSMILL

The Kingsmill Resort is a part of a large development program undertaken by Anheuser-Busch, Inc. just outside of Williamsburg, Virginia. It houses a large convention center and has more meeting square footage than either of the other two properties discussed.

There is so much more to this question concerning service selling vs direct sales than meets the eye that I can only classify the subject as an "explosive issue."

The subject is not just "How is the salesperson best employed?" or "How can management keep salespeople happy?" or "How to reduce costs?," but perhaps should be defined as "Complete client satisfaction ensures rebooking without sales costs." Meeting planners are not sheep, but they need a shepherd to turn to at all times.

Let us, therefore, trace sales procedures, starting with a given company name only, coupled with a reasonable belief that this company would possibly hold meetings.

Salesperson Sells, Then Turns Over To a Convention Service Manager

Sales Step 1: Having been given a cold lead by the sales manager, a sales telephonist is employed to determine the company's meeting plan profile. The information to obtain is broadly as follows:

A.   Meeting frequency
B.   Time(s) of the year
C.   Length of meeting — arrival date and departure date

D. Number of attendees
E. Type of property preferred and why
F. Type of meeting
G. Purchase center and responsible individual
H. Any other attendant information which will help the account executive

Sales Step 2: Having qualified the prospect, the information obtained is then turned over in a written report to the area account executive who then telephones for an appointment, or, if feasible, arranges for the conference planner to participate in a house visit. Sales literature is normally not passed until personal face-to-face contact is made with the potential client.

Sales Step 3: When the verbal sale is made, the client is turned over to the property's conference coordinator, who is responsible for all of the client's needs, preparing the sales contract or letter of agreement, and following through every step of the way to the end of the meeting.

While the conference coordinator has the full responsibility for the smooth running of the client's meeting, and for informing by conference specification sheet, the various department heads concerned, the conference coordinator will, where practical, introduce the client and sit in on discussions with the various department heads (such as food and beverage director, front desk supervisor, conference setup manager, etc.). The client receives a copy of the internal conference specification plan in order that he or she may check that all arrangements have been made in accordance with his or her instructions. The points to be learned by this process are:

A.. The salesperson does not waste his or her time soliciting prospects who would not be suitable for the particular property.
B. The salesperson can devote 100% of his or her time "selling" to live prospects.
C. After the verbal sales has been made, the client is assured that there is a responsible person who will look after his or her needs and who will always be available on the spot, and is, therefore, not "out of town," "will call back later," etc.
D. Management can reduce their number of salespeople needed because the sales people can spend 100% of their time selling to prospects instead of 30% of their time checking internally, 30% making introductions to department heads, and other time setting up meeting rooms.
E. Service promises concerning actual meeting room availability, function areas and times, audiovisual equipment availability, etc. are kept because the service manager will be in the house at the time. How often, in poorly coordinated properties, is a client anguished when he finds a particular meeting room, a function site or a particular piece of equipment promised by the salesperson is not available because it has been committed elsewhere.
F. Furthermore, and equally important, a strong conference coordinator will control the flow of traffic into the main dining room by staggering the times groups break from cocktail parties, banquets and recreational activities. Such planning minimizes the burdens on the chef, the head bartender, and setup people, and provides the client with the type of service anticipated.

In other words, efficient service and attention to small details throughout the length of the meeting is of paramount importance, and, when given, assures that the client will rebook.

JUG END

The Jug End in the Berkshires is a 180-room resort in Massachusetts with about 6,000 square feet in its largest meeting room. It, like the Tamarron, is a mountain resort with winter skiing and summer golf facilities.

In many cases, the servicing of group business depends on the size of the house. If the property has 50 rooms or less, many times the owner/manager can sell and service the property himself (or with the help of his wife)...but when the property is larger than that, I prefer that specialists handle the servicing.

> **Salesperson Sells; Responsibility for Group Based on Size**
>
> Let the salespeople do the selling...get the business "in the house." The reputation of the hotel (and the food service) is mostly dependent on the in-house servicing. With larger groups, the salesperson should be on hand to welcome them, and then, the servicing should be handled by others, preferably by the food staff, since the food staff is so made up that, should one member be unavailable, the whole service operation does not fall apart. I have seen sad situations develop where details have not been properly attended to by the salesperson, and such lack of attention or mishandling reflects poorly on the whole operation.
>
> Should the group planner prefer to deal with the owner/principal of the hotel, we don't object. We will do everything he wants to make him feel at ease. The big thing is not to have a meeting planner come in and feel uneasy...be fearful that the meeting might "bomb out" and so jeopardize his own future in his company. It is also important to let meeting planners know that you recognize their authority and attendant responsibilities and to assure them that you are not going to let them down.
>
> At our property, I always make it a point to meet the head of each group. He has done a great deal of planning for the meeting, has spent thousands of dollars in organizing the meeting, considerable money on transportation, etc., plus what he will spend at our hotel. Consequently, I feel that the head of the hotel has an obligation to the convention group to let them know that the entire staff, from the top right down to the bottom, is interested in making their meeting a success.

and, at many smaller properties, banquet or catering manager. (Chapter 14 offers a thorough discussion of the role of the banquet manager as practiced at most small properties.)

Regardless of the title, the position carries a lot of prestige and a hefty amount of responsibility (see box titled "The Perfect Convention Service Manager"). If any one person can make or break a conference, it is the convention service manager, often referred to as "the person who makes things happen." He or she is the meeting planner's contact person, and so should be readily available to handle all of the convening group's on-the-spot needs. Quite simply, he or she is the single communication link between the meeting planner and the hotel.

The role of convention service manager has grown beyond service to meeting consultant at some hotels. David Kassel, CMP, senior convention service manager, Walt Disney World Dolphin Hotel, states,

> "I try to educate the planner on how to do events with a little more creativity. A lot of my expertise is anticipating needs — having the forethought to put myself in the planner's place. It also means that I find alternatives to save them dollars."[1]

Ideally, the convention service manager has the authority to get the job done and to get it done fast. Meeting planners are able to rest much easier when they have the assurance that their liaison has authority within the hotel as well as the responsibility to fulfill their needs.

Leroy Smith, association executive of the National Automobile Association, has suggested that the convention service department should report directly to the hotel's general manager, not to the director of sales.[2] He suggests that hotels should have an organizational structure that gives the convention service manager line control over the functions of the front desk, housekeeping, banquet, and food and beverage departments as related to conventions.

The working hours of the person in charge of service are often very long. Bill Tobin says of the time he was convention service manager at Caesar's Palace in Las Vegas, "I wanted to give the meeting planner the impression that I never went home." One hour before every function, he checked out the facilities with the group's coordinator. This is a commendable policy, but when there are several groups within the house, one having a late cocktail party and another planning an early-bird breakfast, the convention service manager may find little time for himself. Cutting still further into time off are the preconvention and post-convention meetings often scheduled for weekends.

But there are rewards for these long hours. In addition to the salary paid by the hotel, the convention service manager may receive compensation for long hours in the form of gifts and tips from the meeting planner. Association and corporate executives have been known to be extremely generous in saying thanks for a job well done. Further remuneration is sometimes received from the hotel. The Sheraton Waikiki, recognizing the importance of the convention service manager, has given this individual a suite in the hotel. Sheraton Hotels, like a growing number of chains, has also established advisory boards made up of meeting planners to help the chain respond to the needs and concerns of meeting planners. One of these concerns centers around the role of the convention service manager; in many cases, the advisory boards recommend giving convention service managers more authority to ensure that meeting details can be worked out through a single contact person. Brian Stevens, former Vice President, Sales, Hilton Hotels, agrees,

> "Today, more than ever, hotels need to make sure their customers work
> with the most experienced, most highly trained convention service man-
> agers possible — or there simply won't be any customers after a while."[3]

How does one become a convention service manager? Most have advanced through either the banquet or front office departments, where they were exposed to the problems frequently encountered in group business. Then some alert sponsor placed him or her over the department. Often the next step up the corporate rung is to convention sales. The salesperson who has had experience in group servicing knows what can be promised and what can be delivered, and thus is a most valued employee. However, many are not sure this move to sales is a promotion, and more and more managers are staying with convention services.

Another career move for some is promotion to resident manager. This is not surprising since the convention service manager interacts with virtually all other hotel departments. In a recent speech, Joyce Inderbitzin of Hilton's Corporate Convention Services estimated that 70 percent of Hilton's general managers were convention service managers at one time in their careers.

Increased Recognition

The convention service manager's position has steadily been elevated in status in hotel organizations. The Society of Corporate Meeting Professionals has invited convention service managers to join their ranks and *Successful Meetings* instituted an annual Convention Service Manager of the Year award.

Convention service managers also have their own organization, the Association for Convention Operations Management (ACOM). Membership includes convention service directors, managers and coordinators from hotels, and event service managers from convention centers and convention bureaus. Hotel convention service managers can also join the

Professional Convention Management Association (PCMA). This organization serves the convention industry with educational resources, networking, and an annual meeting that offers nearly 100 educational sessions to meeting planners. The PCMA also offers a Function Space Verification Program for meeting planners and publishes *Convene* magazine, a useful resource for both planners and hotel professionals.

Marketing gurus tell us that the best future customer is the one you've already got, and hotels are placing a heavy emphasis on the convention service manager's role in rebooking. Increasing the authority and responsibility of this department has been used by hotels to show commitment to the meeting business and convention service personnel (see Figure 10.2).

A profile of ACOM's membership supports this contention. The average tenure is five years in their positions, with less than 10 percent going into sales and marketing. Also, a number report directly to the general manager and are members of their hotel's executive committee, along with the directors of marketing, food and beverage, operations and the controller. A number of hotel chains have standardized the position of convention service manager and bring them together annually for networking and idea exchange. Hilton, Hyatt, Marriott and Sheraton have established corporate directors of convention services.

Several chains have made major commitments to training their convention service managers and other convention support staff to better assist meeting planners (see box titled "Training Convention Services Personnel"). As part of its recently introduced "Network Plan," the Marriott chain has committed to staffing each of its convention properties with a minimum of two Certified Meeting Professionals (CMPs). The CMP exam, given by the Convention Industry Council, also figures prominently in the Hyatt chain's "Learning Environment Specialist" (LES) program (passing the CMP exam is a pre-requisite for this advanced training). Developed in association with the Professional Convention Management Association (PCMA), this six-day program offers instruction to help enhance all phases of meeting planning. And, the Hilton Hotel chain has developed its own program, Customer-Focused Convention Service Skills (CFCSS), to sharpen the skills of its convention service managers.

Convention Service Staff

How the convention service department is staffed depends on the size of the hotel, the percentage of occupancy accounted for by convention groups, the size of the groups using the hotel, and the number and size of the property's meeting rooms. Figure 10.3 illustrates a sample organization chart of a convention service department.

Some properties have expanded their convention service departments, creating new positions to better serve meeting planners (see box titled "Introducing the Conference Concierge"). Following are position titles and brief descriptions of the responsibilities of individuals who might work in the convention service department of a large convention oriented property.

Director of Convention Services — oversees, trains and assists the convention staff in all phases of managing meeting accounts. Generally reports to the director of sales/marketing, but at large properties may report directly to the general manager.

Convention Service Manager(s) — services meeting groups as assigned by director of convention services and is the primary contact for assigned groups. There are usually several convention service managers in a large hotel. A sample job description for this position is given in Figure 10.4.

TRAINING CONVENTION SERVICES PERSONNEL

Many hotel chains have recognized the importance of the service function, and have introduced training programs for their convention service managers and other key convention personnel. This increased knowledge and meeting planning expertise helps build the confidence of meeting planners, and is an important selling point in today's highly competitive meetings market.

Figure 10.2. CONVENTION SERVICE PERSONNEL PLAY A PIVOTAL ROLE IN THE SUCCESS OF THEIR HOTELS.

This ad quotes Jonathon M. Tisch, President and CEO of Loews Hotels, as saying he listened to meeting planners and increased the stature of the chain's convention service managers, promoting them to the executive committees of their respective hotels. The executive committee is made up of senior-level hotel managers who report directly to the general manager, and may include the director of food and beverage, the controller, the resident manager, the director of marketing, and the director of convention services.

THE PERFECT CONVENTION SERVICE MANAGER

The Convention Industry Council advises meeting planners that the "perfect" convention service manager is one who: begins working with you as soon as the meeting is booked; knows his or her property and has the respect of people in other departments; has the authority to get things done; anticipates problems and has solutions at hand; offers creative suggestions for set-ups, programs, meals and entertainment; considers himself or herself an extension of your staff; stays in contact with you throughout the planning process to check on your needs; covers your meeting 24 hours a day, personally and through his or her staff; is flexible and honest enough not to over-promise or to under-commit; balances the needs of professionals with the needs of his/her own organization; treats all meeting planners with equal respect.

Source: The Convention Liaison Manual, 6th Edition, p. 66.

Convention Coordinator(s) — entry-level position in convention service department. Primary responsibility is to service small meeting groups and to assist convention service managers.

Floor Manager — responsible for servicing and setup of all meeting room and food and beverage functions. Oversees housepersons to ensure instructions from the specification and function sheets are carried out.

Set-up Crew (sometimes called *Housepersons*) — responsible for the physical setup of all meeting and banquet rooms.

Director of Exhibit Service — works closely with the meeting group's trade show manager when the hotel's exhibition facilities are utilized. This position is only present in hotels with substantial dedicated exhibit space.

Function Book Coordinator — the single person who records entries from the function book reservation forms, responsible for ensuring the accuracy of the function book. This individual works closely with the sales staff, catering, and the convention service manager(s).

Figure 10.3 ORGANIZATIONAL STRUCTURE OF A CONVENTION SERVICE DEPARTMENT IN A LARGE HOTEL.

INTRODUCING THE CONFERENCE CONCIERGE

As the convention industry has grown, the time commitment of the convention service manager has increased. Hotels that once realized 25 percent of their occupancy from meeting groups now look to capture 40-50 percent of their room nights from meetings, which would stretch even the most capable of convention managers too thin to adequately service business.

In response, Starwood Hotels (owner of the Sheraton and Westin brands, Four Points Hotels, the Luxury Collection and the new W hotels) is just one of the chains (Hyatt is another) that have introduced a new position: the *conference concierge*. The conference concierge's responsibilities begin when the group arrives. The concierge stays in constant communication with the planner, improving the level of attention and service planners receive. Typical tasks for the concierge might include getting copies made for the planner at the last minute or assisting with package shipment. With the addition of this position, the planner now has two people on site to assist them, and the level of attention is greatly improved.

The new position also frees up the convention service manger to spend more time with advance planning with groups whose meetings may be months in the future. And, the position offers an opportunity for those wishing to break into convention services.

David Dvorak, Convention Services Vice President for Starwood, says:

"The new title creates a great entry-level position because the concierge sees room setups, how to deal with emergencies and meeting planners, and how to multi-task."

Source of Starwood information: Rayna Katz, "Starwood Makes Top-Level Nod to Convention Services," *Meeting News*, August 7, 2000, p. 1.

Convention Service Secretary(ies) — performs secretarial duties, including typing of correspondence, specification sheets and function sheets for the convention service department.

The Transition

A frequent debate in convention management is, "How and when should meeting planners be turned over to the individual within the hotel who will have charge of coordinating their conference?" Timing depends greatly on the meeting planner, the size and type of the meeting, and how far in advance the meeting has been booked. Four commonly used times for this transition include:

1. *During the site inspection* —The hotel salesperson is the key contact when booking the event, but some planners try to meet the convention service manager during the site inspection visit, saying there is a "reassurance factor" in making early contact with the person who will be handling the details of their meetings.

2. *Right before signing the contract* — Some meeting planners ask for an interview with convention services before signing the contract. This step helps ensure that promises made regarding space, set-ups and meeting services can be met. One meeting planner has stated,

Figure 10.4. SAMPLE JOB DESCRIPTION FOR CONVENTION SERVICE MANAGER.

Job Title: Convention and Conference Service Manager
Reports to: Director of Convention and Conference Service
Department: Convention and Conference Service

Summary of Position

Services all convention and conference groups as assigned by the Director of Convention Service. Plans and coordinates all arrangements, (i.e., golf bookings, audiovisual needs, etc.) related to assigned groups to ensure the success of the convention and to promote repeat business.

Scope

This position is responsible for identifying and communicating the needs of the customer to the hotel departments to ensure proper service throughout the hotel operation for assigned groups.

Objectives/ Responsibilities

A. Plans and executes conventions and conferences as the primary customer contact for assigned groups. *25% of time*

B. Coordinates and distributes all interdepartmental paperwork necessary for the successful implementation of assigned groups. *25% of time*

C. Oversees activities of assigned groups and functions as the onsite contact for the Meeting Planner. *15% of time*

D. Assists with training of Convention and Conference Coordinator as assigned by the Director of Convention and Conference Service. *15% of time*

E. Attends daily and/or weekly meetings as assigned by the Director as well as arranges and conducts Pre-Convention and Conference meetings for assigned convention groups. *15% of time*

F. Assists in preparation of forecasts and budgets. *3% of time*

G. Performs additional tasks as assigned by Director. *2% of time*

Supervision Exercised

Directly supervises: Assigned Clerical Staff
Indirectly supervises: Convention and Conference Coordinator
Floor Manager
Support Staff
Function Book Coordinator

Supervision Received

Responsible to the Director of Convention and Conference Service

Responsibility/ Authority

Employee Relations:
Responsible for communicating and following through with hotel management to ensure that the sales commitment is being fulfilled. Distribute written communications (resumes, event orders) detailing the needs of the customer and the sales commitment. Maintains effective relationship with Sales and Service Staff as well as all department heads.

Materials or Products:
Maintains up-to-date group files to ensure proper coordination of sales commitment as well as customer needs. Maintains trace system for these files.

Equipment:
Assists in proper use and adequate inventory of meeting equipment to properly service all functions.

	Financial: Responsible for maximizing revenues associated with meetings for assigned group files as well as maximizing function space usage.
	Business Contacts: Maintains proper communications between groups, outside vendors and hotel staff. Also responsible for establishing customer relationships that will encourage repeat business.
Preferred Knowledge/ Qualifications	**Equivalent Education Level:** College degree (or equivilent Convention and Conference Service experience) required.
	Experience: A minimum of two years in Convention and Conference Coordination with exposure to office procedures and experience in function room setups and service with strong interpersonal skills and organizational skills.
	Knowledge Required: Function space configuration, room setups, maximizing space, art of negotiating and selling. General knowledge of hotel management, operations and facilities.

"Before signing a contract, I want to meet the convention service manager and let him or her know who I'm bringing in and what my meeting is all about. The salesperson may wine and dine me, but the convention service manager makes it happen. That's the person I'm married to for three days."

3. *Immediately after the point of sale* — If the convention is large and complex, some planners start working with convention services as soon as the contract is signed.
4. *One year before the meeting* — Many planners feel no need to involve convention services before one year in advance to begin the formal planning process. This procedure will not work in the case of short-term bookings that will require immediate contact between the meeting planner and the convention service manager.

It is difficult to divorce the salesperson entirely from the service function. The salesperson who simply dismisses a client after the sale, assuming that the convention service manager will shoulder the burden, will probably not get a rebooking. Jim Hill, Director of Sales at the Inverness Hotel and Golf Club in Englewood, CO, uses a unique approach to ensure that both the salesperson and the convention service manager are known and trusted by the meeting planner:

"What we've introduced is a buddy system. Each sales associate is working with a conference service manager, and they actually work through the sales process together. From day one, we introduce the conference services manager, who the sales associate knows and has been working with throughout the year."[4]

Repeatedly partnering the convention service manager with a specific salesperson creates strong bonds and efficient teamwork. If the sales staff is deployed by market segments, partnering benefits convention service managers by concentrating their work with similar types of groups. For example, working with a salesperson dedicated to medical

Figure 10.5. SAMPLE LETTER OF INTRODUCTION AND TIMELINE SHEET.

February 6, 2002

Ray Harper, President
Harper and Pritchard Construction
611 S. Bridge Street
Columbus, OH 48850

Dear Mr. Harper:

I would like to take this opportunity to introduce myself as your Convention Service Manager for your upcoming meeting which will take place at the Las Vegas Hilton during the dates of September 1-4, 2002. I will be responsible for all aspects of your meeting with the exception of food and beverage arrangements, which will be handled by Gus Moser in our Catering Department.

Below I have noted a few of the key items relating to your meeting. Please bring any discrepances to my attention as soon as possible so the appropriate changes may be made internally.

Room Block — 125 king rooms and 4 suites in the North Tower
Room Rate — $110 guest rooms, $150 suites
Method of Reservations — Rooming list
Billing — Master Account

Additionally, please find enclosed a time line for required information which will assist both of us in planning your upcoming convention. This schedule ensures that your program receives the attention and service that it deserves. Please review the schedule and advise me if any dates seem unattainable.

If you will be shipping any packages to the hotel in conjunction with your meeting, please insure they are addressed to my attention in care of the Las Vegas Hilton Convention Service Department along with your organization's name and date of your function. However, due to storage requirements, we ask that these items be sent as close to the convention as possible.

Sincerely,

Cindy O'Keefe
Executive Director of Convention S

cc: Sean Steward, Sales Manager
     Gus Moser, Catering Manager

TIME LINE

GROUP:	Harper and Pritchard Construction
CONTACT:	Ray Harper, President
MEETING DATES:	September 1-4, 2002

Listed below are areas of concern with review dates that will assist us both to ensure a successful meeting.

ITEM	DUE DATE
Preliminary meeting program	April 1
Final meeting program	May 1
Credit application finalized	July 1
Cut off date	August 1
Meeting & audiovisual requirements	July 15
Food & beverage menus finalized	July 15

Please make any changes as necessary then sign and return the form to me. If these dates seem practical as listed above, I would appreciate your signing and returning this form to me. Thank you.

Ray Harper, President	Cindy O'Keefe
Harper and Pritchard Construction	Executive Director of Convention Services

The convention service manager and meeting planner should communicate often —and in writing — from the time the business is turned over to the convention service department. Today, the convention service manager and the meeting planner also exchange e-mail addresses early in the planning stage. Establishing a written timetable with the customer for pre-planning and communicating the group's requirements is essential to effectively service meeting groups. Most convention service managers tell us that their biggest problems in servicing groups stem from not getting enough information from their planners in a timely manner. A timeline such as this one alleviates that problem by setting dates when specific information is needed.

groups allows the convention service manager to gain an indepth understanding of how to service these types of meetings.

The transition from the salesperson to the convention service manager must be handled smoothly. Frequently the client has dealt exclusively with the salesperson for two or three years and has complete trust in the sales staff. The salesperson's exit can be traumatic if the planner has not been reassured of the service manager's competence.

We recommend that once the sale is made the salesperson step aside and turn the meeting over to the service people. We don't believe, however, that the client should be abandoned by the salesperson. We suggest that the salesperson greet the planner, if possible, when the meeting comes to the hotel and reassure him or her that the meeting is in good hands. Further, the salesperson should keep in touch and reenter as the meeting closes to suggest a rebooking. It just makes good sense for a salesperson to maintain contact with a client who has bought the property as a meeting site, and could, of course, buy again in the future.

Importance of Communication

Convention service managers must be great communicators. Jose Perez, convention service manager at the Sonesta Beach Hotel in Key Biscayne, Florida, says:

> "When the convention is in the planning stage, I find out how the group wants to handle check-in and check-outs, what kind of meeting rooms and audiovisual equipment is needed, how to bill the rooms, what types of recreational activities to plan and what kind of transportation. I call the meeting planner at least once a month, and about 45 days prior to arrival I average speaking with the planner two or three times a week. A week before the group arrives, we talk every day."[5]

Quality as well as frequency of communication is also crucial. Let's consider a fictional situation. The Cannon Corporation, a larger torpedo manufacturer headquartered in the East, has scheduled a convention in a Seattle hotel. The Cannon meeting planner has informed the convention service manager of a heavy 4:00 P.M. check-in on Sunday. The convention service manager included the following instructions to the front desk and the hotel's restaurants:

Attention: Lanny Kingsbury — Front Desk Check-in
This is a major check-in day for Cannon Corp. I recommend you plan to staff the desk to handle the overload during the peak around 4:00 P.M... Traffic should be heavy, with 600 delegates arriving on two charter flights.

Attention: Marney Vartanian — Public Feeding Facilities
I would recommend full staffing by 5:00 P.M. due to the heavy arrival. Food and beverage functions are nonexistent during Sunday evening so delegate traffic will be particularly heavy in all restaurants.

The hotel has made plans to handle the overloads, according to the instructions. At one o'clock Sunday in Seattle — 4:00 P.M. eastern time — 600 delegates arrive at the hotel. The delegates, anxious to get settled, face long lines and a minimum hotel staff. *Someone forgot to communicate* the time change between the east and west coasts. To compound the problem, the delegation has arrived at the peak of the previous day's check-out. The Cannon Corporation is ready to fire its product at the hotel's lobby.

Who is to blame? The meeting planner is outraged. He charges, "We have supplied you with a big piece of business and immediately you blow it." The hotel counters, "We were ready for you. We didn't deliberately try to give you a bad time. You told us four o'clock; we were ready at four o'clock." Whether the fault lies with the meeting planner or the convention service manager, the hotel's image is damaged, perhaps beyond repair.

The convention service manager should not be satisfied with just selling rooms and food. He or she is also in the business of providing service. This means he or she should be a problem solver for the client, not a problem maker. A hotel should request full and detailed information so it can better serve the group. Likewise, the hotel should communicate accurate data to the client. The clearer the communication in the beginning, the less likely there will be disappointments later.

An Overview

Thus far, we've talked about the importance of service, the role of the convention service manager, and his or her position in the hotels' organizational structure. In subsequent chapters, we will cover in detail every facet of this person's job and how he or she works with other departments within the hotel. To give a clearer picture, an overview of the convention service manager's role, step-by-step, follows:

Step No. 1 — Once a group is booked, the convention service manager reviews all correspondence to find out what information has been documented and what information is still required. Many times he or she will review files from two or three years before the date of the convention. A *sales to service turnover data sheet* is now used by many hotels to quickly bring the CSM up to date on the group. This short form summarizes specifics negotiated by the salesperson, including guestroom block, preliminary meeting program, cut-off dates, and so on. With this information, the CSM begins to assemble the *working file* needed for servicing the group.

Step No. 2 — The booking is listed in the function book, and contact is made with the meeting planner through a **letter of introduction** (see Figure 10.5). This letter specifies that the group will be dealing the the convention service manager while in the hotel. At this point, the salesperson goes behind the scenes and the convention service manager begins to get answers to the three basics: *reservations, program and billing*.

Step No. 3 — **Tracing** — using follow-up letters, telephone calls and personal contact with the association executive — is initiated to build a relationship of trust and cooperation between the two parties. Correspondence is made as clear as possible, and includes lots of detail. Technology has made tracing easier, more efficient, and faster. In the past, convention service managers relied on telephones and letters; today, e-mail and faxes are used to speed up the tracing process.

Step No. 4 — Details of the program are formulated in a *personal interview* with the meeting planner at least six months before the event. Reservation requests are also mailed to the delegates at about this time in an effort to determine the number of guestrooms (see Chapter 11 for additional information).

Step No. 5 — A monthly preconvention meeting is held with all department heads to review upcoming groups (see Chapter 12). All *convention specification sheets* and *banquet event orders* are discussed in detail.

Step No.6 — Two or three days before the conference opens, a preconvention meeting is held with the front office manager (see Chapter 12), the supervisor in charge of room setup (see Chapter 13), the catering manager (see Chapter 14), and the meeting planner. The entire program is reviewed, the menus are reaffirmed, and the meeting setups are verified. *Step No. 7* — During the convention, the service manager is on hand as much as possible. He or she will be at each meeting location one hour ahead of time to view the setup, check the audiovisual equipment (see Chapter 15), exhibit setup and check security (these are discussed in Chapters 16 and 17).

Step No. 8 — A post-convention meeting is held at the end of the event (see Chapter 18). All charges to the master account are verified and initialed a second time by the client. The post-convention meeting is a review of the event by those persons in attendance at the preconvention meeting. At this time, the salesperson steps in to sell the group on a repeat convention. When the service department does its job, a rebooking percentage of 70 percent is not uncommon.

Chapter Summary:

Your attitude and professionalism in serving your guests will be what sets you and your property apart from the rest. And the foundation of your professionalism begins with knowledge. You must know what tangible products and services are required by meeting planners and how to deliver the successful meetings and functions that they demand.

In this chapter, we have presented an overview of the convention services structure and the importance of meeting with the planner to ensure that his or her requirements will be met. In the next chapter, we will discuss how to get the meeting or convention off to a good start by discussing the most efficient way to register guests. In subsequent chapters in this section, we will provide a foundation in other elements of service. Armed with this knowledge, you will have the confidence to embark on the most important aspect of your job: building the trust and rapport that results in satisfied customers and repeat business for your property.

Endnotes:

1. Robert Carey, "Leaders of the Pack," *Successful Meetings*, February 1995, p. 115.
2. Speech given at a Hospitality Sales and Marketing Association International (HSMAI) meeting in Las Vegas.
3. Brian Stevens, "A New Commitment to Convention Service," *Convene*, September 1995, p. 25.
4. Connie Goldstein, "Productive Meetings," *Corporate Meetings and Incentives*, October 1995, p. 57.

5. Todd Englander, "Ombudsman-Quarterback-Decorator-Shrink," *Business Travel News*.

Additional References:

- <u>Hospitality Marketing Management, Third Edition</u>, Robert Reid and David Bojanic, John Wiley 2001.

- <u>Marketing for Hospitality and Tourism, Second Edition</u>, Philip Kottler, John Bowen, James Makens, Prentice Hall 1999

Internet Sites:

For additional information on the firms and organizations discussed in this chapter, visit the following Internet sites. The Web addresses listed are current as of January 2001. Addresses may change, however; if a site is not available at the address below, a search engine can be used to access its new location.

Caesars Palace Resort - www.Caesars.com
Four Seasons Regent Hotels and Resorts - www.fshr.com
Hilton Hotels - www.hilton.com
Hyatt Hotels and Resorts - www.hyatt.com
Loews Hotels - www.loewshotels.com
Marriott International - www.marriott.com
Professional Convention Management Association (PCMA) - www.pcma.org
Society of Corporate Meeting Professionals (SCMP) - www.scmp.org
Successful Meetings magazine - www.successmtgs.com

Study Questions:

1. Should sales department personnel become involved with group servicing? Discuss the three approaches used by the Tamarron Resort, the Kingsmill and the Jug End.
2. Where does the convention service manager fit into the hotel organizational structure?
3. What types of programs are available to train convention service managers and their staffs to better assist meeting planners?
4. Describe the titles and duties of the members of the convention services staff.
5. What is meant by the transition? At what four times can transitions take place?

6. What is tracing and how is it used to build a relationship with the meeting planner?

7. Briefly define the eight steps inherent to servicing a group's meeting.

 Key Terms:

Letter of introduction. Letter sent by the convention service manager to the meeting planner. Specifies who the group will be dealing with while in the hotel.

Tracing. Building a relationship with the client by using follow-up letters, telephone calls and personal contact.

APPENDIX

CONVENTION SERVICE CHECKLIST

Detailed checklists serve as planning guides and often prevent the overlooking of important items in staging a successful convention. Numerous checklists exist for helping the meeting planner avoid oversights, but few are available specifically for the convention service manager. This is the format used by the Penta Hotels and is the best checklist of its type that we have seen in the industry.

Penta Hotels
CONVENTION SERVICE CHECKLIST

NAME OF GROUP _____

DATES OF MEETING _____

MEETING PLANNER _____

MASTER ACCOUNT ADDRESS _____

_____

_____

TELEPHONE NUMBER _____

SALES MANAGER _____

BANQUET MANAGER _____

	Completion Date
TWELVE (12) MONTHS AWAY FROM MEETING DUE DATE	
1. Sales manager to turn account file over to Convention Service with a copy of the signed contract, a copy of the approved booking notice, a copy of the approved room block, a copy of the credit form (if credit has not been determined, trace three days and follow-up), and a past history on pick-up for the last two (2) years.	_____
2. Review account file	_____
3. Verify definite program, confirm diary space, meeting room rental, exhibit rental, set-up charges, and date all space hold to be released (if applicable).	_____
4. Confirm room commitments with Front Office and Group Rooms Control for accuracy, based on past history, block VIP suites. Determine when room rate will be established, and trace if not already established.	_____
5. Determine if all exhibit information is complete in contract and remind account of need for floor plans to be approved, exhibitor's contract to be approved, hold harmless clause signed, insurance certificate for $250,000.00.	_____
6. Initial contact and letter of introduction — obtain names of other key meeting personnel.	_____
a) Request most recent convention history.	_____
b) Review credit procedures and billing address.	_____
c) Review reservation procedures, when mailing will go out, clarify need for approval of reservation form if they act as housing bureau.	_____

---

6. d) Check need for hospitality suites, who will use them, their names and addresses, and previous suite number if annual. _____

e) Ask about public relations opportunities, famous people, unusual events, and newsworthy issues. _____

f) Inquire if account is tax exempt; ask for tax exempt form. _____

7. Discuss their needs and requirements for outside security per corporate policy. _____

8. Send Penta meeting planner fact book. _____

9. Send Penta convention kit. _____

10. Order reservation cards (if the salesperson has already done so, obtain a copy of this form.) _____

SIX (6) MONTHS AWAY FROM THE MEETING DUE DATE

1. Contact public relations for coordination of publicity. Place director of Public Relations in contact with the meeting planner. (If this is applicable.) _____

2. Accentuate the need for the accounts to provide detailed instructions at an early date so that proper service may be administered. _____

3. Explain convention resume procedure. _____

4. Reconfirm staff and VIP housing requirements; double check suites blocked. _____

5. Determine audiovisual needs. Discuss how extensive set-ups are. Sell in-house audiovisual company. _____

6. Discuss registration personnel and procedures. Penta needs to maintain integrity of our property. All signs must be professionally printed; no signs allowed on walls. No signs allowed in the main lobby, except by management approval. _____

7. Coordinate contact with banquet representative, give name, telephone number, have banquet representative call account. _____

8. Review account's needs in regard to office equipment, i.e., typewriters, telephones, need for decorations or decorators, florist. _____

9. Request name of drayage company. Review needs of union labor. This is a union house. _____

10. Inquire into anticipated companion programs, anticipated bus tours. Coordinate information regarding bus tour loadings and unloadings.

11. Request finalized meeting and exhibit floor plans for approval. _____

12. Review final meeting schedule and check diary. _____

THREE (3) MONTHS AWAY FROM MEETING DUE DATE

1. Reconfirm required suites and staff requirements with guest and Front Office. _____

2. Review billing arrangements, identify all master accounts and authorized signatures. _____

3. Remind client of cut-off date for rooms. _____

4. If rooms do not materialize, a rental may have to be implemented (if there is not a rental or sliding scale in the contract) by the salesperson. _____

5. Request official printed program. Compare published program to space requirements in regard to time, set-up times, coffee services, etc. _____

SIX (6) WEEKS AWAY FROM MEETING DUE DATE

1. Process letter for VIPs. _____

2. Verify attendance at all functions, establish rental based on contractual agreement and establish master account and billing instructions along with authorized signatures. _____

3. Secure deposit if required, due 30 days prior to arrival date, unless we have devised a payment schedule. _____

4. Review file on the departmental basis to alert key people of heavy or unusual requirements. _____

5. Review microphone requirements. _____

6. Review lighting requirements and any production set-up needs. _____

7. Review room block against pick-up and cut-off date with the convention service manager. _____

8. Review complimentary rooms. If pick-up is below what the client anticipated, causing a comp room assignment problem, confer with Sales Manager and Convention Service Manager to explore best means of satisfying customer. _____

9. Request complete set-up information. _____

10. Review room registration, check-in arrangements. _____

11. Review special housekeeping requirements, if applicable. _____

12. Obtain a copy of authorized signatures for the master account. _____

13. Review cash advance needs. _____

14. Review safe deposit needs. _____

15. Review shipping arrangements of materials. _____

THREE (3) WEEKS AWAY FROM MEETING DUE DATE

1. Forward resume (specification sheet) and check with Catering on menu progress. _____

2. Distribute resume to hotel departments and include affiliated activities. _____

3. Establish date and time for a pre-convention meeting, process in-house memo. _____

4. Inquire if client wishes to guarantee rooms not picked up. _____

TWO (2) WEEKS AWAY FROM MEETING DUE DATE

1. Order limousine if applicable. _____

2. Re-check program with diary for possible quick meeting room turn-over and enter proper times for all events. _____

3. Review complimentary room arrangements. _____

4. Request posting instructions. _____

FORTY-EIGHT (48) HOURS AWAY FROM MEETING DUE DATE

1. Check hospitality and complimentary orders and VIP reservations. _____

DURING MEETING DUE DATES

1. Check setting of meeting rooms (a.m., afternoon, p.m.). _____

2. Public Space Mgr. or Asst. to complete checklist for each function room. _____

3. Assist with restaurant reservations for VIPs. _____

4. Review shipping arrangements for post convention materials. _____

5. Review complimentary room arrangements. _____

6. Compare room pick-up to complimentary list, make necessary adjustments. _____

7. Set up post-convention meeting. _____

8. Verify booth and exhibit hall by walk through with customer. _____

9. Determine exhibit rental charge if determined by booth. _____

10. Determine repeat booking potential and advise Sales Manager. _____

11. Review master account with account credit department at a predetermined meeting. This should be completed each day. _____

IMMEDIATELY AFTER MEETING DUE DATE

1. Call account and send thank you letter. _____

2. Complete report of convention and profit and loss statement and distribute. _____

3. Determine report on abnormal circumstances in the post convention memo. _____

4. Post-convention report to include under "comments" section an objective evaluation of the hotel's performance. _____

5. Turn file over to Convention Service Manager for review. _____

ONE (1) MONTH AFTER MEETING DUE DATE

1. Breakdown working file and return appropriate correspondence to account file. _____

Learning Objectives:

This portion of your text introduces you to the various systems used to make reservations for meeting and convention attendees. We will also take a look at how the room blocks for group meetings are managed, and see how the computer has changed the way in which group reservations are processed. When you have studied this chapter, you will:

- Know the six methods commonly used to make reservations and the advantages and disadvantages of each.

- Be able to detail the factors that affect room assignments and ways to manage a property's room blocks.

- Be able to describe how the computer has changed reservations, registration and room assignments procedures and is being used to facilitate check-in and check-out and billing.

Outline

Reservation Systems
- Postal Reply/Fax Response Cards
- Toll-Free Telephone Numbers
- Hotel Internet Site Reservations
- Rooming Lists
- Convention Center Housing Bureaus
- Third-Party Housing Companies
- Tally Sheets

Room Assignment
- Rate Structures
- Complimentary Arrangements
- Priorities
- Room Types
- Release and Confirmation Dates
- Arrival/Departure Pattern
- Other Hotels

Managing Room Blocks
- No-Shows/Overbooking
- Historical Performance

Check-in/Check-out
- Check-in Procedure
- Check-out Procedure

The Computer Influence
- Reservations
- Registration and Room Assignment
- Check-out and Billing
- Reports and Analysis Applications

A Planner's Perspective on Room Reservations

Sara R. Torrence, CMP
Chief, Special Activities
National Institute of Standards and Technology

"The meetings for which I have been responsible have used a variety of reservations systems — ranging from rooming lists to postal reply cards to call-in reservations, to housing bureaus. We have even used a combination of services, and once created our own housing bureau, through a travel agent, because we were using four hotels for a relatively small international conference (800 attendees — too small to use the CVB housing bureau for the host city)...One of the MOST important points about any reservation system is that the Sales Manager MUST get the details of the convention to the Reservations Department as soon as the contract is signed, and these details must be entered into the computerized reservations system as soon as possible. I cannot tell you how many times I have had attendees call a hotel for a reservation only to find that the Reservations Department has no record of the conference...."

11 Guestrooms

The letter of agreement has been signed and countersigned. The dates are firm. The room block is specified in the contract. At this point, many departments and organizations become involved as the service process branches out into different areas. One area is assigning guestrooms through the front desk. Through cooperation between the convention's housing staff and your own front office and reservations departments, this area plays a strong supportive role in the success of a convention.

Reservation Systems

Guestroom reservation information is sent to the group's membership three to six months before the event. The systems that are primarily used today include postal or fax reply cards, the use of toll-free numbers, making reservations on the hotel's Internet sites, rooming lists, convention center housing bureaus, and third-party housing companies. In addition, the use of other technologies (such as e-mail, which is growing in popularity) is making it easier for meeting attendees and other guests to make their reservations. Making reservations using such technology as fax reply cards and hotel web sites is especially attractive to meeting attendees because of the convenience and speed of making the reservation and the capability for almost instant confirmation (or notification if there is a problem).

Postal Reply/Fax Response Cards

The usual agreement calls for the meeting planner to mail reservation forms to his or her membership along with promotional material about the meeting. These **reply cards**, which are printed by the hotel and sent in bulk to the convention group's headquarters, may be self addressed postal reply cards (see Figure 11.1) or similar information cards that can be faxed back to the hotel. Whatever the format used, a cover letter from the hotel, providing information and instructions, is enclosed with the reply cards.

The convention headquarters then sends its promotional material and the cards to its membership from its mailing list. While postal reply cards have long been used by convention attendees, cards that can be faxed are increasing in popularity with both hotels and attendees. Attendees appreciate the ease of faxing, while hotels are more likely to get an immediate response; there is no need to wait for the mail.

To facilitate this reservations process, an effective form is essential. This form will be used in-house and to confirm reservations for guests, and may be required for coordination with a housing bureau. If you have to develop a form or revise one, look at our sample or start from scratch, keeping the following factors in mind:

Clarity.
- Be concise.
- Ask guests to print or type. Allow enough space for hand printing. Design for standard typewriter spacing whenever possible.
- Use a paper stock that works well with either pencil or pen.
- Use standard-sized forms for easy handling and storage.

Pertinent information.
- Include spaces for responses for all the the information you will need to process the reservation.
- Arrival and departure date.
- Arrival and departure times.
- Rate requests (unless flat rates are part of the agreements).
- Kind(s) of room(s) requested.
- Number in the party.
- Provide enough information for the attendee to understand what is expected by the hotel.
- Eliminate the need for the attendee to have to find and refer to other material.
- Indicate how long rooms will be held.
- Indicate if and how the room may be held past that time (guarantee or deposit).
- Indicate if deposit is required for all reservations.
- Use self-addressed forms or specify where reservation is to be sent.

Keep the form simple.
- Use terms in common usage. Indicate number of bedrooms in suites.
- Don't ask for unnecessary data.
- Test new forms before printing.

If the group uses its own housing form, the hotel must approve the reservation card to assure that all information is communicated to attendees to minimize misunderstandings. The reservation card policy of the Chicago Hilton reads as follows:

"The Chicago Hilton and Towers will supply your organization, at no charge, a reasonable amount of self addressed reservation cards imprinted with the name of your association and the dates of your convention.

"In the event that your company or association plans to use its own housing form or you intend to use the Chicago Convention and Tourism Bureau for housing, the Chicago Hilton and Towers must approve the copy in writing prior to its being printed in its final form and sent to your members or the Bureau to ensure that all information listed on the form pertaining to the Chicago Hilton and Towers is correct and complete, thus eliminating any discrepancies in room rate when your members receive their confirmations."

Toll-Free Telephone Numbers

Many convention delegates opt to use the property's toll-free numbers to make their reservations. If this is the case, they should be notified beforehand that they must indicate that they are attending the convention when making their reservations. Another alternative is for the hotel to offer a special toll-free number for the group's use (especially if the group is a large one or if several groups are meeting at the same time) or to have the group's delegates ask for a specific operator when making a reservation.

Figure 11.1. SAMPLE POSTAL RESERVATION REPLY CARD.

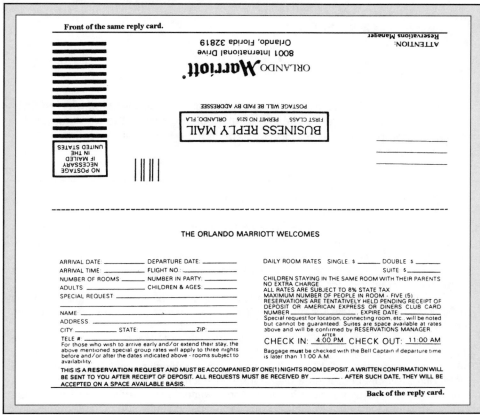

This is a self-addressed postal reply card that is filled out by delegates and returned to the hotel. Other forms of reply cards may include printed return envelopes (usually used when a deposit is required) or a card that may be faxed to the hotel. Whatever form is used, reply cards include such pertinent information as the name and dates of the meeting and room rates. Many associations include such reply cards with their general mailing detailing the convention program, activities, and costs.
Source: Courtesy of the Orlando Marriott.

These measures eliminate several potential problems. Since the hotel and meeting planner agreed to reserve a specific block of rooms, the commitment becomes overestimated if individual reservations are not credited to the group. The hotel may be stuck with unfilled guest rooms and the association will not get credit for the number of complimentary rooms to which it is entitled.

Hotel Internet Site Reservations

The Internet is expected to play an increasingly significant role in convention registration. On-line hotel reservations were ushered in by The Hotel Industry Switch Company (Thisco), offering a TravelWeb site that enabled guests to make reservations with eight major chains using computer terminals. Current screens include only the rates found in properties' central reservation system — not the group's negotiated rates. However, hotels are now creating individual web sites to provide specific convention information and group rates.

Case Study:

City Housing Bureau

When several hotels are used, the convention is commonly called *city-wide* and the reservations are handled by a city housing bureau. We will illustrate this more complicated reservation system with the hypothetical National Popcorn Association case study.

National Popcorn Association

The NPA has an active membership of 3,550 delegates. The association executive and the site selection committee have narrowed down their selection for the upcoming annual convention to Chicago, Miami and Las Vegas. It will be necessary for such a large group to use a number of hotels so the planners have been in touch with the convention bureau of each city.

The NPA staff makes personal visits to each site and picks hotels. It then prepares a list of the desired hotels in each city and asks the convention bureau to request room commitments from each property.

The **bid sheet** used by the Las Vegas Convention and Visitors Authority is shown in Figure 11.3. Upon receiving it, the hotel sales department checks room availability for the dates designated. It then specifies the number of singles, doubles and suites the hotel has available and gives a price range for each. Note that the hotel stipulates a cutoff date by which time the NPA must send a written acceptance of the hotel's offer. The completed form is then mailed back to the convention bureau. The bureau forwards or personally presents the proposal sheets to the association's site selection committee for analysis and a decision.

On the basis of price, location and service, the NPA chooses Las Vegas as the site for the convention. It also selects a headquarters hotel and designates four others as overflow hotels.

Approximately eight months before the convention the NPA association executive requests assistance from the Las Vegas Housing Bureau in setting up a reservation system. The association, in conjunction with the housing bureau, prepares a reservation form (Figure 11.4) to be sent to each member, who in turn completes it, writes out a deposit check, and returns it to the housing bureau. The members each indicated their first, second, third and fourth preferences in hotels, and they have also specified the type of room desired. The housing bureau sorts through the forms and approves reservations on a first-come, first-served basis. As each reservation is approved, the form is returned to the sender specifying which hotel he or she is to stay in during the convention. If none of the choices are available, the form is returned to the member with a note of explanation and a request for new choices.

As each batch of new reservations is approved, it is sent to the respective hotel and processed there by the reservation department. Each week before the convention, a **reservation housing report** (see Figure 11.5) prepared by the housing bureau is sent to the hotels and to the association to indicate the reservation status of the hotel's room blocks. This report is extremely important to the hotel. If a room block is not filling up as expected, the hotel will probably contact the association and ask for an update on its room commitment. Although the housing bureau specifies a thirty-day cutoff, if only half of the 3,550 rooms commited are reserved, the five hotels might have difficulty in booking the remaining guestrooms.

> The handling of the deposit checks by the housing bureau can be avoided if the NPA collects the deposits itself and pays each hotel its respective amount. This procedure is almost the only method some groups use and it is definitely preferred by the hotel.
>
> Once NPA reservations begin to come in, the hotels start convention reservation records and master accounts for the group. Usually a rooming list (Figure 11.2) is developed and each delegate is assigned a room and sub-account under the master. If and when checks are received by the hotel, a credit is added to the sub-account.

Hilton Hotels Corporation, for example, now offers group reservations on its HiltonNet website. A planner who has reserved a room block at a Hilton property can link his or her organization to a special page on Hilton's site. This site not only provides details about the meeting, but attendees are also given a passcode to access the group reservations module. There, they can book a room at the group's designated rates during a specified time. Hilton's system tracks these reservations and planners can view pickup data via a password protected area of the site. The chain also provides a hard copy of room pickup upon request.

While this technology is still in its infancy, Hilton is reporting good results, and other chains, including Sheraton, are testing the concept. Sheraton is also partnering with software companies that will allow for interactive bookings for city-wide conventions.

Rooming Lists

Many hotels prefer to get a consolidated **rooming list** from the planner (see Figure 11.2). When rooming lists are used, reservations are not made with the hotel, but with the housing staff at the planner's headquarters. The meeting planner prepares the rooming list from the reservations received and sends it to the hotel prior to the cutoff date. When the hotel receives the list, the front office assigns attendees rooms from the block that is committed to the group and preregisters attendees.

It is extremely important that the front office knows whether a group's reservations are coming individually or through a list. It is standard operating procedure that the trace file on any group, for which a rooming list is expected, to be brought up in sufficient time to remind the customer that the list is expected.

Rooming lists are most commonly used by corporate accounts and incentive travel groups where attendance is almost always mandatory or highly predictable. The convention service manager should encourage the use of rooming lists, when possible, because it reduces the load on the reservation department.

Convention Center Housing Bureaus

When several hotels are used, the convention is commonly called **city-wide** and the reservations are handled by a convention center **housing bureau** (see box titled "City Housing Bureau Case Study").

Many meeting planners, however, cite several problems with city housing bureaus. Many are understaffed, especially when it comes to handling large conventions. Meeting planners tell "horror stories" of constantly busy phone lines, long delays when calls finally get through, and delayed reservation confirmations. While some CVBs are now offering

Figure 11.2. SAMPLE ROOMING LIST.

Rooming lists are generally used for small corporate meetings for which the corporation will pay room charges and attendees will be responsible for their incidental charges. Some associations, however, also use them rather than having individual delegates contact the hotel for reservations directly. After the meeting planner obtains room information from delegates, he or she prepares a list to be sent to the hotel by an agreed upon date. Information typically includes the names of attendees, the type of room desired (and how many will occupy a room), and arrival and departure dates.
Source: Courtesy of The Hershey Lodge and Convention Center

their housing systems on-line to eliminate some of these problems, a growing number of meeting planners are turning to other outside sources for their housing needs.

Third-Party Housing Companies

Third-party housing providers, private firms that typically use high technology to make housing arrangements for groups, are often used by large organizations that utilize several hotels for city-wide conventions. But associations, who need consistency as they generally rotate their annual conventions geographically, are also turning to third-party providers, citing the inconsistency of housing services offered in CVBs in different cities. And not only are meeting planners using third-party housing companies, many CVBs have recognized the cost savings of using third-party companies and are now outsourcing housing to third-party vendors.

One private firm, ITS Inc., a Deerfield, Illinois-based reservation service, offers both consistency and sufficient staffing. ITS President Steve Martin employs 135 employees, including 55 that take hotel reservations, compared to a dozen dedicated housing staffers at a typical CVB.

Figure 11.3. SAMPLE BID SHEET

LAS VEGAS CONVENTION BUREAU
CONVENTION CENTER - PARADISE ROAD
P.O. BOX 14006
LAS VEGAS, NEVADA 89114

Date: May 15, 19__

FROM: Adam James Stubbs, Convention Sales

SUBJECT: REQUEST FOR ROOM COMMITMENT

THE ___National Popcorn Association___ HAS REQUESTED US TO OBTAIN
TENTATIVE / FIRM ROOM COMMITMENTS FOR THEIR CONVENTION IN LAS VEGAS, NEVADA.
FOR MEETING DATES OF ___Oct. 18, 19___ THROUGH ___Oct. 21, 19___.
THE ___Abbey Hotel___ AGREES TO RESERVE THE FOLLOWING NUMBER OF
SLEEPING ROOMS AT THE RATES SHOWN BELOW: PROVIDING A WRITTEN ACCEPTANCE
BY THE CONVENING ORGANIZATION IS RECEIVED BY THE HOTEL OR MOTEL PRIOR TO
___Sept. 15, 19___.
DATE

NUMBER OF:

SINGLES ___100___   RATE ___$75-85___

DOUBLES ___475___   RATE ___$85-95___

TWINS _____   RATE _____

SUITES ___25___   RATE ___$110 --170___

GRAND TOTAL ROOMS ___600___

ROOM DEPOSIT (IS) (NOT) REQUIRED. (IF REQUIRED, STATE AMOUNT) $75.00

SIGNED BY:

___Chantal Puepke___   ___Abbey Hotel___
NAME   HOTEL OR MOTEL

___Sales Manager___   ___May 20___
TITLE   DATE

* * * * *

PUBLIC SPACE AVAILABLE ___yes___   ___negotiable___
                                          RATE OR GRATIS

PUBLIC SPACE DESCRIBED ON ATTACHMENT (NOTE TO HOTEL: IF APPLICABLE PLEASE
ENCLOSE BROCHURE)

RESERVATIONS FOR PUBLIC SPACE TO BE REQUESTED AND CONFIRMED BY LETTER.

* * * * *

NOTE: TO BE COMPLETED IN TRIPLICATE. MAIL TWO (2) COPIES TO THE LAS VEGAS
CONVENTION BUREAU. HOTEL OR MOTEL TO RETAIN ONE (1) COPY.

When a number of hotels must be used for large conventions, a bid sheet is filled out by individual properties and returned to the city convention bureau. In this case, the form is filled out in triplicate. The hotel keeps one copy, the bureau keeps another, and the third is incorporated into a summary of local hotel rates that is sent to the organization.
Source: Courtesy of the Las Vegas Convention and Visitors Authority.

Figure 11.4. TYPICAL RESERVATION REPLY FORM.

APPLICATION FOR HOTEL ACCOMMODATIONS

MAIL COLORED COPY TO:
NPA Housing Bureau
Las Vegas Convention/Tourist Authority
P.O. Box 14006
Las Vegas, Nevada 89114

October 19-21, 19
Las Vegas Convention Center
Industry Day
October 18th

NPA
COMMITTEE

Send Confirmation to:

Company Name _____

Attention _____

Street Address or P.O. Box _____

City _____ State _____ Zip Code _____

Hotel Preference:

1. _____   3. _____

2. _____   4. _____

Please Reserve The Following Accommodations.   (See reverse side for Rates and Map Locations)

. . . . . . Singles(s) for . . . . persons(s)   Rate Preferred $ . . . . per room

. . . . . . Double(s) for . . . . person(s)   Rate Preferred $ . . . . per room

. . . . . Parlor Suite(s) with . . . . Bedroom(s) for person(s)   Rate Preferred $ . . . . per suite

REMARKS . . . .

. . . .

If Rate Requested Not Available, Next Higher will be Assigned.

List each type of room, its occupants and their arrivals and departures

Type of Room	Names of Occupants	Arrival & Departure Dates & Hours
1.		
2.		
3.		
4.		
5.		
6.		

Please Attach List of Additional Names, if necessary

CONFIRMATION OF THE ABOVE REQUEST WILL BE SENT BY THE HOTEL.
PLEASE MAKE ALL RESERVATION CHANGES DIRECTLY THROUGH THE CONFIRMING HOTEL.

A form such as this one is used when a city housing bureau handles hotel room assignments. The delegate fills out the form and returns it to the housing bureau. The map and hotel rates shown on the next page assist the attendees in indicating their choice of hotels.
Source: Courtesy of the Las Vegas Convention and Visitors Authority.

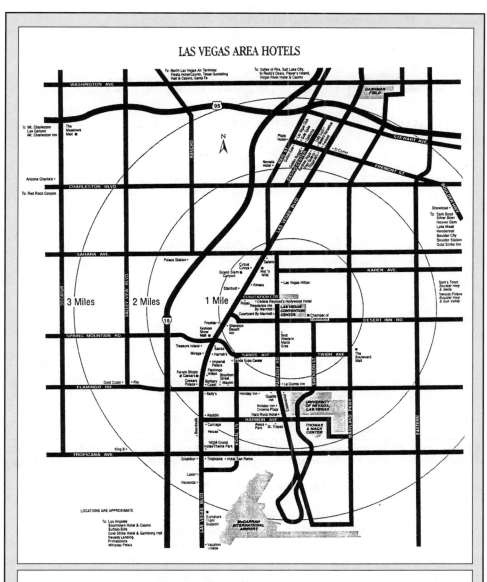

LAS VEGAS AREA HOTELS

Las Vegas Hotel Rates

NPA Industry Day - Oct 18th-Hotel A
NPA Show-Oct 19,20,21 -Convention Center

Room Block	Hotel	King	Double/ Double	Parlor Suites *** 1 Bedroom	Parlor Suites*** 2 Bedroom	
1500	A	$60-72	$60-72	$118-140	$151-185	*One night room deposit required with reservation
	(Hdqtrs)	$77-80	$77-80	$144-175	$198-227	
1000	B*	$66-75	$66-75	$120-130	$155-170	** $50 deposit required with reservation
600	C*	$54-58`	$58-64	$105-120	$133-148	***Hospitality suites available Rates for special hospitality suites on request.
250	D**	$62-68	$62-68	$120-140	$180-210	
200	E*	$50 S/D Occupancy	$50 S/D Occupancy	$50 S/D Occupancy	$50 S/D Occupancy	All rates subject to 8% Clark County Room Tax

Figure 11.5. RESERVATION HOUSING REPORT.

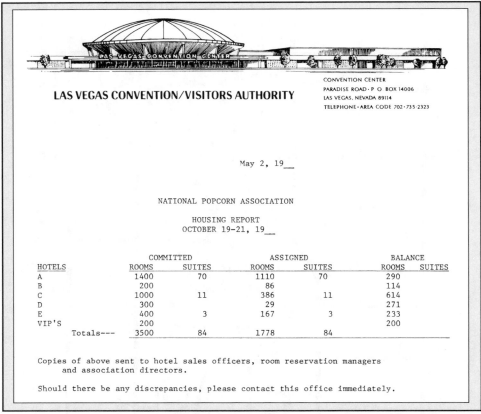

LAS VEGAS CONVENTION/VISITORS AUTHORITY

CONVENTION CENTER
PARADISE ROAD · P O BOX 14006
LAS VEGAS, NEVADA 89114
TELEPHONE · AREA CODE 702·735·2323

May 2, 19___

NATIONAL POPCORN ASSOCIATION

HOUSING REPORT
OCTOBER 19-21, 19___

HOTELS	COMMITTED		ASSIGNED		BALANCE	
	ROOMS	SUITES	ROOMS	SUITES	ROOMS	SUITES
A	1400	70	1110	70	290	
B	200		86		114	
C	1000	11	386	11	614	
D	300		29		271	
E	400	3	167	3	233	
VIP'S	200				200	
Totals---	3500	84	1778	84		

Copies of above sent to hotel sales officers, room reservation managers
and association directors.

Should there be any discrepancies, please contact this office immediately.

A form such as this one is used by the housing bureau to inform hotels of the meeting group's pickup on its room commitment. Reports are sent on a periodic basis to enable the individual hotels to adjust their reservations information.
Source: Courtesy of the Las Vegas Convention and Visitors Authority.

The growth of other third-party providers has been fueled by Internet technology. Internet-based Passkey.com, the largest and best known of the third-party providers, utilizes an accessible centralized database to process housing transactions. Its system also generates confirmations and acknowledgements for attendees and provides reports that enable meeting planners to manage their room blocks. After Passkey received an endorsement from the International Association of Convention and Visitors Bureaus (IACVB) in 1998, it began servicing ten CVBs, including those in Atlanta, Boston, Detroit and Orlando. The system is also marketed to other third-party housing vendors and to tradeshow organizers and meeting planners who formerly made housing arrangements internally.

Planners now have over two dozen third-party housing firms from which to choose, and the competition has resulted in innovation and better service to the planners that use these services. In many cases, meeting attendees still fax or mail in their housing reservations, but the Internet is expected to account for the majority of reservations received by housing companies in the near future. No matter how reservations are received, these third-party providers prepare a rooming list for the hotel.

Third-party housing firms are the "preferred providers" for large conventions and a growing number of smaller meetings, and it is estimated that 50 percent of all multi-hotel events were handled by third-party firms in 2001.[1] There is a downside, however. Private firms, unlike convention and visitors bureau housing services, charge a fee, often as much as 10 percent of the room rate. A CVB will pay this fee when outsourcing its housing, but meeting planners, especially those who have used no-cost CVB housing services, must find a way to pay for housing assistance. In some cases, the meeting planner will negotiate with the hotel to pay the fee of a third-party provider, passing the cost along to the attendees in the form of higher room rates. Some hotels balk at this arrangement and insist that the service be paid for separately, either by the planner or the attendee, to eliminate artificially raised room rates. Some third-party planners negotiate with the hotel to have their fee paid, much as travel agents are compensated.

Tally Sheets

No matter how reservations are made, a breakdown of the precise types of rooms needed must be made and kept current. **Tally sheets** such as the one shown in Figure 11.6 give the hotel a clear picture of each day's convention reservations and group movements and provide an arrival and departure flow study for each group.

From the tally sheet, the hotel's reservation department sends out reservations confirmations (see Figure 11.7). If a housing bureau is handling reservations, a confirmation form by the hotel is a must. Confirmations should be made in any case, but it is particularly crucial when a number of hotels are pressed into use.

Room Assignment

The front desk carries off most convention and trade show room assignments without incident. Problems do arise, however, and must be handled smoothly.

Prior to the meeting, the service manager should review and confirm with the customer:

- the rate structure by category of room.
- the room block, including the types of rooms needed by the group.
- complimentary room assignments.
- guest room priorities for VIPs and speakers.
- the arrival and departure pattern for the group.
- the group's history in regard to guestroom pickup, no-shows and cancellations.

Rate Structures

Rates are extremely important to the planner. If the rates negotiated are beyond the budget of some attendees, they may book sleeping rooms elsewhere (outside the designated room block). This could significantly impact rental agreements for meeting rooms and could result in attrition fees.

Because most large scale conventions are planned well in advance, the hotel will not commit itself to any firm rates. This policy is usually made clear during initial negotiations. It is also included in the final contract.

One of the preliminary decisions to be made in booking a convention is what rates to charge for delegates' rooms. Naturally the rates will vary between hotels and even within the hotel itself. Rates are determined according to a number of factors, including season

Figure 11.6. SAMPLE TALLY SHEET.

HOUSING COUNT TALLY

Name of Organization or Convention _____

Convention Official _____

Address _____ Tel. No. _____

Convention Dates: _____

Number of Rooms Allotted: _____

Breakdown:

Singles	_____
Doubles	_____
Twins	_____
Suites	_____
Total	_____

Arrival and Departure	Day Date	Arr.	Dep.	Arr.	Dep.	Arr.	Dep.	Arr.	Dep.	Arr.	Dep.	Arr.	Dep.	Arr.	Dep.	TOTAL ROOMS USED
Singles																
Doubles																
Twins																
Suites																
Parlors																
Complimentary																
Makeup Suites																
Total Res. per Day		X		X		X		X		X		X		X		
Total Dep. per Day	X		X		X		X		X		X		X			X

A form such as this one provides a hotel with a summary of convention reservations and pickup of the group's rooms. Note that the form is broken down into room type and that arrival and departure times are noted to ensure smooth front desk staffing.
Source: Reprinted with permission from The Convention Liaison Manual, published by the Convention Industry Council.

(busy or slow), days of the week, size of the group, length of stay, type of room, number of persons in the room, and the known attendance and difficulty with the group's past conventions. Of course, the interpretation of these factors is up to the individual property. A resort hotel, for example, fills up with social guests on weekends, so it is not likely to offer discounted rates to a meeting group, while a downtown hotel that realizes the majority of its business during the middle of the week is more likely to offer discounted rates on the weekends.

Many hotels work within the limits of certain rate scales determined by management. The main ones are:

Rack rate. All rates remain as posted, with no discounts or concessions. This is generally preferred by the hotels for easy bookkeeping, but rack rates are rarely used because convention groups are able to negotiate a group rate lower than rack rates.

Run-of-the-house rate. All similar rooms except suites are priced at the average between minimum and maximum rates, despite level or location. All guests pay the same rate. This is also called a *flat-rate arrangement.*

Split rate. Rates are offered to a group based on the room type. For example, regular guestrooms would be offered at a different rate than tower club rooms.

Discounted rate. This type, also called *spread rates,* is used primarily when the result will bring preferred return business, encourage current business, or attract business from the hotel's competition for preferred groups.

It is important to remember that many conventions are planned years in advance, and that rates could vary a great deal over that time. This makes it essential to "peg" a rate of increase to determine the rates that the group will pay in the future.

Figure 11.7. RESERVATION CONFIRMATION FORM.

Name_____ Pr._____

_____

Address _____ (Convention)

_____

Type Room _____ Rate $ _____ to $ _____

Time of _____ A.M.

Arrival: _____ P.M.   Date _____ Departing Date _____

Confirmed by_____ Hotel

Signature _____

Title _____ Date_____

ATTEN: HOTEL MGR. 1. Signature and date to appear legibly on all copies. 2. Separate by holding top and bottom of paper and snap off at perforation. 3. (a) Mail Guest Copy to applicant. (b) Retain two hotel copies. (c) Return Blue & Pink copies to:

HOUSING BUREAU, CONVENTION CENTER, PARADISE ROAD, LAS VEGAS, NEVADA.

GUESTS: PLEASE NOTIFY YOUR HOTEL OF LATE ARRIVALS AND ANY OTHER CHANGES OR CANCELLATIONS. SEND A COPY to the Housing Bureau, Las Vegas Convention/ Visitors Authority, P.O. Box 14006, Las Vegas, Nev. 89114.

PRESENT THIS CONFIRMATION WHEN YOU CHECK INTO YOUR HOTEL.

GUEST COPY   THANK YOU

HOTEL COPY

PRESENT THIS CONFIRMATION W...

HOUSING BUREAU COPY

Forms such as these are sent by the housing bureau to the hotel. The guest, the hotel, and the housing bureau retain copies.
Source: Courtesy of the Las Vegas Convention and Visitors Authority.

In most cases, the hotel's rack room rate is used to find the "peg rate." If, for example, the current rack rate is $75 per night and the group rate is $60 per night, the percentage below the "peg rate" is 20 percent. This percentage would be used to determine room rates at the time of the meeting (attendees would get 20 percent off the rack rate in effect at the time of the function). Other planners insist on more specific room rate guarantees; one planner, for example, specifies the following clause be included in the contract:

"The Hotel guarantees that room rates extended to the Symposium shall not exceed 85 percent of the rack rate and the present applicable rate shall not increase more than 5 percent per year. The final rate shall be established 12 months in advance of the Symposium."

Small groups tend toward the use of flat rates, while large conventions find split or discount rates more to their liking. Rack rates are seldom used for conventions unless the group is small or the hotel is running at high occupancy.

Discounts typically range up to 30 percent of the rack rate. Naturally, the hotel's objective is to ensure that it gets business, but at the highest possible rate. Questions often asked about the group to determine the amount of discount include:

- How much can they be expected to spend? Will they have cocktail parties? Banquets? Requests for meeting and exhibit space?
- What are the opportunities for future business with the group?
- Is the group willing to put down a firm financial hold on its room block?

Regardless of the rate decided upon, it is important to make the rate arrangements clear. If there is a range of rates, the reservation form should indicate the range and serve notice that rooms in the next higher category will be supplied if those at the requested rate are no longer available. Even if the contract calls for rack rates, it is best to indicate those on the reservation form.

Sometimes the association requests that the hotel charge the delegate more than the agreed upon room rate and to refund the excess to the association. Hotels generally decline such requests for obvious ethical reasons, particularly if the convention attendee is unaware of the arrangement.

Complimentary Arrangements

Most hotels offer concessions to get group business. It is common practice to extend one complimentary guestroom (**comp room**) for every 50 rooms used, or one suite for every 100 guestrooms.

A rooming list supplied by the meeting planner should specify who will occupy these rooms. To avoid heated arguments at the cashier's window, it is the planner's responsibility to spell out the extent of the complimentary arrangements to the guest and provide a copy to the hotel.

The meeting planner should tell his or her people, especially if complimentary rooms will be used by speakers and program members, what they must pay for themselves and what may be applied to the master account. It is easiest to use complimentary rooms for staff, but that is at the option of the meeting planner. It doesn't matter so long as everyone knows what is expected of him or her.

Additional concessions are sometimes granted. Some hotels provide a complimentary cocktail party upon arrival, free travel to and from the airport and free meeting space. There is no general guideline. A hotel must use sound judgment and integrity.

Priorities

It is important that the convention planner supply a list of VIPs to the hotel. It is necessary to codify certain types of guests and the accomodations indicated for them. This is certainly important when you have accommodations in different buildings of the hotel. Association officials such as officers, board members and staff usually get special treatment. Exhibitors, speakers and entertainers may also require special attention.

It is important to block rooms so that oceanfront rooms and suites in resort hotels and the "best rooms available" in commercial properties are assigned to VIPs without question, regardless of the occupancy of the house. It is often the responsibility of the convention service manager to see that these reservations are in order. He or she should set up a procedure to check the day before arrival on what type of accommodations are blocked for VIPs and also on the day of arrival to make sure that these accommodations are delivered. In addition, the service manager might find out the VIPs' arrival times.

It is the policy of some hotels to have the sales office see that the VIPs get the proper attention. The feeling is that the salesperson's self-preservation is determined by his or her impression on the association's decision makers, and the decision makers are usually found on the priority list.

The VIP list should also be coded to include the possible supply of fruit, liquor and/or flowers. The allocation of suites is also important, especially if the hotel has a limited number. Discuss this with the convention planner. Some associations have a rule that non-exhibitors cannot maintain hospitality suites.

Take care to hold a small number of rooms in a prime area of the hotel for late priority listings; they inevitably appear late in the game.

Room Types

You must know the number and kinds of rooms to be held. Most agreements with convention planners call for a guarantee of a total *number* of rooms to be used. This may be fine at the negotiating table, but as the event approaches you need to know how many of these are singles, doubles, twins or suites. Don't forget that there is much confusion about suite designation. Some hotels go so far as to indicate suites as having "one bedroom for two people" or "two bedrooms for four people." In addition, people confuse twins and doubles. This can be clarified by indicating "one bed for two people" or "two beds for two people."

Release and Confirmation Dates

Since many conventions are booked far in advance, the number of rooms blocked out is an estimate, based on past conventions. Communication between hotel and planner is vital.

The letter of agreement, as we said in Chapter 9, should indicate a date by which the organization will either confirm or release the rooms. Reservations received after the cutoff date, usually about thirty days, are accepted on a **space available basis** only and often the convention rate is not available to reservations received after the cutoff date. In all cases, the reservations should be confirmed individually, with a copy sent to the meeting planner.

The hotel and association should re-examine the room commitment on several intermediate dates and readjust the number if necessary. Most convention center bureaus and hotels provide weekly room pick-up reports showing the inventory status of the room blocks to meeting planners. Mutual reassurance will reduce the chances of double booking by delegates and overbooking by hotels.

The convention planner must be alert for early signals that might affect meeting attendance. These could be an unusual circumstance, such as the 50th anniversary of the association, an unusually good or bad year, the selection of a prime resort site, or an unusual number of members recruited that year. The smart planners will communicate their apprehensions and revelations to their hotel counterparts so that all attendees may be housed conveniently.

You should not bury your head in the sand and go blithely about your business if you don't receive periodic communiques from your client. D-Day will come and you may face a milling mob around the registration desk or a multitude of unfilled rooms. You cannot afford just to wait hopefully if you don't hear from your client. Keep constant tabs on the reservations being received and interpret how the flow affects the total number of rooms being held.

Constant communication between both parties leads comfortably to the day when the organization executive confirms or releases the number of rooms held. (This is vital to resorts that have little or no business off the street, especially during off-season periods).

The planner and hotel person who keep in touch constantly and adjust room allotments along the way seem to continue to do business together. They execute meetings together without the shock of housing problems at the outset of the event.

Arrival/Departure Pattern

In assigning rooms you need an overall pattern that will indicate when people will arrive and depart. The convention planner may have some idea from previous years, but you will have to finalize detailed patterns when you get the reservations from the guests. Even for corporate meetings, where the meeting planner has greater control, attendees frequently arrive a day or two early because of transportation difficulties, personal travel plans or the attraction of local tourist or recreational facilities.

For example, typical arrivals for a 400 room convention beginning on Monday and concluding on Thursday might look something like this:

Day	Number of Rooms	Flow of Attendance
Friday	20	meeting planner and staff
Saturday	150	early arrivals
Sunday	360	opening of convention
Monday	400	peak convention attendance
Tuesday	400	peak convention attendance
Wednesday	350	early departures
Thursday	30	post convention meetings and extended days

It is also wise to indicate the breakdown of the group's rooms into singles, doubles, twins and suites. Arrival dates are easier to secure than check-out dates, but these too are important to you.

Be especially careful if you designate the availability of a *specific* suite. That extra-special VIP suite may be earmarked for the chairman of the board, who may very well decide to test your golf course and arrive a day or two before the meeting or stay in it several days after the event. Impress on your client that you must have advance notice of such plans to make sure the room is available and that there is no conflict with another group.

You also need to plot the arrival pattern so you can govern your staff's assignments. You need enough desk clerks and bellpersons on hand for a big influx of guests at a particular time. The typical ratio is one bellperson and one front desk receptionist/cashier for every 75 guests arriving or departing. If a group is to arrive or depart en masse, however, one staff person for every 50 guests may be required.

Should the check-in for the group be early afternoon, the hotel may need to set up a hospitality area where attendees can wait until vacated rooms are readied by housekeeping. This is a problem for European hotels because most large planes arrive from the United States in the early morning but check-out time for departing guests is not until noon or so.

Other Hotels

As we mentioned earlier in this chapter, sometimes a number of hotels are to be used for a large convention. In such instances, a competitor becomes a friend. It is nice to have a nearby hotel bail you out with a number of rooms when you may have overbooked. It is just as nice to receive guests from the other hotel when you have a number of rooms available — and to have the favors returned on other occasions. It pays to work together.

Similarly, you may be unable to supply a function room for the convention or for a local customer's banquet. Show the customer that you are interested in his welfare even when you are full by helping him to book the event at another hotel. The other hotel may appreciate the recommendation and reciprocate; your customer appreciates the help and the fact that you didn't turn your back on him when you didn't need the business. Always look to the future. The key to success in the hotel business is a good reputation for expertise and *caring*.

A variation may involve only the use of hotel facilities, such as golf courses or tennis courts. An inter-hotel billing arrangement also must be worked out in the case of multi-hotel involvements, which may bring local bus companies into the act.

Managing Room Blocks

Managing room blocks is a difficult process for both the meeting planner and the hotel. Problems arise because planners don't want to underestimate the availability of rooms for attendees, while hotels lose revenue if room blocks are left unfilled.

Slippage, the difference between the contracted room block and the guestrooms actually utilized by the group, is a key concern for both parties. As discussed in Chapter 9, hotels allow for some slippage, but are now inserting attrition clauses into contracts to protect themselves. Recall attrition fees apply when the meeting group contracts for a specific number of rooms but the total amount of rooms used is below the original contracted block.

Slippage might occur for a number of reasons: the planner inflates the group room block to achieve a better negotiating position; some attendees bypass the group's housing service and the hotel doesn't attribute those reservations to the group's block; or, attendees may book rooms at hotels other than those specified by the meeting planner. This is termed "booking outside the block." Some room blocks also go unfilled because of the "wash factor." The wash factor refers to reservations that weren't realized because of no shows and cancellations.

No-Shows/Overbooking

Two bugaboos of the hotel convention business are those interwoven horrors, the *no-show* (and its cousins, the *early departure* and the *underdeparture),* which is the fault of convention attendees and guests, and *overbooking*, an act of some hotels. Instead of pointing the finger of blame at each other, hotel personnel and hotel users must work together to minimize these annoyances.

No-shows too often result from delegates making multiple reservations because they fear they won't get a room at their first-choice hotel. Because the no-show problem is more significant at high-demand resorts than at commercial properties, resorts have been the leaders in instituting stricter cancellation policies. In an effort to eliminate no-shows and control rooms inventory, some convention hotels have pushed their cancellation deadline to 72 hours before expected check-in.

The Hospitality Sales Marketing Association International strongly recommends the use of deposits as a solution to no-shows. With a **deposit reservation**, the hotel receives payment for at least the first night's lodging prior to the guest's arrival and is obligated to hold the room regardless of the guest's arrival time. Most city and airport hotels get a certain amount of **walk-in** business after five o'clock to fill in no-show vacancies. But resort properties don't have this reserve factor so there is an increasing trend for these properties to insist on deposits. This is appealing, but a hotel that is going to take deposits must also consider the necessary control, the record-keeping, and the possibility of refunds.

Effective Guestrooms Management

Kristine K. Gagliardi
Corporate Director of Convention Services
Hilton Hotels Corporation

"During the past several years, I have had the opportunity to develop and implement standardized quality assurance programs for Hilton Hotels Convention Service Departments corporate-wide...During the initial research phase, all existing hotel-wide guestroom block procedures were examined...Aware that Hilton's system-wide computerized reservation/front office system would jointly benefit the group/hotel alliance by means of technical support, it was our intent to offer meeting groups an effective, accurate guestroom system during every stage of the meeting — pre-planning, on site, and beyond, to post-meeting information.

"Also important to our research was the initial booking process by sales. Was a group's historical data properly checked? Did this information correlate with the current booking? Was the pattern of arrival and departures in line with the group's meeting program? Did the proposed reservation method work to benefit the group and hotel? Did the group's cut-off date give the group and hotel enough time to react to casualty?

"In order to monitor reservations closely, a convention service file activity checklist was developed to systematically track group pick-up and other pertinent group arrangements. By use of this checklist, the convention service managers could trace group block activity and, if warranted, have subsequent discussion with the meeting planner regarding pick-up information...One week prior to the cut-off, the group was contacted again to re-verify all room-related issues...the checklist once again was to be utilized as a primary tool to initiate action ten days before the group's arrival.

"Equipped with valuable customer information regarding check-in/check-out expectations, the hotel could then prepare a strategy to ensure a smooth arrival. Arrival patterns, transportation methods, and peak check-in times are closely reviewed...The pre-registration of rooms, suites, and VIP accommodations would also be accomplished in preparation of the group's arrival...At the conclusion of the meeting, this information would be compiled into a 'meeting report.' Sent directly to the meeting planner, and routed throughout the Hilton system, this report was to cover all aspects of the meeting, including guestroom particulars: reservation method, sequence of hotel reservation pick-up, arrival/departure patterns, final pick-up data, casualty and no-show percentages, suite usage, etc."

Another solution offered is the use of *guaranteed reservations*. A **guaranteed reservation** is a room being held without deposit, but for which payment is guaranteed. In case of a no-show, billing takes place in the usual manner. But many hotels cite difficulties in collecting such payments. It seems there is an educational problem; often the term guaranteed reservation is misinterpreted, with the guest not understanding that he or she is agreeing to guarantee payment regardless of whether or not the room is used.

Early departures can also result in a significant loss of room revenue, as well as food and beverage, incidental, and recreational income. Scott Boone, vice president of sales for Inter-Continental Hotels and Resorts, says,

Figure 11.8. SAMPLE OVERBOOKING/DEPOSIT POLICY.

> Below we have printed the overbooking policy of the famous Greenbrier, a five star resort hotel in White Sulphur Springs, West Virginia.
>
> The Greenbrier, as a firm policy, will not overbook. It does not condone the policy and will exercise every effort to see that the rooms contracted for will be available. There are circumstances, however, when individuals, due to illness or other reasons, will refuse to vacate a room on the date promised. This can result in the Hotel not being able to have that room available to honor a reservation with a deposit. Should that happen, the Greenbrier will be responsible for lodging and transportation costs to the nearest available substitute accommodations in the vicinity of the Greenbrier. Meals, sports facilities and all other services at The Greenbrier will be available at regular guest rates. Immediately upon a room becoming available, the individuals will be notified and transportation (if required) provided back to The Greenbrier. If the individual chooses not to move to The Greenbrier, no further obligation exists on the part of The Greenbrier and transient fees will be charged at The Greenbrier, subject to availability of services. To make the "no overbooking policy" work, The Greenbrier adheres to the following deposit policy.
>
> DEPOSIT:
>
> All requests by individuals for reservations must be accompanied by a $100.00 deposit for each room. Cancellation, failure to "show," late arrival or early departure will cause forfeiture of deposit, unless written cancellation or changes in dates are made 15 days in advance of scheduled arrival date. Checks should be made payable to The Greenbrier. The deposit will be returned to the individual if a written cancellation is received by The Greenbrier 15 days prior to the arrival date. Reservations will be filled in the order in which they are received and must be received no later than 45 days prior to the date of the meeting.

Due to their low walk-in business, resorts have stiffer cancellation and cutoff policies and are more likely to require deposits than city center hotels.
Source: Courtesy of the Greenbrier Hotel.

> "We've noticed an increase in early departures over the past three to four years, especially with convention attendees. Attendees usually book rooms months ahead for the whole conference, then adjust their schedules and neglect to notify the hotel...We just want guests to focus on their departure date so that we in turn will have inventory to offer."[2]

Chains such as Hyatt, Hilton and Westin have initiated *early departure fees* because guests who check-out early leave the hotel with a room that will likely produce no revenue for the night unless the property has a great deal of transient business. Convention guests must indicate at check-in that they will be departing early or they will be charged a fee, generally ranging from $25 to $50. While meeting planners are not thrilled with early departure fees for attendees, the policy does help planners with banquet guarantees by providing firmer counts for their closing banquets.

On the other end of the spectrum, problems may also arise if the guest decides to stay another day; this is called **underdeparture**. The hotel may have set aside a block of 250

SOME ASSOCIATION HOUSING POLICIES CONTRIBUTE TO HOTEL OVERBOOKING

In a perfect world no hotel would ever overbook guest rooms. But hotels can't stop taking reservations when all their rooms "appear" to be sold. Because of "early departures" and "no-shows," hotels that do not confirm more than 100 percent of their rooms run the risk of going 10 percent to 15 percent unsold.

The system is broken, and no one is fixing it. Consider the scenario for city-wide conventions. Attendees return a form indicating which hotel(s) they prefer to be in. Registrants are asked to select their top three to six choices, in case the first choice is sold out.

The housing organization attempts to assign the attendees to their desired hotel. If the No. 1 or No. 2 choice is available, there is a high probability the attendee will use the reservation. However, that likelihood decreases the further down the list you go. When all of an attendee's preferred hotels are sold out, most housing authorities will arbitrarily assign a hotel.

This is where the real trouble begins.

Hotels get notification of reservations from the housing organization without knowing if their hotel was a primary request or if it was an "assigned" reservation. (This information would be helpful because there is traditionally a larger "no-show" factor among attendees who are "assigned" rooms.) Many of these "assigned" attendees do not bother to call the hotel to cancel their reservations. Even advanced deposits made by credit card do not deter this practice because most travelers know that if they challenge a charge, most credit card companies will not pay the deposit to a canceled hotel.

The net result: Hotels that don't overbook during a citywide convention have absolutely no hope of selling out their available rooms.

Another reason for overbooking is when booking many years out, planners tend to be overly optimistic, resulting in hundreds (or even thousands) of excess room nights requested.

If past history doesn't support the block, hotels are caught in a bind. If the group doesn't pick up, many rooms will go unsold. One strategy many hotels employ, whether they admit it or not, is to disregard the contractual block and instead protect a smaller block for the group. This enables the hotel to sell the remaining rooms to any interested buyers, be it other groups or individuals. Ideally, when the cut-off date arrives, the group will be under its contracted block by the same number of rooms that the hotel oversold.

Unfortunately, this is not an ideal world. Walks result when a group picks up beyond its history...or when a hotel sells too deeply into its block. This creates the overbooked situation where some attendees have to be "walked" to a different hotel.

The solution here is to establish realistic room blocks based on past performance. After each year's convention, future room blocks would be adjusted to reflect actual growth (or decline) in attendance. This would create a situation in which, at 12 months out, the room block would be within 3 percent to 4 percent of the previous year's pickup.

This adjustment would give hotels a much tighter comfort level. And, instead of 10 percent to 15 percent, overbooking could drop to 5 percent or less.

Source: Bruce Harris, president of *Conferon,* the nation's largest independent meeting planning company.

---

rooms and if 20 attendees decide to stay another day an overbooking problem may result.

Many hotels require a guest to initial the registration card indicating the day of departure; this institutes a contract between the hotel and the guest. The hotel meets its obligation by providing the room through that date. Once the date has passed, the guest may be considered a "trespasser." The hotel has two options: it can enter a new contract at a different rate (the hotel is not obligated to extend the convention rate); or, the hotel may evict the guest (the problem is that in the vast majority of states the hotel has to take the overstaying guest to court, which obviously is costly and time-consuming).

Overbookings stem from hotel's experience with no-shows and their fear for that perishable commodity, tonight's room bookings (see Figure 11.8). No-show history is a good reason for you to contact hotels previously used by the association. In return, it is a smart meeting planner who checks among his or her peers for the hotel's overbooking pattern. Wise planners also inform their members of the practice of hotels to hold reservations only until a certain hour, such as 5:00 p.m. They urge their members to arrive earlier than that or to guarantee or pre-pay to make sure they get their rooms.

It is the official policy of some hotels to overbook. They use a numerical factor determined by their general performance records, not the record of a particular convention. These hotels accept the difficulties that arise when they have to walk customers to other hotels as a necessity of avoiding empty rooms. This policy reflects on a management that is only too aware that you can't rent yesterday's room. It also reflects on the failure of many guests to appear, despite confirmed reservations. This situation can be improved but only through mutual performance and confidence. Hotels and clients must recognize that undesirable action on their part brings about corresponding reaction from the other.

It takes diplomacy at the registration desk when people arrive late in the evening after their reservations have been released and their rooms are no longer available. Apologies should be extended, along with an explanation of the cutoff hour and the need for it. The clerk should make some effort to arrange for other accommodations. A phone call to a nearby hotel might bring results, and at least indicate to the guest that you are concerned. It is essential that some efforts be made to secure other housing when you are overbooked. Many hotels pay their guests' cab fares to the substitute hotels.

Many of the problems that come up can be handled if both key people in the convention — the convention executive and the hotelier — are honest with one another and communicate regularly. Both the hotel and the meeting planner should monitor guestroom pickup on a regular basis to avoid potential problems.

Historical Performance

Whenever possible, find out where the group met in previous years. It may be best to do this after the contract is signed in order to maintain business security. Don't hesitate at that point to call the sales manager of the hotels used in the past. They will gladly cooperate because they will want to call you sometime for the same reason. See Figure 9.1 for an example of an inquiry questionnaire.

The historical pattern of a convention tells you a great deal. It can inform you early that this group seldom meets its commitments, or that it always does. You may learn that more attendees show up each year than are expected, or that early departures are common. You may find out that the no-show situation is an ever present problem, or just an odd one or two that is not of major significance.

If nothing else, these calls will give you insight into the meeting planners and let you know whether you are dealing with well-organized pros who can be relied on to control their conventions or planners who lack expertise or experience. The more you learn about your customers, the better equipped you are in handling them.

If you do learn that a convention generally fails to fill its quota, don't duck the issue. Call the convention executive and indicate that you know they had problems in previous years and ask him or her to reconsider the number of rooms to be held. Don't just release rooms without telling him because the planner may have good reason to believe it will not reoccur. Corrective steps may have been taken or something may have happened to stimulate attendance. At the very least, you may hasten the room release data and get a more realistic appraisal.

There are a number of industry publications that provide lists of the past and future meeting sites of the majority of corporate and association groups in the United States. Also, members of the International Association of Convention and Visitors Bureaus exchange their experiences with conventions in order to better understand their customers. It is well worth the time spent to research your customers.

The Westin chain uses three interrelated procedures in an effort to assess the accuracy of a convention's commitment by observing its past performance. First, a standard letter of inquiry is sent, along with a questionnaire, to the last two hotels in which the group met. The letter states that the group has booked with a Westin property and asks the hotels to make a post-convention critique of the group. The critiques then are matched with the requirements that have been requested. If there is an indication that the group has exaggerated its needs, the hotel goes back to the customer to clarify the discrepancy.

Westin's second procedure is to question a meeting planner who books a year or more in advance about his or her schedule of upcoming meetings. Through the use of the tickler system, the hotel brings up the file two weeks before the group's next meeting and two weeks after it.

On the first date, the hotel wishes the meeting planner the best with the scheduled meeting and advises the planner of an evaluation questionnaire to be sent in four weeks. The planner usually is impressed with the hotel's meticulous approach to detail, and the hotel can be alerted to any change or trends that might alter the number of guest rooms or function space it is holding for the group.

The third technique used by Westin might be called "preparticipation." When convention groups with complicated programs or unusual requirements are booked, the hotel salesperson and the convention service manager might request to be admitted as observers to the group's next meeting. By observing the meeting process and requirements, the convention service manager is better able to service the group at its forthcoming convention in his or her hotel. And, again, the client is reassured that he or she is in good hands.

When the convention planner and the hotel executive have mutual confidence in each other, they can work things out so that all delegates are housed and no one gets hurt by variations in expectations.

Check-in/Check-out

A hotel should determine in advance when the heaviest influx of delegates can be expected so it can staff accordingly at the front desk. It would be foolhardy to step off on the wrong foot in the beginning. A delegate who is forced to wait in long lines becomes disgruntled and is a likely complainer throughout the stay.

Check-in Procedure

Arrival lines can be noticeably shortened if a distinction is made between guests with and without reservations. By the process of **pre-registration**, rooms are assigned in advance according to the rooming list provided by the group or developed by the reservation clerk based on reservation requests. If a group arrives together, the group representative merely signs and the keys are given in envelopes labeled with the guests' names and their assigned rooms. If the group members are expected to arrive individually, the registration cards are started for them and the keys again put in envelopes marked with their names. All the guests then do is sign for the key and go on their way.

Pre-registration of all guests is being done more frequently. Special receiving desks, and even special lobbies, are being used by some hotels that service extensive group business. Many conventions set up a **housing assistance desk** near the registration area where the meeting planner and members of the housing staff can greet and assist delegates. This desk services attendees who encounter reservation problems. These arrangements minimize lobby confusion, long lines and slow check-in procedures. Whether individual or group check-in is used, the convention service manager should ask that the meeting planner be present at check-in time.

Check-out Procedure

A poor check-out procedure can destroy an otherwise perfectly organized convention. The group may have had a smooth meeting for three or four days, with excellent food and beverage service, but when the delegate arrives at the cashier's window to check-out, he or she is greeted by a long line, or worse, a sharp remark from the cashier. That delegate is very likely to leave with a bad taste, and three or four days of good meetings are out of the window. Group check-out procedure may be one of the little elements of a convention, but it really counts, particularly if it is not handled expeditiously.

Hotels often establish check-out times at noon or 1:00 P.M. If the wrap-up meeting is a luncheon, late check-out service allows the attendees to attend the conference climax. But if guest arrival patterns prohibit late check-outs, guests should be told to sign out before the luncheon session. Their bills should be ready so that the entire group can be processed quickly and their baggage checked in a convenient storage place until departure time. When the company is picking up the rooming tab, let the guest merely drop off the key.

The Computer Influence

One of the most important trends for the lodging industry is the increased use of computers. While an in-depth discussion is beyond the scope of this chapter, we will briefly consider how computers have influenced the servicing of groups, from reservations to check-out and billing.

Reservations

Of all front office operations, reservations are most associated with computers. Computer assisted reservations systems require fewer labor hours and provide higher accuracy than manual systems, allowing reservation clerks to enter, retrieve, modify and question reservations in seconds. Reservation clerks can check availability from meeting room blocks and print confirmations and registration cards on high-speed printers. In addition, various summary reports, including reservation tally sheets which track room pickup against the block, can be generated to assist managers in scheduling and forecasting.

When the reservation department receives a reply form from a delegate, all the information about the guest is typed into the computer and stored. Once the information is entered, there is no need to duplicate the data. The same information is used for confirmation and deposit receipt notices, pre-registration, check-out and billing procedures.

The computer is linked to a printer. At the end of the day, the printer will automatically type out confirmation slips, eliminating a time-consuming manual step. The computer is programmed to call up the number of rooms reserved to date by any convention.This eliminates the onerous task of keeping a tally sheet on each convention.

Figure 11.9. COMPUTER PREPARED ROOMING ENVELOPE FOR A PRE-REGISTERED GUEST.

AS A GUEST OF THE ST. TROPEZ-RAMADA
SUITES YOU CAN ENJOY MANY
DISTINCTIVE FEATURES.
THEY INCLUDE:

- All suite resort in a park-like environment
- Complimentary airport/strip shuttle service
- In room and outdoor jacuzzis
- In room VCR
- Secretarial services
- Complimentary breakfast daily
- Meeting/Banquet facilities
- Concierge service
- Room service
- Exercise suite
- Health and tennis club privileges
- Fully stocked EUROPEAN mini bar
- Dining and entertainment in our Savoia restaurant
- Shopping plaza

455 E. HARMON AVE.
LAS VEGAS, NEVADA 89109
(702) 369-5400

RAMADA® SUITE

St TROPEZ

Welcome to the Ramada Suite-St. Tropez

Welcome to the Ramada-St. Tropez. We are pleased that you decided to stay with us, and will do all that we can to make your visit a thoroughly rewarding one.

Our entire staff is committed to the highest quality service. Whatever your needs, you will find us ready to respond gracefully and efficiently.

We hope you will enjoy the unique amenities offered by the Ramada-St. Tropez that will make your visit to Las Vegas a memorable experience.

Above all, enjoy yourself.

Most Sincerely,

The Management

 RAMADA SUITE
St TROPEZ

CHECK OUT TIME 12:00 PM.

RESERVED FOR	ROOM	ACCOUNT	DEPARTURE
	2207	65400	12/6/9

	ARRIVAL DATE & TIME	NUMBER OF GUESTS	ROOM/TYPE
RYAN, Jon	12/3/90 6:00 pm	1	K-1
DOG WORLD	DEPOSIT DATE		ROOM RATE
200 E. 36th N.			$75
Redland, CO 10001		RATE DESCRIPTION	
	COMMENTS	Conv.	

METHOD OF PAYMENT   EXPIRES

SHARE WITH   ACCOUNT

NOTICE TO GUESTS

The above indicates your name, rate and No. of days of your stay as it appears on our records. If there is an error please notify the room clerk immediately.

There will be a nominal charge for all phone calls made from the Ramada Suites. Safe deposit boxes are available at the front desk for the protection of your valuables. The proprietor will not be responsible for any articles unless they are so deposited. Please lock your car during your stay at the St. Tropez.

NAME _____

COMPANY _____

ADDRESS _____

CITY _____ STATE _____

ZIP _____ PHONE _____

I agree that my liability for this bill is not waived and I agree to be held personally liable in the event that the indicated person, company, or association fails to pay for the full amount of the charges

GUEST SIGNATURE X _____

PLEASE INDICATE FORM OF PAYMENT

☐ DINERS CLUB   ☐ DISCOVER CARD
☐ TRAVELERS' CHECK   ☐ AMERICAN EXPRESS
☐ CASH   ☐ VISA
☐ CARTE BLANCHE   ☐ MASTERCARD

Source: Courtesy of Ramada Suite St. Tropez Hotel.

Figure 11.10. COMPUTER PREPARED GUEST FOLIO.

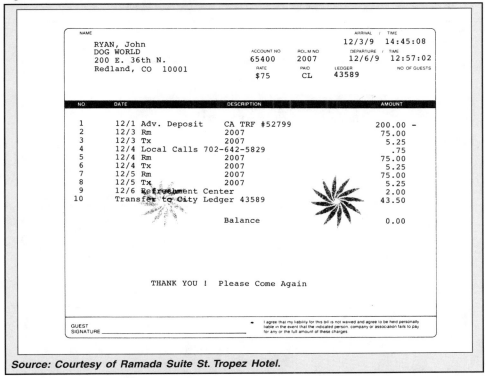

NO.	DATE	DESCRIPTION	AMOUNT
		NAME RYAN, John DOG WORLD 200 E. 36th N. Redland, CO 10001	ARRIVAL / TIME 12/3/9 14:45:08 ACCOUNT NO 65400 ROOM NO 2007 DEPARTURE / TIME 12/6/9 12:57:02 RATE $75 PAID CL LEDGER 43589 NO OF GUESTS
1	12/1	Adv. Deposit CA TRF #52799	200.00 -
2	12/3	Rm 2007	75.00
3	12/3	Tx 2007	5.25
4	12/4	Local Calls 702-642-5829	.75
5	12/4	Rm 2007	75.00
6	12/4	Tx 2007	5.25
7	12/5	Rm 2007	75.00
8	12/5	Tx 2007	5.25
9	12/6	Refreshment Center	2.00
10		Transfer to City Ledger 43589	43.50
		Balance	0.00

THANK YOU ! Please Come Again

GUEST SIGNATURE _____

I agree that my liability for this bill is not waived and agree to be held personally liable in the event that the indicated person, company or association fails to pay for any or the full amount of these charges.

Source: Courtesy of Ramada Suite St. Tropez Hotel.

Registration and Room Assignment

The computer saves considerable time in the preparation of rooming lists and room assignments. Pre-registration of convention attendees, particularly corporate groups, begins the night before the guest arrives; the required rooms are blocked off, registration cards are pretyped for each guest (Figure 11.9), and room keys are sorted. Delegates are listed alphabetically within each convention group and assigned rooms according to the type of accommodation and rate range requested. When delegates arrive, they are given preprinted registration cards, prepared by the computer, which they inspect and sign if all is in order. Some hotels set up separate counters away from the main desk to reduce traffic congestion for pre-registered guests.

To speed check-ins, sophisticated systems are emerging, following the lead of Hyatt Hotels' Touch and Go Instant Check-in Machine. Used much like an ATM machine, these self-service kiosks are located in the hotel lobby, and allow guests with reservations to swipe their credit card through the machine and receive their room key and printed room number in less than 90 seconds, eliminating long waits at the front desk.

Check-out and Billing

Throughout the delegate's stay, charges are posted to an electronic folio, either at the front desk or at several *points-of-sale*. Point-of-sale terminals are located in profit centers throughout the hotel and are linked to the central computer, so guest charges are entered

Figure 11.11. COMPUTER GENERATED BOOKING REPORT.

The Durham Resort

Bookings Report Short Form

For Bookings Arriving Between February 1 to February 7, 1994

Arrival Date	Days	Account Name / (Total RN) Pattern	Booked By	Stat	Funct Space	Average Rate	Total Contribution
2/ 1- 2/ 3/94	Tue Thu	Adams Point Landing (104) 2 102	LMS Post As: Adams Point Landing	D	Y	100.67	10756.00
2/ 1- 2/ 5/94	Tue Sat	Automobile Travelers Association (119) 20 47 44 5 3	LS Post As: Automobile Travelers Assoc.	D	N	95.00	8131.27
2/ 1- 2/ 4/94	Tue Fri	Grant Retirement Party (70) 1 19 42 8	LS Post As: Grant Retirement Party	D	N	79.00	3663.10
2/ 6- 2/ 7/94	Sun Mon	Wed City Anniversary Celebration (45) 20 25	LS Post As: Wed City Anniversary Celeb	D	Y	95.00	3174.85
2/ 6- 2/11/94	Sun Fri	Society Of Technical Writers (905) 8 103 294 272 218 10	AJ Post As: Society Of Technical Writers	T	N	68.62	37964.75
2/ 7- 2/ 7/94	Sat Sat	New England Conservatory (9) 9	LMS Post As: New England Conservatory	D	Y	98.00	641.97

The Durham Resort

Bookings Report Summary by Market Segment

For Bookings Arriving Between February 1 to February 7, 1994

Market Segment	# of Bookings	# of Rm Nights	Guestroom Revenue	Food Revenue	Beverage Revenue	Rooms Rental	Resource Rental	Other Revenue	Total Revenue
National Association	3	180	21600	5400	1345	600	1200	800	30945
Regional Association	2	1024	112640	28160	4525	500	500	800	147125
State Association	3	0	0	5850	890	1500	250	500	8990
National Corporation	1	0	0	2450	580	250	500	400	4180
Local Corporation	2	70	8750	2580	1200	600	600	400	14130
Tour & Travel	7	347	38864	9716	2500	700	660	1200	53640
TOTAL	18	1621	181854	54156	11040	4150	3710	4100	261010

Data entered into the computer system is often used to generate reports such as booking activity by market segment. Producing such reports manually would require hours of labor.
Source: Delphi Reports Sampler, Newmarket Software Systems, Inc., 44 Market Rd., Durham, NH 03824.

directly to the electronic folio instantaneously. Because vouchers do not have to be physically carried from the points-of-sales to the desk for posting, time delay and possible revenue loss are significantly reduced. Folios are often preprinted for convention attendees expected to depart on a given day. As delegates arrive at the cashier's window for departure, the clerk quickly scans the folio on the screen for late charges, prints a new folio only for those needing updating and presents the printed folio (Figure 11.10). When the guest is ready to check out, he or she is given a running account of the transactions. Computer systems also maintain master accounts for the meeting staff and can separate all charges by specific service location.

Reports and Analysis Applications

The applications of the computer to the front desk operation are not the only benefits that are obtained from such a system. Management information, such as marketing reports and control features are additional advantages of an in-house computer. An automated sales office can quickly generate lists and reports that would take hours to produce manually. For example, the *Booking Report* shown in Figure 11.11, allows the sales and rooms departments to select and summarize important marketing criteria such as booking status, arrival dates, room night totals and booking patterns. These statistics are a vital tool to help management plan sales strategies and to give insight into targeting promotional efforts.

The computer frees personnel from laborious bookkeeping and paper shuffling, allowing them to provide convention groups with more prompt service.

Chapter Summary:

A smooth reservations procedure sets the stage for a successful function. Both the hotel and the meeting planner should ensure that communication regarding this crucial area begins at an early stage and that the progress of reservations is monitored on a regular basis to ensure that adjustments can be made. Proper room arrangements and efficient check-in and check-out procedures also add to a delegates favorable impression of the property -- and may result in future business from the meeting planner.

Getting the delegates into the hotel smoothly is just one segment of the servicing process, however. They are coming for a meeting or a function and their expectations are high. In the next chapter, we will see how the convention service manager communicates the numerous details required for the service staff to execute a successful meeting.

Endnotes:

1. "Associations' Use of 3rd-Party Housing Companies Is Soaring," *MeetingNews*, September 20, 1999, p. 2.

2. Linda Humphrey, "Early Check-Out Fees Gaining Momentum," *Business Travel News*, May 6, 1996, p. 1.

Internet Sites:

For additional information on the firms and organizations discussed in this chapter, visit the following Internet sites. The Web addresses listed are current as of January 2001. Addresses may change, however; if a site is not available at address below, a search engine can be used to access its new location.

Greenbrier Hotel - www.greenbrier.com
The Hospitality Sales Marketing Association International (HSMAI) - www.hsmai.org
Hyatt Hotels and Resorts - wwwhyatt.com
International Association of Convention and Visitors Bureaus (IACVB) - www.iacvb.org
Passkey - www.passkey.com
Sheraton Hotels - www.sheraton.com
The Hotel Industry Switch Company (Thisco) - www.thisco.com
Westin - www.westin.com

Study Questions:

 1. Describe in detail the types of reservations systems used to handle group bookings.

 2. Trace the procedures used to service a city-wide convention. Describe the forms used and tell why individual properties make use of a tally sheet to track their reservations.

 3. Distinguish between rack rates, run-of-the house rates, spread rates, and split rates.

4. What three procedures are used by the Westin chain to assess the accuracy of a group's commitment?

 5. What is the relationship between no-shows, under departures, and overbooking?

 6. What factors are taken into consideration to ensure the smooth check-in and check-out of a convention group?

 7. Assess the present-day application of the computer in servicing convention business and project technology's likely role in the future.

Key Terms:

Bid sheet. Form used by local convention bureaus to obtain room commitments and prices from local hotels. The list is later forwarded to the meeting planner or site selection committee.

City-wide. A convention which, because of its size or special requirements, requires accommodations for its delegates in several hotels.

Comp rooms. Complimentary rooms; rooms that the hotel offers at no charge to a group in ratio to the number of rooms occupied by the group. The standard is one comp room per fifty rooms occupied.

Deposit reservation. Payment to the hotel for the first night's lodging prior to arrival. The hotel is obligated to hold the room regardless of the arrival time of the guest.

Discounted rate. The practice of many hotels to mark down normal rates by a percentage or dollar amount as a concession to the group. Usually aimed at a specific type of client or offered at a particular time of the year. Also called a spread rate.

Early departure. An attendee who checks out of the hotel earlier than scheduled. A fee may be charged by the hotel to make up for lost business.

Guaranteed reservation. A reservation that assures the guest a room will be held until check out time of the following day of arrival. The guest guarantees payment for the room, even if it is not used, unless the reservation is properly cancelled.

Housing assistance desk. An area used to provide service to convention attendees who have concerns about their reservations.

Housing bureau. Provided by a city's convention bureau when large conventions are booked to help place the delegates in the city's hotels.

Overbooking. The hotel has committed more rooms that what are actually available for use.

Pre-registration. Often used for group business, the hotel assigns the attendee a room that will be available upon the attendee's arrival.

Rack rate. The standard rate established by a property for a particular category of room. May vary depending upon season.

Reply card. A pre-printed, self-addressed card used for reservations for large conventions. Information on the card includes the name of the group, dates of meeting, and room rates.

Reservation housing report. A report indicating the meeting group's pickup of its room commitment. Sent by a housing bureau to both the hotel and the group.

Rooming list. A list submitted by the meeting planner of the names of attendees who will occupy the previously reserved accommodations.

Run-of-the-house rate. An agreed upon rate for all available rooms except suites. Generally priced at an average figure for group accommodations. Also called a flat rate.

Space available basis. Reservations that have no claim against the block of convention rooms because the request arrived after the official cutoff date.

Split rate. The pricing of guestrooms to groups based on different room types, such as regular guestrooms versus tower rooms.

Tally sheets. A breakdown of each day's convention reservation and group movements. Also provides an arrival and departure flow schedule for each group.

Third-party housing provider. A private company that is contracted to manage the housing of convention delegates.

Under departure. Occurs when a guest scheduled to leave decides to stay longer.

Walk-in. A guest who does not have a reservation but requests accommodations at a hotel. Also called transient business.

Learning Objectives:

In this chapter, we will discuss the specifics of a pre-convention meeting and detail the forms used by the hotel to ensure that departments servicing the event execute it to the planner's specifications. When you have studied this chapter, you will:

- Know the importance of the pre-convention meeting, and its key players

- Be able to distinguish between a specification sheet and a function sheet and tell how each is used.

- Recognize the importance of communication in the execution of an event and be able to describe how the computer is used to communicate meeting details.

Outline

Pre-convention Meeting
- Key Personnel Roster

The Specification Sheet (Resume)

The Function Sheet
(Banquet Event Order)

The Importance of Communication

Communicating Details Electronically

The Importance of Follow-up

The Pre-Con: The Most Critical Meeting on the Program's Agenda

Marilyn McIver
Director of Convention Services
Marriott Desert Springs Resort, Palm Desert

"The Pre-Con meeting is possibly the most critical meeting on the program's agenda!...Executive support is of paramount importance for any event, and General Manager attendance at Pre-Cons is a real plus! After introducing the planner and allowing him/her an opportunity to give a brief of the program, our staff introduces themselves and their departments' roles during the convention...Don't make the mistake of confusing 'pre-con' with 'pre-planning'...By the time you've gathered the 'players' together, the majority of the work has been done via function sheets...I cannot stress enough the importance of detailed function sheets sent by the group, well in advance of the actual event. These sheets are usually transferred to a property format, so both parties should review function sheets to ensure accurate translation...Detailed function sheets, an accurate group resume with a timely distribution and finally a well-run pre-con are all tools we can use to make our joint venture a success."

12   Preparing for the Event

A fter a letter of agreement has been signed by both parties and the reservation cards sent, the event must be planned in great detail. Some conventions are planned a number of years in advance; others, a year or two. Some member of the organization's staff will be the primary coordinator for the group. It may be the executive director for a small or medium-sized association or a convention coordinator for a large organization. It could be a professional convention coordinator who is paid a fee by the association to run the event.

For the hotel, logistics are controlled by the convention service manager. As we discussed, the convention service manager is a most vital person on the hotel staff. He or she is the liaison person with the client and the control person within the hotel. It is not an exaggeration to consider the convention service manager as the key to the success or failure of an event. He or she is responsible for seeing that the event is properly planned and for taking quick, positive action should things go wrong during the event.

In many small hotels, the catering manager may serve as the convention service manager. It is not unusual in such a case for the catering manager also to be active in soliciting banquet business. If this is the case, communication with the sales department and use of the function book must be diligently controlled. This is doubly true when many promises are verbal, and not documented in correspondence or the letter of agreement.

Pre-convention Meeting

A **pre-convention meeting** is essential and goes a long way toward eliminating problems that may surface during conventions. A smart hotel sales executive will arrange for a pre-event meeting to introduce the hotel's convention service personnel and the organization's people. Hotels should make it a firm practice to bring the entire convention staff together for an unhurried pre-convention session with the meeting planner. This get-together gives both parties an opportunity to review the convention agenda item by item to make sure that everyone fully understands what is to take place and to finalize any last-minute details.

Westin's Larry Stephan, former director of sales at the Detroit Plaza, says that his chain services meetings with "Operation Excell." This program begins with a pre-convention meeting held a day or two before the arrival of the group's main delegation. At this time, the meeting planner and his or her staff meet with the convention service manager and the hotel's department heads who are involved in the direct servicing of the group. The upcoming program is thoroughly reviewed.

Attendees at the meeting vary. For simple or one-day meetings, the pre-con may include only the meeting planner and the convention service manager. The following individuals are likely to be in attendance for a large convention with a number of banquets, meetings and complex setups:

- Meeting planner and his or her staff.
- Director of convention services and the convention service manager responsible for servicing the group.
- Salesperson who secured the group and perhaps the director of sales.

- Food and beverage manager, catering/banquet manager and the chef.
- Hotel's general manager and perhaps the comptroller.
- Director of exhibit service, floor manager, and a convention service secretary.
- Representatives from the following departments:
  - front office
  - reservations
  - publicity
  - security
  - uniform services
  - housekeeping
  - telephone
  - recreational facilities
  - audiovisual
- Outside vendors who will play a significant role, such as third-party housing companies, destination management companies or audiovisual firms.

A small ceremony takes place at the end of the pre-convention meeting. The meeting planner and his or her key personnel are given VIP pins, which serve two functions. First, they give distinction to the meeting planner and staff, recognizing that the hotel is aware of their positions and the importance of the meeting. Second, they help the hotel staff single out members who are in charge should there be any last minute changes or requests.

This concept works well for Stephan, who offers a step-by-step review of his chain's "Operation Excell" program used to facilitate the servicing of convention groups in the "Putting It All Together" section at the end of this chapter. The procedure is not put into operation at every convention, nor is it always necessary for all department heads to be present; the convention program determines which department heads will attend. Major conventions and smaller ones with complicated requirements, however, are preceded by such a meeting.

Regardless of who attends the pre-con, from that meeting on, it should be the service manager, not the salesperson, who deals with both the client and the hotel staff. If a hotel wants to suceed with convention business, it must develop good salespeople to bring in the right kind of business, and good convention service people, functioning in-house, to guide that business through to successful completion. In larger convention facilities, a convention service manager would have an assistant and possibly other specialists.

Key Personnel Roster

Meeting planners often request a **key personnel roster** from the convention service manager so they have someone to contact should trouble arise. This roster would list the names and telephone numbers of hotel department heads and other specialists (such as the in-house audiovisual contact). Many convention service managers, however, are hesitant to provide such a list, preferring to have all requests channeled through them. We feel that the wisest course lies between these two positions.

If the convention service manager will *always* be on the scene and available to the meeting planner, it is possible for him or her to receive every request. But if this is not feasible, an assistant should be designated to act in such instances. If this is not practical, department heads should be trained to inform the convention service manager of all requests.

During a convention, a meeting planner will often refuse to wait until the manager can be located before taking action in what he or she deems a crisis. In any case, prompt action on the part of the hotel staff is crucial; communication between key personnel and the convention service manager is obviously essential.

Minita Wescott, past president of both the Chicago Trade Association Executives Forum and the American Trade Association Executives, suggests:

"One person on the hotel staff should be assigned to the convention for the duration of the meeting. This person should be readily available to handle all on-the-spot needs. It makes for a smoother meeting if the executive of the association can meet and get acquainted with all top members of the hotel staff with whom this executive and his staff will have to work."[1]

The Marriott chain has responded to such meeting planners' requests for hotel contact people to act on last-minute needs and further expanded on it with the introduction of its Red Coat service. A number of property convention staff personnel, easily identified by their red jackets, are both trained and empowered to handle last-minute details and crises. This program helps free up the property's convention service manager while still ensuring that immediate help is available to meeting planners who need it. The visibility and accessibility of these trained professionals helps to boost the confidence of even the least experienced meeting planner and demonstrates the chain's commitment to service.

In the pressure cooker of an ongoing convention, meeting planners are most appreciative of reassurance that last minute problems will be dealt with, and promptly. Gestures of such reassurance go a long way towards making a property a favorite of convention planners.

In summary, we feel it a positive action to furnish a roster of key hotel personnel to the client (see Figure 12.1), along with the request that all action be taken through the convention service manager, *whenever possible.*

The Specification Sheet (Resume)

The convention service manager is responsible for writing a detailed schedule for each convention. The title for this schedule may vary. It may be known as the master prospectus, the resume, the bible, the summary, or the specification sheet. We will use the latter term.

Do not confuse the *specification sheet* with the *function sheet*, which is explained in the next section. The **specification sheet** provides a comprehensive overview of the entire program, from pre-convention to post-convention, to the hotel staff. The function sheet details only a single event.

Although they are titled differently, all convention hotels use similarly constructed specification sheets when servicing groups that meet for more than one day. Specification sheets set forth activities day by day and hour by hour, covering meetings, meals, refreshment breaks, cocktails, reservation procedures, billing, exhibit instructions, special events, guest programs, recreational activities, and anything else that needs the hotel staff's attention. It is undoubtedly the single most important element of the convention servicing process, providing a tool for planning and communication between hotel departments.

The specification sheet is prepared by the convention service manager in conjunction with the meeting planner. Much of the information is extracted from correspondence and discussion with the convention group. For larger groups (such as associations that meet annually), the convention service manager may request a copy of the group's previous year's specification sheet. The group's information then is put in the hotel's format and the specification sheet is distributed to all people involved with servicing the convention. This must be done far enough in advance to ensure that departments will have time to staff and prepare appropriately (in most cases, at least a week before the group arrives).

The length of the specification sheet varies, of course, with the size, number of days, and details required for each convention. We have seen some specification sheets that were

Figure 12.1. HOTEL KEY PERSONNEL ROSTER.

HOTEL PERSONNEL

Hotel staff personnel contact for over-all service during the convention of _____

Period	Hours	Name	Title	Phone Extension
Early morning	___a.m. to ___p.m.			
Daytime	___a.m. to ___p.m.			
Evening	___a.m. to ___p.m.			
Saturdays	___a.m. to ___p.m.			
Sundays	___a.m. to ___p.m.			
Holidays	___a.m. to ___p.m.			

Hotel key staff by departments
Check marks on the hotel staff list given below indicate the departmental key personnel with whom the organization will come in contact during the servicing of the convention.

Check	Department	Name	Title	Phone Extension

The meeting planner should have a principal contact on the hotel staff at all times during the day. In addition to key personnel rosters, some planners insist on being supplied with a two-way radio, beeper, pager or cellular phone to ensure immediate contact with the hotel staff.
Source: Reprinted with permission from the Convention Liaison Manual, published by the Convention Industry Council.

more than 40 pages long. Most, however, run eight to 12 pages for a three-day session. Simply put, a specification sheet should be long enough to include all the details (some hotels use legal size sheets to cut down on the number of pages).

The importance of putting every detail in writing cannot be overstated. And the more detailed the better. "Nobody told me," is heard too often in hotels. Putting everything in writing lessens the chance of this occuring.

Figure 12.2 illustrates an abbreviated specification sheet written for a ficticious convention, the Architectural Draftsmen International. Note that the specification sheet opens with a pre-convention setup and closes with a post-convention meeting. The specification sheet begins with a general description of the group and a brief statement informing the hotel staff of the basic purpose and objectives of the meeting. Note that a list of the individuals and departments that receive this information is listed on the left-hand side of the first page. The first page also includes such information as complimentary accommodations, arrival and departure schedules, the reservation procedure, and billing to both master and individual accounts.

The next two pages provide an indication of the detail required in a specification sheet. Every scheduled event is documented and thorough instructions provided regarding room setup and food and beverage arrangements. While reading through the sheet, keep in mind the importance of the meticulous recording required in the preparation of this form.

Figure 12.2. SAMPLE GROUP SPECIFICATION SHEET.

```
* * * * * * * * * * * * * *
      GROUP SPECIFICATION SHEET
* * * * * * * * * * * * * *
```

General Manager
Food/Bev. Dir.
Front Office
Showroom
Exec. Chef
Beverage Mgr. (2)
Coffee Shop
Room Service
Group Billing
Hotel Manager
Asst. Hotel Mgrs. (2)
Food Checker
Reservations
Publicity
Security
Housekeeping
Head Houseman
Head Banquet Waiter
Sales (2)
Food & Bev. Control
Linen Control
Doorman
Benihana Manager
Stage & Sound (2)
Public Porters
Steward
Catering Director
Group Services (4)
Uniform Room
Purchasing

SUBJECT:	Architectural Draftsmen International Attendees are the world's leading architects. The focus of the meeting is on customer service. The theme of the meeting is, "Building Better Relationships with Clients."
DATES:	February 16-20, 20__
CONTACT:	Jay Bryan Master Draftsman 206 Clark - Suite 307 Lakeview, Michigan 48850
HOTEL SALESPERSON:	Larry Kingsbury, National Sales Manager
ARRIVAL/DEPARTURE PATTERN: ROOM RES. MANAGER ASSISTANT MANAGERS FRONT DESK HOTEL CASHIER	300 rooms have been committed to this group. Most are arriving late Sunday, February 16 and departing Thursday, February 20, 20__. Arriving individually - Preregister
	RATES - European Plan $95.00 Single or Double occupancy, plus 6% County room tax, net, non-commissionable.
	SUITE RATES - One Bedroom $100.00 - Petite Suite $120.00 - Deluxe Suite $180.00 - Royal Suite
LOCATION:	DESERT VIEW, FOUNTAIN VIEW, POOLSIDE HEXAGON, CENTRAL TOWER
COMPLIMENTARY ACCOMMODATIONS:	A King Bedroom (North Tower) for Marney Vartanian, Associate Convention Manager ARR: February 15, 20__ DEP: February 20, 20__
	Additional complimentary units to be assigned based upon 1 complimentary unit for every 50 rooms actually occupied. (Names forthcoming)
HOSPITALITY REQUEST FOR:	Ms. Marney Vartanian Dewars Scotch w/setups ARR: February 15, 20__
RESERVATION ACCEPTANCE PROCEDURE:	This group utilized our return reservation cards.
MASTER ACCOUNT:	All Group functions should be billed to the master account. Ms. Marney Vartanian will be the authorized signer.
INDIVIDUAL ACCOUNT:	Room, tax, and incidentals to be paid by individuals.

(continued)

This form for a fictitious convention is similar to those used by hotels to provide an overview of a group's event. At the left is a list of the people and departments that will receive this sheet. In addition, the convention service manager usually sends the specification sheet to the meeting planner well in advance of the pre-convention meeting to ensure that details are correct and that nothing has been overlooked. This saves time during the pre-convention meeting as the major points have already been negotiated and accepted by both parties.

```
* * * * * * * * * *
   SCHEDULED FUNCTIONS
* * * * * * * * * *
```

Saturday, February 15, 20__

  3:00 P.M.   ADI/HOTEL STAFF PRECONVENTION MEETING   Board Room

                             15 persons

  Attn: Set-up Crew   "U" shape

  Attn: Banquet Wtr.   Complimentary coffee, soft drinks, sweet rolls

Sunday, February 16, 20__

  6:00 - 8:00 P.M.   ARCHITECTURAL DRAFTSMEN INTERNATIONAL   Sec. F
                             COCKTAIL RECEPTION
                             Approximately 30 persons. All are convention officials
                             and board members

  Attn: Set-up Crew   Cabaret style

  Attn: Banquet Wtr.,
        Bar Manager   Call brand liquor to include: Beefeater, Johnny Walker Black,
                             Dewars, Smirnoff, Jack Daniels Black, Old Grand Dad, CC,
                             Bristol Cream Sherry @ $26.00 ++ and $30.00 ++. Two bottles
                             Chablis and Pinot Noir @ $7.00 per bottle ++. Beer @ $1.00 ++.

  Attn: Banquet Wtr.,
        Exec. Chef   Following hors d'oeuvres: 5 orders Polynesian Pu-Pus @ $7.50++,
                             5 orders Selection #3 @ $6.75 ++, 10 orders Selection #4 @ $6.75 ++
                             10 orders hot seafood @ $8.00 ++, 10 orders cold seafood @ $8.50 ++,
                             and one shrimp bowl @ $100.00 ++. Hors d'oeuvre table to be
                             decorated with two gold candelabra and 6 silver chafing dishes, white tapers.
                             Cold hors d'oeuvres to be passed by waiters.

  Attn: Accounting   Bill to Texas Instruments - Exhibits Master Account.

Sunday, February 16, 20__

  3:00 - 6:00 P.M.   REGISTRATION   Foyer

  Attn: Set-up Crew   6' draped table rear of registration desk.
                               2 house phones. 1 directory board. Ice water
                               stand. Bb/c/e. (blackboard/chalk/eraser)

Monday, February 17, 20__

  9:00 A.M. - NOON   GENERAL BUSINESS SESSION   Sec. F

                               500 Persons

  Attn: Set-up Crew   Theatre style with stage 12' x 40' x 24'
                               twenty feet out from kitchen wall. Projection platform
                               will be required against kitchen wall for rear screen projection.
                               Size to be determined. Head table for 8 on stage. American
                               Flag stage right. 1 35mm Carousel slide projector. 1 Lantern slide
                               projector. 1 electric pointer. 2 center aisle mikes. Central dimmer
                               to be located at projection platform. 1 projectionist.

  9:30 A.M. - NOON   EXHIBIT HALL SETUP   Exhibit Hall

  Attn: Hall Supervisor   20 - 8' x 10' exhibit booth to be set up by
                               Scott Stubbs Service Company.

(continued)

As you can see, a large volume of information must be entered -- and often changed -- which is not only time-consuming, but may also result in costly errors.

In order to standardize resume data, and to minimize error, technology is being developed with financial backing from the Hyatt, Marriott, and Sheraton chains, along with the ASAE and MPI. The venture, called PlanSoft Ajenis Limited Partnership, uses the Ajenis

```
        12:15 P.M.                          LUNCHEON                                               Sec. B

                                            500 Persons

        Attn:  Set-up Crew                  Rounds of 10 with raised head tables on 32" dais
                                            for 12 centered in south wall.

                                            Lighted table podium mike center of head table.

        Attn:  Banquet Wtr.                 Tickets to be collected except at head table. Linen will probably
               Exec. Chef                   be alternated on this function. This is to be advised.

        Attn:  Banquet Wtr.                 Serve our Group Luncheon Menu #7 with tomato juice
                                            appetizer @ $6.10 ++.

        Attn:  Accounting                   Bill to ADI Master Account.


        Thursday, February 20, 19

        3:00 - 5:00 P.M.                     ADI/HOTEL STAFF POST-CONVENTION MEETING               Board Room

                                            Same setup as on Saturday
```

software to speed up the entry (and any subsequent changing) of meeting data and to eliminate communications problems during meeting planning. The system, which will provide a "one-stop" planning service, will use a database from which planners can choose properties, "view" meeting rooms and call up specifications, and enter and change their meeting specs. A planner using the same property for a subsequent meeting can simply modify such details as dates and attendance.

The Function Sheet (Banquet Event Order)

When the program is finalized, each function should receive individual attention. Such attention to detail translates into service efficiency. This is done by means of the **function sheet**. Figure 12.3 is the form used for our architectural draftsmen convention. The function sheet for the cocktail party gives the reader an understanding of how the function sheet and specification sheet are related. Think of the specification sheet as providing a panorama of the convention and the function sheet as offering a close-up view.

The function sheet, like the specification sheet, has been tagged with a variety of names: event form, worksheet, banquet event order, etc. Function sheets, too, vary from hotel to hotel in the amount of detail required. Individual function forms are generally prepared from the specification sheets and are the working form for the hourly employees. For example, Figure 12.3 is prepared from the specification sheet and is the form from which the bartender, set-up crew and cooks will work while servicing this event.

Ideally, the specification sheet should be completed and two copies sent to the meeting planner two to three weeks in advance of the meeting and prior to distribution to the hotel staff. Function sheets should be accompanied by a letter asking the planner to review the copies, note any changes, and sign and return one copy prior to the meeting.

Whether the function is a general session or a small committee meeting, document it. The basic seating layout, decorations, visual aids, and any other special services required should be detailed on the function sheet. Copies of each function sheet, as with the specification sheet, should be distributed to hotel department heads at least a week prior to the event.

Figure 12.3. FUNCTION SHEET (BANQUET EVENT ORDER).

FUNCTION ORDER - FOOD AND BEVERAGE

EVENT DATE February 16, 19-		DAY Sunday		ORDER NO 126
ORGANIZATION Architectural Draftsman International				FILE NO N-614
POST AS Architectural Draftsman International Cocktail Reception				
BILLING ADDRESS Bill to Master Account Texas Instruments, 120AK, Lakeview, MI 48851				
CONTACT Deanne Pritchard	ON SITE CONTACT Robert Olson		BUS PHONE NO 363-1906	RES PHONE NO
EXPECTED 30	GUARANTEED 30	SET UP 33	BOOKED BY Amber S.	DATE TYPED 2/1

TIME	SETUP REQUIREMENTS	LOCATION	TIME	MENU	LOCATION

SETUP REQUIREMENTS

6:00 PM - 8:00 PM Cocktail   Sec. F

Cabaret Style Set-Up
Draped Cocktail Rounds with ashtrays,
no chairs

MENU

5 orders Polynesion Pu-Pus @ $7.50++,
5 orders selection #3 @ $6.75++,
10 orders selection #4 @ $6.75++,
10 orders hot seafood @ $8.50++,
10 orders cold seafood @ $8.50++,
1 shrimp bowl @ $100.00++

Hors d'oeuvre table to be decorated
with two gold candlabra and 6 silver
chafing dishes. White tapers.
Cold hors d'oeuvres to be passed by
waiters

Food @ $6.75 +T+T
Seafood @ $8.50 +T+T
Shrimp bowl @ $100.00 +T+T

HOTEL TO ORDER

X Decorations
3 Tropical Florals
Charge to Master
___ Entertainment

REFRESHMENT BREAK

AUDIO VISUAL

Time   Location

SPECIAL NOTES

BEVERAGE REQUIREMENTS

RECEPTION

Call Brand Liquor to include: Beefeater,
Johnny Walker Black, Dewars, Smirnoff,
Jack Daniels Black, Old Grand Dad, CC,
Bristol Cream Sherry @ $26.00 ++, $28.00 ++
and $30.00 ++. Two bottles Chablis &
WINE SELECTION   Pinot Noir @ $7.00 ++ per
bottle. Beer @ $1.00 ++.

SUMMARY OF CHARGES

FOOD   See Menu
BEVERAGE   See Beverage Requirements
RENT
LABOR
PARKING
DEPOSIT RECEIVED
METHOD OF PAYMENT
BALANCE DUE DATE

TIME   LOCATION

WE NEED YOUR ASSISTANCE IN MAKING YOUR BANQUET A SUCCESS. PLEASE CONFIRM YOUR ATTENDANCE AT LEAST 3 BUSINESS DAYS IN ADVANCE. IF WE ARE NOT CONTACTED WITHIN THE SPECIFIED TIME, YOUR EXPECTED ATTENDANCE WILL SERVE AS YOUR GUARANTEE. THIS WILL BE CONSIDERED YOUR MINIMUM GUARANTEE. WE WILL ADD THE CUSTOMARY 17% SERVICE CHARGE AND SALES TAX. FOR GROUPS SERVED UNDER 25 THERE WILL BE A $50 LABOR CHARGE. I HAVE READ AND I UNDERSTAND THE REVERSE SIDE OF THIS DOCUMENT.

IF IN AGREEMENT, PLEASE SIGN ONE COPY AND RETURN   X _____

This form is used to detail each convention function listed on the specification sheet.

It is essential that *each program segment* have its own function sheet to ensure that all details will be handled. Document the head table, platform, basic seating layout and all other arrangements. But also have a checklist for small but needed items, such as water glasses, pads and pencils, audiovisual equipment, sound systems, floral arrangements, and so on.

You may find that many well-organized association and corporate meeting planners make their own checklists of what is needed. Some pros will even provide you with a complete *staging guide* of their meeting from which you can prepare your own function sheets, incorporating their itemized requests (see Figure 12.4). Such customers are a delight. Make sure to get copies of their lists. One convention service manager shared with us,

Figure 12.4. STAGING GUIDES.

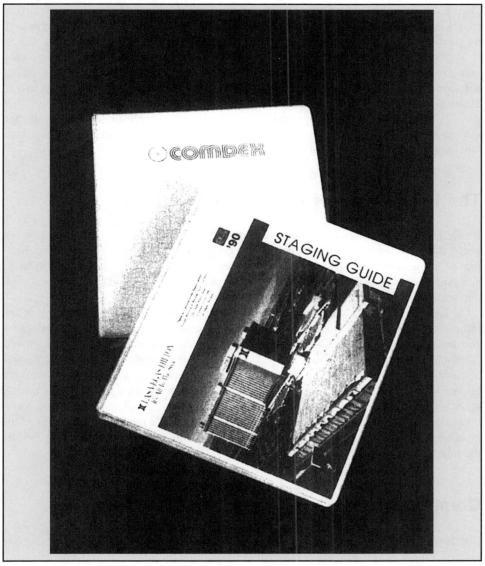

The overriding factor in the success of a meeting is communication. Meeting managers who provide staging guides, detailed instructions for each event or setup in a loose-leaf notebook, facilitate the convention service manager's task of preparing the specification sheet.

> "Most people think that all the convention service manager does is handle the group while it's in-house, but 90 percent of our work is the extraction of details one to two years prior to arrival. My job is to direct, produce and extract information from the meeting planner and in turn pass this information on to various department heads through specification and function sheets."

A master schedule should be made. This will assist you in determining the number of pieces of anything needed anywhere at any particular time. You may have specified on a number of function sheets that a Carousel slide projector is needed, but the master schedule would indicate how many such projectors are needed at the same time.

Many hotel people feel that such details are truly the responsibility of the meeting planner. However, it is the hotel staff that will be called upon under crisis conditions to rectify any oversights. You could avoid those last-minute panics by being well organized; by creating such accurate checks yourself and suggesting them to the client.

If planners are inexperienced and fail to anticipate their needs correctly, they may say you gave them insufficient notice and you may end up as the victim. Given a choice between blaming you and accepting the blame themselves, they may find it all too easy to blame you.

Not only is it important to plan defensively, but your suggestions and organization also will establish your reputation. Clients will retain the memory that meetings at your hotel always run smoothly. That memory is the one you want to leave with clients.

The Importance of Communications

Problems during meetings can be largely eliminated if a "pipeline" of communication has been established from the very beginning. It has been said that "the job of servicing meetings is 95 percent communication and 5 percent service." Securing detailed information and expectations from the meeting planner is one of the most important tasks of the convention service manager.

Letters, telephone calls and personal on-site visits are normally used to get initial information. Another excellent tool to initiate the communication process is to send a **resume questionnaire** (see Chapter Appendix) to the meeting planner. This form consolidates a list of important questions and reduces the frequent telephone calls and exchanges of correspondence on individual items. Other ways to improve communication are for the convention service manager to provide the meeting planner with a formal and mutually agreed upon timetable for communication of meeting details. And, some convention service managers ask to be put on the meeting planner's mailing list, while others will send the meeting planners a sample specification sheet to inform the planner of the format used by the hotel.

Communicating Details Electronically

Computer technology has altered the way specification and function sheet information is created. Figure 12.5 illustrates a computer generated function sheet. Automated sales systems can build a function sheet as information is gathered and input by the salesperson into the client's file. Also, a computerized system allows the creation of a number of forms that

Figure 12.5 COMPUTERIZED FUNCTION SHEET.

The Durham Resort
44 Newmarket Road
Durham, New Hampshire 038244
(603) 868-1500

GROUP NAME: Automobile Travelers Association
POST AS: Annual Meeting
IN CHARGE: Mr. Harry McArthur **FUNCTION ORDER NO: 104**

DAY	DATE	TIME	FUNCTION	ROOM	PEOPLE	RENT
Tue	10/12/96	8:00 AM - 5:00 PM	Lunch Meeting	Cherry Room	75	$250

BEVERAGES

Service: 17.5%   Tax: 9.5%
Bartender Fee: $65.00 each

ARRANGEMENTS

In charge of service: Banquet Service

Chairs (18")
16mm Movie Projector
6' Round Dinner Table for Rounds of 10
Slide Projector with remote control
  capabilities
Rear Screen Projection (10' x 10')

FOOD

Stuffed Pork Chop from 8:00 AM to 5:00 PM
Room: Cherry Room   Attendance: 75

Tender Pork Chop Filled with a Special
  Sausage Stuffing in a Mushroom Sauce
Whipped Potatoes
Vegetable du Jour
Tossed Garden Salad, Choice of Dressing
Assorted Rolls
Coffee, Tea & Decaf
Charge: $18.00 Per Person

Billing: Master Account
Address: 1234 Albany Drive
           Atlanta, GA 01234
Phone: (404) 555-2141

Client Signature:_____ Date:_____
Prepared By: Kathy McDonald_____ Date: June 14, 1996

The contents of the above meet with my approval. I consider our agreement definite and confirmed.
Guarantees must be sumbitted 48 hours in advance of all functions (Monday functions, 72 hours).
Prices are subject to 17.5% gratuity and 9.5% sales tax (where applicable).

This function sheet, generated in an automated sales office, merges important account information and relative booking information on one display screen. This report retrieves the information from the hotel's meetings database.

can be tailored to specific servicing needs. For example, you can create a form that contains just menu information for your chef, or a form containing just setup information for your service staff.

Database management programs also allow meeting information stored in the computer to be isolated, manipulated or sorted to answer specific requests. With just a few keystrokes, the meetings can be sorted by location, time, date, size, and so on. For example, you may wish to ask the computer to list all meetings scheduled in the convention area that require overhead projectors on Monday between 7:00 A.M. and 7:00 P.M. or which rooms require classroom setup this week. This information is available instantly on a computer-ized data management program and would not require searching through numerous typed resumes. Additionally, changes and deletions are made simply by calling up the meeting in question and revising the individual fields or deleting the record.

In addition, new technology processes driven by the Internet and e-commerce will alter the way in which specification and function sheet information is communicated. In the future, this information will be transmitted electronically via a direct Internet link between the meeting planner and the hotel's convention service manager. Each will have all the details on-screen and will be able to make corrections online, eliminating the mail-ing of large amounts of paperwork.

Once approved by the meeting planner, the specification and function sheets will be distributed electronically to departments within the hotel rather than having sheets (even computer generated ones) copied and distributed. With the click of a mouse, the exacting details of the meeting will be distributed to all involved with servicing the group.

The Importance of Follow-up

Follow-up is an important part of showing your commitment to servicing a group's meet-ing. Follow-up, of course, should begin after initial contact with the client, as discussed in the communications section in this chapter. Checking details increases the likelihood that there will be fewer problems during the event.

During the meeting, frequent contact with the meeting planner and/or his or her staff is also important. Checking to ensure that all is going well reassures the meeting planner of your commitment to his or her group.

After an event, a **post-convention meeting** should be held. The same people who met for the pre-convention meeting should meet for an after-the-fact review of the convention. This meeting is an opportunity for both the planner and the hotel staff to assess the success of the event and to address any problems (and determine ways to solve them in the future).

"PUTTING IT ALL TOGETHER"

Westin's "Operation Excell"

It is important for meeting planners and a property to get off to a proper start. A well-organized pre-convention procedure such as Westin's "Operation Excell" eliminates many of the unforseen crises inherent to group meetings and could well mean the difference between a successful convention and one that is plagued by disorganization. The follow-ing, a step-by-step review of the "Operation Excell" checklist, is a concept for servicing meetings that can be used by any size property, whether resort, commercial hotel or motel.

1. A pre-convention date and time is agreed upon by the hotel and the meeting planner. A reminder is sent to all departments involved, with a notation that all department heads are to be there ten minutes before the meeting begins. This is to give the convention service manager a chance to prepare the staff for any unusual characteristics or demands of the convention group. All the normal procedures used in setting up meeting rooms should be applied in planing an Operation Excell meeting. Taking care of details such as

proper seating setup, the right sized meeting room, and comfortable chairs gives the client the impression that the hotel will service his or her meeting as well as it runs its own. Coffee, soft drinks and sweet rolls should be provided so there is an atmosphere of informality. To instill confidence that the hotel knows how to service meetings, the convention service manager should check the room an hour ahead of time for those little things, such as lighting, pads and pencils, and comfortable temperature, that make for a pleasant, attractive meeting setup.

2. An inventory of nameplates of all department heads should be maintained so that the client may relate in the meeting to the key people on the hotel's staff. VIP identification pins are presented to the meeting planner and his or her staff.

3. The meeting format gives department heads a chance to ask questions about matters that relate directly to their roles in servicing the group. The convention service manager then goes over the program event by event. A sample agenda might include:

   - review of the specification sheet and function sheets
   - review of the master account
   - an updated room pick-up report

If there are areas of misunderstanding or changes are needed, the client has an opportunity to inject input. A secretary should be on hand to take note of these changes. These last-minute changes are typed up after the meeting and distributed to all involved.

4. A specification sheet (resume), which covers the entire convention program and is the hotel's in-house communication medium, should be distributed not only to those at the Operation Excell meeting but to every department in the hotel. Each department needs to be kept informed so it can forecast staffing needs. For example, if no luncheons or dinners are scheduled on a particular day, the people in charge of staffing the hotel's coffee shop and restaurants should be alerted to the possibility of extra volume. Likewise, if a late evening activity is scheduled outside the hotel, security personnel should be informed to take extra precautions.

 ## Chapter Summary:

In this chapter, we have seen the necessity of working closely with the planner in the days leading up to a meeting or convention and the necessity of informing all hotel departments of their roles in the event. Pre-convention meetings, detailed specification and function sheets, and communication with both the planner and hotel staff will ensure the success of a meeting and will leave a good impression of the property's commitment to service.

The function sheets discussed in this chapter cover the requirements discussed by the planner and the property to set the tone for and properly execute the planner's event. These details include food and beverge requirements and room setups. In the next chapter, we will take a detailed look at the types of set-ups commonly used for meetings and other functions.

Endnotes:

1. HSMAI Sales Manual.

Additional References:

- Meetings and Conventions: A Planning Guide, Don MacLaurin and Ted Wykes, Meetings Professionals International. www.mpiweb.org

Internet Sites:

For additional information on the firms and organizations discussed in this chapter, visit the following Internet sites. The Web addresses listed are current as of January 2001. Addresses may change, however; if a site is not available at address below, a search engine can be used to access its new location.

Convene - www.pcma.org
Delphi-Newmarket Software - www.newsoft.com
Marriott International - www.marriott.com
Meeting News - www.meetingnews.com
Meetings and Conventions - www.meetings-conventions.com
Westin Hotels - www.westin.com

Study Questions:

1. What is the purpose of the pre-convention meeting? Who should attend?
2. What are the positions of the meeting planner and the convention service manager regarding a key personnel roster? What have some hotels done to compromise?
3. What key information is provided on a specification sheet?
4. How does the function sheet differ from the specification sheet?
5. How is the computer used to facilitate the communication of meeting details?
6. Why is follow-up so important? Describe three key times when hotel personnel commonly follow-up on a meeting.
7. Describe Westin's "Operation Excell." Outline the four stages of this program and discuss why each is important.

Key Terms:

Function sheet. A form that provides a detailed breakdown of a single event. Also called a banquet event order (BEO).

Key personnel roster. A list of the hotel personnel who are available to the meeting planner throughout the day to help service the event.

Post-convention meeting. A meeting held after the completion of a convention or meeting to evaluate the forecasting and planning that preceded the convention and the hotel's performance during the event.

Pre-convention meeting. A meeting held before the convention or event to review the entire program to ensure that the planner and hotel understand each other's requirements and expectations. This meeting is attended by the planner and key hotel people who will be involved in serving the event to eliminate any misunderstandings and ensure a smooth event.

Resume questionnaire. Form on which meeting planners answer questions relating to the upcoming event. Having detailed information readily available reduces the need for frequent contact with the meeting planner and assists hotels in preparing for both the pre-convention meeting and the event itself.

Specification sheet (resume). Form providing a comprehensive overview of the entire convention program. Sent to the various hotel departments, it provides specific instructions to the staff for servicing the convention.

APPENDIX

RESUME (SPECIFICATION SHEET) QUESTIONNAIRE
Resume questionnaire to be completed by the meeting planner.
(By permission, Penta Hotels)

NAME OF ORGANIZATION _____ Page _____

PROGRAM AND SET-UP INSTRUCTIONS

DAY/DATE	FUNCTION	LOCATION	TIME	SET-UP INSTRUCTIONS
Monday, 12/13	Registration	Georgian Foyer	8am-5pm	3 - 6' x 30" tables with 2 chairs each. 2 easels, a corkboard, a wastepaper basket.
	General Session	Georgian Ballroom	9am-5pm	Theater style for 200pp facing a head table for 6pp on a 1' high platform. Provide a table lectern. Audio: Provide a lectern mike. Audiovisual: Provide a Carousel projector with remote control with long cord and screen.
	Refreshment service	Georgian Foyer	10:30am-11am	Please discuss with Banquet Manager.
	Luncheon	Gold Ballroom	12N-1pm	Please discuss with Banquet Manager.
	Refreshment service	Georgian Foyer	3pm-3:30pm	Please discuss with Banquet Manager.
Tuesday, 12/14	Registration	Georgian Foyer	8am-5pm	Set-up: Same as the previous day.
	General Session	Georgian Ballroom	9am-5pm	Set-up: Same as the previous day.
	Refreshment Service	Georgian Foyer	10:30am-11am	Please discuss with Banquet Manager.
	Luncheon	Gold Ballroom	12N-1pm	Please discuss with Banquet Manager.
	Refreshment Service	Georgian Foyer	3pm-3:30pm	Please discuss with Banquet Manager.
etc.				

Penta Hotel

<u>RESUME GUIDELINES</u>

1. EVENT TO BE POSTED AS FOLLOWS:

_____

_____

2. OFFICIAL OFFICERS:

<u>NAME</u>   <u>TITLE</u>

_____

_____

_____

3. AUTHORIZED SIGNATURES:

<u>NAME</u>   <u>SIGNATURES</u>   <u>TITLE</u>

_____

_____

_____

4. MASTER BILLING ADDRESS, TELEPHONE NUMBER AND TO WHOM'S ATTENTION IT SHOULD BE LISTED.
   (Upon approval of credit manager)

_____

_____

_____

5. NEW YORK STATE TAX EXEMPT: _____ YES   _____ NO

   (If your organization is tax exempt, please forward a copy of the certificate to the Convention Service Department.)

6. CONVENTION HEADQUARTERS HOTEL : _____

   OTHER HOTELS USED: _____

   _____   _____

7. EXPECTED CONVENTION REGISTRATION: _____ ADVANCE _____ ON-SITE

8. WILL THERE BE A NECESSITY FOR HOTEL SAFETY BOXES FOR THE CONVENTION OFFICERS? _____ YES _____ NO
   (If yes): HOW MANY? _____ AND WHAT NAMES SHOULD THEY BE LISTED UNDER:

_____

_____

_____

-2-

9. MONEY EXCHANGE: Will there be a necessity for the officers to exchange large bills during the conference? _____YES _____NO
(If yes, in what denominations?)

PENNIES _____   NICKELS _____   DIMES _____   QUARTERS _____

$1 BILLS _____ $5 BILLS _____ $10 BILLS _____ $20 BILLS _____

10. RESERVATIONS: _____ HOTEL FORM   _____ OWN FORM   _____ HOUSING BUREAU

_____ ROOMING LIST   _____ PHONE IN

11. ARRIVALS: Will most of your arrivals be arriving by:

_____AUTOMOBILE   _____TRAIN   _____COMMERCIAL AIRLINE   _____CHARTERED BUS
Note: For bus arrivals, please have the person(s) and/or organization contact our Reservation Manager directly.

12. HOSPITALITY SUITES: Please have the companies who will be sponsoring Hospitality Suites contact our Room Service Manager
directly for their food and beverage needs. Also, our Reservation Manager and Credit Manager should be
contacted to expedite their reservation and billing needs.

13. BUS DEPARTURES: Have you contracted for buses for tours, trips, etc. _____YES _____NO
If yes, please advise us of your schedule in the program and setup instructions.

14. CELEBRITIES: Will any of your speakers attract media attention? _____YES _____NO
If yes, please list their names and speaking date/time below:

_____

_____

_____

15. SECURITY SPEECH: Do you require our Security Department to give a short speech on security tips on this city and the hotel?

_____ YES   _____NO   If yes, it will be conducted at your first General Session.

16. OFFICERS, SPEAKERS AND VIP RESERVATIONS:

NAME: _____   Double - 1 bed

ADDRESS: _____   Twin - 2 single beds

_____

TELEPHONE #: _____

ARRIVAL DATE:_____   ESTIMATED TIME: _____

DEPARTURE DATE:_____   ESTIMATED TIME:_____

ROOM TYPE: _____ SINGLE   _____DOUBLE   _____TWIN

_____ 1 BEDROOM SUITE   _____2 BEDROOM SUITE

(Sharing with: _____)

Arrival: _____ Departure_____

BILLING INSTRUCTIONS: _____ Pays own room, tax and incidental charges

_____ Room and tax to the Master Account

_____ Room, tax and incidentals to the Master Account

SPECIAL REQUIREMENTS: _____

-3-

17. REGISTRATION: (Speakers - Exhibitors - Registrants)

       DAY   DATE   TIME   LOCATIONS

_____

_____

18. ADMISSION: _____

19. EXHIBITS: DAY/DATE   TIME   LOCATION(S)

Drayage setup: _____

_____

Exhibitors Setup: _____

_____

Show Opens: _____

_____

Exhibitors Dismantle: _____

_____

Drayage Dismantle: _____

_____

20. NUMBER OF EXHIBITORS: _____ TYPE OF BOOTHS:_____
      Forward the exhibitors contract to the Convention Service department.

21. HOTEL HOLD HARMLESS CLAUSE: Please sign and return.

22. CONTRACTORS: (Contact, address and telephone number)

      DRAYAGE CONTRACTOR   SECURITY CONTRACTOR

      _____   _____

      _____   _____

      _____   _____

      AUDIOVISUAL CONTRACTOR   TYPEWRITER CONTRACTOR

      _____   _____

      _____   _____

      _____   _____

      SIGN CONTRACTOR   COPY MACHINE/OFFICE EQUIP CONTRACTOR

      _____   _____

      _____   _____

      _____   _____

-4-

SOUND/LIGHTING CONTRACTOR   OTHER CONTRACTORS

_____   _____

_____   _____

_____   _____

23.   CONVENTION BUREAU PERSONNEL USED: _____ YES   _____NO

24.   ROOM SERVICE/RESTAURANTS/BARS: L=Light, M=Moderate, H=Heavy

	BREAKFAST	LUNCH	DINNER	COCKTAILS
Room Service	_L _M _H	_L _M _H	_L _M _H	_L _M _H
Restaurants	_L _M _H	_L _M _H	_L _M _H	_L _M _H
Bars	_L _M _H	_L _M _H	_L _M _H	_L _M _H

25.   TELEPHONE INSTRUCTIONS:

       Will there be a need for outgoing calls?   _____YES   _____NO

       If yes: _____LOCAL   _____LONG DISTANCE   _____BOTH

       The special code word for all outgoing calls will be: _____

26.   CHECKROOM FACILITIES:

       The hotel does have a Main Checkroom located in the lobby. Will you require a second checkroom?   _____YES   _____NO

       (If yes, our checkroom manager will contact you directly for charges incurred.)

27.   PACKAGE ROOM:

       Will you be shipping boxes to the hotel Package Room?   _____YES   _____NO

       If yes, approximately how many?   _____Basic Size   _____Basic Weight

28. PROGRAM AND SET-UP INSTRUCTIONS:

       On the following page, please find an example of the format followed for the Convention Service resume. We suggest this format for simpler communications and easy understanding. For more detailed set-ups, we suggest attaching a diagram.

       This information will be included in the hotel's convention resume, which is distributed to all departments in the hotel.

Learning Objectives:

This portion of your text introduces you to the various types of function rooms and setups used for meetings and food functions. We will also discuss how to manage function room space to best serve the group while maintaining maximum profitability for the hotel. When you have studied this chapter, you will:

- Know the factors that are considered before assigning function space to meeting planners.

- Be able to describe various meeting room setups and tell when each is commonly used.

- Be able to detail how to monitor function room usage and make the most of function space.

Outline

Function Rooms
- Types of Function Rooms
- Function Room Size and Layout
- Meeting Room Plans
- Timetable for Setup and Breakdown

Managing Function Rooms
- Sales Restrictions on Function Space
- Function Room Charges
- Release Dates
- Several Meetings Simultaneously
- Use of Meeting Rooms by Others
- Employee Procedure Manuals

Meeting Setups
- Function Room Furniture
- Basic Meeting Setups
- Setups with Tables

Meeting Rooms of the Future

Monitoring Function Room Usage

How to Assign Meeting Rooms and Determine Meeting Room Setups

David Scherbarth, CMP
Director of Banquets and Convention Service
Sheraton Bal Harbour Beach Resort

"The convention service department is an extension of the sales department and must work closely with the sales manager to maximize function space while providing the group with a comfortable environment to achieve the goals of the meeting...Working closely with the meeting planner on the agenda will allow you to select proper function space so that the space is not too large or small for their meeting...The type of setup and the number expected to attend has a direct impact on how much space you need...You must know the various setups and what the capacity seating of each setup is for every function room in your facility...Other items that need to be considered when assigning function space are: noise conflicts with other meetings or banquets; traffic patterns of associated public space; lighting needs; ceiling heights; decor; electrical needs; competitive groups."

13 Function Rooms and Meeting Setups

Any hotel can supply guestrooms. A convention hotel is one that has a sufficient number of function rooms and the trained staff needed to handle the many different kinds of meetings and conventions.

Function Rooms

When the hotel sales representative originally solicited the convention, he or she presented the client with information about the hotel's meeting rooms. Most larger convention hotels have a number of suitable meeting rooms and often more than are needed for an event. In the case of a smaller meeting, the hotel needs to obtain the release of unneeded meeting rooms as early as possible to enable its staff to sell another event.

Often a convention planner will request that all the convention facilities be held for his or her event, at least until the program is roughed out and it is obvious what facilities are needed. This is rarely possible. Unless the convention is large and virtually sells out the house, the hotel management cannot lock up a precious commodity like meeting rooms for any longer than absolutely necessary.

It is urgent, therefore, for you to get together with the meeting planner to place a hold on the rooms thought to be needed and to urge that planning be done to determine realistically the needs of the event. There is no pressure if you have no other meetings scheduled for those dates, but most sizable hotels handle a number of smaller meetings simultaneously.

Types of Function Rooms

Before assigning rooms, the convention service manager must be aware of what the hotel has to offer. A common mistake is to assume you have only those rooms specifically designed as function rooms. Actually, all public space may be function area depending on the group and its needs.

Some of the most common **function rooms** depicted in the hotel's convention brochure are exhibit halls, ballrooms for banquets, and conference rooms for meetings.

Unless meeting planners are advised otherwise, these are the rooms with which they will work as they lay out their schedules. Foyers and hallways outside the meeting rooms, however, can be used as **pre-function space**. These areas are often ideal for morning and afternoon refreshment breaks and as cocktail areas prior to evening banquets. Other possiblilities include use of the foyer, the parking lot and swimming pool areas for cocktail parties; upper-floor suites equipped with conference tables for small, intimate meetings; and the garden area behind the hotel for an evening party. The possibilities are limited only by the imagination of the convention service manager. The unusual is often what makes a hotel unique, so it is important to keep in mind that all public areas may be used as function space.

A fairly recent trend is the **breakout room**, used when a session divides into small groups for discussion and feedback. The trend toward breakout configurations as a method

One Seal You *KNOW*
You Can Count On

Another Seal You
Will Grow to
Count On

CERTIFIED MEETING SPACE.

Responding to the need to provide meeting planners with the actual dimensions of meeting rooms and their capacities under a wide variety of setups, the Professional Convention Management Association (PCMA) began a program to certify the dimensions of meeting rooms at hospitality properties. Properties that take advantage of this program are given detailed computer printouts of their meeting space and permission to use the PCMA certification seal on promotional literature.

The Hilton chain is among a growing number of properties that offer certified meeting space specifications to meeting planners. In addition to bearing the PCMA certification seal, this ad promotes the Hilton's adherence to Convention Industry Council guidelines to assure meeting planners that they will get the meeting space promised in the chain's promotional materials.

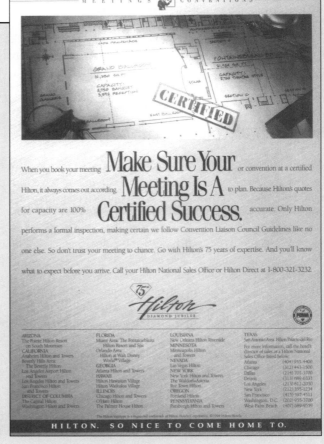

of training has become increasingly popular, so many hotels are making suites available near the main conference room. Others have provided rooms that can be subdivided with movable **air walls** to accommodate these setups.

Function Room Size and Layout

Many factors come into play when discussing meeting room size. First and foremost, of course, is the number expected to attend. Then you must consider the room setup desired and the number and type of audiovisual equipment needed. Additional space may be required for clothes racks, props, or tables to distribute literature. And you must allow more space if refreshment breaks are scheduled.

The basic layout indicates the style of seating. It is wasteful of labor to set each room to utmost capacity, but you obviously must provide enough seating. This is the time to examine the kind of sessions that will go on just before and just after this specific program to make sure the setup is the same or enough time is allotted to make the change. Hotels are frequently able to put similar meetings back to back and thus keep manpower and equipment change-over time to a minimum.

The meeting planner will also have to confer with you about the style and size of the head table. Pads, pencils, folders and printed material may all be placed on chairs and tables. And water glasses and pitchers may be put at a number of tables or stations if tables are not used. Each session has its own requirements; some, for example, call for name signs. Attention to details is the key to service.

Meeting Room Plans

It is important to include meeting room plans on resources used by meeting planners, including the hotel's convention brochure, websites, and directory advertising. For years, convention brochures gave general — often approximate — dimensions of meeting rooms, and meeting planners were often dismayed to find that there was not enough room to stage their functions. To eliminate this problem, the Professional Convention Management Association (PCMA) developed a program to help both properties and meeting planners by actually measuring the dimensions and capacities of meeting rooms. After the rooms are measured with sophisticated laser powered equipment, computer software is used to accurately map out the room and determine room setup capacities. The detailed computer printouts generated are given to the property to be used in presentations. Properties that have had their space certified are provided with gummed seals that can be affixed to current promotional materials, and are given permission to use the PCMA seal in advertising to assure planners that they are getting the space promised (see box titled "Certified Meeting Space").

In addition to the dimensions of rooms, meeting planners need to know the capacity of each under a variety of setups (see Figure 13.1). While planners are made aware of the kinds of rooms available to them during a sales presentation, the convention service manager should be available to help planners decide which function would work best in each room. We will discuss the setups commonly used and how capacity is affected by various setups later in this chapter.

Convention service managers should also be aware of the impact of the Americans with Disabilities Act (ADA) in regard to their property's function space. While there are still a number of "gray areas" in terms of responsibilities of the property, certain physical re-

Figure 13.1. MEETING ROOM CAPACITIES AND DIMENSIONS.

CAPACITIES AND DIMENSIONS*

ROOM	THEATRE	SCHOOL ROOM	BANQUET	RECEPTION	U-SHAPE	HOLLOW SQUARE	EXHIBITS 8x10	EXHIBITS 10x10	SQUARE FEET	DIMENSIONS	CEILING HEIGHT
GRAND SALON	–	–	640	1,373	–	–	28	28	9,612	178'x54'	12'
GRAND BALLROOM	4,556	1,008	3,340	4,556	–	–	307	254	50,112	270'x150'	22'-16'
ADELPHI ROOM	1,896	1,008	1,020	1,929	–	–	85	74	13,500	150'x90'	22'-16'
BROADWAY ROOM	1,120	735	650	1,286	–	–	52	52	9,000	150'x60'	22'-16'
CAPITOL ROOM	1,120	735	660	1,286	–	–	52	52	9,000	150'x60'	22'-16'
RIALTO ROOM	1,120	735	600	1,286	–	–	52	52	9,000	150'x60'	22'-16'
RIALTO 1	150	84	120	264	52	65	–	–	1,850	45'x37'	22'-16'
RIALTO 2	150	84	120	264	52	65	–	–	1,850	45'x37'	22'-16'
RIALTO 3	150	84	120	264	52	65	–	–	1,850	45'x37'	22'-16'
RIALTO 4	150	84	120	264	52	65	–	–	1,850	45'x37'	22'-16'
REGISTRATION OFFICE	–	–	–	–	–	–	–	–	350	14'x25'	10'
GOLDWYN BALLROOM	5,000	3,400	3,400	5,200	–	–	291	237	44,600	180'x240'	10'-23'6" *
GOLDWYN OFFICE	–	–	–	–	–	–	–	–	1,221	37'x33'	10'
GOLDWYN FOYER	–	–	–	–	–	–	–	–	1,232	22'x56'	12'
PALACE ROOM**	–	–	340	462	–	–	24	24	5,082	–	10'
PALACE 1	65	40	40	113	22	34	–	–	792	22'x36'	10'
PALACE 2	96	63	50	113	32	40	–	–	792	22'x36'	10'
PALACE 3	280	154	170	280	70	85	–	–	2,112	32'x66'	10'
PALACE 4	76	54	50	99	32	40	–	–	693	21'x33'	10'
PALACE 5	76	54	50	99	32	40	–	–	693	21'x33'	10'
PALACE 6	84	45	50	102	32	40	–	–	713	23'x31'	10'
PALACE 7	84	45	50	102	32	40	–	–	713	23'x31'	10'
DIRECTOR'S ROOM	Permanent Conference Table Seats 22								1,189	41'x29'	12'-10'
GROUP INFORMATION BOOTH	–	–	–	–	–	–	–	–	196	14'x14'	9'
ASSN. OFFICE 1, 2, 3, 4	–	–	–	–	–	–	–	–	108	9'x12'	9'
CELEBRITY ROOM	Permanent Seating for 1,499								2,640 Stage Dimensions Only	60'x44'	26'
ZIEGFELD ROOM	Permanent Seating for 1,096								5,016 Stage Dimensions Only	88'x57'	30'
METRO PROMENADE	–	–	–	305	–	–	–	–	4,572	254'x18'	12'
METRO 1	175	175	200	175	56	72	–	–	2,623	43'x61'	10'
METRO 2	215	215	200	215	56	72	–	–	2,928	48'x61'	15'-12'
METRO 3	270	270	250	270	60	80	–	–	3,660	60'x61'	15'-12'
METRO 4	155	155	150	155	52	64	–	–	2,074	34'x61'	12'
METRO OFFICE	–	–	–	–	–	–	–	–	384	16'x24'	10'
METRO FOYER	–	–	–	–	–	–	–	–	2,444	94'x26'	10'
METRO 5	480	250	380	615	–	–	–	–	5,600	80'x70'	12'-10'
METRO 6	615	380	420	615	–	–	–	–	6,240	80'x78'	12'-10'
GARLAND BALLROOM	1,446	1,150	980	1,446	–	–	97	79	15,903	210'x70'	12'-15'-17'
GABLE BALLROOM	918	780	672	918	–	–	–	–	10,100	210'x48'	12'-15'-17'
GABLE 1	206	100	100	206	49	58	–	–	1,440	48'x30'	12'-15'-17'
GABLE 2	206	100	100	206	49	58	–	–	1,440	48'x30'	12'-15'-17'
GABLE 3	206	100	100	206	49	58	–	–	1,440	48'x30'	12'-15'-17'
GABLE 4	206	100	100	206	49	58	–	–	1,440	48'x30'	12'-15'-17'
GABLE 5	206	100	100	206	49	58	–	–	1,440	48'x30'	12'-15'-17'
GABLE 6	206	100	100	206	49	58	–	–	1,440	48'x30'	12'-15'-17'
GABLE 7	206	100	100	206	49	58	–	–	1,440	48'x30'	12'-15'-17'

*Capacity figures are subject to change depending on space allocations for head table, dance floor, staging, and catering requirements.
**Palace Room totals do not include Palace 6 and Palace 7.

Source: Courtesy of Bally's Casino Resort, Las Vegas, NV.

quirements must be met by properties offering convention space. These include (but are not limited to) adequate handicapped parking, easy accessibility (ramps, wide doorways, etc.), adapted restroom facilities, and assistive devices for the hearing and visually impaired.

Sometimes, the meeting planner will have additional requirements to meet the needs of attendees at a function. Perhaps wider space will be needed to accommodate wheel chairs or a signer will be needed for the hearing impaired. In some cases, it is not difficult for a property to make the necessary adjustments; in others, it will be up to the property and the meeting planner to determine who is responsible for providing the additional services needed.

Scaled Drawings. If a hotel does not present its meeting rooms in complete detail, it will be necessary to prepare other material. Most properties prepare scaled drawings of each room (see Figure 13.2). These should indicate doors, windows, pillars, elevators, electrical outlets and any obstructions that might affect the setup of the meeting. Meeting planners will probably ask for scaled drawings of each room, so you should have accurately scaled drawings of each function room for your own use and for distribution to customers.

These drawings should be accurate enough to be used to designate meeting or exhibit layouts. If you indicate capacity on the drawings, keep in mind that different setups accommodate widely differing numbers of people. Some properties have simplified room arrangement planning by the use of a magnetic planning board. The setup for a particular room is worked out in advance by using scaled metallic pieces to represent various sizes of furniture. The meeting planner using such a technique is able to get a better feel for the setup suggested by the convention service manager.

In addition, meeting planners also like to visualize the flow of their attendees. Figure 13.3 shows an overall schematic of a facility. While this plan does not provide the detail inherent to scale drawings of the meeting rooms itself, it may prove helpful to the planner in planning his or her program.

Using Computer Technology to Assist Meeting Planners. Many properties are taking advantage of today's computer technology to assist meeting planners in determining the optimum room setups. Using computer programs is far quicker than manually drawing floorplans (often to find that the space does not accommodate the function), and offers the advantages of flexibility (features of a room — pillars, curved spaces, etc. can be considered when determining the best layouts — and a number of room setups can be compared) and storage (selected room setups can be stored and referred to for use in future functions).

The advantages of computerized scale drawings are many. They can show a number of options that the meeting planner (and the convention services staff) may not have previously considered, they enable meeting planners to see at a glance how various setups will work in terms of traffic flow as well as capacity, and they can be stored to enable them to be used for future functions. Many properties, such as the Marriott (which utilizes its own software to offer computerized room drawings to meeting planners as part of its Network Plan) are finding this technology to be an invaluable tool for the varied needs of meeting planners. This technology is expected to be increasingly used by both properties and meeting planners themselves and should be considered as part of your property's program to assist meeting planners with staging a successful function.

We have already mentioned the PCMA computer printouts that provide room capacities for varied setups, but still other software is available, such as MeetingMatrix and Room Viewer, which also "draw" room setups (see box titled "Using Computer Technology to Assist Meeting Planners"). The MeetingMatrix is one software program used to enable meeting planners to see which setups will work best for their functions. After entering such basic information as room dimensions, number of attendees and special requirements (size

Figure 13.2. DETAILED MEETING ROOM PLANS.

Figure 13.3. AN OVERALL FACILITY SCHEMATIC AS A SALES TOOL.

Using a plan as illustrated here, a salesperson can help the meeting planner visualize the attendees'
flow from guestrooms to function rooms.
Source: Courtesy of SunBurst Resort Hotel and Conference Center.

or shape of tables, space needed for exhibits, etc.), the program "draws" one or more possible room configurations, enabling the meeting planner to see which one will be best — and providing the convention services department with a list of function room furniture and equipment needed for the setup chosen.

Monica Cheeks, director of convention services at the Hyatt Newporter in Newport Beach, California, is enthusiastic about the new technology:

> "We use it every day. Previously, we were sketching out meeting setups by hand, which is obviously neither precise nor very fast. Now with Room Viewer, I can plot out a planner's request very quickly and accurately, print it out and give copies back to the planner, as well as to our catering manager. Our sales team uses it in proposals, and it's helped to

Using Computer Technology to Assist Meeting Planners

MeetingMatrix is one software program used to enable meeting planners to see which setups will work best for their functions. After entering such basic information as room dimensions, number of attendees and special requirements (size or shape of tables, space needed for exhibits, etc.), the program "draws" one or more possible room configurations, enabling the meeting planner to see which one will be best — and providing the convention services department with a list of function room furniture and equipment needed for the setup chosen.

Sample Banquet Setup

FUNCTION SPECIFICATION: Meeting name: Sample meeting   Facility name: Sample facility

Function name:	Banquet	Setup items used:	QTY	ITEM	
Room name:	Ballroom		209	18" x 18"	Chairs
Number of people:	209		8	6' x 30"	Rectangular tables
Setup:	Banquet —		3	8' x 30"	Rectangular tables
	10 per 5 foot diameter table		20	5' dia	Round tables
Distance between rows:	75 inches		2	5' dia	Quarter-round tables
Center aisle width:	5.0 feet		9	6' x 30"	Crescent tables
Side aisle width:	5.0 feet		25	3' x 3'	Dance floor squares
Cross aisle width:	5.0 feet				

MEETINGMATRIX is a trademark of SCLM, Inc. Used with permission.

FACTORS TO BE CONSIDERED WHEN ASSIGNING FUNCTION SPACE

David Scherbath, CMP, Director of Banquets and Convention Service at the Sheraton Bal Harbour Beach Resort, says that details are important when deciding how to effectively manage function rooms and meeting setups. Factors that should be considered include:

- Day(s) of meeting. If more than one day, try to keep the meeting in the same room. This minimizes labor and gives the group consistency.
- Beginning and ending times. Accurate times allow the room to be utilized more than once a day — sometimes for as many as three or four times for different functions.
- Setup style and attendance. The type of setup and number expected to attend has a direct impact on how much space is needed.
- Audiovisual & staging requirements. These two items can dramatically alter the size of space needed. A 24-hour hold may be necessary for extensive audiovisual and/or staging requirements.

Working closely with the meeting planner on the agenda will allow you to select proper function space so that the space is not too large or small for their meeting. This is important because the comfort of a meeting room can have an affect on the environment and on the focus of the meeting. This also allows the sales team every opportunity to maximize function space and guestrooms with additional bookings. Releasing space unneeded by one group may allow your sales team to book another group in the hotel, increasing your occupancy and revenues.

---

close deals. It even has six different aisle sizes, so it can conform to our complicated fire codes."[1]

MeetingMatrix is available from SCLM Software Inc., 6 South Main, Stewartstown, Pennsilvania 17363. Room Viewer information and a free demonstration disk can be obtained from TimeSaver Software, 10884 Kimball, Tustin, California 92680.

Timetable for Setup and Breakdown

Most hotel brochures do an adequate job of presenting the basic contours of each meeting room, and many are designed to show how a room is used in a variety of ways. Few, however, tell the convention organizer how much time is required for room setup and breakdown. But there is a great need to communicate that information.

It is very important to know exactly how long it takes a crew to set up each room under the many seating arrangements. Many a meeting program has failed because those planning it did not take into account the time it takes to set up and break down and the program was designed much too tightly to permit good service. The planner would have developed the program more realistically if he or she had some idea of the time needed to perform these services.

Too often, the hotel bears the stigma of failing to perform well, give good service, or show much expertise, so the hotel staff should make the meeting planner aware of such a timetable so that he or she can take it into consideration when the program is mapped out. Most meeting planners would gladly loosen up their timetables if they knew what was involved to assure that their shows ran smoothly and on time.

We strongly recommend that convention service managers have charts made up indicating such requirements. These charts should list the time it takes to set up each room for maximum capacity under each seating arrangement. They should give the time it takes to break them down, plus union regulations regarding workday, hours, overtime charges and any unusual characteristics that may affect costs and time. Specify the number of people needed. Time may be saved by using a larger crew but this will cost more; at times a meeting planner might choose such an option.

Managing Function Rooms

Your hotel function space is a precious asset, and your goal as a convention service manager is to maximize its utilization (see box titled "Factors to be Considered When Assigning Function Space"). Empty rooms, whether guestrooms or function rooms, are a perishable product.

The convention service manager is the person most qualified to assign rooms for specific events. This should be done in communication with the meeting planner. The service manager knows the hotel's facilities; the planner knows the event's characteristics.

In assigning a room, its size, its capacity under a specific layout, the type of event, and the presentation style should be considered. The room size should "match" the expected attendance. Too much space or too many empty seats can create the wrong psychological setting. These fundamental requirements probably were hashed out during the sales presentations, but other factors must be considered, too.

Consider the room's location within the hotel in regard to traffic in corridors, elevators, escalators, parking arrangements and coat check rooms. All program segments must be definitely allocated to specific locations about sixty days before the event, at the latest. This is especially important if a group wishes to reserve their space on a 24-hour basis. According to Maria Dempsey, director of sales and marketing North America for Pan Pacific Hotels and Resorts, this can pose a problem for the hotel:

> "The request for access to public meeting space on a 24-hour basis means no other groups may use those rooms, even if the room is not occupied overnight."[2]

A number of groups, however, wish to reserve their rooms for the duration of their meeting, especially if functions involve exhibits or extensive staging or if there is the possibility that a meeting will not end on schedule. David Kilman, CMP, President of MPI, offers this perspective:

> "There is a tug-of-war between planners and suppliers regarding 24-hour space holds. It all comes down to the total value of the meeting. If a planner expects, or demands, the luxury of a round-the-clock hold on space, there must be an appropriate financial return to the supplier...Once the economic impact of a meeting is resolved, it should be easy to determine if a 24-hour hold is a reasonable request."[3]

When considering a 24-hour hold, therefore, it is vital to analyze the economic impact of the meeting, including the value of the meeting itself and subsequent business from the group, and the time of year. If, for example, the group wishes to book during the Christmas holidays, when you can expect to generate a large volume of lucrative catering business, it may not be a sound business decision to reserve function rooms on a 24-hour basis (see Sales Restrictions section in this chapter). If you decide to reserve the rooms around the clock, a clause should be included in the group's contract guaranteeing the 24-hour hold and any restrictions put upon it by the hotel.

You should get a list from the client of all the people on his or her staff who are authorized to move an event to a different location, should the need arise. Just before the event, and especially during it, it is absolutely essential to know the channels of authority within the convention staff. Time may be too short and the need for action too great to let you double-check any instructions. Cancellations of sessions, changes in timetables and the like may be made at the last minute.

Such a list should be in writing, of course. And the degree of authority should be specified. What can these staff members order? Changes in layout or location can be costly in terms of time and labor.

The list you get from the convention organizer should be similar to the list of your department heads that you give to the organizer. The key people of both the hotel and

Figure 13.4. *GUIDE TO FUNCTION SPACE CHARGES.*

SHERATON FUNCTION SPACE CHARGES

The Sheraton Waikiki charges for function space under the following circumstances:

1. All Exhibits.
2. All function rooms that are held on a 24-hour block.
3. All function space for groups that have meetings only and are holding no sleeping rooms at the Sheraton Waikiki Hotel.
4. All function space when unusual or costly setups are required.
5. All function space when the sleeping rooms decrease proportionately from the original commitment.

FUNCTION SPACE VS. SLEEPING ROOM CONSUMPTION (PROPORTINATE SLIDING SCALE)

Percent of Decrease From Original Block	Amount of Meeting Room Charges
Up to 40% decrease	No charge
41%-60% decrease	50% charge for meeting rooms as listed on "meeting room charge sheet."
61%-80% decrease	75% charge for meeting rooms as listed on "meeting room charge sheet."
81%-100% decrease	100% charge for meeting rooms as listed on "meeting room charge sheet."

In addition to the above "sliding scale,"...the hotel will also take into consideration your definite food and beverage events when determining your meeting room charges.

The Sheraton Waikiki provides meeting planners with the following space pricing policy. Note the charges increase if sleeping rooms slip from the original room block commitment. In determining meeting room charges, many hotels consider "slippage" — when guestroom pickup decreases significantly, the charge for the group's function space increases. Meeting room rental at this 1,900-room property totals over $250,000 annually.

convention group staffs should attend the preconvention meetings. Let them get acquainted before the pressure begins. Discuss possible changes. This is the time to indicate what the hotel staff will need in the way of time and labor to bring about such program alterations.

Because association conventions must cope with optional attendance at both the convention and individual programs, it is often necessary to move workshops and meetings from one room to another to accommodate smaller or larger groups. Airing such possibilities in advance allows your staff and the client's staff to understand such conditions and to react more quickly and constructively in crisis situations.

Sales Restrictions on Function Space

Both the hotel sales staff and the catering department are involved in selling function space. The sales department is responsible for selling space that is used by convention groups requiring sleeping rooms. The catering department is responsible for selling function space to local groups. Since hotels are primarily interested in filling sleeping accommodations because of the high profit margin, the hotel sales department should have preference in booking the available function space.

Therefore, most hotels have local catering sales restrictions. For example, during its peak convention season, a hotel may limit local catering to a short booking cycle. That is, the catering department may only sell function space to local groups after the hotel is assured that the needs of groups needing sleeping rooms have been met. Once the hotel sales staff sells their group room allotment on a given day, any function space still available may be sold by catering.

The further out this commitment is made by convention groups, the greater the opportunity for catering to sell the unused space. This period of time is frequently referred to as the *open sale period*. Holidays are often designated as open sales periods as group guestroom business is traditionally slow around Christmas, Thanksgiving, and the Fourth of July. Any hotel business booked by catering during those times is not likely to displace conventions needing meeting space.

Function Room Charges

How do you determine what to charge for meeting space? Brochures list rates for guest rooms but rarely for meeting rooms. The latter situation is most flexible; it depends on the meeting group, the time, and the space required. If a group uses enough guestrooms, there is often no charge for meeting rooms. In the case of food functions, the cost per person often covers the use of the room.

Properties with unique function space may be able to charge more for their room rental. Function space characteristics that might command a premium include:

- large ballrooms that are free of pillars or other obstructions.
- high ceilings with retractable chandeliers.
- tiered theater-style auditoriums.
- advanced audiovisual equipped rooms.
- meeting rooms that are convenient to guestrooms.

It is important that the meeting planner understands your property's policy regarding function room charges. Many hotels include a clause similar to the one below to eliminate potential misunderstandings:

"Meeting and function space is assigned based on the type of setup and the number of people in attendance. Should advance setup and late teardown or an abnormal amount of meeting space be required, a charge may be incurred. Specified meeting rooms cannot be guaranteed and are subject to change. If the final attendance figures are less than the original estimate, an adjustment to the meeting and function space will become necessary. Any changes requested in your agenda after receipt of this contract are based upon space availability at the time of your request. Any cancellation of food and beverage functions after acceptance of this agreement will result in the organization being charged the full dollar value of that function based on either the actual menu price or an average menu price. Should the hotel be able to resell a function of similar value in the originally scheduled room, there will be no charge assessed."

There may well be circumstances in which the hotel management prefers to charge for a function room. You should consider having a listed price for each room; after all, it looks great when you waive the fee. When you do charge for a function room, a list of charges should be available. Function room rental rates should be determined for each meeting room by time of day. Some properties will list specific rates for morning, afternoon, evening, full-day, and 24-hour weekday hold, and weekend rates.

You might outline a sliding scale arrangement, tying the meeting room fees to the number of guest rooms used for the convention (see Figure 13.4). For example, if the group picks up 200 room nights or more, the $1000 fee for the ballroom could be waived; if 100-199 room nights are used, the cost would be $500; and, if the group uses fewer than 100 room nights, the cost would be $750.

There is a trend today to charge for space. A hotel that handles a number of small meetings would be wise to consider a fee, particularly if the group plans to meet in one room, hold a food function in another, and conduct breakout meetings in another three to five rooms.

In such situations room charges should be stipulated if the guestroom commitment is not enough to cover the labor costs of setting up, servicing, cleaning and tearing down. After all, a hotel is in business to make a profit.

You might also want to charge for meeting rooms when companies participating in a trade show take the opportunity to hold dealer or sales meetings. The people attending may already be registered for the trade show, and the requirements of the trade show would place great strain on the allocation of meeting rooms. Of course, if the food functions of such additional meetings mount up, it may justify not charging for the use of the room. But a room charge may be justified if the food function is only a refreshment break. In final analysis, there is no hard and fast rule on charging for meeting space. A hotel needs to look at the food, at the room, at all the profit areas to determine its rate structure.

Increasingly, hotels are applying traditional guestroom yield management methods to meeting and function rooms. Yield management sets prices based on the forecasted demand for function space. Rental rates are increased or decreased from the established rates depending on the time and date of the meeting and on the total revenue the event brings to the property. Several Hiltons, for example, have begun to determine intricate yield management formulas for pricing their function space. Steve Armitage, senior vice president of sales at Hilton Hotels Corporation states:

"The meeting buyer can expect to see meeting room yield management become more widespread as technology advances." [4]

Release Dates

When a convention buys out the house, a request to hold all rooms seems reasonable. *All space blocks* requests are typical from large groups who are booking two to three years out. But a request to "hold all function space" is difficult for a hotel, especially in periods of high demand. Groups requesting an all space block on your function space should be closely monitored, and all space blocks should be negotiated with reasonable release date increments, such as one year, nine months or six months, to allow your property to sell the space with some lead time should the large group not materialize as anticipated.

Release dates should be set in every letter of agreement. At some early date when a rough program is available, the room assignments can be tentatively made. At this point, *some* function rooms can be released if there seems to be more than enough. The convention in the house should have a priority for meeting rooms, but you may get other calls. Here again, it is obvious why there is a need to have just one function book, under one person's control.

At a somewhat later date, when a detailed program is worked out, try to get unneeded rooms released. Planners often to try to hold onto every room indefinitely, to have a reserve for some occasion that may come up. But the practice can inhibit your other sales efforts.

Many properties specify their release date policies in meeting contracts. The following clause spells out one property's policy:

"In order to ensure that adequate space is available for your meeting, please provide the Convention Service Department with a tentative function schedule six months prior to your meeting/convention, or as soon as possible. A final program is required no later than 90 days prior to the start of your convention. Space not assigned at 90 days will be released to the hotel for scheduling of other functions, as required."

Several Meetings Simultaneously

Most meetings are small. More than 75 percent of all corporate meetings have fewer than 100 in attendance. To do much business in meetings, you must be able to house more than one simultaneously. Naturally, this is not the case when you virtually sell out the house, but most often the function book fills up with a number of more modest events.

Handling several smaller meetings calls for careful planning. You cannot negotiate with all groups at the same time, so you must take care not to commit all your public space to one group, leaving you with no facilities for the other. Traffic patterns must be carefully planned to avoid confusion and congestion. Give thought, too, to the proximity of different kinds of groups. Don't forget to find out what will be going on in the room next door. Holding a training session next door to a college reunion is asking for trouble; a rock band next door to a speech could be disastrous. And even a seemingly ordinary meeting can become quite noisy merely by adding a sound film.

You may find it extremely profitable to go after smaller meetings. To begin with, there are more of them. And smaller meeting organizers are generally not as demanding of price and concessions, often can offer much repeat business, and tax your staff less in serving them. It is tempting to hit that home run by bagging a full house convention. But a steady stream of good base hits in the form of modest size meetings often wins the ball game by providing what every hotel wants — profitable business.

Use of Meeting Rooms by Others

Some organizations ask, or demand, that all requests by other groups for meeting facilities in the hotel at the time of their event be cleared with them. They are trying to control the entire environment of their event and they don't want rival organizations meeting at the same time under the same roof. Apprehensions of industrial security cannot be dismissed lightly.

The hotel must be careful about this. Imagine an IBM research seminar in the house at the same time as Control Data or Honeywell meetings! When a competitive organization appears on the scene, the usually easygoing meeting planner gets quite uptight. And you may find yourself needing strict security systems for a relatively easy, small seminar.

And should you be concerned about only the exact date of the meeting, or must you worry, too, about the days immediately before and after the event?

Small properties that can handle only one average-sized group at a time can use such situations to sell themselves. In the off season the small resort can claim that walk-in business from competitive personnel is highly unlikely. The meeting organizer is assured of receiving all your facility and attention and need not worry about traffic pattern and unwanted guests.

The convention organizer may want to veto a meeting held in the hotel during his or her dates. Many companies hold dealer meetings at trade shows. Most association executives have no objections, and many feel that it adds importance to their event. But many worry that the timing of such meetings may pull delegates away from the main sessions or events.

It is safe to say that you can expect meeting planners to be interested in who and what is scheduled in the hotel during *their* time.

Employee Procedure Manuals

Convention service managers, as we have said, are the in-house coordinators of the convention. They work with virtually every department in the hotel. Their authority in dealing with these departments is to a great extent determined by their character and the respect they have earned from those with whom they work. In many hotels, convention service managers do not have direct line authority over rooms or food and beverage departments. This often necessitates that they use tact and discretion in getting the job done.

However, they do have line authority within their own department and must function as managers there. Serving under them are three to ten housepersons who set up the function rooms. Each of these people should be trained in the various types of meeting setups. Our experience shows this is best accomplished with the use of an **employee procedure manual**.

A procedure manual is not a job description. A procedure manual tells the employee how to do the job, whereas the job description is prepared primarily for management and states the job's responsibility and authority. Ideally, the procedure manual should include illustrations or drawings. For example, setup illustrations similar to those used in this chapter should be included. The manual also should include a step-by-step outline of the houseperson's job.

The procedure manual will have the same importance for employees in the convention service department as the master recipe card does for a cook. Successful restaurants are largely successful because of consistency; the same should be true for convention servicing. A procedure manual will help ensure that setups will not be done in a slightly different way each day.

It is often difficult for employees to recall each procedure in a setup and all the required supplies. The manual eliminates the exclusion of certain setups, as well as serving as a valuable training tool for new employees. Manuals might also include rules and regulations that apply to the setup houseperson.

Efforts should be made to personalize the manual. It should be published in a small booklet form that can easily fit into a shirt pocket for quick reference.

No such manual is permanent. On the contrary, new tables, chairs and operating techniques will necessitate updating. Hopefully, the employees themselves may suggest ways to perform certain aspects of the job better.

Meeting Setups

The physical arrangement of chairs and tables plays an important role in meetings. Convention planners know that the atmosphere of a meeting can be enhanced or destroyed by the size of the room and the manner in which it is arranged. Thus it is essential that you have an orderly presentation for each of your facility's meeting rooms, giving its dimensions and its capacities under a variety of layout designs.

Function Room Furniture

Hotel function rooms get heavy use. Often a number of functions are scheduled on one day for a single room, with only an hour or two between events. These events are usually quite different, and housepersons must work quickly to set up a variety of functions — business meetings, lectures, training sessions, fashion shows, banquets and others. The only flexibility the room can provide is through the use of air walls or folding division doors. The major change must be provided by the equipment and setup.

Function room furniture is the term coined for equipment used in meeting and banquet rooms. Jacob Felsenstein of King Arthur Incorporated, a leading supplier of such furniture to the hotel industry, has suggested four general features to look for in function room furniture.

Strength and durability. Watch for the weakest link such as mechanical folding devices which are easily broken, or strong components which may depend on a weak hinge or spring. Safety of guests is a foremost consideration. There are simple and effective folding devices that minimize the possibility of failure. Keep in mind, frequency of use means frequency of cleaning. Parts in contact with the floor must be made to withstand and facilitate frequent scrubbing, waxings and vacuuming.

Ease of handling. All folding or knock-down equipment should be simple to set up. Equipment which is light in weight may not be the most durable. There are a variety of carriers such as dollies and trucks which are designed to aid in handling.

Ease of storage. Equipment should be able to be stacked so that one piece does not mar the next, and in a manner which prevents vulnerable parts from protruding. In choosing dollies or trucks, check to see that they are designed to handle the particular piece of equipment in your particular setting.

Flexibility. It may be advisable to buy function room furniture which serves two or more purposes in order to avoid extra handling or storage. For example, a Knockdown Cabaret Table allows for the different-sized tops to be used interchangeably with one column and base, enabling it to fill many different needs; one Dual Height Folding Platform serves two different levels, many different purposes, can save up to 50 percent on initial outlay and an additional 50 percent on handling costs and storage space.[5]

Chairs and Tables. Meeting room chairs and tables vary a great deal, but there are certain types and sizes that are used most frequently. We will use these basic types when we present layouts and schematics for setups. Your capacity figures should be based on such equipment, and will vary when you use other than the standard. Most variations are used in small meeting setups, such as board room facsimiles; we have relaxed during many such meetings in posh swivel chairs. Conference centers frequently boast ergonomic chairs, which are bigger than a regular chair, upholstered in leather, come with a cushion seat and swivel and are said to be comfortable for 18 hours at a stretch.

Most chairs used for meetings are 18 inches wide by 18 inches deep by 17 inches high. Stacking armchairs (not the deluxe type mentioned in the previous paragraph) are slightly larger, such as 20 by 20 by 17. Most folding chairs are smaller and not as comfortable, and are generally used for last-minute overflow accommodations. Planners want their attendees comfortable so they can concentrate on the program.

Rigid chairs are recommended for food functions. They are more comfortable than folding chairs, which are smaller and lower.

The standard height for tables is 30 inches; the standard depth, either 30 or 18 inches. When people are to be seated opposite each other, the 30-inch table is required. When people sit on only one side of the table, as we shall discuss in *schoolroom* setups, the 18-inch depth is sufficient and saves much space. There is a growing use of 15-inch tables to save even more space. The 30-inch-deep rectangular table, however, is used most frequently for head tables, even when people are seated on only one side. This deeper table is also used for display tables, exhibit stands and other purposes. It is most versatile and comes in lengths of four, six and eight feet so that a variety of total lengths may be achieved easily.

Round tables are used for many food functions and also for some kinds of meeting sessions. They most often are five, five and one-half, or six feet in diameter. Comfortable seating calls for a five-foot round table for six to eight people; a five and one-half foot table for eight to ten guests; and a six-foot table for ten to 12. A cocktail round of about three feet in diameter is used for receptions, and can accommodate up to four people comfortably.

An almost infinite number of variations can be created by using half-rounds and quarter-rounds. The more imaginative curved serpentine tables are commonly used for buffets. You are restricted only by your imagination in developing unique buffet arrangements.

Tablecloths, mitered on the corners, are used on tables because most banquet and meeting room tables are damaged and unsightly from continual breakdown and storage. Several companies have begun to market folding tables that are attractive and not easily damaged, and they can be used without tablecloths, saving on laundry and labor costs. Such tables, however, are expensive and fail to provide the warmth and color of tablecloths.

Head tables, as well as display and buffet tables, require special drapery. Traditionally, pins and tacks have been used to attach floor-length linens for such setups, but velcro is now being used by many hotels.

Snap-drape skirting is also available. Plastic clips are fitted along the top edge of platforms and tables, and grippers sewn into the upper pleat of the skirting are snapped into place quickly. Snap-drape skirting is made of permanent-crease polyester and fiberglass, making it easy to clean and wrinkle-free.

Platforms. Folding platforms are used in many ways; they elevate head tables for banquets and speakers. They come in different sizes, with different names: platform, riser, stage, **dais**, podium or rostrum. You must construct them to size. Check local safety regulations carefully. The usual heights are six, eight, 12 and 16 inches, plus a 32-inch high *riser*. Lengths may be four, six or eight feet, or any combination of these. Widths vary from four to six feet. If you maintain adequate stocks, a variety of combinations can be created. If the platforms are old and unsightly, put pleated skirting around the bottom and perhaps carpeting on top.

Lecterns. Lecterns are reading desks used to hold the speaker's papers and come in two basic types. The smaller *table lecterns* are placed on tables, while full-size *floor lecterns* are set on the floor. Both sizes should feature built-in light fixtures and enough connecting wire to reach wall outlets.

Many a room becomes difficult to set up because the wall outlets are on the same circuits as the overhead lights and are controlled by a common switch. Make sure the lectern's light unit is connected to a wall outlet that will not be cut off with the overhead lights. House lights are often dimmed for effect or for greater visibility of audiovisual presentations. Check each setup carefully; smart meeting planners will double-check such items themselves.

Permanent stages allow you to develop more sophisticated lecterns with full audiovisual controls. Such units don't lend themselves to the temporary setups of most meeting rooms, but they are received most enthusiastically by program members. Consider these units whenever a permanent installation is possible. A must item that is most versatile for temporary setups is a portable lectern with a built-in sound system that plugs into an ordinary outlet.

Basic Meeting Setups

A number of basic seating arrangements have evolved. Be sure that your customer is using the terminology correctly. Layout or schematic sheets will help in this area.

Auditorium or Theater Style. One of the most common seating arrangements, termed the **auditorium/theater style**, calls for chairs to be set up in rows facing the speaker, stage or head table. Good for lecture sessions with limited note taking (see Figure 13.5), it is used in both large and small meetings.

To set auditorium style, place two chairs first to position the aisle. Two inches, called the *space*, must be left between chairs side by side. The *distance* is the dimension from a chair to the one in front of it. Minimum distance is 36 inches from chair center to center.

When chairs have been positioned to indicate the aisles, the bulk of the chairs can be placed. One-square-foot carpet patterns is the most popular with hotel people because it helps to align setups. If there is no carpeting, the lines in hardwood floors might guide you.

Aisle sizes and numbers are regulated by local fire departments. If you have any doubts, get the specifications from the fire department. Most regulations call for aisles to be six feet wide if 400 or more people are involved; aisles of four or five feet are sufficient for smaller groups.. Double aisles are preferred if the meeting format calls for questions from the floor or anything that will result in back-and-forth movement of people or passing of objects such as microphones.

Figure 13.5. VARIATIONS OF THE AUDITORIUM STYLE SEATING ARRANGEMENT.

Straight

Senate

Semi-circular

V-shape

Many planners prefer the V-shape or semi-circular rather than the straight setup because attendees will have a more direct line of sight to the speaker. Aisles are generally four to six feet wide and when possible should align with exit doors. Aisles are required across the front and rear of the room as well as along the sides. When attendance is large, requiring several rows of chairs, cross aisles should be placed for every 15 rows.

Source: Reprinted with permission from Function Room Set-Up Manual by Gerhard M. Peter; published by the Hospitality Sales and Marketing Association International.

Figure 13.6. THE SCHOOLROOM STYLE ARRANGEMENT AND VARIATIONS.

Straight

Perpendicular

Crescent-round

V-shape

The V-shape schoolroom allows the best sight-lines between attendees and towards the speaker. If attendees are expected to use laptops, 30-inch wide tables are preferred rather than the standard 18-inch wide tables. The crescent-round setup is often used when a planner wishes to follow a meal function with a presentation and desires to keep participants in the same room. Once the meal is finished and tables are cleared, attendees are seated on on side of the round, facing the speaker.
Source: Reprinted with permission from Function Room Set-Up Manual.

The first row of chairs should be about six feet from the front edge of the head table or platform. The most popular auditorium style uses a center aisle but many experienced planners avoid a middle aisle because the presenter is facing an empty space. Many planners prefer to divide the seating area into three sections with two aisles of four feet. In larger halls, fire departments may require aisles across the front and back of the room and an additional horizontal aisle halfway down. It pays to check and to keep a record of local fire regulations.

Keep in mind the number of chairs in a row. It is extremely uncomfortable for an attendee to have to make his or her way across fifteen people to find a seat in the middle of the row. Many planners opt for a "mini row" of no more than seven seats.

There are variations, but they require more room. One is *auditorium style, semicircular, center aisle.* You need at least 12 feet from the head table or platform to the front row of chairs. Set the outside chair where you want it. Use a piece of string tied loosely between the two ends of the curved row. Line up the rest of the rows measured from the first one.

Auditorium, V-shape (sometimes referred to as *chevron*) sets up similarly; the side sections form an angle to the center aisle.

Space and distance vary from the norm when armchairs with writing arms are used. Because of the bigger dimensions of these chairs, use three-inch spacing and 35 inch distance from chair center to center. Tablet chairs are usually used in auditorium style, but they can be used in any of the other variations as well.

When on a dais, regardless of the floor arrangement, make sure that the head tables are draped down to the floor. Place water and glasses at the lectern and on the head table. Use one water carafe for every two people seated on the stage.

Setups with Tables

A great many meetings and most food functions require tables as well as chairs. In this section, we will take a look at some of the most commonly used setups and their variations.

Schoolroom Style. One of the most popular setups among both large and small groups is the **schoolroom/classroom style** (see Figure 13.6). In the most common arrangement, people sit on just one side of the table. In such cases, use the 18-inch-deep rectangular tables and, most of the time, allow for a center aisle. The recommended distance from table center to table center is 48 inches, but allow several inches more whenever possible. Allow about 24 inches of space for each person.

Schoolroom tables are either six or eight feet in length. Six-foot tables can seat two or three persons per table; eight foot tables seat three or four. For groups requiring space to spread out, the smaller number should be set for each table.

The 30-inch-deep tables are usually too wasteful to use in schoolroom setups because people are seated on only one side. But there are instances when you do have to use them, especially if a great deal of paperwork is to be done. In such cases, allow 60 inches from center of table to center of table. The length of each row depends on the room size and attendance.

The tables should be draped. Place pads and pencils at each setting, plus water pitchers for every 16 persons. You can put a glass at each setting or provide a tray with ten or 12 glasses for every 16 persons.

A variation is *schoolroom, perpendicular style.* In this arrangement, the rows of tables are perpendicular to the speaker's table. The 30-inch-deep tables are used because people will be seated on both sides. It is necessary to allow additional room for each person

Figure 13.7. THE U-SHAPE SEATING ARRANGEMENT.

Figure 13.8. THE HORSESHOE ARRANGEMENT.

Source: Reprinted with permission from Function Room Set-Up Manual.

because the seats must be turned somewhat to face the speaker. Allow 30 inches of table space per person instead of 24 for the wide table and 60 inches from center of table to center of table. Tables should be six feet from the head table, with six-foot aisles on both sides of the room and a four-foot horizontal aisle in the center.

Schoolroom setups may also be *V-shape*, off a center aisle. Schoolrom styles may also be setup using round tables. The crescent-round setup uses either 60, 66 or 72-inch diameter rounds. Seating is used on only one side so all attendees can face the speaker.

Many groups schedule a break if a meeting is longer than two hours. The break should be programmed so that your staff could take the opportunity to refresh the meeting room. When the meeting breaks, housepersons should refill ice water pitchers, replace dirty glasses with clean ones, replace soiled or wet linen, straighten all chairs and pick up all obvious trash on the tables and floor. Such procedures help project a positive image of the hotel.

U-Shape. Smaller meetings prefer to set up in a more face-to-face arrangement, making the **U-shape setup** popular (see Figure 13.7). Use 30-inch rectangular tables if people will be seated on both sides; use 18-inch-deep tables if only the outer sides will be used.

The usual per-person allowance is 24 inches, but training and technical groups may need more space for material so often specify 30-inch tables. Drape the front part of the U all the way to the floor. When the tables are draped, make sure the crease is straight so that it runs continuously along the center of the table.

Horseshoe. The **horseshoe setup** is just like the U-shape except the head table is connected to both legs with serpentine sections to soften the corners (see Figure 13.8). The U-shape and horseshoe arrangements are good for board meetings and idea exchange and lend themselves well to audiovisual presentations. The horseshoe and U-shape setups are ideal

Figure 13.9. THE HOLLOW SQUARE AND HOLLOW CIRCULAR ARRANGEMENTS.

Figure 13.10. THE E-SHAPE AND T-SHAPE ARRANGEMENTS AND VARIATIONS.

Used for groups that do not want a head table concept.
Source: Reprinted with permission from Function Room Set-Up Manual.

for training meetings in which the speaker needs access to the participants. These setups allow all participants to see and hear each other, but the size of the group is limited to approximately 40 persons.

Hollow Square and Hollow Circular. The **hollow square setup** and the **hollow circular setup** are preferred by meeting planners who want to do away with the head table concept (see Figure 13.9). They are formed like the U-shape or the horseshoe except that the open

Figure 13.11. THE BOARD OF DIRECTORS SETUP.

Popular seating arrangement for small meetings shown with its oval variation.
Source: Reprinted with permission from Function Room Set-Up Manual.

Figure 13.12. ROUND TABLE ARRANGEMENTS.

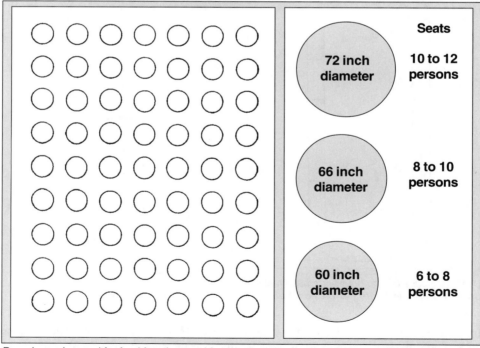

Rounds can be used for food functions and for meetings that break up into smaller discussion groups. Seventy-two inch rounds seat ten to 12 people. Sixty-inch rounds seat six to eight persons. There are also sixty-six-inch rounds, that seat eight to ten. For greatest comfort, the lesser number of seats is preferred. When spacing tables it is important to remember than 60-inch rounds require ten linear feet. This takes into account the amount of space needed for both seated guests and the aisles between tables to facilitate seating and service.
Source: Reprinted with permission from Function Room Set-Up Manual.

end is filled in. Naturally, chairs are placed only on the outside. The hollow square and the hollow circular are popular for small meetings. Both arrangements should be skirted on the inside and are usually constructed to accommodate up to 40 persons.

Variations. The **E-shape setup style** is a variation of the U-shape (see Figure 13.10). You need about four feet between the backs of the chairs to facilitate traffic. The *T-shape setup* has a head table 30 inches deep. A single leg extends from the center of the head table for as long as is needed. The leg is often set with double tables to make a 60-inch solid rectangular unit.

Figure 13.13. THE CIRCULAR BUFFET TABLE ARRANGEMENT AND VARIATIONS.

Source: Reprinted with permission from Function Room Set-Up Manual.

Board of Directors. The **board of directors setup** is a popular arrangement for small meetings. It calls for a single column of double tables making a draped table of 60 inches by as long as necessary (see Figure 13.11). Allow 24 inches of table space per person. The board of directors arrangement is so popular with meeting planners that many convention hotels have permanent setups with fine wooden tables and deluxe executive-type chairs. Suites equipped with such permanent fixtures are versatile small meeting rooms.

The *board of directors oval setup* is simply the board setup with a 60-inch half-round table at each end of the long table. Chairs may be set at the curved end.

Round Tables. *Round tables* (see Figure 13.12) can be used when meetings break up into smaller discussion groups without leaving the room. Round tables are also used most often for food functions.

Use the design in the carpet or lines in the floor to align the tables in neat rows. Allow at least nine feet from center of table to center of table.

Waiters need 24 inches between chairs and walls. Place chairs near the tables and position after the waiters have set the tables. The front edge of the chair should just touch the tablecloth. Afterwards, stack the chairs immediately to facilitate cleanup and break-down.

Circular Buffet Table. The *circular buffet table*, most useful at food functions, is made by using four serpentines and four 30-inch deep four foot tables (see Figure 13.13). This makes up a 20-by-20-foot buffet table. A round center table can be used for flowers or a display. Tier arrangements can be made with risers.

Many variations can be made by using tables of various shapes. You are limited only by imagination, time and space. If you design one you particularly like, draw a schematic of it. You can show this to a prospective client and use it for future reference.

Breakdown of Function Rooms

After a meeting or party is completed, housepersons should break down the room and clean it. The reason for this is obvious. Business could be lost, or a poor impression given, if a prospective customer saw an untidy meeting room while walking through the convention area.

Chairs and tables need to be stacked. Function chairs probably receive more damage than any other furnishings in a hotel. Housepersons who display more speed than caution in setup and dismantling should be instructed to avoid such carelessness.

If the meeting room isn't scheduled for immediate use, tables and chairs may need to be stored. Storage is a common headache to convention servicing. Hotels unfortunately often do not allot adequate and accessible storage space for function room equipment. Space that is too small or is too difficult to maneuver in shortens the life of the equipment. Furniture that is "forced" into storage is often damaged.

Some properties keep formal control over the location and storage of their equipment. In large convention hotels where the volume justifies it, a requisition system is used for issuing equipment and supplies. An inventory is taken periodically and all articles are locked up when not in use.

Meeting Rooms of the Future

As we entered the 21st century, dramatic changes were already taking place in how meeting rooms were designed and equipped. The Hyatt Hotels, for example, replaced drywall construction with open-structured ceilings in their ballrooms, providing greater versatility as well as faster setup time. In its meeting rooms, the chain installed infrared lighting controls, giving the speaker the ability to make instant adjustments to the lighting system. Distracting noises were eliminated by adding light and sound vestibules between public areas and the actual meeting space and by creating double walls between the subdivisions of the ballroom to eliminate noises from adjacent meetings. The chain also installed permanent state-of-the-art communications systems featuring fiber-optic cable, Category 5 data cable and ample telephone wiring.[6]

Another development for meeting rooms of the future is the use of plasma screens. These three-inch thick, self-contained units will not only change the way in which presentations are made, but will also change the shape of meeting rooms. As plasma screens become the dominant feature in meeting rooms, lighting requirements will change -- and the sizes of the rooms themselves will have to be adjusted to accommodate the new wide screens. Acording to Martin Dempsey, director of the media and business center at the Scottsdale Conference Center in Arizona, "Ambient light is not an issue with the plasma screen."[7] There is no need to dim lights to see the image.

Other changes cited by architects in the field include changes in table shapes, room decor, and simplifying controls used for presentations. Tomorrow's tables, although they will have the look of heavy wooden tables, will be hollow, light and easily moved. Rooms will be white or light colored to provide for better contrast when video cameras are used, while rooms in which plasma screens are dominant can be painted in lively hues. While high technology will continue to play a major part in presentations, it is expected that control panels will become less visible (concealed yet readily accessible).

Despite these exciting innovations, there is, conversely, a trend toward a traditional look for boardroom setups. Cindy Carney, an interior designer with Debra Myers Associates, says,

"Five years ago, everyone wanted laminates and a techy look."[8]

Now, clients want a more conservative, throwback style. Wood paneling, leather seating, and traditional light fixtures add to the trend toward a masculine, conservative, "clubby" atmosphere.

Whatever trends finally emerge as dominant, it is important that hotels keep abreast of the latest innovations but make decisions concerning design and function with the actual needs of the meeting planners they are serving in mind. If a hotel caters primarily to SMERF segments, for example, a large investment in plasma screens and other high-tech gadgets would be a waste of money. Corporate groups, however, would demand the latest in technology.

Monitoring Function Room Usage

It is important you understand the dollar value of function room space. One chain calculated that meeting space cost $.08 per square foot per day when it was not being utilized. In other words, a 10,000 square foot ballroom costs $800 per day just sitting vacant. To get a handle on function space utilization, it is useful to track and monitor the following:

- Function room occupancy by meal period
- Types of functions
- Use of guestrooms by function groups
- Popularity of individual banquet menu items
- Sales revenue per square foot of function space
- Average banquet check by type of function
- Pattern of unused times and days
- Average number of persons by type of function

Reporting function room statistics can be revealing. While the hotel's function rooms may seem very busy, during certain times of the year only one function per day is often booked in each of the meeting rooms. Keeping track of function room business can disclose soft spots and help the department sell and schedule banquet and meeting room business when it is most needed.

PUTTING IT ALL TOGETHER

This time, *you* will be using the information that you have learned in this chapter to demonstrate how a property's meeting space can be utilized to its maximum potential. You have been named convention service manager of a hotel with fairly limited meeting space (see diagram). It is your job to fill this space as effectively as possible, so you have booked a number of functions. On Thursday of next week, your property will be hosting:

1. A morning (9:00 a.m.-12:00 p.m.) training seminar for 50 distributors of a multi-level marketing company. The distributors will need to check in and will receive packets of information before entering the training room. A refreshment break will be taken at 10:30 a.m.
2. An afternoon (1:00 p.m.) press conference for a local official announcing her candidacy for Congress. Attendance is projected to include approximately 20 news reporters, three television crews, and the candidate's key staff of nine people. In addition, the candidate has requested the provision of additional seating in the event the public wishes to attend. She has also requested the availability of floor microphones for a question and answer session.
3. A two-hour afternoon (2:00 p.m. - 4:00 p.m.) meeting of twelve directors of the board of the community's hospital.
4. A local charity's evening fund-raising dinner. A cocktail reception will be held from 6:00 p.m.- 6:30 p.m., with dinner following at 7:00 p.m. Dancing will follow from 8:30 p.m. until midnight. Expected attendance is 300 people. Special requirements include a head table for 20 VIPs and the availability of an area for ticket collection and the viewing of prizes that will be raffled throughout the evening.

The following morning, another training session will be held from 9:00 a.m.-12:00 p.m., and you will want the room set up before the staff goes on overtime at 1:00 p.m.

1. Which room(s) would be most suitable for each meeting? What factors did you take into consideration in making your decision?
2. What style of seating would you choose for each meeting? Draw up a sample floorplan for each function.

3. Develop sample function sheets that detail the special needs for each function and how these requirements will be met.

Chapter Summary:

In this chapter, we have taken a look at the various types of function rooms and the setups that are commonly used when servicing convention groups. We have discussed the importance of assigning function rooms for maximum efficiency and revenue and detailed the factors that should be considered when assigning function room space. We have also seen that the use of function rooms must be monitored to ensure maximum profitablilty for your hotel. In the next chapter, we will take a look at how some of the function room setups we have discussed are used when servicing one part of the convention business: food functions.

Endnotes:

1. Bryant Rousseau, "Low-Cost Software for Room Layouts," *Meeting News*, April 22, 1996, p. 9.
2. M. Jill Wien, "Holiday Holds," *The Meeting Manager*, December 1995, p. 37.
3. Ibid.
4. Chris Davis, *Business Travel News*, May 15, 2000, p. 39.
5. Guide to Function-Room Furniture, Jacob Felsenstein; King Arthur Incorporated, Pennsauken, NJ.
6. Doug Fox, "Hyatt's Improvements Upgrade Presentations," *Convene*, February 1999, p. 57.
7. Justin Henderson, "21st Century Box," *Successful Meetings*, January 2000, p. 20.
8. Ibid, p. 21.

Additional References:

The Convention Industry Council Manual, 7th Edition, Susan Krug, Executive Director, 2000

Internet Sites:

For additional information on the firms and organizations discussed in this chapter, visit the following Internet sites. The Web addresses listed are current as of January 2001. Addresses may change, however; if a site is not available at the address below, a search engine can be used to access its new location.

Meeting Matrix International - www.meetingmatrix.com
TimeSaver Software - Room Viewer - www.timesaversoftware.com
3D Event Designer - www.eventsoft.com
Event Sketch - www.timesaver.com

Study Questions:

1. What is a function room? List the basic types of function rooms.
2. What is mean by the statement: "All public space may be function area depending on the group and its needs." What other areas can be used to host functions?
3. What factors must be considered in charging a group for meeting space? For assigning meeting rooms?
4. List the basic styles of meeting room setups and tell when each is used. What styles are commonly used for food functions?
5. What is "function room furniture"? What features should you look for when selecting function room furniture?
6. How will meeting rooms of the future differ from today's meeting space?
7. What methods are used to monitor function room space?

Key Terms:

Air walls. Moveable barriers that partition large areas into smaller ones. Not necessarily soundproof.

Auditorium/theater style. Chairs set up in rows facing head table, stage or speaker. Number of aisles may vary. Some variations are V-set up and semicircular.

Board of directors setup. One wide table or series of tables set up in a rectangular shape with chairs on both sides and at the end. Some hotels have permanent board setups featuring expensive furniture and executive chairs. Oval setup is also used.

Breakout room. Smaller meeting room used when larger sessions divide into smaller groups for discussions and group work. Usually planners request that these rooms be located near the main meeting facilities.

Dais. Raised platform on which the head table is placed.

Employee procedure manual. Instructions for employees to do job. Often includes illustrations or drawings. Helps ensure consistent setups.

E-shape setup style. Tables set in the shape of an E with chairs on the outside of the closed ends and on both sides of each leg.

Function rooms. Rooms specifically designed to house meetings or social gatherings.

Hollow circular setup. Same as horseshoe setup except both ends are closed; chairs placed on the outside.

Hollow square setup. Tables set in a square with a hollow middle; chairs placed only on the outside.

Horseshoe setup. Similar to U-shape style; set in shape of a horseshoe. Chairs can be placed around both the inside and outside.

Lectern. A reading desk used to hold the speaker's papers. Either rests on the floor (full size) or on the table.

Pre-function space. Area adjacent to the main event room; used to assemble attendees prior to a function.

Schoolroom/classroom style. Tables six feet by 18 inches are lined up in rows on each side of a good sized center aisle. Usually six chairs to two tables. All tables and chairs face the head table. Variations are the V-shape and perpendicular style.

U-shape setup. Tables set up in the shape of the block letter U; usually used for smaller meetings. Chairs are placed on the outside of the closed end and on both sides of each leg.

Learning Objectives:

This portion of your text introduces you to the various types of food and beverage functions typically held at a convention hotel. When you have studied this chapter, you will:

- Know the different types of table service and when each is commonly used.

- Be able to describe several types of beverage service and tell how beverage service is billed.

- Be able to detail the factors that are taken into consideration when staging food and beverage functions and describe how hotel departments work together to ensure successful events.

Outline

Food Service
- Types of Food Functions
- Themed Events
- Changing Tastes
- Types of Service
- Pricing Food Functions
- Attendance
- Attrition
- Function Rooms
- Control Procedures
- Staffing
- Uniserve or Duoserve

Beverage Service
- Types of Setups
- Hospitality Suites
- Brands
- Pricing Methods
- Beverage Control

Post-Function Actions

In-House Coordination: Large vs. Small Properties
- Role of the Catering Manager
- Servicing and Selling
- Communication and Cooperation

Planning Food Functions

Gene Meoni
Director of Food and Beverage
Grand Traverse Resort Village, Michigan

"The catering or conventions services department is the most profitable division of any hotel food and beverage operation provided the proper planning, controls, service and creativity are utilized for an event, be it a refreshment break for 20 or a five course gala dinner for 1,000...When planning meetings, conventions or catered events, you must utilize the controls planned to guarantee service to your guests and the profitability of your operation. Function sheets for food and beverage products and services must be detailed and specific...When setting up for a convention, meeting or catered event, organization and pre-planning are necessary for a successful execution...The plans, controls and teamwork involved in food and beverage service are immense. But, if effective, will lead to operational success, which I define as exceeding guest expectations, motivated employees who take pride in their accomplishments, and exceeding budgeted bottom line profits."

14   Food and Beverage Service

Food and beverage functions play an important part in convention programs. The kinds of functions can vary greatly, from a hospitality suite serving soft drinks and liquor, plus some peanuts and pretzels, to a full-scale banquet. But all food functions are important, and they represent another area where close communication and cooperation are needed.

Food Service

Banquets, parties, and other business or social functions involving food and beverage can produce additional, often high, revenues for your hotel. Bill Carlin, managing editor of Nation's Restaurant News, states,

> "Banquets are the most profitable area of hotel food and beverage operations."[1]

Successful banquets can contribute greatly to the overall profitability because the profit margin on sales for banquets often runs 35-40 percent, as opposed to 10-15 percent for hotel restaurants. There are several reasons for this difference.

In convention oriented hotels, banquet sales volume often exceeds restaurant volume by as much as two to one.

Banquets allow flexibility in pricing. A New York steak dinner priced at $20 on the restaurant menu may bring $35 on the banquet menu. The justification for this difference is the cost of setting up and tearing down the banquet area and also the short time allowed for serving a large number of people in one seating.

Food costs are lower due to volume preparation and no large inventory is needed since ordering can be done as needed and all attendees normally receive identical meals.

Beverage profits are high because beverage costs are easily controlled and revenues are greater because of pricing flexibility.

Labor costs are significantly lower because banquet servers and bartenders are often part-time employees used on an as-needed basis. The cost of restaurant employees, in contrast, is largely fixed because a regular staff member must be maintained even during slow periods.

Employee productivity is high since staffing levels can be set for a predetermined, guaranteed attendance.

Types of Food Functions

Meetings may call for breakfasts, luncheons, dinners, dinners with entertainment and/or dancing, refreshment breaks, bars, receptions, buffets and continuous hospitality setups in suites, meeting rooms or exhibit halls. Gene Meoni, Director of Food and Beverage at the Grand Traverse Resort Village, says that banquet menus should be varied in selection and price range to meet your market segments. Menus should include regional specialties, property specialties and upgraded menus that have been executed during past events.

Group menus come in a variety of forms and sizes. For convenience, we recommend a small bound booklet, such as used by the Radisson Hotels (see Figure 14.1). The Radisson booklet gives both sit-down and buffet suggestions for breakfast, lunch and dinner.

Two other types of food functions held in conjunction with beverage service are refreshment breaks and cocktail receptions with hors d'oeuvres. Refreshment breaks ideally should be set up in a room adjacent to the meeting room. If this is not possible, the beverages and other items should be carted outside of the meeting room and served when the person in charge of the group gives the signal for the waiters to enter (see box titled "Refreshment Break Guidelines").

Figure 14.1. SAMPLE MENUS FROM THE GROUP MENU BOOKLET USED BY THE RADISSON HOTEL.

Breakfasts

The aroma of freshly brewed coffee. Fresh juices, pastries, muffins and breads warm from the oven.

Launch a successful day at the Radisson Hotel St. Paul with breakfast full of homemade American goodness.

Chef's Breakfast Recommendations

The French Connection $6.75
Grapefruit Juice or Orange Juice, Egg Dipped French Toast Topped with Apples, Bananas, Pecans and Maple Whipped Butter. Canadian Bacon or Sausage. Freshly Ground and Brewed Guatemalan Antigua Coffee or Colombian Supremo Decaffeinated Coffee. Granola Bars and Assortment of Whole Fresh Fruit Basket.

Midwestern Sunrise $6.95
Vegetable Juice or Cherry Cider. Scrambled Eggs with Wisconsin Cojack Cheese, Fresh Chives, Canadian Bacon or Smoked Ham Steak and Sautéed Red Potatoes. Blueberry Muffin Basket. Freshly Ground and Brewed Guatemalan Antigua Coffee or Colombian Supremo Decaffeinated Coffee.

The All American $6.50
Grapefruit Juice or Orange Juice, Scrambled Eggs, Bacon, Hash Brown Potatoes, Assorted Breakfast-Bakeries, Butter, Jams and Marmalades, Freshly Ground and Brewed Guatemalan Antigua Coffee or Colombian Supremo Decaffeinated Coffee, Assorted Herbal and Premium Teas

Breakfast Buffets (minimum 50 people)

Sunrise Buffet $7.95
Orange Juice, Grapefruit Juice, Fresh Fruit Medley, Scrambled Eggs, Home Fried Potatoes, Bacon and Sausage, Assorted Muffins and Pastries, Beverage

Northwoods Buffet $11.50
Apple Cider, Orange and Vegetable Juice. Country Style Eggs Scrambled. Display of Seasonal Fruits and Berries. Homemade Granola, Smoked Fish and Cheese Platters, Hickory Smoked Ham. Flapjacks with Blueberry Compote, Grilled Homefried Potatoes. Assorted Muffins and Pastries, Beverage.

Omelette Bar (maximum 75 people) $11.95
Orange Juice, Apple Juice, Fresh Fruit Medley, Omelettes or Eggs cooked to order, Home Fried Potatoes, Hickory Smoked Ham, Yogurts, Granolas and Muffins.

*Low Cholesterol Eggs Available

A la Carte Breakfasts

FRUITS AND JUICES (Choice of One)
Half Grapefruit, Grapefruit Juice or Orange Juice, Fresh Fruit Medley, Chilled Melon

COMBINATIONS
Served with Basket of Muffins and Breads, Butter, Jams, Marmalades and Beverage

Scrambled Eggs, Sausage or Bacon Strips $6.50
Home Fried Potatoes

Scrambled Eggs, Ham or Canadian Bacon $6.90
Home Fried Potatoes

Ham and Cheese Egg Croissant $7.50
Home Fried Potatoes

Roast Beef Hash with Poached Eggs $7.50
Home Fried Potatoes

Grilled Tenderloin Steak with Scrambled Eggs $9.95
Home Fried Potatoes

Figure 14.1. SAMPLE MENUS FROM THE GROUP MENU BOOKLET USED BY THE RADISSON HOTEL.

Lunch

Take a memorable mid-day break. Introduce the occasion with our Chef's creative soups of the day or a picture-perfect salad. Select one of our savory main courses. Then top off the meal with a dessert guaranteed to set your guests to talking.

Chef's Luncheon Recommendations

Chicken Salad Plate with Fresh Fruit $9.95
Soup of the Day, Breadsticks, Beverage

Roasted Top Sirloin of Beef $10.50
Mushroom Sauce, Tossed Green Salad, Fresh Vegetable, Potato, Rolls and Butter, Beverage

Grilled Breast of Chicken $10.95
Basil Cream Sauce, Fresh Fruit Salad, Fresh Vegetable, Three Rice Blend, Rolls and Butter, Beverage

Deli Platter $9.95
Soup of the Day, Roast Beef, Turkey, Ham and Salami, Assorted Cheeses, Relishes, Potato Salad, Assorted Breads in a Basket, Beverage

Tuna Salad, Canteloupe $9.95
Soup of the Day, Hard Boiled Egg, Cottage Cheese, Relishes. Rolls and Butter, Beverage

Roast Breast of Turkey $9.95
Gravy and Dressing, Apple, Orange Waldorf Salad, Fresh Vegetable, Whipped Potatoes, Rolls and Butter, Beverage

Baked Chicken Breast $11.95
Mustard Sauce, Filled with Spinach Wild Rice and Jarlsburg Cheese, Fresh Vegetables, Rolls and Butter, Tossed Green Salad, Beverage.

Grilled Chicken & Shrimp Stirfry $10.95
Florentine Rice, Peapods and Carrots, Luncheon Salad, Rolls and Butter, Beverage

Broiled Orange Roughy $10.50
Fresh Dill Sauce, Danish Cucumber Tomato Salad, Three Blend Rice, Fresh Vegetables, Rolls and Butter, Beverage

Grilled Salmon Filet $11.50
Dilled Salsa Verde, Butter Lettuce Salad, Three Rice Blend, Steamed Broccoli, Rolls and Butter, Beverage

Desserts A La Carte $1.75
Chocolate Fudge Cake, Vanilla Ice Cream with Berries in Season, Chocolate Rum Mousse, Carrot Cake, Apple Pie, Cheesecake, Pound Cake Compote

Hearty Deli Box Lunches $9.50
Choice of One in Each Category:
Mustard Glazed Ham, Roasted Turkey Breast, or Lean Roast Beef
Cheddar, Smoked Gouda or Swiss
Onion Bun, Whole Wheat Bun or Pumpernickel Bread
Marinated Vegetable Salad, Pasta Salad or Dill Potato Salad
Granola Bar, Chocolate Chip Cookie, Peanut Butter Brownie, Banana or Apple
Soda or Spring Water

LUNCHEON BUFFETS

New York Deli $12.50
Soup of the Day, Roast Beef, Turkey, Ham and Salami, Assorted Cheeses, A Variety of Breads, Condiments, Salads, Relish Platter, Cheesecake, Beverage

Picnic Time (minimum 25 people) $10.95
Sliced Tomatoes, Sliced Cucumbers, Potato Salad, Southern Style Fried Chicken, Rolls and Butter, Apple Pie, Beverage

Boulevard Buffet $15.00 (minimum 75 people)
Tossed Green Salad, Fresh Fruit Medley, Soup of the Day, Sliced Tomatoes, Sliced Cucumbers, Relish Platter, Potato Salad, Salad Dressings, Breads and Butter, Assorted Cold Cuts, Assorted Cheeses
Select Any Two:
Fish and Chips, Grilled Chopped Sirloin, Roast Top Sirloin, Fried Chicken, Baked Ham, Roast Half Chicken
Chef's Select Fresh Vegetable, Potato,
Carrot Cake, Apple Pie, Chocolate Rum Mousse, Beverage

The cocktail reception with hors d'oeuvres should create a carnival atmosphere that will carry over to dinner. It also gets the dinner guests together so that you can start to serve dinner on schedule. Suggest a one-hour maximum for such events to the meeting planner.

Two basic methods are used in charging for hors d'oeuvres and finger food: by the person per hour and by the bowl or tray. Figure 14.2 shows these two methods.

Each function should be dealt with separately to make sure of details. As we stressed in Chapter 12, a function sheet (banquet event order) should be filled out for each event, listing all the information needed for smooth execution.

Themed Events

Every meeting planner tries to do something different at each event. Most conventions have a high percentage of people who repeatedly attend, so the planners want to "add a new twist" to the program, from adding flair to the cocktail party to staging a themed banquet.

Experienced meeting planners disguise the same old cocktail party by introducing a different theme each year. Theme events, both large and small, are very propular and are remembered by the attendees. In addition, themed events do much to enhance the reputation of the hotel. Photographs taken during such events are a great help in selling other business and can stimulate the thinking of meeting planners.

Figure 14.1. SAMPLE MENUS FROM THE GROUP MENU BOOKLET USED BY THE RADISSON HOTEL.

Dinner

Select menus to round out the day's events . . . or a beginning to your evening's production. A leisurely ambiance of taste and imagination.

Chef's Dinner Recommendations

Roast Prime Rib of Beef $19.50
Caesar Salad, Potato, Fresh Vegetable, Rolls and Butter, Chocolate Cheese Cake, Beverage

Char-broiled Pacific Salmon $19.50
Mustard Dill Sauce, Tossed Garden Greens, Fresh Vegetables, Wild Rice Blend, Rolls and Butter, Chocolate Chip Cheesecake, Beverage

New York Cut Strip Sirloin $19.50
Peppercorn Sauce, Caesar Salad, Potato, Fresh Vegetable, Rolls and Butter, Four Layer Chocolate Cake, Beverage

Char-broiled Center Cut Pork Chop $17.00
Apple, Orange Waldorf Salad, Potato, Fresh Vegetable, Rolls and Butter, Carrot Cake, Beverage

Roasted Top Sirloin of Beef $16.50
Mushroom Sauce, Caesar Salad, Potato, Fresh Vegetable, Rolls and Butter, Chocolate Chip Cheesecake, Beverage

Grilled Breast of Chicken $15.00
Spicy Tomato Sauce, Tossed Garden Greens, Fresh Vegetables, Fettucini, Rolls and Butter, Pound Cake Compote, Beverage

Hardwood Grilled Chicken Breast and Beef Tenderloin Filet $18.95
Peach Chutney, Tossed Garden Greens, Brown Rice and Lentils, Fresh Vegetables, Rolls and Butter, Irish Cream Mousse Cake, Beverage

Grilled Swordfish $19.50
Minted Tomato Sauce, Caesar Salad, Potato Gnocchi, Fresh Vegetables, Rolls and Butter, Bread Pudding with Caramel Sauce, Beverage

Chicken Breast Porcini $16.95
Mushroom Cream Sauce, Tossed Garden Greens, Wild Mushroom Chicken Mousse, Fresh Spinach, Wild Rice, Fresh Vegetables, Rolls and Butter, Cheesecake with Amaretto Cream Sauce, Beverage

Stuffed Pork Loin $15.95
Pistachio Apple Brandy Sauce, Caesar Salad, Sweet Potato Tart, Fresh Vegetables, Rolls and Butter, Dutch Apple Pie, Beverage

Grilled Chicken Breast and Shrimp Marinara $18.95
Caesar Salad, Fettucini, Fresh Vegetables, Rolls and Butter, Four Layer Chocolate Cake, Beverage

Midwestern Grill $22.00
Four Season Salad, Beef, Veal and Lamb Chop Grilled to Perfection, Potato Au Gratin, Fresh Vegetables, Rolls and Butter, Irish Cream Torte, Beverage

Hardwood Grilled Tenderloin and Baked Salmon Filet $22.00
Peppercorn Sauce, Caesar Salad, Lentil Brown Rice, Fresh Vegetables, Rolls and Butter, Amaretto Cheesecake, Beverage

Sliced Tenderloin and Grilled Shrimp $24.95
Port Wine Cherry Sauce, Marinated Tomato and Spinach Salad, Wild Rice, Fresh Vegetables, Rolls and Butter, Walnut Layer Cake, Beverage

Dinner Buffet $18.95 (minimum 75 people)

Tossed Green Salad, Fresh Fruit Medley, Sliced Tomatoes, Sliced Cucumbers, Relish Platter, Potato Salad, Salad Dressing, Breads and Butter

Select Any Two:
Roast Loin of Pork, Natural Gravy; Breast of Chicken, Cordon Bleu; Roast Half Chicken; Rainbow Trout Almondine; Grilled Pacific Salmon, Orange Butter; Roasted Top Sirloin of Beef, Mushroom Sauce; Baked Ham; Roast Breast of Turkey, Gravy and Dressing

Vegetables and Starches to Complement Buffet

Assortment of Pies, Cakes and Mousse, Beverages

Dinner Grand Buffet $24.00 (minimum 75 people)

Tossed Garden Greens, Fresh Fruit Medley, Marinated Mushroom Tomato Salad, Danish Cucumber Salad, Antipasta Salad, Relishes, Bread Display

Carver Attended: Select One
Roast Prime Rib of Beef or Baked Ham

Select Any Three:
Roast Loin of Pork, Breast of Chicken Cordon Bleu, Roasted Chicken, Sole Roulades, Seafood Creole, Roasted Breast of Turkey.

Vegetables and Starches to Complement Buffet
Grand Dessert Display, Beverages

The focal point of any such function is the menu. Hotels that have theme or ethnic banquet suggestions are a step ahead. In presenting theme menus, be honest about your capabilities and suggest what you do best. It is better to refuse a request than to fail with a theme your staff is unable to handle.

In addition to special menus, decorations, costumes and entertainment are used to carry out the theme. Most convention planners love theme setups, but many cannot afford a one-time use of a theme or they lack the imagination or staff to develop one. A property

Figure 14.2. PRICING CATERED ITEMS.

Canapes and Hors D'Oeuvres

No.1: $6.50 per person	No. 2:
Hot Grilled Cocktail Franks, Mustard Sauce Swedish Savory Meatballs Knishes Chinese Egg Rolls Butterfly Shrimp, Cocktail Sauce	**Cold Canapes** Large Tray...**$68.50** (Serves approximately 25 persons) Medium Tray...**$46.00** (Serves approximately 15 persons)
Cold Canapes Savory Cheese Spread, Pimento Cornets of Imported Genoa Salami Smoked Nova Scotia Salmon Deviled Eggs with Anchovies	Selection: A variety of Assorted Cold Canapes including Stuffed Eggs Moscovite

---

This hors d'oeuvres menu shows two methods of pricing: by the person per hour and by the tray or bowl. While the eating habits of groups may vary, the industry standard for a two-hour reception is eight pieces per person for the first hour and four per person during the second hour.

that has a store of props, costumes or centerpieces has a better chance of landing theme party business.

You can be the catalyst for better and more exciting events. When you help a client develop a theme, manufactured pieces such as signs and art work can be stored for future use at a reduced cost. You may also build an inventory of themed props by asking airlines or vendors to supply posters or decorations (most beverage vendors, for example, offer "game themed" props, such as Super Bowl decorations).

The hotel can also add "atmosphere" to a theme party in a number of ways, including using costumed food servers, "sound scapes" (tapes of sounds, such as ocean waves), lighting, and other low-cost effects (bubble machines, fog machines and so on). If a particular item is not immediately available, the convention service staff should be able to recommend sources, such as wholesale suppliers or third-party party providers of props, entertainment, and other needed items.

Clients will likely respond to your suggestions, especially if you have successfully staged themed events. Hotel people should be the pros, the ones to supply the expertise, the material, or at the very least, the suggestions. More, and bigger and better, parties result and everyone benefits.

Changing Tastes

Banquet menus should reflect meeting attendees' desire for a more healthful diet. People are increasingly conscious that the food they eat and the way it is prepared has an impact on their overall health. Hotels have responded by offering lighter, low-cholesterol items. Alter-

---

Refreshment Break Guidelines

1. Breaks normally last 15 to 30 minutes.

2. Space stations so bottlenecks are kept to a minimum.

3. Open stations farthest from the main entrance first to draw people into the room.

4. Separate coffee and soda stations

5. Identify each hot beverage with a sign.

REFRESHMENT BREAK ESTIMATES FOR 200 PEOPLE

A.M.		P.M.	
Coffee	65% x 200 = 130 cups = 6.5 gals	Coffee	35% x 200 = 70 cups = 3.5 gals
Decaf	30% x 200 = 60 cups = 3 gals	Decaf	20% x 200 = 40 cups = 2 gals
Tea	10% x 200 = 20 cups = 1 gal	Tea	10% x 200 = 20 cups = 1 gal
Soda	25% x 200 = 50 drinks = 50 sodas	Soda	70% x 200 = 140 drinks = 140 sodas

6. Lay out stations for quick service: coffee cups, followed by regular coffee, decaf, tea bags and hot water. Accessories, cream, sugar, sweetener and spoons should be available on a separate table a short distance from the beverage station.

7. Set one beverage station per 75 to 100 attendees.

8. Staff one server per 100 people for refreshment breaks; one server per 50 people at receptions and buffets.

9. Figure 20 six-ounce cups of coffee in a gallon.

10. "Marry" (combine) coffee stations toward the end of the break.

---

native menus for people with dietary or religious restrictions are now available to meeting planners.

The biggest change in eating habits has occurred at breakfast. Eggs, potatoes, bacon and sausage have given way to a variety of lighter, health-conscious offerings such as whole grain muffins and rolls, low calorie yogurt, fresh fruits and low-fat dairy products. Hot oatmeal, cooked wheat cereal and shredded wheat are very popular alternatives to the traditional fare. Lunches and dinners have also become less formal. Diet-conscious attendees appreciate extensive salad bars featuring fresh vegetables and low-calorie dressings. Poultry, fish, veal and lean pork entrees, grilled rather than fried, are popular with fitness conscious attendees. Heavy meals promote sleepiness, so offer moderate portions and food groups that are high in protein.

Today, new technology is being used to assist planners in making their decisions — and to improve the quality and variety of food and beverages offered to meeting and function guests. Sheraton's "Sheraton Cuisine," the umbrella name for the chain's hotel kitchen software, provides colored pictures of the 365 dishes offered in its "Cuisine of the Americas" menu, along with the recipes and a breakdown of the nutritional content of each entree. Scott Geraghty, director of culinary services for the Sheraton New York Hotel Complex, is enthusiastic about this program and its next phase, which calculates nutritional content after substitutions have been made. He states:

> "A catering manager will be able to sit down with a meeting planner, call up a color picture of what a plated dish would look like, and make substitutions like: 'What would this dish look like with carrotts instead of zucchini?'"[2]

Refreshment breaks no longer require doughnuts, Danish and other surgary bakery items. Health conscious participants know that simple sugars provide few nutrients and play havoc with the waistline. Fruit juices, flavored mineral waters, yogurt, muffins, fresh fruits such as pineapple, melon and strawberries plus decaffeinated coffee and hot tea are popular items.

Smoking has become a social issue. Some meeting planners request designated special smoking and nonsmoking areas, clearly marked.

Types of Service

An important planning decision is the type of service to be used at food functions. The kind of banquet service selected influences pricing, staffing and the overall effect of the function.

Plate service, also known as *American Service,* is the most common form of banquet service. The food is assembled in the kitchen and waiters deliver plates to the tables. Cold food may be plated ahead of time and stored in refrigerators. Hot food is plated just prior to delivery and is sometimes served from a number of stations set up in the kitchen. Guests are served food from the left and beverages from the right. All items are picked up from the right at the end of the course. Plate service requires the least skill on the part of the service personnel.

With **Russian service**, food is served from platters and waiters work as teams, placing the food items individually on the diners' plates. Russian service, or *platter service,* requires more space between tables for waiters to move freely and a larger and skilled labor force.

French service, also called *cart or tableside service,* requires sufficient space between tables for waiters to move about freely. More experienced waiters are required for this type of service as much of the food is prepared tableside on a gueridon (rolling cart).

Pre-set service is frequently used for luncheons where faster service is needed. The first course of soup, salad or appetizer is set on the table prior to the guests' arrival; occasionally the dessert may also be pre-set. While pre-set service works well when the schedule is tight, pre-set food is rarely as attractive as food delivered in courses during the meal.

Buffet service is a presentation of several food items from which the attendee makes a selection. Buffet service is efficient because a large number of people can be served in a short period of time with a small serving staff. A combination of service styles is sometimes used with buffets. For example, receptions may feature a buffet of appetizers and then a sit-down dinner served plate style. Or the first and dessert courses may be served by waiters, while the main dish is presented buffet-style.

Another trend in food functions is **a la carte catering**, which offers more options to both planners and diners. Under the a la carte system, catering departments develop menus offering two or three items from which guests can choose or unique combinations of entrees to suit more palates (a *combination* of meat and seafood or creative vegetarian entrees, for example).

The Marriott chain has made extensive use of a la carte catering, even offering seated guests a menu to give more of a sense of fine dining. The Peabody Orlando, which has offered a choice between beef and chicken for some time, has extended its a la carte service to include duo and trio entree choices in its regionally-oriented banquet dishes (such as jerk chicken and Caribbean-style pork). Karl Edlbauer, executive chef of the hotel explains:

> "The clientele is looking for more upscale menus that are daring, but with a classical presentation."[3]

Many hotels host a "tasting dinner" to enable planners to sample the banquet dishes so they'll know in advance how the food will look and taste. Chef Gordon Marr of the Hilton Washington in Washington, DC recommends that the tasting meal be an exact replica of the banquet meal and that it should approximate the meal service.

Pricing Food Functions

Many convention planners prefer to complete all negotiations in detail before signing the letter of agreement. Some even want to go so far as to select menus and agree on prices. A planner would prefer this because it makes budget projections so much easier. But with conventions planned years in advance, it is not possible for a hotel to make accurate quotations.

Most hotels will gladly say what they charge for menus currently in use, feeling that this is a sufficient guide for meeting planners. There is obvious danger in pricing a menu so far in advance. Most meeting planners with any experience at all realize that any such agreements may have to be modified because of rising costs. If you examine the dollar values of the past fifty years, you see constant inflation. When the spiral goes up sharply, everyone recognizes the inflation, but in reality there has been a steady curve upwards over the years.

You must be very careful when you have to make price guarantees for dates several years ahead. Most hotels have adopted a policy of quoting room rates not more than one year in advance and firm menu prices not more than six months before the event. Some hotels even quote a more restricted policy. For example, the Orlando Marriott contract reads:

Menu prices cannot be confirmed more than 60 days prior to the function due to the daily fluctuation of market prices. The organization grants the hotel the right to make reasonable substitutions on the menu to meet increased market prices or commodity shortages.

You cannot avoid such a policy unless you have no need to be competitive and can build in a fat reserve in your quotations. But few of us have such prerogatives. To be competitive, you figure prices closely and cannot absorb inflationary additions to cost.

You will find some exceptions, but most meeting planners understand such limitations and are concerned about unduly squeezing a hotel. After all, each event is a custom production and the planners are concerned with the quality of what they will receive. If they *are* obliged to set an early price on tickets, they understand that a flexible attitude on the menu can enable them to carry out the meal function while allowing the hotel a fair profit. Some astute meeting planners attach a copy of the hotel's current menu to the contract and specify that prices cannot be raised "more than X percent per year" over current prices.

All agreements on menus, prices and terms must be made in writing and signed by both parties. This eliminates misunderstandings.

Attendance

The planner initially will estimate attendance at a food function. This is vital as it indicates the scope of the event. The figure is only for preliminary preparations, and must be reviewed.

The convention planner owes it to the facility to keep it informed of the closest possible estimates of attendance at each food event. The planner may not know for sure, but a time will be set by which a firm guarantee must be given in order to prepare for the event.

Properties doing banquet business face the problem of determining a fair and workable **guarantee** policy. No one policy is applicable to all hotels or all situations. However, the Hospitality Sales Marketing Association International surveyed a number of hotels and found that most adhere strictly to their guarantee policies. Those surveyed stressed the importance of explaining the guarantee and working with the planner to set a realistic attendance figure.

Most hotels require a guarantee either 48 or 72 hours before a food function. The meeting planner then agrees to pay for the guaranteed number of people whether or not that many appear. If 200 people are guaranteed for luncheon at a per-head charge and only 185 show up, the organization will pay for all 200. It is a touchy situation, but the obligation is clear-cut.

What happens when more show up? The experienced planner will ask that places be set for more than the guaranteed number; an overset safety margin of five percent is common. It is to the advantage of both the hotel and the convening group to avoid last minute scrambling with chairs, tables, and place settings.

Often the guarantee is included in the function sheet and is signed by both the hotel and a convention representative. Any agreement between the hotel and client is binding. If the guarantee calls for 200 and the hotel agrees to set for 5 percent over, the hotel sets tables and chairs for 210. If 210 show up, all is in readiness and the bill indicates 210. If 230 show up, the hotel is allowed to substitute 20 meals of a quickly prepared item.

Be careful about circumstances that may affect the timing of the guarantee. The hotel may require a greater lead time before a weekend or holiday because a full staff may not be working then. Kitchen purchases and preparations may then be possible only on an overtime basis.

Another guarantee method suggested by meeting planners, but seldom used, is to guarantee only labor. If only 185 of the guaranteed 200 showed up, the association would pay for only the cost of one waiter and not the extra fifteen meals prepared. Obviously, a hotel should never consent to this unless the extra meals can be used somewhere else.

The organization must designate, in writing, who is authorized to make changes in attendance estimates, menus and prices. A guarantee sheet (see Figure 14.3) summarizing the functions and the guarantees for each day is printed daily and distributed to appropriate staff.

Attrition

Food and beverage attrition clauses have become increasingly common in recent years. When hotels book a piece of business, they often base the room rate quoted to the group on the amount of food and beverage and room rental anticipated. Typically, hotels look at the type and size of functions planned for the convention, put a dollar value on each one, add up the numbers and then allow about 20 percent of that number for attrition (slippage). The resulting number is the minimum amount the group is expected to spend on food and beverage. If the group fails to spend this amount because of poor attendance or the need to cancel banquets, the attrition clause in the contract allows the hotel to collect damages for lost profits.

Figure 14.3. GUARANTEE SHEET.

The Durham Resort
Guarantee Sheet
For February 8, 20_

Time	BEO #	Room	Func.	GTD	Set	Sources	Post As
4:00A-4:00A	121	Madison	EXHB	25	28	DJ/AO/JH/CH	Kopykat Sales
7:00A-9:00A	378	Monroe	BMTG	150	165	AO/AO/JH/JH	Auto Travelers Assn
7:00A-9:00A	127	Grant	BMTG	100	110	DJ/DJ/AO/AO	Auto Travelers Assn
7:00-11:00A	382	Ballroom J	RECP	200	220	KZ/KZ/JH/JH	Kopykat Sales
7:30A-8:00A	352	Ballroom J	CONT	50	55	AO/AO/JH/JH	Kopykat Sales
8:00A-4:00P	482	Ballroom A	EXHB	20	22	ML/ML/MW/MW	Auto Travelers Assn
8:00A-6:00P	482	Ballroom A	EXHB	20	22	DJ/DJ/AO/AO	Auto Travelers Assn
8:00A-6:00P	371	Webster	EXHB	20	22	AO/AO/JH/JH	Auto Travelers Assn
8:00A-12:00P	487	Coolidge	REG	20	22	AO/AO/JH/JH	Auto Travelers Assn
8:00A-5:00P	877	Washington	GS	80	88	DJ/DJ/AO/AO	Kopykat Sales
10:30A-4:30P	472	Jackson	MTG	75	85	JH/JH/DJ/DJ	Kopykat Sales

This computer printout lists all food functions on a particular day. Copies of the form are generally distributed to the Executive Chef, Banquet Chef, Executive Steward, Food and Beverage Control, Function Book Coordinator, Banquet Manager, and Convention Service Manager.

Function Rooms

The type of function room to be used for a food event depends on the nature of the session, its location in relation to other functions and the hotel traffic flow, and the kind of seating arrangement desired. Pay attention, too, to the decor, lighting and other decoration requested. And, thought must be given to heating and cooling controls.

All these factors must be considered when the convention service manager sits down with his or her counterpart in the convention organization to select a room for the function. Priorities may dictate that the most suitable room go to another event, but any room used for a food function must be able to provide satisfactory results (see Figure 14.4).

A reminder is in order here to note the time it takes to set up the food function room and clean it up afterwards. It is important to know whether the cleanup noises will disturb the meeting session going on next door. It may not be possible to avoid such proximity, but it shouldn't come about because no one thought about it. The clash of silver and china can be most distracting at a serious meeting and can reflect on the hotel's image.

On one occasion, the Salvation Army had a meeting scheduled next door to a luncheon for the governor of Hawaii. As the governor was presenting his opening remarks, the Salvation Army opened its meeting in the traditional way with a song to the resounding beat of the bass drum. Needless to say, the hotel's convention service manager gave greater consideration to a group's program after this incident.

Control Procedures

Most food functions are charged on a per-head basis. Every hotel should devise a head-count procedure to determine the actual number of **covers** (meals) served. Guesswork has no place in banquet billing. The charges should be agreed to in writing, and the menu selection should be indicated.

Many meeting planners prefer to use coupons or tickets. The delegate at registration is issued a coupon book with tear-out tickets for each function. There is need for caution if this system is suggested. Here are the two most common methods of ticket collection:

At the door — A table should be set up with a representative from the association and one from the hotel there to collect tickets.

At the banquet table — In this case, the waiter collects the tickets. This can be a touchy area if delegates do not have their tickets. A common delegate response is, "I left my ticket in my room." This is a difficult situation to police; if the hotel is paid for only the tickets collected, the waiter is forced to refuse service. Hotel personnel should be instructed what to do if a conferee shows up without the proper ticket.

Counting the dishes expected to be used in advance is another method of determining the number of covers served. The chef or convention service manager then counts the number of dishes that were not used and subtracts this from the first figure. Perhaps the best system is to totally count the people seated. The convention service manager and the meeting planner should both take counts. This should be done immediately after the entree has been served.

Some food functions, such as refreshment breaks and hospitality centers, obviously cannot be charged in this way. Spell out clearly the formula used. You may charge for coffee by the cup or by the gallon, fruit juice by the gallon, Danish pastry by the piece or by the tray.

Some canny sales managers will give away hors d'oeuvres or favors. In such cases, it enables them to close the deal at higher rates for rooms or meals. Psychologically, the

Figure 14.4. AD PROMOTING THE PROXIMITY OF THE KITCHEN TO MEETING SPACE.

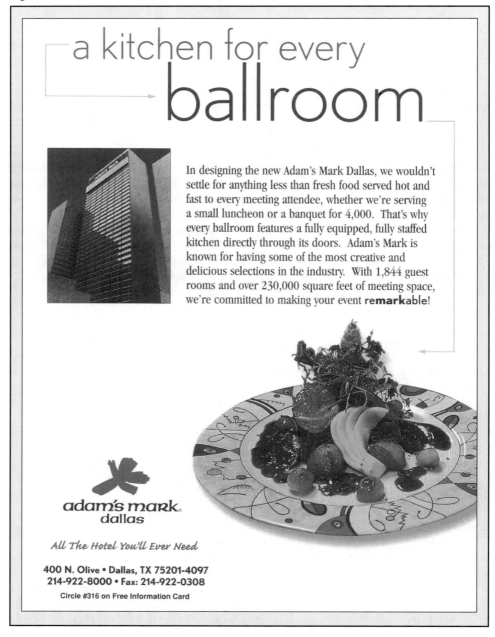

practice may make for a better presentation, and economically, it may represent less than the price advantage. In addition, the higher rate will bring in a further dividend should more people attend. The buffet and hors d'oeuvres are fixed costs on your part, while the higher rate for additional guests adds to your profit.

Small food functions are often tagged with additional charges. If the function is not large enough to cover labor and setup costs, hotels frequently add on to the bill. Figure 14.5 provides an example of banquet labor and miscellaneous charges.

Staffing

Hotels generally provide more waiters per guest as the price per cover increases. The minimum wait service for standard plated dinners is one waiter per 20 guests (at rounds of ten, one waiter per two tables; at rounds of eight, two waiters per five tables). French and Russian service generally require one server for every ten guests. For buffet meals, the standard is one wait staff to 40 persons for breakfast and one wait staff for 30 persons at lunch and dinner.

When price and service warrant it, the ratio may go as low as one to 12. If the menu calls for wine service poured by wait staff, the minimum is one waiter per 16 guests. For large parties, there should be one captain for every 150 guests.

Pre-meal briefings should be conducted by the captains for all large banquets. Menus, special service requirements, station assignments and other pertinent items should be reviewed. The setup and service of the head table should be assigned to the captains. Special attention is paid to silverware, glasses and proper arrangement of place settings.

Finally, the times for serving must be carefully controlled. It is necessary to adhere closely to scheduled meal times, so extension of cocktail parties should be kept to a minimum.

Figure 14.5. MISCELLANEOUS FUNCTION CHARGES.

Banquet Labor and Miscellaneous Charges

I. Food

A. Waiter Labor Charge...........$30.00
All functions with less than 20 guests

B. Overtime Charge, Waiter...$9.00/hr
Breakfast over 2 hours
Lunch over 3 hours
Dinner over 4 hours

C. Service Charge $10.00/extra table
For setting less than 10 covers per table.

D. Carver (Chef).............. $30.00/hour
After 2 hours

E. Housepersons.............$12.00/hour
4 hours minimum

F. Early Setup of Banquet
Rooms........$12.00/hour per waiter
Prior to meal functions

G. Porter....................$80.00/8 hours
If no food functions and meeting room complimentary.

II. Beverage

A. Bartender Charge —
If less than $150 sales, labor charge
....$70.00

B. Bar Supplies — If group supplies liquor
Cocktail Napkins
Stir Sticks $1.00/person
Assorted Bar Fruit
Mix - Sodas $2.50/quart
Bloody Mary Mix, Orange Juice
and Sweet and Sour........$8.00/quart
Blenders......................$10.00/each

C. Extra Bartender Charge $15.00/hour
4 hour minimum

D. Extra Barback Charge $74.00/8 hrs
8 hour minimum

Hotels frequently add on to the bill if the food function is not large enough to cover labor and setup costs.

Should Hotel Catering and Convention Services Departments Be Combined?
by Nora May, Assistant Director Convention Services, Sheraton Tucson El Conquistador

"UNISERVE" — the word used by the Sheraton Tucson El Conquistador to define a manager who specializes in catering AND convention services.

When it was announced that our hotel would be switching to the Uniserve concept, there was a definite concern that arose in my mind on how a person could "do it all!" After all, in my experience as Assistant Catering Director, catering alone took all of my time, including my personal family time, and now they want to add to my responsibilities? It seemed almost impossible.

Several years have passed since the Uniserve concept was put into action, and there is no doubt in my mind that this is THE BEST way to run the business. The positive aspects of this concept outweigh the negative aspects. As a matter of fact, I can't think of a negative aspect. These are the positives.

1. **Efficiency!** The meeting planner benefits from working with just one person. It simplifies the job. Plus it saves on communication time for the meeting planner and the Uniserve Convention Service Manager. When working the split method, often times I would get little notes on my desk from convention services that said something like, "Spoke with ABC Company on the phone. They want to add a continental breakfast to the meeting on Monday." It is incredible how much time it takes to find out exactly what this message means. Which meeting? There are 3 breakouts and a board meeting scheduled. How many people? First you go the the convention services person to obtain more details, and usually you have to call the client to confirm. Uniserve eliminates this type of time waste.

2. **Control!** As a sole person handling all of the group's conference requirements, one has a grasp of the whole picture. The Uniserve CSM is responsible for every detail of the Conference.

3. **Rewarding!** Opportunities and challenges continuously arise prior to a group's conference and during the conference. There is no getting around the problem-solving issues that tend to keep our blood flowing in the hospitality industry. That is what makes our jobs so interesting, exciting and sometimes exhausting. In Uniserve, when the group departs and the guests are grinning from ear-to-ear, sending compliments in every direction and the meeting planner re-books for the following year on the condition that YOU are assigned to work their file... rewarding? You bet!

4. **Free Time!** It's the best part of Uniserve! Prior to Uniserve, I literally spent 90% of my time at work. Family life barely existed. And although this type of job can be addicting, everyone has a right to a personal life. Uniserve permits a personal life. I say this with caution as this is dependent on a number of things.

(continued)

A. Adequate staffing is necessary in the Uniserve department. The Sheraton El Conquistador convention services department consists of four Uniserve people who handle the convention groups, one local catering manager, and a one-stop-shop manager who blocks, contracts and caters to groups of 20 sleeping rooms and under. Of course staffing varies from hotel to hotel and is dependent on the type of market the hotel pulls.

B. The convention files must be assigned strategically between managers to allow adequate days for paperwork between groups and allowing for *days off*.

C. The Banquet Manager, Banquet Captains and Conference Floor Manager *must* be trained to handle problem solving situations effectively and with confidence. The same captain should handle as many of the group's meal functions as possible so that the Meeting Planner can feel comfortable with familiar faces. It is the Uniserve Convention Services Manager's responsibility to introduce the client to the Banquet Manager, Captain and Conference Floor Manager prior to the function. After introductions are made and the banquet room is checked for details, the Uniserve CSM can depart if the Banquet Manager/Captain/Client are comfortable. If a client seems uncomfortable, or you personally know of a problem that might arise, the Uniserve CSM MUST be in attendance.

D. A daily meeting with the hotel staff to include the Chef, Banquet Manager, Conference Floor Manager and Uniserve CSMs is a MUST! The purpose of the daily meeting is to cover all functions in the hotel for the upcoming three days. Any questions about group's meetings and banquet functions should be brought up at this meeting and solved so that there are no questions as to room setups or service. This system prevents the necessity of constantly putting out fires prior to or during functions. With this type of detailing, the Uniserve CSM can feel confident when turning the functions over to the Banquet Manager, Captain and Conference Floor Manager.

I cannot claim that the Uniserve system will work for all hotels. However, I believe there are many hotels who could use this system and it would relieve many of those catering and convention service managers who are "burned out."

Uniserve or Duoserve

The food and beverage service is generally handled in one of two ways by hotels. In a **uniserve** system, the meeting planner makes all arrangements for both function space and food and beverage through one service contact, the convention service manager. In this system the banquet/catering department reports to convention services. With a **duoserve** system, the food and beverage responsibilities are separated from the scheduling of function space. In this case meeting planners must work with the banquet/catering department for their food and beverage requests and with the convention services department for their function room needs. When the duoserve approach is used the banquet/catering personnel generally report to the food and beverage director. As we indicated earlier, most meeting planners want to deal with only one contact person at a hotel. The assistant director of convention services at the Sheraton Tucson El Conquistador makes a strong case for the uniserve system (see box titled "Should Hotel Catering and Convention Services Departments Be Combined?").

Beverage Service

More discontent has been voiced over beverage service and charges than over most factors of a convention. Of all the price policies at a convention, the liquor arrangement brings the loudest and most frequent outcry.

Unfortunately, meeting planners or the hosts at hospitality suites usually specify their favorite brands of liquor, and they are familiar with package store prices. Many planners and hosts resent what they consider to be unfair markups on name-brand liquor by the hotel. Some hotels have taken to charging the same prices as local liquor stores, but most have a much higher rate — two or three times the cost. This is a management decision. The additional revenue gained by marking up must be weighed against the frequent ill will engendered.

Types of Setups

A number of beverage arrangements are used in catering to private parties. We will discuss the four most common procedures specified by meeting planners.

The first and most typical type of bar is the **host bar**, where the guests are free to drink the beverages and the host pays the bill at the end of the function. Also called an *open bar*, this is most frequently used by corporate meeting planners. This type of bar is stocked to prepare for all types of drinks and is staffed by a bartender. A purchase amount is almost always guaranteed. If, for example, at least $300 worth of beverage is not consumed, the host will pay for what was consumed, plus an additional amount to cover labor. Figure 14.5 shows typical labor costs for beverage service.

The second most common arrangement is the **cash bar**, also called the *C.O.D. Bar* and a *no-host bar*. Each person pays for his or her own drinks. A minimum guarantee is also specified by the hotel in this case.

Coupon sales are used at many private parties. Delegates buy tickets or coupons ahead of time and give them to the bartender when the drinks are served. The coupons may be sold by the hotel management or the host organization. Coupon sales eliminate the use of cash and the need for a cashier at the function.

Stanley Stearman, executive vice-president of the National Society of Public Accountants, said of the use of coupons for beverage functions:

> "We give everyone two drink tickets along with their banquet ticket. They are actually perforated stubs which are turned in to the bartender in return for drinks. Not only does this method limit consumption to two drinks per person, but it gives me control over my liquor costs. I pay a certain amount for each stub that has been turned in. The only disadvantage to me is that I have to pay full price even if someone redeems his stub for a soft drink."[4]

The South Coast Plaza in Costa Mesa, California, uses still a different method in servicing private parties. The **captain's bar** is a self-service or make-your-own drink bar that has been stocked with full bottles of liquor and mixes needed to make all the basic bar drinks. This bar is always hosted. The meeting planner and the convention service manager inventory the bar before and after the party, and the association is charged for how much is consumed. There is no guarantee on this type of setup because there is no bartender labor cost.

Hospitality Suites

Sales prospects are drawn by complimentary beverages at the end of a day to exhibitor's hospitality suites. A **hospitality suite** may also be hosted by the planner as a way to build good will.

Some meeting planners and exhibitors wish to avoid what they consider to be excessive prices charged by the hotel by bringing in liquor purchased outside the hotel. They then order mixers, ice and glasses from room service. Hotels have varying policies regarding such action. Some hotels have a **corkage** charge to cover the use of liquor that is purchased elsewhere. Some have two sets of prices for the setups — a higher rate if the order is not accompanied by liquor orders; a lower rate if it is. It eliminates many arguments if the policy is clearly spelled out to the meeting planner and the guests.

Union regulations often dictate the circumstances under which a bartender must be employed. Tell your client in advance about such regulations. Explain the hours involved, overtime charges and other pertinent details. Spell out the circumstances under which no such help is required. The choice should be the customer's. Include information about gratuities and taxes.

Brands

Most hotels offer a selection of standard (house) brands to the meeting planner. Upon request, special brands may be used. This depends on suitable notice and the agreement of the hotel. When a hotel uses house brands, there should be clear notification. Sometimes, there is a different price for house brands than for a **call brand**; sometimes the prices are the same. But the meeting planner must be informed and involved in the decision. This is another example of a frequent complaint that could be avoided through timely communication.

Pricing Methods

Liquor charges can be figured *by the hour, by the bottle* or *by the individual drink*. Whichever is used, make sure that someone on the convention staff has been designated to tally up after the affair with a designated member of the hotel staff. This will help avoid misunderstandings after the event and avoid last minute searching for someone of authority on the convention management staff to corroborate the tally.

Meeting planners often ask advice on how much liquor will be needed. The consumption of liquor varies, of course, with the makeup of the attendees. A chart such as the one shown in Figure 14.6 should prove helpful to you and your customers in making such decisions.

By the Hour. When liquor is priced *by the hour*, a flat rate is charged for each person present during a specified period of time. Sometimes a flat rate is charged for a cocktail party of a specified time period and additional time is charged on an hourly basis. At other times the rate is given only as an hourly charge. If food is to be served, what kind and how much must be discussed and listed in the agreement.

From the meeting planner's perspective, this flat rate per person can be the simplest, but not necessarily the cheapest pricing method. Unless the group has a lot of drinkers, this is usually an expensive plan.

If your hourly charge is based also on the number in attendance, you will need a way to determine the accuracy of the count. Collecting tickets or invitations at the door is one way to do this.

Extension of the time period and the admission of people who do not have tickets require approval by an authorized person. The head count and the time period should be acknowledged immediately after the event by having the authorized person initial the tally.

By the Bottle. The convention organizer may prefer to pay *by the bottle* consumed. Liquor by the bottle can be cost-effective for large groups. If you are charging $3.00 per drink and serving one-ounce drinks from a fifth, the meeting group pays $75.00 for the bottle (25 drinks per fifth). Whereas a by the bottle charge is generally $40 to $50.

The by-the-bottle system is very popular for hospitality suites, both with and without bartenders. This system calls for charges on all bottles opened regardless of how much of the contents is consumed. Some hotels permit the host to keep the opened bottles; others do not. Some hotels agree to store opened bottles of liquor from one reception and use them for the group's next reception. Obviously, the bartender must be made aware of the arrangement, and it must be made part of the work order for the beverage event.

Sometimes the charges for the bartender are part of the per-bottle price. If so, this should be indicated in the work order or agreement; if not, list the rates and hours.

Make sure that the liquor supply given is stored securely. Good hotel people assist their guests in arranging storage. It is imperative that both the hotel and the convention organization have people designated to tally and record the number of bottles used and returned for credit. In some cases, meeting planners will personally count the number of bottles prior to the start of the reception and affix a stamp or pressure sensitive label to each bottle to prevent paying for empties that were not from the group.

When buying liquor by the bottle, meeting planners often request the banquet bars be closed in staggered order, moving the partials from one to the other (this is termed *marrying* the bars). Their instructions also frequently call for the bartenders to pour measured drinks, as bartenders could pad the bill by overpouring.

Food may be served, but is charged separately. And, under certain conditions, there may be a room charge. Much depends on the anticipated volume and the basic agreement under which the event takes place.

By the Drink. Charges can also be made *by the drink* on the basis of the individual drinks served. There should be an agreement on the size of the drink to be poured, and the bartenders so instructed. These rates include the mandatory use of bartender service. No less than one bartender for every 75 guests is the rule of thumb.

This arrangement is used by many meeting planners, especially those planning for small groups. Most meeting planners feel the most economical bar for receptions of under 100 persons is by the drink; for over 100 persons, by the bottle. The chart in Figure 14.6 is helpful if estimates are requested, but be sure to point out that these are only *estimates*.

Figure 14.6. GUIDE TO HELP ESTIMATE THE AMOUNT OF LIQUOR AND SERVICE NEEDED FOR A BEVERAGE FUNCTION.

Reception Drink and Service Estimator

Based on an all-male attendance and easy access to bars. With 50% female attendance, average is 2 1/2 to 3 per hour; with 100% female attendance, average is 2 to 2 1/2 per hour.

Number of Guests	1/2 hr	3/4 hr	One hr	1 1/4 hrs	1 1/2 hrs	1 3/4 hrs	Two hrs
25-55	2	3	3 3/4	4	4 1/4	4 1/2	4 3/4
60-104	2	3	3 3/4	4	4	4 1/2	4 3/4
105-225	1 3/4	2 1/2	3	3 1/2	4	4	4 1/2
230-300	1 1/2	2	2 1/2	2 3/4	3	3 1/4	3 1/2
315 & up	1 1/2	2	2 1/2	2 3/4	3	3 1/4	3 1/2

Reception Service Estimator

Number of Guests	Number of bartenders	Number of waiters with food	Number of waiters without food
25-100	1	2	1
105-205	2	3	2
215-325	3	3	2
350-475	4	4	3

Drink Estimator

Bottle size	Drink size	Number of drinks
4/5 quart	1 oz.	25
4/5 quart	1 1/4 oz.	20
4/5 quart	1 1/2 oz.	17
Quart	1 oz.	31
Quart	1 1/4 oz.	25
Quart	1 1/2 oz.	21

Source: Reprinted with permission from The Schenley Guide to Professional Hosting. Published by Schenley Affiliated Brands Corp.

The guests may pay for drinks in cash or prepaid coupons, or the host may pay for it all. Food charges are a separate item, and there may be a room charge. Give the meeting planner advance notice of gratuities, taxes and a schedule of bartenders' work regulations.

Beverage Control

Rigid procedures for issuing liquor and the use of it should be maintained. The banquet department is generally responsible for issuing the liquor. Since it is impossible to judge how much or what kind of liquor will be preferred, it is customary to stock 25 percent over what the group is estimated to consume. This policy eliminates shortages, but it must be controlled.

The excess must be returned to the storeroom at the end of the function. Special banquet requisition forms are used for private parties, showing all the bottles issued, consumed and returned. Immediately after each function all bottles — full, empty and partially used — should be accounted for.

The Renaissance Hotel uses the requisition form shown in Figure 14.7. The banquet manager uses this form for each function, showing the number of bottles originally issued, any additional issues, and all returns. Each bottle issued is marked with a distinctive means of identification. At the end of the party, the banquet manager totals the requisition by determining the amount of each item consumed and its price and then making the appropriate extensions. The total is transferred to the banquet guest check, which is verified and signed by the meeting planner. A percentage of the check total is usually added to the bill as a gratuity for the staff.

Host Bar Control. Because cash is not taken with host or open bars, they are easiest to control. Opened bottles of liquor may either be returned to the storeroom for credit or bought by the meeting planner. If the meeting planner takes the open bottles, this should be noted on the requisition sheet, along with the name of the guest. Some groups buy the "cracked" bottles but prefer that the hotel hold the bottles in storage for them. Such bottles should be clearly marked and given to the guest upon request.

Cash Bar Control. This arrangement requires the most rigid controls. A bartender should not be allowed to take cash, as he would then be controlling both cash receipts and the issuing of liquor. A less-than-honest bartender could pour smaller than average drinks and pocket the cash on every fourth or fifth drink without being detected. An accurate count requires a control system.

Cash bars necessitate at least two employees — a bartender and a cashier. At the end of the party, cash sales should be equated with the amount of merchandise consumed. This system also enables the bartender to concentrate on pouring drinks and giving rapid service.

Coupon Sales Control. A cashier is not necessary if the meeting planner issues tickets prior to the event. The bartenders collect tickets for the drinks and turn them over to the banquet manager. The manager, in turn, inventories the bar before and after the function and compares the consumption of liquor with the tickets collected.

If tickets are to be sold at the party, a cashier will be needed, and cash banks must be issued. The banquet manager should issue numbered tickets to the cashier and get them back, along with the cash, when the function is completed. He can then verify the number of tickets issued with the cash receipts.

Automated Bars. Several hotels are making use of automated bar systems. A long-standing complaint of meeting planners is the tendency of bartenders to over-pour in host bar setups. They feel the staff members are encouraged to pour on the heavy side because their tips are figured as a percentage of sales. Another problem area is the counting and storing of open bottles. Both of these problems are eliminated with automated bars.

Automated bars operate much like soda bars, with individual push buttons for each liquor item — vodka, gin, bourbon, scotch, rye, etc. Quart bottles are placed upside down in the wells and dispensed by a vacuum system. Each bottle has its own dispensing unit and meter. The size of the drink is determined by the meeting planner, and the dispensing unit is set accordingly. The meters are checked and recorded before and after the party, with the difference being the amount consumed.

The control feature offered by the metered bars is what makes them attractive to both the meeting planner and the hotel. They provide a consistent drink and eliminate overpouring, but they are not without their limitations. The machine dispenses only the alcohol; mixed and blended drinks still must be prepared by a bartender. And only eight

Figure 14.7. BAR REQUISITION FORM.

RAMADA RENAISSANCE HOTEL

BANQUET WINE/LIQUOR REQUISITION

NO. 001399

DATE *8-25-*   DAY OF WEEK *MONDAY*   TIME *6:00 PM*

FUNCTION *RECEPTION*   ROOM *Foyer / Renaissance Ballroom*

ORGANIZATION NAME *Singer*

BANQUET CHECK # *06272*

BANQUET EVENT ORDER # *02135*

TENDERS IN CHARGE *Bill / Cheryle*

CLIENT'S ACCOUNT # *12948*

NUMBER OF GUESTS *275*

MANNER OF SALE: ☑ BY DRINK ☐ BY BOTTLE ☐ BY HOUR

TYPE OF BEVERAGE: ☐ PREMIUM ☑ HOUSE ☐ SPECIAL LIST

TYPE OF SALE: ☑ HOSTED ☐ CASH BAR

COST

CODE	DESCRIPTION	ISSUED QUANT.	ISSUED SIZE	RETD BOTT.	USED BOTT.	NO. DRINKS	DRINK PRICE	TOTAL	LIQUOR	WINE	MISC	% POT.
	HOUSE BOURBON	3		1.7	1.3	43	3.00	129.00	8.35			6.5%
	HOUSE SCOTCH	3		1.9	1.1							
	HOUSE GIN	4		2.4	1.6							
	HOUSE VODKA	4		1.1	29							
	HOUSE BRANDY	2		1.8	.2							
	HOUSE RUM	2		1.6	.4							
	HOUSE TEQUILA	2		1.3	.7							
	HOUSE WHISKEY	2		1.8	.2							
	HOUSE WHITE WINE	18		2	16							
	HOUSE RED WINE	6		3	3							
	MILLER LITE BEER	24		5	19							
	HEINEKEN BEER											
	PREMIUM BOURBON											
	PREMIUM SCOTCH											
	PREMIUM GIN											
	PREMIUM VODKA											
	PREMIUM BRANDY											
	PREMIUM WHISKEY											
	PREMIUM TEQUILA											
	PREMIUM RUM											
TOTALS												

ISSUED BY _____ RETURNED BY _____ APPROVED BY _____

RECEIVED BY _____ RECEIVED BY _____

WHITE - FOOD AND BEVERAGE CONTROL   CANARY - BANQUET MAITRE D'   GOLDEN ROD - BEVERAGE MGR.

This form details the number of bottles issued, consumed, and returned. The form also specifies the pricing method to be used (by drink, by bottle, by hour), the type of brand (premium, house, special list), and the type of setup (hosted, cash bar).

bottles can be filled on most units, limiting the choice of drinks. Some observers also say that metered bars are impersonal, lending a mechanical atmosphere to cocktail parties.

Liquor Liability. Can a hotel be held liable to an innocent third party for wrongful acts of an intoxicated attendee? The answer depends on the individual state, but due to alcohol related automobile accidents, many states have passed acts that impose liability on the dispenser of alcohol sold illegally, terming a sale is illegal if to a minor, intoxicated person or known alcoholic. Management must take reasonable care in serving alcoholic beverages at functions. Managers should be trained to be alert to potential problems with intoxicated patrons and how to deal with unruly meeting attendees. A typical contract clause might read:

If alcoholic beverages are to be served on the Hotel premises (or elsewhere under the Hotel's alcoholic beverage license) the Hotel will require that beverages be dispensed only by Hotel servers and bartenders. The Hotel's license requires the Hotel to (1) request identification (Photo ID) of any person of questionable age and refuse service if the person is either under age or proper identification cannot be produced and (2) refuse alcoholic beverage service to any person who, in the Hotel's judgment, appears intoxicated.

Some provisions are stricter, prohibiting attendees from bringing alcoholic beverages into the hotel from outside:

Alcoholic beverages may not be brought into the hotel from outside sources. The sales, service and consumption of alcoholic beverages are regulated by the State Alcoholic Beverage Commission. The Hotel, as a licensee, is subject to the regulations promulgated by the Commission, violations of which may jeopardize the Hotel's license. Consequently, it is the Hotel's policy that alcoholic beverages may not be brought into the hotel from outside sources.

Staffing and Logistics. Staff one bartender per 75 to 100 people. When food is served at receptions, staff one server per 50 people, and one waiter per 100 people for receptions without food service.

Bar locations will vary according to the room's dimensions and the placement of other provisions such as staging, dance floors and buffet tables. Generally, one bar station is required for every 75-100 guests. Avoid grouping bars too close together. With large receptions requiring several beverage stations, open those bars farthest from the entrance first in order to bring people into the room. This helps to spread the crowds.

Meeting planners often request that multi-station bars be consolidated or "married." One or two stations might be closed 10 to 15 minutes before the party ends and partials taken to one of the others.

Post-Function Actions

Prompt action must be taken at the end of each food function to eliminate possible billing difficulties and to bring each function segment to a satisfactory close.

If billing is based on attendance, the captain in charge should tally the number of persons served or the number of tickets collected and have the authorized convention person sign an acknowledgment of the total. Make sure the person signing is designated in writing.

If beverages were served, tally the unopened bottles of liquor and/or soft drinks and have the amount acknowledged by signature. Bottles to be returned for credit must be signed for.

Most convention groups use a master billing account for the food functions. If the terms are cash, the money or check should be presented when the tally is certified as correct. If cash is collected by the organization, the hotel should provide a safe place for it or accept it in payment and give a suitable receipt.

Place a summary of the food functions in the file folder for the analysis of the convention.

In-House Coodination: Large vs. Small

We have referred to the convention service manager as the person who coordinates the convention. This person, however, does not do it all; many departments are involved. The competence of the department heads determines the extent to which the convention service manager becomes involved. If the reservations, front-desk and catering managers are on top of their jobs, the convention service manager's headaches are minimized. If not, the convention service manager must spend more time overseeing the operation.

Role of the Catering Manager

The in-house coordination at *small properties* is generally not handled the same way as at larger properties; the major difference is the role played by the *catering manager.* At larger properties catering managers are only in charge of food and beverage; seldom do they become involved in sales and seldom are they required to account for more than the food and beverage service. But at small properties, their areas of responsibility branch out.

A property with insufficient sales volume to justify carrying a convention coordinator must nevertheless give one person that responsibility. Usually, it is the banquet or catering manager who wears two hats: head of his or her department and head of group business.

What distinguishes a large property from a small one? There is no definition, but hotels with fewer than 250 guest rooms might well handle servicing differently than larger ones.

Figure 14.8 gives a catering manager's job description adapted from the operating manual of Doubletree Hotels, whose hotels range from 140 to 300 guest rooms and are typical of such properties whose catering managers double as convention service managers.

Servicing and Selling

The division between servicing and selling is less pronounced at small hotels than at large ones. As we discussed in Chapter 10, there is wide variation among hotels in the extent to which the sales department participates in servicing.

At smaller hotels, servicing and sales, particularly of food and beverage functions, are more likely to be handled by the same person. Part of the catering manager's job might be to actively solicit and schedule group banquet business. Often the catering manager is

Figure 14.8. JOB DESCRIPTION OF A CATERING MANAGER.

Catering Manager's Job Description

1. Basic Function
To service all phases of group meeting/banquet functions; coordinate these activities on a daily basis; assist clients in program planning and menu selection; solicit local group catering business.

2. General Responsibility
To maintain the services and reputation of Doubletree and act as management representative to group clients.

3. Specific Responsibilities

a. To maintain function book. Coordinate the booking of all meeting space with the Sales Department.
b. To solicit local food and beverage functions.
c. To coordinate with all group meeting/banquet planners their specific group requirements with the services and facilities offered.
d. To confirm all details relative to group functions with meeting/banquet planners.
e. To distribute to the necessary inter-hotel departments detailed information relative to group activities.
f. To supervise and coordinate all phases of catering, hiring and training programs.
g. To supervise and coordinate daily operation of meeting/banquet setups and service.
h. To assist in menu planning, preparation and pricing.
i. To assist in referrals to the Sales Department and in booking group activities.
j. To set up and maintain catering files.
k. To be responsive to group requests/needs while in the hotel.
l. To work toward achieving Annual Plan figures relating to the Catering Department (revenues, labor percentages, average checks, covers, etc.)
m. To handle all scheduling and coverage for the servicing of catering functions.

4. Organizational Relationship and Authority
Is directly responsible and accountable to the Food and Beverage Manager. Responsible for coordination with kitchen, catering service personnel and accounting.

As seen by these duties detailed by the Doubletree Hotels, the catering manager often serves as the convention service manager at small properties.
Source: Courtesy of Doubletree, Inc.

given charge of the function book. This is fine as long as the lines of authority, responsibility and communication are clearly understood.

The problem arises when the left hand does not know what the right hand is doing; when the sales department books a convention that conflicts with the catering department's efforts. The problem is likely to be acute when the two departments are located in different areas of the hotel. In this case, the sales department rarely sees the function book and must rely on the phone or memos to communicate with the catering department. There may even be inter-departmental rivalry for function space, with each trying to show greater sales and profit.

Communication and Cooperation

Servicing requires clear communication channels at small properties. When the property has a convention service manager, there is generally good cooperation, with one independent person coordinating the efforts of other departments. But when the catering manager serves as the coordinator, there seems to be more autonomy of departments. The catering manager may be unfamiliar with the problems in the front of the house; reservation and front office departments lack understanding of the handling of food and beverage.

Such a situation is not necessarily detrimental, as long as each department does its job and there is good inter-departmental communication. The difficulty may arise when the association executive questions the hotel's handling of his or her membership's registration. If the catering manager is the planner's contact in the hotel, the planner may find little relief for the problem. Perhaps the catering manager is too busy with the upcoming dinner or has not been schooled in the procedure of registering guests. Or perhaps — and this is a more common problem — the catering manager doesn't have the authority to go to the rooms department to straighten out the situation. The meeting planner's nightmare is a contact without the muscle to get the job done.

The autonomy of departments also leads to the lack of specification sheets, which we mentioned in Chapter 12 as the backbone of control and communication in servicing. Substituting for the specification sheets are memos from the sales department to the rooms department and individual function sheets prepared by the catering manager for all meeting room and food and beverage setups. Memos and function sheets are fine ways of communicating, but a comprehensive schedule of the overall convention program is still needed.

"PUTTING IT ALL TOGETHER"

Your property has been approached by the corporate office of a large multi-level marketing company that wishes to hold a convention for approximately 600 distributors and spouses. While funds are unlimited, the meeting planner is totally inexperienced and will need your help to plan a successful function.

At this time, plans are sketchy. The meeting planner does want to incorporate the company's "Pot of Gold" promotion into an Awards Banquet and to stage a luau to celebrate the vacations won by the company's top five distributors. The meeting planner is open to your suggestions regarding creative menus for these two functions, but wants to serve traditional American fare for the buffets and other meal functions.

The convention will run from Wednesday afternoon through Sunday afternoon. Events currently being considered are:

Wednesday	(Afternoon)	**Registration**
	(Evening)	Registration and **Hospitality Suite**
		Dinner on own

Thursday	(Morning)	**Three seminars** (Approx. 100 people each room.) **Refreshment Break**
	(Afternoon)	**Three seminars** (Approx.100 people each room) **Refreshment Break**
	(Evening)	**Buffet Dinner** (Approx. 500 attendees)
Friday	(Morning)	Same as Thursday
	(Afternoon)	**Buffet lunch** (Approx. 500 attendees)
	(Afternoon)	Same as Thursday
	(Evening)	**Directors Dinner** (24 in attendance) Other attendees: optional dinner show (on own)
Saturday	(Morning)	**President's Breakfast** (approx. 300 attendees) **General Session** (600 attendees) Lunch on own
	(Afternoon)	**Continuation of General Session**
	(Evening)	**Awards Banquet**, **Entertainment** (music and dancing) (600 attendees)
Sunday	(Morning)	Breakfast on own
	(Afternoon)	**Farewell Luau** (Approx. 350 attendees)

Using what you have learned in Chapters 12, 13 and 14, develop a presentation that you will use in your pre-convention planning session with the meeting planner. Cover the following areas:

1. A proposal detailing what food and beverages could be offered at the food functions (hospitality suite, refreshment breaks, buffet lunch and dinner, the directors dinner, president's breakfast, the awards banquet and luau). Include how the client could be charged for each function.
2. An outline of what your property can offer in the way of decorations, staffing, and meeting requirements (musicians, additional entertainment, staging, lighting, etc.) for the awards banquet and the luau. Provide room set-up plans detailing suggested seating, food service and entertainment area options.
3. A sample room set-up for the seminars and the general session. Include the style of seating, a list of available audiovisual equipment, and staffing (set-up, registration personnel, etc.) that your property can provide.

Chapter Summary:

Food functions are an integral part of most meetings, and, as we learned in Chapters 4 and 5, both association and corporate meeting planners rate the quality of foodservice as "very important" in their selection of meeting facilities. And, food and beverage functions are second only to guestrooms in generating revenue at most convention hotels.

So, while hotel sales and service people are generally primarily concerned with filling guestrooms, it is imperative that convention sales and service managers also be knowledgeable in the food and beverage area.

In addition to food and beverage functions, the success of a meeting is often judged by its impact on attendees. In today's world of high technology, it is a rare delegate who leaves a meeting whose highlight was a simple flip chart presentation. In the next chapter, we will take a look at how hotels are using today's sophisticated audiovisual equipment to enhance both large and small meetings and generate repeat sales for the property.

Endnotes:

1. *Meetings and Conventions*, March 1999, p. 21.
2. Jeanne O'Brien, "Sheraton Reveals New Food & Beverage Program," *Meeting News*, June 12, 1995, p. 10.
3. Toni Giovanetti, "A La Carte Catering Emerges as the Favored Choice of Meeting Planners," *Hotel Business*, August 7-20, pps. 25-27.
4. Bob Skalnik, "Liquor Control," *Association and Society Manager*. Copyright Barrington Publications.

Additional References:

• <u>On-Premise Catering,</u> Patti Shock and John Stefanelli, John Wiley and Sons, 2001.
  www.hospitality@wiley.com
• Controlling Alcohol Risks Effectively (CARE).
  www.ei-ahla-org/care.index.htm

Internet Sites:

For additional information on the firms and organizations discussed in this chapter, visit the following Internet sites. The Web addresses listed are current as of January 2001. Addresses may change, however; if a site is not available at address below, a search engine can be used to access its new location.

The Catering Connection - www.caterconnect.com
Chef's Store - www.chefstore.com
Cuisine - www. cuisinenet.com
Food Net - www.foodnet.com
Internet Food Channel - www.foodchannel.com
National Association of Catering Executives (NACE) - www.nace.net
Training for Intervention Procedures by Servers of Alcohol (TIPS) - www.gettips.com
Virtual Vineyards - www.virtualvin.com

Study Questions:

1. Name several types of food and beverage functions commonly requested by meeting planners. Why is it necessary to have a separate function sheet for each?
2. What trends have affected the types of food served at functions? How have hotels responded to these trends?
3. What types of service are used for food functions? What factors determine the most effective type of service for a function?
4. Discuss the procedures used in establishing a guarantee for food functions. In what ways is attendance monitored to ensure the guarantee has been met?
5. What three different pricing methods are used to bill for liquor? How is control maintained for billing purposes?
6. Discuss the staffing and logistics common to beverage functions.
7. How does control of the food and beverage function differ between large and small properties? Distinguish between the role of catering manager and convention service manager.

Key Terms:

Á la carte catering. Catered events in which guests may choose from a number of entrees.

Buffet service. A presentation of several food items from which the guests choose and serve themselves.

Call brand. Brand name liquor, distinguished from "house brand," selected by customer according to personal preference.

Captain's bar. Self service bar where guests make their own drinks. This type of bar is always hosted.

Cash bar. Also called a no-host bar, at which all participants pay for their own drinks.

Corkage. Charge that covers the use of liquor that is not purchased on the property. This charge usually includes cost of labor, ice, glassware and mixers.

Coupon sales. Delegates at a function buy drink tickets from the hotel or from the host organization.

Covers. The number of meals served at a meal function.

Duoserve. A meeting service system in which food and beverage responsibilities are handled by catering while other aspects of servicing the group are handled by the convention service manager. Because responsibilities are separated, meeting planners have two hotel contacts.

French service. Food service in which items are prepared tableside from a cart or gueridon.

Guarantee. The minimum number of meals to be paid for by the client, even if some are not consumed. Usually the hotel requires the planner to set this number 48 hours prior to the event.

Hospitality suite. Guestroom/suite used for receptions and entertainment. Usually stocked with beverages and light food. Often used by exhibitors at trade shows to entertain and sell delegates on their firm's products.

Host bar. Beverage plan for banquets or other functions in which the guests do not pay for drinks; the host is charged either by the drink or by the bottle. Also called an open bar.

Plate service. Food is arranged on plates in the kitchen and brought to the guests.

Pre-set service. Placement of some foods on banquet tables prior to the seating of the guests.

Russian Service. Food is served on platters to guests at their tables.

Uniserve. A meeting service system in which the meeting planner makes arrangement for both function space and food and beverage through one service contact, the conventiozn service manager.

Learning Objectives:

This portion of your text introduces you to the wide variety of audiovisual equipment available to meeting planners today. We will also discuss the best options for meeting AV needs and provide guidelines for charging for audiovisual equipment and service. When you have studied this chapter, you will:

- Be able to describe the common types of audiovisual equipment and tell when each type is commonly used.

- Be able to detail the advantages and disadvantages of owning expensive audiovisual equipment versus contracting with outside sources for audiovisual needs.

- Understand how signs and notices are used by meeting planners and be able to discuss hotel procedures used to price and control the use of signage.

Outline

Outside or Inside ?
- Audiovisual Specialists
- In-House Equipment

Types of Audiovisual Equipment
- Sound Systems
- Lighting
- Lecterns
- Screens
- Slide Projectors
- Overhead Projectors
- Rearview Projection
- Motion Picture Film Projectors
- Videotape Projectors
- Projection Systems for Computer Presentations
- Projector Stands
- Multimedia Presentations
- Simultaneous Interpretations
- Virtual Conferencing
- Spare Parts
- Other Presentation Devices

Charging for Audiovisual Equipment

Union Regulations

Signs and Notices
- Hotel Rules
- Sign Responsibility
- Price Schedule
- Locations

Understanding Audiovisual Requirements

Lee Sterbens
Director of Sales, Creative Services Division
Greyhound Exposition Services

"In the field of communications and information exchange, equipment and the technology used to operate it are changing rapidly. More and more people are using computers interfaced with monitors and video projectors to exchange information, compared to a few years ago when slides and transparencies were the norm. While convention service managers are rarely expected to be expert audiovisual technicians, they should be able to assist meeting planners with the selection of appropriate space and proper audiovisual equipment. Having a basic understanding of what equipment is required to achieve the desired goal will allow you to better serve your meeting groups and yourself."

15

Audiovisual Requiremnets

I
t is a rare meeting today that doesn't incorporate an audiovisual presentation some-where in its program. The more sophisticated users of AV systems require little help from the hotel staff. They know precisely what equipment they need and what is required in the facility. They bring their own equipment or contact an AV service company for support.

In the past, most meeting needs were fairly simple. Meeting planners simply re-quested a few microphones, a slide projector and screen, a few flip charts and an occasional movie projector. Over the past two decades, however, technological developments in com-munication have led to audiovisual equipment and techniques that have greatly enhanced the meetings market. And today's sophisticated meeting planners want to take full advan-tage of these advanced capabilities (see Figure 15.1). It is not unusual for a meeting planner to request teleconferencing equipment, videocassette players, personal computers and even multivisual synthesizers, quadraphonic sound and total immersion environments.

The meeting planner who is less knowledgeable about audiovisual systems will need support. Someone on the hotel staff should at least be familiar with, if not expert at, AV systems to provide such service or to help the planner get it locally. It is not realistic to expect convention sales and service personnel to be expert in every facet of the convention business, but all, especially the convention service manager, should keep abreast of new developments as well as be conversant in the terminology and requirements of today's AV technology.

Outside or Inside?

Since audiovisual equipment plays such a vital part in today's meetings business, proper-ties are faced with the dilemma of how to make AV equipment available. Is it feasible to maintain a large in-house inventory, and, if so, what should be stocked? Or, would it be more cost-effective to have an outside AV firm provide the requested equipment? Or, as yet a third alternative, should the most commonly used items be stocked and outside AV firms be called upon to supply any special equipment requested by the meeting planner? In this section, we will take a look at the advantages and disadvantages of supplying AV equip-ment from outside sources or in-house (see box titled "Outside or Inside") and look at what factors figure into a property's decision on meeting AV requirements.

Audiovisual Specialists

Many hotel managers prefer to use a local AV service organization rather than cope with this area in-house. Outside rental firms are used when:

- the hotel lacks adequate storage space.
- equipment is used so infrequently that investment in a piece cannot be justified.
- the call for certain equipment, such as video projectors, is so heavy that it is not feasible for a hotel to inventory so many pieces.

Figure 15.1. TODAY'S "WIRED" MEETING ROOMS.

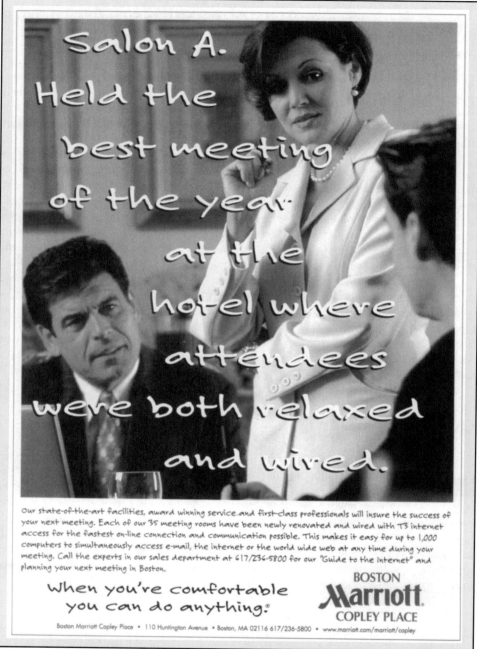

Today's hotels are advertising their ability to meet the needs of meeting planners with meeting rooms and equipment designed for the high-tech meetings common today. Note that this ad promotes T3 Internet access to enable attendees to access e-mail and the Web during the meeting.

When an outside firm is used, many convention service managers prefer to order the equipment themselves rather than have the association do it. There are three reasons for this. First, they are assured that the equipment will arrive in plenty of time to set it up. Second, they can determine how large to set the stage, since the screen is often placed on a raised platform. A third, not so admirable, reason is that AV companies often pay a commission to hotels that book them instead of the competition.

An outside company offers the hotel's client a specialist with a full staff and inventory of equipment. An expert staff can be relied upon to maintain the equipment and to handle any on-the-scene malfunctions. Many hotel managers have said that they would install an inventory of such equipment only when the volume of such rental would enable them to hire at least one full-time specialist to manage a small department. That person would assist in planning, setup, operation and service.

This is sound thinking when the hotel is in an area with good service companies. But in the more remote resort areas, the nearest AV dealer may be some distance away. If that is the case, last-minute malfunctions or additional needs can constitute a severe problem. Large conventions often contract with AV service companies that will go anywhere to handle the convention. The fees they charge are usually a small price for the convention organization to pay for a smooth AV presentation.

But it is not practical to call in such organizations for the small meeting. Yet some meetings, particularly training ones, use a great deal of such equipment and need some assistance.

Outside or Inside

Hotels are faced with the decision of either owning AV equipment and leasing it to the meeting group or entrusting the AV needs of a group to an outside firm. The final decision will vary depending on individual property needs, and the following factors should be taken into consideration when making that decision.

Advantages of Using an AV Company Outside the Hotel

1. Audiovisual equipment is expensive. In the event of theft or lost items, the outside firm, rather than the hotel, would incur the loss.
2. Many audiovisual pieces are used so infrequently that the cost of maintaining an inventory would be prohibitive.
3. The cost of maintaining and repairing equipment is expensive and may not justify the hiring of a staff specialist to service audiovisual items.
4. With advances in audiovisual equipment, some items may become obsolete and require additional expenditure by the hotel.

Advantages of Owning AV Equipment and Leasing it to the Meeting Group

1. There may be a lack of suppliers in the area, or it may be difficult to rent a particular piece.
2. The property can purchase pieces that best meet its need rather than have to rely on an outside contractor whose equipment may not be adequate.
3. The property has greater control over the quality of equipment if it owns it. Rental property may have been misused and may not function properly.
4. The property directly benefits from renting its own equipment to meeting groups, rather than turning the profits over to an outside firm.

In-House Equipment

If an arrangement with a local AV service company cannot be made, a hotel may decide to stock at least the basic AV requirements. Rick Stanfield, senior vice president of Opryland Lodging Group, cautions:

> "It is essential to track usage before investing in equipment. Do you have enough demand? Who will coordinate the AV service? These are important questions to answer. Go through a year's worth of records to see how often certain equipment is rented and calculate how many rentals will be necessary to break even. Look carefully, plot it on a graph because it's hard to get payback if your equipment is sitting on a shelf."[1]

The question might well be asked, "If a hotel is going to have its own equipment, what types and how much of each must be stocked?" Naturally, the type and quantity vary from hotel to hotel. Figure 15.2 shows the AV equipment supplied by a well-known resort

Figure 15.2. SAMPLE AUDIOVISUAL EQUIPMENT RATES.

AUDIO VISUAL

PROJECTORS
- Overhead Projector $30.00
- 35mm Slide Projector $30.00
- 35mm 50% Brighter $75.00

SCREENS
- 6' Tripod Screen $30.00
- 8' Tripod Screen $40.00
- 12' Cradle Screen $65.00

MICROPHONES
- Handheld Podium Mic. ... $15.00
- Wireless Lavalier $60.00
- Wireless Handheld $60.00

SPEAKER PHONES
- Speaker Phone
  (6 people) $30.00
- Polycom System
  (20 people) $75.00
- Gentner System
  (large groups) $250.00

TAPE RECORDERS
- Portable Cassette $15.00
- Stereo Cassette $40.00
- CD Player $40.00

VIDEO CAMERAS
- Camcorder $100.00
- Digital Video Camera $550.00

VIDEO MONITORS & TVs
- 25" Monitor $80.00
- 31" Monitor $150.00
- 51" Monitor $275.00

VIDEO PLAYERS/RECORDERS
- 1/2" VHS $50.00
- Beta SP $400.00

DATA & VIDEO PROJECTION
- LCD for Computer $350.00
- LCD for Video $400.00
- LCD 2000 Lumens $550.00

PRESENTATION AIDS
- Easel Only $10.00
- Flipchart (pad & easel) $25.00
- Whiteboard $20.00
- Corkboard $15.00

CARTS & STANDS
- Projection Carts $15.00
- TV/VCR Cart $20.00
- Safe Lock Stand
  (adjustable) $10.00

Additional Information:
Please call (435) 655-9898
Fax (435) 655-9899

WASATCH AUDIO VISUAL BUSINESS CENTER

Equipment is supplied and serviced by our on-site audio visual specialists, Wasatch A/V Business Center.

An experienced event consultant will preview your needs and arrange for hardware and technical support. This could range from the latest in giant screen projection from video or computer sources to an overhead projector and screen or a simple flipchart with colored markers.

Prices subject to change.   Equipment subject to availability.   This is a partial list only.

Source: Courtesy of Yarrow Hotel, Park City, Utah.

hotel. But no one list or rate schedule can be applied to every hotel; a hotel must consider the needs of its clients in offering the proper assortment of AV equipment.

Some hotels are reluctant to bring in local companies on a one-time rental basis for fear that the service may not be up to their own staff's standards. But if you call on a local company frequently, you have the muscle to demand *excellent service*, rather than the business-as-usual kind. After all, the malfunctions generally happen on the weekend or at night. If you can achieve a good working relationship with an alert and eager AV company, your problems are solved. If not, you had better set up some sort of department of your own.

Several hotels now contract with an AV company to set up an office at the hotel and store equipment there. The in-house AV firm is often provided space rent-free but is required to pay a commission to the hotel when meeting planners contract for AV equipment. Bauer Audio Visual Inc. provides in-house services at 80 hotels. Other companies, such as AVW Audio Visual, have signed corporation-wide contracts with hotel chains. These AV firms know the facility and what will and won't work in each meeting room. Last-minute needs can be met quickly from the on-site storage of AV equipment. And, in-house companies provide convenient, consolidated billing for the planner.

Equipment used at a convention, then, can come from any of three sources — the *convening organization*, the *hotel* or an *outside AV specialist* hired by either the convention organization or the hotel. And equipment can come from any combination of the three.

The first need is to coordinate service. Another is to identify hotel equipment permanently to facilitate sorting equipment afterward. Use decals or permanent stencil imprints in paint.

Your own equipment will fare better from security and maintenance standpoints if responsibility for it is assigned to specific individuals. These people should receive special training in the care and operation of such material. Everyone in convention sales and service should be at home with the kind of equipment needed for most meetings. The dealer from whom the merchandise is purchased should agree to train your personnel; it requires merely some demonstration, not a lengthy course. And technical representatives of AV equipment manufacturers can be reached through the dealer to provide advice and training assistance.

Many properties with in-house audiovisual departments are utilizing *bar coding* to both inventory equipment and to facilitate billing. Each type of equipment is labeled with its own bar code that can be scanned to generate reports as to where and how much is used, and charges can be instantly calculated and posted to the client's account.

Types of Audiovisual Equipment

The audiovisual equipment used for today's meetings can range from a simple flip chart to a sophisticated computer-generated multi-media presentation. In this section, we will take a look at the various types of AV equipment commonly used by meeting planners and see how each can be used to help stage a successful meeting.

Sound Systems

A sound system is the kind of AV system that most hotels own. A supply of microphones, microphone stands, amplifiers and speakers is the first purchased by a hotel staff.

Top-quality **amplifier** systems are a must. Speakers should be distributed so that there are no "dead spots" in sound. When sound systems are used with projection equipment, they should be located in the same area as the screen. Studies have shown that people tend to comprehend better when the sound and the visuals come from the same direction.

You need a variety of microphones, stands and long extension cables to handle meeting situations. It may be necessary to supply a mike for every one or two panelists at the head table or speakers at lecterns, and/or to have several microphones on the floor for questions from the audience. Ideally, the moderator and each speaker on a panel should have a microphone; if this is too costly, only then should microphones be limited to one for every two or three panelists...and they should be reminded beforehand to speak into the nearest microphone.

If you join any but a brand new facility, take inventory and have a list ready of what is available for use, in good working order. Call in a consultant on sound systems and find out what constitutes a basic inventory. Discuss this with experienced convention coordinators too.

Any basic inventory should include a variety of microphones. A **lavaliere microphone** is popular with speakers because it hooks around the neck with a ribbon or cord, leaving the hands free. It is always properly positioned. This type of mike has a variety of optional positions such as the lapel of a business suit. It is also called a *lapel, neck,* or *pendant* microphone.

It is important that all microphones used with public address systems (lectern, table and floor mikes) be unidirectional. A **unidirectional microphone** picks up sound from only one direction (the speaker) and background noise (sounds coming from the sides and back of the microphone) is rejected. Windscreens (porous covers) also reduce the possibility of distracting sounds, such as blowing or popping.

Floor stands for microphones are free-standing and adjustable, with a sleeve or collar into which a mikes slips easily. A **roving microphone** may be equipped with a floor stand, but it also needs a long cable to reach out to different parts of the audience. A table microphone has a short stand that rests on a table, desk or lectern. Some meeting planners use a *cordless/wireless microphone* when roving mikes are required. There are two types of cordless mikes: UHF (ultra high frequency) and VHF (very high frequency). UHF is preferred, but both work well.

These should be tested in each room to make sure the signal doesn't come through neighboring amplifiers. Cordless microphones should only be used in situations where freedom of movement is important, as they can cause problems. Signal interference is possible from a number of sources: metal structures in the room, wire mesh in the walls, and even suspended ceiling framework can cause disruptions or distortion in the sound. And even the more expensive models can face such problems as weak signals and quality as batteries wear down. If wireless microphones are used, then, it is wise to have a backup system (such as a wired lavaliere microphone) immediately available.

All cables should be taped to the floor or carpet to avoid accidents in a darkened room. Avoid at all costs cables that run across the dais. Run such connectors along the front of the stage, hiding them in the draped skirting.

Have an attendant available during conventions. It helps to have the person on hand for the larger events and available for troubleshooting at smaller events such as workshops.

All systems should be set up and *tested* before the meeting. And spare microphones should be available; equipment is not indestructible. Find out if the meeting group plans to have someone in charge of volume control and distribution of microphones. The amplification system is crucial to the success of the meeting, and is an important part of the testing process. In cases where multiple microphones will be used, or when proceedings will be recorded, a sound technician will be needed to run a **mixer board**; the mixer board raises and lowers the volume from each input source, and will be located in the audience to enable the technician to hear exactly what the audience is hearing. In general, one mixer is required for two to four microphones and two mixers should be used for five to eight mikes.

If the hotel uses Muzak or similar background music or a paging system, make sure you can control or eliminate such distractions in each meeting room. This is essential. And many times larger rooms are subdivided by temporary walls and the controls are in only one segment. The meeting planner may not know which subdivision has the controls. Orient the convening organization staff to such control locations.

Lighting

Lighting requirements should be handled by a specialist. If the hotel has a permanent stage, a professional service company should equip it for versatile lighting. But most often, platforms are temporary and lights must be furnished on stands. If platforms are always placed in the same position in certain rooms, a permanent lighting booth may be constructed and equipped. Even smaller rooms need skillful light placement to improve visibility of screened presentations.

While the technical details should be left to a lighting professional, the convention service manager should have a working knowledge of the basic types and uses of lighting equipment.

Lighting requirements for small rooms are simple; for large rooms and audioriums they are more complex. Union regulations recognize this. Attendants are required for spotlight use when large rooms use stage lighting, and so on. They are usually not required for simple setups in small rooms. Don't forget to tell the client about union regulations and rates.

Some of the basic types of lighting include profile spots, follow spots, floodlights, and special effects lighting. *Profile spots* are also known as ellipsoidal spots or lekos, and are ceiling mounted with a range from 500 to 1,000 watts. Employing a halogen lamp, they are used to light lecterns, signs and the area of the stage nearest the audience to project background light patterns (colored filters are often used for this effect). Profile spots can also project gobo patterns, pre-cut designs that fit over the projected light to form light shapes, such as a company logo.

Follow-spots are cannon-shaped, movable lighting devices that are usually located to the rear of the auditorium. They are used to highlight and follow the speaker or performer, and require the services of a technician to ensure this added visibility is maintained. These lights are extremely brilliant, and may also be used with colored filters for a variety of effects.

Floodlights are usually used to light objects rather than people, and are often used to light backdrops (known as cycloramas) that serve as neutral backgrounds for the speakers. Floodlights are used to project a diffused, even light, and feature frames that can accommodate color filters for different effects.

Special effects lighting is used both for illumination and to "create the mood." Ballroom globes, strobe lights, ultraviolet lighting and laser lighting can be used to create a number of effects that enhance special functions — and can serve as visual centerpieces.

Dimmer switches on house lights are a must for meeting rooms. Delegates need partial illumination to take notes, while still being able to see the projection on the screen clearly. A control board is used to balance lighting to achieve the desired effect, and, depending on the complexity of the board, it may require lighting personnel or a lighting technician.

Lecterns

A **lectern** (discussed in Chapter 13) is a speaker's stand that holds notes and papers and has suitable illumination. More sophisticated lecterns have controls to enable the speaker to manipulate lighting and audiovisual equipment directly.

You should have a good inventory of table lecterns, floor models and some with self-contained sound systems. It is helpful if the lectern has a flat area that securely holds at least a water glass. This area should be large enough so that writing implements such as a pen, pencil, chalk or an electric pointer can be stored.

Lecterns should be easily accessible. They often must be approached in a relatively darkened room, so the access path must have some illumination. Cables must be taped, like those of microphones or light units. Tripping the guest speaker is not a recommended way to start a session.

Most hotels have their names or logos painted on the lectern faces. Because speakers are commonly televised and photographed, the hotel name can result in much publicity through local and national news media. It is often necessary to show some goodwill gestures to the TV people so they will compose the scene large enough to include the hotel logo.

Screens

Projection screens are often purchased by hotels. Larger ones must be tailor-made for the larger rooms, especially those hampered by a low ceiling. The charts in Figure 15.3 offer a guide to screen size selection under a variety of conditions and can help you decide where to place the projection stands when setting up.

There are several formulas used for determining seating capacity and screen placement. The two most commonly used are the *five feet rule* and the *one by six rule.*

The five feet rule states that the minimum distance from the bottom of the screen to the floor is five feet, while the average height of a seated person is four feet, six inches. Therefore, to view the screen clearly, the bottom of the screen must be a minimum of five feet off the floor.

The one by six rule states that no one should be seated closer to the screen than one times the screen's width nor farther from the screen than six times the screen's width. For example, if the meeting room's ceiling height is 15 feet, the maximum height for the projection screen is 10 feet, and if a 7-1/2 ft. high by 10 ft. wide screen is used, the farthest seat from the screen should be no more than 60 feet and the closest seat no closer than ten feet.

There are many types of screens available. The most popular of the larger screens is the **fastfold**, available in sizes up to 30 ft. high. The screen comes with adjustable legs to vary the height of placement off the floor (or it may be hung from the ceiling). They last a long time when taken care of and the smaller fastfolds represent a relatively minor investment. Local AV dealers may have a hard time supplying the huge screens, but no trouble supplying any number of small units.

Wall or *ceiling screens* come in a variety of sizes and are designed to be hung from hooks or lines or mounted on the wall or ceiling. They are inexpensive and the metal tube casings make for easy storage. They are activated like the old-fashioned window shades.

Tripod screens, in a metal tube like the wall screen, are mounted permanently on folding tripod stands so that they can be placed anywhere. Light, portable, versatile, and inexpensive, they are extremely useful in smaller meetings. Tripod screens should be tilted

Figure 15.3. GUIDE TO SCREEN SIZE SELECTION AND SEATING DISTANCE FROM SCREEN.

Choosing a screen size that takes full advantage of the specific type of projector and room size is as important as choosing the proper screen surface. Today's shorter projection lenses and larger rooms permit bigger, more lifelike projecting than ever. Now, for example, a 4" lens projects a 35mm slide to 60" height and width from a distance of only fifteen feet. And the zoom projectors need big screens to make the most of their capabilities. These charts are accurate guides to screen size selection. Make sure the screen selected is on the basis of the largest size slides or movies intended for projection.

16mm Movies

Lens Focal Length	Projance	Screen Width			
		40"	50"	60"	70"
1"	D i s t a n c e	9'	11'	13'	16'
1 1/2"		13'	17'	20'	23'
2"		18'	22'	26'	31'
2 1/2"		22'	27'	33'	38'
3"		26'	33'	40'	46'
3 1/2"		31'	38'	46'	54'
4"		35'	44'	53'	61'

35mm Slides

Lens Focal Length	Projance	Screen Width			
		40"	50"	60"	70"
3"	D i s t a n c e	7'	9'	11'	13'
4"		10'	12'	15'	17'
5"		12'	16'	19'	22'
6"		15'	19'	22'	26'
7"		17'	22'	26'	30'
8"		20'	25'	30'	35'

Audience Capacity

Farthest Seat — 6 times screen width. First consideration when picking ideal screen for any room. (Assuming choice of lenses)

Closest Seat — Equal to screen width.

Audience Capacity — 6 sq. ft. per person after aisle space is deducted. (Assumes ideal seating arrangement)

Screen Size	Farthest Seat from Screen	Closest Seat to Screen	Audience Capacity	Square Feet Seating Space
43" x 58"	30'	5'	88	531
54" x 74"	36'	6'	125	755
63" x 84"	42'	7'	169	1,018
72" x 96"	48'	8'	224	1,345
7 1/2' x 10'	60'	10'	350	2,100
9' x 12'	72'	12'	502	3,010
10 1/2' x 14'	84'	14'	684	4,110
13 1/2' x 18'	108'	18'	1,175	7,050
15' x 20'	120'	20'	1,400	8,400

Source: Reprinted from Basic Requirements for Meeting Room Facilities. Used with permission by the Association of National Advertisers.

forward at the top to avoid **keystoning**, an effect in which an image appears noticeably wider at the top than at the bottom and appears unfocused. And, for a more professional image, the bottom of the screen should be skirted.

There is a variety of screen fabric in use today. A favorite is *glass-beaded* (white), which offers great brilliance. Smooth white *matte-surface* screens offer consistent brilliance from a wider angle, which is important in small rooms where some seats may be at a sharp angle to the screen, and are the most commonly used types of screens. *Silver metallic* and *lenticular* surfaces combine the best features of both types, offering maximum brilliance and wide-angle light consistency. They are somewhat more costly than the others. Any local AV dealer can assist you in selecting the proper ones for your facility.

Slide Projectors

Slide projectors have improved tremendously over the years. The most popular tray is an 80-slide **carousel projector**. A 140-slide carousel is also in use, but it is preferable to use the 80-slide tray as much as possible; the 140-slide tray has the same diameter as the 80-slide tray, so the narrower width per slide often leads to jammed or damaged slides. Once a slide is positioned properly in the round slide tray that attaches to the top of the projector, it remains properly oriented and is not handled again. Of course, lack of rehearsals and careless tray filling still produce mishaps, but they are diminishing.

It is unfortunate that each brand of projector seems to take a different tray and the trays are not interchangeable. The situation is not as chaotic as it may seem because the Kodak Carousel slide projector is used by the vast majority of meeting presenters. It is extremely dependable and requires little maintenance and service other than lamp replacement. Spare lamps, fuses and extension cords should be on hand.

If it chooses to stock any slide projector, a hotel should select this one. There are various models under the Carousel designation but all take the common tray. Should a presenter use another brand of projector, he or she would have to specify it to an AV dealer who may be able to supply it, or just unload the trays and reload into Carousel trays, which every AV dealer has. This is a non-technical chore needing no tools and taking but a few minutes.

Such projectors are called 2 by 2 or 35mm size. They are so termed because they are designed for 35mm slide film mounted in standard frames measuring two inches by two inches. Happily, this is an industry standard. You may occasionally get a call for a projector to handle larger slide film such as 2-1/4 by 2-1/4 or 3 by 4 inch lantern slides, but not frequently.

A remote control device is often used for slide projectors. Both wired remotes and cordless remotes are available, with the wireless device giving the speaker additional mobility. When a remote device is used, it is advisable to have an assistant near the machine in case of a malfunction.

Many slide projectors can also be connected to an audiosync tape recorder. A silent electronic "cue" is added to a tape that provides music or a narrative accompaniment. As "cues" are processed, slides are automatically advanced.

A **dissolve unit** is required when two or more projectors are used in combination. A dissolve unit activates fade-in and fade-out of slides and is widely used by meeting planners to avoid the light flash between slides when only one projector is used. When multiple slide projectors are used, a prerecorded tape may be synchronized with the slide sequence. The signal from the tape will activate the slide projector at the right moment.

To ensure proper functioning of equipment, the convention service manager should also have a working knowledge of the components of slide projector systems. Lenses, for example, are commonly a 4-to-6 zoom lens, but larger lenses are available if there is a need to project over longer distances. Specialized lenses are often quite expensive, but may be available from an AV company if there is a need for a non-standard lens.

Most slide projectors use a quartz-halogen bulb, but xenon bulbs are also available in cases where increased brilliance is required (when projecting over long distances, for example). The xenon bulb can be dangerous, however; it is filled with a high pressure gas, and its use and care is best left in the hands of an experienced operator. The availability of bulbs can be crucial to a presentation; it is wise to ensure that replacement bulbs are readily available in the event of a blowout during a presentation.

Overhead Projectors

An **overhead projector** is very popular for instructional use. Figure 15.4 illustrates how a speaker may draw or write on blank forms as he talks to his audience. The projector is positioned at the speaker and projects behind him onto a screen. Overhead projectors handle any brands of transparencies up to nine by nine inches. Such units are relatively inexpensive, rarely break, and are in great demand. Popular brands are the 3M Company, Singer, Beseler, and many others.

One of the most versatile developments in the field of overhead technology is the **computer projection panel** (also known as the LCD — liquid crystal display). This new development is an electronic device that is used instead of a transparency. The special

Figure 15.4. OVERHEAD PROJECTORS.

With an overhead projector, there is no need for the speaker to look at the screen to see the image being projected. The visual on the projector stage enables the speaker to see it exactly as the audience sees it. This enables the speaker to face the listeners and maintain eye contact, which stimulates audience reaction.
Source: Courtesy of the 3M Company.

attachment is attached to a personal computer, projecting whatever is on the computer monitor to the projection screen. Not only does this device make the image large enough for easy audience viewing, but it can also store and select data at the operator's command (see Figure 15.5)

Although most meeting planners are well versed in the layout of meeting rooms, occasionally the convention service manager will be called upon to advise in the placement of audiovisual equipment. Few things can destroy the effectiveness of a meeting more than the improper positioning of projectors and screens. No one wants to look down the back of someone's neck while the speaker explains the visuals. Obscured views can be prevented with a simple understanding of AV layout.

Figure 15.6 illustrates the proper positioning of an overhead projector so that the speaker does not block the audience's view. Figure 15.7 shows the best positioning of an overhead projector, a slide or filmstrip projector, and a movie projector. Review these illustrations thoroughly. Good visibility is foremost in communicating with visual techniques.

Figure 15.5. LIQUID CRYSTAL DISPLY (LCD) TECHNOLOGY.

An image may be projected from a computer monitor to a larger screen with the use of Liquid Crystal Display (LCD) technology. The LCD panel is used with an overhead projector; the LCD projector has a built-in light source.

Rearview Projection

A relatively new technique in visual presentation that is receiving wide use is **rearview projection**. The term "rearview" is somewhat of a misnomer because the audience still views the picture (slides, film or video visuals can be projected) from the front (see Figure 15.8). The projector, however, is set up behind the screen. By using a curtain or similar room divider, hotels can cut off one part of a room from the other. The audience sits on one side of the partition, the projector on the other. A translucent rear-projection screen is framed by the curtain, and the projection equipment is hidden on the darkened rear side.

Three of the most commonly used self-contained rear-projection units are Telex's Caramate, Kodak's Audioviewer, and Bell & Howell's Ringmaster. These units resemble

Figure 15.6. SEATING ARRANGEMENTS WHEN USING OVERHEAD PROJECTORS.

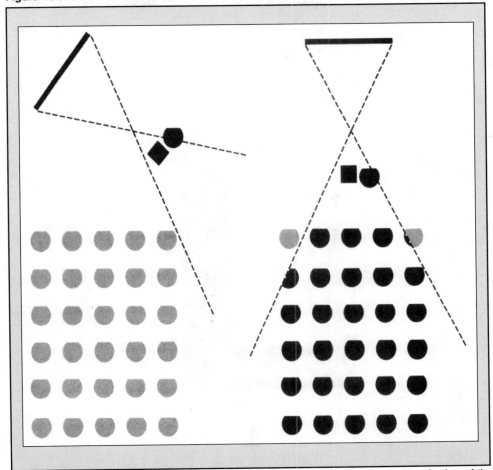

When using an overhead projector, the room should be arranged so that the audience's view of the screen is not blocked by the speaker and the projector.
Source: Courtesy of the 3M Company.

small television sets with a slide tray on top; slides can be advanced manually or through the use of an audio tape programmed with silent "cues" (pulses).

The primary advantage of this technique is that all projection equipment is hidden from the audience, eliminating the need for an aisle. The disadvantage is that the room cannot be fully used for seating (rearview projection reduces the available square footage for seating up to one-third). Another disadvantage is that rear projection requires an almost completely dark projection area behind the screen, requiring complete draping of the screen -- sides, bottom and top (the area of the room where the audience is seated does not need to be darkened). In addition, if space behind the screen is limited, a more expensive wide-angle lens may be required. On the positive side, however, rearview projection can be effective as it allows the speaker more freedom of movement and the presentation can appear more dramatic as the image seems to appear out of nowhere.

Figure 15.7. MULTIMEDIA ARRANGEMENTS IN U-SHAPED SETUP.

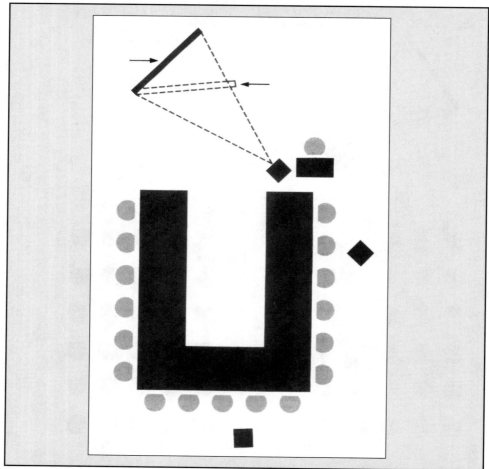

This diagram illustrates the best position for an overhead, slide or filmstrip projector in a U-shape table arrangement.

Motion Picture Film Projectors

When movies are shown at meetings, they are most frequently the 16mm size. Fortunately, any 16mm film, sound or silent, black & white or color, can be shown on any 16mm projector. There are a number of brands on the market, and such variations as the slide trays discussed earlier for slide projectors are not found in motion picture projectors. The projectors can be used interchangeably.

The sound system built into motion picture projectors is often poor; in larger meeting rooms, an independent subsidiary sound hookup should be used. The sound from a 16mm projector can be "patched" into the property's built-in sound system for greater clarity.

Motion picture film projectors require an operator to thread the film into the projector, although some have an automatic feeding system (preferred by most convention service departments). To be on the safe side, however, a trained projectionist should be available in the event of a malfunction in the automatic system.

Another consideration when dealing with motion picture projectors is the lamp system. As with slide projectors, a higher intensity bulb is required when images must be

436

Figure 15.8. COMPARISON OF COMMON PROJECTION SYSTEMS.

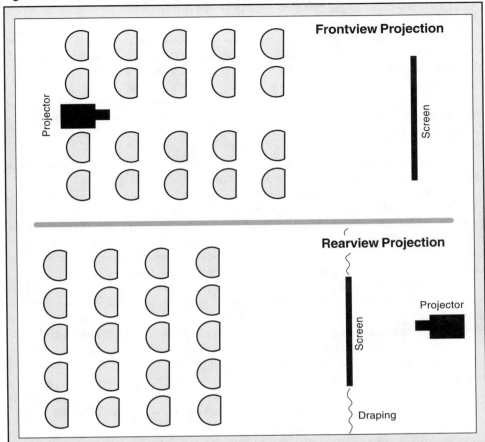

Rearview projection equipment is hidden behind the screen and drapes. This allows for more dramatic presentations and eliminates the need for a center aisle. Frontview projection however offers more squared footage for seating.

projected over longer distances. A MARC (mazda closed arc) projector can be used when greater clarity is required, while a Xenon 16mm projector is the most powerful projector for long-distance projection (a professional projectionist is required for this equipment).

It is wise for the convention service manager to check out the room setup and the audiovisual equipment supplied before the meeting starts. He or she should check:

- the *screen*, to see if it is above the audience's heads so that all will be able to see clearly from where they sit.
- the *projector*, to see that it is secure on the stand and that an extra lamp is available.
- the *speaker*, to see that it is near the screen; and
- the *electrical cords,* to be sure they are out of the aisle and hidden.

Videotape Projectors

With the growing use of videotape for meeting presentations, many properties are finding it imperative to provide video playback equipment and support.

Video projectors are essential for viewing videotapes in all but small groups. A self-contained video projector has a curved six-foot screen that can easily be seen by audiences of up to 100 people.

While several of these units can be used for larger groups, it is usually more effective to use a detached video projector and a fastfold projector screen in larger rooms. This equipment offers a quality image 12 feet wide, and can be used for both front or rear projection.

For arenas and other larger areas, light-valve video projectors must be used. This type of projector projects up to 400 feet and creates an image roughly 40 feet wide. It may not be feasible to purchase this type of projector. It is more practical to rent them when the need arises.

On the other end of the meetings spectrum, television sets can be used to service small meetings. Television falls into two categories: monitors and receivers.

A **monitor** has no tuner, and interprets signals directly from a videotape player or video camera. Monitors are more costly than television receivers, but are often requested by meeting planners due to the crisper image they produce. The next level of video monitors is high definition television (HDTV) and plasma screens. These monitors are only six inches thick and up to 50 inches in size. While available, these monitors are costly and, as yet, are not used as extensively by meeting planners.

Receivers are used to interpret and reproduce television signals, but cannot play videotapes without the use of a videotape player. And, while television receivers have built-in audio systems, these are usually of a mediocre quality; it is advisable to patch sound into the property's sound system rather than to rely on the units' audio systems.

Signals from videotapes can be split to feed a number of monitors and television receivers, and the number of units needed will depend on the size of the audience. A general rule of thumb is 25 viewers per 19-inch set and 50 viewers per 25-inch set.

Since video is widely used, it is important that the property have compatible tape equipment readily available. The basic formats available in the United States are:

- VHS — uses 1/2-inch tape and is the most popular variety of tape with meeting planners.
- Betacam, Beta SP — is the common video format for presentation graphics and is the most widely used format in today's meetings market.
- U-Matic or Industrial — uses 3/4-inch tape and generates a better image than VHS. These formats are generally used for educational tapes.
- Broadcast video — 1 or 2-inch tape, used primarily by television stations and production houses; will rarely be requested by meeting planners.
- Video 8 — another Sony product that uses small cassettes (only slightly larger than standard audio cassettes). This format is rarely used, but may be found in exhibits, where space is at a premium.

It is important to note that none of these tape formats is compatible with any of the others. And, problems may also arise if speakers or presenters are from foreign countries. A NTSC standard is used for tapes in the United States, while Europe, Africa, Australia and Southeast Asia use a PAL standard, and the SECAM standard is used in Russia, France and the Middle East. It is usually impractical to stock equipment to accommodate foreign standard tapes, but the convention services department would be wise to locate audiovisual suppliers that can provide this equipment when needed.

Projection Systems for Computer Presentations

Throughout the meetings industry there has been a very rapid movement to computer-driven presentations. Slide, film, and overhead transparency projection is being replaced by computer projection at many gatherings.

There are two primary types of projection systems available for personal computer-based presentations: liquid crystal display (LCD) computer panels and computer projectors.

Liquid crystal display computer panels, discussed in the previous sections, are units that sit atop an overhead projector. The LCD panels are connected to a computer, and images on the computer screen are then displayed on the overhead projector.

A more recent innovation, and one that is preferred by many meeting planners, is the **computer projector**. These stand alone projectors are equipped with their own built in light source into which the computer plugs directly. There is no need for an overhead projector when using this device.

There are two computer display projectors used in today's meetings market: the LCD projector and the new digital light processing (DLP) projector. DLP-based projectors are lighter (five to ten pounds is common) and more portable, brighter, and have a better image quality.

Projector Stands

Projectors have to be placed on something. It may be a table or desk, but it is more versatile and convenient to have special projection tables or stands. These come in folding and rigid types. Some have casters for easy movement; with these stands projectors may be placed anywhere in a room.

There are two basic types of projector stands: the Safelock and the rolling cart. The Safelock is ideal for large projectors, and has four telescoping legs that adjust to heights up to 56 inches. Rolling carts come in several fixed heights, with the 32-inch and the 54-inch the most commonly used. The 32-inch rolling cart is ideal for overhead projectors, while the 54-inch cart is usually used for television monitors. When using rolling carts, regardless of height, they should be skirted for a professional, finished look.

Permanent projection booths can be constructed for larger rooms. The screen chart in Figure 15.3 will help you choose the proper lens to fill the screen from such a fixed position. Lenses of extra-long focal lengths for long projection distance may not always be in stock but can be ordered from local AV dealers. Check local fire and union regulations regarding projection booth operations.

Multimedia Presentations

This concept uses several types of audio and visual equipment to create total sight/sound environments. **Multimedia** can range from the very simple to highly sophisticated systems, and convention service managers should have a working knowledge of the basic types of equipment commonly requested by meeting planners.

The simplest form of multimedia is the sound/slide synchronizer. This type of equipment was mentioned in the slide projector section of this chapter. It uses a sound tape that automatically advances the slides and provides music or narration during the slide presentation.

Slide projectors can also be teamed with dissolve units. Dissolve units alternate two or three slide projectors focused on the same screen. These units fade and overlap images to create a smooth multimedia presentation.

Programmers are the ultimate in multimedia equipment. The computerized control can be used to synchronize sound tracks and multiple slide projectors on multiple screens (and can even turn the lights off in the room) for a stunning audiovisual performance. And, as video continues to become a popular alternative to slides, multimedia is becoming even more exciting as a motivational and communications tool.

Simultaneous Interpretations

As meetings become more international in scope, many properties have found it necessary to provide **simultaneous interpretation** facilities. This involves having a speaker's words translated into the language(s) of the meeting participants, and requires specialized equipment and personnel.

In most cases, the speaker addresses the group and an interpreter (or interpreters) in soundproof booth(s) relays what the speaker has said to the attendees via wireless headsets. The number of booths and headsets needed will depend on the number of languages required for the meeting.

Today's technology has enhanced this process. Loop antennas can be used within certain areas to enable attendees to hear their language within that area. And, infrared signals are also used to beam a language to attendees. Another development is multiple channel selection, which enables attendees to channel back and forth between different languages.

While simultaneous interpretation can be costly, both in terms of equipment (sound booths, headsets, antennas or infrared radiators) and personnel (interpreters and technicians), more meeting planners will require this service in today's increasingly international business world, and the properties that offer this capability can capture a share of this growing — and lucrative — market.

Virtual Conferencing

In an increasing number of cases, meeting planners have found that it is virtually impossible — or too costly — to bring all persons that should be involved in a meeting together in person. Conflicting schedules and the high cost of travel are the prime factors for the use of **virtual conferencing**.

Virtual conferencing can be broadly defined as the electronic linking of more than two people at different sites, and falls into four basic categories: audio, audiographic, video and web conferencing.

Audio conferencing, the most basic form, is generally used when budget is a major consideration. Audio conferencing simply utilizes the telephone lines and speaker phones to connect several parties. A speaker can give a presentation to meeting "attendees" at several locations via speaker phones or special microphones and amplifier systems tied directly to the telephone lines of the participating properties or alternate remote sites.

Audiographic conferencing is generally used for planning sessions, project reviews and briefings because it combines both audio interaction and visual capabilities. Specially designed conference rooms offer the ability to "show" documents, slides, and objects via television monitors at the remote sites.

Video conferencing provides full-motion, "face-to-face" networking, and is the most expensive — and the most sophisticated form of virtual conferencing. Remote sites are "linked" through the use of satellite technology, and many properties now offer this type of conferencing network.

Video conferencing involves considerable expense. First, it is necessary to provide full video production, which involves multiple video cameras, technicians and special effects equipment. Second, it is necessary to provide a playback system at each location. This equipment includes multiple video monitors or video projectors. Third, uplink/down-link and satellite facilities are required. Special equipment (telephone lines, cable or a microwave system) sends the signal from the origination point to a satellite dish ("uplink" or "earth station") which beams the image to the satellite (22,000 miles or more above the earth). The signal is received by a transponder (an access point on the satellite), the frequency is changed, and the signal is beamed down to satellite dishes ("downlink") at each remote location before it travels, again via telephone line, cable or microwave system, to the remote receivers.

While this process requires a large initial investment, many properties have found it worthwhile to purchase or lease uplink systems. The investment may pay future dividends, as adverse circumstances — a fuel crisis, worsening economic trends, or other negative shifts in the business world — make video conferencing a viable alternative to costly meeting travel and accommodations.

The newest alternative to face-to-face meetings is *web conferencing*. Web conferencing refers to conducting meetings, events and seminars over the Internet. Web-based presentations utilize an Internet connection rather than satellites.

There are a number of different ways that speakers can connect to the Internet. The easiest, least expensive, but slowest connection is through a telephone line. Many planners find this access too slow and prefer the high speed connections possible with ISDN or TI data lines. These lines ensure Web information will appear very quickly on computers and projection screens. Therefore, many hotels, conference facilities and convention centers are now installing these types of lines throughout their meeting space. A recent survey found that 73 percent of the facilities polled had ISDN data lines available and 51 percent had installed TI lines for Internet transmission.

Spare Parts

If you have your own projectors — slide, movie, video, computer-based or overhead — you should maintain a stock of spare lamps. Keep fuses at hand if the hotel is not wired with circuit breakers. Someone on the convention service staff should know how to select the proper lamps, replace burnt-out ones, and instruct others in the operation of the projectors. This attention to detail can be very important to meeting planners (see Figure 15.9)

Other Presentation Devices

Not all presentation is done by film, of course. Many speakers use *chalkboards*. Some call them *blackboards*, but most of them are green these days. These may be permanently installed, hung on a wall, or used on a tripod **easel**. Make sure the chalkboard is washed clean and that chalk and *clean* erasers are supplied. To enliven the presentation, an assortment of colored chalk is preferable to white or yellow chalk only. It is the hotel's responsi-

Figure 15.9. SOLVING PROBLEMS FOR MEETING PLANNERS.

Many meeting planners worry about small details. This ad featuring Holiday Inns' "No Excuses" meeting guarantee assures meeting planners that each property is ready to handle any problem that might arise — including having spare lamps on hand to ensure that presentations can go on as planned.

bility to provide the meeting planner with first-class chalkboards, blackboards and easel charts. Such equipment that is in need of repair is unsightly and difficult to work with.

A *whiteboard* is cleaner and more convenient than a chalkboard, and can be used as an impromptu projector screen as well as for easy-to-read, readily correctable presentations.

Advantages and Disadvantages of Popular AV Equipment

Advantages	Disadvantages
Slide Projectors 1. Can be operated with wireless remote control device. 2. Can be connected with audio-sync tape. 3. Excellent color reproduction on slides. 4. Can be computer programmed for multi-image productions. 5. Can project a larger image.	1. Limited motion capabilities compared to video. 2. Fan noise can be distracting.
Motion Picture Projectors 1. Full motion capabilities. 2. Excellent color rendition. 3. Can project large, quality images.	1. Difficult to feed unless equipment has automatic threading mechanism. 2. Built-in speakers are often of poor quality; sound may have to be "patched" to the facility's sound system.
Flip Charts and Chalkboards 1. Very inexpensive. 2. Take up very little seating space. 3. Ideal for "brainstorming" and training meetings.	1. Limited to small audiences (50 persons or less). 2. Messy and often difficult to erase.
Computer Based Projectors 1. Most are compatible with laptop computers. 2. Powerpoint and electronic graphics make for powerful presentations. 3. Possible to provide Internet connection.	1. Resolution (sharpness of image) doesn't match slides or film. 2. Technology changes about every 18 months so equipment can become obsolete. 3. Not as bright as overhead projectors so glass-beaded screens may be needed to provide a brisker image.
Overhead Projectors 1. Can be used in a lighted room. 2. Simple to operate, and transparencies can be produced quickly on a copy machine. 3. Speaker can control presentation by highlighting or marking on transparency during presentation. 4. Speakers can face audience and do not have to turn their backs (as is the case with chalkboards or flip charts).	1. Noise from built-in fans can be a distraction. 2. Limited color reproduction.
Video Projectors 1. Instant playback capabilities. 2. Full motion and color capabilities. 3. Simple to operate. 4. Video display of computer-generated information is possible.	1. Various formats of playback equipment are incompatible. 2. Difficult to project for large audiences.

Instead of chalk, dry-erase markers are used, and many whiteboards are marked like graph paper, making it easy for a speaker to write or draw in a straight line.

Whiteboards are also available in electronic versions. One model, Panasonic's Panofax, reproduces everything written on it or taped to it. When desired, a photocopy of everything on the board can be made with the push of a button. This eliminates extensive note-taking, which often distracts attendees from what the speaker is saying.

The Gemini Blackboard is another technological improvement of the whiteboard. This device has capabilities to send materials written on it to another board (sometimes thousands of miles away) via a telephone line. This application has become increasingly popular as more meeting planners are turning to teleconferences.

Paper easel pads or **flip charts** are commonly used with broad soft-point pens, markers or crayons. These are always portable, using handy tripod easels. There are special cabinets to house them. If you have rooms used extensively for training classrooms, you may find it convenient to mount such flip-charts. The Oravisual Company has a selection of these, which are readily available from audiovisual and art supply dealers.

Flip charts are generally 27x34 inches in size, and should be limited to use in small meeting rooms. When ordering flip charts, the convention services department needs to specify "flip chart easel with pad;" this will differentiate from the order for "tripod easels," which support signs but not the heavy flip chart pads. Some properties charge extra for pads and markers and supply the easels only; others include all materials needed for the presentation in the basic charge— easel, pad, and specified colors of markers.

Pointers have become more sophisticated since the days of long wooden ones. Many speakers use metal pointers that telescope down to ball-point pen size. There are also electric hand-held laser pointers that can project an arrowhead onto the screen from 100 feet away, allowing a greater freedom of movement for the speaker.

Another device, which is used for presentations, communication, and training, is the personal computer. Most meeting planners realize that computers can easily become damaged in transit, and look for properties that can supply personal computers for workshops and training sessions (as well as for on-site convention registration).

While the cost of stocking computers may be prohibitive, many properties make arrangements with a local computer rental center when needed. Other properties have found that the establishment of computer systems has generated sufficient bookings to prove profitable. Yet a third alternative is for the property to "link up" with a nearby computer facility.

If the property does decide to make use of computers as an attraction for meeting planners, it should be aware of several requirements. First, computers must be kept cool; a computer center or computerized meeting room must have the capability of being climate controlled for maximum efficiency. Second, computers require a great deal of electricity, and since most meeting planners require a classroom setup for computer workshops and training classes, the property must have sufficient electricity in the middle of the room as well as on the room's perimeters. Third, computers take up a great deal of space; at least 60 square feet should be allowed for each computer and operator. Lastly, it is important to remember that computer printers are generally noisy; they need to be placed away from groups requiring quiet.

Hotels are not expected to supply the gear for sophisticated AV presentations such as multi-screen extravaganzas. These are usually handled by specialists. Local AV dealers or service organizations can handle such needs if you get requests for such sources.

It is usually enough for hotels to be able to supply on short notice such basics as slide projectors, overhead projectors, 16mm sound projectors, screens, chalkboards, and easel pads. Beyond this, advance notice should be given and a specialist dealer called in. A meeting planner should supply a list of all AV needs in advance.

To sum up, a hotel should have a good working relationship with a local audiovisual dealer/service organization. If such a company is not available, the hotel may decide to stock a department of its own. In either case, a hotel may choose to stock a minimum number of basic items and train staff people to maintain and operate them.

Sample AV Equipment List/Price Sheet

A listing such as this one can be used to give the meeting planner an at-a-glance look at exactly what audiovisual equipment will be used for a meeting or function and its overall costs. This list can also be helpful to the property's convention service department, as it provides an overview of the equipment that will be in use on specific days. (Source: Bill Masheter, "AV Bids," *Association Meetings*, April, 1991, page 28. Used with permission.)

AV Flowsheet

Meeting: **American Association of Widget Waxers**
Property: **Hotel Unique**
City: **Heartland**

Room: **All**
Session:
Dates: **March 14–20, 199**

EQUIPMENT	BASE COST	Day/Date Thu 14 (QTY)	Day/Date Fri 15	Day/Date Sat 16	Day/Date Sun 17	Day/Date Mon 18	Day/Date Tues 19	Day/Date Wed 20	TOTAL
Tripod screen 70" x 70"	$18.00		5 / $90.00	8 / $144.00	6 / $108.00	6 / $108.00	7 / $126.00		$576.00
Tripod screen 84" x 84"	$24.00		1 / $24.00	1 / $24.00	1 / $24.00	1 / $24.00	2 / $48.00	1 / $24.00	$168.00
Tripod screen 96" x 96"	$30.00							2 / $60.00	$60.00
CPE fastfold screen 10' x 10' front	$55.00		2 / $110.00	1 / $55.00	1 / $55.00	1 / $55.00	2 / $110.00		$385.00
CPE fastfold screen 12' x 12' front	$85.00		1 / $85.00	2 / $170.00	2 / $170.00	2 / $170.00	2 / $170.00	1 / $85.00	$850.00
2 x 2–35mm slide projector Kodak EKIII	$27.50		4 / $110.00	7 / $192.50	6 / $165.00	5 / $137.50	8 / $220.00		$825.00
2 x 2–35mm slide projector Kodak EKIII Britelite projector	$48.00		4 / $192.00	3 / $144.00	2 / $96.00	3 / $144.00	2 / $96.00	4 / $192.00	$864.00
2 x 2–35mm slide projector 500w xenon	$200.00			1 / $200.00	2 / $400.00	1 / $200.00	2 / $400.00		$1200.00
2 x 2 long lens	$15.00		7 / $105.00	7 / $105.00	7 / $105.00	7 / $105.00	8 / $120.00	4 / $60.00	$600.00
Safelock stand	$10.00		5 / $50.00	9 / $90.00	7 / $70.00	6 / $60.00	8 / $80.00	1 / $10.00	$360.00
Overhead projector	$27.50		5 / $137.50	10 / $275.00	6 / $165.00	5 / $137.50	8 / $220.00		$935.00
32" cart w/drape	$15.00		5 / $75.00	10 / $150.00	4 / $60.00	8 / $120.00	11 / $165.00	3 / $45.00	$615.00
16mm projector	$35.00		1 / $35.00				1 / $35.00		$70.00

Charging for Audiovisual Equipment

No single rule can be established for how much a hotel should charge for AV equipment. Competition and the availability of outside firms, the number of guest rooms occupied, the extent of food and beverage functions, and the amount invested in equipment are some of the variables that must be considered in establishing a policy.

In some cases, the client deals directly with the AV supplier if an outside supplier is used. In other cases, you may contract with the outside service and pass the charges along to the client. Whether you use outside services or provide in-house equipment, you should supply a list of your prices to the client. A form detailing the specific equipment to be used and the cost for each piece is commonly used to provide an at-a-glance overview of AV charges (see box titled "Sample AV Equipment List/Price Sheet").

Remember when figuring your prices to include any additional charges, such as delivery costs, set-up charges, labor requirements (technician, sound mixer, etc.), and other miscellaneous fees (the cost of bringing extra electricity to a room, for example). These costs may be figured into the price of the equipment, in which case you may wish to add a notation to that effect on your form. Or, additional costs may be listed separately on your form.

In any case, it is bad business to surprise the meeting planner with hidden costs; he or she must often work within an AV budget and should know exactly what will be charged for the entire meeting beforehand.

A logbook should be used to control the rental of audiovisual equipment. The log should contain the date ordered, the item, the delivery date, the guest billed, and the banquet check number. If an outside agency is billing the hotel, each invoice should be approved by the convention service manager and recorded in the logbook before sending it to accounting.

Union Regulations

One of the biggest complaints of meeting planners is the influence that unions have on the operation of audiovisual equipment. When AV equipment is ordered from outside firms, technicians are often part of the package. Projectionists, sound recording engineers, spotlight operators and other specialists with expertise in complicated equipment are required. The problem arises when the services of a projectionist really aren't needed, but the union contract calls for such a person whenever the equipment is used. One convention manager told us:

> "One of the biggest complaints by convention groups coming to our city is the requirement to pay the high union scale for some person to sit idly by and run a machine that anyone can operate. In some cities the meeting planner or his people can't even plug the equipment in, but must wait for a union projectionist."

While this may seem a little farfetched, the situation is actually becoming more common. And it is unlikely that union restrictions will be eased. Hotels should inform meeting planners of such rigid union regulations; a violation can lead to work stoppage and a crisis in the convention.

Figure 15.10. HOTEL SIGN POLICIES.

- All signs must be professionally printed or painted. Handwritten signs are not permitted.
- All signs must be displayed from easels.
- Placement of signs is restricted to meeting room area.
- No signs allowed in main lobby or guest room corridors. The hotel has an electronic event board in the lobby for daily meeting room and registration information, as well as electronic signs outside of each function room.
- No pins, tacks or adhesives of any sort are permitted on any hotel wall or door.
- No tape or glue permitted on painted walls. We realize that visual aids have to be displayed occasionally on the vinyl walls of our meeting rooms, but please check with your convention service manager on the type of tape to use on vinyl walls.
- The hotel's staff will be happy to assist in hanging any banners or large signs. Please check with your convention service manager for any restrictions.
- Please be advised that you will be held liable for damages if the above mentioned policies are not adhered to.

This is a typical hotel policy regarding the placement of signs.

Signs and Notices

Only the simplest meeting can make do without *signs* and *notices*. They are most obvious when absent. The convention organization has a great stake in making sure that all goes smoothly, and signs are a great help within the convention area. Many convention planners are inexperienced, so the hotel must stand ready to advise and supply. Unless you want to scramble at the last moment, you should remind the client of the need for such signs and notices and expedite the creation of them.

Hotel Rules

Hotel and convention facilities need rules about the use of signs to avoid damage to walls and doors by indiscriminate use of tapes and tacks. It is a wise hotel that builds sign holders in crucial areas of its convention space.

The best kind are permanent frames on or near doors of meeting rooms that hold standard-sized card stock for signs. Bulletin boards and other movable signboards are handled easily on short notice. Those reliable tripod easels make great sign holders and are most versatile.

A printed form outlining the hotel rules on signs should be submitted to the convention organizers to be included in their convention manuals (see Figure 15.10).

Hotel rules regarding distribution of notices also should be outlined clearly. Companies at trade conventions frequently request to distribute printed material at strategic points within the hotel or even to place them at the door of each delegate's room. Daily convention newspapers, newsletters and advertising material are distributed in this manner.

The hotel should inform the organization if it is willing and able to undertake such distribution and if it charges for the service. The convention organizer should be directed to inform the participants about the recommended procedure to follow for such service.

It is important to learn if the convening organization has any policy about signs and distribution of newspapers, magazines, newsletters, advertising materials or any other printed matter. The policy should be aided by the hotel staff's compliance, and all such requests should be referred to the convention staff. Hotel personnel should either handle or supervise the hanging of posters or signs.

Sign Responsibility

It is the convening organization's responsibility to create signs. The convention service manager should be alert and advise when he or she notices that they are not being planned. A discussion of signs is helpful. The inexperienced meeting planner will appreciate it; the old pro won't mind the reminder.

The program indicates the need for signs. If the organization supplies them, the hotel is freed from the responsibility. We would suggest documenting that decision with a memo or letter. Most often, however, it is easier for the organization to have the signs made through the hotel to save the bother of transporting them.

Regardless of who accepts the responsibility of supplying signs, invariably a few more are needed at the last minute. Some arrangement must be made for such service. If the hotel cannot do the job in-house, a local sign painter must be on call. In view of the fact that setup usually is on weekends and evenings, it is a wise convention hotel that sets up in-house.

Price Schedule

Establish a price schedule for all sign work, whether the hotel has an in-house shop or farms the work out. A work order should be made out for each sign; its location, if predetermined, should be noted. No verbal orders should be taken. State whether the hotel will bill the organization or the group will deal directly with a local sign company

Locations

The purpose of signs is to give information, direct pedestrian traffic and activity, and assure a smoothly flowing meeting. Thus signs are needed in logical locations. Trace the progress of attendees step by step to determine what signs are needed and where.

Start with the lobby. Large banners may be placed outside the hotel entrance or over the marquee. The goals are to prevent delegates from milling around and to direct traffic.

Notices on the bulletin board in the lobby, in elevators, and at crucial places in the corridors will help facilitate movement of people. The hotel staff also must be informed about events so it can answer questions intelligently. Such informed staff people should include the assistant manager, the bell captains, the door attendants and front desk person-nel.

At some properties, the creation and placement of signs and notices may come under union contract. In this case, the client should be notified about any union jurisdiction to avoid difficulties.

Today's technology is also being used to convey convention information. Many hotels have an in-house television channel that is programmed to display meeting information (in most cases, there is no charge for scheduling information, and the convention organizer or vendors have the option to purchase time for additional messages or advertisements approved by the hotel). When guests awaken, they merely turn on the TV to access the schedule of events for the day. This method of communication is especially useful when last-minute changes have been made in the convention program.

Chapter Summary:

Convention programs are becoming more sophisticated and often involve the services of both the hotel and a number of outside suppliers to carry them out. Today's hotels must have -- or be able to obtain -- the latest in presentation devices in addition to the traditional flipcharts and slide projectors used in the past. Today's meeting and convention attendees expect a professional presentation and come to the meeting with high expectations. In the next chapter, we will take a look at servicing meeting attendees. We will see how admission systems are set up and detail the wide variety of support services that are being used to make the convention or meeting a memorable event for all concerned.

Endnotes:

1.   Vicki Meade, "Picture This," *Lodging*, September 2000, p. 94.

Additional References:

The Boston Handbook on Meeting Technology, Doug Fox,
City of Boston and PCMA.
Contact PCMA at (877) 827-7262.

"What is Videoconferencing," *Videoconferencing Insight*, October 1999.
www.videoconferencing.co.uk

Internet Sites:

For additional information on the firms and organizations discussed in this chapter, visit the following Internet sites. The Web addresses listed are current as of January 2001. Addresses may change, however; if a site is not available at address below, a search engine can be used to access its new location.

AVW Audio Visual - www.avw.com
American Society of Training and Development - www.astd.org
Aspen Productions, Inc. - www.aspenproductions.com
Bauer Audio Visual, Inc. - www.bauerav.com
CP Communications - www.cpcom.com
In Concert Productions, Inc. - www.in-concert.com
International Webcasting Assocation - www.webcasters.org
Kodak - Meeting in a Box - www.kodak.com/90/mpi
Presentations.com - www.presentations.com
Projection Presentation Technology, Inc. - www.projection.com
Opryland Lodging Group - www.opryhotel.com

Study Questions:

1. In what cases would a hotel prefer an outside AV specialist rather than coping with in-house service? What have some hotels done to offer on-site service without the expense of purchasing AV equipment?
2. Discuss the types of sound systems, lighting, lecterns and projection screens usually offered by hotels.
3. What types of projectors are commonly used in meeting presentations? When is each type typically used?
4. How has technology changed the presentation of information? What high-tech AV equipment is used today?
5. How do union regulations affect meeting presentations?
6. What factors are considered when hotels determine charges for AV equipment?
7. How do signs and notices improve convention traffic flow? Where is signage commonly posted to enhance the convention experience? What other methods are used to provide information to convention delegates?

Key Terms:

Amplifier. A device that enables sound signals to be intensified.

Carousel projector. Most popular 2 by 2 (35mm) slide projector. Projects images from slides in mounts measuring 2 by 2 inches, presorted in round trays.

Computer projection panel (LCD). A device that projects the image on a computer monitor onto a screen.

Computer projector. Similar to LCD panels used with an overhead projector, except uses its own light source to project the computer image onto the screen.

Cordless/wireless microphone. Small, portable microphone that operates without any direct electrical connection.

Dissolve unit. Device that activates fade-in and fade-out of slides; can be used with several projectors. Used to create a "seamless" slide presentation.

Easel. Portable three-legged stand used to hold signs, boards, posters, etc.

Fastfold. Most popular of large viewing screens. Available in sizes up to 30 feet high.

Flip charts. Large pads on a tripod stand. Used by a speaker for illustration and drawings.

Keystoning. Distortion of a projected image; corrected by tilting screen.

Lavaliere microphone. A microphone that hands around the neck, leaving the hands free. Also called a lapel, neck or pendant microphone.

Lectern. A speaker's stand that holds papers; most are wired to provide suitable illumination.

Mixer board. Regulates the sound from multiple microphones.

Monitor. Device used to view a video or computer image.

Multi-media. Refers to the use of two or more audiovisual devices for a presentation.

Overhead projector. Projects transparency onto a screen. Speaker can write on transparencies as they are projected.

Rearview projection. Image projected from a projector positioned behind the screen onto the back of a screen placed between the viewer and the projector.

Roving microphone. Hand microphone with long cord that allows speaker to move around more freely.

Simultaneous interpretation. The interpretation of the presentation into another language while the speech is in progress.

Table microphone. Microphone attached to a small stand placed on a table, desk or lectern.

Unidirectional microphone. A microphone that picks up sound from only one direction. Used for speeches, it is different from omnidirectional devices, which pick up sound from all directions.

Virtual conferencing. Allows people at different sites to communicate by electronic linkage.

Learning Objectives:

This portion of your text introduces you to a number of the details inherent to a successful meeting or convention. We will discuss convention admission systems and security, additional services provided by the hotel to enhance the events, and ways to build attendance by offering special programs for the adult guests and/or children of attendees or delegates. When you have studied this chapter, you will:

- Be able to describe the various types of convention registrations commonly used and detail the security systems that are put in place to control attendance at events.

- Know the other services typically provided to convention groups by a hotel or selected suppliers.

- Be able to detail various programs that are arranged to entertain the attendees' companions or children while the meeting or convention is in progress.

Outline

Convention Registration

Convention Security
- Controlled Admission
- Ticket Arrangements
- Uncontrolled Admission
- Exhibit Security

Other Services
- Convention Headquarters Room
- Convention Hospitality Suites
- Guest Packages
- Telephones
- Printing and Duplication
- Decorations
- Entertainment
- Preferred Suppliers

Guest/Companion Programs
- Building Guest/Companion Attendance
- Activities for the Attendees' Guests
- Shopping Trips
- Sightseeing and City Tours
- Guest Lectures
- Other Activities
- Activities for Children

Checklists

Building Attendance: Mixing Business with Pleasure

Alan T. Brenner, CMP
Manager, Monterey Conference Center
Monterey, California

"*Mixing pleasure into business is an attendance-builder...if the program includes pleasure along with the work, with leisure time activities and entertainment arranged and scheduled just for the fun of it...well now, there's a meeting with some of the drudgery taken out of it...Getting together just for the fun of it does more than just entertain. It refreshes the mind and uplifts the spirit...The fun times promote a different level of exchange: unstructured, open, less risky, easier to be heard, more attentive, even confidential...Managers and planners should... arrange good times ahead of time. As the working sessions march along, it's good business to mix in some pleasure!*"

16

Admission Systems and Other Services

Admission at most conventions is controlled through registration of delegates. It is restricted for many reasons, such as membership, security and exclusivity. The convening organization sets the admission policy; the hotel's obligation is to help carry it out.

Convention Registration

Convention registration is different than room registration. As discussed in Chapter 11, when delegates register for guestrooms they are given room keys and account folios to which the hotel staff will post the delegates' charges. But in the **convention registration** process, delegates receive packets outlining the convention program and pay their registration fees to the convention's sponsoring organization. In most cases, a convention registration desk is set up away from the room registration area.

The hotel's convention service manager has little control over convention registration, and yet it is extremely important that things run smoothly. The delegate who has to wait may come away with a poor image of the hotel, even if it is not the hotel's fault.

Thus convention registration is a hospitality function, as well as a control function. The delegate's first impressions of the hotel are formulated at this desk.

Registration also serves as a source of information. Robert Paluzzi of Caesars Palace in Las Vegas, speaking before a class of ours, defined the convention registration desk as "the headquarters place for the meeting." A directory board is placed here, listing all the meetings of the day in chronological order, and a message board for memos and last minute changes.

The facility's convention service manager must be perceptive about the traffic flow and layout of this area and understand the problems that the meeting planner might face. Poorly trained registration help, a shortage of supplies, such as badges, computers or printers, and inadequate directional signs that lead to traffic bottlenecks are just a few of the potential problems. The convention service manager should try to keep these headaches from arising.

The registration area is generally broken into three areas: the packet pickup area, where the delegate receives the convention agenda; an area for the actual registration, where money changes hands and the delegate is given a badge; and an area where information and literature about tours and special services is available.

The packet pickup may occur in one of three ways. Packets may be picked up at the front desk when the delegates register for their rooms. Or after preregistering and preassigning rooms, the hotels may leave the packets inside the guest rooms. The most popular method is to hand out the packets at a convention desk independently of the guestroom registration.

Included in the delegate's packet are complete details of the convention and instructions for registering. A prudent convention service manager can make this packet really pay off for the hotel; it is an excellent method of informing and promoting in-house sales.

Among the items the association might include in the packet are:

- a list of scheduled events
- coupon tickets for all functions
- an introductory letter stating the purposes and aims of the meeting
- information about speakers and entertainers

The hotel should also provide the meeting planner with material for inclusion, such as:

- the hotel facilities available to the guest
- the times the hospitality suites and restaurants are open, and their locations
- procedures for handling hotel bills and check-out
- special favors, such as notebooks and pens with the hotel's logo

The second area in the registration process, the point where the actual registration takes place, is handled almost exclusively by the meeting planner. Three to four secretaries are normally required for large groups. Many cities provide secretaries free of charge through their convention bureaus; at other times, the hotel may be requested to find registration help, or the association may bring its own.

Figure 16.1 shows a typical example of the third stop in the registration process, the tour and special service desk. City tours, trips to local attractions, exhibit setup instructions, and similar services are provided at this point.

Figure 16.1. TOUR AND TRAVEL DESK.

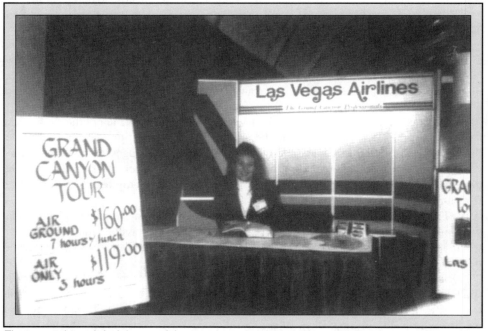

The tour and travel desk is one of the stopping points in the delegate registration process.

Convention Security

Another important area of concern to meeting planners is staging a worry-free event. Meeting planners want to ensure that their attendees and exhibitors don't have to worry about their personal safety or their property. Hotels have responded to this requirement for greater

454

security by installing electronic door locks, providing well-lighted parking and public areas, and offering high-tech alarm and surveillance systems in their exhibit halls.

The meeting planner can also contribute to a hassle-free meeting by controlling access to the group's functions. There are a number of ways in which this can be accomplished. The following pages will offer some insight into methods of controlling access to the event.

Controlled Admission

Most conventions insist upon registering all attendees, even when there are no charges for admission. At the very least, good mailing lists are derived from the data collected at the registration desk.

Admission often is limited to people with particular jobs or professions. People are screened at a central registration desk, fees are collected, and some sort of credential, usually a **badge**, is presented. The registrant's name and affiliation are typed, printed, or written on the badge, which then is usually placed in a plastic holder of some kind. Some holders are pinned to a garment; others clip or slip into a jacket pocket. Some conventions use a self-adhering badge for one-time use.

A more sophisticated type of badge is a plastic card embossed with the registrant's name and address, similar to a charge card. Exhibitors are supplied with "lead retrieval" devices that scan the badges of the attendees. At the end of the show, the exhibitor returns the machine to the lead retrieval company and receives a printout of all the attendees who visited the booth. (Exhibitors use trade shows to develop new trade contacts, and follow-up of these new contacts may result in additional business. That's the system that feeds the exhibits, which certainly support the entire convention.)

More sophisticated systems include bar coded badges, which can be used not only for on-site registration to identify guests, but also for billing purposes. Some registrants, for example, are coded to authorize the rental of audiovisual equipment or meals and special services. The bar codes will permit instant access to these charges, making cost-accounting far more accurate and up-to-date.

The convention service manager should be able to supply the names of local companies that stock different kinds of badges. However, it is generally not the hotel's responsibility to supply badges. This is the job of the convening organization. One innovative hotel stepped over this rule and designed a combination convention badge-service directory as a giveaway item. The badge-directory could be put into a suit coat pocket. The top of the badge provided space for the delegate's name and organization, and the bottom had the directory of the hotel's services.

Badges are often color-coded to sort out the different categories of registrants. In some cases, all but exhibitors are barred from the exhibit hall area except during certain show hours, and the color-coding helps the security guards police this policy. Color-coding also helps the exhibitors recognize prospective customers.

Ticket Arrangements

As discussed in Chapter 14, tickets provide a simple way of presenting evidence on which to base charges. If the agreement is to charge ten dollars for each person served at a luncheon, each of those lunch tickets represents a ten-dollar bill. The tickets must be counted immediately after the affair, and the number verified by an authorized person from the convention staff.

Systems for collecting tickets are simple enough, but nothing should be left for the staff to improvise. Suggest one system.

If the admission is to be by ticket, a small table or two, with chairs, is set up to handle the transactions. The table is especially needed if tickets may be purchased at the door and not merely presented. Sometimes tickets or badges are to be claimed at such a table. If you expect a crowd, you'll need several table stations. It is easier to bring up the subject and discuss it in advance than to scramble for tables and chairs at the last minute.

The tables and chairs may be placed just outside or just inside the door of the function room. Space is a consideration in deciding where to put the tables.

Waiters can collect tickets at a sit-down meal, while a hotel employee can collect tickets at the door for a buffet. It is worth repeating that a person on the convention staff should be at the door, too, to troubleshoot and to identify and greet VIPs. The tables also serve as a focal point for those who have questions, for notices to be placed, and for material to be picked up.

Tickets are often sold in advance by convention organizers. The associations make money from such functions in many ways. The price they charge might be more than they pay the hotel. In addition, not every ticket is used and no refunds are made. This happens especially when the convention sells a package of tickets for all the meals of the event at a flat fee.

Lots of ruffled feathers can be avoided if the hotel staff meets with the convention staff to decide what to do when delegates lose or forget their tickets. Don't expect a security guard or a waiter to improvise in such cases. If a convention executive is authorized to approve admission at each function, make some provision for recording that number. The simplest way is for the convention executive to have extra tickets to supply when he or she sees fit to do so.

Sometimes, the count must be verified and the bill submitted to someone other than the convention organization. Many companies sponsor food functions as a way of helping an organization and to promote their image within that industry. The procedures are all the same except that you deal with another person. Arrangements should be made to ascertain who should be billed — the convention organization or the sponsor. And an authorized person should be designated to verify counts. Payment arrangements should be spelled out.

Uncontrolled Admission

There are times when the doors are open to all who care to enter. However, this is relatively rare. But it is common to permit all who have badges to enter, allowing a free flow of people into and out of the meeting and function areas. This is where color-coding helps a great deal. When admission requires only a badge, and the badge is readily available, a security guard or other hotel person, such as a captain, stationed at the door may be all that is needed.

In such uncontrolled arrangements, it is most common for all liquor and food to be paid for with cash or coupons.

Exhibit Security

Conventions accompanied by exhibitions pose a number of potential problems that can be both embarrassing and costly to a hotel. Communication is needed between the convention service manager and the person responsible for security. Coordination and cooperation are necessary to provide the protection required.

When exhibitors are involved, the hotel's security force may have to be beefed up with outside help. The extra cost should be figured into the selling price and absorbed by the association. There are a number of national security companies that might be called in. However, many hotels maintain an on-call list of reliable off-duty police and fire officers. They have been trained in basic security procedures and are an excellent source of help.

All security personnel, whether part-time or full-time, experienced or inexperienced, should go through a training session and orientation of the hotel's facilities. A job description such as that shown in Figure 16.2 might be given to each guard. It outlines the guard's duties and responsibilities as an employee of the hotel.

Security in the modern hotel is becoming a more complex problem. There are four critical periods involved in security: move-in; open show hours; closed show hours; and move-out. Each is different.

Move-in and move-out periods are the most critical times because of the many transitory, poorly identified persons who have access to exhibits and displays. People have been known to take anything from calculators to operating tables. Security personnel must be wary of anyone who looks suspicious. For example, it is strange to see someone wearing an overcoat when it is quite hot outside. The security guard should make tactful inquiries of such people immediately. Security guards must be alert and observant to spot the unusual.

Tight security is essential at the loading docks and truck entries during move-in. Any materials or displays that go in and out of the door should have a pass-check from show management. Security personnel often encourage exhibitors during move-in to put their display goods in a "safe room," if one is available. If it is not available, they are encouraged to put their displays under their booths, away from the view of passing persons. This will help to eliminate theft.

Figure 16.2. A TYPICAL JOB DESCRIPTION FOR HOTEL SECURITY GUARDS.

Hotel Security Personnel Job Duties and Responsibility

1. *Help take care of an antagonist calmly.* Security must know how to take care of troublemakers through the use of logic or force without attracting too much attention from the guests.
2. *Watch for fire.* Security must know what to do about extinguishing small fires when fire trucks are still in transit.
3. *Report accidents.* A report must be presented to the hotel office for insurance purposes.
4. *Know how to take care of bomb threats.* Security must learn how to warn guests of bomb threats without making them panic.
5. *Emergency evacuation plan.* Security must know the hotel's exits so that in an emergency, they can direct people.
6. *Crowd control.* Security guards must know how to handle crowds during a mass panic.
7. *Policing loading areas.* Loading areas must be checked for stolen hotel property or stolen exhibits.

And in addition to these duties, a security officer must have a law enforcement background and be familiar with local and state laws.

It is advisable to have a roving officer rather than one who merely stands at the door; this more often is a psychological deterrent to would-be thieves.

During the show or exhibit, much of the responsibility for guarding the booths falls on the exhibitors themselves rather than the security guards; this is especially true of large conventions, where it is just not feasible to have a security guard at each exhibit. Exhibitors who decide to leave their booths for any period of time should have replacements so the booths are never left unattended.

When Burns Security Institute surveyed exhibitors and show personnel across the nation about exhibit hall security problems, more than 200 responded. According to the survey, exhibitors feel that one of the primary problems in exhibit areas is internal pilferage, with both hall workers and exhibit workers taking advantage of management trust and stealing items.

Likely times for employees to steal is during dismantling. Security needs are crucial at this time because so much is going on in the hall. The employee knows the hotel, its hiding places, and the exits that are unguarded. Because of this, employee thefts are often successful.

Exhibits are also very vulnerable to theft during the evening when exhibitors are gone. Exhibitors often leave in a hurry to join the merriment without putting expensive exhibits in the security rooms, if they are available.

Electronic surveillance is a new feature of hotel security systems. Burglar alarms and closed-circuit television are used now, but not to the extent that people might believe. Certainly there is going to be better control with such equipment, but there will be a greater expense, which the association will have to bear. Thus many conventions will decide not to use such surveillance because of their tight budgets. If, however, the exhibition is a large one with highly valued items, this electronic equipment will be used.

Other Services

There are a number of other services that may have to be arranged by the convening organization or that will require your input and assistance to execute. Press facilities may have to be designated, and a source of typewriter or computer rentals found for the convention staff. Local modeling agencies, public stenographers and similar services may have to called in. Most of these services do not require special handling, just advance notice and some thought.

Convention Headquarters Room

The administration of a large convention often requires a staff of five to ten people, so the association needs a room to work out of as an office. Hotels recognize this need and usually provide such a room free as part of the package. Ideally, this room should be adjacent to the meeting rooms and equipped with tables, typewriters, duplicating machines and perhaps a stenographer. Naturally, the hotel will charge for any such equipment supplied.

The Sonesta Hotel chain has gone a step further. A secretary is assigned to large groups free of charge to work in the headquarters room. The secretary's functions might include typing, handling messages, and arranging show tickets, among others.

Convention Hospitality Suites

Planning something for the evening hours is sometimes a real problem for meeting sponsors. One solution a convention manager might suggest to a client is a company hospitality suite. This calls for coffee, a bartender, card table, television — in general, a lounging atmosphere where the members may congregate informally. The advantage to the hotel is that the delegates stay in the hotel and spend their money there rather than being out on the town.

Another service provided by the hotel is what might be called "controlled hospitality suites." There is a tremendous demand for hospitality suites when a large convention and exhibition move into a hotel. Exhibitors rush for these rooms as places to entertain and transact sales. But the association executive also needs these suites for board and convention officials. When the demand for hospitality suites is greater than the number available, *the hotel's first obligation is to the meeting planner.*

Meeting planners are specific about the assigning of suites. Ground rules often state that:

- exhibitors are not to have their hospitality suites open while meetings are scheduled.
- non-exhibitors will not be allowed to have hospitality suites.

Guest Packages

Convention exhibitors and convention delegates frequently bring samples and promotional material that they would like to distribute at the meeting. Procedures for accepting these guest packages must be determined and communicated to the employees involved. If adequate storage space is available, packages are generally stored free. But it should not be a hotel's practice to store large packages or any packages for an extended period of time.

To avoid any misunderstandings, the hotel's policy can be stated in a clause, such as the following, in the organization's contract:

Storage of Exhibit Materials

The Hotel cannot accept and store shipments of exhibit materials in advance of a show. Due to County fire department regulations, crates, boxes, and other items to be used for the storage of exhibit materials cannot be stored on the Hotel premises during a show. It will be necessary for you to make arrangements with your exhibitor service to receive and store exhibits for delivery to the Hotel on the move-in date. These arrangements must also include the removal of empty crates, their storage during the show, and their subsequent return to the Hotel on the move-out date. Should any property not be removed by the designated move-out date, the Hotel management may store, or cause to be stored, any such property and your organization or the exhibitor will be charged a reasonable fee for all expenses incurred.

A package logbook should be maintained, showing the date of receipt, where a package is stored, and both the addressee and addresser.

Exhibitors occasionally misdirect packages to the hotel. Such packages should be referred to the decorator's warehouse for later delivery. If exhibitors ask the hotel at the end of the convention to wrap and send out packages, the service should be provided at a charge.

Telephones

Telephone service should be discussed with the convention staff before the event; it may be necessary to bring in telephone company representatives. Many conventions want provisions made for incoming calls to meeting rooms and exhibit areas. Outgoing telephone service from meeting rooms can be abused if it is not controlled. If outgoing service is requested, it must be planned. You should discuss who is to pay and when.

Printing and Duplication

Most printing is done by the organization before the event, but last-minute work is often needed. You should be able to supply the names of cooperative printers nearby who have proved their reliability. Some hotels have in-house print shops.

You should inform the convention staff of what types of duplication you can handle, what the lead time is, the costs, and the kinds of material you can handle. Have a fee schedule printed and presented beforehand or on display. You may have an in-house shop with offset printing capability, a stencil or spirit duplicator, or one of the more sophisticated models of office copiers. All of these can handle notices and the like. The convening organization is not the only one to seek such services. Many of the exhibitors look for last minute printing to fill needs of their exhibits and/or the sales meetings that are frequently held in conjunction with the convention.

Decorations

From time to time you will get calls for special draperies, flowers and plants, and special flags and banners. Exhibit decorators usually handle such items; they have the expertise and the trained personnel to take care of these things.

Hospitality suites may need floral decorations. You should have an arrangement with a florist to facilitate service and billing. Make clear to your clients whether they are to pay you or to deal directly with the florist. Unless you have an arrangement with a florist for exclusive business, you really shouldn't care if the florist and your clients make their own arrangements. Often, clients are happy to be steered to firms in the house or recommended by the hotel so that they can feel sure of prompt service, especially when they are not obliged to use that particular vendor.

Entertainment

There are union regulations and tax liabilities to be considered when live entertainment is used. This varies from area to area and should be part of the general information included in the letter of agreement and discussed at the pre-event meetings.

Live entertainment will also affect your table and chair setups. Bands may call for raised platforms. Entertainers have different requirements, too. The entire stage area should be discussed to make sure you have enough space and meet all specifications.

Hotels are often called upon to supply dressing rooms for entertainers. A problem is that entertainers prefer to rehearse on the scene, which may not be possible because the room may be in use for other convention events. This should be taken into consideration when the program is arranged and rooms selected. It may not be possible to honor such requests.

Preferred Suppliers

Because meetings and conventions have gotten so sophisticated and complex, it is not always possible for the planner to make the necessary arrangements for each of the services described in this section. In this case, the help of an outside party is often sought. Convention decorators, drayage companies, florists, printers and duplicators, photographers, ground handlers and audiovisual specialists are a few of the outside organizations that can be used. Over the years, the increasing use—and success of—other private services, called *destination management companies,* has led a number of properties to establish their own DMCs (see box titled "Destination Management Companies").

This can also be the case when dealing with some of the larger convention hotels. Nashville's Opryland Hotel and the Pointe Hilton Resorts, for example, own and operate services outright rather than deal with outside suppliers. They have even formed in-house destination management companies (DMCs) to keep as much as possible of the convention group's spending coming into the hotel — and offering planners the benefit of "one-stop shopping."

Receptive agents, who perform such services for delegates as guided tours and local transportation, are also extremely important to the success of a convention, as are local talent and modeling agencies, speakers bureaus, and temporary personnel services. Most hotels maintain a list of *preferred suppliers* who can provide specific services to meeting

---

DESTINATION MANAGEMENT COMPANIES

Marriott has led the way in offering in-house destination management services. Destinations by Marriott, a new division of Marriott Lodging, has been established at several properties. Resort properties were the first to offer in-house event planning, but now a growing number of city hotels are adding it as well.

The trend toward more elaborate meetings and conventions has been on a collision course with company downsizing, forcing more meeting planners to rely on outside help for planning the myriad details associated with group functions. More and more, planners have been turning to help at the scene of their functions—destination management companies (DMCs) that can arrange for everything from ground transportation to decorations to elaborate theme perties.

Many properties, who see this type of service as a logical extension of the sales effort, are getting into the act as well; either offering hotel office space to outside DMCs or setting up their own in house DMCs. This enables the hotel to offer everything required by the meeting planner—from planning through execution of the function—with the added benefits of consolidating deposits and posting all charges to the group's master account.

Naturally, the entry of hotels into this area has sparked some resentment from private DMCs. They claim that the DMC staff at the hotel may not have the experience—or contacts—of established DMCs. But the entry of hotels into this arena can only make things better for meeting planners—there will be increased competition for business, resulting in even more creative options—and better service.

Meeting planners are not required to use the services of an in-house DMC; a property's service bids for the business just as outside services do. Many meeting planners, however, appreciate this "one-stop shopping" option, making it likely that the number of in-house DMCs will continue to grow—and offer more and better service to stay competitive.

Preferred Suppliers: What Meeting Planners Have To Say

"The value of a preferred supplier list depends on where my meeting is located. In my home area — Greater Chicago — I have my own resources and preferred suppliers. I have had experience with most suppliers or know someone else who has used the vendors and service providers.

"Away from my home base, I'd welcome a preferred supplier list to tell me who does a good job in the area, but I still would do my own calling to compare prices. I wouldn't be bound to using that list, but I would appreciate that the hotel offered it."

Roseanne M. Hoban, Account Executive, Association Management Systems Naperville, IL

"I like to find my own suppliers and negotiate with them directly. I think you get a better price. If you go through the hotel to book your photographer, for example, there's going to be an added cost. The hotel is going to make some money. But it takes a lot of time to find suppliers on your own. The advantage of using a hotel's preferred suppliers are that they are familiar with the property's quirks and are likely to do a good job because their position with the hotel is at stake. And even if a planner is working with an in-house supplier, he or she can still negotiate with them directly and pay them directly."

Pat Fagan, Conference Service Manager, Sun Life of Canada Wellesley Hills, MA

"The issue of preferred suppliers is a hot one right now. More and more hotels are doing it, and I have even heard of hotels that are telling meeting planners that there will be a 15 percent surcharge if they do not use a preferred supplier. That's because the hotels are getting a commission from suppliers they recommend.

"I don't like it. I want to be able to choose the decorating firm, the florist, and the audiovisual company I use for my meetings. Now, if I am in a city where I have no contacts, a list of preferred suppliers might be helpful. But I don't want to be bound by it.

"Hotels that tell planners which suppliers they should use — or penalize them with a surcharge — should realize that the practice is going to cut into their business...for example, our association has a decorator we've used for the past seven or eight years. He knows our show and travels with us on site visits to cities we'll be using. While I am negotiating with the hotel, he meets with local decorators to explain exactly what we need and to find someone to contract for the job. I want his advice, not that of the hotel.

"Other groups have two- or three-year contracts with audiovisual people who will go to their meeting sites and run locally rented equipment to make sure the show goes the way it's supposed to. Now, if the hotel insists the planner employ a preferred supplier, the association is still bound to a contract with its own audiovisual firm and duplicate services could get very expensive."

Janet Balletto, National Meetings Coordinator, American Mathematical Society

---

planners. In many cases, the hotel receives a commission for recommending these suppliers.

Many times, hotels allow their preferred suppliers to maintain an on-site office. In this case, the supplier has a greater chance of getting most of the convention business, and pays the hotel rent and a percentage of sales. While some meeting planners appreciate the convenience of such on-site service, many are expressing concern over the growing number of properties that insist that the convening organizations use the property's preferred supplier (see box titled "Preferred Suppliers: What Meeting Planners Have to Say").

When hotels have *exclusives* with outside suppliers or their own DMCs, this should be clearly spelled out during the negotiation process. Exclusives, while not illegal, are not popular with meeting planners, and they should know about them in advance. In some cases, hotels are willing to compromise to secure the business (allowing the convening organization to bring in its own decorator if it agrees to use the property's photographer, for example).

Guest/Companion Programs

Many hotels have neglected a potentially profitable market in not promoting guest attendance at conventions. The average convention delegate spends approximately $200 per day in the hotel. If the delegate brought a guest the expenditures for both might well exceed $250 per day. It is a general conclusion that members stay longer and spend more money when a spouse or guest is along; both result in more money for the hotel. This is added revenue for the hotel and doesn't require the selling of another guestroom. For a 500-delegate convention, this could mean an *additional* $25,000 a day in sales, no small sum for any hotel.

More often than not, attendance at today's conventions includes the spouse or a guest. According to the most recent *Meetings & Conventions* Meetings Market Report, over 11 million spouses or guests attend conventions and association meetings each year. And for some groups the annual convention has become a family affair. Convention service people should make provisions for entertaining these additional guests. Special programs are usually arranged that are no different than any other program segment, as far as the hotel is concerned.

The first step, after recognizing the significance of attendance by spouses, is to sell the idea of a **guest/companion program** to the meeting planner, who after all must increase the convention budget if these programs are part of the plan. Point out that the presence of spouses and guests may be healthy for the meeting. The attendees are less likely to come to the morning session bleary-eyed after a late night on the town if their spouses or guests are accompanying them. Sessions will probably be more businesslike and delegates more alert, attentive and receptive. In addition, ticket sales for food and social functions will increase markedly with positive effects on the meeting planner's anticipated revenue.

Suggest to the meeting planner that they often determine the attendance figure. If delegates anticipate they'll have a good time, they encourage their mates or guests to attend the convention. Spouse and guest attendance at conventions fosters a close-knit family feeling, which improves the company's image. This is a strong factor in corporate decisions to invite the spouse or a guest to attend.

In summary, if a poll were taken, it would probably show that the most successful meetings were those where both the husband and wife attend.

Building Guest/Companion Attendance

Once a meeting planner is convinced of the value of inviting guests, much can be done by hotels to promote their attendance. Working in conjunction with the association, the con-

Developing Attendance With Guest/Companion Programs

Janet H. Wright, CEM
President, The Wright Organization, Inc.

"One of the most challenging aspects of meeting and exposition management is developing memorable recreational and social programs for both attendees and spouses and guests. In order to do so, you must know what the local area has to offer, and, equally important, know your audience...In some recreational areas, such as Orlando, Anaheim, etc., it is foolish to plan tours that compete with existing recreation. In those cases, we try to negotiate discounted tickets, line passes, etc. Yet in many locals where there is an abundance of activities we have found our more successful activities are those which we have created with the help of a convention service manager or a destination management company...Since we know our audience, the broad strokes of an idea are normally generated by us, with the convention service manager supplying the details and implementation. For example, one of our corporate meetings featured a 'Beach Olympics.' Since it was obvious we would lose attendees to the beach in the afternoon anyway, we made the beach part of the Corporate program...The event consisted of surfing, volleyball, sand castle building, hula dancing contests, and, during rest periods, participants heard a brief — and usually humorous, always instructive — message from the sponsor...With the tightening of tax laws, it is imperative that these supplementary activities fall within IRS guidelines as education rather than recreation to be considered tax-deductible...."

vention service manager should suggest ways to create interest and thus increase attendance. The following methods might be used:

- Supply the association with the hotel's brochures and internal pieces and suggest that the meeting planner include them with group mailings. Include such items as menus, pictures of the hotel and highlights of the city.
- In addition, you might secure a complete and up-to-date membership mailing list from the meeting planner and send personalized letters describing the planned activities. Also tell potential guests about the climate and offer suggestions on appropriate attire.
- Suggest that the association designate a chairperson for a guest/companion pro gram. Offer to work with this person in arranging shows, sight-seeing and other interesting programs.
- Advertise in the popular trade journals of the conferring group. Your ad should extol the virtues of having the delegates' guests come along.

Activities for the Attendees' Guests

Hotels have recently taken positive steps to increase spouse and guest attendance; a few properties have even created guest/companion service departments with directors to meet

Figure 16.3. GUEST PROGRAMS.

Guest Entertainment

Fashion Show: A very popular attraction for the ladies — and men also — It is usually staged at the Cabana Club or Boca West Country Club at the conclusion of luncheon. A very fine show can be put on by the Hotel dress shop with eight to ten professional models.

Backgammon: Beginners' and advanced play. Matched play or Round Robin tournaments available on request.

Brushless Painting Demonstration: A nationally known artist, lecturer and teacher with a flick of her hands and arms creates graceful rhythmical and delicate shadings of color magic. This is an enjoyable as well as entirely different kind of entertainment which captures every audience. Most interesting as well as creative program. Original work done during the demonstration will be given to members of the audience. The demonstration runs approximately 45 minutes. Arrangements can also be made for groups to participate or for private lessons in painting if desired. (Available December 1 - April 1).

Golf and Tennis Clinics: Information available upon request.

Boat Trip on Inland Waterway: Many groups plan a boat trip either north or south on the inland waterway. Various boats are usually available upon advance notice. A boat from Fort Lauderdale carries 400 people. A musical combo may be taken along on one boat for dancing aboard. Bar and soft drinks are available.

Shopping Trip: Many groups enjoy a shopping trip combined with luncheon. A trip can be arranged via air conditioned 41-passenger buses to Palm Beach with a stop for luncheon at one of the nice restaurants in Palm Beach, and a few hours shopping on beautiful Worth Avenue. Prices quoted on request. Such a trip would require one hour each way and another three hours for luncheon and shopping for a total of five hours.

The Flagler Museum: A complete tour of this famous museum located in Palm Beach. Luncheon arrangements can be made at one of the fine restaurants or hotels there.

Horse Racing: Spend a delightful afternoon complete with lunch at the world famous Calder Race Track. Arrangements made through the social hostess.

Arrangements for any of the above programs can be made through the
Convention Sales Department, Boca Raton Hotel and Club.

To build attendance, guest/companion programs are often offered. This list of activities appears in the convention brochure of the Boca Raton Hotel and Club.
Source: Courtesy of the Boca Raton Hotel and Club, Boca Raton, Florida.

the needs of the these attendees. Working alongside the convention service manager, the program's director helps convention committees plan and coordinate interesting programs.

Most hotels cannot afford to staff a special director for spouses and guests, but every hotel dealing in group business should at least prepare a directory of possible activities for them. This directory should be freely distributed to meeting planners. Figure 16.3 shows a list used by the prestigious Boca Raton Hotel and Club in Florida.

Shopping Trips. A very popular event that promotes goodwill is the shopping trip. Proper planning is very important. Normally, chartered buses take care of the transportation. A store guide should be scheduled to greet the attendees and, if possible, the group should be shown behind the scenes.

Timing is important. Often the attendees will break into smaller groups to go through different stores, so a rendezvous time should be clearly communicated. Also be sure that the attendees are back at the hotel in time to get ready for the evening's festivities.

Figure 16.4. GUEST AND CHILDREN'S PROGRAMS.

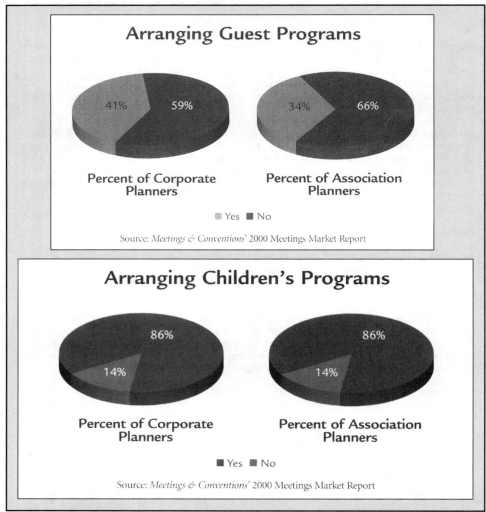

The most recent "Meetings Market Report" conducted by Meetings and Conventions *magazine shows the extent to which corporation and association planners accommodate guests and children at meetings.*

Sight-seeing and City Tours. Sight-seeing and tours are also popular. A competent guide is paramount. The convention service manager should have a list of sight-seeing and tour agencies contacted in advance.

All cities have points of interest: colleges, historic spots, gardens, and so on. One of the best-received tours is the home and garden type. Local residents open their homes for conventioneers' guests, often in an effort to raise money for charity. Generally five homes for viewing is ample. As in the case of shopping trips, timing is important. Discourage the use of cars; go by bus to keep the group together.

Guest Lecturers. Many guest/companion programs present speeches by professional people, such as doctors, lawyers, chefs, company executives and psychiatrists; questions and answers follow. Perhaps there are local speakers you might suggest to the organization. The range of these lectures is great, from flower arranging and dancing lessons to how to prepare a will.

Other Activities. Certainly the list of possibilities is nearly inexhaustible. Other suggestions gleaned from our readings and discussions with convention service managers are theaters and concerts, special business meetings for spouses and guests only, and finale parties. Local cultural activities, "behind-the-scenes" tours of the property and nearby attractions, and self-improvement courses (time management, stress reduction, dress for success, etc.) are other popular activities.

When planning guest activities, however, it is important to know your audience and gear your program to their specific interests and tastes. For example, the Hudson Valley Resort and Spa in Kerhonkson, New York, has developed a "menu" of ideas to customize activities to match the interests and personalities of the meeting group. Planners can choose from indoor and/or outdoor activities. A sampling of offers includes paintball battles, rock climbing excursions, and wine or antiquing tours. If possible, find our what was done in previous years (you won't want to duplicate last year's program) and gauge which activities were most favorably received.

You will also want to schedule activities carefully. Also keep in mind that many spouse and guests consider conventions as vacations and like to sleep in; suggest that guest/companion programs be scheduled in the afternoons. And, spouses and guests often dislike being rushed from one activity to the next; ample free time should be allotted.

Activities for Children

Many organizations are also seeing the value of inviting the entire family to conventions as a way to boost attendance (see Figure 16.4). Smart meeting planners are aware that working parents want to spend more time with their children and that combining business meetings with family vacations is both practical and economical. Having to plan activities and supervision for children of varying ages, however, can prove to be a challenge.

Some hotels have established in-house programs for junior attendees. The Hyatt chain, for example, offers Camp Hyatt, a program that offers structured recreation and learning activities for several age groups. The Walt Disney World Swan offers Camp Swan, with activities (featuring Disney characters) available until midnight. There are properties that offer licensed child care facilities or lists of registered babysitters for the youngest children.

Other properties (or the sponsoring organization) look to outside sources to provide daycare and activities for children. Some of these groups, such as KiddieCorp, provide temporary childcare for conventions, while others, such as Kids Along, develop special events and programs to entertain various age groups.

There are a wide variety of choices available, from on-site supervised recreational activities to field trips to local attractions. The wise meeting planner will schedule both children's activities to entertain young guests while their parents are tied up in meetings and activities for the entire family to enjoy together (one organization, for example, stages a variety show for the entire family, while others may arrange for discounted family passes to nearby attractions).

No matter which avenue is chosen, there are a number of factors to consider when hosting family-oriented groups. First and foremost is liability. The hotel must protect itself (and its guests) in regard to the safety of facilities used and the personnel supervising children. All childcare facilities should carry a minimum of $1 million in liability coverage, and most require that parents sign a waiver when dropping off children; this should also be done for any in-house programs, and especially for any field trips off-site. Background checks should be performed on all personnel having direct contact with children, and the hotel should ensure that there is a small ratio of children to staffers to ensure adequate supervision.

When the details have been worked out, it should be up to the meeting planner to communicate to the attendees exactly what will be offered—and who is responsible for paying for various activities and programs. This will eliminate any misunderstanding by participants, ensure a happier time for all involved, and establish the hotel as a family-friendly property that will likely be considered for future group activities and family vacations.

Checklists

As you can see, there are numerous details that must be worked out to ensure a successful meeting or convention. The use of checklists can help to avoid overlooking important items, and can assist in contracting for the special services that will be needed.

There should be an overall checklist giving an overview of the entire meeting as well as for each function. Many properties, such as the Sheraton Hotels, offer meeting planners' guides that include these types of checklists (see Figure 16.5). Save good checklists that you run across in your travels and adapt them to meet the needs of your convention clients.

Figure 16.5. CONVENTION CHECKLISTS.

Convention Planning Guide and Check List

1. ATTENDANCE
    Total number of convention registrants expected

2. DATES
- ☐ Date majority of group arriving
- ☐ Date majority of group departing
- ☐ Date uncommitted guest rooms to be released

3. ACCOMMODATIONS
- ☐ Approximate number of guest rooms needed, with breakdown on singles, doubles and suites
- ☐ Room rates for convention members
- ☐ Reservations confirmation: to delegate, group chairman or association secretary
- ☐ Copies of reservations to:_____

4. COMPLIMENTARY ACCOMMODATIONS AND SUITES
- ☐ Hospitality suites needed — rates
- ☐ Bars, snacks, service time and dates
- ☐ Names of contacts for hospitality suites, address and phone
- ☐ Check rooms, gratuities

5. GUESTS
- ☐ Have local dignitaries been invited and acceptance received?
- ☐ Provided with tickets
- ☐ Transportation for speakers and local dignitaries
- ☐ If expected to speak, even briefly, have they been forewarned?
- ☐ Arrangements made to welcome them upon arrival

6. EQUIPMENT AND FACILITIES
- ☐ Special notes to be placed in guest boxes
- ☐ Equipment availability list and prices furnished
- ☐ Signs for registration desk, hospitality rooms, members only, tours, welcome, etc.
- ☐ Lighting—spots, floods, operators
- ☐ Staging—size
- ☐ Blackboards, flannel boards, magnetic boards
- ☐ Chart stands and easels
- ☐ Lighted lectern, Teleprompter, gavel, block
- ☐ P.A. System—microphones, type, number
- ☐ Recording equipment, operator
- ☐ Projection equipment, blackout switch, operator
- ☐ Special flowers and plants
- ☐ Piano (tuned), organ
- ☐ Phonograph and records

- ☐ Printed services
- ☐ Dressing rooms for entertainers
- ☐ Parking, garage facilities
- ☐ Decorations—check fire regulations
- ☐ Special equipment
- ☐ Agreement on total cost of extra services
- ☐ Telephones
- ☐ Photographer
- ☐ Stenographer
- ☐ Flags, banners. Hotel furnishes U.S., Canadian, State flags
- ☐ Radio and TV broadcasting
- ☐ Live and engineering charges
- ☐ Closed circuit TV

7. MEETINGS
    (Check prior to convention)
- ☐ Floor plans furnished
- ☐ Correct date and time for each session
- ☐ Room assigned for each session; rental
- ☐ Headquarters room
- ☐ Seating number, seating plans for each session and speakers' table
- ☐ Meetings scheduled, staggered, for best traffic flow, including elevator service
- ☐ Staging required—size
- ☐ Equipment for each session (Check against Equipment and Facilities list)
- ☐ Other special requirements
    (Immediately prior to meeting, Check)
- ☐ Check room open and staffed
- ☐ Seating style as ordered
- ☐ Enough seating for all conferees
- ☐ Cooling, heating system operating
- ☐ P.A. System operating, mikes as ordered
- ☐ Recording equipment operating
- ☐ Microphones; number, type as ordered
- ☐ Lectern in place, light operating
- ☐ Gavel, block
- ☐ Water pitcher, water, glass at lectern
- ☐ Water pitcher, water, glasses for conferees
- ☐ Guard service at entrance door
- ☐ Ash trays, stands, matches
- ☐ Projector, screen, stand, projectionist on hand
- ☐ Teleprompter operating
- ☐ Pencils, notepads, paper
- ☐ Chart stands, easels, blackboards, related equipment
- ☐ Piano, Organ
- ☐ Signs, flags, banners
- ☐ Lighting ordered

Many chains offer planning kits that include checklists that the meeting planner can use to ensure that all the details of his or her meeting or event have been covered.
Source: Courtesy of the Sheraton Corporation.

☐ Special flowers, plants, as ordered
☐ Any other special facilities
☐ Directional sign if meeting room difficult to locate
☐ If meeting room change, post notice conspicuously
☐ Stenographer present
☐ Photographer present
    (Immediately after meeting, assign someone who will)
☐ Remove organizational property
☐ Check for forgotten property

8. EXHIBIT INFORMATION
☐ Number of exhibits and floor plans
☐ Hours of exhibits
☐ Set up date
☐ Dismantle date
☐ Rooms to be used for exhibits
☐ Name of booth company
☐ Rental per day
☐ Directional signs
☐ Labor charges
☐ Electricians and carpenter services
☐ Electrical, power, steam, gas, water , waste lines
☐ Electrical charges
☐ Partitions, backdrops
☐ Storage of shipping cases
☐ Guard service

9. REGISTRATION
☐ Time and days required
☐ Registration cards; content, number
☐ Tables; number, size
☐ Tables for filling out forms; number, size
☐ Chairs
☐ Ash trays
☐ Typewriters, number, type
☐ Personnel—own or convention bureau
☐ Water pitchers, glasses
☐ Lighting
☐ Bulletion board, number, size
☐ Signs
☐ Note paper, pens, pencils, sundries
☐ Cash drawers, number, size
☐ File boxes, number, size
☐ Safe deposit box
    (immediately prior to opening, check)
☐ Personnel, their knowledge of procedure
☐ File boxes, number, size

☐ Safe deposit box
☐ Policy on accepting checks
☐ Policy on refunds
☐ Information desired on registration card
☐ Information on badges
☐ Ticket prices, policies
☐ Handling of guests, dignitaries
☐ Program, other material in place
☐ Single ticket sales
☐ Emergency housing
☐ Hospitality desk
☐ Wastebaskets
☐ Mimeograph registration lists
    (if delegates fill out own registration cards)
☐ Set up tables away from desk
☐ Cards, pencils in place
☐ Instructions conveniently posted
☐ Tables properly lighted
(During registration, have someone available to)
☐ Render policy decisions
☐ Check out funds at closing time
☐ Accommodate members registering after desk has closed

10. MUSIC
For ☐ reception   recorded or live
    ☐ banquet   recorded or live
    ☐ special events   recorded or live
    ☐ shows   recorded or live
    ☐ entertainers and orchestra rehearsal
☐ Music stands provided by band or orchestra

11. MISCELLANEOUS
☐ Has an interesting entertainment program been planned for men, women and children?
☐ Baby sitters
☐ Arrange sightseeing trips
☐ Car rentals

12. PUBLICITY
☐ Press room, typewriters and telephone
☐ Has an effective publicity committee been set up?
☐ Personally called on city editors and radio and TV program directors
☐ Prepared an integrated attendance-building publicity program
☐ Prepared news-worthy releases
☐ Made arrangements for photographs for organizations and for publicity
☐ Copies of speeches in advance

Chapter Summary:

Hotel personnel are often involved in a number of activities to ensure that convention programs run smoothly. When servicing a large convention, the convention service department may be involved in everything from suggesting effective admissions systems to providing security to delegates and exhibits to arranging for in-house or outsourced decorations, entertainment, and printing services. To be effective, your property must be willing to "go the extra mile" in assisting the meeting planner with these details -- as well as helping to build attendance through guest/companion and/or children's programs.

Building your skills in these areas will enable you to handle any type of meeting -- including the largest of conventions and trade shows. In the next chapter, we will take a closer look at the trade show, which provides a true test of a hotel's ability to organize and execute minute details.

Additional References:

• Special Events: The Best Practices in Modern Event Management, 2nd Edition, by Joe Jeff Goldblatt, John Wiley and Sons, 2000.
www.hospitality@wiley.com

• The Convention Industry Council Manual, 7th Edition, Susan Krug, Executive Editor, 2000.

• The Dictionary of Event Management, by Joe Jeff Goldblatt and Kathy Nelson, John Wiley and Sons, 2001.
www.hospitality@wiley.com

Internet Sites:

For additional information on the firms and organizations discussed in this chapter, visit the following Internet sites. The Web addresses listed are current as of January 2001. Addresses may change, however; if a site is not available at address below, a search engine can be used to access its new location.

Global Event Partners - Destination Management Companies -
www.globaleventspartners.com
Marriott Hotels, Resorts and Suites - www.marriott.com
nternational Special Events Society (ISES) - www.ises.com
Association of Destination Management Executives - www.adme.org
PC/NAMETAG - www.pcnametag.com

National Speakers Association - www.nsaspeaker.org
The DMC Network - www.dmcnetwork.com
Kiddie Corp - www.kiddiecorp.com

Study Questions:

1. What is the difference between hotel registration and convention registration? What three methods are used to distribute delegates' convention packets?
2. There are four critical periods for convention exhibit security. Identify them and detail the methods for control of each.
3. List at least three services that can be directly provided to conventions by the hotel. List at least three services that can be provided to conventions either by the hotel or by outside suppliers.
4. Why is it important for hotels to work with or to be able to recommend reliable outside suppliers? How do these arrangements benefit: the hotel? the meeting planner? the outside supplier?
5. Discuss the importance of guest/companion attendance at conventions. List possible programs for encouraging adult attendance.
6. Many conventions are planned at vacation resorts or other "family friendly" locations so delegates can bring their children along. What activities are typically planned to entertain children while their parent(s) are occupied with convention business?
7. Review the convention planning guide and checklist used by the Sheraton Hotels. What are the benefits of such a checklist? Design a similar checklist for a property with which you are familiar.

Key Terms:

Badge. ID card given out during convention registration with registrant's name and affiliation printed on it for control and security reasons.

Convention registration. Process where attendees receive packets outlining the convention program and pay convention registration fees.

Guest/Companion program. Entertainment/activities, such as sightseeing, shopping and lectures, planned for guests and companions attending conventions.

Learning Objectives:

This portion of your text introduces one of the most lucrative — and most detailed — segments of the meetings and conventions industry: the exhibit and trade shows market. Trade shows require extensive planning in a number of areas, which we will cover in this chapter. When you have studied this chapter, you will:

- Be able to describe the importance of the trade show to associations, hotels, and local businesses and tell what personnel are typically involved in staging trade shows.

- Be able to detail the areas that are considered when planning for trade show events, including show hours and room assignments, labor regulations, handling of exhibits, and insurance.

- Be able to describe how trade shows are billed and what factors are considered when billing for exhibit space and setup.

Outline

The Scope of Exhibits and Trade Shows
- Types of Exhibits
- Exhibit Assignments

Exhibit Planning
- Key Trade Show and Exhibit Personnel
  - The Trade Show Manager
  - Exposition Service Contractors/Decorators
  - Exhibitors
- Scaled Drawings
- Layouts
- Photo File
- Timetable
- Show Hours and Room Assignments
- Labor Regulations
- Insurance

Exhibit Billing Procedures
- Hotel's Rental Charge
- Exposition Service Contractor's Fee

Convention Shipping and Receiving
- Exhibit Shipping
- Recommended Address Terminology
- Shipping Methods
- Incoming Shipping Costs

Exhibitions Require a Team Effort

Sam Lippman
President
Integrated Show Management and Marketing

"Producing trade shows is an exciting, demanding, complex challenge that requires teamwork and communications...The trade show industry is completely interdependent. Associations depend on the income generated by trade shows to keep their membership fees low and still offer their members many benefits and services. Show managers depend on their trade show team for the success of their trade's show. Trade show contractors depend on healthy trade shows for their livelihood. Facility managers depend on accurate floor plans to deliver their services to the correct booths. Exhibitors depend on qualified labor to set up and dismantle their displays. Because of this interdependency, successful trade shows have a commitment to communications. Trade show managers communicate early and constantly with their exposition contractors, facilities, labor and exhibitors. This constant, interactive communication among all members of the trade show team helps to create shows that provide a cost-efficient marketing and education forum for exhibitors and attendees."

17

Exhibits and Trade Shows

T he exhibit is a very important part of the convention business. It is a key element in most trade conventions, with over 80 percent including an exhibition in their annual meeting, and a very important part of technical, scientific and professional conferences as well. Associations see exhibits both as a way to attract attendance and as a very essential revenue producer.

Exhibitors, in turn, consider exhibitions as unique opportunities to market their products. There is no other way they could reach so many buyers so quickly, and face to face. Most of the attendees present at the shows are decision makers, so much effort is put into exhibits as marketing tools.

The Scope of Exhibits and Trade Shows

Exhibits and trade shows are a lucrative and fast-growing segment of today's convention and meetings market. Growing at an annual rate of over four percent, an increasing number of companies are taking advantage of this excellent marketing opportunity, and some trade shows are becoming major international events (see Figure 17.1).

We explained in Chapter 4, "Selling the Association Market," that the association makes a profit from exhibits by charging exhibitors for booth space. Exhibits also offer the association a cash flow, which helps finance the convention planning. The exhibitor's reservation for booth space is usually accompanied by a check for half the cost of the space. The rest is sent in later, but still in advance of the convention.

The association's only costs at this stage have been for promotion of the event and payroll, a year-round burden. This advance money from exhibitors amounts to a great deal, and it literally finances the convention. The only additional revenue of any consequence comes from admission and registration fees. It, too, is solicited in advance for the same reason.

The importance of the trade show is reflected in the development of hotels with considerable convention space. These hotels have had great success in going after conventions with exhibits.

It is a rare convention organizer who does not prefer to house the entire convention under one roof. When this is not possible, separate exhibit centers are often used in conjunction with neighboring hotels. The largest exhibits use huge convention centers such as McCormick Place in Chicago, which has 2,200,000 square feet, and the Las Vegas Convention Center, which boasts over 1.3 million square feet of space.

Convention hotels with built-in exhibit areas are successful even in a city with a giant convention center. In Las Vegas, for example, the attraction of a one-house event brings lots of business to individual properties, even with the convention center available. While the very largest conventions would use the convention center and several hotels near it, a somewhat smaller event might turn to the MGM Grand Hotel (5,009 room and 150,000 square feet of exhibit space), Caesars Palace (1,508 rooms and 91,000 square feet of exhibit space), or the Mirage Hotel (3,044 rooms and an exhibit area of 60,000 square feet). All have the necessary supporting meeting rooms, as do other hotels in the city that can accommodate conventions with exhibits.

Figure 17.1. TRADE SHOW MARKET OVERVIEW.

Trade Show Market Overview
1989 - 2000

Year	Number of Shows	Number of Attendees	Number of Exhibiting Companies	Number of Net Sq. Ft. Used
1989	3,289	60 million	1 million	270 million
1990	3,738	75 million	1.1 million	330 million
1991	3,887	71 million	1.2 million	331 million
1992	4,066	77 million	1.2 million	366 million
1993	4,172	73 million	1.2 million	387 million
1994	4,316	85 million	1.3 million	400 million
1995	4,380	116 million	1.3 million	448 million
1996	4,400	101 million	1.25 million	448 million
1997	4,336	110 million	1.26 million	445 million
2000*	4,781	140 million	1.5 million	550 million
Average Annual Growth Rate to Year 2000	4.1%	12.1%	4.5%	9.4%

Source: *Tradeshow Week, Inc.*

Source: Convene, July 1998, p. 34.

Las Vegas enjoys as much event business as it does because of its excellent convention facilities and tourist attractions. However, trade show business is not limited to large properties only. Smaller hotels around the country use in-house exhibit areas as an asset in selling convention business and as a lucrative source of revenue. Research by the Center for Exhibition Research reveals that approximately one-third of the conventions involving trade shows have fewer than 50 exhibits per convention. A common rule of thumb is that twice the amount of space is needed for each square foot of booth space. For example, 50 eight-by-ten-foot booths need 4,000 square feet of space for the actual booths plus an additional 4,000 square feet of space for aisles, entrance and exit areas, and registration desks.[1]

Types of Exhibits

There are three basic types of exhibits: a **table top exhibit**, that is often used when there are few exhibitors or space is limited; an **area exhibit**, in which the exhibitor is assigned a specific floor space for displaying large, tall equipment or two-tier displays; and, a **booth exhibit**, which is usually constructed with **pipe and drape**.

The most common arrangement is the booth plan. Exhibit booths are ten feet wide by eight feet deep or ten feet wide by ten feet deep and limited in height to eight feet or 12 feet along the back wall with three-foot high side dividers. There are four basic types of booths: 1) standard booths (also known as in-line booths) are placed back-to-back with adjacent booths on the sides and have maximum heights of eight feet; 2) perimeter booths are located on outside walls and maximum heights of 12 feet are allowed; 3) peninsula booths consist of four or more spaces and are bordered on three sides with aisles; and 4) island booths are bordered on all four sides by aisles and include four or more spaces.

Exhibit Assignments

Not only is the size and type of booth important to exhibitors, but also its location on the trade show floor. Exhibitors are eager to acquire prime spots near the entrance that are likely to provide the highest foot traffic.

Space can be assigned to exhibitors by four different methods. One of the most commonly used systems is the *first-come, first-served* approach. While many exhibitors feel this is the fairest system, this approach must be carefully planned. The association must first ensure that all potential exhibitors receive an exhibitor prospectus at the same time and that a firm date is set for the receiving of space reservations. The association will also need to assign staff members to check postmarks to ensure that space is indeed awarded on a first-come, first-served basis.

The *point system* is also used by a number of trade show organizers. Under this system, points are given to potential exhibitors based on a number of factors — exhibition in previous years, advertising pages in the association's monthly magazine, donations to the organization, etc. This type of system, however, can cause drawbacks for new or small companies that find it difficult to compete with more established exhibitors and for the organization itself; waiting for former exhibitors to claim their space may result in delays before a general sale of remaining exhibit space can be initiated.

A *lottery system* in which numbers are drawn for a position to select exhibit space can also be used. Under this system, space is awarded to exhibitors based on the numerical order of the lot drawn. While this system may be fair, it, too, can pose problems. A large exhibitor, for example, may draw a high number and find itself relegated to a "back corner" — and withdraw from future exhibitions. To combat this problem, some organizations hold two separate lotteries — one for exhibitors who require multiple spaces and one for small exhibitors requiring only one or two booths.

The fourth method, *advance sale*, takes place at a current exhibition. Exhibitors present can make their future site selection from a floorplan of the upcoming event. This may be done at a specified time, which allows everyone an equal chance to make space reservations, or may be done throughout the show on a first-come, first-served basis.

This method does have several disadvantages. Perhaps a previous exhibitor has not been able to attend the current show or the exhibitor's representatives have no authority to make reservations on behalf of their company. Another drawback is that this method works against potential new exhibitors who are not showing at the current show.

No matter what method the convening group decides upon to assign exhibit space, firm criteria should be used to avert ill feelings — and potential liability. Methods used to assign space should be clearly documented: postmarked envelopes should be kept when selling space on a first-come, first-served basis; guidelines for awarding points should be clearly spelled out and followed; lists of lots drawn in a lottery system should be kept; and, procedures should be implemented to ensure fairness in an advance sale situation. The method of selection and any pertinent information should be clearly spelled out in an **exhibit prospectus** to avoid misunderstanding. This information kit, which is sent to potential exhibitors (and will be discussed in greater detail later in the chapter), outlines general information, such as space reservation methods and deadlines and payment methods.

Exhibit Planning

Normally the trade show is held in conjunction with the professional or trade association's annual meeting, but other groups or corporations may also sponsor a trade show as a profit making venture. The association or corporation may manage the trade show from in-house, using its own personnel, or may hire an outside show manager to plan, organize, market and operate the show.

Both trade show managers who work directly for a particular association and those who work as independents are represented by the International Association for Exposition Management (IAEM), a professional association of approximately 3,000 show managers.

As mentioned in Chapter 10, some hotels with substantial dedicated exhibit space may staff a director of exhibit service. This person functions as the principal liaison between the hotel's convention service manager and the meeting group's show manager. There is a wide range of professionalism in show management. Local committees generally have little background in exposition management, while association and corporate meeting planners responsible for annual shows have developed considerable expertise in conducting a show. Hotels committed to the trade show market are well advised to employ a knowledgeable director of exhibit service with a good understanding of exhibit and trade show jargon to assist committees and meeting planners in producing a successful event.

Key Trade Show and Exhibit Personnel

Trade shows provide a forum at which companies can exhibit their products and services to convention attendees. They are, essentially, a "live" marketing event, with about sixty percent of today's trade shows held in conjunction with an association convention and forty percent sponsored by independent corporations. No matter how an exhibit is managed, if your property plays host to such an event, you will be working with a number of different people, including:

- trade show managers,
- exposition service contractors, and
- exhibitors.

Trade Show Manager. The **trade show manager** (also called the show producer or show organizer) produces and manages the exhibition. He or she is responsible for developing a list of potential exhibitors, marketing the show to both exhibitors and attendees, contracting with an exposition service contractor, and overseeing all logistical planning. The trade show managers you work with will be employed in one of two ways:

- directly for the association, serving as an in-house staff member assigned to organize, market and manage the show for the association (the National Restaurant Association operates in this manner). Or, the trade show manager may be an outside individual or firm contracting with the association to oversee the trade show aspect of the convention.
- as a private entrepreneur or corporate entity, organizing an independent trade show for profit. For example, Comdex, the world's largest computer show, is owned and managed by Softbank. A recent trend is for associations to either sell their trade show and use the invested funds to benefit the association or partner with a multimanagement trade show firm and get a percentage of the profits. Examples of such trade shows include the sale of the American Booksellers Association's trade show to Reed Exhibition Companies and the sale of the National Sporting Goods show to Miller Freeman, Inc.

The show manager's first priority is to sell floor space to exhibitors. To attract exhibitors, the trade show manager prepares an *exhibit prospectus* that includes the location and dates of the show, a profile of prospective and past attendees, floor rental prices, and other pertinent information to assist potential exhibitors in making a decision as to whether to participate. High attendance figures from past shows are particularly important in recruiting exhibitors.

Exposition Service Contractors/Decorators. It is customary for the hotel to furnish the basic exhibit area, perhaps with a floor covering, but perhaps with nothing. The trade show manager usually selects an exposition service company to work as an "official" **exposition service contractor** (decorator) for the event. While the trade show manager will contract with an exposition service firm, this does not generally preclude exhibitors from using an outside contractor for the installation and dismantling of their booths. Some companies have contractual arrangements with firms that travel around the country setting up the corporation's exhibits. These firms are called *exhibitor appointed contractors*. Show management and the "official" contractor require a letter of intent to use an outside contractor.

Sam Lippman, who is quoted at the start of this chapter, considers the exposition service contractor the most important member of the trade show team. He says:

> "The exposition service contractor's account executive is the show manager's 'eyes and ears' on the exhibit floor, allowing the show managers to focus on their many other responsibilities. From the unloading of the first truck to the dismantling of the last exhibit, a happy exhibitor is

the goal of both the show manager and the exposition service contractor. Exhibitors that have a successful show will increase their budget for the next show, for more exhibit space and more complex displays, which means more revenues for both show management and their exposition service contractor."[2]

The contract with the show manager generally calls for general decorating of the exhibit hall (includes entrance signage, aisle carpeting, and basic construction of pipe and drape booths), the design of the **exhibition floor plan**, and on-site coordination for the show.

It is the exposition service contractor's job to organize, coordinate and execute all the services required to set up the exhibit area. The old-time decorator was basically a window trimmer, carpenter and sign painter whose function was to construct eight-by-ten foot booths. Decorators' work today is much more encompassing. They are in charge of labor, plumbing, electrical work, signs, cleaning, telephones, florists, booth hostesses, audiovisual information and drayage (shipping and warehouse storage of exhibits).

In fact, exposition service contractors are key persons in the convention process. They work with meeting planners from the pre-show planning until the exhibit hall is cleaned and all the exhibitors' equipment is returned to the home offices. Decorators prepare floor plans for approval by local fire marshals. They contract with a number of suppliers, such as audiovisual dealers and florists, removing this task from the meeting planners. They provide floor managers to supervise and control the setup and dismantling of exhibit booths.

Equally important, they consult with hotel convention sales and service staffs in an effort to bring about understanding and acceptance of each other's procedures and responsibilities (see box titled "Do's and Don'ts of Exhibit Planning). This mutual understanding is best facilitated through a pre-event meeting or a series of meetings between the decorator and the convention service manager.

The exposition service company's contract with the exhibitors is initiated through the **exhibitor's service kit**. This kit or manual provides information, pricing and order forms for booth items including floor coverings, signage, janitorial services, electrical services, furniture rental, shipping of materials and so on. The service contractor of today frequently uses the power of technology to carry on business with exhibitors. Using the Internet, the exposition service contractor can display the floor plan, allowing exhibitors to determine space availability. Additional linking allows the exhibitor to browse the exhibitor's service kit and complete forms for drayage, carpet, phone lines, and other needs on-line.

Often, the exposition service contractor will subcontract special services, such as floral, catering and audiovisual, to specialty contractors. But, regardless, the exhibitor normally contracts directly with the exposition service contractor for all services.

The exposition service manager oversees the move-in, set-up and tear down of the trade show and is present throughout the event to service any last minute needs of either the exhibitors or the trade show manager.

Because of the tremendous coordination required in staging an annual show, many associations and independent trade show sponsors seek multi-year contracts with an exposition service company. A good working relationship between the sponsoring organization and the exposition service contractor is of obvious importance and should receive the very highest priority by all parties.

Exhibitors. The **exhibitor,** who can be an individual or a firm, sees the trade show as an opportunity to demonstrate products or services to prime decision makers and is therefore diligent in selecting and participating in what he or she considers to be most important events.

Exhibitors are first contacted by the trade show manager through the prospectus. After deciding to participate, they rent floor space from the trade show manager. The exhibitors are then introduced to the exposition service contractor via the exhibitors service kit and buy (or rent) other services and materials, such as booth signage and decorating from the exposition service contractor.

Many participating companies appoint an exhibit manager to coordinate the exhibit. Large companies who participate in several shows throughout the year may assign a corporate exhibit manager to coordinate their company's exhibit. Smaller companies give sales managers or sales staff managers the additional part-time responsibility of organizing the exhibit and selling at trade shows.

While the property will not usually deal directly with exhibitors, they can have an enormous impact on the property. They require guestrooms, patronize food and beverage outlets, and often host hospitality suites. It is a wise convention service manager that works with a show organizer to ensure that the organization's overall plan includes analyzing how exhibitors will affect the overall strategy for the function.

In some cases, for example, a limited amount of guestrooms may be available at the host property, and an overabundance of exhibitors may result in convention attendees being forced to find lodging elsewhere. The convention service manager may suggest that exhibitor registration be limited to ensure that enough guestrooms are available for convention delegates. Or, the convention service manager may work with the trade show manager to find alternate accommodations for exhibitors.

Scaled Drawings

We have discussed the need for the hotel to have scaled drawings of its meeting rooms. Obviously, the same need exists for the exhibit area (see Figure 17.2). Large, accurate drawings to scale should note the presence of columns, doors, windows, obstructions of any kind, the **floor load** capacity, and ceiling heights. The latter two factors are essential because some displays rise high in the air and some merchandise is heavy.

Supply the drawings to association clients in sizes that make good work sheets. It is important to keep drawings to scale. Many office copiers reduce the image to save paper or to increase sharpness. Some do it slightly; some, a great deal. But reduction destroys the key to the scale. If the scale is given as one-quarter inch equaling one foot, a *reduced* drawing carries such a notice, but a rule laid across the drawing would give a false reading. Imagine setup day with a layout that was planned on the basis of such a false print!

If you have your scaled drawings printed, perhaps in a fair quantity by the offset printing process in a convention booklet, be sure to inform your printer of the need to maintain the strict scale. Usually, printers reproduce your copy exactly as it is presented, but it doesn't hurt to make sure. Sometimes, a slight reduction in overall size helps the job get done on a specific size sheet of paper, and it usually does not affect the overall quality of a job. But not in your case. If the printer knows the importance of maintaining your scale, you might eliminate costly and aggravating problems later on.

Do's and Don'ts of Exhibit Planning

Exposition service contractors do find fault with hotels. GES Exposition Services, a leading decorator with offices nationwide, has outlined the following hotel problem areas from actual convention situations:

1. Poor Planning for Exhibit Layout

How many times has an exhibitor walked into his assigned booth space to find a beautiful gigantic and low-hanging chandelier right smack in the middle of the booth — or a column or similar obstruction? Reason? The convention sales personnel just pulled out a basic stock floor plan and submitted it to the client — without consulting the exposition service contractor— and nowhere did the plan indicate the column or chandelier.

2. Plumbing

Neither the plumbing contractor nor the exhibitors will ever be the same after this session — 140 booths in 30,000 sq. ft. of exhibit space...and two water and drain outlets from which to supply all the plumbing lines and connections required by the exhibitors.

3. Electrical

This was an electronics show; power load was so great that existing equipment in the hotel was inadequate to provide half the required current. Additional lines had to be brought in by the utility company at the time of the show move-in. An electronics show obviously involves a heavy power load, and the hotel could have saved everybody a lot of headaches if this had been taken into consideration while booking the show — balancing requirements against electrical facilities available — and increasing the power in advance.

4. Outdoor Tent or Patio Shows

No one at GES mentions "Patio Shows" to our production supervisor who handled this one. The exhibit area consisted of canvas carport-type awnings, on the oceanside patio of the hotel...on the windiest day of the year. A case of man against the elements...and I'm afraid "man" came out a very poor second best. It can be done, but only on a cost plus basis.

5. Labor

How many times have we set up a one hundred or two hundred booth show, all custom constructed displays, and found we would be allowed six hours for dismantle, pack-up and move out from the area? This unreasonable rush causes breakage and damage to property, misdirected shipments, and worst of all, an unhappy client who will not do business with you again.

6. Freight Move-in and Move-out

We handled a big show, involving snack food exhibits, which began dismantle at 5:00 p.m., with exhibitors for another show scheduled to begin set-up the following morning, in the same room, with different color booth drapery. The schedule didn't allow enough time for dismantle of the outgoing show, let alone the massive clean-up a food show involves with popcorn, hotdogs, mustard, ice cream and soft drink syrups on carpets and floors. We pulled out the carpet for cleaning, of course, but those slippery floors had to be scrubbed, and scrubbed thoroughly after dismantle, recrating and move-out of all freight was complete. So we worked all through the night, and throughout the morning, while the impatient incoming exhibitors watched in fascination.

7.   Heavy Equipment

Heavy equipment shows do not belong on ballroom floors, nor should this heavyweight material have to be moved over marble or plush carpet. Further, the live load limit of a floor is not equal to the static load limit. One of the machines exhibited in a ballroom weighed 12,800 pounds, in a single unit 12' long and 8' wide. Not only that, but there was another part meant to be attached to the machine, weighing an additional 6,000 pounds all by itself, which was to be hoisted and attached to the top of the machine, to complete the unit, to a total height of 20'. We regret to say the hotel took a dim view of the whole operation, and refused to allow use of the hoisting rig necessary to raise the 6,000 pound attachment, so the show went on without it. A perfect show for a concrete floor, but never a ballroom.

8.   Crane and Hoisting

Here is a beautiful hotel, conceived as a convention facility, with no loading dock. The primary exhibit area is on the third floor, with freight access through a removable plate glass window, also three stories above the ground. The hotel is ideal for holding a gift show, where small freight can be moved in through the receiving room and service elevators, but our show consisted of construction materials. The only way to get the freight in was to park our loaded trailers right smack under the canopy, at the hotel's main entrance, unload the freight onto specially constructed sling platforms, and hoist it up into that third floor access window by means of a two-ton crane.

9.   Control of Dock

Here, we meet the drayage contractor's most serious problem. The most important single function of the drayage contractor is to get the exhibit freight in and out on schedule, a schedule not determined by him, for his convenience, but predetermined by the association and the hotel. No hotel has unlimited facilities for receiving, storing and handling tons of exhibit freight. Most have limited dock space. Some much tighter than others, but none so extensive that they can accommodate miscellaneous common carriers, display house vans and independent exhibitors' vehicles, out of control of the official drayage contractor. The official drayage contractor assumes the responsibility for prompt, orderly move-in and move-out of all freight for the show, and the only way he can fulfill this obligation is by being allowed absolute control of the loading dock, and with all freight movement through his hands

As we said, a meeting of the convention service manager and the decorator before showtime is a must. Most of the difficulties outlined above could be resolved through communication and joint cooperation.

Layouts

You should also offer a convention planner a variety of layout schemes for a specific hall (see Figure 17.3). An exhibit in a hall seemingly too large for it looks awful — it carries the stigma of failure on the part of the association to attract enough exhibitors. A different layout might provide wider aisles, or conference or rest areas; or perhaps the exhibitors could be spaced out to make for a better looking, more efficient exhibit. Screens (run-off drapes) or temporary walls could be used to block off unoccupied areas. The appearance of the exhibit is important to the hotel as well as to the convention planner. It is in your interest to make the exhibit look great.

The schematics should be presented to the convention executive early enough to help him or her prepare convention solicitation brochures. After all, the executive sells specific areas designated by numbers, not general space. It is difficult to change the layout

Figure 17.2. SCALED DRAWINGS.

This scaled drawing for the Boca Raton Hotel and Club provides information on ceiling heights, sizes of door openings, and floor load limits. Note that although a scale is provided it is approximate.
Source: Courtesy of the Boca Raton Hotel and Club, Boca Raton, Florida.

after positions have been assigned. Exposition service contractors might be helpful in supplying these exhibit layouts for your hall.

The service contractor will know the local fire regulations in regard to aisle width, room capacity, access to exits and anything peculiar to the area. In many places, the local fire inspector must approve exhibit layout and setup. It is so much easier to conform to local fire regulations from the very onset of the planning of the exhibit. It avoids those headache-provoking late changes and explanations that can plague a planner.

Photo File

It is also helpful to maintain a file of photographs of conventions held previously in your establishment. The convention executive can check out aisle width, exhibit heights and overall appearance from the photos. All too often, printed material shows only open rooms. Besides guiding the planner for his or her layout, the photos carry the endorsement of past patronage by convention organizations.

Guide the photographer by listing the characteristics you want shown clearly in the photographs. Build a file of floor setups with and without people in the scene.

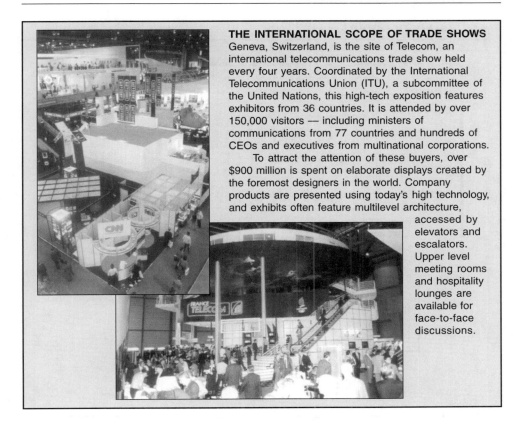

THE INTERNATIONAL SCOPE OF TRADE SHOWS
Geneva, Switzerland, is the site of Telecom, an international telecommunications trade show held every four years. Coordinated by the International Telecommunications Union (ITU), a subcommittee of the United Nations, this high-tech exposition features exhibitors from 36 countries. It is attended by over 150,000 visitors — including ministers of communications from 77 countries and hundreds of CEOs and executives from multinational corporations.

To attract the attention of these buyers, over $900 million is spent on elaborate displays created by the foremost designers in the world. Company products are presented using today's high technology, and exhibits often feature multilevel architecture, accessed by elevators and escalators. Upper level meeting rooms and hospitality lounges are available for face-to-face discussions.

Timetable

When planning for the exhibit, it is necessary to block out the time that each exhibit area will be in use. This includes the time needed to bring in the exhibit material, remove it from the crates, set it up, remove the packing cases, and clean up before the exhibit opens.

After the event, the exposition contractor must plan the logistics of bringing in the packing cases, delivering them to the individual booth areas, arranging for shipping or storage of the units, and cleaning up in time for the next exhibit to move in.

A day or two is needed for both setup and teardown with most exhibitions. Labor charges are important in this process. The most common complaint of exhibitors is the need to use high-priced labor at overtime rates. In an effort to negotiate the improvements they feel are needed, exhibitors have joined together to form their own trade associations.

Exhibitors in the health care industry are represented by the Healthcare Convention and Exhibitors Association (HCEA). The International Association for Exhibition Management (IAEM) is another professional association of exhibit managers. Companies and individuals who design and produce the exhibits are represented by the Exhibit Designers and Producers Association (EDPA).

Show Hours and Room Assignments

Two other common complaints of exhibitors are the hours the exhibit hall is scheduled to be open and the method in which guestrooms are assigned. Actually, both of these are

Figure 17.3. BOOTH LAYOUTS.

RIALTO 1

RIALTO 2

RIALTO 3

RIALTO 4

GRAND SALON

phones

bar

regis-
tration
desk

Booth Size: 8' x 10'
Aisle Width: 7' 6''
Number of Booths: 235

phones

bar

regis-
tration
desk

Booth Size: 8' x 10'
Aisle Width: 8'
Number of Booths: 313

(continued)

These graphics from the Bally Grand Hotel's convention brochure show a variety of booth layouts for the same room.
Source: Courtesy of the Bally Grand Hotel, Las Vegas.

RIALTO 1

RIALTO 2

RIALTO 3

RIALTO 4

GRAND SALON

phones

bar

regis-
tration
desk

Booth Size : 8' x 10'
Aisle Width : 7' 6''
Number of Booths : 235

phones

bar

regis-
tration
desk

Booth Size : 8' x 10'
Aisle Width : 8'
Number of Booths : 313

487

determined by the association, not the hotel, but it is important for the convention service manager at least to be aware that there are complaints.

Exhibitors feel that delegates should have free time from meetings during the day to browse through the exhibit area. Many are annoyed at the long days of sitting in their booths with little delegate traffic flow. They maintain that they are too tired after sitting all day and that there is too little time left to make their important business appointments, which is why they came to the convention.

How does this all relate to the convention service manager? Bill Tobin of Caesars Palace said to a class of ours: "If I notice there is a particularly busy meeting and function schedule, I will tactfully encourage the meeting planner to give exhibitors more exposure."

The assigning of guestrooms is another source of exhibitor discontent. One of the services provided to the association by the hotel is "controlled hospitality suites," which means the association gets first choice on all hotel rooms and suites it needs. After all, it is the association's meeting. Exhibitors would like to see less of this policy, however, because it leaves many of them in hotels other than the headquarters hotel. And when forced to stay in a different hotel other than the delegates, the exhibitors naturally find it more difficult to transact, and close, important evening sales.

So what can the hotel do? One solution is for the hotel to rent its smaller meeting rooms to exhibitors for evening hours. This arrangement would help delegates, exhibitors and hotels.

Labor Regulations

The trend of trade shows beginning on Sunday has made it difficult to avoid night and weekend labor charges. This overtime, added to what many exhibitors consider already exorbitant labor rates, has caused some to reconsider their commitment to exhibitions. Whenever possible, a hotel should allow exhibitors to set up early to avoid such charges.

Labor regulations in some cities prohibit exhibitors from even plugging in a projector or pounding a nail. The labor contractor does all the work, even the simple jobs that the exhibitor could easily do. Ed Johnson, past Trade Show Exhibitors Association (TSEA) president, says of this situation:

> "Every show contract specifies an official contractor and spells out certain functions the official contractor will perform exclusively. Usually these services are limited to plumbing, electrical work and drayage, but some contracts include carpenters, model agencies and photographers. We believe the exhibitor should be able to select his own florist, photographer and models rather than have to be forced to use someone who may not suit his needs. (Often these subcontracted services lead to a kickback situation.) We want to make it clear, however, that if we use someone besides the official contractor, he will be a bonafide contractor located in the show or convention city. Associations are afraid the exhibitor wants to bring in non-union help, and that just isn't true."[3]

Labor regulations vary a great deal throughout the country. Convention service managers should not close their eyes to the varying restrictions and trust to luck. Remind the association to alert its exhibitors to the labor regulations that apply to your hall. You must live with the labor contracts in your city. Most experienced convention executives are aware of the labor situations and have learned to live with them, but be wary of the inexperienced client.

Insurance

Accidents do happen, and claims do come up, so insurance coverage is absolutely essential. It should be provided by the convening organization, and smart exhibitors will carry their own as well.

The convention organization should be encouraged to contact its own insurance agents to provide full coverage for liability, fire, theft and breakage. In turn, if notified early, the convention staff should pass along such advice to exhibitors.

Too often the subject is not discussed until the need for coverage is at hand. Then someone says that he thought the hotel was covered. This is another area in which the hotel must be wary of inexperienced convention personnel.

For the protection of the hotel, each exhibitor should be presented with a contract releasing the hotel from liability should there be an injury, loss or breakage. And if exhibitors damage hotel property, they should be held liable for repair charges (see Figure 17.4).

Figure 17.4. INSURANCE AND HOLD HARMLESS CLAUSE.

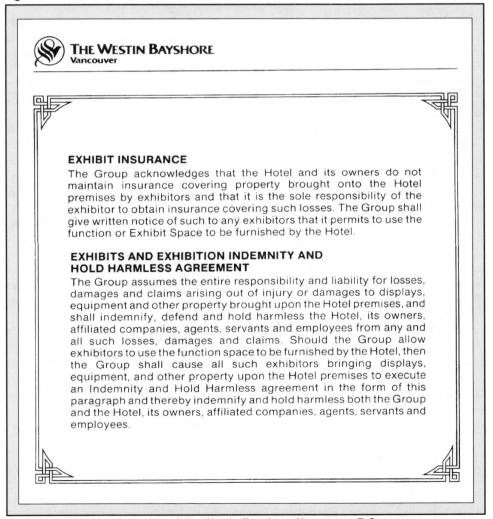

THE WESTIN BAYSHORE
Vancouver

EXHIBIT INSURANCE
The Group acknowledges that the Hotel and its owners do not maintain insurance covering property brought onto the Hotel premises by exhibitors and that it is the sole responsibility of the exhibitor to obtain insurance covering such losses. The Group shall give written notice of such to any exhibitors that it permits to use the function or Exhibit Space to be furnished by the Hotel.

EXHIBITS AND EXHIBITION INDEMNITY AND HOLD HARMLESS AGREEMENT
The Group assumes the entire responsibility and liability for losses, damages and claims arising out of injury or damages to displays, equipment and other property brought upon the Hotel premises, and shall indemnify, defend and hold harmless the Hotel, its owners, affiliated companies, agents, servants and employees from any and all such losses, damages and claims. Should the Group allow exhibitors to use the function space to be furnished by the Hotel, then the Group shall cause all such exhibitors bringing displays, equipment, and other property upon the Hotel premises to execute an Indemnity and Hold Harmless agreement in the form of this paragraph and thereby indemnify and hold harmless both the Group and the Hotel, its owners, affiliated companies, agents, servants and employees.

Source: Used with permission of the Westin Bayshore, Vancouver, B.C.

Exhibit Billing Procedures

What does the hotel charge for? There is no reason why a hotel cannot set its own policy regarding any aspect of the exhibit, providing, of course, that the client agrees to it (see Figure 17.5).

Common trade practice calls for the hotel to make a basic charge for the room. This charge may be a flat fee or it may be based on the number of booths sold. The booth unit fee is based on the minimum booth offered by the convention organization to exhibitors, usually an eight-by-ten foot area. Large units are figured on multiples of the basic one.

This latter method of pricing is popular with meeting planners because it protects them from a poor showing by exhibitors. Of course, it means that the hotel is locked into the convention's success, or lack of it, in selling exhibit space. And the hotel's role in such sales efforts is necessarily a passive one.

Hotel's Rental Charge

Hotels historically have been paid for guestrooms and food and beverage, but only recently have they capitalized on the sale of exhibit space. Exhibitions more and more frequently are held concurrently with conventions, and hotels with adequate exhibit areas are in the best position to book these groups. Some hotels have not only been able to show profits from the rental of their exhibit areas, but they have also taken on the role of decorator, providing booths, furniture, drapery etc., for which there is an additional rental fee. This is not the rule, however; most associations use independent decorating firms. There are two common types of exhibit arrangements for shows held within a hotel — the exhibit held concurrently with a convention and the exhibit held as part of a trade show. The first is sometimes termed a private trade show, with preregistration required and attendance restricted to individuals within the association. The latter, often called a **consumer show**, is open to the public and targeted directly to consumers. These categories require different considerations in determining rental charges.

The exhibit held concurrently with a convention is the more common type of arrangement, and rental charges vary to a greater extent. As we mentioned, it is a common hotel practice to make a basic charge for the exhibit area. Associations, which make a sizable profit reselling the space to exhibitors, are willing to pay a reasonable fee. While there are no hard numbers and fees vary from city to city, time of year and demand, it is common for the facility to charge the association or trade show company from $1.00 to $3.00 per square foot. The association or trade show company then resells the space for considerably more – in the $10-$20 per square foot range or even more.

Hotels frequently establish a figure from which they are willing to negotiate. Each group must be analyzed individually. Various factors must be considered in arriving at an agreed rate, just as in determining the charges for meeting rooms. Here are some of the considerations:

- What is the extent of the group's guestroom commitment? Its meeting room commitment?
- How much can the members be expected to spend for food and beverage?
- Is there the possibility of repeat business with this group?
- Are there any unusual problems in catering to this group (e.g., a large electronics show)?
- How great is the demand from other groups for these particular days?
- How much of an exhibit area will the group need?

Figure 17.5. EXHIBIT AND DECORATOR'S CHARGES.

Exhibit and Decorator's Charges

There are *two charges* that you should be aware of for your budget purposes:
   A)   *Hotel Exhibit Charge*   B)   *Decorator Charge*

A. Hotel Exhibit Charge

Sheraton-Waikiki exhibit charge is on a *Sliding Scale Per Room basis. Sliding Scale* is based on a *Per Booth Basis Per Room Per Day*, as follows (When we use the terminology "Booth", we are speaking of an 8' x 10' area):

Sliding Scale

Number of Booths in a Room Respectively	Per Room Respectively Kauai/Maui/Molokai/Lanai
35 - 44	$30.00 per 8' x 10' booth per day.
26 - 34	$35.00 per 8' x 10' booth per day.
18 - 25	$40.00 per 8' x 10' booth per day.
10 - 17	$60.00 per 8' x 10' booth per day.
05 - 09	$180.00 per 8' x 10' booth per day.

All Foyer booths $30.00 per 8' x 10' booth per day. Entrance and exit days are full price on Fridays and Saturdays. One-half (1/2) price on Sunday through Thursday.

   Exhibit Pavilion: $2000.00 each day, plus 4.16% tax Daily charges include set-up days and exit days.

All above subject to 4.16% sales tax.

There are two *money-saving opportunities* contained in the above:
a)   By careful planning of your entrance and exit dates and time, you can save money.
b)   By containing your exhibits to the capacities that the respective rooms will hold offers money savings.

Kauai Room	(44) 8' x 10' exhibits	Maui Room	(44) 8' x 10' exhibits
Molokai Room	(44) 8' x 10' exhibits	Lanai Room	(37) 8' x 10' exhibits
2nd Floor Foyer	(28) 8' x 10' exhibits		

B. Decorator Charge

The decorator, when selected, also has a booth charge which includes rod and drape, electrical outlets and other specific equipment as negotiated between the decorator and the association.

The hotel agreement with the decorator is as follows:

a)   The decorator will provide all chairs and tables negotiated with the association. The hotel cannot provide the tables and chairs for exhibits.
b)   The respective booth electrical specifications, including spotlights, are negotiated between the decorator and the association. The hotel is not involved.
c)   Storage equipment responsibility rests with the decorator. Equipment is stored in the decorator's warehouse prior to and after each convention.
d)   Drayage — The decorator is responsible for the following:
    1. Receipt of exhibits from the mainland.
    2. Storing of goods.
    3. Transfer to hotel.
    4. Transfer to second floor exhibit area.
    5. Removal of exhibits back to warehouse.
    6. Shipping to mainland.

Source: Courtesy of the Sheraton Waikiki.

The exhibit held as part of a trade show is often open to the public, as in the cases of boat, gem and antique shows. In other cases, such as the National Ski Show, the exhibit is restricted to dealers. Trade show organizers are primarily in the business for a profit and fully intend to make their profit from subleasing the hotel exhibit space. In this case, the mark up for exhibit space is considerable. For example, when Softbank stages the Comdex computer show, their space is sublet to exhibitors for a minimum of $50 per square foot; prime exhibit locations command an even greater cost per square foot.

Hotels can generally command a bigger rental charge for trade show exhibitions than those used in conjunction with conventions. Meeting rooms are seldom used by trade shows, and there is no assurance that attendees will stay in the hotel guestrooms. A case we know of is when antique dealers were booked into the Las Vegas Hilton. Most of the dealers were not financially able to pay the Hilton's high room rates, so they stayed in nearby budget motels.

Another consideration justifying a higher rental charge is the likelihood of damage to the hotel with the increased traffic flow. Such business, however, might well provide the hotel with increased food and beverage revenue in its restaurants and lounges.

Exposition Service Contractor's Fee

The exhibition service contractor usually receives a flat fee of $75 to $100 for setting up each booth, using pipe frame dividers and drapery for separation on the back and sides. The service contractor charges the exhibitor extra for such furnishings as tables, chairs and wastepaper baskets.

The fees the hotel charges for the room usually include the overall lighting (but not that for individual exhibits), heating and air conditioning, and cleaning services. The individual exhibitor orders from the decorator and pays directly for extra lighting, booth decorations, the furnishings described above, electrical connections, water and gas connections, telephone service and installation, extra signs, graphics, floral decoration and photography.

Convention Shipping and Receiving

The convention service manager can avoid many frayed tempers and difficulties by advising the convention organization about shipping procedures. Such advice should be given early enough for the convention executive to include it in mailings to exhibitors.

Exhibit Shipping

Many hotels do not have adequate storage space to receive and store exhibit material prior to the event, especially since they hope to have other exhibits both before and after the event. A **drayage company** thus plays an essential role in the flow of exhibit material.

The drayage company receives all the exhibit material. It has adequate storage facilities in another part of town, probably where real estate is less expensive and zoning allows large warehousing operations. It also has adequate trucking equipment to move the material from its storage area to the convention site within a day or two of setup time. It is the aim of every exhibition hall manager to reduce to an absolute minimum the time the hall is not

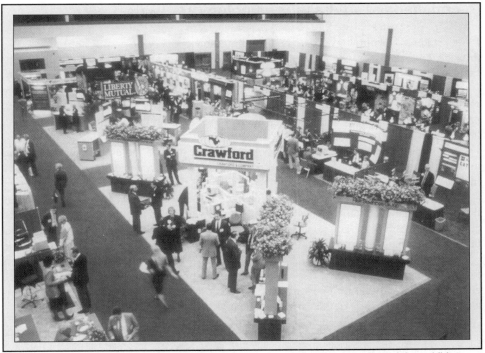

Pictured are exhibits using only a portion of the more than 218,000 square feet of the exhibit space available at the John B. Hynes Veterans Memorial Convention Center in Boston, Massachusetts. Source: Courtesy of the Massachusetts Convention Center Authority.

used for an active exhibit. When setup day comes, the manager wants the material moved in quickly.

Exhibit handling and storage are paid for by the exhibitors. When the exhibitor doesn't understand that the drayage company is to store all material, cases start coming to the hotel. But if the drayage company is selected early enough, such shipments are rerouted to the drayage company facility. And the drayage company can have the convention organizer include its facility as the proper shipping address for the exhibit crates. The exhibitor then ships directly to the drayage company, which accepts the material, stores it, and starts to deliver all the crates to the convention site on setup day. When the time comes to break down, the entire process works in reverse.

Frequently, the decorator will handle all the drayage. He or she will send the exhibitor labels for any freight that will be sent to the convention. The labels are pre-stamped with the name of the convention to ensure that the service company gets the freight to the right show. The service company sometimes gives exhibitors thirty days of free storage prior to the convention; this is to make sure all freight arrives in time.

Drayage material will be delivered to the booths prior to the show. After the convention, the service company delivers the freight to a common carrier or other means of transportation, such as air or padded van.

It is important that the decorator know the truck line and invoice number of the shipment in order to trace freight if it is not received in time. Reforwarding instructions are also required by the service company.

Recommended Address Terminology

Proper address terminology facilitates handling and delivery of crates and parcels. If a drayage company is used, have all shipments addressed and consigned directly to its facility.

The *event* the shipment is intended for and the *dates* of the event should be marked clearly. This is essential even if in-house storage is provided. It is also important for small parcels sent through the mail, so there can be a logical grouping and storage within your hotel package room.

A convention service manager often will prefer to have the association address its material marked to his or her attention. Lost or misplaced crates create havoc; the first inquiries made by exhibitors are often in regard to their crates and parcels.

It is important to set up a procedure on handling material addressed to the hotel. Even if the exhibitors' manual instructed that shipments were to be sent directly to the drayage company, you'll always get some sent to the hotel. How you handle such shipments depends on how much room you have at the hotel and how much time is left before the event.

Lost shipments are always a problem. It is difficult for convention service managers to help when cases are lost en route, but they should do what they can to calm concerned and aggravated exhibitors. They, of course, should help exhibitors trace their shipments and expedite installation at the earliest moment after arrival.

Shipping Methods

You help your client and you help yourself if you indicate a preferred shipping method in your area, if there is one. From your vantage point, a preferred carrier or trucking company may mean smooth delivery of many shipments. The client is assured of delivery with little trouble.

Local companies don't all offer the same degree of service. Some truckers may have a larger installation in your city, or more trucks, or perhaps just a better, more concerned traffic manager. One desirable characteristic is delivery on weekends. Whatever the reason, recommended firms with consistently good performances ease the bottlenecks that appear on setup day. Good local trucking arrangements help a great deal.

Incoming Shipping Costs

Some arrangements must be made to handle shipments that come in with postage or freight charges due. Drivers are not empowered to leave shipments when money is due. Without a clear arrangement, a truck might remain at the loading platform, keeping others from unloading and generally causing havoc.

Exhibitors should be advised to prepay all shipping charges, but inevitably a number of cases and cartons arrive with some money due. A procedure should be set up to pay such charges and arrange for reimbursement. This responsibility clearly belongs to the convention organization, but the hotel should make sure that some sort of system is set up. When it isn't, the hotel is generally blamed as being unable to handle incoming shipments without trouble.

Outgoing shipments should be handled properly, too. One reason so many shipments come in with charges due is the ease of shipping that way, eliminating the need to weigh and evaluate shipping costs on the scene. If exhibitors prefer to ship that way from your hotel, keep in mind that those shipments may not be going back home. Many go to other events. Similarly, the exhibit cases you receive may be coming from another event freight-collect.

Working with good shipping companies can ease your outgoing shipment problem. Alert them to the breakdown schedule of the show, and they can arrange for the trucks and drivers to be there. Those companies that work well with you to clear the cases out of your hotel are very likely the companies you'll be recommending for incoming shipments. Good local service companies are a comfort to a convention service manager, and they should be cultivated carefully.

Inform the convention staff of the time needed to set up the exhibit and to break it down. Reminding exhibitors about overtime charges works well. Some exhibitors rush to get ready for the exhibit but have to be prodded to get out quickly.

 ## Chapter Summary:

Trade shows can be a lucrative business for hotels that are willing to make the effort to organize for them. This involves developing a capable sales and service staff that understands the needs of both the trade show organizer and the exhibitor. While a hotel's role in the trade show may vary, it is important that its staff be able to assist associations or trade show companies as needed. This may involve contracting exposition service contractors or other outside services, such as florists, security staff, personnel to set up and dismantle booths, and drayage companies, or directly assisting with specific requirements. No matter what the hotel's involvement, the property has a stake in the success of a trade show. Trade shows bring in guestroom and food and beverage business, and satisfied exhibitors and trade show organizers often result in repeat business -- not only for future trade shows but also for other meetings and leisure stays.

 ## Endnotes:

1. Total number of booths = 50 booths
    Size of each booth (8'x10') = 80 square feet
    Total number of booths multiplied by the size of booths
    80 square feet x 50 booths = 4,000 net square feet
    Net square feet multiplied by 2 = 8,000 gross square feet
2. From correspondence with Sam Lippman. Used with permission.
3. Jane Chase, "Exhibitors Have Their Say," *Association & Society Manager*, copyright by Barrington Publications.

Additional References:

- The Art of the Show, by Sandra Morrow, Association for Exhibition Management Foundation
  www.iacm.org
- Exhibit Marketing: A Success Guide for Managers, by Edward Chapman, McGraw Hill.
- Expositions and Trade Shows, by Deborah Robbe, John Wiley and Sons: 2000.
  www.hospitality@wiley.com

Internet Sites:

For additional information on the firms and organizations discussed in this chapter, visit the following Internet sites. The Web addresses listed are current as of January 2001. Addresses may change, however; if a site is not available at address below, a search engine can be used to access its new location.

Center for Exposition Industry Research - www.ceir.org
Exhibit Designers and Producers Association - www.edpa.com
Exhibitor Magazine - www.exhibitornet.com
Exhibitor Appointed Contractors Association - www.eaca.com
Expo Magazine - www.expoweb.com
Expo Net: Tradeshow Marketing Resource Network - www.exponet.com
Exposition Service Contractors Association - www.esca.org
The Freeman Companies - www.freemanco.com
GES Exposition Services - www.gesexpo.com
Healthcare Convention and Exhibitors Association - www.hcea.org
International Association for Exposition Management - www.iaem.org
Society of Independent Show Organizers - www.siso.org
Trade Show Exhibitors Association - www.tsea.org
Tradeshow Week - www.tradeshowweek.com

Study Questions:

1. Why are trade shows important to both meeting planners and hotels?
2. What are the three types of exhibits used at trade shows? What methods are used to assign space for these exhibits?
3. Who are the key personnel responsible for executing trade shows? What is the role of each?
4. Review Figure 17.2, noting the detail of Boca Raton's scaled drawing. What is the difference between this scaled drawing and a layout? How is each used?

5. Discuss how such factors as labor regulations and insurance coverage affect exhibitors.
6. What are the billing procedures typically used by hotels to bill trade show participants? What factors play a part in determining hotel charges?
7. Discuss the shipping of exhibits, including address terminology, shipping methods, and shipping costs.

 ## Key Terms:

Area exhibit. Exhibitors are assigned specific floor space for displaying equipment and other displays.

Booth exhibit. A standard unit of exhibit space (usually 8 ft. by 10 ft.) occupied by an exhibitor. Usually constructed of pipe and draping.

Consumer show. Show open to the general public. Not generally connected to any convention or meeting.

Drayage company. Company that receives all exhibit material, stores it and transports it to the convention site a day or two before setup starts, re-crates at end of show and returns exhibit material to sender.

Exhibition floor plan. To-scale plan showing spacing of booths, aisles and design of the exhibition. Prepared by the exposition service contractor for the show manager and approved by the fire marshal.

Exhibit prospectus. Detailed guide to the exposition prepared by the show management. Serves as a selling tool, inviting exhibitors to participate.

Exhibitor. Person representing and responsible for a company's or group's exhibit.

Exhibitor's service kit. Contains information about the services needed by the exhibitor for a successful convention.

Exposition service contractor. Independent firm or individual responsible for organizing, coordinating and executing all the services necessary to set up the exhibit. Sometimes referred to as a decorator. Usually contracted by the planner's organization. If the sole agent, said to be the *exclusive contractor*.

Floor load. Weight per square foot that the exhibit can safely accommodate.

Pipe and drape. Tubing draped with fabric to create separate exhibit booths.

Table top exhibit. Used where space is limited or where there is a limited number of exhibitors.

Trade show manager. Individual who plans, organizes and operates the trade show. Responsible for renting the site and soliciting exhibitors. May work directly for the association or corporation, or as an independent. Also termed the *show organizer* or *show producer*.

CHAPTER APPENDIX

A Behind the Scenes Look at a Trade Show

The Consumer Electronics Show (CES), held in January in Las Vegas, is the premier trade show for the consumer electronics industry. Sponsored by the Electronics Industries Association/Consumer Electronics Group, this trade show features audio and video-based products, multimedia, home computing, interactive, electronic gaming and cellular products. The large number of displays require the use of several facilities, including the exhibit halls of the Las Vegas Convention Center, the Convention Center parking lot, and several hotels that offer exhibit space.

Naturally, a show of this magnitude requires extensive planning and pre-show preparation. In the following photographs, we will take a "behind the scenes" look at the steps taken to prepare just one hall for this trade show.

Exhibit Hall S2 has been cleaned after a prior event and spaces for the CES exhibitors' booths have been marked and numbered. The Winter CES show will utilize over 1 million square feet of exhibit space and will host more than 1800 exhibitors

On December 28 & 29, trucks begin moving in cargos of freight, including construction material that may be used to build exhibitor booths and displays. These crates will be stacked prior to booth construction and removed as booth construction progresses.

On December 30, additional freight, including the exhibitors' merchandise and components for the display continues to arrive, the first overhead directional and exhibitor signs are hung, and booth decorating, including the laying of individual booth carpet, begins.

On January 3, booths are beginning to take shape.

By January 4, booth construction is well underway, as is booth and hall decorating, including the draping of booth and exhibit hall walls.

On January 5, the last of the freight, including rental furniture and last-minute decorating items (such as plants and flowers), is moved in. Later that evening, the aisle carpet will be laid in preparation for the next day's opening.

On January 6, the four-day show opens. Over 100,000 people, including buyers, international, and editorial press will attend.

On January 10, the day after the show, dismantling is already in progress. Aisle carpet was rolled up immediately after the show's close to facilitate the removal of freight, crates are returned for the packing of show merchandise, and booth dismantling begins.

By January 11, most of the show has been crated and is in the process of being removed from the exhibit hall.

Photographs courtesy of Stephen A. Stoney. Special thanks to the Las Vegas Convention and Visitors Bureau and the Electronic Industries Association/Consumer Electronics Shows for their help in the preparation of this Appendix.

Learning Objectives:

This portion of your text introduces you to how meetings and conventions are billed and the need for post-convention or meeting follow up to assess the performance of both the group and your property. When you have studied this chapter you will:

- Be able to detail the areas that must be covered when establishing a billing procedure for a group or a meeting.

- Know the difference between the various types of folios commonly used to bill groups.

- Recognize the need for post-event follow up and be able to describe the two types of meetings typically held and know why each is important.

Outline

Convention Billing
- The Master Account
- Time of Payment
- Guest Credit
- Tips and Gratuities
- HSMAI's Suggested Payment Schedule

Post-Convention Review
- Comparison with Projections
- Function Attendance
- Special Services
- Individual Comments
- Post-convention Reporting
- Final Appraisal

Establishing Convention Billing Procedures

Karen Hudson
Sales Manager, Four Seasons Hotel
Newport Beach, California

"At the Four Seasons Hotel, convention billing procedures are set up prior to the meeting. Once a contract is signed and the group requests direct billing of charges, a credit application is forwarded to the client...If the credit manager approves the credit application, a master account is established for the group. In the event credit is not approved, a deposit is then required either immediately or at some point prior to group arrival...When a master account is established in the computer system, any and all charges that the company or association is responsible for are posted to that account. These charges are processed through the front desk, which posts these charges daily. Once the group checks out, charges are collected by the credit department and compiled into one bill...If the group uses outside vendors such as entertainment or special flowers or plants, it is the responsibility of the conference service manager to post the supplier or vendor charges to the group's master account...."

18

Convention Billing and Post-Convention Review

A fter a booking has "gone definite," the convention service manager begins to collect information from the meeting planner about various aspects of the convention so that he or she can prepare the specification sheet. (As we explained in Chapter 12, the specification sheet, or resume, is the major internal means of communication for hotel personnel involved with the convention.) There are three basic areas that every convention service manager looks at as he or she puts together the specification sheet: reservations, program and billing.

Open and honest communication is paramount in all three of these areas. We have already discussed the reservations and program segments. Now let's deal with the many questions about *billing* that need to be answered.

Convention Billing

Convention billing is much too important to be handled haphazardly. Ranking near the top of the list of meeting planners' pet peeves are surprise billing charges. Open communications can help tremendously to have the event end on a happy note. When it is clear who pays for what, everything seems to go more smoothly.

As with most aspects of convention planning, the time to avoid billing problems is at the beginning and not at the end. Billing policy is usually established months before the group gets into the hotel, not at the end of the convention, and should address:

- What areas does the master account cover?
- How are the delegates' charges to be handled?
- Will there be more than one master account?
- Who is authorized to sign?
- What about tips and gratuities?
- How should early arrivals and late departures be handled?
- Should the hotel or the group be billed by outside service companies, such as florists and audiovisual suppliers?
- What are the charges for the various types of guestrooms? Meeting rooms? Exhibit area?
- What are the arrangements for food and beverage?
- How are transportation charges to be handled? How are special events, such as golf tournaments and tours, to be priced?
- What are the arrangements for audiovisual, electrical, and phone charges?
- Will there be a charge for security and other labor provided by the hotel?
- How does the meeting planner want the bill broken down?
- Are deposits required?
- Who will prepare and collect chits? Tickets? Banquet checks?

All of these aspects need to be prearranged, and each detail should be clearly spelled out. Billing requirements for each function should be clearly outlined in the specification sheet (see Figure 18.1). The accounting department, as well as the other service departments in the hotel, wants explicit instructions on the billing procedure. You definitely want to avoid the problems that arise at the check-out desk when the specification sheet doesn't deal in detail with billing arrangements.

Figure 18.1. CORPORATION AND ASSOCIATION BILLING EXAMPLES.

Example I — Arizona Biltmore Hotel, Phoenix

_____**Corporation**

Controller: Corporation will guarantee all personal checks up to $250 for all members.
Reserve suites 67-66-63-62-61-59-58 from 4/28. Charge 6 to Master Account — other 2 to be complimentary.

Billing: MASTER ACCOUNT to cover American plan room rate, tax and service charge of all guests.
Master Account also to cover: receptions, surcharges, recreational activities on tournament day, breakfast trail ride, cowboy hats, bandanas, refreshment breaks, entertainment, hostesses, etc.
PREPARE INCIDENTAL FOLIO for each guest. Post all incidental charges to their respective accounts. To be paid prior to departure. (LIST IN ACCOUNTING OFFICE OF ENTIRE ACCOUNTS TO BE TRANSFERRED TO M/A).

Night Auditor: NOTE: Extend $4.50 inclusive credit per person for those taking shopping tour on 4/4 or leaving prior to luncheon on 4/5. MUST NOTIFY CASHIER 24 HOURS IN ADVANCE IN ORDER TO RECEIVE THIS CREDIT. THIS CREDIT GOES TO MASTER ACCOUNT — NOT INCIDENTAL ACCOUNT.

Example II — Caesars Palace, Las Vegas

_____**Association**

Master Account I: All group functions should be added to the master account.
Mr. _____ and Ms. _____ will be the authorized signers.
NOTE: Please post a charge in the total amount of $250 to this group's master account. This charge is for the purchase of 250 Caesars Palace medallions at a cost of $1.00 per medallion.

Master Account II: A second master account is to be set up. To this master, charge the entire accounts of all _____ Association Directors and Staff.
Mr. John M. _____ will be the authorized signer.

Individual Account: Rooms, tax, and incidentals to be paid by the individuals.

Billing instructions from actual specification sheets for a corporate meeting and an association convention.
Source: Courtesy of the Arizona Biltmore Hotel and Caesar's Palace.

The Master Account

The biggest problem when working with convention billing is usually unclear communication. Therefore, an understanding of billing procedures begins with terminology.

A *folio* is a collection of charges incurred by an individual or an organization. There are three types of folios to which charges are posted:

- **Master Account Folio** — charges are paid entirely by the sponsoring organization.
- Individual **Guest Folio** — charges are paid entirely by the individual guest.
- **Split Folio** — charges are paid partially by the sponsoring organization and partially by the individual guest. Most meetings in hotels are accounted for as split folios.

A master account is generally set up to facilitate billing to the convention organization. The hotel executive and the convention executive should discuss the charges that should be billed to this account. All other charges are billed to the guests on their individual accounts.

Additional master accounts may be set up for individual program segments upon request. For example, many groups will specifiy a separate master account for group food and beverage functions, another for audiovisual, and still another for miscellaneous items such as telephone and business center use. Sometimes a participating company will sponsor a program event, such as a luncheon or cocktail party, and a separate master account is set up for this affair.

It is imperative that the convention organization put down in writing all people authorized to charge to the master account. These usually are the convention staff personnel. If *all* their charges are to be allowed on the master account, say so. The understanding is that these people are also authorized to sign charges. If this area of authority is to be limited in any way, those limitations should be spelled out.

Failure to detail the extent of charges to the master account can lead to difficulties in the case of convention guests, speakers and program presenters. The hotel doesn't care who pays what or how, so long as it is made clear who is to pay. It is the convention staff's responsibility to inform its guests about the extent of the hospitality, but it is your desk clerk or cashier who must face these people when they check out.

Ask the convention staff to inform you, as well as the guests, who will pay for rooms, food, beverage, telephone, valet charges, and other incidentals. It helps to inform the guest when he or she checks in that the room charges will be paid for by the association, but many hotels feel that this is the convention staff's task. Unfortunately, it is surprising how infrequently the convention staff follows through to tell its guests the extent to which they are responsible for charges. Bringing the matter to the attention of convention executives will at least alert them to potential embarrassing problems and maybe move them to set policy.

Such arrangements apply to corporate meetings as well those of associations, since corporate meetings may be attended by persons other than company employees. The arrangements should be spelled out completely. This applies to corporate personnel, too. Some companies pay *all* charges through the master account, while some pay only room and food charges, with the rest paid through individual expense accounts. All variations will be encountered.

The hotel should have no policy of its own, but should merely follow the *clear* instructions of the company meeting planner. These instructions should be in writing. Generally speaking, if you get the meeting planner to spell it out to you in writing, the

Figure 18.2. MASTER ACCOUNT BILLING AUTHORIZATION FORM.

ICP MASTER ACCOUNT BILLING AUTHORIZATION

Convention
Name_____
Dates_____
Food Plan_____

NOTE: Please post charges as indicated below. Master Account charges noted here apply only on meeting dates. See separate letter for exceptions and additional Master Account information.

ROOM & FOOD PLAN	MA	IND	HOTEL SERVICES	MA	IND	SPORTS	MA	IND
Room & Tax			Telephone • Local			Golf Greens Fees		
MAP (FAP)* Guest			• Long Distance			Golf Lessons		
MAP(FAP)* Spouse			Parking			Golf Driving Range		
Other			Valet & Laundry			Golf • Caddie Fee		
			Bellmen			Golf • Cart Rental		
FOOD & BEVERAGE			Maids			Tennis • Court Fees		
			Pool/Beach Attendants			Tennis • Lessons		
Restaurant • Food			TV Movies			Tennis • Racquet Rentals		
Restaurant • Bar			Beauty Salon			Sports Merchandise		
Room Service • Food			Barber Shop			Spa/Health Club		
Room Service • Bar			Merchandise Shops			Stables		
Bar Charges			Other			Other		
Cover Charge								
Other			MISCELLANEOUS			TOURNAMENTS		
BANQUET CHARGES			Airport Transfers			Refreshments		
			Other			Club/Racquet Rental		
						Golf/Tennis Balls		
						Greens Fees		
						Cart Rental		
						Caddie Fees		
						Court Fees		
						Other		

*Including tax & Service Charge, if any.

The _____Company
    (Sponsor Organization)

1. (Is/Is not) responsible for payment of delinquent charges to individual accounts.
2. (Will/Will not) guarantee payment of its attendees' hotel bill whether paid by check or charge card.
3. (Will/Will not) guarantee personal checks cashed by its attendees up to $_____.
4. Some persons (list attached) will have entire room and incidental accounts posted to Master. These persons should be preregistered and will not check themselves out. Their room bills will be reviewed and signed by the sponsor organization's planner.
5. Authorizes these signatures (Type) _____ _____ _____
    for its MA charges   (Sign)_____ _____ _____
The hotel should consider these billing instructions definite and authorized by_____
                                            (Planner/ Date/Telephone Number)

The meeting planner uses this form to provide the hotel with a comprehensive set of instructions on how specific charges are to be billed.
Source: Courtesy of the Insurance Conference Planners Association.

corporate personnel stand a much better chance of receiving detailed instructional memos telling them how to check out.

The Insurance Conference Planners Association has prepared a guide providing possible solutions to problems usually associated with master account billing to be used by meeting planners and hoteliers alike. Two forms from this guide are illustrated in this chapter. Figure 18.2 illustrates a **master account billing authorization form**, which provides a comprehensive set of instructions on:

- How hotel charges are to be posted (master account or individual guest's room folio).
- The limit of financial responsibility the meeting group will accept.
- The names and specimen signatures of those who are authorized to sign for any master account expenses (only those with an **authorized signature** are permitted to sign for group charges).

Figure 18.3 illustrates a **rates and charges bulletin**, which communicates to the convention attendees the specific rates for rooms, meals, **incidental charges** and billing procedures as agreed to by the convening group and the hotel. The bulletin is sent to the convention attendees one month prior to the convention date. Use of this communication bulletin reduces disputes and speeds guest check-out.

Time of Payment

Methods and time of payment vary a great deal, depending on the policy of the hotel, the credit and reputation of the convening organization, past history, the frequency of group business and other factors.

Master accounts can add up to a considerable amount of money, and it is hard to blame hotel managers if they try to get as much of it as possible up front. This is not only because of concern about being paid, but also because of a desire to accelerate time of payment and to ease the hotel's cash flow.

The usual practice in the trade is a payment when the contract is signed, a pre-convention payment at an agreed date, on-the-scene payments, and a final one. The final payment can be broken into two parts — one at the end of the event, and a final settlement later.

Hotels have been known to be flexible about payments, depending on what they know about the client. Political organizations certainly should not be allowed to run up large bills because the payment may be uncertain or delayed. But a prestigious local corporation that has dealt with you many times may cause your controller little concern about the bill.

Many meeting planners insist on talking with someone from the hotel's accounting department before the convention begins. The standard policy for the Hyatt Hotel chain is to take the meeting planner to the accounting office at the first mutually convenient time to go over billing procedure. The understanding agreed upon earlier is reinforced and problems are solved before the service is performed.

Convention organizers frequently complain that hotels cannot present the final accounting at the end of the event, while the convention staff is still on the premises and memories are fresh. If complete billing is not ready, they can still review the charges and initial approval. Some charges lag, but at least the bulk of the account can be settled.

A good practice, endorsed by many convention service managers, is to arrange for the meeting planner to meet with the property controller daily to go over the previous day's charges on the master account. Any discrepancies and questons can be addressed at that time. Then, upon check-out most charges will have been settled and, ideally, the master account can be presented before the organizers leave.

The hotel doesn't want the entire account held up while a relatively minor matter is adjudicated, of course. One suggestion is to set this amount aside pending further investigation and/or discussion while the rest of the bill is settled. Some meeting planners ask that a certain amount be held back after the event to handle any adjustments. The amount of

Figure 18.3. SPECIMEN RATES AND CHARGES BULLETIN.

SPECIMEN RATES AND CHARGES BULLETIN

To. Convention Attendees

The following rates and charges, which have been agreed to by ABC Company and the XYZ Hotel, will be in effect during your stay at the XYZ Hotel. The rates listed in this bulletin represent the maximum you should be charged for the listed services during the length of your stay at this convention.

DAILY ROOM RATE: Modified American Plan (2 meals)

$ 70.00 Per Person, per day plus
     5.50 Per Person,
           daily service charge* plus
     2.27 Daily state tax (3%)
	$ 115.00 Per Person, per day plus
	     5.50 Per Person,
	           daily service charge* plus
	     3.62 Daily state tax (3%)

$ 77.77 Daily Total	$ 124.12 Daily Total

These Rates: Include Lodging, breakfast & dinner daily, and gratuities for maids and MAP dining room personnel.

Don't include Bellman, doorman or limo driver gratuities, parlor charges or incidental charges.

MAP CREDITS

Tavern Room   A credit of $8.00 per person will apply and the balance would be charged at a la carte prices.

Golf Club   Dinner in Golf Club carries a surcharge depending on items selected.

Main Dining Room A few items are a la carte, depending on items selected.

All Extra Meals   (A la carte) charges will be billed to your individual hotel account.

Room Service   A room service charge of $2.00 per person ($2.50 in cottages) will apply to all room service orders.

NOTE: MAP includes dinner on check-in day, and breakfast on check-out day. Should you dine in a group, be certain that all room numbers are listed or only that person who signs will get the total charges for the group.

TRANSPORTATION

Airport to Hotel $6.50 per person
                $3.25 per person (small children)

*Applicable if the hotel imposes a Service Charge

One month prior to the convention, a listing of specific rates and charges is sent to the convention attendee by the meeting planner. This type of communication clearly spells out exactly what is covered by the convening group and what charges the individual attendee will be responsible for, greatly reducing the chances of any misunderstandings at the time of the meeting or convention.
Source: Courtesy of the Insurance Conference Planners Association.

money held back and the time allowed should be part of the letter of agreement or other correspondence. Otherwise, the entire bill might be held up and perhaps used unfairly for leverage.

At some conventions, a considerable amount of cash is generated through registration and ticket sales. Some arrangements should be made to count this money and keep it safe. If such cash is applied against the master account, receipts should be issued for all payments. If agreed-upon payments have been made on schedule, organizations may request checks from the hotel in return for such cash. Clear such arrangements with the hotel controller.

The increasing use of the computer for accounting functions has greatly enhanced the billing process. But in addition to more efficient billing (some charges can be added instantaneously if the property uses point of sales terminals), computers increase the speed with which hotels can analyze convention groups for future billing.

One hotel sales executive sees technology helping both the hotel and the meeting planner:

> "Among the things that are different these days are that you can see the arrival/departure pattern of a group. You can see what food and beverage sales are per occupied room because they play a role in what's charged for meeting and sleeping rooms. Now the planner can get a report that will show the exact value of his or her group to the hotel. We still need to offer good meeting space, but now a lot of the competition is going to revolve around who can make the planner's job easier. And technology is helping us to accomplish that."[1]

Of course, a few hotels cannot afford the benefits of a computer, but more and more properties are making the investment. With computer systems, the bill can be broken down for each function and quickly tallied to provide the total charge within an hour of the last meeting. Confusion and long hours of labor are minimized, and the bill can be reviewed and finalized while details are still fresh in the minds of the hotel people and the meeting planner.

Guest Credit

Another matter to be discussed by the hotel staff and the meeting planner is **guest credit**. With national credit cards, it is simply a matter of saying which cards the hotel will accept. If the hotel limits the cards it will take, this information should be given in time for inclusion in the convention brochure so the guests will be forewarned. But most national and international cards are accepted in most hotels, so this seldom constitutes much of a problem.

The extension of credit directly to the guest is more of a risk. The convention executive should be told if this is contrary to hotel policy. Then the recommended procedure by which a guest could establish credit with the hotel might be outlined.

The hotel should also state its policy about cashing checks for guests. Maximum amounts should be made clear. Cashing checks for people with no established credit is a courtesy, not an obligation. Many associations, and certainly corporations, guarantee the checks cashed for members or employees. A maximum limit, if any, should be indicated.

Tips and Gratuities

Tips and gratuities are a generally accepted part of convention costs. They are covered in all sales proposals and later in the letter of agreement. Yet, few areas of convention management seem to cause as much controversy. It is important to note that while the terms tips and gratuities are used interchangeably, they are different. A tip is a voluntary gift given for excellent service. A gratuity (sometimes called a service charge) is a fixed, mandatory amount given to service personnel.

Meeting planners are often confused about how much to tip, who should be tipped, and when the tip should be given. One hotelier states:

> "The end of tipping is a long way off in America. I feel the planner should settle the gratuities subject in advance. If he or she feels uncomfortable with the amount specified, he or she should go to another hotel. Likewise, if he or she feels there is dissatisfaction with the amount of the gratuities, he or she should think twice about returning to that hotel. Most of the problems with gratuities are the result of not discussing the matter with the hotel convention staff — in the beginning, when everything else is being settled. Nobody should ever feel strange about asking the hotel for advice on this matter."[2]

When hotels are approached for advice on the amounts considered fair, tipping guidelines should be suggested. Wisdom, however, should be used. Meeting planners are naturally offended by the suggestion that their gratuities are a form of remuneration rather than an expression of appreciation for good or exceptional service.

Tips and gratuities can be categorized into four distinct groupings:

- Tips for hotel hourly personnel, such as bellpersons, food servers, housekeepers, and door attendants.
- Gratuities for group functions and banquets. These are termed fixed gratuities and generally figured as a percentage of the bill and added to the check.
- Blanket gratuities. The gratuity is added to the room charge and delegates are not encumbered with further tipping.
- Special tips given to management personnel, such as the convention service manager, banquet manager and head houseperson.

Because the issue of tips and gratuities is often confusing to meeting planners, Howard Feiertag of the Center for Hospitality Research and Service suggests that the planner set aside one percent of the total convention costs for tips (the industry standard is one to two percent). When attendees pay tips themselves, however, there may be even more confusion. According to Feiertag, the following general guidelines apply when tipping hourly service personnel, our first classification:

Bartenders:	15 percent at the bar; 20 percent at your table
Bell Staff:	$1 per bag
Concierge:	Varies in relation to the service provided
Door Attendant:	$1 for hailing a cab or carrying bags
Housekeeping Staff:	$1 per room per night
Restaurant Server:	15 to 20 percent of the check
Room Service Staff:	15 percent unless tip is included in room charge
Valets:	$1 when your car is delivered
Wine Steward:	10 to 20 percent of the cost of the wine

Gratuities for group meals and banquets, our second classification, seem to present the most problems. Many meeting planners justifiably decry the practice of a 15 percent gratuity regardless of the quality of the service. However, the hotel is often following the terms of a union contract, which should be explained in the initial negotiations with the meeting planner. The flat percentage gratuity is 15 to 20 percent in most cities.

It is important to note that in some states the amount will be subject to sales tax if it is listed as a service charge rather than a gratuity. If a planner hosts a lunch for 100 people at $25 per person, for example, and a gratuity of 18 percent ($450) was added, the resulting total of $2,950 would be subject to the state's sales tax—not just the original cost of $2,500.

To combat this problem, some hotel eliminate the term *service charge* and replace it with *gratuity*. A gratuity can legally be added to the bill after the state sales tax has been levied on the cost of meals only. This results in major savings for meeting planners, and most of them prefer to be charged in this way.

No matter which approach is used, it is important that your hotel clearly spells out its policy to eliminate unpleasant surprises for the meeting planner. If mandatory service charges on food and beverage functions or sleeping rooms can legally be replaced with agreed-upon gratuities not subject to state taxes, this arrangement should be spelled out in the convention contract.

When there is a flat percentage on food and beverage setups, the hotel normally distributes the gratuity among the service personnel. Many planners will ask the convention service manager for a breakdown of who shares in the distribution. Policies vary. While the bulk of any mandated gratuity will go to the workers servicing the function, it is not uncommon for a portion to be used by management to offset labor costs. For example, one director of convention services at a well-known San Francisco hotel says:

> "The union contract specifies the apportionment of the 19 percent gratuity. No part goes to convention service staff, banquet managers, or room setup; but just 75 percent is equally distributed among the waiters -- the people who worked the function. The other 25 percent is allocated to a category called "salaries recovered", reducing labor costs on the profit and loss statement."[3]

Blanket gratuities, our third classification, are becoming common. Planners and delegates often favor this form of tipping; it means they tip only once -- when they register -- and are not faced wih it again. Some resorts have used this method for years, and now commercial convention hotels are trying the system. The **American plan** has a single charge for rooms, meals and gratuities. The more common **European plan** prices rooms, meals and tips separately.

If a blanket tipping policy is to be used, this must be communicated to the delegates. Often the meeting planner will point out the policy in the registration packet. Notices declaring "Your gratuities are completely covered in the room charge; do not tip hotel personnel" are common. Similarly, the hotel must communicate this procedure to its employees and discourage them from accepting tips. Again, the specification sheet is the medium whereby the tipping policy is communicated internally.

To help clarify blanket tipping charges, we have outlined below the policies of two well-known resorts:

- The Greenbrier
  White Sulphur Springs, West Virginia

  In lieu of gratuities for housekeeping and Modified American Plan food service personnel, a service charge of $5.00 per person is added daily to guests' accounts.

Bellmen, doormen, and others who render personal services are not included in the service charge.

- Boca Raton Hotel and Club
  Boca Raton, Florida

For the convenience of the convention group, the hotel adds $4.50 per day per person to cover the following hotel personnel:

- front door and parking attendants
- handling of luggage on arrival and departure
- chamber maids
- dining room personnel for meals served under the meal plan

For a la carte food and beverages an automatic gratuity of 15 percent is added to the check. Other personnel are tipped at the convention group's discretion.

The final type of gratuity is that used in rewarding special personnel. Meeting planners may ask the hotel about the accepted practice and internal policies for giving such tips. Hotels that do recommend tipping for special services will offer a suggested minimum scale. Figure 18.4 shows the results of a survey of meeting planners regarding how they tipped special service personnel.

In conclusion, the handling of gratuities, as with all elements of convention management, should be carefully reviewed and understood by both the meeting planner and the convention service manager. Even though tipping is a touchy area, no difficulties should arise if guidelines are clearly established at the outset.

HSMAI's Suggested Payment Schedule

The Hospitality Sales & Marketing Association International offers a list of standardized procedures which help reduce problems in convention accounting. Here are the guidelines:

- Establish a formal procedure for the hotel and the meeting planner to review periodically the room block arrangements before the meeting. The recommended schedule: up to one year before the meeting; six months before; then every month; and, with one month to go, weekly. The use of rooming lists is encouraged.
- Meeting room usage and charges should be thoroughly reviewed before the meeting.
- The hotel should clearly specify what credit cards are accepted and the maximum that can be charged.
- A master statement of all functions should be organized daily.
- Night auditors and cashiers should be instructed about the details of posting convention charges.
- It is desirable to have corporate meeting planners guarantee all attendees' bills.
- The hotel should inform the company of any delinquent accounts after thirty days.
- A representative from accounting, the head cashier, and perhaps the accounts receivable department head should also attend the pre-convention meeting.

- The specification sheet and individual function forms are to be supplied to the meeting planner before the convention; charges to be clearly specified in advance.
- At the conclusion of each function, a copy of the master statement and supporting vouchers should be furnished to the meeting planner for his or her signature.
- It is recommended that the master account be submitted in full no more than five days after the event. Prepayment of a portion of the master account is encouraged.

The emphasis of this checklist is communication. Every aspect of billing must be clearly and concisely communicated to the accounting department and the meeting planner.

Post-Convention Review

It is wise to review a job when it is completed. Much can be learned. Such a review should be done with an eye toward constructive improvement. The purpose of a review is to evaluate performance during the event and the forecasting and planning that preceded the convention. The goal is to improve technique so that the next event will go even smoother.

A convention service manager we interviewed about post-convention meetings said:

> "A good, thorough pre-convention meeting can lead to a very short and satisfying post-convention wrap-up."

We recommend two review sessions. The first, an intra-staff meeting, should involve the hotel staff only. The second, termed a post-convention, should be attended by both the hotel staff and the meeting planning staff.

The hotel meeting should include the hotel sales manager, convention service manager, and all departments involved in servicing the group. The purposes of this meeting are

Post-Convention Reporting

Mike Gamble
Sr. Vice President, Sales and Marketing
Philadelphia Convention & Visitors Bureau

"Post-convention reporting has become one of the overlooked, underrated, and irritating duties that convention professionals face everyday. Cities and hotels are still faced with inaccurate reporting of history and typically do not have the adequate information available to make a good business decision on whether or not to book a group or convention. With the fast pace of the hospitality industry, it is easy to move on to the next meeting or convention and forget about the one that has just finished....A thorough Post Convention Report...will give a much better picture of the overall value of the meeting that most times is not conveyed. During the qualifying and pre-sales activities, the hotels and convention bureaus often ask for an extraordinary amount of information about the group's history, buying habits, and ancillary spending...The irony is that typically hotels and cities are unable to provide the same amount of information back to the planner once the meeting is completed...."

Figure 18.4. GRATUITY STRUCTURE FOR SPECIAL TIPS.

Gratuities Vary Based On Hotel Staff Positions

Q. Assume that the following hotel personnel have been equally attentive. Indicate whether you would give them a gratuity, and if so, how much:

PERSONNEL	YES	NO	HIGH	LOW	AVERAGE
Convention Service Director (main contact)	75%	25%	$500	$25	$125
Food and Beverage Manager	68%	32%	$500	$15	$ 88
Assistant Convention Services Director	65%	35%	$150	$15	$ 58
Setup Crew Supervisor	62%	13%	$200	$10	$ 44
Hotel General Manager	0%	100%	—	—	—
Convention Sales Manager	10%	90%	$200	$35	$ 69
Account Executive on your convention	17%	83%	$400	$15	$ 80
Catering Manager	63%	37%	$400	$20	$ 78
Front Desk Supervisor*	69%	31%	$100	$10	$ 36
Head Banquet Waiter**	82%	18%	$125	$10	$ 42
Audio Visual Operator	41%	59%	$200	$ 5	$ 44
Switchboard Operator***	39%	61%	$ 50	$10	22

* Other gratuity: candy (1)
** Other gratuity: $10 per event (1); $20 per function (1)
***Other gratuity: $10 for each operator (1); $250 to PBX Fund (1); $150 to include operators (1); candy (4); and gift (1)

Mentioned By 10 Or Fewer Respondents	Average Amount
Accounting Manager	$ 23
A/V Supervisor	$ 25
Banquet Captains	$ 40
Bell Captain	$ 33
Chef	$ 90
Sales, Convention Services & Catering Secretaries	$ 38
Executive Suite Maid	$ 20
Front Desk Personnel	$ 25
Group Reservations Coordinator	$ 75
Head Housekeeper	$ 33
Maids for Staff Rooms	$ 20
Master Account Coordinator	$ 50
Package Room Supervisor	$ 37
Pastry Chef	$ 25
Reservations Assistant	$100
Reservations Manager	$163
Reservations Personnel	$ 5
Room Service Supervisor	$ 75
Sous Chefs	$ 35
Tennis and Golf Pros	$ 62
Transportation Director	$ 25

In a recent survey, Meeting News *asked meeting planners which hotel personnel they tipped for special service and the average amount of such tips.*
Source: Courtesy of Meeting News.

to review the meeting's rough spots, to discuss how the event could have been expedited, and to recognize any efforts that went well as examples for the future. Often in such a meeting an internal report, called a **performance report**, is prepared. Kirby Smith, vice president of sales skills training for Marriott says his company takes post-meeting performance reports seriously:

> "We use one form that's designed to hold people accountable in every
> facet of a hotel's operation, channeling to them with our bonus system.
> The form is broken down into the sales process -- pre-event, event, and
> post-event phases -- and addresses transitions from sales to service."[4]

The second meeting should involve both the meeting planner and his or her staff and the hotel staff. If the convention is a city-wide, the convention bureau, exposition service contractor, destination management company, and audiovisual supplier may be invited. This meeting is also held to go over the many things that happened at the convention while they are fresh in everyone's mind. A good time to hold this meeting is when the master account gets its final review and approval. Everyone is in the hotel and relaxed after the great effort.

Don't duck discussions about the rough spots. Talk them out and try to agree on how they can be handled in the future. Both teams learn much from these inter-staff meetings.

This is also a time to begin the pitch for more business. Many hotel staff people are reluctant to start selling at this time, but if all went well, it may very well be the best time to make the pitch. If not for the convention itself, for other types of meetings. Corporations hold meetings all the time, and you should make your bid for more of their business.

Every aspect of the meeting should be reviewed and discussed candidly. Association executives should feel free to express their views on the staff's service and performance. Meeting planners appreciate having the opportunity to share their comments. If they sense the hotel is honestly concerned about improvement, they will more readily book future business.

Comparison with Projections

Compare what happened with what was expected to happen. Compare the number of rooms originally blocked out with the number actually used. Review the flow into and out of the hotel. Did you have adequate help on hand to receive the guests. Were no-shows a problem? Did you overbook? If so, how did you handle it? Compare attendance with that of other years.

Early departures wreak havoc with hotel income. Yet they generally reflect at least as much on the convention programing as on the hotel attractions. If early departures were greater than in previous years, the program could be at fault; but the hotel still might give some thought to what it can do to make its facilities or area more inviting.

If this convention continually has a problem with early departures, the executive should make some effort to get members to estimate their stays more accurately and honestly. Most convention executives realize that healthy hotels are their concern, too.

Late departures create a different problem when they interfere with other group commitments that are beginning. There is enough evidence of intentional overbooking by hotels that late departures add fuel to the fire. Late departures are a problem, of course, only when the house is overfilled. Otherwise, it's a pleasant bonus.

The entire projection of arrival and departure patterns should be reviewed. The mix of rooms used — single, doubles, twins and suites — should be compared with what was blocked out in order to polish the technique for the next time. Compare the pattern with the work schedule of your front desk people and other personnel needed for heavy arrival traffic.

Function Attendance

Both the hotel people and the convention executive are most interested in how actual attendance at special functions compared with expectations. Guarantees at food functions don't tell the whole story. If actual attendance fell below the guarantee, the convention executive still has to pay for the full number guaranteed or try to persuade the hotel to accept payment for only those served. On the other hand, if more than an extra five percent showed up, the hotel is hard pressed to seat and serve them. The convention organization is chagrined not to serve its members; the hotel is undeservedly shown in a bad light.

Review function room allocations. It is difficult to conduct a meeting in a room only 30 percent filled. A smaller room would have helped, if one were available. If not, dividers and screens could have helped. Perhaps the larger room could have been used for something else.

Special Services

Feedback on the hotel's services also is of interest. Each convention is different, but the hotel can learn from each one about room service, the restaurants, the play at the athletic facilities, the elevator service. Keep an eye on these services because hotel reputations depend on them. It is an interesting phenomenon that the people who shape the image in the hotel business are the ones who get the least pay. The telephone operator and the front desk people probably have more contact with hotel guests than anyone else on the staff. If they have been congenial throughout the convention, the customer probably will carry away a good image of the hotel.

Individual Comments

A very different picture may emerge if you take the trouble to invite comments from your own staff, too. Staff members have a different vantage point than the convention service manager. Ask the bell staff, housekeepers, and front desk people how they think the convention went.

Stand near the cashier at check-out time to get candid comments from guests. Some hotels make post-event mailings to guests. The benefits are twofold: the hotel projects a sincere desire to render good service, and it is often able to detect unspotted problem areas.

Doubletree Inns, for example, uses a service evaluation form (see Figure 18.5) to quiz the respondent on all service aspects of the meeting. An analysis of the results has proven to be very advantageous when it comes to booking repeat business.

Hyatt Hotels recently employed third-party telemarketing assistance to receive feedback from planners about service delivery. Fred Shea, vice president of sales operations, says:

> "Nobody can tell you what to do better than your customers. Hyatt commissioned the Gallup polling organization to survey meeting planners

Figure 18.5. SERVICE EVALUATION QUESTIONNAIRE.

DOUBLETREE INN

SERVICE EVALUATION

COMPANY/GROUP NAME _____

EVALUATOR'S NAME _____

FRONT OFFICE	Exlt	Good	Fair	Poor	Comments
Registration					
Bellman Service					
Telephone Service					
Desk Clerk Service					
Employee's Attitude					

RESTAURANTS & LOUNGE					
Coffee Shop					
Food & Beverage Quality					
Food & Beverage Service					
Dining Room					
Food & Beverage Quality					
Food & Beverage Service					
Lounge					
Entertainment Quality					
Beverage Quality					
Beverage Service					
Room Service					
Food & Beverage Quality					
Food & Beverage Service					

HOUSEKEEPING					
Guest Rooms					
Restaurants & Lounge					
Public Areas					
Meeting & Banquet Rooms					

MEETING & BANQUET FACILITIES					
Room Set-up					
On Time?					
Banquet Meal Service					
Food & Beverage Quality					
Food & Beverage Service					
Coffee Breaks					
Employee Attitudes					
Sales/Catering Staff					
Service Staff					
Air Conditioning/Heat					
Lighting					
Necessary Equipment Provided					

MISCELLANEOUS					
Courtesy Car Service					
Parking					

ADDITIONAL COMMENTS _____
_____
_____

FUTURE RESERVATIONS:

Are there future meeting or banquet dates presently in the planning stage? _____

Can dates be held on tentative basis? _____

I would like additional information on Doubletree facilities in the following cities: _____
_____

132   987-5

Asks delegates for a rating of the hotel's performance. (By permission of the Doubletree Inn).

by telephone. With results of the canvassing, the company is making changes it its culture that are tied to service accountability."[5]

Whatever your approach, some effort should be made to determine the staff's and guests' feelings about how the event went and how the hotel fared.

Post-convention Reporting

Post-convention reporting has become one of the most discussed topics in today's meetings market, as accurate and thorough reports are important to both planners and hoteliers.

Meeting planners know that information is power, and when it comes to negotiating a thorough meetings history provides leverage in ensuring better rates. Catherine Roper, director of meetings for the Health Industry Distributors Association says:

> "As a planner, I need help from the hotel in knowing the value of my business. This is so I have a history to bring to negotiations. For instance, my people are in the gift shops, the restaurants, playing golf and tennis and using the spa. I want to know the total picture of my meeting's value."[6]

Hotels, likewise, recognize that post-convention reports allow them to more accurately evaluate and qualify business. Convention bureaus need accurate histories when trying to establish room blocks for city-wide conventions, and hotels need them to determine their level of participation.

Accurate post-convention reports also lead to better service. For example, the convention service manager can staff to handle peak arrivals based on past experience.

To ensure they receive post-convention reports, some planners are stipulating in the contract that they won't pay until they get an accurate report. Planners are also asking hotels to provide post-convention information on **ancillary business** -- affiliates and sub-groups as well as exhibitors. Planners recognize that the ancillary revenue to hotels from associations with exhibits can be huge. Not only do exhibitors utilize guestrooms, but many also hold events ranging from meals to hospitality suites to meetings.

Responding to the need for post-convention reports, most major hotel chains now have a company-wide standardized system for post-convention reporting. Hyatt, Hilton, and Marriott automatically provide post-convention reports for all groups using 100 rooms or more on peak nights.

Many in the meetings industry would like to see an industry-wide, single database of post-convention information. One possibility proposed by industry groups is to have post-convention information submitted by hotels to their convention bureaus. The information would then be stored in the **CINET** (the Convention Industry Network) system, a database developed by the International Association of Convention and Visitors Bureaus, which is accessible on the Internet.

Since it is so important to get accurate meeting statistics, there has been a growing consensus within the industry that standardized forms would facilitate the process. In response, the Convention Industry Council (CIC), developed both a long form and a short form to be used for post-convention analysis (see Chapter Appendix). These forms are not only available on paper, but on computer disks and on-line as well, making it easy to enter data and get an almost immediate picture of the convention's success.

Final Appraisal

Before breaking down the working file and returning appropriate correspondence to the account file, ask if you could do a better job if the clock could be turned back to give you another chance. That question should be considered with complete frankness in the cold light of post-convention experience. If the answer discloses areas of difficulty, you should take steps to eliminate the problems in the future. The problems could deal with personnel or facilities. Solving them could help the sales manager set priorities on the kind of business you want and can handle. If the answers please you, don't forget to send a thank-you letter to the meeting planner, and to put that name in your follow-up file for some time in the very near future.

Chapter Summary:

As we have seen throughout this text, selling to and servicing the conventions and meetings market requires careful planning and attention to details. The convention billing process and post-convention follow-up are important factors in building a group's goodwill and generating future business. A property must clearly spell out billing procedures and make it easy and convenient for the meeting planner to keep abreast of meeting charges. And, after the convention or meeting, follow-up is necessary to determine areas of strengths and weaknesses and to build a group history that can be used in the future to negotiate additional events.

Endnotes:

1. Don Nichols, "High-Tech Comes to Hotels," *Association Meetings*, January 1997, p. 46.
2. Roger Sonnabend, "The Hotelier Looks at the Business of Meetings," *3M Business Press*.
3. Julie Barker, "The Ultimate Guide to Tipping and Gratuities," *Successful Meetings*, July 1997, p. 46.
4. Ruth Hill, "Planner's Lament," *Lodging*, September 1999, p. 80.
5. Ibid.
6. Ruth Hill, "Confronting the Bull in Today's Market," *HSMAI Marketing Review*, Winter 1998, p. 35.

Additional References:

S.R. Torrance, "To Tip or Not to Tip?," *Convene*, December 1988, p. 85-87.

Internet Sites:

For additional information on the firms and organizations discussed in this chapter, visit the following Internet sites. The Web addresses listed are current as of January

2001. Addresses may change, however; if a site is not available at address below, a search engine can be used to access its new location.

Caesars Palace - www.caesars.com

Convention Industry Council - www.conventionindustry.org

Philadelphia Convention and Visitors Bureau - www.libertynet.org/phila-visitor

Insurance Conference Planners - www.icpanet.com

Hospitality Sales and Marketing Association International (HSMAI) - www.hsmai.org

 Study Questions:

1. Discuss the statement "As with most aspects of convention planning, the time to avoid billing problems is in the beginning and not at the end." What procedures are recommended for avoiding billing problems?
2. What are the three different folios that can be used for a meeting or convention? Who pays the charges for each?
3. What factors should be considered when determining a time of payment for a meeting group? When are charges typically billed?
4. List the four groupings for service gratuities and distinguish between blanket gratuities and special tipping.
5. Outline the HSMAI's suggested payment schedule.
6. Why is a post-convention review important? Who should attend post-convention review meetings?
7. What should be included in the post-convention report? What are the benefits of post-convention reports? Design a sample report that would help your hotel to gauge the success of a convention.

 Key Terms:

American plan. Charge includes room, food and beverage, and gratuities. Includes three meals per day.

Ancillary business. Affiliates and subgroups, such as exhibitors, who contribute to the overall value of the meeting.

Authorized signature. Signature of person(s) with authority to charge to a group master account.

Blanket gratuities. Gratuities added into the room charge so the attendees do not have to tip during their stay. Mostly used with the American Plan (AP) system.

CINET. An online database of meeting profiles maintained by the International Association of Convention and Visitors Bureaus.

European plan. Prices rooms and food/beverage separately.

Guest credit. Credit extended to the guest based on information collected by the hotel's credit department. This is a courtesy of the hotel, not an obligation.

Guest folio. An account on which all individual guest charges not covered by the master account will be posted and paid by the individual guest.

Incidental charges. Expenses other than the guestroom charge and taxes. Billed to a guest's folio.

Master account folio. An account on which all charges incurred by the delegates are accumulated and paid by the sponsoring organization. The charges to be posted to this account should be agreed upon in advance.

Master account billing authorization form. A form that provides instructions on the types of folios to be established, limits of financial responsibility, and the names and signatures of personnel authorized to sign for group charges.

Performance report. An internal report used by hotels to evaluate a convention. The hotel can use this research to determine how the convention facilities matched the client's needs.

Rates and charges bulletin. Communicates specific rates for rooms, meals, gratuities and billing procedures agreed upon by the various parties involved.

Split folio. Charges are paid partially by the sponsoring organization and partially by the guest. Communication is needed to ensure that all parties involved understand who is responsible for specific charges.

Chapter Appendix

CONVENTION LIAISON COUNCIL

OFFICIAL POST-CONVENTION REPORT

Short Form

ACCOUNT INFORMATION

ORGANIZATION:	
Division:	
Meeting Dates:	
Contact:	
Title:	
Address:	
Phone Number:	Fax Number:

HOTEL NAME:	
Sales Mgr:	
Conv Svcs Mgr:	
Catering Mgr:	

INTERMEDIARY:	
Contact:	
Title:	
Address:	
Phone Number:	Fax Number:

ATTENDANCE	
Members:	
Spouses:	
Speakers/Guests:	
TOTAL:	

☐ Individual
☐ Rooming List
☐ Other

OVERFLOW HOTEL(S) NAME	PEAK ROOMS

AVERAGE LENGTH OF STAY	
PEOPLE PER ROOM RATIO	

COMMISSIONABLE: ___ Yes ___ No

TO WHOM: _____

Group Rate OK after Cut-off Date? ___ Yes ___ No

Rooms Guaranteed by Group? ___ Yes ___ No

CLC/PCR - 7 93

168

(continued)

CONVENTION INDUSTRY COUNDIL'S STANDARDIZED POST-CONVENTION REPORT

ROOM PICK-UP REPORT

DAY										
DATE										
ORIGINAL BLOCK										
REVISED BLOCK										
6 MONTH BLOCK										
3 MONTH PICK-UP										
6 WEEK PICK-UP										
CUTOFF PICK-UP										
FINAL PICK-UP										
SINGLE										
DOUBLE										
TRIPLE										
QUAD										
1 BEDROOM SUITE										
2 BEDROOM SUITE										
PRESIDENTIAL										

GROUP FOOD & BEVERAGE FUNCTION REPORT
(Catering)

DAY/DATE	NAME OF ORGANIZATION	FUNCTION	# OF PEOPLE			AFFILIATE
			ORIGINAL	GUARANTEE	ACTUAL	
TOTAL FOOD & BEVERAGE						

MEETING INFORMATION

Date Final Agenda/Program Received	
Largest Single Meeting (# of people)	
Largest # of Concurrent Meetings	

24-HOUR HOLD MEETING ROOMS

REASON	QUANTITY
Rear Screen Projection	
Offices	
Exhibits	
Computers	

CLC/PCR - 7/93

169

The CIC developed post-convention report forms (depicted here is part of the three-page short version) in an effort to standardize the collection of convention data throughout the industry. The CIC felt that using standardized forms (available on paper, disk, and online) would facilitate analyzing pertinent convention information and would provide "accurate, reliable, and verifiable historical data."

The exchange of group history on post-convention reports can become a problem if actual dollar amounts are released. It is a violation of antitrust law to exchange pricing information such as room rates or banquet charges. Exchanging number of rooms blocked, rooms picked up, number and size of food functions, and describing room service and restaurant volume as light, moderate or heavy is an acceptable practice.

Appendix I

Directory of U.S. Trade Organizations and Publications

**American Hotel & Lodging Association
(AH&LA)**
1201 New York Avenue, NW, Suite 600
Washington, DC 20005
(202) 289-3100
Fax (202) 289-3199
www.ahla.com

**American Society of Association
Executives
(ASAE)**
1575 Eye Street, NW
Washington, DC 20005
(202) 626-2741
Fax (202) 371-0870
www.asaenet.org

**American Society for Training and
Development
(ASTD)**
1640 King Street/P.O. Box 1443
Alexandria, VA 22313
(703) 683-8100
www.astd.org

**American Society of Travel Agents
(ASTA)**
1101 King Street, Suite 200
Alexandria, VA 22314
(703) 739-2782
Fax (703) 684-8319
www.astanet.com

**Association for Convention Marketing
Executives
(ACME)**
2965 Flowers Road S., Suite 105
Atlanta, GA 30341
(770) 454-6111
Fax (770) 458-3314
www.acmenet.org

**Association for Convention Operations
Management
(ACOM)**
1819 Peachtree Street, N.E., Suite 712
Atlanta, GA 30309
(770) 454-9411
(770) 458-3314

**Association of Corporate Travel
Executives
(ACTE)**
515 King Street, Suite 330
Alexandria, VA 22314
800-ACTE NOW
www.acte.org

***Association Management* (Publication)**
1575 Eye Street, NW
Washington, DC 20005
(202) 626-2711
www.asaenet.org/publications

***Association Meetings* (Publication)**
63 Great Road
Maynard, MA 01754
(508) 897-5552
www.meetingsnet.com

***Business Travel News* (Publication)**
1515 Broadway
New York, NY 10036
(212) 869-1300
www.btnonline.com

Center for Exhibition Industry Research
2301 Lake Shore Drive, Suite E1002
Chicago, IL 60616
(312) 808-2347
Fax (312) 949-3472
www.ceir.org

**Convention Industry Council
(CIC)**
Dept. 4490, P.O. Box 85080
Richmond, VA 23285
(703) 610-9030
Fax (703) 610-9005
www.conventionindustry.org

Corporate & Incentive Travel
(Publication)
488 Madison Avenue
New York, NY 10022
(212) 888-1500

Corporate Meetings & Incentives
(Publication)
43 L Nason Street
Maynard, MA 01754
(978) 897-5552

Convene **(Publication)**
2301 S. Lake Shore Drive
Chicago, IL 60616
(312) 423-7262
www.pcma.org/pub

**Exhibit Designers and Producers
Association
(EDPA)**
5775-G Peachtree-Dudwoody Road
Atlanta, GA 30342
(404) 303-7310
Fax (404) 252-0774
www.edpa@assnhq.com

**Expositions Service Contractors
Association
(ESCA)**
400 S. Houston Street, Suite 210
Dallas, TX 75202
(214) 742-9217
Fax (214) 741-2519
www.esca.org

**Healthcare Convention Exhibitors
Association
(HCEA)**
5775 Peachtree-Dunwoody Road
Atlanta, GA 30342
(404) 252-3663
Fax (404) 252-0774
www.hcea.org

**Hospitality Sales and Marketing
Association International
(HSMAI)**
1300 L Street, NW, Suite 1020
Washington, DC 20005
(202) 789-0089
Fax (202) 789-1725
www.hsmai.org

HSMAI Marketing Review **(Publication)**
1300 L Street NW, Suite 1020
Washington, DC 20005
(202) 789-0089
Fax (202) 789-1725
www.hsmai.org

**Institute of Association Management
Companies
(IAMC)**
104 Wilmot Road, Suite 201
Deerfield, IL 60015-5195

Insurance Conference Planner
(Publication)
43 L Nason Street
Maynard, MA 01754
(978) 897-5552
Fax (978) 897-6824

**International Association of Assembly
Managers
(IAAM)**
635 Fritz
Coppell, TX 75019
(972) 255-8020
Fax (972) 255-9582
www.iaam.org

International Association of Conference Centers
(IACC)
243 N. Lindbergh, Suite 315
St. Louis, MO 63141
(314) 993-8575
Fax (314) 993-8919
www.iacconline.com

International Association of Convention & Visitors Bureaus
(IACVB)
2025 M Street, NW, Suite 500
Washington, DC 20036
(202) 296-7888
Fax (202) 296-7889
www.iacvb.org

International Association for Exposition Management
(IAEM)
5001 LBJ Freeway, Suite 350
Dallas, TX 57244
(972) 458-8002
(972) 458-8119
www.iaem.org

International Association of Fairs & Expositions
(IAFE)
P.O. Box 985
Springfield, MO 65801
(417) 862-5771
Fax (417) 862-0156

Medical Meetings **(Publication)**
43 L Nason Street
Maynard, MA 01754
(978) 897-5552

Meeting News **(Publication)**
1515 Broadway
New York, NY 10036
(212) 869-1300
www.meetingsnews.com

Meeting Professionals International
(MPI)
4455 LBJ Freeway, Suite 1200
Dallas, TX 54244
(972) 702-3000
(972) 702-3036
www.mpiweb.org

Meetings & Conventions **(Publication)**
500 Plaza Drive
Secaucus, NJ 07094
(201) 902-1700
www.meetings-conventions.com

Meetings & Incentives **(Publication)**
See Appendix II.

National Coalition of Black Meeting Planners
(NCBMP)
8630 Fenton Street, Suite 126
Silver Spring, MD 20910
(202) 628-3952
Fax (301) 588-0011
www.ncbmp.com

National Association of Catering Executives
(NACE)
5565 Sterrett Drive, Suite 328
Columbia, MD 21045
(410) 997-9055
Fax (410) 997-8834
www.nace.net

National Business Travel Association
(NBTA)
1560 King Street, Suite 301
Alexandria, VA 22314
(703) 684-0836
www.mbta.org

Official Meeting Facilities Guide
(Publication)
500 Plaza Drive
Secaucus, NJ 07094
(201) 902-1700
Fax (201) 319-1685

Professional Convention Management Association
(PCMA)
2301 S. Lake Shore Drive
Chicago, IL 60616
(312) 423-7262
Fax (312) 423-7222
www.pcma.org

Religious Conference Management Association
(RCMA)
1 RCA Dome, Suite 120
Indianapolis, IN 46225
(317) 632-1888
Fax (317) 632-7909
www.meetingsnet.com

Religious Conference Manager
(Publication)
43 L Nason Street
Maynard, MA 01754
(978) 897-5552

Sales and Marketing Management
(Publication)
777 Broadway
New York, NY 10003
(646) 654-7323

Society of Corporate Meeting Professionals
(SCMP)
2965 Flowers Road, Suite 105
Atlanta, GA 30341
(770) 457-9212
Fax (770) 458-3314
www.scmp.org

Society of Government Meeting Planners
(SGMP)
908 King Street
Alexandria, VA 22314
(703) 549-0892
Fax (703) 549-0708
www.sgmp.org

Society of Incentive Travel Executives
(SITE)
21 West 38th Street
New York, NY 10018
(212) 575-0910
Fax (212) 575-1838
www.site-intl.org

Successful Meetings **(Publication)**
633 Third Avenue
New York, NY 10017
(212) 986-4800
www.successmtgs.com

Trade Show Exhibitors Association
(TSEA)
5501 Backlick Road, Suite 105
Springfield, VA 22151
(703) 941-3725
Fax (703) 941-8275
www.tsea.org

Travel Industry Association of America
(TIAA)
1100 New York Avenue, NW
Washington, DC 20005
(202) 408-8422
Fax (202) 408-1255

Appendix II

Directory of Canadian Trade Organizations and Publications

Canadian Association of Convention & Visitors Bureaus
c/o Tourism Winnipeg
279 Portage Avenue
Winnipeg, Manitoba, Canada, R3B 2B4
(204) 943-1970
Fax: (204) 942-4043

Canadian Association of Exposition Management
Box 82, 6900 Airport Road, Suite 239-A
Mississauga, Ontario, Canada L4V 1E8
(905) 678-9377
Fax (905) 678-9578

Canadian Association of Fairs & Exhibitions
Box 1172, Station Main
Edmonton, Alberta, Canada T5J 2M4
(780) 474-1902
Fax (780) 471-4981

Canadian Association of Professional Speakers
Box 294, 10435 Islington Avenue
Kleinburg, Ontario, Canada L0J 1C0
(905) 893-1689
Fax (905) 893-2392

Canadian Business Travel Association
5988 du Bocage
Montreal, Quebec, Canada H1M 1X2
(514) 353-4681, (888) 990-2540
Fax (514) 353-5736

Canadian Hotel Marketing & Sales Executives
84 Seventh Street
Toronto, Ontario, Canada M8V 3B4
(416) 252-9800
Fax (416) 252-7071

Canadian Society of Association Executives
10 King Street E., Suite 1100
Toronto, Ontario, Canada M5C 1C3
(416) 363-3555
Fax (416) 363-3630

Exhibit & Display Association of Canada
51A Esna Park Drive, Unit 2
Markham, Ontario, Canada L3R 1O9
(905) 943-9548
Fax (905) 943-9547

Hotel Association of Canada
130 Albert Street, Suite 1016
Ottawa, Ontario, Canada K1P 5G4
(613) 237-7149
Fax (613) 237-8928

Independent Meeting Planners Association of Canada
324 Glen Manor Drive
Toronto, Ontario, Canada M4E 2X7
(416) 686-5266
Fax (416) 686-5277

Insurance Conference Planners Association
106-206 West Esplanade
Vancouver, British Columbia, Canada V7M 3G7
(604) 988-2054
Fax (604) 988-4743

Meeting Professionals International
Box 11, 329 March Road, Suite 232
Kanata, Ontario, Canada K2K 2E1
(613) 271-8901
Fax (613) 599-7027

Meetings and Incentive Travel
(Publication)
777 Bay Street
Toronto, Ontario, Canada M5W 1A7
(416) 596-5640
Fax (416) 593-3193

Professional Convention Management Association
Canada East
2 Bloor Street W., Suite 1902
Toronto, Ontario, Canada M4W 3E2
(416) 923-2324
Fax (416) 923-7264

Canada West
1665 West Broadway
Vancouver, British Columbia, Canada V6J 1X1
(604) 736-1877
Fax (604) 736-4675

Society of Incentive & Travel Executives, Canadian Chapter
6519-B Mississauga Road
Mississauga, Ontario, Canada L5N 1A6
(905) 567-7190
Fax (905) 567-719

Index

A

a la carte catering 400
AV equipment list/price
    sheet 426
Account file 92
Account management 85
Account master card 89, 90
Account responsibility 84
ACOM 287, 292
Action plans 37, 52
Action steps 53, 63
Activities for children 467
Activities for spouses 464
ADA 363
Admission systems 455
Advance sale 478
Advantages and disadvan-
    tages of popular AV
    equipment 443
Advantages of automation
    101
Advantages of owning AV
    equipment 425
Advantages of using an AV
    company 425
Advertising 222
Advertising agencies 249
Advertising and sales pro-
    motion manager 76
Advertising strategy 243
Advertising to planners of
    small meetings 78
Advertising to the meeting
    planner 223
Affordable Meetings Expo-
    sition and Conference
    170
African-American fraternal
    organizations 177
AIDA 223
Air walls 390
All-suite hotel 16
Alpha Omega 177

Alternative dispute resolu-
    tion 274
American Meetings Data-
    bank 132
American Bar Association
    12
American Legion 177
American Management
    Association 17
American Medical Associa-
    tion 14
American plan 520
American service 399
American Society for Train-
    ing and Development 524
American Society of Asso-
    ciation Executives 190,
    524
American Society of Travel
    Agents 524
Americans with Disabilities
    Act 363
Analysis 38
    Competitive 38
    Marketplace 38
    Property 38
Anatole Hotel 271
Annual conventions 118
Application for direct bill-
    ing 270
Arbitration 274
Area exhibit 477
Arrival/departure pattern
    264
ASAE 190, 524
Asian Business and Incen-
    tive Show 186
Assigning account responsi-
    bility 88
Association and Society
    Manager 524
Association director 127
Association Directory &
    Buying Guide 131
Association Executive 129

Association for Convention
    Operations Management
    287, 292
Association housing poli-
    cies 315, 316
Association Management
    524
Association management
    companies 23
Association meetings
    Characteristics 122
    Importance 113
    Kinds 118
    Trends 115
Association of Corporate
    Travel Executives 524
Association of Independent
    Meeting Planners 524
Association president and
    vice president 129
Associations 13
    Educational 14
    Professional 14
    Scientific 14
    Technical 14
    Trade 13
    Veterans and Military
        15
ASTA 524
ASTD 524
Attrition clause 273
Audio teleconferencing 440
Audiosync tape recorder
    430
Audiovisual equipment 422
Advantages and disadvan-
    tages of popular 443
Advantages of owning 425
Advantages of using an AV
    service company 425
    Charging 446
    Comparison 443
Audiovisual requirements
    422
Audiovisual specialists 422

Auditorium style 380
Authorized signature 508
Automated bars 412

B

Backdrop 477
Badge 455
Ballrooms for banquets 403
Banquet business 393
Banquet Event Order (BEO) 347
Banquet food and beverage revenue 393
Banquet/catering department 393
Bar requisition form 413
Basic meeting setups
  Auditorium style 380
    Variations 380
Bed taxes 214
Behind the scenes look at a trade show 498
Best's Insurance Convention Guide 524
Beverage control 411
Beverage service 408
Bid sheet 261
Billing 503
Blackboards 411, 412
Blanket gratuities 510
Blue Book of College Athletics 175
Board and committee meetings 122
Board of Directors 130
Board of Directors set-up 384
Booking forms, definite 91
Booth exhibit 477
Boy Scouts 169
Break-out session 353
Breakdown of function rooms 386
Bring-up file 91
Broadcast Fax 232
Broadcast video 438
Brochures 233
Budget

Sample marketing budget form 59
Budgeting 58
Buffet service 399
Building spouse attendance 463
Business class rooms 143
Business publications 162
Business status and trends summaries 44, 45
Business Travel News 524
By the bottle 409
By the drink 410
By the hour 410

C

Call brand 409
Call report 207
Camp Hyatt 467
Cancellation form 98
Cancellation policies 271
Captain's bar 409
Carousel projector 432
Cart service 399
Cash bar 408
Cash bar control 412
Catering manager's job description 416
Catering/convention services manager 407
CD-ROMs 234
CD-ROM presentations 234
Certified Meeting Professional 6
Certified meeting space 363
Chairs 376
Chalkboards 411, 412
Change form 98
Characteristics of association meetings 122
Charging for audiovisual equipment 446
Check-in/Check-out 332
Checklists 469
Choosing a screen size 431
CINET 132
Circular buffet table 385
City housing bureau 315

Classroom style 381
Clinic 9
Close-ended question 200
Closing and follow up 202
Cocktail receptions 408
Cold calls 198
Collateral material 232
Company meetings
  Kinds 145
Comparison of association and corporate meetings 142
Comparison of audiovisual equipment 443
Competition analysis 38
Competitive rate analysis 47
Complete meeting package 20
Complimentary and reduced rate rooms 265
Computer generated booking report 97
Computer influence 333
Computer prepared guest folio 335
Computer projected image 439
Computer systems 97
Computerized master files 100
Computerized reports 101
Computerized systems 338
Computerized trace report 144
Computers in guestroom booking 145
Concurrent session 118
Conducting market research 38
Conferences 9
Conference center 17
Confirmation dates 312
Congress 9
Consumer show 490
Continuing Medical Education 188
Contract 259
Contract standardization 278
Controlled admission 455

Convention 10
Convention and visitors
bureau 214
Convention billing 503
Convention brochure 232
Convention bureau housing
bureaus 315
Convention checklists 469
Convention hospitality
suites 409
Convention income 114
Convention rates 322
Convention registration 453
Convention sales manager
78, 79, 80
Convention security 454
Convention service check-
list 306
Convention service depart-
ment 76
Convention service man-
ager
Job description 298
Convention service person-
nel 293
Convention service secre-
tary 295
Convention service staff
293
Convention services 288
Convention shipping and
receiving 492
Cooperative advertising
248
Corkage 409
Corporate and incentive
travel 524
Corporate meeting planners
157
Corporate meetings 12
Corporate Meetings &
Incentives 524
Corporate sales staffs 81
Corporate travel profes-
sional 160
Coupon sales control 412
Coupon sales/bars 412
Customer-focused conven-
tion service skills 293
Cut-off date 264
Cut-off requirements 264

D

Dais 378
Databank information 132
Databases 132
Dealer meetings 147
Decorator 479
Decorator charge 492
Decorators/Exhibition
service contractors 479
Definite booking form 100
Delphi reports 97
Departure pattern 264
Deposit policy 325
Destination management
companies 461
Destination marketing 216
Developing a marketing
plan 33
Developing action plans 53
Difference between sales
and marketing 33
Direct billing, application
270
Direct mail 237
Direct mail campaigns 240
Direct mail "gimmicks" 241
Direct mail marketing 239
Direct mail series 238
Director of advertising 76
Director of convention
services 293
Directory of corporate meet-
ing planners 162
Director of exhibit service
296
Director of marketing 75
Discounted rates 322
Dissolve unit 432
Drayage 492
Dun and Bradstreet's Mil-
lion Dollar Directory 162
Duoserve 407

E

Early arrival 327
Early departure 328
Easel 447

Economic impact of con-
ventions, expositions,
meetings 5
Educational associations 14
Effective check-in and
check-out 332
Electronic mail 231
Employee procedure
manual 375
Encyclopedia of Associa-
tions 131
E-shape 383
European Incentive Busi-
ness Travel Meetings
Expo 186
European plan 511
Evaluating sales effort 87
Exchange trade advertising
247
Exhibit and decorator's
charges 492
Exhibit and marketplace
trade shows 490
Exhibit assignments 477
Exhibit billing procedures
490
Exhibit planning 478
Exhibit security 456
Exhibit shipping, handling
and storage 492
Exhibiting at trade shows
211
Exhibition service contrac-
tors 479
Exhibitor prospectus 478
Exhibitor's service kit 488
Exposition 478
Exposition service contrac-
tor 479

F

Facility schematic 367
Familiarization (fam) tour
217
Fastfold 430
Fax-on-demand 232
Feeder cities 43

Filing systems 88
   Account master card 89
   Hotel systems 89
Final appraisal 518
Flat-rate arrangement 322
Flip charts and chalk boards
   411, 412
Floodlights 429
Floor load 481
Floor manager 296
Folding platforms 378
Folio 505
Follow-up file 91
Food and beverage control
   393
Food and beverage service
   393
Forecasted demand 106
Forum 9
Fraternal Executives
   Association 177
Fraternal market 175
Fraternal meetings 175
Free pour 412
French service 399
Full-time meeting planner
   158
Function attendance 516
Function book 91
Function book coordinator
   296
Function book reservation
   sheet 95
Function room breakdown
   386
Function room charges 371
Function room furniture
   376
Function room plans 363
Function room size and
   layout 363
Function sheet 347
Function space charges 371
Funding of convention and
   visitors bureaus 241

G

Gemini blackboard 444

General session 118
Geographic file 92
Geographic index of asso-
   ciations 131
Geographic origin of group
   bookings 43
Geographic origin study 42
Geographic restrictions 124
Getting prospect involve-
   ment 200
Globalization 20
Government travel business
   179
      Federal travel directory
      179
Government executive 179
Government Services Ad
   ministration 179
      Society of Government
      Meeting Planners 179
      United States Govern
      ment Manual 179
Government agencies 179
Government meetings mar-
   ket at a glance 179
Gratuity structure for spe-
   cial tips 514
Group allotment 93
Group room night by mar-
   ket segment 45
Growing importance of the
   convention service man-
   ager 292
Guarantee method 403
Guarantee sheet 402
Guaranteed reservations
   328
Guest credit 509
Guest folio 505
Guest history analysis 46
Guestrooms control book
   93
Guide for reunion planners
   172
Guide to American Directo-
   ries 170
Guide to screen size 431

H

Handling objections 202
Historical pattern 331
Historical performance 331
History of convention ser-
   vices 287
Hold harmless 489
Hold harmless clause 489
Hollow circular 383
Hollow square set-up 383
Horseshoe arrangement 382
Horseshoe set-up 382
Hospitality suites 409
Host bar 408
Host bar control 412
Hotel key personnel roster
   342
Hotel marketing plan 32
Hotel negotiation policies
   and practices 258
Hotel's rental charge 490
Houseperson 296
Housing bureau 315
Housing policies, associa-
   tion 330
How CVBs can market your
   property 213
How to find associations
   131
How the sales office inter-
   faces with other depart-
   ments 72
How to develop and
   implement a hotel mar-
   keting plan 35

I

Impact of association and
   corporate meetings 114
Importance of attracting
   meetings market business
   5
Importance of marketing 34
Importance of price 35
Importance of team effort
   for successful exhibitions
   474

Importance of the association market 113
Importance of the convention service department 76
Importance of the trade show 475
In-house coordination: large vs. small 415
In-house equipment 425
In-room technology 24
Incentive meetings
    Important factors 183
    Top 10 users 184
Incentive travel
    Asian Business and Incentive Show 186
    Canadian Travel Expo 186
Incentive travel ad 185
Incentive travel and meeting executives show 186
Incentive travel houses 24
    S and H Travel Awards 186
Incentive travel planners 182
Incidentals 506
Inclusive 503
Incoming shipping costs 494
Indemnification 275
Independent hotel representatives 81
Independent meeting planners 24
Individual guest file 505
Industry standardization 277
Inquiry questionnaire 262
Insurance 187
Insurance company decision makers 187
Insurance Conference Planner 188
Insurance Conference Planner Association 188
Insurance meetings 187
Insurance/indemnification 275
Interest charges 509

International Association of Conference Centers 17
International Association of Convention & Visitors Bureaus 213
International scope of trade shows 475
Internet 229
Invitation for bids 263

J

Job descriptions 78, 298

K

Key account management 86
Key personnel roster 342
Key trade show and exhibit personnel 478
Kinds of association meetings 124
Kinds of company meetings 153

L

Labor unions 182
Laptop computers 105
Lateral referral 164
LCD (liquid crystal display) 433
LCD projector 434
Lead time 124
Lecterns 430
Lecture 9
Letter of agreement 260
Letter of introduction 302
Liability 275
Life Insurance Marketing Research Association 187
Lighting 429
LIMRA 187
Liquid crystal display 433
Liquor liability 414

Local influences 130
Lost business report 101
Lottery system 477

M

Major close 203
Management meetings 148
Managing the sales effort 83
MARC (mazda closed arc) projector 436
Market research 37
Market segment plan 63
Market segments 63
    Sample budget form 59
Marketing and sales services manager 159
Marketing budget form 59
Marketing mix 34
Marketing objectives 52
Marketing plan 37
    Putting into action 60
    Monitoring 58
Marketplace analysis 47
Magazine space options 227
Master account 505
Master account billing authorization form 506
Master account folio 505
Master card 89
Media chart 244
Medical and scientific meetings 188
Meeting calendars 230
Meeting pattern of associations 123
Meeting planner profile 25
Meeting planner's corporate position 158
Meeting planning associations
    American Society of Association Executives 190
    Insurance Meeting Planners Association 190

Meeting Professionals International 190
National Coalition of Black Meeting Planners 190
Professional Convention Planners Association 190
Religious Conference Management Association 190
Society of Corporate Meeting Professionals 190
Society of Government Meeting Planners 190
Society of Incentive Travel Executives 190
Meeting Professionals International 190
Meeting room capacities and dimensions 364
Meeting room plans 363
Meeting room set-ups 376
Meeting terminology 9
Meetings 10
Comparison of association and corporate meetings 142
Impact 142
Menu prices 396
Menus 396, 397, 398
Method of payment 269
Microphones 428
Midweek business year round 150
Military and other reunions 171
Military Reunion News 172
Monitoring function room usage 372
Motion picture projectors 436
Multi-booking potential 157
Multimedia presentations 439
Multiple association management 121
Multiple-meeting contracts 278

N

National and regional sales meetings 146
National Association of Catering Executives 529
National Association of Reunion Planners 174
National Coalition of Black Meeting Planners 190
National conventions 117
National Director of College Athletics 174
National Interfraternity Conference 177
National Panhellenic Conference 177
Negotiations 259
Net square feet 476
New product introduction 147
No-host bar 408
No-shows 327
Nonprofit organizations 14
North American Free Trade Agreement 19
Notices 447

O

Official dates 264
Official Meeting Facilities Guide 227
On-site connection 288
Open bar 408
Open-ended questions 200
Opening the sales call 196
Operation Excell 352
Option 98
Option date 98
Organizing for convention sales 70
Organizing the sales office 70
Outline for property fact book 198
Overbooking 327
Overhead projectors 433

P

PAL standard 438
Panel 9
Panhellenic Conference 177
Panofax 443
Paper easel pads 444
Passenger traffic/corporate travel manager 160
Per-diem 180
Performance report 515
Personal sales calls 195
Piggybacking 12
Pipe and drape 477
Planning an advertising strategy 243
Planning food functions 393
Plate service 399
Platforms 378
Platter service 399
Podium 378
Point system 477
Positioning the property 49
Post-convention meeting 513
Post-convention report 514
Post-convention review 514
Postal reply cards 311
Postal reply forms 330
Pre-call planning 195
Pre-Con 340
Pre-convention meeting 341
Pre-function space 381
Pre-set service 399
Preferred suppliers 461
Presentation devices 233
Presenting your property 201
Press kit 253
Press release 253
Price 35
Pricing food functions 400
Pricing methods 409
Print ads for meeting planners 224
Print advertising 224
Printing and duplication 460
Prior visits 266

Procedure manual 375
Professional and scientific associations 14
Projection screens 430
Projector stands 440
Property analysis 39
Property fact book 196
Property newsletter 238
Proposal letter 261
Public relations and publicity 251
Publicity 251
Putting a marketing plan into action 60

Q

Quartz-halogen bulb 432

R

Rack rates 322
Rates 322
 Discounted 322
Rates and charges bulletin 508
Reach 343
Reader file 87
Rearview projection 434
Reception drink and service estimator 411
Reciprocal advertising 247
Refreshment break guidelines 398
Refreshment breaks 393
Regional sales office 81
Registration and room assignment 335
Relationship marketing 110
Release and confirmation dates 370
Religious conference manager 175
Religious conferences 176
Religious meetings 176
Request for proposal 263
Reservation confirmation form 323

Reservation housing report 321
Reservation reply card 313
Reservation reply form 313
Reservation systems
 Postal reply cards 313
 Rooming list 315
 Toll-free telephone reservations 316
Resume 345
Retreat 9
Reunion network 172
Reunions market 171
Reunions, the magazine 172
Revenue producers 113
Reviewing and monitoring the marketing plan 59
RFP 263
Role of the catering manager 406
Rooming lists 315
Rooms control bible 92
Run-of-the-house rates 322
Russian service 399

S

Sales 68
 Authority 71
 Convention sales manager 74
 Differences between large and small properties 70
 Difference between sales and marketing 34
 Director of marketing 74
 Director of sales 73
 Evaluating effort 87
 Positions 73
Sales blitz 210
Sales call 194
 Six steps 195
 Opening the sales call 199
 Closing and follow up 209

Getting prospect involvement 200
Handling objections 202
Presenting your property 201
Turning features into benefits 203
Pre-call planning 195
Sales letters 231
Sales office 71
 Clerical staff 71
 Function 73
 Independent hotel representatives 80
 Interface with other departments 72
 Physical layout 71
 Regional sales offices 80
 Sales staff 73
Sales office automation 101
Sales prospect card 211
Sales records and filing systems 87
Sales staff 73
Sales within the hotel framework 73
Sample property analysis form 40
Sample script for a telephone appointment call 204
Sample "Tip sheet" 205
Schoolroom 381
Screen size selection 430
Screens 429
Second-tier cities 21
Selecting an ad agency 249
Selling 194
 Familiarization tours 194
 Personal sales calls 194
 Sales blitzes 194
 Site inspection selling 194
 Telephone selling 194
 Trade show selling 194
Selling to the association market 112

Selling to the corporate meetings market 141
Selling to the meetings market 194
Selling with convention bureaus 216
Seminars and workshops 9
Serpentine tables 385
Service Evaluation Questionnaire 517
Setting appointments by phone 204
Shoulder 259
Shoulder and value season group 259
Show manager 479
Simultaneous interpretation 440
Site inspection selling/ familiarization tours 217
Slide projectors 432
SMERF 168
    Educational 170
    Fraternal 175
    Military 171
    Religious 175
    Social 169
Society of Corporate Meeting Professionals 190
Society of Government Meeting Planners 190
Society of Travel Agents in Government 181
Specialty items (premiums) 236
Specification sheet 343
Specification sheet questionnaire 345
Specimen rates and charges bulletin 508
Split folio 505
Spouse program 463
    Building spouse attendance 465
Spread rates 322
Staging guides 349
Standard operating procedures 83
Standardized post-convention report 522

State and regional association market 121
State and regional associations occupancy chart 121
State and regional conventions 121
Stockholder/public meetings 149
Supplemental sales staff 82
Symposium 9

T

T-shape 383
Table microphone 426
Tabletop exhibit 476
Telemarketing 208
Telephone sales call follow up 206
Telephone selling 202
Tentative booking form 99
Tentative booking sheet 99
Theater style 374
Themes 396
Tickler file 91
Timetable for setup and breakdown 363
Total account management 164
Tour and travel desk 454
Tracer file 91
Trade magazines 223
Trade show 474, 479
    Behind the scenes look 498
    Importance 473
Trade show and exhibit manager 479
Trade show selling 211
Trade-out advertising 247
Training meetings 148
Trial close 203
Turning features into benefits 201
Types of exhibits 477

U

U-shape 381
U-shape seating 382
Union meetings 182
Uniserve 407

V

Video brochures 234
Video conferencing 440
Videotape projectors 437
Virtual office 103
Virtual sales manager 105

W

Walk in 327
Warranty of authority 275
Web pages 230
Whiteboard 442
Who services? 289
Working file 89
Writing effective sales letters 266

X

Xenon 16mm projector 436
Xenon bulbs 435

Y

Yield management 106

Z

Zero-based budget 58